Thelma & Louise and
Women in Hollywood

Thelma & Louise and Women in Hollywood

GINA FOURNIER

McFarland & Company, Inc., Publishers
Jefferson, North Carolina, and London

LIBRARY OF CONGRESS CATALOGUING-IN-PUBLICATION DATA

Fournier, Gina, 1963–
    Thelma & Louise and women in Hollywood / Gina Fournier.
        p.   cm.
    Includes bibliographical references and index.

    ISBN-13: 978-0-7864-2313-2
    ISBN 10: 0-7864-2313-7
    (softcover : 50# alkaline paper) ∞

    1. Thelma & Louise (Motion picture)   2. Women in motion pic-
tures.   I. Title.
PN1997.T43F68   2007
791.43'72 — dc22   2006012357

British Library cataloguing data are available

Cover photograph: *Thelma & Louise*, 1991 (MGM Photofest)

Manufactured in the United States of America

McFarland & Company, Inc., Publishers
    Box 611, Jefferson, North Carolina 28640
    www.mcfarlandpub.com

This book is dedicated to waitresses everywhere.
To those they serve, remember: tip big and tip often.

Acknowledgments

I couldn't have kept my sanity and completed this project without the kindness of strangers and the assistance of those around me. Thank you to the people who helped, especially my mother, who has given me so much for so long, and my brother Rod, for continually passing along essential computer parts. I'd like to extend a special thank you to my mentor, sculptor and painter Connie Mississippi, for teaching me the artists' way of life. Friends and family stood by me for the better part of a decade as I repeatedly begged off, "I can't... the book." A sincere bow to those I don't know personally, such as mail clerks and customer service operators, who nonetheless endured my lapses in proper decorum as a result of feeling overwhelmed. (No excuses, just apologies.) And, for his example of strength, deep well of support and steady belief in me, I'd like to share a world of gratitude with my best friend, mate and the most beautiful man I know, Christopher Allen. Thank you for walking out of that building.

The going wasn't always easy, but not finishing was never an option.

Contents

Preface

Thelma & Louise *and Women in Hollywood* examines the film's importance to Hollywood and beyond. The MGM/Pathé Entertainment release is truly a landmark film as evidenced by the surprising and considerable stir it created. Since the dynamic duo of *Thelma & Louise* hit movie screens nationwide on May 24, 1991, women have been slowly gaining ground toward employment and representational parity in Hollywood, but there's still much room for improvement.

Those of us working on behalf of women in film look forward to a day when female storytellers and deserving stories starring women are equally accepted and genuinely welcomed alongside of male storytellers and worthwhile stories starring men — without the kind of resistance that was aimed at *Thelma & Louise*. With that goal in mind, this book is designed to spur fresh thought and conscientious action within film studios and at the box office.

To set the scene for a discussion about women in film, the introduction goes back to the beginning of women in media studies, Virginia Woolf's *A Room of One's Own*. The challenge of discussing gender issues begins with the first of many questions: Why Isolate Women? The first part of the book looks at the relevance of *Thelma & Louise*, a film written by a woman, Callie Khouri, which stars two women, Susan Sarandon and Geena Davis, minus any male leads. Chapter 1, "The Primary Insult," provides readers with a big picture look at the status of women working in Hollywood, both in front of the camera and behind the scenes. The discussion regarding the on-screen representation of women continues in Chapter 2, "Woolf Passes the Pen to Khouri," which recognizes the connection between two important female writers and establishes the film's revolutionary nature. With *Thelma & Louise* in mind, Chapter 3, "The Bloody Truth About Women in Hollywood Films," investigates why women are underrepresented in Hollywood. Before engaging the many voices of the great debate over *Thelma & Louise*, Chapter 4, "The Remarkable Thelma and Louise," pinpoints what's so special about the women's story.

1

Thelma & Louise *and Women in Hollywood* also pays tribute to an important piece of cinematic history. Because an incredible amount of press coverage surrounded the release, the second part of the book reviews the film's fiery public reception. Chapter 5, "The Great Debate," takes an up-close look at the controversy involving the film primarily through point/counterpoints that appeared in *The Boston Globe* and *The Los Angeles Times*. Chapter 6, "Rape Downgraded to a 'Minor Plot Point,'" focuses on the movie's initial wave of reviews. To check the pulse of the entire country, I purposefully make room for a wide range of critical voices from across the United States. Chapter 7, "Second Wave," tracks the second wave of op/eds that followed initial critiques. Spanning a 10-year period from 1991 to 2001, "Deep Impact," Chapter 8, catalogues the many ways in which the film continued to garner the attention of journalists, newspaper readers and the country at large. The picture sparked a wide scattering of smaller fires, from greeting card campaigns to political metaphors. The impact was so deep, this conversation continues in Chapter 9, "The *Thelma & Louise*-ing of American Culture." Chapter 10, "Thelma and Louise Reunite — In Jail," pays special attention to the widespread trend of naming real-life criminals after the title duo.

In the third and final part, to make the case that the film matters more than most Hollywood releases, chapters 11 through 19 closely detail press coverage invoking *Thelma & Louise* found in specific newspapers across the United States. This selection of 10-year case studies surveying the post–*Thelma & Louise* decade comprises the largest portion of the book in order to include a fair sampling of cities representing the Midwest, Inner Mountain West, South, Mid-Atlantic region, West Coast, New England and the Heartland.

Wrapping things up, Chapter 20, "Conclusion: Too Many Bogus Years," updates the figures for women's employment in Hollywood and takes a final look at the current scene for women in film and their fans. With the help of film historians Molly Haskell and Jeanine Basinger, the chapter presents a brief history of women's representation in film from the early sound era, through Hollywood's many misleading "Year of the Women," to the present.

The great debate over the film has been solved by time: *Thelma & Louise* is worth all the fuss it caused. Today's thoughtful observer can find traces of it in numerous films produced since 1991. More so than any other major motion picture in recent memory, *Thelma & Louise* positively affected the culture's attitude toward women and their ability to lead.

Thelma & Louise *and Women in Hollywood* sets out to prove that the film greatly influenced popular culture and, in a meaningful manner, the way people think about men and women. Attitudes toward Callie Khouri's creation reflect attitudes toward women's greater progress in society and what is too often considered the "battle" between the sexes. However, reactions to both the film and feminism are complex and uncontrollable. For those who dislike the movie and the idea of women ranging free, *Thelma & Louise* may have cemented misogynist beliefs. This study reiterates what many already realize: the country is split along ideological lines. Some factions are more socially advanced than others as revealed in local presses and the greater story of *Thelma & Louise*.

Nothing worth keeping comes without dedication and sweat. This book began in graduate school as a short paper. Over the course of a decade or so, it developed into its present form. Through *Thelma & Louise*, I found passage from naïve, Midwestern Catholic schoolgirl to proud feminist. Early in the process, I finally figured out why my younger self loved reading and watching the television program *Little House on the Prairie* and, conversely, why as young woman with aspirations *Bonanza* held no appeal for me. Like Louise, I've waited on tables to earn a living; years before meeting Thelma, I, too, walked around in a daze, not realizing women's place in the world or the effect I could have on my own life. While writing this book, ever in hope of a better tomorrow, I've imagined readers similar to myself, who love good films and hard, sweet life, and want to better understand how the world works.

This project began in the Boston area, where both film critics and the public embraced the picture. Living in New England, I routinely encountered strangers and Store 24 clerks who loved the movie and showed interest in my project. However, the book was completed in metropolitan Detroit, which offered *Thelma & Louise* a much cooler reaction. Returning home to the Midwest, to my surprise, and for the first time, I heard people trash the picture. Here, former classmates, family members and 7–11 check-out clerks make comments like "I never saw *Thelma & Louise*" or "I didn't like it." At first their words made me feel like a bewildered Dorothy lost in Oz. Now I better understand why studies like this one are necessary. Though personal perspective is subjective and open to great variances in taste, nevertheless I hope a wide cross section of individuals will give the film a second thought.

Gina Fournier
Fall 2006

Introduction:
Why Isolate Women?

So many questions surround *Thelma & Louise*. Is it good for women in film? Is *Thelma & Louise* guilty of male-bashing? Is the picture worth all the fuss it received? What to make of the ending? Especially for those who saw the film in the summer of 1991 and remember the heated controversy that followed, a book about the movie definitely needs to supply answers, yet investigating the full story of *Thelma & Louise* opens up more questions. What does *Thelma & Louise* have to do with women in films above other films? Why segregate women in Hollywood films from men in Hollywood films? Why isolate women?

Virginia Woolf tackled similar questions (then about women and fiction) posed to her some eighty years ago in England, where she lived. There were no easy answers then, either.

> When you asked me to speak about women and fiction I sat down on the banks of a river and began to wonder what the words meant.... The title women and fiction might mean, and you may have meant it to mean, women and what they are like; or it might mean women and the fiction that they write; or it might mean women and the fiction that is written about them; or it might mean that somehow all three are inextricably mixed together and you want me to consider them in that light.[1]

Born in Victorian times, Woolf represents the beginning of women in media studies. She became one of the first proponents of a woman's professional involvement in the arts before terms like "mass communications" and "the media" existed. As movies acquired sound, Woolf began to investigate the inequities facing her gender within the writing profession. In her work, Woolf analyzed the depiction of fictional women compared to fictional men. Unlike anyone before her, Woolf demonstrated particular concern for the employment — or lack thereof— of women writers in comparison with male writers. These issues and Woolf's views have very much to do with *Thelma & Louise*, a film written by a woman, Callie Khouri, about two women, which inspired a huge public debate over gender issues. If Hollywood told more stories about women, which the public gladly received, Khouri's creation would not have caused such a sensation.

Now that women have created a place for themselves in the general workforce and broken the often described "glass ceiling" in some fields, women naturally want greater access to positions writing and directing movies. Woolf might be very happy to see how far women have advanced in the publishing world. However, in Hollywood, women have much more catching up to do. Penny Marshall and Nora Ephron are two among a very small group of female Hollywood film directors who work and enjoy name recognition. According to *Variety* in 2001, there were only 3,536 women and/or members of minority groups among the 12,000 members of the Director's Guild. Because far fewer than one in four working directors are female, the entertainment industry newspaper commented, "The glass ceiling is alive and well in Hollywood, and almost as impregnable as ever."[2] Applying Woolf's theory about fiction to Hollywood, when more women write screenplays and make movies, then conditions and depictions of women in film will improve.

Expanding upon Woolf's earlier goals for women in fiction, the aims for women in film have become even more crucial because things have changed considerably. For the most part, today's women must work. They want to do the work men do, and they need to earn the money men earn. There's no question that women deserve equal access to the same professions and similar, fair compensation.

But when will we elect a woman President of the United States? When will we finally recognize a female Steven Spielberg? The goal is for women to lead culture like men do by becoming society's top artists, as well as leading politicians. As fans of women in the arts already understand, American society needs more honored female storytellers and revered female-led stories — and not just in the action-adventure genre. We need a greater diversity of successful female creators whom current and future generations can look up to and admire, particularly in the mainstream. Although the film industry often caters to viewers under 25, largely ignoring adults, few industries attract a crowd like Hollywood does.

I want to share my enthusiasm for *Thelma & Louise* while exposing the truth about the status of women in the motion picture industry. In 1991, *Thelma & Louise* presented a new kind of movie: combining genres, adding women and breaking new ground. Likewise, this is a new kind of book investigating the story of women acting in Hollywood and their fans (or lack thereof) through *Thelma & Louise*. In her 1929 book *A Room of One's Own*, Woolf reasoned that women need their own money and a private place to work if they are to write and influence fiction. Three-quarters of a century later, the lack of parity in employment opportunities and pay for women in film compared to men is uniquely addressed through a discussion about two fictionalized, controversial women, Thelma Dickerson and Louise Sawyer. Callie Khouri was able to ascend the ranks, rise above the crowd of hopefuls and deliver her characters thanks to the stir in consciousness attributable in part to Virginia Woolf.

Because responsibility is a web that connects everyone, there is no single direction in which to point an accusatory finger of blame. The big picture of women in the movies — what has gone well and what has gone awry — is complicated. This book investigates how the Hollywood machine has supported women's confinement but does not ignore the contributions of viewers as consumers. I will not cry on your shoulder, but I will ask you to take your part as moviegoer and member of society seriously. Although you may hear me bemoan the status quo, my aim is to inspire — further action, anger, whatever. The choice is, of course, yours.

PART I. A FILM OF THEIR OWN

1. The Primary Insult

To help adjust the usual imbalance of history told minus women's contributions, Thelma & Louise *and Women in Hollywood* begins with a little help and historical insight from Virginia Woolf because mentors are invaluable. While preparing to speak at Newnham and Girton colleges, Woolf scrutinized her assigned subject in the first paragraph of *A Room of One's Own*, the thin but powerful collection of her speeches. There was something precarious about the title "women and fiction." Soon after women won the right to vote in the United States and Great Britain, the topic was not an easy matter to approach. Something nagged, hanging in the air unsaid. Carefully choosing her words, Woolf worried that she could never come to an absolute conclusion about the "true nature" of women or fiction due to fluctuating individual opinion.

This lack of resolution is similar to the way in which Thelma and Louise are suspended in flight and visually saved from a troublesome double suicide at the close of the film. Cinematically, the women don't clearly live or die. For some viewers, the film's ending made for a frustrating conclusion to an otherwise riveting tale. As there was no easy out for Thelma and Louise, there is no easy way out of the dilemma surrounding women in the arts. Even today, discussing the topic is still tricky.

Caution, calm and close consideration were necessary in Woolf's time, as there was no corollary topic then either, no discussion about the special situation of "men and fiction." Like men in Hollywood today, men writing fiction in the early days of the twentieth century were predominate, ubiquitous and undoubtedly quite content with (or perhaps not fully unconscious of) their privileged positions. The similar conditions for women writing fiction in the not too distant past and conditions for women in Hollywood at present tell us that the fight to change the world for the better is not yet over. Unfortunately, too many assume that a battle exists between the sexes. Rather, the tension lies between backward and forward thinking mindsets.

Juxtaposing then and now, "women and fiction" and "women in film" are not as clear-cut, dull, whiny or overly self-righteous as they may at first sound to those unaccustomed to feminist discussion. Rather, the need for these special topics remains the primary insult. "That collar I have spoke of, women and fiction," Woolf admits, "the need of coming to some conclusion on a subject that raises all sorts of prejudices and passions, bowed my head to the ground." Woolf apologizes dramatically, for instead of clearing up questions on behalf of her audience, she could only present "one minor point." Demurring slyly, Woolf makes history by stating the obvious: "a woman must have money and a room of her own if she is to write fiction."[1]

Her theory sounds simple. It's straightforward and difficult to argue against. Writers need space, time and funding in order to write. However, in Woolf's day, not that long ago, demanding solitude and a salary was asking quite a lot, much more than most women could hope for as they cared for their homes, husbands and children in the years between two world wars. Beyond the necessary concerns of quiet office space and ample time to work, most critically Woolf recognized women as the poorer half of the two sexes. Finally, this was the greatest cause of difference between the output of male writers and the far less prodigious output of female writers. Unequivocally, Woolf knew women must improve their economic standing if their artistic and intellectual work was to equal men's.

A similar, uneven distribution of wealth affects women starring in Hollywood films today.

Julia Roberts earned $20 million to star in *Erin Brockovich* (2000), making her the highest paid actress in the business.[2] Often, when I discussed the plight of women in film with strangers like checkout clerks at Store 24, they invariably rushed to point out, *"But Julia Roberts makes $20 million!"* As if her salary alone balances out the scale, which is otherwise heavily tipped toward men.

"Yeah," I replied, *"but Tom Cruise, Jim Carrey, Harrison Ford, Sylvester Stallone, Arnold Schwarzenegger and Mel Gibson all made $20 million first!"*[3]

Here's a good example of the different treatment afforded to men and women acting in Hollywood. Meg Ryan and Tom Hanks were reunited in director Nora Ephron's *You've Got Mail* (1998) based on their earlier success in Ephron's *Sleepless in Seattle* (1993). Ephron's co-producer for *Mail*, Lauren Shuler Donner, described the filmmakers' casting cues. Donner gushed, "We always had them in mind. I think when you say romantic comedy, you go 'Tom Hanks–Meg Ryan.'"[4] So why did Hanks earn more money? In 1998, before *You've Got Mail* was released during the Christmas season, *Variety* reported that Hanks' "current asking price" was in the "neighborhood" of $20 million.[5] Three months earlier, *The Hollywood Reporter* noted that Ryan's salary for her next film, *Hanging Up* (2000), produced and co-written by sisters Nora and Delia Ephron, totaled just over half of what Hanks was said to earn at $10.5 million.[6] If these figures accurately indicate what the players received for *You've Got Mail*, Hanks was paid roughly twice what his leading lady brought home. "Mature females" were "wildly excited over this reteaming of the principals from the 1993 hit," according to *The Hollywood Reporter*.[7] Yet Ryan was compensated far less to fall equally in love, and female moviegoers shelled out just as much to see the picture as did their male counterparts, perhaps without realizing the imbalance they supported.

Even queen of the pack Julia Roberts hasn't been immune to this kind of treatment. To star in *Conspiracy Theory* (1997), Mel Gibson signed a contract for $20 million up front and 15 percent of the film's gross on the back end, while Roberts settled for $11 million total.[8] Gibson received top billing, played the largest part and earned more money. Roberts occupied the lead female position in the film, but in Hollywood that means lower pay and a part that reads more like a supporting role. Even critically acclaimed movies like Oscar-winning *American Beauty* (1999), with Kevin Spacey and Annette Benning, follow a familiar pattern. The guy shines as the star, while the girl orbits around him. Although they're counted as lead roles by producers reporting to the Screen Actors Guild, women who co-star with men often fill less substantial parts and almost always earn less money.

One afternoon a few years ago I found myself responding to a poll over the phone about yet-to-be-released summer movies of 1999. The solicitor inquired about the movies I might see in the near future based on the industry-generated hype. I divulged my bias and asked questions of my own.

"Got any movies with lead females on your list?"

The woman on the other end had trouble doing so, but came up with *Notting Hill* and *Runaway Bride*.

I pushed further. "Any movies with lead females on your list besides Julia Roberts?"

She shyly suggested, "*Stepmom*?"

"No," I replied with a growl, losing my friendly composure. "That was a 1998 Christmas release! *Stepmom* is not on your list, plus Julia Roberts was in it!"

It's difficult to be a fan of women in film and not carry at least a tiny grudge against Roberts because of the part that powered her rise to the top of stardom's female heap: a sugar-coated prostitute, but a hooker nonetheless, in Disney/Buena Vista's *Pretty Woman* (1990). Too few people seem to realize the need for and lament the terrible absence of a-stereotypical, commanding and compelling female subjects in Hollywood films. Upon further conversation, even this Hollywood pollster hadn't realized the disparity of film roles awarded by gender.

Many of us see movies; we recognize them readily and digest them easily, but on the whole we don't often talk about what makes them good or bad, how they're products to be bought or ignored, supported or boycotted. There's little exchange between critics read in the newspapers and the everyday people at home who comprise audiences. Video stores don't foster conversations about films like libraries encourage conversations about books. Writers and readers have discussed what makes good literature for centuries, in schools, book clubs and other interested groups, but film lovers lack a similar dialogue. Both filmmakers and filmgoers could benefit from more in-depth discussions regarding one of our favorite national pastimes. With greater attention to and focus on the subject, more people might become aware of the disparity between the treatment of men and women in Hollywood films.

The nature of movies is inextricably linked to the topic of women in film. Filmgoers are just another group of consumers, women included, of course. Although it often appears that females *must* support Hollywood in smaller numbers compared to males, apparently in this regard, too, looks can be deceiving. Women represent 50 percent of the moviegoing audience, according to Alec Gallup of the Gallup Organization, which has tracked Hollywood numbers for over 60 years. "For all the years we've been doing polling, and despite the hypotheses and superstitions you hear," Gallup contended in 1997, "the gender breakdown has been roughly 50/50." Who's responsible for propagating the problems of women in Hollywood? Among others, women are.[9]

I came of age in the early 1980s, and as an adult I haven't ever witnessed Hollywood excite a discussion about feminism like happened with *Thelma & Louise*. In many ways, from the moment the film came out it has elevated the topic of women in film. Finally, a mainstream, Hollywood picture that tackles tough issues, including rape, class, gender and quality of life, while catching a few smiles and laughs along the way. Heavy topics generally don't get much attention from major film studios, particularly from a down-to-earth duo, female point of view. With Geena Davis and Susan Sarandon in the title roles, *Thelma & Louise* sets a fine example for Hollywood hiring practices. Two women are better than one, and yet the characters don't have to compete in order to make the picture a success. Hire talented women as leads in riveting, well-crafted motion pictures, the reception of *Thelma & Louise* suggests, and people will come to the theater. Commenting just a couple of weeks after *Thelma & Louise* was released, Memorial Day weekend 1991, *The Hollywood Reporter* admonished producers: "Clearly, adult females are demonstrating that as a group they're ready, willing and able to do a lot of summer moviegoing if there's product playing that they want to see."[10]

Callie Khouri's first big screen effort earned the Best Original Screenplay Oscar, the Golden Globe Best Screenplay award and the Writers Guild prize for Best Screenplay Written Directly for the Screen, and inspired the female leads to turn in once-in-a-lifetime performances. Sarandon and Davis shared honors together, receiving kudos from the National Board of Review for Best Actress and the David di Donatello Awards for Best Foreign Actress

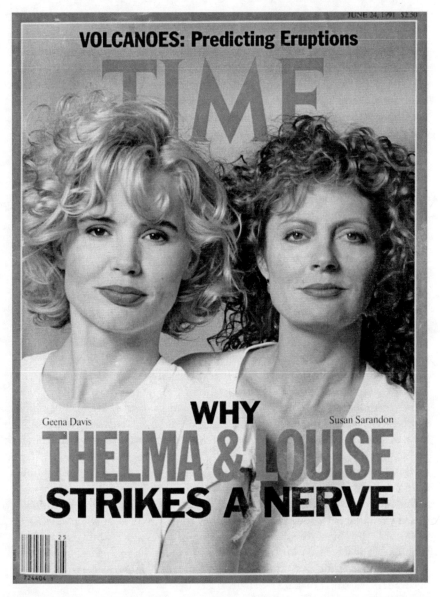

VOLCANOES: Predicting Eruptions

JUNE 24, 1991 $2.50

TIME

Geena Davis

WHY

Susan Sarandon

THELMA & LOUISE
STRIKES A NERVE

724404

Due to the great debate following the film's reception, Geena Davis and Susan Sarandon, the stars of *Thelma & Louise*, landed on the June 24, 1991, cover of *Time* (reprinted by permission of Time Life Pictures/Getty Images).

(Italy's equivalent of the Oscar). Sarandon won the London Film Critics Circle Awards Actress of the Year title, Davis snagged the Boston Society of Film Critics' Best Actress prize, and both women were nominated for Best Actress Oscars.

To recognize his cinematic guidance, the motion picture academies in

both the United States and England nominated Ridley Scott for Best Director. Not previously known as a director who could deliver pretty pictures,
special effects and well-developed characters, Scott took home the London
Film Critics Circle award for Director of the Year. With his irreplaceable help,
the film's dynamic duo soon achieved extra visibility and demonstrable pop
culture status. Sarandon and Davis together appeared on the cover of *Time*
magazine on June 24, 1991, exactly one month after the movie debuted.[11]

Thanks to all the filmmakers involved in the production, Davis as
Thelma Dickerson and Sarandon as Louise Sawyer together inflated their roles
into larger than real-life proportions. That's an unusual quality for female
film characters these days, which are usually so slim, both in body and substance. Women in film rarely land meaty roles, which brings the discussion
back to Julia Roberts. She's appeared in over 25 films and starred in over 20,
yet *Erin Brockovich* offered her first autonomous lead role and is the only part
she has played where her character alone drives the movie. In recognition of
her performance, Roberts was awarded the Best Actress Oscar, her first, for
her portrayal of the title character, a real life, working class, single mother
turned class action advocate.

My favorite Roberts movies find her in roles like *Erin Brockovich*, where
the story isn't just about her getting the guy and living happily ever after (cutting out all the sticky marriage stuff that invariably follows the honeymoon).
Roberts is a famous movie star who falls in love with an average guy who
shows the good sense to initially turn her down in *Notting Hill* (1999). She's
a younger, pretty woman who makes peace and even tentative friends with
her fiancé's dying ex-wife in *Stepmom* (1998). Roles like these in which Roberts
plays complex characters who are usually deemed unattractive (wicked stepmother) or beyond sympathy (big star with troubles) are more engaging than
roles that rely solely on the actress' good looks and her subsequent worth as
a love interest. Working against the tendency to brand stars and continually
repeat the same performance over and over from movie to movie, *Mary Reilly*
(1996) dared to break the mold by featuring Roberts as a plainly dressed Victorian servant who falls for both Jekyll and Hyde. Though the film wasn't a
critical success, amid gray and grimy old England, Roberts doesn't ever flash
her trademark smile or flare her hair to get by.

The beginning of Roberts' career is marked by one of her most humble
and endearing roles. In *Mystic Pizza* (1988), her first major screen appearance, Roberts debuts as a working class waitress looking for a way out of a
small seaside town. But she's concerned with more than geography, and seeks
to escape the confines of class and gender. Unlike her college-bound little sister and her best girlfriend, who decides to marry her high school sweetheart,
Roberts' character lacks future plans. Not wanting to serve pizza her whole
life, Roberts believes that her greatest asset is her appearance, yet one drunken
night she realizes that rewards based entirely on looks represent little conso-

lation and no real opportunity. As a result, when tested, Roberts puts integrity ahead of romantic pursuits by refusing to become involved in the power play between a rich boyfriend and his father. Instead, she shines conviction from the inside out despite her bimbo big hair and working class curves, as yet untamed by star power. After *Mystic Pizza*, rarely would the actress play a member of the lower class who stays there.

In her less inviting roles, Roberts' good looks are forefronted, not her character's inner development. She stands in as attorney/love object opposite Mel Gibson's CIA guinea pig conspiracy geek in the otherwise charming and campy *Conspiracy Theory*. Too bad Roberts' lead female role was passive, smaller and less interesting than Gibson's character, which was positioned at the center of the film. Watching *Conspiracy Theory*, audiences are asked to believe that a reasonable woman would tolerate without much hesitation or clear motivation a likeable but potentially dangerous stalker.

To serve the plot, Robert's character performs quick-of-hand coin tricks. A flashback showing her murdered father teaching her a trick would be nice, but in *Conspiracy Theory* there aren't many scenes devoted to the female lead that aren't shaped by the male lead. The film doesn't spend much time unfolding Roberts' motivation because her reason for being is more superficial rather than substantive. At the very end of the film, we are told in quickly revealed snippets the hidden emotional connection between Gibson and Roberts: Gibson's character may have murdered Roberts' father. When the picture's almost over, we finally learn why the she cares, why she runs so much, why she puts up with a possible nut case. Although she's trying to figure out who's responsible for father's death, the filmmakers aren't particularly concerned with developing Roberts' internal world.

In *I Love Trouble* (1994), Roberts plays a smart, young journalist opposite Nick Nolte. The picture revives classics like *His Girl Friday* (1940), but few fans came to the theater, possibly because the film's jumbled formulas failed to create a strong hybrid. Perhaps the picture's biggest detraction was the age difference between the co-stars. In 1994, Roberts was 27 years old, while her on-screen rival and love interest Nolte had seen almost twice her days at 53. To reinforce this disparity, Nolte ruled Roberts as if he were her father. *I Love Trouble* may have sprung from good intentions, but the film fails to support women in film. Academy Award winning actress Olympia Dukakis and Marsha Mason merely flash on screen in itsy-bitsy, token roles as secretary and senator, while three less lauded actors playing bad guys and bosses receive more screen time and juicier lines.

Too often Roberts' roles revolve around her appearance and glossed-over, unrealistic romantic relationships with men while declining to offer anything else for discriminating viewers to mull over. The trouble is that this formula works. "Here's how to make a $100 million," quipped the *South China Morning Post*, according to *The Hollywood Reporter* in 1998. "Force

Julia Roberts to grow her hair long, give her a set of curlers and make her smile in a light romantic comedy."[12] Along these lines, Roberts wears padded clothes to portray an overweight woman who stops eating bread, loses weight and steals her sister's boyfriend in *America's Sweethearts* (2001). Before she embodied the indecisiveness that plagues her character in *Runaway Bride* (1999), which reunited the *Pretty Woman*–starring duo, Roberts played a jealous, confused and inexplicably wishy-washy food critic in *My Best Friend's Wedding* (1997). In this outing, Roberts freaks out, sinks low and relies on her new gay best friend when her old straight best friend weds up-and-coming Cameron Diaz. Roberts' work often deals with the institution of marriage and the traditional expectations society places on women. In *Michael Collins* (1996), an Irish history bio epic, Roberts fills in as a standard Hollywood love interest to Liam Neison and Aidan Quinn.

In *Something to Talk About* (1995), Callie Khouri's disappointing screenplay following *Thelma & Louise*, Roberts regrets her decision not to pursue an interest in veterinary medicine. To suppress her unhappiness as a wife and mother without outside interests, she immerses herself in an upper-class equestrian lifestyle and encourages her young daughter to compete in that world. Meanwhile, she catches her husband, Dennis Quaid, and father, Robert Duvall, fooling around, yet forgives them both. Instead of confronting their behavior in a meaningful manner, she tries to have an affair, too, but is unable to follow through. *Something to Talk About* would have been much stronger if the women in the film were given better and bigger parts. Although Quaid and Duvall are fine actors worthy of screen time, the story's most interesting tension exists between the women, not between the sexes. Occupying smaller roles than Duvall, Gena Rowlands plays mother to Roberts, and Kyra Sedgewick plays her sister. Unlike her tougher and more resolute sibling, Roberts accepts her fate submissively, as does her mother. Instead of being allowed to balance the family's weaknesses, Sedgewick's character's comparative strength is reduced to brief screen time and saucy one-liners. Had the film's emphasis been shifted, *Something to Talk About* might have made good on its promise and better addressed the question of why, generation after generation, women put up with disrespect.

Oftentimes, Hollywood tries to looks more hip than it actually is, like when producers cast women in exclusive job titles such as lawyer, then proceed with business as usual, neglecting to give female characters a full spine and seven layers of skin. In *The Pelican Brief* (1993), Denzel Washington is cast as a journalist opposite law student Roberts. The film trounces racial divisions, but the lead characters aren't written any thicker than the corrugated cardboard from which they are cut, suggesting tokenism. Although Roberts' character is central to the action (she plays "the little lady who started this whole brouhaha," as described by one of the film's many white guys in suits), she's practically the only woman in *The Pelican Brief*. When the camera isn't focusing on her face as she reacts to the many men who hunt her down, tons of males pack the screen, playing politicians in the Oval Office, FBI and CIA agents, lawyers and journalists.

In one of her earliest roles, Roberts plays a sprite who, like a good girl, always considers the central male character's wishes ahead of her own. In *Hook* (1991), as Tinkerbell, Roberts recreates a storyline for women as old as fairy tales, in which mothers often died in order to let father and daughter spend more quality time together. On the rebound in *Dying Young* (1991), Roberts nurses and falls in love with a fatally ill Ivy Leaguer. Her dedication to the young man reveals what a good sport she is, but more importantly, she matches his physical ideal of what a lovable woman looks like. What a waste of Academy Award winning actress Ellen Burstyn and Colleen Dewhurst. In *Dying Young*, each receives just a few seconds of screen time and a mere couple of lines playing stereotypical crones: one a childish doll collector, the other a wise but perhaps dangerous widow who has buried three husbands in the maze out back. Taken together, these bi-polar bit roles provide two unattractive alternatives for women who don't die young. The film's nosy but concerned butler, played by George Martin II, enjoys as much screen time as Burstyn and Dewhurst combined.

Arguably her most manipulating and infuriating film, *Sleeping with the Enemy* (1991) casts Roberts as a battered wife who fakes her own death in order to escape a violent husband. Again, as in *Conspiracy Theory*, what gives this movie's sympathies away stems from an old dictum. To reveal character and meaning, writers are constantly instructed to "show, not tell." In *Sleeping with the Enemy*, the filmmakers spend much more time showing Roberts scared, abused and hunted down than anything else. Halfway through the film, Roberts' character explains in a brief voice-over, accompanied by a quick flashback, how all along she planned to break away from her abusive mate by secretly taking swimming classes. While most of the movie targets her as prey, viewers are to believe that she's been very busy plotting to fake her own drowning when the opportunity presents itself. Other than this flash of steel, the majority of the film's screen time is devoted to Roberts' entrapment. Her character is either boxed inside a glass house, controlled by her husband and conveniently located by the ocean, or contained in her new home far away, where he soon tracks her down. Through this emphasis, what becomes clear in *Sleeping with the Enemy* is that the filmmakers care more about Roberts' visible vulnerability than her secret, hidden strengths. Same thing in *Steel Magnolias* (1989), where Roberts blossoms as a sickly, selfish Southern belle who loves the color pink, wants to have a child above all else and throws one hell of a diabetic fit.

A quick analysis of the roles Roberts has filled exemplifies in a brush stroke the M.I.A. status of women in film. Too often women play less important, stereotypical and uninteresting supporting characters while their male co-stars occupy more riveting and vital central roles.

Between roughly 1950 to the present, right before our eyes, the numbers of women appearing in Hollywood films and the figures for how much they are paid have slipped far enough behind those of men to sound an alarm. (And, no big surprise, the news for black actresses and those from other minorities is worse than it is for white women pursuing dreams of the silver screen.) For proof, look at the movie section of your Sunday newspaper. Count the leads advertised by gender. Although the situation has improved since the debut of *Thelma & Louise*, male thespians still come out ahead, week by week, year after year, and with little public attention focused on the imbalance. Unfortunately, not enough people seem to be listening or care.

The problem is even worse behind the camera. In 1998, the American Film Institute (AFI), dedicated to advancing and preserving film art, premiered its list of the top 100 movies of the past 100 years. None were directed by women. None were filmed by women. On both sides of the camera, the percentages for women's participation in Hollywood moviemaking are disparaging.

According to the AFI, in the 20th century women fared infinitesimally better as writers than they did as directors or cinematographers. Only one film out of the supposed top 100 ever made, *E.T.—The Extraterrestrial* (1982), number 25, is credited to one woman writing alone, Melissa Mathison. Otherwise, at best women were allowed to collaborate with men on films such as *The Wizard of Oz* (1939), number six, which was written by Florence Ryerson and 15 male co-screenwriters.

Women showed up best on the AFI's list behind the scenes as editors. Twelve films that appeared among the top 100 were edited by women who received sole credit for their work, including Anne V. Coates, editor of *Lawrence of Arabia* (1962), number five; Thelma Schoonmaker, editor of *Raging Bull* (1980), number 24; Dede Allen, editor of *Bonnie and Clyde* (1967), number 27; Claire Simpson, editor of *Platoon* (1986), number 83; Margaret Booth, editor of *Mutiny on the Bounty* (1936), number 35; and Sally Menke, editor of *Pulp Fiction* (1994), number 95. An anomaly for her day, Adrienne Fazan received sole editing credit for two films on the list, numbers 10 and 68, *Singin' in the Rain* (1952) and *American in Paris* (1951). Cutting and pasting with 23 male cohorts at a ratio of two men for every one woman, 12 females co-edited some of the pictures that made the grade, including Martin Scorcese's longtime associate Schoonmaker, who co-edited *Taxi Driver* (1976), number 47, and *Goodfellas* (1990), number 94.

Given general knowledge about the work world, one might expect the number of women employed on the set to be lower for earlier films, which is the case in terms of the early sound era. Women are almost non-existent among crew for films made in the 1930s, 40s and 50s. Interested individuals can check for themselves. Internet Movie Database (www.imdb.com) credits 95 people with forging *Gone with the Wind* (1939), number four on the AFI's list. From the looks of their names, only 10 crew members were women, and they held lowly positions: an uncredited hair stylist and associate make-up artist, two stunt doubles, a stunt person, a script clerk, a color consultant, a scenario assistant, a technical advisor, an uncredited script clerk and an uncredited landscape designer (Lila Finn, Aileen Goodwin, Hazel Rogers, Elaine Goodman, Connie Earl, Natalie Kalmus, Barbara Keon, Susan Myrick, Lydia Schiller and Florence Yoch, respectively). Likewise, when Disney created *Fantasia* (1940), number 58, of the 11 directors employed, none were female. Twenty-five writers were required, yet only two were women, Sylvia Moberly Holland and Bianca Majolie, who both worked on the "Nutcracker Suite" segment. Of 24 art directors, only one, Kay Nielsen, was female. Many movies on the list produced during the so-called "golden period" failed to invite any women to participate behind the camera.

From the days of classic Hollywood to the renegade, troubled sixties, things didn't improve much though fans of women in film might have hoped otherwise. The only woman involved in the production of *Easy Rider* (1969), number 88, was Joyce King, the script supervisor. *Butch Cassidy and the Sundance Kid* (1969), number 50, at most permitted women to design costumes and apply makeup, in this case, Edith Head and Edith London. (The most prolific female Oscar winner of all time, Edith Head was responsible for dressing eight of the AFI's top 100 films.) Bucking trends, Lynn H. Guthrie served as an uncredited assistant director on *The Graduate* (1960), number seven, but during her long career she never progressed to the top of a production. According to her imdb.com profile, Guthrie racked up 54 assistant director positions between 1959 and 1990 without ever advancing in the ranks beyond an occasional first assistant director position.

Eventually the situation must improve, but when? For *E. T.—The Extra-Terrestrial*, number 25, the visual effects team numbered 53 and favored men by retaining only 11 women and two persons of indeterminate gender based on their names. A large sound crew of 45 was gathered for another one of Steven Spielberg's noted releases, *Schindler's List* (1993), number nine, which employed 35 men, eight women and two persons of indeterminate gender. More than any other director, Spielberg had five films celebrated by the AFI, including *Jaws* (1975), number 48, *Close Encounters of the Third Kind* (1977), number 64, and *Raiders of the Lost Ark* (1981), number 60.

Studying the full crew credits of the films on the AFI's top 100 list, apart from a little writing and editing, one finds women costuming movies released through the 1950s and casting, doing make-up and providing art direction for movies made in the later half of the century. Increasingly, in movies made in the 70s, 80s, and 90s, women lent a hand in producing. Though women rarely served as executive producer, they did occasionally perform as assistant director. Outnumbered by 42 male co-workers, 12 women served as producers for AFI top 100 films. *Taxi Driver* (1976), number 47, and *Close Encounters of the Third Kind* (1977), number 64, were both produced by Julia Phillips, who collaborated with three other males including her ex-husband Michael Phillips II.

Women's ideas and input have always been sought in Hollywood, just not in remotely even numbers compared to men. "Traditionally, writing was one area, along with editing and costume design, through which women might be able to scale the studio gates," *The Hollywood Reporter* explained in 1997.[13] Among others, the work of writers Margaret Mitchell, Harper Lee, Emily Brontë, Edna Ferber and Mary Shelley have been adapted for the screen; each conceived material found on the AFI's list.

However, by concentrating on films from the sound era, which started in the late 1920s, the AFI's list ignores the movies' nascent days. Strange as it may sound, women enjoyed a greater percentage of screenwriting credits in the silent era. According to Cari Beauchamp in *Without Lying Down: Frances Marion and the Powerful Women of Early Hollywood*, "Half of all the films copyrighted between 1911 and 1925 were written by women."[14] When the movie business was born and began to grow, women filled a greater percentage of behind the scenes positions than they have in later years; they were more easily able to work their way into film production. "Little conspired against women in the early days of the medium and work was easy to find," explains film historian Lizze Francke in *Script Girls: Women Screenwriters in Hollywood.*[15]

Spurred by the excitement of a new century, eager young women hunting for employment were hired by the blossoming industry as performers and secretaries. Amidst chaos and boom, daring women could pitch in and fill additional job duties. In the spirit of cooperation, women gained wider experience and exerted more influence, particularly those working for a powerful, open-minded boss. One such example was writer and director Lois Weber, who made films for Carl Laemmle's Universal Studios.[16] A prolific screenwriter from 1915 to 1953 and a protégé of Weber's, Frances Marion commented that she was indebted to other women in the business for her "greatest success." Marion, who was Mary Pickford's favorite scribe, believed, "Contrary to the assertion that women do all in their power to hinder one another's progress, I have found that it has always been one of my own sex who has given me a helping hand when I needed it."[17] Unfortunately, modern film fans are unlikely to recognize Marion's name or her contributions.

Not a big surprise, the atmosphere of openness and flexibility present at the start of the movie business changed as the major film studios solidified and matured. As the years progressed, women couldn't help other women if they weren't in any position to do so. After the Depression and two world wars, attitudes regarding women in the workforce further deteriorated. As indicated by authors like Susan Faludi, various backlashes have occurred over time restricting the numbers of women working across the spectrum of professions. According to *The Hollywood Reporter*, "The records show Academy Awards nominations for women in writing categories was practically a yearly occurrence from the inception of the awards in 1927 through the end of World War II, after which they became less routine, with each one bringing pronouncements of gender gains."[18] Apparently, those gains were made by men.

Often tucked away out of sight, writers, editors and visual designers occupy non-threatening positions. These quiet, segregated outposts leave the decision making about which stories to shoot and how to depict characters to the more visible and powerful positions such as producers and directors. In Hollywood, writers are notoriously treated as underlings, but female screenwriters face a double dose of hard knocks. After she graduated from the world of misogynistic music videos and segued into writing major motion pictures, Callie Khouri was not allowed to remain on the set while her work was filmed, nor did she attend the screening of *Thelma & Louise* at the Cannes Film Festival, despite her requests.[19] Rachel Abramowitz, a reporter for *Premiere* magazine, interviewed Khouri regarding her role in the production. Abramowitz later compiled her interviews with women in Hollywood in her 2000 book, *Women's Experience of Power in Hollywood: Is That a Gun in Your Pocket?*

> Once filming started, Khouri was relegated to being persona non grata. "It was weird to go from spending every day with Ridley to being completely and utterly excommunicated," she says. Even to be allowed to visit the set took several days of negotiation. "It was humiliating, and it changed me forever, because I was treated like a nonbeing. I think it was because of Mimi. [Mimi Polk, producer of *Thelma & Louise*] Mimi actually said to me, 'Darling, that's how it is. The writer never gets to do blah blah blah,' " says Khouri. She wasn't invited to any preview screenings.... Khouri paid her own way to New York to attend one screening, then watched as Scott, Polk and the studio brass went off to discuss the results. She wasn't invited to the New York premiere. "It was closing-night of the Cannes Film Festival. I was prohibited from going," says Khouri. "It is the way writers are typically treated. I had a typical experience, and it made me vehement that I would never go through it again. After the movie came out, everybody wanted to talk to me. Before, they all pretended like Geena and Susan and Ridley made the whole thing up.[20]

As much as celebrities may try, they can only affect the world to a limited degree by changing clothes and dying hair. Though necessary work on a movie set, the tasks of selecting wardrobe and painting faces fail to sway the culture as much as a person directing pictures can. Regrettably, even when Hollywood welcomed female writers like Frances Marion, the door was already closed to women directors. "By 1927," *Variety* extolled, "when it came apparent that movies were much more than a fad and were in fact big business, [Dorothy] Azner was the only woman director left in Hollywood."[21] Not well known, Azner stood out with Ida Lupino as the only female figures among Hollywood directors until Barbra Streisand directed *Yentl* decades later in 1983.

What's been going on here? Women were not responsible for creating most of the images of men, women, or anything appearing in all the many popular films made in the 20th century. If people lived as long as Yoda, Virginia Woolf would definitely have something to say about this situation. Like an archeologist on a dig, Woolf, in her essay about "women and fiction," set out to discover why books by women weren't published throughout history alongside of books written by men. In pursuit of a more gender-balanced perspective, she walks through centuries of library shelves stacked with books primarily written by men, and it takes Woolf centuries to reach books written by other women. Adding injury to the primary insult of second-class citizenship, many books she browses publicly deplore the capabilities of all women, presenting an altogether depressing outlook.

Three-quarters of a century later, even after the invention of the automatic washing machine, the passage of civil rights legislation and the waning popularity of the Miss America pageant, the stigmas working against women have not yet been obliterated. Gender bias is alive and well, particularly in Hollywood. Among its many pleasures and uses, *Thelma & Louise* reminds audiences how far women have to go in their fight for economic and cultural equality.

2. Woolf Passes the Pen to Khouri

Despite her daunting task and reluctance to take it on, in *A Room of One's Own*, Virginia Woolf does mark literary history with indelible impressions about both womanhood and fiction:

- She recognizes that fiction shares life's values but feels that any judgment of how well a writer accomplishes her task is bound to start an argument.
- She finds books to exist on a literary continuum with no book an island.
- She points to patriarchy's rule and believes that both men and women suffer when one sex lives life subordinate to the other. In Woolf's view, when women cease to be the "protected sex," then women will be free, to exalt themselves or possibly to ruin themselves, to do whatever they choose. "Anything may happen when womanhood has ceased to be a protected occupation," Woolf noted with anticipation and warning.[1]

Woolf's thoughts about unavoidable arguments, connections between works of art, and the joys and pitfalls of freedom also apply here:

- The "great debate" (as coined by *The Boston Globe*) over *Thelma & Louise* consumed critics and the general public. From the time of its release to the present, people have not come to a consensus about *Thelma & Louise*.
- *Thelma & Louise* reflects the pertinent films that precede it. If we review the history of women starring in Hollywood films, a timeline emerges. If we study the film as well as the hype, *Thelma & Louise* implores moviegoers to focus on the struggling lifeline of movies employing women as leads. Films that preceded, which featured strong female leads, women acting on their own behalf, women breaking genre barriers, male buddies, fugitive crime sprees, car chases and car crashes, rape, revenge, female buddies and femme fatales, all paved the way for *Thelma & Louise*. The film would not

exist without pictures such as *The Wizard of Oz* (1939), *Gone with the Wind* (1939), *Woman of the Year* (1942), *Bonnie and Clyde* (1967), *The Odd Couple* (1968), *Butch Cassidy and the Sundance Kid* (1969), *The Sugarland Express* (1974), *The Turning Point* (1977), *Aliens* (1979), *The Blues Brothers* (1980), *9 to 5* (1980), *The Accused* (1988), *Lethal Weapon* (1987), *Fatal Attraction* (1987) and *Blue Steel* (1990), which came before. Likewise, *Thelma & Louise* opened the door for a number of subsequent releases in a variety of genres. To cite just a few examples, *Bad Girls* (1994) followed up *Thelma & Louise*'s western setting. *Boys on the Side* (1995) copied the film's focus on women's friendship. *First Wives Club* (1996) continued what some viewers recognize as a "revenge against men" theme. *Set It Off* (1996) copied the film's women in crime aspect, and *Charlie's Angels* (2000) and *Lara Croft: Tomb Raider* (2001) capitalized on the idea of women starring in action films.

• Once they decide to take charge, Thelma and Louise (who probably would not have been familiar with Virginia Woolf's work) assert their freedom unfettered. While many of their decisions on the road are desperate and misguided, the title characters spontaneously choose to leave home, dance with a cowboy, commit murder, run away, spend the night with a sexy stranger, turn down a marriage proposal, rip off a convenience store, hassle a trucker, become best friends and together jump off a cliff because nothing tied them down.

Though freedom as practiced by Thelma and Louise is far too coarse and uncivilized for the real world, the drama reminds us that women today can truly do just about anything — except outnumber or even equal men's employment figures for their work acting in Hollywood films.

How many other mainstream pictures produced in the United States can you name that feature two female leads minus any major parts for males? Grappling to find a few? I can think of *Whatever Happened to Baby Jane* (1962), *The Miracle Worker* (1962), *Julia* (1977), *The Turning Point* (1977), *Rich and Famous* (1981), *'Night Mother* (1986), *Black Widow* (1987), *Outrageous Fortune* (1987), *The Accused* (1988), *Beaches* (1988), *Postcards from the Edge* (1990), *Fried Green Tomatoes* (1991), *Leaving Normal* (1991), *Passion Fish* (1992), *Single White Female* (1992), *Walking and Talking* (1996), *Romy & Michele's High School Reunion* (1997), *Anywhere But Here* (1999) and *Tumbleweeds* (1999). However, this list is pretty short considering the vast numbers of films produced since the 1960s.

On the other hand, there are plenty of films from the same period starring only men, in twos, threes and more. Most Hollywood films prefer male characters, designating a single small supporting role for a female serving traditionally as wife, mother, girlfriend or prostitute and, increasingly, as sidekick. Domestically produced films made since the 1960s that feature two lead males minus any truly lead females include *Analyze This* (1999), *Analyze That* (2002), *Anger Management* (2003), *Arlington Road* (1999), *Bill & Ted's Excellent Adventure* (1989), *Bill & Ted's Bogus Journey* (1991), *Birdy* (1984), *The Color of Money* (1986), *Colors* (1988), *Dumb & Dumber* (1994), *Dumb and Dumber: When Harry Met Lloyd* (2003), *48 Hrs.* (1982), *Another 48 Hours* (1990), *The Falcon and the Snowman* (1985), *The Fisher King* (1991), *Grumpy Old Men* (1993), *Grumpier Old Men* (1995), *Ishtar* (1987), the four films in the *Lethal Weapon* series (1987, 1989, 1992, 1998), *Men in Black* (1997), *Men in Black II* (2002), *Midnight Cowboy* (1969), *Nothing to Lose* (1997), *The Odd Couple* (1968), *The Odd Couple II* (1998), *Tango and Cash* (1989), *Twins* (1988), *Wayne's World* (1992), *Wayne's World 2* (1993) and *White Men Can't Jump* (1992).

While neither list is complete, more films could be added to the men's longer list than to the women's shorter list. Notice the plethora of sequels on the second list, indicating that the films led by men are seen by more people and therefore make more money, warranting follow-ups. Another difference is that the male buddy tradition got a much earlier start. Bud Abbott and Lou Costello collaborated on over 30 films from 1940 to 1956. The vaudeville-inspired comedy team of Bob Hope and Bing Crosby pursued Dorothy Lamour around the globe in eight films beginning with *The Road to Singapore* (1940) and ending with *The Road to Hong Kong* (1962). Dean Martin and his wacky sidekick Jerry Lewis starred together in nine films, from *At War with the Army* (1950) to *Hollywood or Bust* (1956). More recently, Cheech Marin and Tommy Chong put out six pictures as gentle, wayward pot smokers Cheech & Chong, starting with *Cheech & Chong's Up in Smoke* (1979) and ending with *Cheech & Chong's The Corsican Brothers* (1984).[2]

While women's pairings tend to receive little attention or support, Hollywood encourages men to partner up, on screen and behind the scenes. Although women rarely get the chance to write and direct, teams of filmmaking brothers have become popular lately. Peter and Bobby Farrelly were responsible for *There's Something About Mary* (1998), in which Cameron Diaz plays a ditzy brain surgeon, and *Shallow Hal* (2001), which purveyed the notion that overweight women could be loved as long as they looked as lovely as Gwyneth Paltrow. Among other films, such as *Raising Arizona* (1987) and *Fargo* (1996), Joel and Ethan Cohen penned and directed *O, Brother, Where Art Thou?* (2000). Compared to her Oscar winning role in *The Piano* (1993), Holly Hunter's part in *O, Brother, Where Art Thou?* (staying home with the kids while her husband pursues adventures on the road) is minute, thoroughly inconsequential and a total waste of her talents. The Wachowski brothers, Andy and Larry, brought *The Matrix* (1999) to theaters. The Keanu Reeves cyber-adventure followed their disingenuous debut *Bound* (1996), which pretended to care about its two female leads, Gina Gershon and Jennifer Tilly, but really just wanted to watch them kiss and grope. *Bound* focuses on the numerous male Mafiosoes written into the picture more than the film's early titillating sex scenes.

The AFI's list of the 100 top films contains dozens of movies starring mostly men, including (from top to bottom) *The Godfather* (1972), *Lawrence of Arabia* (1962), *On the Waterfront* (1954), *The Bridge on the River Kwai* (1957), *Star Wars* (1977), *One Flew Over the Cuckoos Nest* (1975), *2001: A Space Odyssey* (1968), *Raging Bull* (1980), *Dr. Strangelove* (1964), *Apocalypse Now* (1979), *The Treasure of the Sierra Madre* (1948), *The Godfather Part II* (1974), *High Noon* (1952), *Midnight Cowboy* (1969), *A Clockwork Orange* (1971), *Jaws* (1971), *Butch Cassidy and the Sundance Kid* (1969), *All Quiet on the Western Front* (1930), *Mash* (1970), *The Third Man* (1949), *The French Connection* (1971), *Ben-Hur* (1959), *Dances with Wolves* (1990), *Rocky* (1976), *The Deer Hunter* (1978), *The Wild Bunch* (1969), *Platoon* (1986), *Mutiny on the Bounty* (1935), *Easy Rider* (1969), *Patton* (1970), *Goodfellas* (1990), *Pulp Fiction* (1994), and *Unforgiven* (1992).

Although the AFI's list includes hordes of movies driven by an ensemble of males, accounting for nearly a third of the total films, of the 100 selected, none feature a cast populated primarily by women. Apparently *Snow White* made the list only due to the presence of the seven dwarfs. What makes *Mutiny on the Bounty* (1935) any better than the many film versions of Louisa May Alcott's *Little Women?* Does the mere fact that a man's world is depicted rather than a woman's automatically render a film qualitatively better? The AFI's list leads me to believe that our perceptions are askew when it comes to judging the merit of films — including *Thelma & Louise*— and Meryl Streep agrees.

At Women in Film's 1998 Crystal Awards in Los Angeles, where she was presented with a Lifetime Achievement Award, Streep had this to say about the AFI's list:

> The protagonist of a film is the person who drives the plot, carries the action, impels the drama of the story being told. Of the best 100 films of this century as chosen by the American Film Institute, more than sixty have a male protagonist. About thirty have what I call a balanced cast (yin and yang in nice apposition), like "Casablanca," or "Gone with the Wind" or "The African Queen." Seventeen of them have pretty much no women in them at all, like "The Wild Bunch," "Platoon," "Mutiny on the Bounty," etc. And of the 100 best films of this century, the number with female protagonists is four. One's a cartoon, "Snow White," one's a child, Dorothy in the "Wizard of Oz," and there are two women: Julie Andrews in "The Sound of Music" and Bette Davis in "All About Eve." One sings, the other doesn't.[3]

No matter how you slice the pie, counting leads vs. supporting roles or scanning for protagonists, the status of women in Hollywood films trails behind men's more esteemed and commanding position.

Female-friendly casting is the main reason why *Thelma & Louise* caused such a stir. By simply featuring two adult female leads, the picture stands apart.

Thelma & Louise is a rarity because the movie's title characters exist to complement and contrast one another, resulting in a total expression of womanhood that is varied and individualistic rather than stereotypical. In contrast to most films, *Thelma & Louise* personifies rather than plunders the goals of wom*en* in film (plural, as in more than one per picture), as if directly answering Woolf's concerns. While pondering the topic of "women and fiction," she questioned:

> All these relationships between women, I thought, rapidly recalling the splendid gallery of fictitious women, are too simple. So much has been left out, unattempted. And I tried to remember any case in the course of my reading where two women are represented as friends.... It was strange to think that all the great women of fiction were, until Jane Austen's day, not only seen by the other sex, but seen only in relation to the other sex. And how small a part of a woman's life is that....[4]

Perhaps what's most remarkable about the production is that the filmmakers did not heed the usual practice of casting a major male character opposite the women. *Thelma & Louise* bypassed hiring some guy to serve as alpha dog, someone the women might fight over or revolve around.

Leaving their respective men behind, Thelma and Louise strike out on their own. Forging a fierce friendship based on renewed faith in themselves and each other, they search out space in which to develop apart from men, a task they find very difficult to do. Although the film's ending implies that women can't escape a male controlled world without dying, *Thelma & Louise* still differs from typical movies starring women, in which female protagonists seek out and share the stage with men. In standard Hollywood films, even when women receive lead roles and top billing, their male supporting co-stars tend to play sizable, key roles. This patronizing arrangement reflects the outdated notion that women are a weaker sex who cannot do a thing without the guiding influences of men.

In 1983, Shirley MacLaine and Debra Winger played a memorable mother and daughter team in *Terms of Endearment*. MacLaine and Winger shared the marquee with an ensemble cast, including Jack Nicholson, who was billed above Winger although he played a smaller role as McLaine's next-door neighbor and ex-astronaut love interest, John Lithgow, with whom Winger has an affair, and Jeff Daniels, Winger's husband. Today *Terms of Endearment* represents an average Hollywood story: men cast opposite lead women serve as necessary catalysts and vital magnets. In *Rambling Rose* (1991), houseguest Laura Dern and hostess Diane Ladd skirt around patriarch Robert Duvall. In *Death Becomes Her* (1992), competing sorceresses Meryl Streep and Goldie Hawn battle over the attention of mortal Bruce Willis. The memory of a sexually abusive, alcoholic (and thankfully deceased) husband and father, played by David Strathairn, as well as the actions of revenge-seeking detective Christopher Plummer, reconnect estranged mother Kathy Bates and daughter Jennifer Jason Leigh in *Dolores Claiborne* (1994). The hunt for serial killer Harry Connick Jr. brings detectives Holly Hunter and Sigourney Weaver together in *Copycat* (1995). A remake of *Cyrano De Bergerac* with the gender roles reversed, *The Truth About Cats & Dogs* (1996) connects radio talk show host Janeane Garofalo to dumb blonde Uma Thurman via love interest Ben Chaplin. Although *Ever After* (1998), based on the Cinderella fairy tale, reinvigorates the traditional plot, the attentions of the prince, Dougray Scott, further divide Drew Barrymore and her wicked stepmother Angelica Huston. Witch sisters Sandra Bullock and Nicole Kidman can cast spells but have trouble keeping their mates alive, which lures single detective Aidan Quinn into their deadly and competitive lair in *Practical Magic* (1998). The tie that binds ex-wife Susan Sarandon and new girlfriend Julia Roberts in *Stepmom* (1998) is Ed Harris, the father of Sarandon's children and Roberts' fiancé. In *Dick* (1999), with Kirsten Dunst and Michelle Williams, if it wasn't for Richard Nixon, there'd be no silly political satire.

Flip positions and the opposite situation does not hold true: women rarely serve as integral and important supporting co-stars in male-led films. In *48 Hrs.*, cop Nick Nolte and convict Eddie Murphy work together to track down criminals, as do law enforcement partners Mel Gibson and Danny Glover in the *Lethal Weapon* movies. In both cases, women like Annette O'Toole and Rene Russo (who appears as an afterthought to Gibson and Glover in the third and fourth installments in the *Lethal Weapon* series) are tangential to the buddies' important work. Women in these successful film series serve as plucky subordinate co-workers, lovers, prostitutes, dead muses and women in waiting, but never big screen equals. The odd couple, mobster Robert De Niro and psychiatrist Billy Crystal, don't need Crystal's wife, Lisa Kudrow, to conduct their sessions or alleviate De Niro's stress in *Analyze This* and *Analyze That*. Likewise, teenagers Bill and Ted, who just want to pass their history final, time-travel the world without asking their mothers' permission in *Bill & Ted's Excellent Adventure*. Of the eight historical figures they meet, only one, Joan of Arc, is a woman. In *Grumpy Old Men*, Jack Lemmon and Walter Matthau compete and drool over new neighbor Ann-Margret, who serves as eye candy, just as Sophia Loren does in the following picture, *Grumpier Old Men*. Male buddy films starring actors like Jack Nickolson, Adam Sandler, Jeff Bridges, Tim Robbins, Paul Newman, Tom Cruise, Robert Duvall, Sean Penn, Jim Carrey, Jeff Daniels, Robin Williams, Jeff Bridges, Dustin Hoffman, Warren Beatty, Sylvester Stallone, Kurt Russell, Martin Lawrence, Tommy Lee Jones, Will Smith, Arnold Schwarzenegger, Danny DeVito, Dana Carvey, Mike Myers, Wesley Snipes and Woody Harrelson provide for women minor supporting parts as token females and beautiful sex objects embodied by actresses such as Marisa Tomei, Joan Cusak, Mary Elizabeth Mastrantonio, Maria Conchito Alonso, Lauren Holly, Mercedes Ruehl, Isabella Adjani, Teri Hatcher, Linda Fiorentino, Lara Flynn

Boyle, Kelly Preston, Tia Carrere and Rosie Perez. Even as big league stars, these women aren't allowed to take charge of the screen like the males under whom they stand.

In contrast, in female buddy films men manage to play a pivotal role and determine what the women ranking above them do throughout the picture. Like Thelma and Louise, women in female buddy pictures have no choice but to deal with a male-controlled universe. The pursuit for lying boyfriend Peter Coyote unites Shelley Long and Bette Midler in *Outrageous Fortune*. Gang rape introduces assistant district attorney Kelly McGillis to victim Jodie Foster in *The Accused*. The two sets of girlfriends in *Fried Green Tomatoes* maneuver around abusive and uncaring mates. Roommates Jennifer Jason Leigh and Bridget Fonda in *Single White Female* compete for the position of most desirable, which they cannot share and Leigh cannot win through healthy means.

For daring to shine the spotlight on two women as they try to break away from men, *Thelma & Louise* was bravely conceived. By casting two lead females who for the most part eschew men, the filmmakers took a considerable financial risk. Strong opening weekends led to impressive ticket sales, yet according to *Variety*, reporting in 1996, "The conventional wisdom is that a big name actor can buy an opening weekend"—not a big name actress unless you're Julia Roberts, who's racked up well over a six pack of $100 million domestic assaults.[5] None of the movies featuring two top-billed women listed here made that much, and doubling up on lead women generally diminishes a film's draw. Even *Stepmom*, starring Roberts along with Susan Sarandon and Ed Harris, earned only $91 million domestically. Conversely, half of the films on the male buddy list released in 1990 or after took in over $100 million (the general definition of a blockbuster). The budgets for some of the later male buddy movies named in this chapter tallied multiple times what many of the films on the women's buddy list earned in total. *Analyze This* cost $30 million (then attracted $106 million domestically during its theatrical run), while *Black Widow*, *Leaving Normal*, *Passion Fish*, *Dolores Claiborne*, *Walking and Walking*, *Romy & Michele's High School Reunion*, *Anywhere But Here* and *Tumbleweeds* all returned less. Even the duds among men's films, *Ishtar* and *Arlington Road* (domestically rounding up $14 million and $24 million respectively, in ticket sales), beat or matched the trickle of money generated by many of these films featuring females.

Released in 1969, *Midnight Cowboy*, a drama about the odd friendship formed between a young, green hustler from Texas and one of New York City's forgotten faces, accounted for $44 million in U.S. receipts. Despite drastically lower ticket prices, the Dustin Hoffman and Jon Voight drama outperformed all but five female buddy films excluding *Thelma & Louise*, *Outrageous Fortune*, *Beaches*, *Fried Green Tomatoes* and *Single White Female*. More recently, that group's total gross earnings were far outpaced by the two *Men in Black* films, which together sopped up $440 million. Made for less than $20 million back in 1991 before foreign market grosses ballooned to colossal sizes, *Thelma & Louise* chalked up a modest but respectable $47 million from its theatrical stateside take making it the least successful female buddy film compared to *Outrageous Fortune*, $53 million, *Beaches*, $57 million, *Fried Green Tomatoes*, $80 million and *Single White Female*, $49 million.

As a demanding presence and profitable venture starring two women, *Thelma & Louise* is an isolated phenomenon. That explains why three-quarters of a century after *A Room of One's Own* was written, Meryl Streep, who constitutes virtual Hollywood royalty,[6] still yearns for Virginia Woolf's vision to be realized in Hollywood and accepted by the general public. Still, *Thelma & Louise* did not make the AFI's final cut for top films of the century (although it was one of 400 films nominated[7]), and neither did any films in which Streep has played a starring role. *The Deer Hunter*, number 79 on the AFI's list, prompted Streep's first Academy Award nomination for Best Supporting Actress. In the picture, which did not provide any lead roles for women, she plays a meek girlfriend to blue collar worker Christopher Walken, who leaves the steel mill to fight in Vietnam. When Walken fails to return to the States, Streep indecisively switches allegiance to become Robert De Niro's romantic interest. Outside of relationships with men, including her abusive father, Streep's character lacks a personal identity. Streep's larger, more well-known lead roles, such as Sophie in *Sophie's Choice* (1982) and Karen Silkwood in *Silkwood* (1983), did not register on the AFI's list.

Blazing the cineplexes with palpable excitement, the release of *Thelma & Louise* presented unprecedented opportunities. The film gives female film viewers the rare chance of paying to view two average (at least at the outset), flawed but ascendant, power-seeking, vibrant female leads. Seeing *Thelma & Louise*, women may recognize some aspect of their own lives within the characters. Meanwhile, male film viewers get to know fully realized female protagonists who are not social psychotics and are not plagued by social psychotics as are the female leads in *The Hand That Rocks the Cradle*, *Basic Instinct*, and *The Silence of the Lambs*, other films from the 1991-1992 season. As blockbuster films earning over $100 million at the U.S. box office, they each sold more admissions and were seen by more people. However, none caused a commotion as big as *Thelma & Louise* did.

If you missed the contentious, unsolved mystery of *Thelma & Louise* the first time around, take a look at most any newspaper or magazine from the summer of 1991 and you can see that *Thelma & Louise* debuted as a very controversial film. Here is a diverse sampling of critical responses interested moviegoers could read at the time:

"Despite some very rough spots," *Thelma & Louise* is a "mostly comic adventure about two cute, lovable outlaws who have seen the gritty side of life but never run out of pithy things to say as they flee through the rugged

Southwest landscape that has backed thousands of Westerns."—Ted Mahar, *The Oregonian*[8]

Thelma & Louise "is just one of the current bumper crop of woman-kills-man movies, but it is clearly the most upsetting."—John Leo, *U.S. News & World Report*[9]

"From this film you might think all white guys fell into two categories: leering macho pigs-at-large and the domesticated version of that wild creature, the cretinous sports addict."—Deborah J. Funk, *The St. Paul Pioneer Press*[10]

"The men escape stereotype over and over."—David Denby, *New York*[11]

Sarandon and Davis "are triumphant in an end-of-the-road finale that may shock feminists (and others) but it is true to the mythic nature of a big-hearted movie."—Jack Kroll, *Newsweek*[12]

Thelma & Louise "is the bleak-est of adventure-comedies, and perhaps as nihilistic a view of the way-between-the-sexes as has ever appeared on screen."—William Arnold, *The Seattle Post-Intelligencer*[13]

"To my way of thinking (and not everyone will agree), the worst thing about *Thelma & Louise* is its ending."—Robert Denerstein, *The Rocky Mountain News*[14]

"The ending is enough to take your breath away."—Linda Deutsch, for the Associated Press in *The Memphis Commercial Appeal*[15]

"I really want you to see this film, because I think its execution is lovely and you'll make a tight emotional connection with the story and the characters."—Jeff Millar, *The Houston Chronicle*[16]

"The two lead characters, played by Geena Davis and Susan Sarandon, are appealing at the start but become tiresome as they move along."—Lou Cedrone, *The Baltimore Sun*[17]

"*Thelma & Louise* is a feminist buddy movie, a Hollywood rarity in which women take charge of their destiny."—Hal Lipper, *The St. Petersburg Times*[18]

Thelma & Louise "proves that Hollywood still has a long way to go before its feminist credentials can be called respectable."—David Sterritt, *The Christian Science Monitor*[19]

In the U.S., the polarity of reactions surrounding the film anticipated the political divisiveness that has since evolved into "red" and "blue" state designations. Still, the gender issues that surround *Thelma & Louise* can be confusing no matter an individual's perspective. As a society, we still have trouble discussing feminism, particularly how it plays out in every day life. Even at this point over a decade after the film's release, not every viewer would agree that *Thelma & Louise* honors positive qualities about women or that it advances women in film. Not everyone who saw the movie (especially those who saw it only once) would concede that Thelma and Louise are not deranged psychotics.

Callie Khouri's creation hit a raw nerve. One of the fantastic things about the picture is the way it exploded preconceived notions about women *and* film. Though she wasn't a contemporary of Khouri, Woolf, who was avant-garde in her own work, would have understood the flack Khouri received. The great grandmother of women in media realized that contemporary art made people feel uneasy by presenting new views instead of the old, comfortable ones.

3. The Bloody Truth about Women in Hollywood Films

Apart from all the uproar surrounding its release, *Thelma & Louise* urges viewers to face the bloody truth about women acting in Hollywood films: women are underemployed and underpaid compared to their male counterparts. Overall, they're treated like second-class citizens, and the movie-going public is largely responsible.

It's difficult to catch up to men and get ahead when you're part of the economic underclass because of prejudice. The bad news for fans of women acting in Hollywood films is that Hollywood patrons — men, women, children and teenagers — do not support films led by women as readily as they support films led by men. *Variety*, *The Hollywood Reporter* and the various industry guilds keep tabs on the bottom line and consumer trends. Movies starring men and employing more men than women make more money. Actors get more jobs, land more fulfilling roles and earn more money than actresses do because men in film sell more admissions.

Since the late 1980s, the Screen Actors Guild has monitored employment trends in Hollywood as they affect the group's membership. A 1989 study conducted by the SAG's Affirmative Action office reported that in the year of the study, SAG members were cast in a total of 9,440 feature film roles. Women were granted fewer than 30 percent of those roles (29.1 percent). Presenting the study to SAG members in their membership publication *Screen Actor*, Ms. Timothy Blake, chair of SAG's National Women's Committee, announced, "Men earn twice the total money that women do, and have consistently higher average earnings."

After the release of *Thelma & Louise*, SAG completed another casting study mid-decade. The numbers for women acting in Hollywood films

WOMEN IN AMERICA EARN ONLY 2/3 OF WHAT MEN DO.
WOMEN ARTISTS EARN ONLY 1/3 OF WHAT MEN DO.

A PUBLIC SERVICE MESSAGE FROM **GUERRILLA GIRLS** CONSCIENCE OF THE ART WORLD

Virginia Woolf's dictum that a woman artist "must have money and a room of her own" still holds true today. "Women have never gained economic equality by just working hard and being good girls," the Guerrilla Girls explain on their website (www.guerrillagirls.com). Aiming their wit at the art world, the Guerrilla Girls have been "reinventing the 'f' word" through actions and appearances since 1985. (Copyright 1985, 1995 by the Guerrilla Girls, Inc. Reprinted with permission.)

showed gains. However, this more recent data combined television and film roles, possibly making things for women in film appear as though they were improving more than the actually were. Between 1991 and 1995, women's numbers for all roles cast in films and on television jumped a tad (2 percent), from 34 percent to 36 percent, with men's hold consequently dropping by the same margin, from 66 percent to 64 percent. Furthermore, between the same span of years, the percentage of lead roles awarded to women also increased, from 36 percent to 40 percent, while lead roles for men fell from 64 percent to 60 percent domination.

Despite these gains, the mid–1990s figures for female thespians don't remain partially sunny for long. Darker clouds roll in when the numbers are analyzed along an age axis. The increase in parts granted to women over 40 as a beleaguered sub-group within the larger minority was only 1 percent (among all roles cast over 40) from 26 percent in 1991 to 27 percent in 1995.

Men over 40 endured the same minute decrease during the same five-year period, from 74 percent in 1991 to 73 percent in 1995. Culturally speaking, Richard Gere's gray hair is dignified while a woman's gray hair signifies that she is a worthless hag, which is why no women in Hollywood who want to continue working would dare age naturally. By the last year of this mid-decade study, 39 percent of all male roles cast were bestowed upon men 40 and over, while only 26 percent of all female roles cast went to the same age group of women. These numbers, which reveal an age bias in addition to a gender bias, are due to Hollywood's propensity for pairing older men and younger women, but not the reverse.[2]

By 1997 and the next SAG study, the numbers barely changed. Men still controlled two-thirds of the characters featured in television and film; 64 percent of all television and film roles went to men, while 36 percent were set aside for women. Peering deeper, however, reveals that conditions for women in film were more devastating than the numbers indicated. As the SAG report explained, the employment figures for men compared to women were "slightly closer for lead roles (61 percent v. 39 percent) and slightly worse for supporting roles (66 percent v. 34 percent)." Given the overall deplorable conditions, the fact that women landed a greater percentage of lead roles over supporting roles may sound preferable to the opposite outcome until fans of women in film recall movies like *Conspiracy Theory*, with Mel Gibson and Julia Roberts. In today's Hollywood, "lead" doesn't mean equal time for the top-billed male and female parts. In *American Beauty*, Annette Benning's role as wife, mother and real estate agent was secondary and smaller than Kevin Spacey's part as husband and father, yet disingenuously both were considered leads. This disparity between what is considered a man's lead role versus a woman's lead role isn't reflected in SAG's accounting. Though moviegoers may be inclined to shrug off and accept the lower percentage of supporting roles allotted to women, the figures for small and bit parts are especially disconcerting when you think about how many movies load up on males (especially war, crime and action films) and practically skip women.[3]

No surprise in a youth-centric culture, older actors in Hollywood get less screen time. In 1997, the percentage of all roles awarded to men 40 and over dropped a percentage point accounting for 38 percent of all men's roles. Meanwhile, the same numbers for women 40 and over happened to also dip by the same amount. Nearing the end of the twentieth century, women 40 and over received only 25 percent of all women's roles appearing on the big screen. Within that age group herself, no wonder Meryl Streep has been upset. She's too young to retire gracefully.

One of our most beloved screen performers, at least among mature viewers, Streep was voted number one among actresses in a 1999 *USA Today* poll.[4] She placed one spot ahead of Julia Roberts, "who came in a distant second," though Streep is paid less money per film because fewer people venture out to the theater to see her perform. Streep's 1999 effort, *Music of the Heart*, was a financial disappointment. In terms of domestic ticket sales, it fell far behind Roberts' two releases that year, *Runaway Bride* and *Notting Hill*. Receiving an Oscar nomination for her efforts didn't help Streep because the people who read *USA Today* and voted for her as their favorite actress declined to support *Music of the Heart* at the box office. The story of New York City violin teacher Roberta Guaspari, who brought classical music to poor kids, made just under $15 million in the U.S. and under $2 million outside of the country, while *Runaway Bride* nabbed $35 million over its opening weekend and $152 million in total domestic ticket sales. Roberts' other 1999 film, *Notting Hill*, performed somewhat worse in the U.S. but largely recouped its sales dip in the U.K., undoubtedly due to British leading guy Hugh Grant. The romantic comedy set in London grossed 116 million pounds west of the Atlantic and $30 million in the States. Comparatively, *Runaway Bride* captured only 7 million pounds across the pond, yet all together *Runaway Bride* and *Notting Hill* walloped *Music of the Heart*, which failed to break even. The disparity between what potential patrons supposedly like and what actual patrons pay to see worked against Streep's otherwise valiant effort.

On May 3, 1999, SAG issued a press release revealing its 1998 employment figures, which analyzed the breakdown of roles awarded by ethnicity as well as gender and age, but did the word get out to the public? Did your hometown news agencies cover the story?

The news was certainly striking and relevant enough. As the bulletin sent to the press said, "SAG previously released data showing that in 1998 two out of three SAG jobs went to performers under 40. However, the numbers for men and women are quite different." Two years shy of the new century, roles devoted to characters of both genders 40 and over were still on the decrease: 37 percent of all roles cast in television and film went to men 40 and over while just 24 percent the year's work was dolled out to women in the same age group. Opposing the general trend for female performers under 40 (who land a greater percentage of supposed lead roles and fewer supporting roles), the numbers for Hollywood's senior citizens (especially women) worsened when it came to lead roles. Just 21 percent of female lead roles employed women age 40 and over, while 34 percent of male lead roles were written for men age 40 and over. Contrasting reality against Hollywood, SAG pointed out that "according to the U.S. Bureau of the Census, approximately 42 percent of Americans are 40 years old or older," meaning that big budget films don't reflect the country's make up by gender or age, yet the actor's union stressed that situation was worse for women. Looking at the total figures, "merely 8 percent of all leading roles went to women 40 or older," the industry watchdog analyzed.[5]

Weekend box earnings figures are reported regularly by cable and network television, online resources and print newspapers across the country. Why aren't these hiring disparities a big story too?

The answer relates in part to the inbred nature of business relations between media entities. As of this writing, AOL/Time Warner owns CNN (Cable News Network), New Line Cinema (movie studio), Time Warner Cable (home cable service), TBS (another top cable station), HBO (yet another premium cable station) and the media hybrid *Entertainment Weekly* (television programming, magazine and website). Because New Line Cinema produced *The Lord of the Rings: The Fellowship of the Ring* (2001), in December 2001, interested Internet surfers could find a great deal of *Rings* content on the CNN website, cnn.com, including a review, a connection to the film's official website, copyrighted pictures, an explanation of *Rings* terms, a biography of author J.R.R. Tolkien and message boards devoted to discussion about the film. Simultaneously, on the *Entertainment Tonight* website, ew.com, the coverage of *Rings* was greater than the coverage of Columbia's *Ali*, which was released at the same time.

Even though some films reap gobs of money, like *The Lord of the Rings: The Fellowship of the Ring*, which grossed over $300 million in U.S. ticket sales, most releases are not blockbusters. With millions and potentially billions of dollars at stake, the pressure on artists and producers to churn out mega hits for financiers can be intense. "MGM is just a movie company," worried *The Thomas Crown Affair* director John McTiernan in 1999. "Everyone else in the field is a movie company with a television network, a major publishing house, a magazine chain, an Internet connection and all sorts of other things," he complained. Although his film turned a modest profit by Hollywood standards, tallying $69 million in domestic box office receipts, before its release McTiernan told *Variety* that the "prospect of actually trying to market a movie when you're just a little movie company is terrifying."[6]

Quite conceivably, a viewer can come home from school or work, watch cable, go online, read a magazine and never leave the realm of a single corporate entity. Consumers can choose to see a film on the weekend, such as *Lord of the Rings*, in response to advertisements and news coverage paid for and broadcasted by the entertainment conglomerate that produced the film. As a result, AOL/TimeWarner's CNN and EW find it more profitable — more profitable for New Line Cinema — to discuss weekend box office figures rather than SAG employment statistics because such coverage also provides advertising for goods produced by the conglomerate. On December 30, 2001, the lead story on the entertainment page of cnn.com celebrated, "'Rings' Lifts Hollywood to a Big Finish for 2001," encouraging viewers to see the picture. Women acting in Hollywood film could use similar alliances.

In 1998, at the dawn of the 21st century, women filled only 37 percent of all SAG jobs, no matter what size. Male thespians still cornered nearly two-thirds of the work that year, playing 63 percent of all roles created. SAG summarized that its 1998 results were "similar to the gender split recorded every year since 1992," when women captured 34 percent of all parts versus men's take of 66 percent, reflecting slight improvement (3 percent growth) over the course of the decade. The Guild again highlighted the difference between the number of lead and supporting roles given to women, but no one seemed to be listening. SAG stipulated that women continued to "fare slightly better" in lead roles, but as far as I can tell, for the most part the mainstream media didn't care to analyze what these figures meant. The SAG's 1998 report claimed that men took 60 percent of lead roles leaving women the other 40 percent. This was "the same split that was recorded last year," the union stated, rounding off its previous figures.

Since the release of *Thelma & Louise*, women in Hollywood have been making gains — but in tiny steps as if made by persons with bound feet. Depending on whether you're a glass half-empty or glass half-full person, these figures present depressing statistics or evidence of hope, as women's percentages slowly climb from a quarter, to a third, creeping up hopefully toward an equitable half of all roles cast. Women are "Half the People," as PBS put it so succinctly in its labeling of the episode focused on the women's movement in their series *People's Century*, but women don't earn half of Hollywood's starring and supporting roles.[7]

Even if they don't tell the whole story, the employment figures for women in Hollywood films don't lie. If women acting in Hollywood can't reach the employment levels and earnings figures of men acting in Hollywood films, what does that say about women trying to make it at the office or in school? The furor brought on by *Thelma & Louise* is a good indication of the powerful opposition, whether it is premeditated or not, that still hinders women's advancement.

The problems plaguing women in film stem from more than one cause. The bind they are in is not simply the result of men who are unwilling to relinquish some of their power to women. Hollywood's male actors, producers, directors, writers and cinematographers are not working in cahoots, consciously conspiring to keep women down, though many may choose to work with men and men's stories over women and women's stories. It seems that pornography and the so-called "adult market" is the only genre that desperately needs women, though only in the most superficial and degrading way. Demonstrating the impersonal quality of the sex industry, one entertainment analyst was elated because "one porn movie is like another porn movie, they're infinitely reusable." In other words, women utilized as sex objects result in a product that is "exploitable" throughout the world.[8]

The "multibillion-dollar" adult video industry, a lucrative market, according to *Variety*, released approximately 7,000 titles in 1997,[9] at an average cost between $10,000 and $25,000.[10] (Comparatively, *USA Today* reported in 1999 that the average price tag of a Hollywood movie topped $50 million, according to the Motion Picture Association of America, although two years later, *The Lord of the Rings: The Fellowship of the Ring* required $109 million to bring the fantasy to the screen.[11]) Profits of pornographic pay-per-view purveyors skyrocketed in the 1990s when brands such as Playboy TV, Hot Network and Hot Zone, which broadcast inexpensive adult programming, came into a greater number of homes through developing entertainment avenues like digital cable and satellite television.[12] As a result, interested consumers no longer have to leave their homes in order to watch consenting adults have sex, but independent video stores have discovered that renting adult titles is the only way to stay in business. According to *The Hollywood Reporter* and a representative from *Adult Video News*, "As the national video chains gobble up market share through studio-direct revenue-sharing business models that give them thousands of new releases at pennies on the dollar," mom and pop video stores "have found that their survival depends upon the highly profitable porn market. "[13] Considering widespread demand and all the many methods of access available to consumers, there's clearly a sizable, thriving market open to women in film, if they're willing to appear naked and have sex.

Concurrent with the rise of the Christian right and incessant talk about "family values," sex continues to sell. In the fall of 1992, *The St. Petersburg Times* ran an Associated Press story revealing that Penthouse videos *The Great Pet Hunt, Part 1* and *Ready to Ride* outsold top-selling Hollywood titles like MGM's *Thelma & Louise* and Disney's *Fantasia*. Playing up the story's business angle, the newspaper printed the story under the headline "Magazines Find Video Helps With Exposure." Circulation for both *Playboy* and *Penthouse* magazines was down from peak sales in the 1970s and 1980s, but video revenues for the same companies were growing.[14] In 2000, west of Florida, *The Houston Chronicle* also provided up-to-date coverage of the pornography industry, legitimizing the venture. "Playboy, Penthouse 'Bare' Down on Video" noted that *Playboy* and *Penthouse* produced 10 of the top 40 videos on *Billboard's* list of top sellers. Having fun with the provocative nature of the business, the Texas newspaper informed readers "Made-for-video features such as *Playboy Sexy Lingerie III* are rubbing naked shoulders with such Disney fare as *The Jungle Book*."[15]

Meanwhile, as people purchase pornography in the privacy of their own homes and newspapers cover the sex industry like they do other less controversial businesses, the line between pornography and "legitimate" films is eroding. In 1993, the Video Software Dealer's Association Homer Award for best adult video went to the Sharon Stone vehicle *Basic Instinct: Original Uncut Director's Version*, beating *Emmanuelle 5*, *Husbands and Lovers*, *The Lover's Guide to Sexual Ecstasy* and *Wild Orchid*.[16] Capitalizing on this success, in 1995, MGM/UA Home Video distributed 250,000 free copies of an eight-minute "teaser" for NC-17 rated *Showgirls* (from the *Basic Instinct* director-writer team of Paul Verhoeven and Joe Eszterhas) to select video retailers. Adapting the concept of packaging inexpensive plastic toys promoting a film within fast food meals sold for children, savvy marketers bypassed a free popcorn giveaway for what some might call free soft porn.[17]

The real kicker is how some executives in the adult market are diversifying their view of employable and desirable women ahead of their counterparts running major movie studios. Jim English of Playboy Television Networks shared his mindset upon becoming the network's president: "It was pretty clear from the research on hand ... that the Playmates had a limiting following from a graying, 40-plus audience." Unlike Hollywood, *Playboy* seeks every male demographic except 18 and under. Sounding like a character actress' dream come true, English explained to *The Hollywood Reporter* in 1997 his philosophy regarding women in erotic films. From the start of his tenure, English believed that attractive women "who weren't as drop-dead gorgeous as the Playmates" had a place in adult films. Since Hollywood tends to hire only the world's most thin and extraordinary looking women, the message here is that average women interested in a movie career might eschew the big screen and develop instead their ability to fake an orgasm.[18]

The consumer plays an important part in this story choosing whether or not to buy what *Playboy* or Hollywood offers for sale. As it stands now, current Hollywood patrons more often choose movie fare featuring the likes of sophomoric comedian Adam Sandler, romping around in such movies as *Big Daddy* (1999) and *The Waterboy* (1998), rather than more challenging and meaningful films like *Beloved* (1998), which was based on Nobel Prize–winner Toni Morrison's novel. Both of Sandler's efforts earned over $160 million domestically, while *Beloved* brought in under $23 million. Despite Oprah Winfrey's massive television audience and honored director Johnathan Demme's special touch, *Beloved* was a financial disaster during its theatrical run, losing as much as *Thelma & Louise* made. It's unfortunate, but popular taste runs shallow, toward a narrow band of stories about men and told by men, who are usually white and upper middle class.

In her keynote speech delivered to the SAG's first national women's conference in August of 1990 and published in the Guild's member magazine, Meryl Streep mused insightfully, "It's interesting that everybody knows who goes to the movies now, but there's not a lot of data on who is deliberately staying home."[19] According to a 2001 Gallup poll, 34 percent of adults 18 and older never go to the movies at all in a year's time. A whopping 58 percent of respondents claimed to trek to the theater only once or twice in a year, or not at all.[20] In contrast, "the average moviegoer in 1946, the peak year for movie attendance, went to the movies three times a month," according to film historian Robert Sklar.[21] Over the passing decades of the 20th century, domestic movie attendance declined dramatically as widespread interest in the product dropped and other entertainment mediums sprung up. At the start of the 1990s, Streep presented her idea of a business plan Hollywood might adopt. She surmised that if she ran a studio[22] and appetite for male-led action adventure blockbusters ever fell, indicating the need to find new avenues for revenue (unlikely as that is), she would "certainly" look for other worldwide markets, meaning women and all fans of women in film.

It is especially true in the western world that women work and earn their own money, making them viable consumers. Yet women are under-represented inside Hollywood films and behind the camera, as if they are a minority within the stateside audience when they really aren't. Studio wisdom turns on the truism that men will only see pictures led by men, but so will women, for the most part. On the whole, consumers — including women, which is particularly frustrating — shun women led films. The 2001 Gallup poll results regarding frequency of movie attendance showed that while 36 percent of male respondents stated that they never go to the movies on average in a 12 month period, only 31 percent of women admitted the same. In other words, women do leave the house and head to the cineplex, but they venture out to see men on screen (maybe because they're sick of a Julia Roberts–only diet). These figures raise the question whether there is anything playing at the cineplex starring women that mature adults, both women and men, want to see.

In her 1990 essay "When Women Were in the Movies," which was distributed to SAG members, Streep explicated another reason why women are under-represented in Hollywood films: the financing of movies by foreign pre-sales. In search of capital, producers pitch foreign exhibitors storylines and filmmaking teams in order to test the financial waters before a film is made. Pre-selling can determine whether a story will ever make it to the big screen through up-front fees paid to secure attractive product. Action-adventure films, generally the bastion of men in film, traditionally fare the best. "You don't have to understand what little English is contained in a film to know that something is exploding and enjoy the spectacle," Streep elaborated. Foreseeing the upcoming decade and beyond, she summarized, "The big scramble is now on for international money."

During the 1990s, the international market for Hollywood films exploded. In 1990, foreign markets represented $3 billion or about 38 percent of the total box office draw.[23] Actor Sylvester Stallone, who crossed the $20 million mark a close second to first place runner Jim Carey (who did so as the *Cable Guy*, which came out in 1996), forged a $60 million, three picture deal with Universal in 1995 based on his box office appeal abroad.[24] As anticipated by Streep and others, early in the decade foreign box office receipts began to outperform domestic returns. Foreign revenues surpassed domestic intake for the first time in 1993, finished a close second in 1995 and retook the lead in 1996.[25] The top money-making movie to date of this writing, *Titanic* (1997), earned an incredible $600 million domestically and three times that figure — a total of $1.8 billion — around the globe.[26] In late 1999, a *Variety* article analyzing the worldwide foreign market opened with a tease. "The formula is etched in Palm Pilots all over Hollywood: Earn at least $100 million on a pic domestically," the industry daily formulated, "and you'll do at least as much, if not more, overseas." Because the foreign market is composed of over 50 diverse markets, few films besides "breakout films" such as *The Mummy* (1999), *Notting Hill* (1999), *The Matrix* (1999) and *Shakespeare in Love* (1998) appeal to moviegoers around the globe. As a result, producers try to pick stories that will appeal to the largest global audience, who may not share much in common except the basics: a little romance, but primarily sex and violence.[27]

To look at the forces that drive ticket sales, go back to 1990 when Streep reasoned that the target audience for films seemed to be 16- to 25-year-old-males, plenty of whom derive excitement from aggression, as evidenced in the U.S. by the popularity of so-called "wrestling" among the same demographic.[28] However, as with so much in Hollywood, the term "violence," like "lead," changes when applied separately to men and women. Apparently, violent displays are only desirable when men like Stallone engineer the blasts but are otherwise troublesome and distasteful when women follow suit. Thelma and Louise blow up a trucker's 18-wheeler, causing a modest but respectable explosion as far as standard Hollywood action-adventure goes. But many people — people who might otherwise easily accept the destruction in movies by the likes of Arnold Schwarzenegger and James Cameron — complained that the blast in *Thelma & Louise* was gratuitous.

Frustrated by the proliferation of violence in movies that don't reap nearly as much press or cause such a stir (in other words, movies starring men) as *Thelma & Louise* did, Callie Khouri explained to *The Richmond Times Dispatch*, "I was putting women into an accepted genre." Exasperated, she said, "One rapist got shot, one truck got blown up and people say *Thelma & Louise* is a violent movie." Compared to *Terminator 2*, where "they go around shooting people's kneecaps off," Khouri argued, her script is pretty tame.[29] In his book *Zen and the Art of Screen Writing: Insights and Interviews*, William Froug elicits this defense from Khouri. In search of open minds, Khouri repeats the same point: "I think that *Thelma and Louise* had a kind of violence, even though I don't think of it as violence. Even blowing up the truck wasn't really violent. The way they took the driver out of the truck — they didn't kill him, they didn't shoot him in the knee."[30]

Speaking from a similar, sympathetic viewpoint in *Where the Girls Are: Growing Up Female with the Mass Media*, media commentator Susan Douglas shares her take, combining a couple of the issues that affront women in Hollywood:

> Why do Clint Eastwood, Robert Redford, Sean Connery, Richard Dreyfuss, and other men in their fifties, sixties and even seventies continue to work and get great parts while terrific actresses over the age of forty, like Sally Fields, Jessica Lange, Meryl Streep, Diane Keaton, Kathleen Turner, Susan Sarandon, and others search in vain for decent roles and have had to set up their own produc-

tion companies to ensure that they can still work? Movies in which these same aging men kill about fifty-eight people are praised as terrific thrillers while *Thelma and Louise* was denounced as virulent feminism laden with dire social consequences."[31]

Women in films can't seem to win on any front, either at the box office or within public discourse.

If Hollywood executives could make as much money producing thoughtful women-led stories, they would certainly find a way to crank them out in droves. The underlying causes preventing a solution are multifold. The men in control of movies aren't consciously involved in a nefarious conspiracy to keep half the world in its place. Neither female nor foreign moviegoers are solely to blame. American men and teenage boys don't deserve the entire rap for the lack of women in film. In community with happenstance, all members of the moviegoing public are complicit.

Young males and the young women who may want to appease them don't explain the comparatively low number of women in film, although youth does rule the movie marketplace. According to the same 2001 Gallup poll cited earlier, only 14 percent of respondents age 18 to 29 reportedly avoided movies altogether. Compared to a larger group of adults age 18 and older who were also polled, the younger set's average rate of refraining was 20 percentage points lower, supporting the picture of youth-driven domestic market. Over half of the respondents who took part and reported that they ignore movie theaters were age 50 and over. In contrast, as the story went at the time, teenage girls were enthralled with Leonardo DiCaprio in *Titanic*. However, I suggest that they were equally enthralled with Kate Winslet and the love story at the center, though DiCaprio received more press and greater credit for selling the film. Whether they desired or lived vicariously through either of the characters, teenage girls were responsible for the blockbuster's enormous national success through their revenue-increasing repeat business.[32]

This discussion doesn't end with a possible Hollywood's men's club, cultural preference for stories led by men (globally, the most common denominator) or the U.S. preoccupation with youth. Producer Robert Evans is associated with a famous analogy between movies and parachutes: "If it doesn't open, you're dead."[33] Opening weekend is crucial to Hollywood success. Waiting and later renting the interesting women-led films that come out on video doesn't carry much weight with Hollywood executives and Wall Street financiers. To keep their pictures running in a competitive marketplace, studios look for instant hits to dominate and control the cineplexes, which milk higher ticket prices compared to home rentals.

Over opening weekend 1999, more people left home to see Oliver Stone's *Any Given Sunday*, a film about football with a supporting part for Cameron Diaz, and skipped or saved for later actress/producer Winona Ryder's *Girl, Interrupted*, about young women, including Ryder and Angelina Jolie, passing the late 1960s in a mental hospital. *Any Given Sunday* scored over $75 million at the box office domestically, while *Girl, Interrupted* finished a distant second, grossing under $25 million. While neither film made noteworthy millions outside of the U.S., *Any Given Sunday* opened on over two thousand screens, roaring to the tune of some $13 million during its first stateside weekend. Debuting with far lower expectations and appearing on only nine screens, within the same time frame *Girl, Interrupted* collected a meager $100,000. When the nuances of character compete against the warlike game of football, it's easy to predict who will win the largest audience. As with any picture, word of mouth may have helped better sell the women-led film, but its limited release, as well as its loony-bin story content, greatly undercut that possibility.

As the Gallup Organization contends, women do show up at theaters on opening weekend — largely to see big-budget productions starring men, more than smaller films marketed to females. Whether women obediently and selflessly follow their boyfriends and husbands to male-led action adventure flicks or charge to the theater to see these same stories with true delight on their own makes no difference to those reaping the profits. As Susan Douglas puts it, speaking as a female audience member, "We are tired of blockbuster movies that glorify beefy, rippled men who speak monosyllabically and carry extremely well-endowed sticks." However, she admitted, "we go to them anyway, nursing our fury and enjoying catharsis."[34] Meanwhile, no matter what gender, nationality or age, a majority of audience members are content to watch women trail male stars.

Over two thousand years ago, Aristotle concluded that action best revealed character. The validity of his notion is reflected in the saying "actions speak louder than words." This seems to explain why moviegoers the world over prefer male-led action films to female-led psychological dramas like NASCAR events outpace Broadway ticket sales. Advancement or not, but thanks in part to *Thelma & Louise*, today women occasionally star in action-adventure thrillers, too. Angelina Jolie brought video game action heroine Lara Croft to life in *Lara Croft: Tomb Raider* (2001), which sauntered across the big screen to the tune of $131 million in ticket sales in the U.S. in the wake of *Charlie's Angels* (2000), a remake of a television show which lured in $125 million. However, because *Lara Croft* cost $80 million to produce and *Charlie's Angels* was billed for $92 million, these big-budget female-led films made less domestically than their gross earnings might suggest. Comparatively, the budget for *Thelma & Louise* leveled out at approximately $17 million. After bringing in around $47 million at domestic box offices, Khouri's first screenplay netted about $30 million in the U.S., for a total not much less than *Charlie's Angels*. However, foreign box offices made a huge difference between the 1991 release and the two pictures that followed a decade later. While imdb.com and variety.com more readily supply foreign figures for films made in the latter part of the 1990s, apparently *Thelma & Louise* drew a modest international audience, attracting six million British pounds, according to *Variety*. Providing much grander financial rewards, *Charlie's Angels* and *Lara Croft* triumphed outside of the U.S. The Drew Barrymore, Cameron Diaz and Lucy Liu outing ensnared over $264 million worldwide but *Lara Croft* did even better, reaping over $274 million the globe over.

In the relatively new genre of women's action films, women are more visible, but still, in too many movies, women matter less than men. If they're lucky enough to make the main course, actresses serve as side dishes. A familiar face to moviegoers, Rene Russo played girlfriend, wife or female sidekick to a host of males in a string of male-led movies throughout two-thirds of the 1990s. In the 40 and over column along with her male co-stars, Russo was billed second best or less to Pierce Brosnan in *The Thomas Crown Affair* (1999), Mel Gibson, Danny Glover and Joe Pesci in *Lethal Weapon 3* and *4* (1992 and 1998), Mel Gibson again in *Ransom* (1996), Kevin Costner in *Tin Cup* (1996), John Travolta and Gene Hackman in *Get Shorty* (1995), Dustin Hoffman in *Outbreak* (1995), and Clint Eastwood and John Malkovich in *In the Line of Fire* (1993). The one movie Russo was allowed to carry, *Buddy* (1997), directed and co-written by Caroline Thompson and aimed at families, concerned the real-life story of an eccentric socialite who raised wild animals (including the film's namesake gorilla) inside her mansion home. Lacking media attention, a big budget and some say a decent script, the effort failed to ignite the public interest and grossed only $10 million at the box office.

Occasionally, a film starring women does break the blockbuster threshold. The 1997 Women in Film Crystal Awards honored Diane Keaton, Bette Midler and Goldie Hawn for the $100 million-plus box office success of *The First Wives Club* (1996). At the event, Joe Roth, representing Walt Disney Studios, sought to placate attendees. Roth commented from "the movie side, the war is over." He claimed the phrase "Should we have a woman do this picture?" is "completely out" of his vocabulary. The inequitable situation for women in Hollywood is not personal, he insinuated. Instead, Roth spoke plainly: "It's totally about selling tickets, not about gender."[35]

To improve the status of women in film, concerned audiences around the world must turn the tide of studio production, as Meryl Streep charged over a decade ago, by how and where we spend our hard-earned money. "If it's not in the financial interest of the studios to change the status quo, then I don't have much hope it will change," she concluded sadly. The power to demand equality for women in film lies in the hands of the consumers. Want to better support women in films? Vote at the box office. Applying Virginia Woolf's theory to the world of motion pictures, because Hollywood is a business, the problems of women acting in film boil down to economics.

More so than any other actor that I've run across, throughout the nineties, Streep consistently went on record and spoke frankly about poor working conditions for women in Hollywood. At the 1997 WIF event, however, when speaking to colleagues inside the industry, she encouraged the crowd:

> It's up to us. Our job is to put our heads down, hold our hands out, and work like mad for all our girls, to put their stories and dreams, where they're important, on-screen. To dispel the myth that it's a good fantasy for a girl to want to grow up, stop eating, and at twenty-five marry a sixty year-old and have a fabulous ten years escorting him into his dotage. That's a time-honored fantasy for him; WHAT'S HERS? It's up to us. We will paint the landscape of their dreams and aspirations. We will light them as well.[36]

Sounds great, but the effort to build the audience for films starring women must come from monumental forces even more pervasive than Hollywood. In order for women in films to prosper, people the world over must enlarge their idea of what women can do. Society must learn to appreciate the full array of women's lives more readily and with greater enthusiasm.

Even before *Charlie's Angels* and *Lara Croft: Tomb Raider*, and due to interest in producing a higher quality and quantity of roles for women in film, a few filmmakers turned to the novels of Charlotte Brontë (*Jane Eyre*, 1996) and Jane Austen (*Sense and Sensibility*, 1995, *Emma*, 1996, *Mansfield Park*, 1999). When producers in the middle to late 1990s wanted to attract a female audience, they sought the female writers Virginia Woolf had first noticed publishing fiction. This urge to tell reality-based stories about women and also written by women represented a more substantive reaction to *Thelma & Louise* than making a little room for women wearing tight, sexy clothes within the superficial action-adventure genre. *Thelma & Louise* marked a new start for women acting in Hollywood films. The most meaningful places to go for material were naturally the first stories told about women in their own words. However, these films based on the work of female English novelists failed to make much money. *Sense & Sensibility* did the best, collecting $42 million at U.S. box offices, but, added together, *Jane Eyre*, *Emma* and *Mansfield Park* didn't draw $50 million.

In 2002, Nicole Kidman, Julianne Moore and Meryl Streep starred in *The Hours*, based on Michael Cunningham's novel of the same name. Cunningham's ambitious and complicated manuscript, which deals with the lives of three women across three separate time periods, depends on Virginia Woolf's 1923 novel *Mrs. Dalloway*. In the film version of *The Hours*, Kidman plays Woolf as she writes her novel, Moore plays a woman reading the novel in the 1950s and Streep plays a modern woman who evokes Woolf's title character. Despite the film's impressive gathering of female talent, and Kidman's Oscar-winning performance, *The Hours* was one of those pictures that reaped more talk and kudos than cash; it rang up under $42 million in ticket sales in the U.S. and about $15 million outside of the States. An even worse showing of *Mrs. Dalloway* was in 1997, when Vanessa Redgrave starred as Woolf's title character in a film adaptation of the novel. Though the picture was well received by critics such as Roger Ebert of *The Chicago Sun Times* and Kevin Thomas of *The Los Angeles Times*, the women-led picture bombed at the box office, earning less than $4 million in the U.S.

Despite successes earned by the various waves of feminism, in the biggest Hollywood films too often women are pushed to the side. Behind the scenes, women don't appear often on the front-line. On screen, mostly they're held to unattainable standards of beauty or reduced to sex object as a primary vocation, with any actual job coming second, and by now this type of treatment constitutes a very tired story.

Moviegoers are so unused to seeing women's lives on screen that they sometimes don't know how to handle themselves when they do. In *Thelma & Louise*, Harlan bloodies Thelma's face as he beats and tries to rape her in the Silver Bullet parking lot; at the end of the controversial film, the women decline to die on screen but nevertheless drive off a cliff. Thanks to their filmmakers, the title characters never hit bottom, sparing viewers the sight of any blood. Ironically, precious little attention from the onslaught of talk surrounding the picture concentrated on sexual violence, yet people couldn't argue enough about the antiseptic ending.

To improve and better balance future SAG employment figures, audiences need to reevaluate their movie-going habits, keeping the bloody truth about women in Hollywood films in mind. Meanwhile, Hollywood might review its moviemaking practices.

4. The Remarkable Thelma and Louise

Thelma & Louise: buddy film, road movie, crime spree flick, comedy-drama, set in the west. Up until the film's release, Hollywood women had never before led a film that covered such an array of genres.

The story: Two friends from Arkansas set out on a weekend getaway to the mountains. Intending to teach their men back home a lesson, Thelma doesn't ask permission from her controlling husband, and Louise leaves without informing her musician boyfriend. Friday night, a quick drink at a honky-tonk called the Silver Bullet alters their original plan. The women can no longer enjoy their short vacation at a borrowed cabin with vague thoughts of fishing after a lousy suitor from the bar attempts to rape Thelma in the parking lot. To make matters much worse, Louise interrupts and shoots him dead — not because he doesn't stop attacking Thelma (who sobers up too late), but because he caps off his physical assault with a verbal blow: "I should have gone ahead and fucked her." Harlan's scorn provokes a deep vein of angry rage, as Louise can't believe what she hears. Because of her violent outburst, viewers are led to believe that Louise has been raped in the past.

Suddenly in serious trouble, the women do not turn to the police because they fear the stigma surrounding rape and the added trauma rape survivors must contend with in court. Plus, Louise has just killed a man so they return to the open road and choose to become fugitives instead. Given the desperate circumstances, the women's cumulative decision is reaffirmed in the end as their best option.

In transit to an uncertain future, two ordinary women become best friends and learn a great deal about themselves with the dubious help of gender-inspired roadblocks. Instead of facing a judge and jail time, Thelma and Louise set out for the legendary freedom of Mexico but do not make it.

The film forewarns viewers of a dire ending from the very start. *Thelma & Louise* opens with the camera pointed at a rugged mountain, which is set deeply to appear both foreboding and entrancing. Viewers are pulled toward the summit by a road headed straight up the middle. The same shot reappears twice: it marks the close of the film's third act where it stands as a bridge to the film's finale, and it appears within the final police chase but in this instance with an added element. Reinforcing the women's imminent doom, a police car drives toward the camera as if released from the forces of the mountain. The primary placement and repetition of the image tells viewers that *Thelma & Louise* is not about the protagonists' victory flight across the border. *Thelma & Louise* is about what happens on the road, not about reaching the women's dream destination.

The problem: Crime begets more crime muddling issues and viewpoints. In reaction to a thick tangle of circumstances, many questions arise. Which crime began their doom? Harlan's near-rape of Thelma or Louise's murderous revenge? Was Louise's mysterious past in Texas to blame for her reaction? Was Thelma to blame for dancing and drinking with Harlan prior to his attack? Did Harlan get what he deserved? Is society at all to blame for a man's aggression or a woman's victimhood? Does the film treat men fairly? Is the film's portrayal of women positive or negative? Does *Thelma & Louise* advance gender discussions or confuse them?

The audience: Viewers rightly felt pressured as they watched *Thelma & Louise*. In choosing to pay the price of admission, we were simultaneously assigned the job of figuring out who was responsible for what. We were asked to sit in judgment and draw conclusions. Unlike most major Hollywood movies, *Thelma & Louise* forced viewers to take an active role. Some audience members, perhaps accustomed to more passive viewing, found interaction with rape and retribution distressing. Others got into the film's more positive energy about breaking loose of the ties that bind.

The title characters: Thelma Dickerson has been married to domineering, immature Darryl since she was a teenager. She enters the film's escapades lacking experience and with no sense of self-worth. Floundering in a void with no career, no children and no respect or loving regard from her husband, ironically, Thelma's foremost asset is her charming fecklessness. Once Darryl, a carpet salesman, leaves for work Friday morning (not to return home for dinner anyway, as it turns out), her biggest worry switches from asking his permission — which she avoids — to packing for the weekend trip. Rather than sensible clothes like thick socks and a warm jacket, Thelma wants to bring whatever supplies will ward off "pyscho killers." On the lookout for a protector, when Louise arrives in her 1966 green Thunderbird convertible, a big smile of relief crosses Thelma's face.

Louise Sawyer is unmarried and lives by herself. Compared to Thelma, who's never been on her own, Louise is streetwise, fiercely independent and

Laugh Lines: If you, like many women, are in a profession that demands smiles and unwavering sweetness — human resources, food service, or retail, for example — you may be making other people's days better at the expense of your own. According to Dr. Alicia A. Grandey at Pennsylvania State University, "emotional labor" that requires you to make nice on the job causes major stress. And that leads to absenteeism, decreased productivity, fatigue, burnout, and physical ailments. "The physiological bottling up of emotions taxes the body overworking the cardiovascular and nervous systems and weakening the immune system," says Grandey.— Jennifer Block (Jennifer Block's caption reprinted by permission of *Ms.* magazine, photograph ©2000 Hulton Archive/Getty Images.)

In Woody Allen's *Deconstructing Harry* (1997), the title character (played by Allen) asks a prostitute whom he's hired, "Don't you ever get depressed? Doesn't your work ever get you down?" She replies, "It beats the hell out of waitressing." Woody's Harry muses, "You know, it's funny. Every hooker that I ever speak to tells me it's beats the hell out of waitressing." Incredulous, he guesses, "It's got to be the worst fucking job in the world."

The realities of prostitution aside, this author agrees that waitressing is far too hard on the feet and hell on the nerves. My last waitressing job found me serving surf and turf in a tony suburb outside of Boston. Repeatedly asking "Baked potato, french fries, rice pilaf or coleslaw?" often to every single person at each table drove me mad. Apart from Louise's rape experience in Texas, waiting on tables alone is enough to make a person want to kill. "Laugh Lines" appeared in the June/July 2000 issue of *Ms.*

more tightly wound. Louise serves her friend as a mother figure, sister and mentor, but she's an imperfect role model. Laboring in the lower class as a waitress, she carries fatal emotional baggage from something in her past she keeps secret, something very similar to Thelma and Louise's present day circumstances of rape and gun-toting revenge. Although it's not clear how long they've known each other, Louise's preoccupation and reserve strain the friendship between the two women. Louise is further isolated by her boyfriend Jimmy being out of town when the women depart. A musician who goes out on the road performing at Ramada Inns, Jimmy is unavailable for Louise, physically and emotionally, making him a fair match for her standoffish nature.

The bittersweet payoff: Because the women stick to their outlandish plan until their demise, they earn their adventures. In other words, they get what's coming to them. Even better, they realize a greater understanding of themselves. Perhaps most important to women in film and everywhere else, Thelma and Louise find solidarity in their strengthening friendship.

And then they die.

But, first, each woman experiences growth particular to her character. Thelma gains some grit and Louise loosens up, but greater maturity only arrives after learning hard lessons brought on by the other's influence.

To erase the memories of both Darryl and Harlan, Thelma finally "lets her hair down" and "gets laid properly." Meanwhile, when Louise asks for his assistance, Jimmy finally pulls through. Without knowing why he's been asked to do so, he delivers Louise's life savings, $6,700, which she is fully prepared to share with Thelma. Louise's hard work tallies an impressive sum considering the way she's earned it: waiting on tables presumably her entire adult life. Unfortunately, on Thelma's watch, her hitchhiker lover J.D. steals the money, leaving the women with nothing.

A tremendous blow, J.D.'s thievery eradicates Louise's last shred of steely self-confidence. Curled on the floor in a fetal position, she's forced to open up and co-captain the trip. When Louise hits this emotional rock bottom, Thelma's promotion becomes necessary but also welcome. As any optimist will attest, some good does come out of any setback. Louise's weakened state provides Thelma with the opportunity to exercise her own decisive power for the first time. Thelma embraces her new role in earnest, bearing the criminal imprint she acquires during her risky interlude with J.D. Although her modus operandi is suspect, Thelma flowers as a hold-up artist.

Sharing command compels Louise to relax her close-clutched privacy, yet she never completely releases her tight grip. Because she focuses more closely on all the trouble they encounter, Louise doesn't have as much fun on their "vacation" as Thelma, who enjoys her new sense of freedom, no matter the cost. By nature, Louise is more serious though she does face her grief and lighten her load during a brief moment when she stands still and alone. As a result of Thelma's partnership, Louise realizes that strength and independence are not necessarily synonymous with loneliness and isolation.

Although the women become close and exchange traits, they retain their individuality. Louise looks internally for forgiveness and freedom while Thelma displays liberation in her expression and carriage. Louise confronts her murderous misdeed privately in the nighttime desert, while Thelma ranges out in broad daylight with renewed vigor and purpose.

Even though they both make huge mistakes, time after time the women choose staying together over separation or killing each other. Thelma and Louise learn to trust and love another woman's friendship, which should be considered for the revolutionary depiction it is. Film critic Molly Haskell, in her ground-breaking work *From Reverence to Rape: The Treatment of Women in the Movies* (first published in 1973), asks

> Where, oh where, is the camaraderie, the much-vaunted mutual support among women? It was there, without advertising itself, in the twenties: among Griffith's women, with Clara Bow and her college pals; in the thirties, among the gold diggers, with Kay Francis and Aline MacMahon and Eve Arden, and in the advice and support of older women like Binnie Banes and Billie Burke; in the forties, with Bette Davis and her female co-stars; even in the fifties, with Marilyn Monroe and her millionaire-hunting friends. But where, in the movies and out, are their modern equivalents?[1]

Virginia Woolf and Molly Haskell uncovered the same need. Even though they made their comments nearly 50 years apart, both writers lamented the lack of positive depictions of women as individuals as well as companions. Spanning the first wave of feminism, just after women earned the right to vote, to the second wave, when women won equal pay and equal access to employment (at least on paper), their words unite the aims of women in fiction and in film. This unity is crucial, for when Hollywood keeps women apart in the movies, the message sent encourages society to separate women in real life, too. Addressing this historic dearth of female solidarity is what makes *Thelma & Louise* a landmark feminist film. Thelma and Louise's adventures are carried out in relation to many supporting males and a few bit females but in varied terms, and in many expressions, not only sexual or competitive in nature.

The men in the film: Most of the men in *Thelma & Louise* inhabit positions of authority; take, for instance, the numerous male police officers and FBI agents on the duo's trail. Reflecting their counterparts in the real world, some of the men in *Thelma & Louise* wield themselves as if their own freedom is more privileged and more important than a woman's. Darryl Dickerson commands Thelma as if he is his wife's keeper. Harlan Puckett, the worst behaved of the bunch as the would-be rapist, abuses his own independence by criminally intruding on Thelma's.

Importantly, however, the male characters in *Thelma & Louise* aren't completely unsympathetic. Louise's co-worker offers use of his cabin though he doesn't clearly appear in the film. The police officer on their trail, Detective Hal Slocumbe from the Arkansas State Police, enforces the law with a caring attitude. He shows genuine concern for the women's well-being. The highway robber, J.D., who steals Thelma's heart for the night, respectfully shares his charms before he rips the women off. Louise's boyfriend Jimmy isn't a bad person; he's simply an unchallenging and unfulfilling match. Even the truck-driving slob who falls prey to the women's last criminal act isn't all rotten, though he practices out-dated machismo. While he emanates excessive rudeness with his cat calls and suggestively wagging tongue, the trucker is at least thoughtful enough to pack prophylactics. Although he doesn't help the stranded New Mexican police officer (who, like Slocumbe, was just doing his job), the briefly seen biking Rastafarian exudes serenity as he flaunts his marijuana stash.

Seen collectively, the men in *Thelma & Louise* aren't all good, bad or thoroughly stereotypical. They flirt with Thelma and Louise and loan them a cottage, but they also belittle the women and take them for granted. They pursue Thelma and Louise in a variety of ways: violently, passively, passionately, desperately and professionally. They attempt to rape Thelma *and* to understand the duo's motivation. The men try to help the women. They propose to, bed, rip-off, hunt, stand before in awe, pull over and insult Thelma and Louise; in one scene, they are called "bitches from hell." The men attempt to save, feel compassion for and finally threaten to shoot the two fugitives if the women refuse to give up.

The women: Thelma and Louise respond to the men by grabbing the weekend cabin offer and taking off. At the start, the two acquaintances aim to shrewdly manipulate Darryl and Jimmy by suddenly disappearing, but the women can't control the full flow of events that follow. Inside the Silver Bullet, Thelma and Louise play the game and hide behind their looks. They socialize, stand tall and dance, one with drunken abandon, the other with her "jaded" wits ready. Thelma takes a courageous first step away from Darryl's dominance, then walks right into another predator's arms. Because of his rude remarks and unwanted advances toward her, Louise kills him and then throws up, but she's not angry with all men. Once they are on the lam, the women offer thanks to males who approach them politely, particularly the ones who show respect and good timing. Only when men cross the line of acceptable behavior do Thelma and Louise courteously entomb and vengefully humiliate their foes, in part by disabling the men's vehicles. They even invite in, exchange bodily fluids and trade goods with the opposite sex. When appropriate, the picture's title pair curtly hang-up, refuse gently, extend trust and say goodbye.

Together, Thelma and Louise chat, plan, argue, sing, laugh, discuss and dream. Each curses in anger, cries in anguish and swears with renewed determination, upset by Harlan, Darryl, J.D. and themselves. When they do part ways one evening, Thelma finally experiences an orgasm but loses their getaway fund and resorts to armed robbery to make up for the loss. Meanwhile, Louise kisses Jimmy good-bye, not wanting to entangle him in her problems.

The women run from their pasts, their crimes and the authorities chasing them. They find new selves and remain true to those selves even when the going gets tough, even though they've made irreparable judgement errors. They doubt their decisions and turn towards one another for reassurance, comfort, love and joy. They travel and do most everything together. Side by side they resist capture forcefully, pursue revenge aggressively and finally choose to commit suicide rather than face imprisonment.

As we've seen, and will see, the list of actions and relations between the sexes in *Thelma & Louise* is multitudinous with good and bad qualities represented on both sides of the gender fence. The film's roles for both men and women are more detailed and complex than most Hollywood films, even a popular, Oscar-winning production like *The Silence of the Lambs*. Released in the same year as *Thelma & Louise*, *The Silence of the Lambs* was considered to be an outright pro-women film by many because of Clarice Starling's unusual position as an FBI agent who emerges triumphant in her battle against a horrifying male adversary. While trying to do her job, Clarice Starling encounters battles within the FBI that occur because she's a woman working in a traditionally male reserve. Ironically, the picture's antagonist, the cannibal Hannibal Lector, best understands her difficulties. Still phenomenal actors, Jodie Foster and Anthony Hopkins were not extended the opportunity to address as many gender barriers. Upon its release *The Silence of the Lambs* did not stir debate about feminism the way *Thelma & Louise* did with its issues of gender, class, power, rebellion, rape and other acts of violence all converging.[2]

The controversial ending: Thelma wants so badly to exercise her newfound powerful self—free from the chase, her husband and her old way of life, when she allowed herself to be controlled by others—so she increasingly chooses fantasy over fact. She daydreams of reaching Mexico and working at Club Med. Once she starts living in the moment, she's more comfortable as an outlaw and much happier with surface appearances. She does, however, operate on more than one level. Thelma learns to approach life with her eyes open and her mind ready. When necessary, she digs down and gathers strength from within.

Louise is more complicated. Instead of celebrating her new outlaw existence like Thelma does, Louise experiences a private epiphany during which she faces up to her past and reconciles her wrong turns. On the last night of her life, when she and Thelma stop and stare at the stars, Louise confronts the fact that they won't reach Mexico. Because murder is inexcusable as well as irreversible, the women face an ominous future instead of freedom. After this realization Louise is scared, but facing facts gives her a sense of relief amid impeding doom. She increasingly doubts the duo's chances for survival, but outwardly she keeps the faith, at least for her partner's sake.

After a dramatic chase, the authorities finally catch up with the women. When Thelma robs a liquor store, her performance mocking J.D. is caught on tape. Further on down the road, an unfortunate police officer pulls them over, but they are too busy and too pressed for time to deal with him properly. They lock him in the trunk of his own squad car, although the women otherwise handle him respectfully. In a last act of revenge, Thelma and Louise blow up the rig of a disrespectful trucker.

Surrounded by a herd of authorities pointing firearms, in their final moments the women wait and weigh their alternatives as they sit inside Louise's convertible, which is perched on the rim of what passes as the Grand Canyon. Her defenses down and so truly scared, Louise is reduced to desperate determination. She cocks a firearm and says she'll keep fighting, but Thelma looks into the canyon with a knowing look and a mitigating smile, intimating that perhaps she isn't as dumb as she acted. She suggests with a nod and unprecedented wisdom (or what some might prefer to call delusion) that they "just keep going." Following Thelma's lead, Louise puts the pedal to the metal and aims for the edge of the cliff. Tanned, wind-blown and covered in dust, together the women face death with jittery smiles and tears in their eyes. A hug and a kiss for one another constitute their parting act. Thelma and Louise jump together first as friends and secondly as companion fugitives going down with the ship.

Finally, in the film's last shot the title characters are frozen in flight to forever float above their final demise. Through the magic of film, they're saved from crashing by the hopes and wires of their creators. In an attempt for Thelma and Louise to become mythical or angelic, the creators spare viewers the sight of what would have been the duo's true bloody finale because the Thunderbird never lands. Test audiences voted thumbs down to the original ending available on DVD, in which the women miraculously drive away after an unbelievably lucky nosedive. Instead, in the version released theatrically to audiences around the world, the filmmakers leave Thelma and Louise hanging in mid-air and close the film by replaying a series of soft-focus flashbacks featuring smiling and triumphant depictions, borrowed from earlier in their adventure, of Thelma and Louise alive. Most annoyingly, a chorus of angels hums in the background until the soundtrack's most syrupy song replays.

The problem with the ending is not so much the women's implied joint suicide. Death does fit the plotline and follows in the tradition of *Bonnie and Clyde*, *Butch Cassidy and the Sundance Kid* and *The Sugarland Express*. Rather, the film language employed to illustrate the close of Thelma and Louise's story is objectionable. The problem isn't what happens but what's shown.

"Thelma & Louise Live" bumper stickers can be found on vehicles across the nation. Bumper sticker available through the National Organization for Women's website (now.org).

After all their troubles and adventures, the women die, while the softer ending emphasizes the lighter moments they shared while they are alive. When the camera closes in on a smiling, carefree snapshot the women took of themselves at the beginning of their adventure, visually Thelma and Louise are reduced to approximations no more substantial than porcelain dolls. Diehard fans want them to become more than sentimental relics, attic storage or memorabilia. After all the women have been through they deserve better treatment.

Thelma and Louise's contribution to women in film is that they are ordinary, flawed characters who die as they lived on screen, as antiheroines, not perfect little angels. If the filmmakers had depicted the ending of Thelma and Louise's lives as the painful reality it truly would have been, a serious and sad event, audiences may have left the theater in a more reflective mood and in a better position to digest the film. Death urges people to look at the deceased's contribution to the world. A grittier denouement might have helped viewers focus more on the women's lives, friendship and growth rather than the film's violence. Thelma and Louise achieve limited heroism by dying for what they believed in — their newfound selves — but the lightweight ending distracts viewers from that conclusion. Since the filmmakers avoid a more graphic conclusion, cinematically Thelma and Louise never really die. Hence the bumper sticker "Thelma and Louise Live."

Despite the film's objectionable ending, Thelma and Louise become martyrs on behalf of women in film. They symbolize human possibility as well as Hollywood's shortcomings. Contrary to some of the critical responses aimed at *Thelma & Louise*, of course it's okay to tell stories about women who try too late, screw up and die in the end, especially when the story emits so much meaning and points to a better way for the future.

PART II. PUBLIC RECEPTION

5. The Great Debate

For a film starring two top-billed actresses, *Thelma & Louise* wasn't the biggest box office hit in the summer of 1991, according to *The Roanoke Times*, "but it was, hands down, the most talked about," due to the question of feminism surrounding the film.[1]

There are certain topics that people do not discuss easily or calmly. Over 30 years since civil rights legislation was first used to advance legal and cultural equality between genders, feminism is still the f word society stumbles around. Since the second wave of the feminist movement in the 1970s, changes in law and society have not necessarily signaled changes in people's attitudes. The split between what businesses can do legally and what managers may think in private exemplifies the nature of backlashes against the movement. In order to rouse the general public and affect further progress, particularly in outlooks, communication is needed. *Thelma & Louise* provided people in the early 1990s with an opportunity to talk and even urged action, but with all the bluntness of a hammer hitting a nerve.

The upside of a surprise blow is that it works to gain attention. Awarding the film tremendous presence and power, a syndicated Knight-Ridder newspaper article from August 1991 credited *Thelma & Louise* with the rebirth of feminism. The piece appeared in publications such as *The Houston Chronicle* and *The Times-Union* of Albany, New York. Running under the headlines "New Era Begins in Fight Against Sexism at Work" and "Psychologist Sees Women Waking Up to Sexism," Michalene Busico's story began with the film: "First it was Thelma and Louise battling sexism across the southwest. Then it was Dr. Frances Conley blowing the whistle on harassment at Stanford University Medical School." Referring to relentless media prater questioning the status of feminism, Busico asked if anyone still thought the feminist movement was dead. In her view, *Thelma & Louise* was a Rorschach test initiating a renewed conversation about the cliched "battle of the sexes."

According to Busico, feminists saw the film as the launch of a new era. Busico also connected *Thelma & Louise* with women's second place status in

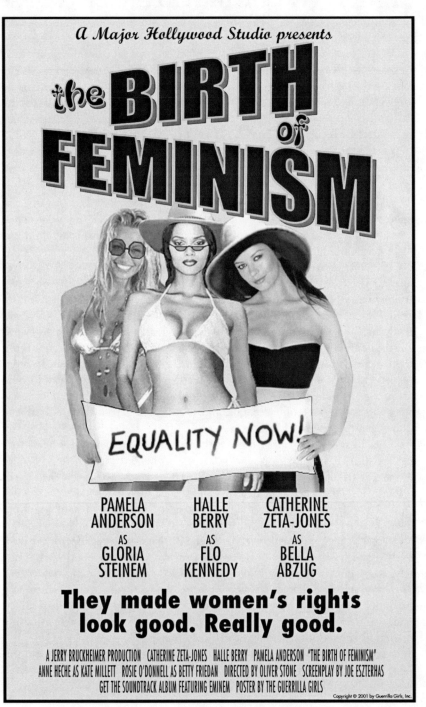

the workplace and interviewed everyday women who felt discriminated against because of their gender, including a Stanford graduate who worked in the San Francisco mayor's office, a Harvard graduate who solicited donations for non-profit groups and a hospital social worker. Citing 1990 Department of Labor statistics, Busico reported that women accounted for a paltry 3 percent of top managers, an encouraging 39 percent of executives and administrators, and an overwhelming 84 percent of information and service jobs, including waitress positions like Louise's.[2]

Well after the film was released and the 1990s ended, Thelma and Louise remained on people's minds as feminist icons. To coincide with the Feminist Expo 2000 held in Baltimore, *The Baltimore Sun* offered readers a time line. Highlighting "notable stops on the ride to equality," the journey began with the 1848 women's rights convention in Seneca Falls, New York, which initiated the arduous fight for women's suffrage. In "Milestones on the March to Equality," Tamara Ikenberg and Andrea Diconi commemorated the year 1991 with two items: Susan Faludi's *Backlash* and *Thelma & Louise*, summarized as a "much-discussed" film about two "fiercely" independent women. The film took its place among such remarkable advances as the first woman to win the Nobel Prize (Marie Curie, 1903), the first black woman to write a play to be performed on Broadway (Lorraine Hansberry, "A Raisin in the Sun," 1959) and the first woman to be appointed to the Supreme Court (Sandra Day O'Connor, 1981).[3]

A connection between *Thelma & Louise* and feminism appeared in newspapers all around the country. Back in May 1992, under the headline "U.S. Depends on Its Stars to Spark Debate," *The Salt Lake Tribune*, with help from Knight-Ridder News Service, credited media products with the power to initiate national discussions. One year after the film's release in theaters, the wire service release contended that television and movies provide material for debate. For examples, a Knight-Ridder article turned to Archie Bunker "provoking arguments about bigotry" and *Thelma & Louise* "sparking talk about feminism."[4]

In February 1992, to the southeast of Salt Lake City, *The Austin American-Statesman* told a murkier but related story, one a bit cooler to feminism. In "Magazines Explore Effects of Recent Events on Feminism: Mainstream May Not Relate to Movement," Michael MacCambridge recalled the hot topics of the early 1990s: Anita Hill, *Thelma & Louise*, Patricia Bowman and Desiree Washington. The film was grouped with the law professor who

Opposite: Among all the true stories Hollywood has adapted for the screen, one glaring omission stands out. Despite the fact that America loves stories about underdogs and women represent the largest minority in the world, screenplays about the first and second waves of feminism in the United States have never made it to the big screen. This 2001 Guerrilla Girls' poster mocks the usual Hollywood treatment of women's lives and contemplates the possibilities. (Copyright 2001 by the Guerrilla Girls, Inc. Reprinted with permission.)

challenged Supreme Court nominee Clarence Thomas on grounds of sexual harassment and two women who gained the media spotlight due to their claims of rape by high-profile figures. MacCambridge alleged that ever since the women's notoriety, magazines had been "clogged" with articles about sexual harassment and queries about the long-term effect of these "resonant public events" on feminism.

Though *Thelma & Louise* was more than a movie to MacCambridge, politically he sided more with *Time*'s sensational 1998 cover piece on the purported death of feminism than the pro-feminist National Organization for Women. MacCambridge predicted the movement's slim chance of gaining momentum as a result of cultural shake-ups. He warned that despite the era's "deep-seated and widespread female frustration," feminism's supposed marginalization and purported lack of appeal for housewives, mothers and professionals might retard social advances.[5]

Although his argument opposes rational thinking since all women need money and security just as much as all men do, some might say that MacCambridge was right. Across the country, *Thelma & Louise* got people all stirred up and talking, but the energy it inspired wasn't channeled into great, sweeping tides of public reaction, only mini-streams and a few select inroads. No subsequent event in one stroke greatly benefited (or negatively affected) women in film, yet SAG employment statistics do indicate some marginal progress over the course of the decade. The country hasn't elected a woman president or established a universal child care system, yet among the listings after 1991 on *The Baltimore Sun*'s compendium of "milestones," 1992 was represented by the so-called "Year of the Woman," named by journalists because of the record-breaking numbers of women who ran for and won political office.[6] In 1993, the Family Medical Leave Act went into effect. In 1995, Shannon Faulkner enrolled in but soon dropped out of the state-supported Citadel military school in South Carolina, publicly and painfully opening the way for other women after her. In the second half of the 1990s, women excelled in music and sports. In 1997, Sarah McLachlan's Lilith Fair proved that female rockers could be "commercially viable," according to the Maryland newspaper. Women's teams won gold medals in gymnastics, basketball, soccer and softball at the 1996 Olympics in Atlanta. Three years later, in 1999, the U.S. women's soccer team won the World Cup.

Bad press and a lack of understanding beleaguer feminism, but it's definitely not dead or else women acting in Hollywood films would have disappeared from the screen by now. Though it may be struggling, feminism is alive and still kicking even in Hollywood. Many women in the industry must have heeded the words of Meryl Streep. In 1990, to warn against impending doom, Streep extrapolated some dire forecasts based on then current SAG employment figures, which thankfully have not come true:

Three years ago, women were down to performing only one-third of all roles in feature films. In 1989, that number slipped to 20 percent. Of course, that was before the figures for this year were tabulated. Just wait till they factor in our contributions to *Total Recall, RoboCop II, Days of Thunder, Die Hard 2, The Hunt for Red October, The Abyss, Young Guns II, Miami Blues, Last Exit to Brooklyn, Dick Tracy* and *The Adventures of Ford Fairlane.* We snagged a good six or seven major roles in those movies. If the trend continues, by the year 2000 women will represent 13 percent of all roles. And in 20 years, we will have been eliminated from movies entirely.[7]

Copying what has worked on men's behalf for thousands of years, and following the examples set by Lois Weber, Frances Marion and Mary Pickford in the first half of the twentieth century, women in film today are building networks of associates. In Hollywood, women are making strides as producers and hiring more women as crew. A 2000 study of the top domestic grossing films of the year by Dr. Martha M. Lauzen of San Diego State University found that films crediting female executive producers and directors employed "significantly" greater percentages of women than films listing exclusively male executive producers and directors. In fact, releases directed by women employed 146 percent more females than efforts directed by men, though there were few hit films directed by women that year. Lauzen's research also found that films produced by at least one female executive producer (a substantially larger category than female directors) employed 28 percent more women than films produced solely by men. Like brotherhood, if people give it a chance, sisterhood works.[8]

With its marginal casting, meaning its employment of female leads, *Thelma & Louise* was not expected to do so well up against other summer of 1991 releases like *What About Bob?, Backdraft, City Slickers, Robin Hood: Prince of Thieves, Naked Gun 2½, Boyz 'N the Hood, Regarding Henry, Hot Shots* and the omnipresent *Terminator 2: Judgement Day,* which earned over $500 million worldwide. All of these male-led films (except *Regarding Henry*) raked in more money than *Thelma & Louise* while none featured a top-billed female. Low budget compared to the $100 million James Cameron required to direct Arnold Schwarzenegger in *T 2, Thelma & Louise* cost approximately $17 million to produce. During its 19-week theatrical release from May 24 to October 3, according to *The Hollywood Reporter, Thelma & Louise* earned $44 million in domestic box office ticket sales.[9]

The movie's producers were delighted. For a film that did not have "all the ingredients of mass appeal" or a big budget, analyzed Alan Friedberg, chairmen of Loews Theaters, *Thelma & Louise* had "all the ingredients of having legs." As reported in *The New York Times* on June 3, Friedberg accurately predicted that the film's theatrical earnings would hover around $50 million.[10] MGM/Pathé distribution chief Jack Foley gushed to *Variety* a week later on June 17, "*Thelma & Louise* is defying gravity."[11] Three months later, on September 19, Jack Gordon, president of international distribution for MGM/UA Home Video, agreed that the sensation surrounding *Thelma & Louise* sold the picture and resulted in a "strong" overseas performance.[12]

Describing the surprise hit's brisk after-market rental business, in February 1993, MGM/UA Home Video senior vice president and general manager George Feltenstein boasted, "*Thelma & Louise* did about $44 million at the box office." However, Feltenstein informed *The Hollywood Reporter*, "We positioned it like a $100 million blockbuster, and that's how it sold."[13] MGM/UA invested $2 million into the film's after-market advertising campaign, representing the distributor's most hopeful effort since *Rain Man* (1988) debuted on video in August 1989. In an unusual move, the picture was released in letterbox and standard television formats, catering to both art crowds and less demanding general interest viewers.[14] Following responsive videocassette business, the laserdisc version of *Thelma & Louise* ranked number one as the company's best seller in 1992, at 36,000 units.[15]

Though not a box office bonanza, *Thelma & Louise* did turn a respectable profit. More memorably, *Thelma & Louise* earned a place in history. Instead of receiving acclaim for blockbuster sales figures, the movie built a reputation based on content. Fueled by its fiery reception, within a few years *Thelma & Louise* took its place among other time-honored classics. In late 1994, MGM/UA Home Video planned to put three major titles, *West Side Story* (1961), *Rain Main*, and *Thelma & Louise*, on moratorium, according to *The Hollywood Reporter*. The titles would be released at a new lower price, $19.98, and then immediately removed from distribution. As the industry newspaper glossed, such a strategy forces retailers and distributors to anticipate consumer demand. By loading the marketplace with inventory, MGM sought to capitalize on the controversy buoying the film. Subsequently, taking *Thelma & Louise* out of circulation reinforced the film's status as a must-have rarity.[16]

Late in the decade, when MGM was weathering financial troubles, *Thelma & Louise* came to the company's aid. In 1999, MGM's international television arm signed a multi-year, multi-billion dollar licensing agreement with Britain's two commercial networks, ITV and Channel Four. According to a British television executive who spoke with *Variety*, the $40 million deal was forged with the "best loved" film franchise due to the strength of its film library, which included by name *Thelma & Louise*.[17] Capping off the decade, in 2000, *Variety* covered MGM's exclusive deal with India's Zee Telefilms. Again, *Variety* singled out *Thelma & Louise*, listing it first among other prized titles such as *Rain Man* and *Midnight Cowboy* (1969).[18]

The film's momentum kept rolling into the next century, in 2001 beginning a second decade of popularity. In September, under the headline "DVD Releases: A Pack O' Pix Redux," *Variety* discussed the re-release of "mini-platters" in souped-up special editions, which would include extra features like commentary from filmmakers and omitted scenes. To exemplify MGM/

UA's impressive array, *Thelma & Louise* shared the spotlight with *The Producers* (1968), *Blue Velvet* (1986), *Mad Max* (1980) and *The Princess Bride* (1987).[19] In October 2001, the same newspaper reported the deal between MGM and Starz Encore Group to run classic titles on pay TV without commercial interruption. This deal was slated for an American market, and *Thelma & Louise* ranked beside *Dances with Wolves* (1990), *The Silence of the Lambs* (1991), *The Apartment* (1960) and *Some Like It Hot* (1959).[20] Of that grouping, only *Thelma & Louise* failed to make the AFI's list of top 100 American films.

Too stunning to slink by unnoticed, the picture's Memorial Day weekend release jump-started the summer of 1991. *Thelma & Louise* built "considerable" momentum thanks to "extraordinary" reviews and word-of-mouth advertising, reported *Variety*. Less than a month into its theatrical run, the industry newspaper knew the picture was something special. Considered both for women and against them, *Thelma & Louise* benefited from the kind of media attention that transforms a movie into a cultural "phenomenon," the show business gazette opined.[21]

The free publicity provided by "The Great Debate over Thelma and Louise," as the stir was labeled by *The Boston Globe*, undoubtedly enhanced the film's total revenues. Newspapers across the country stoked the interest of viewers who caught the show in order to hash out its meaning and worth. Ticket sales grew, and so did the commotion.

Reactions to the picture varied wildly. *Thelma & Louise* moved people to extreme views and passionate remarks. When some commentators fired verbal ballistics, the heated exchange between sides further elevated the picture's name recognition. Essentially, participants in the controversy questioned the movie's relationship to feminism, a term which confuses many. To sort through the "great debate," on June 14, *The Boston Globe* wondered, as did many observers, is *Thelma & Louise* "evil man-bashing or liberating fantasy?"[22]

When the film debuted so loudly, everyone within earshot had to notice. To keep up with current cultural events, film lovers felt the need to go to the theater and make up their minds. Once inside the cineplex, viewers encountered a fresh, sometimes startling story. *Thelma & Louise*'s "snowball" of events tended to overwhelm and cloud the mind. Trying to think amid the clatter of dispute, back in 1991 it was easy to overlook the work's inherent messages.

Both shocked and exhilarated by the experience of seeing *Thelma & Louise* playing on the big screen, like so many others, I got caught up in the picture's confusion of feminism and violence. I liked what I saw, but I wasn't sure how I felt in full or what viewpoints I should adopt. Initially, I wasn't sure if I should support the picture. Rather than rush to judgment, I needed time to figure out my reaction.

Now, looking back calmly, meaning can be found and the controversy settled. *Thelma & Louise* contains all the clues necessary to communicate clear statements about violence and the film's two female protagonists. As it turns out, the real world is confused, not the film.

Since the dawn of cinema, this question has been raised: do movies merely reflect reality, or do they contribute to societal problems in any measure? More exuberant critics tried to shame Hollywood for the ongoing human woes contained in Callie Khouri's screenplay. The picture's welcome reopened a tired what-came-first, chicken-or-egg style investigation, but pointed to an uncomfortable answer: the movie-going public is complicit in whatever Hollywood does. *Thelma & Louise* demonstrates how viewers hold accountability in the media's proliferation of violence because of the entertainment consumers support.

Since the passing of Hollywood's heavy-duty self-censorship, modern viewers who attend R rated films are expected to look for underlying, more thoughtful messages in violent films like Oliver Stone's *Natural Born Killers* (1994). But there's no telling whether viewers do so, and there's no guarantee that such depth actually exists. Those who abhor senseless acts of violence generally know or can guess which movies, filmmakers and other entertainment mediums to stay away from, but *Thelma & Louise* was an unanticipated event. Even though the picture presents a rather timid showing for an R rating compared to the competition, people did not expect the aggressive content they witnessed. Many viewers didn't know what to make of two average women turned fugitives due to the ugly surprise of sexual attack.

Feminism, the basic belief that women are capable, independent people, too, is a monumental change that society has resisted and continues to resist, so *Thelma & Louise* was bound to encounter trouble. *Rape, women and guns, women and violence against men, women acting violently against themselves, all combined in one picture? All this friction in a celebratory film about women breaking free? Breaking free of what? The mean old world or their lesser selves?* All of this aggravated most members of the audience to some degree. The fact that Thelma and Louise escape both their own past bad decisions and a slanted world ruled by men, some nasty, some nice, most a bit of both, jarred people. Never before had the big screen projected a pair of likeable, friendly female protagonists, who make unsuitable role models because they are criminals but achieve adulation from fans anyway.

Because of its fresh take on gender, *Thelma & Louise* surprised patrons by shifting and intensifying a situation that has become paradoxical. Too much of the violence seen on TV and in films is portrayed irresponsibly for shock value, we complain, yet acceptance of murder, blood, guts and destruction is widespread. Female filmmakers wouldn't necessarily act any better given the chance, but still, especially in the early 1990s, before *Thelma & Louise* came out, most often random violence was crafted and committed by males, who to this day continue to attract rather than repel general audiences.

A script grounded in a strong female perspective, thanks to the film's female screenwriter, and women placed in the driver and front passenger seats of an action movie, though it contained minimal violence, upset the status quo by highlighting lingering problems. *Thelma & Louise* opened people's eyes, but it overwhelmed many viewers in the process because the film forced movie-goers to look at themselves and the world.

Since the film's release, time has settled the "great debate." The violence in *Thelma & Louise* is presented responsibly. The picture holds individuals accountable for their actions without basking in an excess of blood and debris. No crime goes unpunished. Despite the furious reaction the movie received, *Thelma & Louise* is not a woman's call to arms nor does it signal a woman's rightful turn to kill.

Thelma & Louise reminds audiences that freedom includes the possibility of committing violent crime, distasteful as that thought is. If men can wreak bloody havoc, so can the opposite sex. However, the goal isn't to fill men and women's prisons equally but to evolve society, so that both genders can live together harmoniously with equal access, hope and respect. To some, the film's violence — particularly the violence committed *by* Thelma and Louise — overshadowed its character element but not because explosions and murder receive more screen time. Ultimately, what's most important about *Thelma & Louise* and what the filmmakers clearly emphasize is its focus on women's lives.

Human beings are still learning what it means to recognize all creeds, colors and genders without bias. In both fact and fiction, a woman trying to steer her own destiny remains a new and developing trend. Because of this fact of real life, forces outside of their control complicate Thelma's and Louise's lives as well as the film's reception. One element is crucial to the wider story: their experiences back in Texas and in the Silver Bullet parking lot would not have happened if Thelma and Louise were men named Ted and Larry. Differences between men and women should be celebrated and bring us together, not create further conflict and drive us apart. Their respective ideals and class confine Thelma and Louise, but essentially Khouri's characters are trapped in existences particular to women, existences that haven't received much onscreen attention, despite cinema's century of filmmaking. The title characters' demise is attributable to their sex because of the special circumstances of rape, a topic too many commentators avoided.

Although the films contain many similarities, *Thelma & Louise* is not simply a female version of *Butch Cassidy and the Sundance Kid*, its leads cloaked in drag, as many critics dismissed. Because of the nature of the crime committed *against* the women, *Thelma & Louise* is not a gender-reversible or gender-neutral film. Sure, men could fill the role of mistreated, ignored mate, but no man could play a role equivalent to Thelma Dickerson, caged, "sedate" housewife. And no man could fill a role directly comparable with "jaded" waitress Louise Sawyer, either. Traditionally speaking, in the land of Denny's, Bob's Big Boy and Bickfords, men manage; women wait on tables, often while hoping for marriage proposals or winning lottery tickets to rescue them from drudgery. The world is changing, thanks in part to the film. Now men do take orders and balance trays in burger joints and greasy spoons, but onscreen, a baggage-bearing regular joe wearing an apron and snapping gum would mean a whole new kind of film inspired by the bold exploration of freedom found in *Thelma & Louise.*

Like Virginia Woolf did in real life, Thelma and Louise commit suicide, their final act of self-determination and violence, which drove some viewers wild with questions. How could the women escape justice in such a cowardly fashion? non-supporters complained. Years later we can make some informed guesses about what made Woolf walk into a river with rocks weighting down her skirt pockets, but of course we'll never know her mindset exactly. We do know that she'd lived through one world war and was encountering a horrible second one. Bombs were exploding all over London, wrecking her own urban home. Moreover, Woolf had always been overly sensitive and had endured a history of mental illness. In the end, she was nearly 60 years old and hearing voices again. Feeling she wouldn't recover from her current bout of madness, Woolf wrote her husband Leonard a final letter and then ended her life.

The film's heroines share Woolf's hopelessness and desire to escape. Perched precariously at the edge of the world, Thelma and Louise don't stand a chance. They can't surrender to the army of police surrounding them without spending a lot of time in jail, one place they don't want to go. Still, fans watch the women quickly decide to "just keep going" with sadness and disbelief. As individuals, Thelma and Louise come so far yet forsake it all.

As symbols, however, they have the opportunity to live forever. Out of love and admiration, the filmmakers shy away from explicitly killing off their creations. In a similar mode of thought, Woolf once said to a friend, "Death is the one experience I shall never describe."[23]

Of course, I've taken more time to reflect and build my reaction to the *Thelma & Louise*, quite unlike the many professionals in the media who enlivened the "great debate."

Two newspapers on opposite sides of the country helped to explode national coverage and inflame argument. Setting the style and tone for a decade of talk to follow, *The Los Angeles Times* asked Peter Rainer and Sheila Benson to lead the battle. *The Boston Globe*, which gave the controversy a name, employed columnists Diane White and John Robinson to wage war over a movie.

The Boston Globe sensationalized its coverage with separate designations. The gender-segregated, side-by-side columns set the stage for a virtual three-round battle of the wits: "She loves it" vs. "He hates it." Considering Robinson's review, "hate" was an understatement. To steer his course in a time of great turbulence, Robinson first admitted his belief that male bashing had long been a remote problem, "once the sport of hairy women in denim jackets and combat boots." According to Robinson, luckily for the culture at large, this marginal and negative societal element was largely restricted to academic papers, as well as other insidious but minor means of dispersion such as women's magazines and novels read only by the elite. In other words, feminism had been avoidable because it stayed out of the mainstream.

However, Khouri's screenplay took male bashing to new heights and brought feminism to the masses, which upset Robinson's world order. Blurring the line between camp and chomp, Robinson complained, "'Thelma and Louise' takes aim at the center of mass culture, grievously escalating the war between the sexes." Whether expounding sarcastically, staking a claim seriously or perhaps responding with a combination of both, Robinson declared that the movie demanded a reply. Someone had to say "enough is enough," and Robinson stepped forward to fill that need.

Thelma & Louise hit Robinson hard. As a man, he felt guilty, targeted, beat up and bruised. Waving the white flag on behalf of his gender, Robinson asked for mercy on behalf of all men, who he claimed were "fed up." Torn between recognizing feminism's righteousness and a wish for the old status quo, the past won Robinson over. He had accepted the validity of feminism in theory, but seeing the film moved him to denounce feminist expression in action. He labeled inequality between the sexes "the imbalance of nature," as in *tough luck, just deal with it.* Resolutely disgusted with the likes of feminism as he recognized it, Robinson believed that *Thelma & Louise* was "the last straw."

Listening to Robinson, White couldn't believe all the fuss. As cool and collected as Mae West, she replied, "Really, boys. Calm yourselves." White reminded readers of the obvious: *Thelma & Louise* is just a movie "and a comedy at that." She wondered what to call the collection of angry male outcries she'd heard, and finally decided on "stupid overreaction." Labels such as "toxic feminism," "man-bashing," "man-hating," "male-baiting" and "fascism" surprised White. She thought men would enjoy the picture because it was "a bang-bang, shoot-'em-up buddy movie" starring two attractive women.

Like her debate partner had done, White grouped men together as if the entire gender shared one mind about the movie, which wasn't true. Contrary to widespread assumption, no matter how often people tried to divide and classify respondents by sex, reactions to *Thelma & Louise* defied such simplistic categorization. In fact, perhaps the greatest lesson to come from the film is that the world is no longer served, if it ever was, by stereotypes assigned rigidly by gender, which in all cases eventually run out of gas or hit a wall and turn up false.

Both *Boston Globe* commentators looked at the picture while caught in outdated grooves. While Robinson spoke as an authority figure who sought to put women in their place, White teased men for their overblown reaction, ignoring women who did the same. Working up a big chortle, she pointed out the notion that men (but not women) thought the picture was too violent. White responded to her opponent about the fictional women being role models, an idea she easily rejected. Mean-spiritedness and violence are staples in many genres of male-led films, she implied, signaling a double standard. She wasn't surprised by this blind spot, but the suggestion that any film characters — male or female — might be revered indicated excessive silliness to White. "Gee, I know whenever I'm looking for a role model I run right out to the movies," she mocked.

In round two, Robinson, writing in defense of manhood, played the martyr and sounded like a sympathizer for the Independent Women's Forum, a conservative, anti-feminist organization. He announced with a flourish, "Since the dawn of feminism, most men have suffered in manly silence the slanders and outrages of an aggrieved female majority." One man among a legion of proud but mute heroes, sanctimoniously Robinson pointed to bra-burning as the start of all the trouble. He briefly credited the undeniable righteousness of feminism's claims, but was more taken with the much-maligned demonstration outside the 1968 Miss America beauty pageant in Atlantic City. He recognized the non-event as the first strike aimed against men, who kept quiet and watched in horror as women moved into power.

Unfortunately, a man's work putting up with women is never done in Robinson's tale. He rambled on about the shock of female body hair, and the need to make room for women in private and professional circles. Faced with threats of lost privacy and increased job competition, Robinson's mounting anger on behalf of his gender was palpable.

Stoically, though showing signs he was ready to blow, Robinson related that until the present men had been silent because of their guilt, yet *Thelma & Louise* disturbed this deceptive peace. Building to an explosive climax, Robinson said that he could "accept" the murder of a rapist, deal with a "loutish" husband and even handle the "beefcake" hitchhiker. However, Robinson could not accept the undone highway patrolman, who starts "blubbering" about having a wife and kids at home. Robinson's patience finally disintegrated. No longer should men put up with the wiles of women. For bringing a man to tears in public, *Thelma & Louise* made war between the sexes inevitable.

Robinson commented rashly, "*Thelma & Louise* would have the world believe that a good man is an exception, and that a bad woman is an oxymoron," so of course he objected — vehemently. In his outrage, Robinson couldn't accept a picture with two female anti-heroines who make mistakes *and* earn the audience's sympathy.

Robinson took for granted a large cast of males and was appalled that there was only one good guy in *Thelma & Louise*. Blinded by passion, Robinson figured that Jimmy equaled the sole sympathetic male in the story. Conveniently, when assessing good guys, Robinson completely overlooked the screenplay's other sensitive men: Detective Slocumbe, who shares Louise's secret and tries to save the women, and the New Mexico state police officer. Contrary to Robinson's complaint, the undone highway patrolman is also likeable, or at least his isn't unlikable. He politely goes about doing his job in a no-nonsense fashion. He pulls over a car clocked at 110 mph, only to have Thelma put a gun to his head. The officer's cries on behalf of his family are campy and played for laughs, but Robinson took his display of tears seriously and personally. Embarrassed, he deemed the officer unworthy of manhood.

A perspective twisted by anger prevented Robinson from seeing the story as it appeared on screen. While Robinson's reaction to the men in *Thelma & Louise* was overblown, his reaction to the film's women was underdeveloped. Throughout his article, Robinson failed to show any genuine sympathy for the female point of view, as if he was jealous of all the attention Thelma and Louise receive as lead characters. Contrary to Robinson's assumption, the film doesn't cast the title characters as angels. Only at the very end, leading to the credits, do Thelma and Louise fly through the air levitated by a heavenly chorus. Throughout the rest of the film, Thelma and Louise exhibit human traits both good and bad. Collectively, so do the supporting male characters.

Because of his averted gaze, Robinson was completely blind to the limited roles that women in film usually endure, and he also overlooked the abundance of roles that men in film generally enjoy. *Thelma & Louise* features a generous 10 parts for male characters ranging from supporting roles to bit walk-ons. In order of appearance:

1. Albert, the respectfully flirtatious busboy
2. Darryl, Thelma's "loutish" husband
3. Harlan, Thelma's attempted rapist
4. Detective Slocumbe, the sympathetic Arkansas cop
5. Max, the cold-hearted FBI agent
6. Jimmy, Louise's sympathetic though too often absent boyfriend
7. J.D., the "beefcake hitchhiker," who rips the women off but operates with better manners than either Darryl or Harlan
8. the undone New Mexico highway patrolman
9. the rude trucker
10. the desert biker, who doesn't stop to help the officer who is locked in his own trunk but does share his joint

Robinson didn't seem to realize that any film featuring a whopping 10 parts for women — even if all were truly stereotypical and highly objectionable — would represent a tremendous boon to employment figures.

White returned to the ring snickering about the issue of violence. She's no fan of excessive aggression passing as entertainment and certainly not a supporter of real life retribution and murder. However, she believed that what rattled some men was not that Thelma and Louise lock the undone highway patrolman in the trunk of his squad car, but that in the film women play the perpetrators while men play the victims, reversing the usual interplay. This didn't bother White — just the opposite. She would have liked even more male bashing. As long as it's just a movie and not real life, White wished the woman had "nailed" the "little weasel" who stole their money. If things were left to her, White would have also taken out Thelma's "toad-like yupster" husband.

White looked at the wider world of film that year, including *Mortal Thoughts* and *Drowning by Numbers*, and noted that women killing men translated to good box office totals. In White's outlook, this trend undoubtedly catered to female moviegoers who wanted to escape the real world where men more often attack women rather than the other way around. The reason for *Thelma & Louise*'s popularity was simple. "Women are getting really fed up with always being the bashees," White suggested, "and want to do a little of the bashing for a change."

Softening his charge while heightening his use of sarcasm, in the third round Robinson tried to butter up female readers. He argued that no man who loves his mother "would deny the essential saintliness and innocence of womankind." Yet overdone platitudes failed to divert attention from Robinson's turgid condemnation of the picture and his total trashing of feminism, joking or not.

Robinson mistakenly assumed that Thelma and Louise spoke for all feminists, as if women were only available in limited array of makes and models. As a result, Robinson was deeply dismayed. Extrapolating out of control, he contended that the film belies the goal of equality and decried the "New Girl Network." Citing "domination or death" as the only feminist alternatives, Robinson conjectured in direct opposition to Michalene Busico that *Thelma & Louise* signals the death of feminism, "dying, not with a bang, but a bashing." Robinson finally assumed the ability to declare the end for the entire feminist movement. Such a display of conceited bravado and stammering rage could not have been the columnist's best moment, even if he was trying to get a rise out of the audience.

White got serious (but only temporarily) in the last round. She wasn't concerned about the movie, though, because it wasn't real. She was more interested in discussing current events and pointed to recent violent crimes in the local news. While Robinson primarily worried about men's hurt feelings, White worried about husbands who kill their wives, and males who stab and strangle unfamiliar females.

In the end, however, White switched gears and returned to a more upbeat mood. She described the audience with whom she saw the picture, which was populated with more women than men. She recalled a lot of cheering when Louise "plugged" Harlan and even more cheering when the trucker's rig exploded. Based on this evidence, White decided that *Thelma & Louise* is a cathartic movie and "a bit of wish fulfillment" for women. Where her co-worker saw the death of feminism, White recognized familiar female experience.

Reviewing *Thelma & Louise* from two distinct vantage points, *The Boston Globe*'s "great debate" made it seem as if Robinson and White had caught completely different movies. While Robinson sounded like he'd rather have teeth pulled minus novocaine rather than see the picture again, White refused to be undone by a mere comedy and preferred to join the fun, even though doing so precipitated a much darker admission. She confided to readers that she knew what it was like to be "so brutalized and humiliated by a man you'd like to murder him." In her own case, however, White didn't resort to violence out of respect for life. Adding a final comedic touch, White said, "Besides, unlike Louise, I didn't have a gun handy."

While White won her match with Robinson, at least in this judge's opinion, her nonchalant take on the film fell short of adequately explicating the whole. White tranquilized Robinson's histrionic distress through sarcasm, which is often used to relax tensions. Her tone was quite appropriate because among the film's many poses *Thelma & Louise* is also a comedy. Often the women resort to one liners in order to distance themselves from doom, but their film is a hybrid, gracefully combining comedy with drama. By downplaying the serious side of what she agrees is the picture's cathartic effect, White discredited the possibility that *Thelma & Louise* or any movie holds meaning or worth, which is definitely not helpful.

At one point, White read the film as a reflection of real women's frustrations, but then she caught herself and retreated. Relating movies to the real world made her uneasy because she didn't like viewing cinema in political terms. When she shared her own experience but then backed off, White sounded a little like Louise refusing to talk about Texas. Her willingness to be placed opposite Robinson in defense of the film is commendable, especially since neither writers are film critics, but White's approach isn't the best way to handle the many ramifications of *Thelma & Louise*. Still, *The Boston Globe*'s "great debate" entertained readers, as it was no doubt intended to do, and also helped promote the picture.

Avoid the mistake that ensnared many great debaters: don't assume that people took sides evenly divided by gender, girls for *Thelma & Louise*, boys against. On the West Coast, predating *The Boston Globe*'s "great debate," *The Los Angeles Times* pitted Sheila Benson against Peter Rainer in "True or False: Thelma & Louise Just Good Ol' Boys?"[25] Reversing the breakdown that occurred in Massachusetts, two weeks earlier in California, on May 31, "he" appreciated the picture more than "she" did. However, neither columnist loved the picture.

Unlike *The Boston Globe* critics, Rainer at least understood the importance of *Thelma & Louise* to the film industry because he lived in Los Angeles. In terms of the film's relation to feminism, however, like Robinson, Rainer heard a death rattle, though he felt slightly more sympathetic towards the movement than his East Coast peer did. He didn't think it was an exceptionally well-made "outlaw-on-the-run" picture, but Rainer was glad that the film's violence wasn't eroticized, which would have belittled the female leads (like happened later in *Bound*). Comparing *Thelma & Louise* with *Mortal Thoughts*, he allowed that both films delivered "a sort of post-feminist howl." Instead of sensationalizing women, in his view the two films punctuate the male preserve. Still, Rainer didn't locate any inspiration in *Thelma & Louise*. He believed that Khouri's brainchild signaled that the expectations of feminism have "gone bust." Reacting to that disappointment, *Thelma & Louise* replaced the hope for equality with "a righteous, self-immolating fury."

To Rainer, at best, while Thelma and Louise self-sacrifice, the film offsets the usual obstacles confronting women in Hollywood. Employing automobile metaphors, a natural tendency when writing about a road film, Rainer related without much enthusiasm that females occupy "the driver seat" in *Thelma & Louise*. As if he thought that Hollywood had changed forever but without improving, Rainer explained that in the film men "along the roadside" are downsized to the kind of "piddling cameos" women previously inhabited. Though he found fault with the production, calling it "rigged," "goofy" and "problematic," Rainer reluctantly realized the picture was a cultural landmark. Because of the "dinky" subordinate roles awarded to most actresses and their resulting anger, he asserted that a movie like *Thelma & Louise* was "inevitable." In Rainer's view, the film not only struck a chord with women working in Hollywood, it also reverberated within greater society.

Rainer took sympathy with the plight of women in film, yet he couldn't fully support *Thelma & Louise* because of the story's violence. He called casting women in action-adventure parts following in the footsteps of men a "sick joke." He contended that in many cases the roles given aren't worth playing and referred to *Aliens* (1979), *Blue Steel* (1990), *Red Sonja* (1985). "Where is the glory in being the female Arnold Schwarzenegger or Bruce Willis?" he demanded.

Of course, the answer to his question is clear: the glory lies in playing a lead role. No doubt Arnold and Bruce would say that saving the world is great work, if you can get it. Yet Rainer was rightly critical of the ghetto created by the female action hero genre, which Hollywood has increasingly turned to as a lucrative alternative to traditional women's films. These new roles may be superficially attractive, but like the parts written for male action heroes, they usually lack substance. Big on questions, Rainer wondered if combining women and guns to command attention at the box office wasn't just another form of subordination. He wasn't prepared to celebrate *Thelma & Louise*, but Rainer did defend women in the industry.

Though Rainer championed women in film, he made some missteps, too, by treating men and women as different species. More comfortable in a male milieu, he was presumptuous regarding the film's female audience. He unfairly assumed that women "are supposed to deplore violence in the movies," and then questioned the motives of women who enjoyed the picture. He put female audience members on the defensive and backed them into a corner, as if women who liked the film were caught changing their minds about violent content at the movies. Robinson noted that "a lot of women seem to be charged up by this film" and queried, "Could it be that violence is OK as long as the object of that violence is appropriately scummy?" Rainer posited the existence of a double standard on the part of female viewers only and implied that women (but not men) should feel guilty for enjoying the picture.

Rainer's limited sympathies toward women were especially evident when he neglected to look closely at the two female leads. Lumping women together, he reported that females in "crypto-male" action roles reinforce each other's "rage," while in the film Thelma runs her course without exhibiting any rage. She corrals the maturity to leave her childish husband, the energy to engage in a kinetic one-night stand and the proper attitude to adopt a criminal life, all during one long weekend. But rather than rage and beyond her initial status as a "fun-loving ditz," as Rainer described her, youthful excitement, a relentlessly positive outlook and a growing loss of naivete better explain Thelma. She becomes steelier as the journey progresses but not just through "gun-toting," as Rainer suggests.

Uncontrolled anger is an emotion that Louise better understands, yet Rainer didn't delve into her character much, either. Too quickly sweeping the duo aside, he took for granted similarities between the title characters that don't exist. He questioned the lack of "psychological horror" evident in the women as they descend into criminal behavior, while in the film Louise is so horrified by what she's done that she quickly throws up. Finding a speck of Harlan's blood on her cheek greatly agitates the ex-waitress and keeps her running. Louise doesn't go to sleep after she kills Thelma's attacker as if she fears nightmares, and because she does regret her murderous actions, she refuses to laugh with her less serious pal at the thought of Harlan's last words. Deciding that "retribution is all" in *Thelma & Louise*, Rainer failed to focus on the most important part of the movie: two women who grow symbiotically. The connection between the characters played by Sarandon and Davis, not the animosity between genders, is the bond emphasized up front in the title and throughout the story. As the film progresses, working better and better as a team, Thelma and Louise battle jerks who happen to be men.

Rainer described *Thelma & Louise* only in terms of its renegade nature and ignored the women's individuality and deepening friendship. He didn't see the tale of two developing and changing women who learn to stick together. As if vigilantism and heart were mutually exclusive in a dramatic world, Rainer registered *Thelma & Louise* a crime story "as vague and negligent as any macho shoot 'em up." He might have talked about the many ways Thelma is characterized as flighty and the numerous times Louise is drawn in opposition, as a more controlled and meticulous personality, but he didn't. Further straying from the core of the picture, he imagined the tale would have been more complex and thoughtful if Thelma or Louise had accidentally shot a woman. Obviously, Rainer missed the point emblemized by the title ampersand. Accidentally shooting a woman is out of the question because *Thelma & Louise* isn't about murder or furthering hostilities between women.

Rainer was cognizant of the unequal situation for women in Hollywood, but he was less understanding and respectful of women in general. After short-changing the title characters and dismissing the basis of the film's plot, he bypassed the actresses' performances. Instead, he applauded only their appearance and physical allure. Rainer insisted that the leads' "glamour" is "part of the polemic," and furthermore that the women's ability to spellbind men is "crucial" to the film's storyline. In other words, if Thelma and Louise were unattractive, in Rainer's analysis they would not have been believable targets for rape, robbery, close-ups or love scenes. Although the film doesn't objectify its lead characters, Rainer did.

Throughout his article, Rainer operated under the assumption that life naturally and rightfully assigns totally separate procedures and evaluations for men and women. While Rainer mishandled women's involvement with the picture, he was too presumptuous and tender on the subject of men, both featured in the picture and sitting in the audience. Attempting to limit reaction by gender like the commentators in Boston, Rainer determined that the picture affords male viewers the thrill of a "masochistic joy ride." Rainer didn't criticize men for enjoying the show because they're supposed to like violence. His division and classification of the audience by sex also ruled out the possibility of men enjoying the non-violent aspects of the women's lives, which Rainer thought fell short of convincing drama and stirring characterization anyway. Simultaneously, Rainer was critical of the few strokes that rendered the men in the picture "louts," which he addressed at length, while he downgraded and largely ignored the "small details" about women's lives — like the way Thelma recklessly packs the gun or the much neater manner in which Louise cleans her apartment as she prepares for the trip — which he largely ignored.

Even though his reaction wasn't as spirited as Robinson's, Rainer also miscounted the number of likable male characters appearing in the film. The undone highway patrolman didn't fall in his sympathetic category, either, and Rainer dismissed him for being a "wimpering simp." Except for Detective

Slocumbe, all of the men in the film are drawn in a "prejudicial" manner to Rainer, who mocked the political agenda he detected in the film. "The Land of the Louts game plan," the critic chided, "functions like fast-food feminism." They way Rainer presented it, in a conscious but bungled effort to persuade audiences to reject men and champion women's rights, *Thelma & Louise* served up "scrupulously" detailed stereotypical supporting men and underdeveloped, too-masculine lead women. Despite his understanding of the film industry, Rainer was uncomfortable with a production that nixed the usual approach and instead infused the screen with a new and bold female point of view, one that refused to acquiesce to the wishes of others.

Diane White was right. What really seemed to throw a lot of people off is the way the usual inequality of lead roles and the imbalance of male to female characters is jumbled up and exaggerated in *Thelma & Louise*, where two female leads play opposite 10 minor to supporting male roles. So far, there's been a good deal of talk about how men and women both inside and outside of the film handled the acts of violence perpetrated *by* Thelma and Louise. However, three out of four critics have largely ignored the "psychological horror" of rape and its effects *on* Thelma and Louise.

In Los Angeles, neither Rainer nor Benson embraced the film. Benson wasn't able to pledge her support, but unlike Rainer she found no redemptive value in the film at all. "Call *Thelma & Louise* anything you want but please don't call it *feminism*," Benson pleaded. She understood the word to represent "responsibility, equality, sensitivity, understanding," not "revenge, retribution, or sadistic behavior." Although the picture contains both responsibility and revenge, therefore replicating the complexity of real life, Benson was preoccupied and looked elsewhere. While the title cued viewers to sympathize with Thelma and Louise, Benson pitied the men ranking below them on the marquee.

Benson hated *Thelma & Louise* as much as Robinson did, but for a slightly different reason. In Massachusetts, Robinson was appalled by the opposite sex's behavior; in California, Benson was disgusted by the way Thelma and Louise represent her own gender. Thelma's undying rosy outlook didn't charm Benson, who called her a "moral midget." Benson charged that the filmmakers make it difficult "for an audience with a conscience" to get behind either of the women. Blaming the filmmakers for a no-win plot and anti-feminist film, Benson was more prepared to defend manhood than identify with the main characters.

Rather than commiserate with the protagonists in any measure for the pain each carries, Benson preferred to discuss her disbelief that most of the men in the picture treat Thelma and Louise poorly, which in the critic's view reflected an "awful contempt" for the entire male gender. Benson denounced the explosion of the rude trucker's rig and the undone highway patrolman's incarceration in the trunk of his own squad car as "despicable," reiterating Rainer's argument. Commenting on the combination of retribution and violence, she pleaded, "Why should it be any more acceptable when it's done by women? Because it's our 'turn'?"

Blinded by passion, like Robinson, Benson overlooked a lot. Somehow she missed the fact that no one in the film gets away with any transgression, but even worse, she managed to forget that art shouldn't be held to the same standards as life. Benson objected to a lack of logic in the picture, expecting a movie to duplicate reality. Despite her profession, Benson forgot the role of symbolism in drama.

In retrospect, one can see where fury obstructed Benson's reception of the picture. Mistakenly, she rejected Thelma and Louise as "heroines," when in fact, as criminals and failures, they are better understood as anti-heroines who hark back to Hollywood filmmaking in the late 1960s and early 1970s, in films such as *Midnight Cowboy* (1969), *Taxi Driver* (1976) and *Badlands* (1973).[26] With good intentions, Benson attacked the idea that the film be considered feminist because, in her view, the women's fate is "determined" by men, delivering a film incompatible with an assertion of women's rights, but even that argument is flawed. Unaware of any other alternatives, Thelma chooses her husband, her girlfriend and her future. Surprised and subject to confusion, Louise opts for murder, escape and death rather than imprisonment. To deny the women self-agency suggests that feminism could never be about making the wrong choices.

But Benson preferred to answer her own questions. Declining the invitation to enjoy *Thelma & Louise*, Benson cried in disbelief, "Are we so starved for 'strong' women's roles that this revenge, and the pell-mell, lunatic flight that follows, fits anyone's definition of *strength*, or even more peculiarly, of *neo-feminism?*"

In short, yes. Although Benson's criticisms are recognizable and in a limited sense sound, for one thing, like other critics she also missed the filmmakers' emphasis on character. The film focuses primarily on the women, who unfold and ironically flower as their friendship intensifies. Portrayed by Davis and Sarandon, rooted in Khouri's script, the story's main characters are fonts of emerging strength and the point from which support for the film springs. The movie's main concern is not violence, although that element sometimes appeared to leave a stronger impression on many.

Unlike the previous critics, at least Benson did address the issue of rape even though her discussion didn't offer any sympathy. Benson could not accept the way Thelma follows her attempted rape and Louise's murder of the perpetrator with a one-night stand approximately 24 hours later. Benson argued, "To write such perky bounce-back doesn't suggest resilience, it suggests that no one's home emotionally." Benson's criticism might be true if the fictional character was a real person, which, of course, Khouri's Thelma is not.

The women's weekend ride does proceed briskly, packing a lot of action and reaction into a short span of time. The film's head-turning, jaw dropping pace was unsettling and unacceptable to some viewers, while exhilarating and plausible to others. To accept Thelma's decision, first viewers need to realize they're watching a drama, not the evening news, then recognize the difference between the aggression of rape and the legitimacy of consensual sex. While all this is going on, audiences need to settle comfortably in the chaos of modern life. J.D. is trustworthy because he looks Thelma in the eye and listens to her, because he's polite in contrast to the attempted rapist and her loutish husband. Ironically, she takes a chance on him because he respects her enough to share his true identity and skills as an "outlaw."

Contrary to the disapproving tone accompanying Peter Rainer's use of the word, Thelma describes J.D. as an "outlaw" with awe. Sure, trusting a criminal is not smart in a rational sense. However, a one-night stand with dangerous but alluring J.D. is enticing to Thelma because she's looking for adventurous alternatives to her actual circumstances. Happily transforming from mousy housewife to trailblazing "outlaw," Thelma welcomes change with an open smile, a coping mechanism which some viewers did find infectious.

It's awfully peculiar how a film about women as made plain in the title evoked so much concern for men. Like Robinson and Rainer, Benson also miscounted the number of sympathetic male characters who aren't fabricated in order to be "toppled." She protested that Khouri made *all* the men "cartoons." Benson amended but did not rescind her statement by noting two major exceptions, the sympathetic cop who's overly sympathetic in her view (she described Slocumbe as an "absolute Greek chorus of empathy") and Louise's "long-term" boyfriend. These miscounts and misjudgments of male characters reveal reviewers on the wrong path. Benson's scathing reaction failed to recognize the bigger picture: the movie's importance in relation to employment figures for women in film. At least in terms of hiring lead roles, *Thelma & Louise* is irrefutably pro-women, and yet the picture offers fans of women in film so much more.

In a night and day world, with so much negative feedback coming from some quarters, naturally there were those who just as passionately embraced the film. On a considerably lighter note than John Robinson, Peter Rainer, Sheila Benson and even Diane White, Cynthia Heimel, in her *Village Voice* column "Tongue in Chic," roasted the "great debate" with thick sarcasm. Heimel, playing a satirical advice columnist, the Problem Lady, counseled fictional follower Sally, who wrote asking to borrow an opinion about *Thelma & Louise*.

Like potential viewers across the country, Sally was totally confused by the onslaught of questions and heated dialogue surrounding the film. Speaking for many, she wondered whether the movie was feminist. She wanted to know if the picture's violence was good or bad for women. She needed to know what to think about the suicide ending. Speechless, Sally had no mind of her own. Exasperated, she confessed that when she actually saw the show she "might as well have had electrodes attached to my head I was monitoring my feelings so closely." Sally asked for help analyzing *Thelma & Louise* so she wouldn't look like a fool.

Playing the Problem Lady, Heimel calmed Sally's fears and provided answers. Through the mock exchange, Heimel slyly let readers know where she stood: people argued so fiercely about the movie precisely because it was worthwhile and long overdue. Without hesitation, Heimel pegged *Thelma & Louise* a "really good movie" and one that should have come out 20 years before in the 1970s. Because current audiences were accustomed to seeing women in Hollywood film play only love interests with few consequential lines, the picture got people all worked up. Reminiscent of Diane White's last line, Heimel dryly teased the touchiness surrounding the film:

> If someone tries to tell you that this movie is bad for feminism and that it provides terrible role models for women, remind them sweetly that men get to play all sorts of horribly complicated messes in movies whenever they want. Then pull out a gun and shoot them.[27]

In shorter form, Heimel understood what Sheila Benson and others missed. Where some saw only bad choices, Heimel recognized struggling female spirit. More effective than any sweeping dismissal, Heimel's relaxed criticism about the picture's timing is persuasive. The storyline in *Thelma & Louise* — women leave home and get into trouble — does sound retrospective of the 1970s, when listing jobs by sex was finally outlawed, a woman could better control her reproductive future and Bea Arthur broke similar new ground on television in Norman Lear's *All in the Family* spin-off, *Maude*. In terms of its story, *Thelma & Louise* takes two steps backwards past the inception of the *Aliens* series starring Sigourney Weaver (*Alien*, 1979, and *Aliens*, 1986, directed by James Cameron, cinematography by Adrian Biddle) to female-led movies such as *Alice Doesn't Live Here Anymore* (1974), *Klute* (1971), *Looking for Mr. Goodbar* (1977) and *The Sugarland Express* (1974). Playing upon the growing interest in women filling traditionally male roles, after *Thelma & Louise*, two more editions to the *Aliens* series were released, *Alien 3*, in 1992, and *Alien: Resurrection*, in 1997, which added Winona Ryder into the sci-fi/horror mix.

Thelma & Louise reminds both fans and critics that foundational changes affecting women's power and progress have been building very slowly since the righteous days of the second wave of feminism — particularly in Hollywood. As Meryl Streep and Susan Faludi have pointed out, the tide of advancement for which feminists have worked so hard has sometimes retreated. As a result, the arrival of *Thelma & Louise* reinforced the regrettable need for an ongoing women's movement and a special focus on women in film.

Arguments aside, however, there is no getting around taste. As a controversial film invoking feminism, the picture didn't play as well in more conservative areas of the country. "While the picture is doing gangbusters in all the sophisticated urban areas you'd expect," noted *Variety*, "it's a wash in Chicago and many parts of the Midwest and the South." "It doesn't have a mainstream sensibility," one Disney production executive explained, adding the picture "offended people slightly."

Greg Morrison, MGM/Pathé marketing chief, emphasized that although the film initially attracted female viewers, attendance analyzed by gender moved from a 70 to 30 female-male spilt in its opening weeks to 55 percent to 60 percent female less than a month later. Though females formed the majority of audience members, men became interested in the picture so they could form an opinion. Still, positive media spin couldn't overcome general opposition in the interior from both genders. "In some places like New York," MGM/Pathé distribution chief Jack Foley stated, *Thelma & Louise* box office soared "beyond our wildest dreams," while smaller towns like Oklahoma City weren't "ready" for it.[28]

In January 1992, *The Salt Lake Tribune* published a guest editorial from *The Boston Globe*'s Steven Stark under the headline "Is Snob a Synonym for Liberal?" Stark speculated a "growing dissonance" between the nation's cultural elite (those John Robinson sneered at for reading feminist novels) and the majority of Americans. While "one side," including Hollywood, "debates the merits of *Thelma and Louise*," he outlined, "the other, when it goes to the movies at all, catches *Terminator 2*." To exemplify his point, Stark looked to Oliver Stone's controversial film *JFK* (1991), which caused a splash among a select audience but created few waves at the box office. Members of the media and intellectuals cared to relive the Kennedy assassination, but the general public did not. "The same thing happened with *Thelma and Louise* last summer," Stark contended. Members of the cultural elite were compelled by the "great debate," but the general public was not.

Nearly a decade before George W. Bush took office for two terms in a big land described by states deemed distinctly "red" or "blue," Stark described a split with far-reaching implications. In America, divergent tastes and varied outlooks had assumed a "political significance," and one that "strongly benefited" conservatives. Fair or not, much of the public discredits members of mass media for operating with an elitist bias, Stark contended. Because newspaper sales and active literacy rates had been in decline for decades, he believed that remaining print media subscribers tended to be better-educated and more liberal on cultural issues such as feminism.

Stark implied that journalists may not operate with elitist attitudes as much as they serve a smaller, more thoughtful customer base, especially when the subject is art or ideas. In regards to Hollywood, the intellectual schism Stark detected seems to explain the *Thelma & Louise* audience. Even more prescriptive than gender or geography, moviegoers most likely to read the picture's reviews represented the film's strongest base of support.[29]

In general, the reaction to *Thelma & Louise* from smaller, low-profile cities and towns and their newspapers, which tend not to cover the film industry much, was less enthusiastic and less supportive than the reaction from fans and journalists in major cities such as Washington D.C., Los Angeles and Boston — but not without exceptions. Those exceptions represent some of the most interesting examples from the tornado of talk surrounding *Thelma & Louise*.

In August 1991, *The Baltimore Sun* ran "Creator of 'Summer Oscars' picks 'Thelma & Louise' as Best Picture." Film critic Jay Boyar didn't have any trouble determining the best picture released between mid-May and the end of August. In his words, there was "no contest." *Thelma & Louise* won even though this "wild and wonderful movie may have inspired some of the most annoying pyschobabble since Harry met Sally." A true fan, Boyar awarded Geena Davis and Susan Sarandon Best Actress, Ridley Scott Best Director and Callie Khouri Best Screenplay. Furthermore, all the men in the picture came in as runners-ups in Boyar's Oscars in July Best Supporting Actor category. The East Coast loved the picture, except in this case the East Coast refers to Florida, as the article originated in *The Orlando Sentinel*.[30]

A more disinterested outlook informed *The Memphis Commercial Appeal*'s January 1992 article "Stores Stock Up, See No Rush for 'Thelma, Louise.'" In Memphis, although one video store manager felt the film's controversy would help sales, another video store owner claimed, "I haven't had as much interest expressed as I expected." The palpable excitement Jay Boyar felt in Florida was not evident in Tennessee.

To clue in unaware readers, *The Commercial Appeal* described the movie as a "departure" for Hollywood. *Thelma & Louise* is "a buddy movie with strong women as the leads," the Mississippi river newspaper politely explained, yet its coverage was colored. Talk about a possible "bad example" set by violence associated with women was purveyed without offering any positive attribution to strike a fair balance.[31] As the local newspaper both predicted and emphasized, negative press hurt video sales in the area.

A January 1992 article in *The Oklahoman*, "Art Films Find Tough Market in City," reinforced the comment made six months earlier by the chief of distribution for MGM/Pathé about smaller towns such as Oklahoma City not being ready for edgy films. The Heartland newspaper pointed out, "The art cinema idea has been tried in Oklahoma City, but so far without success." Three failed attempts to turn a profit were mentioned, with a fourth set to end operations. In defense of the local scene, one hopeful art film supporter argued that a lack of promotion and too short runs hurt smaller films, which might fare better with greater exposure. Specialty films disappear quickly when people don't hear about them, either through marketing or word of mouth. An advertising executive commented that for any art house to work in Oklahoma City, the theater owner must be a "tireless promoter," and the media must "cooperate" by informing people about these films. Consequently, fans must rush out to see specialty pictures immediately to ensure that they don't close. Whatever the cause, lack of interest, lack of advertising or both, the situation certainly sounds tough for fans of film living in Oklahoma City, in large measure due to a lack of opportunity. Half the movies on *Chicago Tribune* critic Roger Ebert's 10 best list for 1991 had not yet played in the area six months after the year had ended. However, nine of the movies picked by a Knight-Ridder newspaper's film critic as the worst films of 1991 had.[32]

At least one city's reported attitude toward the film became a point of pride. In Minneapolis, *The Star Tribune* had to laugh at a piece in *The Los Angeles Times* published early enough in the summer of 1991 to affect ticket sales. Paraphrasing the California newspaper on June 28, a month after *Thelma & Louise* opened, *The Star Tribune* snickered that *Thelma & Louise* is "too sophisticated" for audiences in Chicago. However, according to *The Los Angeles Times* article cited, apparently *Thelma & Louise* "is going gang-busters in all the areas you'd expect, places like New York, L.A. and Minneapolis." As *The Star Tribune*'s Jeff Strickler expressed to fellow upper Midwesterners, "How can you not like a movie that lets us look down our noses at Chicago Bears fans?"[33] Readers internalized comments like these and figured they better see *Thelma & Louise* to keep up with what's happening.

Considering the great debate in its myriad forms, like fictional Sally, potential viewers across the country wondered if the film should be taken seriously or seen at all. Among those who braved *Thelma & Louise*, some audience members found the movie to be a refreshing break from the usual cineplex choices. These happy viewers lived vicariously, stamping out abusive male rule and figuratively stuffing themselves on the entrails along with Thelma and Louise, in a spirit similar to Diane White's counterpoint and Cynthia Heimel's column. Moviegoers of this ilk were also able to look on the light side and shift focus from the less-than-positive elements of the film in order to celebrate alongside Thelma and Louise over their more positive and uproarious developments. Other more reluctant viewers were appalled at the violent measures employed by the protagonists, as were John Robinson, Peter Rainer and Sheila Benson. They could not support the film or support findings that the film was pro much of anything.

Disparate attendees could point to the movie's violence, particularly the conclusion, the protagonists' drive into what appears to be the Grand Canyon (although the scene was shot in Utah), and claim righteousness. Pointing to what would be the wreck below, dismissive viewers responded in disgust. For some, the suicide ending alone ruined the entire film-going experience. At the same time, more enthralled viewers followed the filmmaker's cue and ignored the bloody implications of the women's death leap. Instead of showing the women's crash landing, the filmmakers replay the women's good times through flashbacks. In place of destruction and gore, the film features peppy close-ups of Polaroid snapshots taken before any of the duo's criminal troubles begin — a decision that further complicates any discussion about the suicide ending. Encouraged by the filmmakers, enthusiastic fans relished the experiences leading up to the foregone conclusion of Thelma and Louise's unavoidably messy mutual deaths. Gazing at what was on screen, those who admired the women could rejoice and smile.

Although these two camps aren't the only options available, whatever opinion one adopts about *Thelma & Louise* depends on how the film is interpreted. Undeniably, if not explicitly, a film's story is expressed through the language of cinema, which individuals decode differently to suit their own purposes. In the decade plus since its release, *Thelma & Louise* has been reviewed extensively because its complexities provide many options for attachment. As feminist film scholar Karen Hollinger explains in *In the Company of Women: Contemporary Female Friendship Films*, "Critics have pointed to the film as demonstrating qualities characteristic of an enormous number of genres: the male buddy film, outlaw film, road movie, deadly doll film, western, melodrama, gangster film, screwball comedy and action/adventure film as well as a female friendship film." One of many academics to comment on the film, Hollinger elaborates that "as a multigeneric hybrid, *Thelma & Louise* manages a remarkably broad address."[34] Naturally, people take away from a picture with "many scripts" the one that strikes them the hardest.

6. Rape Downgraded to a "Minor Plot Point": The Nation Reacts to Two Women Characters

Fifteen years after its release, now that the film has settled into the "classic" and "favorites" sections of video stores, readers may not recall how *Thelma & Louise* was the hot topic of the summer of 1991. Like Cynthia Heimel's fictional Sally, people who wanted to take part in the controversy needed to form opinions about the picture, preferably right away. As with any current event, urgency surrounded the great debate. By the looks of things, viewers and reviewers didn't always take the time to sit back, reflect and calmly compose their thoughts. Some commentators didn't even bother to see the picture before passing judgment.

The film caused such a stir, public reaction came in waves. The first wave of reviews, published in most newspapers on May 24, 1991, showed rash, confused and insightful reactions. The second wave took the form of opinion pieces. As talk continued, throughout the summer many magazines and newspapers and other publications come out with additional commentaries following their initial review so they wouldn't miss out on the big story. By this point, criticism began to further crystallize into camps. There were those who didn't like the film's depiction of men, women, feminism and/or violence. Some people picked on the filmmakers. Others complained about details like the stars' accents. There were those who loved the film without reservation and those who liked the film a great deal — except for a few glaring points, such as the suicide ending, the explosion of the trucker's rig and the New Mexico police officer's live burial.

Later waves of public reaction in newspapers in the decade following the film's release included frequent references to the production. As time progressed and *Thelma & Louise* took its place as a revered but still controversial film, the Internet supported commentary and conversations between "regular" viewers who sometimes but now always made more sense than the professionals. In 1999, one message board response on salon.com categorized rape as one of a few "minor plot points" that would simply need revising in order to change the leads from female to male and then prove that the picture wasn't very good. Perhaps thinking that women's lives were a lousy material from which to make a movie, the observer believed that *Thelma & Louise* was only "relevant" because of the main characters' gender and that the film would fall apart if the sex roles were reversed. While his point *is* true — the film couldn't survive as *Ted & Larry*— casting women in lead roles isn't necessarily a bad thing. In the time since the title was released, at least one thing has remained constant: to appreciate *Thelma & Louise*, one must be able to empathize with the film's lead female characters.

In terms of professional opinions, despite loud cries those who hated the movie comprised the minority. If numbers settle the issue, people who supported *Thelma & Louise* won the great debate. According to a count published in *Variety* on May 27, 1991, critical responses culled from newspapers, magazines, radio and television stations in New York, Los Angles, Chicago and Washington, D.C., tallied seven "con," seven "mixed" and 48 "pro" reviews.[1] The majority of initial reactions from high profile cities were positive. Critics who opposed the movie were simply noisier and received more attention.

To dig deeper into the full story of *Thelma & Louise*, however, a wider survey of film reviews is necessary. Between 1991 and 2001, the development of online newspaper archives provided a means to research coverage of *Thelma & Louise* in regions not usually catalogued at libraries outside of their immediate areas. Including smaller cities like Austin, Knoxville and St. Paul with newspaper and magazine articles coming out of larger cities like New York and Los Angeles creates a more representative sampling of the nation's reaction to the film.[2] Studying a more diverse mix of U.S. cities also shows that the number of reviews per column — pro, con and mixed — evens out some. Still, despite the subjective nature of categorizing reviews, those in favor of *Thelma & Louise* continue to outnumber the rest.

Con (7)

The Baltimore Sun (2)	*Newsday*
The Columbus Dispatch	*The Oklahoman*
The Knoxville News	*U.S. News & World Report*

Mixed (14)

The Christian Science Monitor	*St. Petersburg Times*
The Nation	*The State-Journal Register* (Springfield, IL)

The New Yorker	*The Times Union* (Albany, NY)
Village Voice	*The Tulsa World*
Richmond News Leader	*USA Today*
The Roanoke Times	*The Wall Street Journal*
St. Paul Pioneer Press	*The Wichita Eagle*

Pro (21)

The Arizona Daily Star	*Newsweek*
The Arkansas Democrat Gazette	*New York*
Austin American-Statesman	*The New York Times*
The Buffalo News	*The Oregonian*
The Seattle Post-Intelligencer	*The Richmond Times-Dispatch*
The Dallas News	*The Rocky Mountain News*
The Denver Post	*The St. Louis Post Dispatch*
The Houston Chronicle	*Sojourner*
The Memphis Commercial Appeal	*Time*
The Miami Herald	*Variety*
The Minneapolis Star Tribune	

Con

Newspapers and magazines that printed con reviews noted major flaws and little good in the picture. These critics were uneasy with women filling the traditionally male roles — bad guys and best friends united against the world. The film's unbridled anger coupled with expressions of freedom and joy by women created demonstrable confusion among those who weren't ready for the picture. Negative responses often demonstrated a lack of enthusiasm for the release in their headlines: "Female Buddy Film *Thelma & Louise* Filled with Miss-Takes," "Superficially Politically Correct, *Thelma & Louise* Has Terrifying Theme," "Toxic Feminism on the Big Screen," "*Thelma & Louise* a Good Road Film That Ultimately Goes Too Far," and "*Thelma & Louise* Sails Around Curves, Falls Victim to Plot."

Looking back with the benefit of time on my side, I wonder if the film's few ardent detractors would stick by their original reviews. Frank Gabrenya of *The Columbus Dispatch* labeled the picture a "pseudo" breakthrough for women in film that sunk instead of elevating its lead characters. Buying into the simple gender-reversal theory like the viewer posting to a discussion on salon.com, Gabrenya objected to the way the female-centric movie "tips way over in the other direction" by presenting "so many unreal dirtbags." Though he commiserated with Thelma and Louise to a point, Gabrenya still disapproved of the picture's negative depiction of males and the way the story "gives in to the romanticism of lawlessness." Missing the friendship at the film's core, he sarcastically attributed the movie's power to "the exhilaration of law-breaking, the tingling excitement of a loaded revolver, the unbridled joy of causing huge explosions, and the inner peace that comes from unnecessary self-destruction." In order to trounce the film, Gabrenya ignored the women's inner growth and instead focused on the film's many men and few acts of violence.[3]

Stephen Hunter of *The Baltimore Sun* discredited the film for hiding behind political correctness. He recognized but disdained what he understood as the film's "fashionable feminist subtext." Hunter felt confident assuming widespread popularity of feminism despite the public's noticeable reluctance to embrace the "f word." Like Frank Gabrenya, Hunter found the picture "terrifying" because of "the degree to which violence is seen as liberation." A close analysis of the film, however, reveals that the women each take a good look at themselves and act decisively in a variety of ways including leaving their mates and recognizing their own mistakes. Each in her own way, Thelma and Louise range beyond aggression but Hunter didn't recognize this. For instance, he stated that the women "love the power the guns give them," yet in the story Thelma and Louise learn to care for themselves and each other, not the weapons they use. Far from flat, stock characters, Thelma and Louise fully embody very human traits and are rich with quirks and contradictions, meaning the film and its title characters are not as easy to categorize as this commentator tried to imply. True to their natures, the women handle firearms in a variety of conflicting ways, but they never truly "love" firearms. Instead, they brandish a loaded pistol with shaking hands, point weapons authoritatively and play with Darryl's empty gun like a toy. Hunter looked to the bottom of the canyon and saw what the filmmakers chose not to reveal: Thelma and Louise "smashed to pulp on the rocks," "reduced to meat and blood," hence "a lunch for flies." Like Sheila Benson, Hunter was not won over.[4]

Writing for *U.S. News and World Report,* John Leo became famous for saying basically the same thing as Frank Gabrenya and Stephen Hunter. Like his fellow critics, Leo condemned the film's violence. Particularly, he discredited the way the movie's aggression is enacted by female hands while it also evokes feminism. In a longer, headier piece laced with a greater amount of venom than the reviews from Gabrenya and Hunter distributed in Ohio and Maryland, for the nation Leo tagged the film "cynical propaganda." He charged, "Here we have an explicit fascist theme, wedded to the bleakest form of feminism and buried (shallowly) in a genuinely funny buddy movie." With a cavalier generosity, Leo accepted the film's "resolute" male-bashing because of Hollywood's "long and honored tradition of misogyny," but he adamantly objected to the presence of "transformative" violence and the suggestion that it is the only hope for women trapped in man's world. Leo fumed over the opinions of critics who applauded the film, particularly Jack Kroll of *News-*

week. Leo corrected Kroll's pro stance by saying that *Thelma & Louise* is a "small-hearted, extremely toxic film, about as morally and intellectually screwed up as you can get."

One problem with each of these reviews is the way they miss the filmmaker's emphasis on character development over action. Leo informed readers that killing Harlan makes Louise "momentarily ill" but eventually "stronger, giving her, finally, the power to ditch her insufferable boyfriend," yet his criticism doesn't match the picture. First of all, "insufferable" is too strong a word to accurately describe Jimmy. Secondly, and more importantly, committing murder makes Louise come undone emotionally. She only builds herself back up with Thelma's help. Rather than "ditch" Jimmy, Louise declines to make him an accomplice and promises with bittersweet deception that they may meet up again "later on down the road." Instead of seeing what was on the screen, Leo let his personal anger cloud his view of the picture.

To compound his mishandling of the film, Leo insulted the audience. He wasn't unnerved by the amount of violence on screen, calling *Thelma & Louise* "ballistically underdeveloped" compared to *Butch Cassidy and the Sundance Kid*. Instead, he was concerned about the effect of the film's violence on viewers. Like male critics Gabrenya and Hunter, Leo worried that women would read the film literally, but he took his concern a step further by patronizing female viewers.

> The problem, I think, is the dissonance created by manipulation of the audience. Once we identify with likeable Thelma and Louise and the legitimacy of their complaints about men, we are led step by step to accept the nihilistic and self-destructive values they come to embody. By the time this becomes clear it is very difficult for moviegoers, particularly women, to bail out emotionally and distance themselves from the apocalyptic craziness that the script is hurtling towards.

Leo assumed that women — but not men — wouldn't be able to tell the difference between dramatic fiction and real life.[5]

Rather than harp on the film's feminist or violent content directly, other reviewers who couldn't tolerate *Thelma & Louise* stepped back to criticize major components of the filmmaking and blame the filmmakers. Lou Cedrone, a colleague of Stephen Hunter's at *The Baltimore Sun*, thought that the movie was "handsomely photographed" by cinematographer Adrian Biddle. Yet he subtracted so many points for Callie Khouri's script that the movie "fails," in his view, "because the viewer eventually loses sympathy with the leads," who become "tiresome." After the incident with the policeman, Cedrone lost respect for the main characters, which he never recovered. Interestingly, despite his negative reaction to Thelma and Louise and the story they are given, Cedrone did concede that the film exhibited "some strong acting." Cedrone admitted that the actresses playing them are compelling, which requires an awkward stretch for anyone trying to follow his argument against the picture. Adhering to the perception of women as competitors instead of partners, he pitted the leads against each other to declare that Susan Sarandon was "almost as good" as Geena Davis.[6]

Though he submitted a thumbs down review, Jack Mathews of *Newsday* actually liked parts of the picture, which he cast as a "liberating cross-country flight from the law." Mathews thought that the leads were "great fun," he enjoyed the film's female point of view and he recognized that "big roles" for actresses are "rare." But what Mathews couldn't abide was Ridley Scott's direction, which he considered "heavy handed." Mathews stopped at two and half stars because he thought the film pushed too hard and he disapproved of the "narrative arrows" aimed at the film's "feminist" views. Though he didn't phrase his objection as male-bashing, Mathews was appalled with the "cretinous, tongue-flicking truck driver," whose characterization is so overblown that "he stops the movie in its tracks," turning *Thelma & Louise* from road movie to a *Roadrunner* cartoon.

Mathews is exemplary of viewers who were strangely affected by the film. Once he worked up steam explaining how the movie disappointed him, Mathews backtracked from his initial warm response toward the women and began zigzagging between positions. Ignoring the film's depth of character, Louise's distinct style and Thelma's criminal flair, he described as the duo as "simple and unsophisticated." Mathews liked the notion of Louise's Texas past causing the women to flee, but thought her Mexico plan was too stupid to believe — an opinion that broke Khouri's narrative in two. Despite his feeling that some aspects of the film were over-emphasized, ironically the ending surprised Matthews, who felt unprepared for the outcome. Showing signs of critical fatigue, his review said nothing about the repeated mountain imagery that was designed to prime viewers for the conclusion (but to be fair, neither did most of the other critics surveyed). Overall, Mathews was jarred by the picture's powerful mix of drama and comedy, so he had trouble following the film's rhythm.[7]

Another commentator who experienced difficulty when trying to make sense of her own positive reaction to the picture was Betsy Pickle of *The Knoxville News* who joined Jack Mathews in his widespread appreciation for individual aspects of the picture yet shared his overall condemnation of the finished product. Sounding like a fan, she applauded Sarandon and Davis, noted the title characters' developing friendship as the film's backbone and understood the film's men as "peripheral but crucial." Pickle approved of Khouri's screenplay and Scott's direction. Drawing her detractions more narrowly (and more obliquely), she found one "fatal" error and two "frustrating" ones. Pickle blamed Thelma's behavior after the rape attempt for doing in the picture, though she doesn't make clear how Thelma screws up more than Louise does. She also pegged the incident with the "lewd" trucker and "something" (she doesn't give away what) "in common with the *Smokey and the Bandit* series" as unacceptably annoying. Falling short of specifics, Pickle turned to metaphor and compared the film to a slow-leaking tire with a puncture wound that "takes the pleasure out of an enjoyable ride." Pickle was torn between simultaneously wanting to like and tear down the film, and she concluded that *Thelma & Louise* was a "brilliant failure."[8]

While addressing commentary from the heartland alongside major urban centers is a democratic approach, some of the reviews printed in lower-profile newspapers reinforce the idea that higher-profile newspapers earn their more prestigious stature. Avoiding larger, more germane issues such as gender and rape, Chuck Davis' review in *The Oklahoman* instead worked the local angle. To engage or possibly enrage readers, Davis began by condescendingly commending Scott for doing his homework. When Louise buys a newspaper at the Vagabond Motel, she pulls out "not any newspaper, mind you, but a copy of *The Oklahoman*." Davis didn't want the Hollywood film directed by an Englishman to get the best of the state, so he attempted to cut down *Thelma & Louise* but without precision. The scenes purported to take place in Oklahoma City were shot in Bakersfield, Davis informed readers, adding with a disdainful nudge, "That right there tells you a lot about the film itself."

To his discredit, Davis' response packed more emotion than meaning. His comparisons — "Bakersfield does a good job passing for Oklahoma" and "*Thelma & Louise* does a good job at passing for a movie that could have been a lot better than it is" — advanced a foggy point. Davis recalled Bob Hope and Bing Crosby pictures more fondly, as if he was overwhelmed by the women's far more modern adventures. Ultimately, the lack of clarity in "*Thelma & Louise* Interesting" stemmed from Davis' confusion over the story. *Thelma & Louise* features a "neat and tidy" ending, he allowed, but it "doesn't make a whole heck of a lot of sense." Writing the entire film off out of frustration, he decided abruptly, "This whole movie doesn't make a whole heck of a lot of sense. Sort of like finding a copy of *The Oklahoman* in Bakersfield, Calif." In the end, even more than Jack Mathews, Davis was unprepared to suspend disbelief and go with the filmmaker's dramatic flow.[9]

Mixed

The critics who wrote mixed reviews represented twice as many responses as the con reviews and totaled one-third of the critiques gathered. Like a food review that complains about indigestion following a meal but still recommends the restaurant, mixed reviews united positive and negative remarks sometimes to a confounding degree yet recommended the picture. In this category, the relationship between *Thelma & Louise* and feminism is most clear: the public is uneasy with both. The headlines accompanying these articles projected their position on the fence and enticed readers to see the film: "Ladies on the Lam," "A Driving Movie with Women at the Wheel," "Outlaw Princesses," "Borderline," "Women Hit the Road to Freedom," "Duo's Bright Talents Make This Women's Buddy Picture Work," "*Thelma & Louise* Fun Times in Boonies," "These Girls Offer a Great Times on the Road," "*Thelma*' Makes Road to Hilarity Harrowing Ride," "A Road Show, but a Good One," and "Hit the Road, Jill."

Both con and mixed critics had problems with the film's employment of violence, gender and feminism, but the difference between the two categories was a critic's degree of tolerance. Tagging the film as "slightly offputting," Julie Salamon of *The Wall Street Journal* teetered toward a more negative con review but grooved with *Thelma & Louise* too much to write it off. Defining the picture as "pop feminist," Salamon got closer to the story and the title characters than critics who objected vehemently to the film's characters and main themes. She understood that "freedom," not violence, transforms Thelma, and noticed that Louise "worries" about the impossibility of reaching Mexico.

Salamon took a wrong turn, however, by expecting the women to become heroines. As a result, she was disappointed by the way the film trapped Thelma and Louise between victimhood and doom. Though most of the time the women "don't seem like bullies," she realized, Salamon abhorred the "horrible" revenge the partners enact. Targeting retribution rather than violence as the problem, she too lost sympathy with the duo, who "come off not as victims but as the worst kind of bullies, weak people who trample on somebody else the first time they get the chance." Despite these drawbacks, Salamon described the film's overall appeal in pleasant terms and concluded by recommending the picture. According to Salamon, *Thelma & Louise* "bounces along purely on the byplay between Ms. Davis and Ms. Sarandon, and for the most part that's enough."[10] Mixed reviews like this one effectively upheld society's ambivalence toward women by making the reader feel like a child standing between opposing parents.

Like con critic Jack Mathews, David Sterrit of *The Christian Science Monitor* blamed Scott's direction for failing to unite the film's various "moods." Like Julie Salamon's conflicted piece, Sterrit's review also came close to falling in the con column, but he recognized enough merit in the picture to submit a truly mixed review. "Well-acted" and engaging, he allowed, still what might have been a "slam-bang feminist manifesto becomes just another action picture with too many cheap thrills," including sexual objectification, sex after rape and purposeless explosions. Championing both genders, Sterrit located the false dichotomy of "devils or angels" usually applied to women evident in the film's depiction of men, although Jimmy cannot be fairly characterized as a devil or an angel. Though Sterrit felt that the film fell short of its aims, he congratulated the filmmakers' efforts, especially compared to the usual

Hollywood fare. Empathetic to both detractors and supporters, Sterrit found *Thelma & Louise* "interesting," especially for viewers who might appreciate an "attempt" to address the mainstream box office with an exploration of feminist issues.[11] Like many critics in this split group, while Sterrit snapped at the picture, he simultaneously felt obligated to credit the film for its revolutionary nature.

Longer and more involved than John Leo's angry piece in *U.S. News and World Report*, Terrence Rafferty's much more relaxed review in *The New Yorker* magazine first laid out the movie's shortcomings, particularly the script's "series of leaps" and opportunistic reliance on feminism. However, after deriding Khouri's effort, Rafferty shared well-supported enthusiasm for the film as a whole. Although he pegged the production "an outlaw fantasy, and a mighty shameless one," Rafferty noted that the "funny thing about *Thelma & Louise* is that you can recognize the crudeness of the script's devices and still have an awfully good time." Unlike Jack Mathews and David Sterrit, Rafferty welcomed Scott's direction, which he felt gives the picture's stripped-bare, working-class locales a "luminous expressiveness." Yet Rafferty continued to downplay Khouri's contribution as "gimmicky" and "rabble-rousing."

Like Rafferty, many critics seemed to find fault with the script for little concrete reason. Subconsciously, what may have bugged these folks was Khouri's gender and female perspective. Ironically, Rafferty particularly enjoyed the film's "casual" moments in between key scenes when the characters grow and develop their friendship, which originated in Khouri's screenplay. Like Julie Salamon, Rafferty credited Davis and Sarandon with carrying the picture, playing roles so "vivid" and "likable" that the film's plusses outweigh its minuses.[12] In the case of *Thelma & Louise*, the public's tendency to applaud the actresses but degrade the screenwriter says a lot about attitudes toward women. Society accepts female performers, whom people can watch and appreciate foremost in physical form. At the same time, there is a reluctance to embrace the notion of female creation because of its greater impact and control over art and the world.

Mixed review critics found something wrong with the film even if they were forced to make something up. While Terrence Rafferty objected to "leaps" in Khouri's script, such as the decision to flee to Mexico, Stuart Klawans at *The Nation* rejected Scott's "laboriously prepared moments," such as the build-up to the "preordained" rape. Unfortunately, Klawans doesn't support his position with explicit criticism. But despite his boredom with the Silver Bullet scenes, which is difficult to fathom without greater explanation, Klawans relished the film just as much if not more than Terrence Rafferty. Unlike Julie Salamon, Frank Gabrenya and Stephen Hunter, who were shocked and appalled by the women's tendency for revenge, Klawans thought the film's feminist comeuppance was "worth the price of the ticket." Like most of the reviewers regardless of category, Klawans got a kick out of the leads and narrowed the picture's "strength" to Sarandon and Davis. In particular, Klawans was excited by the way the women physically inhabited their roles. Sarandon stares out through "the most knowing eyes in American film since Bette Davis," and "best of all, Davis gets to swagger," convincing viewers that Thelma should have taken "long, cocky strides" her whole life.

Although he didn't dig deeply into what the women's appearances revealed about their inner characters, Klawans did investigate the film's overall meaning and worth. Questioning the film's appeal, he attributed at best a "lite-feminist fizz" to *Thelma & Louise*. In the wake of the Supreme Court rolling back abortion rights in *Rust v. Sullivan*, Klawans limited his excitement for depictions of freedom occurring in a world where women's bodies are "in chains," which sounds like the kind of political correctness Stephen Hunter objected to in the con column. Yet just the fact that a Hollywood movie would induce a serious and passionate political discussion represents the "empowerment" Klawans thought films lack.[13]

While the reviews in higher-profile specialty publications tend to be longer and wordier, they don't always say more, especially when style is played up as much as or more than substance. To critique the film, J. Hoberman of the *Village Voice* bandied about a series of loquacious phrases and widely plucked references. Labeling *Thelma & Louise* a "buddy film cum road movie given a heady feminist spin," Hoberman summarized the film with hip turns, like referring to the movie's pace as a "chugga-chugga insistence." Three-quarters of the way through "Borderline," which aimed for wit as much as wisdom, Hoberman enlightened readers that "the most subversive aspect of the movie is its representation of the male principle." Instead of finding the women hemmed in by men, Hoberman found the men "trapped in their defensive postures." This situation only bothered the critic a little bit when Thelma's act of retribution against the cop becomes "disarmingly school-marmish," a description which mixes awkwardly with Thelma's newly cultivated propensity for sex, alcohol and the criminal life.

For the most part, however, Hoberman didn't take the movie too seriously. As if he were talking to an acquaintance at a cocktail reception, he gushed, "The actresses both look great." Dubbing *Thelma & Louise* a "party film," Hoberman recalled the façade of the Hard Rock Café when describing the women's cliff dive. Throughout his review, Hoberman called on disparate artists (Robert Frank and Ansel Adams), mythical characters (the Marlboro Man and Ali Baba) and historical figures (Abe Lincoln and Anne Rutledge) to help inflate his pumped-up piece.[14]

Compared to Hoberman, mixed criticism from less urbane sources stuck closer to the source. Hal Lipper from *The St. Petersburg Times* conveyed his delight as well as his criticisms in more targeted (though still effusive) language, even when he contradicted himself. Like many critics, Lipper first categorized the film to set his course, and described *Thelma & Louise* as a "gender-bender road movie." He reported that audiences would discover "a smart, funny, heart-felt tale exploring the status of lower-middle-class women in backwater America" as well as an "allegory about taking control of your life," though later in the review his enthusiasm wobbled. Although he figured that men could "watch and laugh at the caricatures of themselves," Lipper was bothered by the movie's "stereotypical treatment" of male characters, opining that they were handled in a manner "normally accorded" to women. Even those who liked the film and film's portrayal of men still had trouble fully accepting *Thelma & Louise.* Lipper wasn't threatened by the women's antics with the cop or the trucker, contending that the "harder" the women "push," the "better *Thelma & Louise* becomes," yet Lipper was critical of the "bossy lout" of a husband, an "utterly directionless" boyfriend and "sweet-talking poison" wrapped up in a one-night stand against whom the women push off. When he felt that the film spent too much time in "Dogpatch locales," both "celebrating" and "ridiculing" the countryside's "poor-white-trash existence," Lipper held Khouri and Scott equally accountable but let them both off the hook for their energetic exploration of class and gender. Lipper granted the movie four stars, commending the actresses and the soundtrack, but, to cap off his review, which felt a little like a taffy-pull, he described the movie as both "predictable" and a "joy to watch."[15]

Many of the "mixed" responses wanted to retain a large part of the finished product yet somehow restructure some of its glaring appendages. The odd wish to keep the film the same yet importantly change *Thelma & Louise* grew out of uneasiness with the film's edgy collaborations. Tom Alesia of the *State Journal Register* of Springfield, Illinois, criticized the film's promotional tagline, which promised a "comic misadventure" despite the fact that the film delivered "heavy-handed action scenes," starting with Harlan's attempted rape. Under the headline "Duo's Bright Talents Make This Women's Buddy Picture Work," he stated his belief that Sarandon and Davis "almost" make the picture work (talk about misleading promotions), but Alesia would have preferred that *Thelma & Louise* remain totally lighthearted. Grouping the picture with *Sleeping with the Enemy* and *Mortal Thoughts,* Alesia was disappointed in female characters who "violently confront abusive men," though he was aware that Hollywood doesn't offer women many quality roles. His review, which granted the film two and a half stars, wasn't long enough to explain how *Thelma & Louise* might have developed without dark undercurrents, sexual violence and retribution.[16]

Bob Curtright's review in *The Wichita Eagle* presented the picture with three stars, kudos and a lot of complaints, potentially confusing his readers in Kansas. Calling *Thelma & Louise* "Bonnie and Bonnie," Curtright figured that the film was "probably the epitome of the female buddy movie that Hollywood's actresses say they have salivated over for decades." In the abstract, the notion of women sitting at the helm sat well with Curtright, but Khouri's script annoyed him by turning "irritatingly suicidal" and "stupid." He wanted the fictional women to "logically" address their predicament, perhaps by going to the police. Because they don't do what might have pleased him, Thelma and Louise lost Curtright's sympathy by "enjoying their anarchy too much." His review essentially a con at the start, Curtright warned that the women don't run "toward anything, only away," but in the next sentence, not long after he calls them "dumb," Curtright switched tactics to proclaim the title pairing "catchy, compelling and sometimes explosive."

In contrast to more cutting remarks directed at Khouri, Curtright elevated Scott as a "magnificent stylist." Paying closer attention to the director's work than Khouri's, he commented that the film's "perpetual orange-glow" conveys the feeling that Thelma and Louise are "at both the dawning and twilight of their beings which, in a way, they are"—conditions that were created first in the script. Taken more by the way the film's appearance connected with its meaning than the genesis of those ideas, Curtright also commended Adrian Biddle's "operatic" cinematography. By the end, Curtright's review sided with men in control and preferred women who take direction. Meanwhile, "*Thelma & Louise* Compelling, Dramatic" conditioned readers to assume a contradictory viewing experience.[17]

Reviews from Daniel Neman of *The Richmond News Leader*, Dennis King of *The Tulsa World* and Martin Moynihan of the Albany, New York, *Times-Union* repeated some of the splintered criticisms already seen. Neman's divided his review between accolades and annoyance. He relished how "good" and "likeable" a "road" movie *Thelma & Louise* is but complained that "it zips you past a few too many flaws and errors of logic to bring you finally to its preordained destination." Though the movie seemed shorter than its two hour plus running time because it was "expertly made," in Neman's view, the scene with the trucker was "unnecessary" and "ridiculous." According to Neman, who apparently doesn't watch national weather reports, throughout the picture "mistakes in continuity abound." An example is the juxtaposition of desert sunshine and Arkansas rain. In addition, the movie's soundtrack, which features celebrated performers such as B. B. King, Smokey Robinson, Glenn Fry, Kelly Willis and Charlie Sexton, was "mediocre," attempting to replace dialogue. However, by the end of his uplifting review, Newman recommended a drive, not a walk, to see *Thelma & Louise*.[18]

Equally perplexed, Dennis King couldn't rectify Adrian Biddle's "sun-dappled scenic shots" with rape and murder or Scott's "grizzled characters along the roadside" with character development and liberation. Unable to wrap the film up in one blanket description and understand it as a whole, King resorted to seeing *Thelma & Louise* through other pictures. As a result, he ended up denigrating the title characters' gender and ignoring the story's important themes. "At its best," he concluded, the movie "has marks of such compelling outlaw pictures as *Bonnie and Clyde* and *Badlands*." However, "at its worst," he leveled, "it plays like a distaff *Smokey and the Bandit.*" King was another critic who enjoyed gazing at the screen but did not want to consider the film's ideas as much as its look. Because the film is "largely saved" by its leads, King said, Sarandon and Davis are "great fun to watch," but their story is "chaotic and off-kilter," not "great" but somehow "appealing."[19]

Describing the release a "girl-buddy movie" (and later further patronizing the opposite sex by predicting that "women will undoubtedly like this movie more than men"), Martin Moynihan shook his head at the way the film "stretches credibility," a criticism shared with Dennis King and others. However, Moynihan quickly discarded the need for credibility because in his view the story becomes a "fable" that "plugs into the way women resent their treatment by loutish men," who in the film are portrayed "mercilessly and astutely." Sounding like a fan, Moynihan was impressed by the characterization of Darryl, Jimmy, J.D., and Harlan because they "represent at least one trait well known to irritate women" (as opposed to traits that society finds unacceptable). But Moynihan eventually tripped over himself when he returned full circle to chide Scott for reminding audiences, "Remember folks, this is a fable," in part by painting pretty pictures. After establishing the film as a piece of art, Moynihan discredited Scott as if reinforcing a filmmaker's purported mode is a bad thing and "landscapes that look like oil paintings" necessarily wreck a film.

Like many of his peers, Moynihan's critique was a tad bi-polar. Finding the plot unbelievable, Moynihan objected to the four encounters with the truck driver, though he understood the filmmaker's reason for returning to the character and building tension. He explained that the trucker's reappearance functions as a set-up for an "unconventional climax that some will love and some will hate," yet the critic conceded that the ending rightly followed the genre's tradition. Unable to elaborate why he found *Thelma & Louise* so "entertaining," Moynihan belittled the picture and inadvertently anticipated Khouri's next screenplay. "Unlike most summer entertainment, this one gives you something to talk about later," Moynihan teased, "maybe until September." Soon after his review, *The Times Union* published a series of articles that heightened the newspaper's considerable ambivalence to the film.[20]

Deborah J. Funk, writing for *The St. Paul Pioneer Press*, couldn't decide if the film is an "assault" on men or "a fine time out in the boonies." She protested that *Thelma & Louise* is "derivative" and "something of a cheat," but nevertheless Funk felt the picture was "fun." Joining the crowd, Funk recognized Sarandon and Davis as the "best" part of *Thelma & Louise*. High regard for the actresses playing the title roles was the most common element among all the reviews collected, even though many of them overlooked how good acting reflects a tightly balanced script and a well-made picture. Trying to play fortune teller, Funk forecasted that Michael Madsen, who played Jimmy, had the "right stuff," though Brad Pitt, whom she ignored as J.D., went on to become the bigger star.[21]

Mike Mayo's prediction in *The Roanoke Times* was more accurate than Deborah J. Funk's. His review was also less fragmented, hedging a line between mixed and pro critics. Among just a few derogatory remarks, Mayo discredited Davis' Arkansas accent, commenting that it sounds "like her dentures need to be refitted." He sided with the majority, however, and believed that it was "easy" to overlook the film's flaws because the acting is "excellent" and Khouri's script "wisely leaves some things to the imagination." Helped by a thought-provoking conclusion, the movie's staying power was clear to Mayo from the start. *Thelma & Louise* "may not fare so well" among the competition playing that summer in cineplexes, he forewarned, "but in the long run, it will be fondly remembered and often watched."[22]

Not all of the mixed critics disagreed with the filmmaker's choices. Some simply grew a bit bored. Siding with Mayo, who commented that the "trip does get a little slow," Mike Clark of *USA Today* concurred that the "yarn does sag a tad in the middle," but he was taken with the film's potential to "strike a nerve." In a brief but generous review, he awarded *Thelma & Louise* three and a half stars out of four. To summarize the picture's spirit, he pointed to audience reaction. When Clark saw the picture, an "otherwise civil" crowd cheered when Louise shot Harlan. In his discussion of the movie's plot, he alluded to a rather upbeat "body count" not including the year's "most unforgettable" finale, thus keeping the ending a secret. According to the *USA Today* critic, who described the R-rated film in rather pleasant PG terms, "one would-be rapist and a million bugs squashed on the windshield of a '66 T-Bird" constitute the film's fatalities, making the film relatively tame compared to other offerings in the action and adventure genre. Anticipating the great debate, Clark enticed readers to "pick this film apart (though not its leads)," and afterward "savor it as popular entertainment reflecting life as lived."[23]

Pro

Two-thirds of the reviews gathered fall into the pro category, where critics leaned noticeably toward optimism and excitement. Even when pro reviews noted a few drawbacks, the good points they brought up outweighed detractions without creating excess contradiction. For pro commentators, no one flaw overpowered the film's power, artistry and allure. Supportive reviewers also unabashedly gushed their zeal for the picture and urged people to go see it. Many headlines in this group sounded as if they were written by MGM's marketing department: "*Thelma & Louise:* All Roads Lead to a Solid Movie," "*Thelma & Louise* Makes Bang-Up Buddy Movie," "Wit, Wisdom from a Dynamic Duo: Acting Sparkles in *Thelma & Louise*," "*Thelma & Louise* Weaves Bewitchment," "*Thelma & Louise* Two Women on the Run Take a Wildly Joyous Ride," "*Thelma & Louise* a Must-See Movie," "The T-Bird

Fugitives; *Thelma & Louise*, in the Great American Tradition," "*Thelma & Louise* an Exhilarating Taste of Freedom," "At Last, a Feminist Buddy Picture," "Take a Wonderful Ride with *Thelma & Louise.*"

Similar to the critics who wrote con and mixed reviews, critics in the pro category wrote reviews that stretched — from slightly wavering to firmly fanatic. Nearly succumbing to the temptation to see *Thelma & Louise* purely in terms of existing movies, Jack Kroll of *Newsweek* came close to filing a mixed review. However, in his final analysis, what seems like an obvious gender-bender switches "into second gear," as Khouri and Scott "fuse" their talents to create a "genuine pop myth." Like Kroll, reviewers in the pro column watched closely, remained relatively calm and let the women take their place next to men. Although imperfect, the picture becomes its own "big-hearted" movie in Kroll's opinion (soliciting John Leo's reprimand) because of the women's warm and complex sisterhood and the picture's fresh approach to "the old frayed idea of the outlaw as spiritual redeemer."[24]

Citing misleading promotions (along with Tom Alesia of the *State Journal Register*), William Arnold of *The Seattle-Post Intelligencer* adjusted the impression of a "rollicking, good-time comedy" portrayed in ads for the film. To more accurately preview the picture, in "All Roads Lead to a Solid Movie" he clued readers into the picture's "nihilistic" view of gender relations but added that *Thelma & Louise* is also "more substantial" than suggested, with sound writing, acting and directing. To a point, Arnold agreed with naysayers who argued that the film's feminist development is "contrived" and "heavy-handed," yet he concluded "it's hard not to feel good" about a Hollywood film with "very few compromises," true surprises and "bite."[25]

Looking at the film's lighter side, Ted Mahar of *The Oregonian* took in a "mostly comic buddy adventure" starring two "cute, lovable outlaws." A pragmatist, Mahar didn't buy the plot, which he said "goes farther south than the characters," but caring for Thelma and Louise like he did meant he was not prepared to trash the entire picture. With the sympathy of a father, he realized that Butch and Sundance "had outlived their time," while Thelma and Louise "have never come into theirs." Because of his understanding nature and sympathetic point of view, Mahar was able to get past the film's "music video feel" to see the women as individuals. He looked away from Thelma's means and instead recognized her growth. "Some women come into their own with their first job or their first child," he lamented, going on to deadpan that Thelma matures with her "first armed robbery."[26]

Critics who got into *Thelma & Louise* reveled in aspects that con critics berated even when fans detected weak spots in the picture. Rather than thoroughly discredit the film for its elevation of gender, Robert Denerstein of *The Rocky Mountain News* took the film's "pre-digested, market-orientated feminism" in stride (though not without a quick sarcastic comment) and congratulated the film's "celebratory spirit." Putting aside any hesitancy, he suggested that if the "mark of the male buddy movie is resignation, its female counter-part is distinguished by delight in daring and discovery." Like many in the film industry who abuse writers, Denerstein bypassed Khouri by name except to comment that more than once the script "makes a sham of credulity," and, although he subtracted points for what he considered stereotypical flaws of excess frequently found in male buddy movies (in particular "too much bick-ering, too many scenes in cars, too much of everything"), Denerstein con-sidered the film a "fun" comedy and gave *Thelma & Louise* a "B." Though he didn't like the ending, Denerstein recognized a "new chapter in film history." He cheered Sarandon and Davis for accelerating their characters "past pop-ularity and directly into legend," as if film weren't a collaborative effort and the actresses were entirely responsible for the finished product.[27] Alas, even pro critics revealed uneasiness with women's advancement.

Although Michael MacCambridge of *The Austin American Statesman* detected "bits of a dozen other films" within *Thelma & Louise*, the film's nod to predecessors didn't dissuade his distinct, positive response. Just the oppo-site, MacCambridge crowned the movie "the first great buddy picture to star women, the ultimate female revenge film and a dead-on social commentary on the residue of sexism in the 90s." In a review loaded with insights, Mac-Cambridge's discussion of the murder stands out as particularly Texan in its outlook. He described Louise's reaction as a "crime that's technically indefen-sible and at the same time about as justified as anything illegal could possibly be." Unlike critics such as Betsey Pickle and Dennis King, MacCambridge claimed Sarandon and Davis "keep a rein on credibility" and prevent "the more madcap segments from descending to *Smokey and the Bandit* depths." Further contradicting negative responses, he appreciated Khouri's perceptive command of "fully realized" male characters, which, in his opinion, included "some truly sensitive, three-dimensional portraits." He ultimately decided that the picture fell short of classic stature due to Louise's secretive nature and the conclusion's car chase, but he did tell readers that the film was a "can't miss" experience. MacCambridge would give a critical look at feminism's hope for the future in "Magazines Explore Effects of Recent Events on Feminism," which ran in the newspaper nine months later, but in his review he guessed that *Thelma & Louise* would please crowds and "appeal to both sexes."[28]

In terms of professional journalists, fans of the film spanned the coun-try. However, some critics from the Southwest seemed to embrace the film with a special fondness and an almost insider's understanding. Robert S. Cau-thorn of *The Arizona Daily Star* shared MacCambridge's thoughtful appreci-ation of the picture as a whole and in particular his sympathetic look at Louise's rage.

> Louise has done what most women who have faced rape want to do: She offed the creep. The difference is that most people would ultimately stay the deathly

blow. Louise's lack of self-restraint is an act of complete honesty, and slowly, it liberates both women. Poetic truth at least visits their non-poetic world.

Cauthorn carefully read *Thelma & Louise* and judged the film's success, not based on established standards and worn expectations, but on its own merits as a new kind of film story starring women. Some critics lambasted the production for its expression of feminism, as if moving into uncharted territory was a crime; others attacked the film for daring to treat men off-handedly. In contrast, realizing that the story centers on "changes," not violence, Cauthorn felt that the hybrid film works due to even-handedness, "clever ironies" and a "quirky grace." A true fan, Cauthorn adored the ending. He described it as "one of the most unusual visions of triumph seen in many years." The only problem he uncovered existed in the narrative and dealt with the intricacies of character development.

> The only flaw appears when the film pauses for an unnecessary interlude with Louise's ex-boyfriend. We already know about her life; it's written in her eyes and the clipped weariness of her lines. We don't need a lesson on it from Louise's old boyfriend.[29]

Unlike many of his peers, Cauthorn didn't object to the film's portrayal of men. Instead, he didn't see much need for them at all.

Writing for a wider, national audience, Richard Schickel of *Time* magazine expressed thoughts similar to Michael MacCambridge's and Robert S. Cauthorn's. Schickel also regarded the film's landmark nature but with more big-city detachment. Due to the "sexism" suffered by the women, viewers are encouraged to see Thelma and Louise "not as public enemies but as public victims," Schickel expounded. He perceived the film's widely applicable theme of responsibility and related that according to Scott, Khouri and convention, "an unfeeling society" is responsible for the "wicked deeds" the women commit. Schickel viewed the film as a piece of art with symbolic representations. Looking at the release through an urbane and liberal perspective, he did not anticipate the great debate that would follow the film's release. Instead, he predicted a large following for *Thelma & Louise* as a "morally firm yet very entertaining fable that reaches out to an audience far larger than its natural feminist constituency."[30] In retrospect, Schikel's ironic naivete coming out of New York City is heart-warming to those who are like-minded, as it beckons a wish for better days ahead. When the world fully recognizes women, women in film will no longer require and elicit this kind of special consideration that *Thelma & Louise* stirred up.

Critics who sat back in amazement and accepted what the picture offered without giving in to fear and rejection at the sight of something new and different often relished details that other critics missed. Janet Maslin of *The New York Times* was one of very few critics to mention the repeated mountain image, recalling it as a "haunting dawn-to-nightfall title image that anticipates the story's trajectory." She also touched on the little details that marked the title characters, such as "the way Thelma insists on drinking her liquor from tiny bottles, or the way a weary Louise considers using lipstick after a few days in the desert but then disgustedly throws the thing away." To Maslin, hesitant critics missed the mark. In her view, *Thelma & Louise* "reimagines the buddy film with such freshness and vigor that the genre seems positively new." In moving from the minute to the big picture, Maslin better positioned herself to sum up the film. As she phrased it, *Thelma & Louise* wasn't about the "romanticism of lawlessness" but instead illustrated "that life can be richer than one may have previously realized," which aptly encapsulates the positive charm many fans found irresistible.[31]

Unlike reviewers who objected to the film's treatment of gender, David Denby of *New York* magazine didn't take offense at the film's portrayal of men or women. Unafraid to confront dramatic depictions, he opined that the men were "interesting," escaping stereotype "over and over," and that the women were "the greatest subject in the world." Furthermore, from his perspective, the men were "measured" by how they treated women. Rather than seeing the women's actions as mere reactions to a rightfully male centered world, Denby let Thelma and Louise run the show without protest. "Watching the movie," he recounted with amazement and a touch of guilt, "is a little like peeping into someone's diary and discovering an intimate and critical impression ... of yourself."

However, like Stuart Klawans and others, Denby analyzed the leads' performances most passionately in terms of their physical presence, a practice that, if overdone, can become a bit uncomfortable. According to Denby, while Thelma accommodates Darryl "out of habit," Geena Davis

> can be masklike and extremely beautiful, but she's also a bit cockeyed, a woman with a streak of humor, natural and unforced, running right through big puffy lips, apple cheeks, and tinny laugh. She's as tall as a goddess, but she's too loose and funny to be a regulation movie queen.

Denby also characterized Louise separately from Susan Sarandon. Due to the nature of the profession, it does make a certain amount of sense that inner characteristics to Louise are revealed through Sarandon's performance. However, while Denby handled Louise with care and respect, calling her a "man's woman," he ranged dangerously close to objectification when he described the actress portraying her.

> Large and voluminous, with flashing eyes that once seemed to pop out of her head, Sarandon has much greater concentration now, a new hardness around her mouth that plays off nicely against the fleshy softness of the rest of her.

A thespian's physical presence is fair game for critics, yet Denby went too far. He compared Sarandon to Meryl Streep, who didn't appear in the picture. In his view, while Sarandon had become "the voice and image of experience in American movies," Streep, though a "great technician," appeared "lightweight and merely skillful." (In what? Why bring her into his review?) For readers who read his piece through to the end, Denby unnecessarily created an undeserving competition between Sarandon and Streep, which undercut his previous positive assessments, not about *Thelma & Louise* but about women.[32]

Deep into the pro column, reviewers were not afraid to take a stand and say clearly, even enthusiastically, that the movie was good. Look up *Thelma & Louise* on *Variety*'s website (www.variety.com) and you'll find the picture labeled in distinctly positive terms without backstepping:

> Despite some delectably funny scenes between the sexes, Ridley Scott's pic isn't about women vs. men. It's about freedom, like any good road picture. In that sense, and in many others, it's a classic.[33]

Thinking along the same lines, five months into the year Phillip Wuntch of *The Dallas Morning News* christened the film "one of the year's best" and a "superior work of art," which can't be "pigeonholed."[34] South of Dallas, Jeff Millar of *The Houston Chronicle* conversed with readers like he was a used car salesman trying to close a deal. As if he was in position to earn a commission, Millar asked, "What's it going to take to sell *Thelma & Louise* to you?" Pitching wholeheartedly, he continued in convincing terms: "I really want you to see this film, because I think its execution is lovely and you'll make a tight emotional connection with the story and the characters."[35] Anticipating a "big hit," Bill Cosford of *The Miami Herald* gleefully appointed *Thelma & Louise* "the first gal-buddy existential road movie" as well as a "butt-kicking feminist manifesto."[36] Harper Barnes of *The St. Louis Dispatch* bookended his review with equally high praise designating *Thelma & Louise* "one of the great American road movies" and concluding that the ending, "which is original and yet echoes the ending of all great outlaw-road movies, is perfect." Barnes expanded his analysis, going on to add, "In fact the whole movie is darn near perfect."[37] Linda Deutsch of the Associated Press, whose review appeared in *The Memphis Commercial Appeal* among other newspapers, seconded Barnes' opinion. She appraised the film's feminist views as "uncompromising" and finished her sparkling comments with a terse but dramatic come-on. In a one-sentence concluding paragraph she said, "The ending is enough to take your breath away."[38]

The most enamored of the pro reviews beamed their support for the picture with no downsides to relate, at least none within the picture. Championing what he thought was a "wonderful" buddy film worthy of four stars, Jeff Simon of *The Buffalo News* worried that *Thelma & Louise* would get lost in the "summertime shuffle of action, adolescence and asininity." He contrasted Hollywood circa 1974 with Hollywood circa 1991 to provide the historical perspective necessary to appreciate the film's worth. Refashioning the view of *Village Voice* columnist Cynthia Heimel minus her feminist perspective, Simon longed for the days of films with meaning and welcomed *Thelma & Louise* as anachronism.

> If you want to know how punk and egregious is the movie era we're living in, consider this: If *Thelma & Louise* had come out in 1974, it wouldn't have seemed all that rare. It would have been an entertaining and beguiling film about the American landscape and the roles frantic people play. But in a time of drastically contracted movie expectations, this sumptuous and lovable road ramble seems as rare and precious and unexpected as a meteorite from Mars.[39]

A rare bird herself among so many male reviewers (steering at least 32 of 42 reviews), Carole Krass of *The Richmond Times-Dispatch* played ornithologist. *Thelma & Louise* "is a rare bird," she wrote, featuring women in a "buddy picture, a road picture, a picture about pals on the run, fugitives from justice." Perhaps becoming a bit bird-brained in her appraisal, Krass got cozy with the picture's female side but forget or failed to realize that men can identify with female characters, too. She asserted that the film "is for red-blooded women" and "every man who wants to understand them."[40]

Critics who loved the picture were perfectly willing to forgive the women's crimes. Some didn't even bother to maintain any objective distance. Diane Carman of *The Denver Post* shared her movie going experience in narrative rather than analytical terms. She saw the picture with her 70-year-old mother, and both walked out of theater moved to elation, eager to talk and ready to reflect.

> On the way home we talked about our favorite scenes and over the next several days we talked more about what the movie meant. *Thelma & Louise* had become part of our consciousness. It spoke to us. Mom and I knew what it was like to feel like Thelma, who was afraid to ask her husband is she could spend a weekend away with a friend. We knew exactly how it felt to be leered at and harassed by an obscene, vulgar truck driver. And we both knew that if it had been us in that parking lot, even if we didn't shoot the rapist, we would have wished to hell we'd had the guts to do it.

As if responding to John Leo's concerns that women would take the film literally and consider a life of crime of their own, Carman distinctly separated fantasy from real life. Even though she's "such a rabid anti-gun nut" that she denied her children make-believe weapons, exploding the trucker's rig was still Carman's favorite scene because of the catharsis it offered. Purposefully engaging the great debate, Carman addressed the notion that film's violence was overly suggestive:

> So even if we'd never in a million years pack a gun and run away to Mexico, what's wrong with spending two hours caught up in a funny, poignant, beautifully acted movie about two women who play out our fantasies of comeuppance

against obnoxious, controlling people who happen to be men? What's wrong with a little vicarious freedom?[41]

Thelma & Louise opened people up, sometimes revealing blind spots, even within glowing reviews. Jerry Bokamper of *The Arkansas Democrat Gazette* hailed the movie as a "dynamite piece of entertainment," which Scott "pulls off with hardly a hitch," but also reduced the film to "the old buddy movie formula" with "breasts." Revealing his own biased predilections (men have breasts, too), Bokhamper snickered that the film "probably had studio executives squirming even while they were relishing it."[42]

Kathy Maio, a film reviewer for the feminist newspaper *Sojourner*, was just as sexist as Bokhamper when she alleged that "men who have seen *Thelma & Louise* are just as likely to label it a no-see" as women are likely to label it a "must-see." Maio ignored the possibility that men in numbers might enjoy the show and that more than a few women might view the picture in far more harsh terms than her own. A fan caught up in her own viewing experience, Maio claimed to speak for a large but segregated section of the audience. The film "puts most women watching it in touch with their hatred of male violence and oppression," Maio explained, "and, just as importantly, their love of other women."[43]

Jeff Stricker's giddy reaction to *Thelma & Louise* caused *The Minneapolis Star Tribune* critic to become downright silly, though he struck out new territory for the great debate, territory in which feminism was accepted without argument or comment. He insinuated that the film encountered resistance not due to its treatment of gender but for excelling beyond the expectations of genre. Where Diane Carman relied on narrative to sell the picture, Strickler's imagination and fancy kicked in, and he created a group he called Supercilious Nabobs Opposed to Box-office Success (SNOBS). Strickler informed members of "a menace afoot that threatens the sanctity of our most cherished belief: the doctrine that genre pictures, by their very nature, are unsatisfying and meaningless." Of course, *Thelma & Louise* was the culprit in question because it "rises above" the usual "buddy road movie" with expert filmmaking, layered character development, worthwhile depth and striking social relevance. Speaking as the group's leader, Strickler warned:

> In short, this movie must not be allowed to find acceptance among the general public, who may not appreciate the importance of cinematic elitism. For those of us who depend on our ostentatious sense of superiority, *Thelma & Louise* is a disaster.[44]

7. Second Wave

After the initial wave of reviews, the *Thelma & Louise* buzz grew louder as print publications followed expected criticism with additional commentary. What transpired in *The Charleston Gazette* between June 6, 1991, and August 19, 1991, was indicative of the wide spectrum of arguments exchanged across the country — the film moved people from unwarranted hatred to thoughtful reflection. At the beginning of June, syndicated columnist Rheta Grimsley Johnson weighed in with her opinion. "Let me jump into the fray," she announced, then queried antagonistically, "Feminist or frightful? Deep or dumb?"

Aiming for answers (though never quite supplying them), Johnson recapped her viewing experience. She "felt great" when Louise murdered Harlan and Thelma ditched Darryl. Later, when the women exploded the trucker's rig, she "hooted." After she left the theater, however, she began to reconsider what she'd seen. Johnson's "main problem" was that none of the film's "feel-good" feminism could be replicated in real life.

> Things that make us feel good in a movie don't necessarily make good sense for real life. There are gray areas, more subtle solutions. Courts and lawyers and marriage counseling come before Smith & Wesson. Few jump off a cliff until they've exhausted other options. There are fewer chase scenes in life, too.

Despite her reservations, Johnson still enjoyed watching the movie because of the story's focus on female characters. "As a woman," she explained, "you have to like it when a bird of your feather finds her wings." Avoiding her own questions, Johnson paraphrased Susan Sarandon. The critic agreed that there wouldn't be a great debate if the title duo consisted of two men or ying-yang couple.[1]

In response to Johnson's column, *The Charleston Gazette* printed at least five letters from readers who addressed either her piece, "3D *Thelma & Louise*: Women's Feel-Good Film," the comments of other readers about her piece, the film or the great debate. On August 2, one man wrote to the newspaper to express his outrage. Unfamiliarity with the film didn't stop him from mouthing an opinion about other people's reactions. "I have not seen the film yet," he admitted, "so I can't say anything about it." Nevertheless, he called the feminist response to *Thelma & Louise* "shocking."[2] A letter from a second man sharing a plea for peace was published on August 7. Violence "by either sex is not in society's interest," he reminded.[3] Three days later, on August 10, a third man responded to the first, pointing out information that was overlooked. Referring to the history of violence toward women in films, he argued it was time a movie "showed women winning" and that no man "should feel threatened" by *Thelma & Louise*.[4] The vehement opinions of a fourth man appeared on August 12, reprimanding the newspaper for printing Johnson's article. Calling her presence a "disservice," his tirade sunk to the level of an ad hominem attack.

> Lesbianism is nothing new; and therefore, does not need to be featured in a newspaper. Printing this trash puts *The Charleston Gazette* in the same league with *The National Enquirer*. A lengthy review of *Deep Throat* or a "snuff" movie would merit more time and space than Johnson's childishly inappropriate verbal diarrhea.[5]

On August 19, a woman's rejoinder sought to quell the fourth man's comments. Labeling his remarks "sexist gibberish," she too pointed to Hollywood's history of "exaggerated" female stereotypes and lack of a similar uproar. As with so many voices of the great debate, she asked questions to advance her views: "Why is that so many men have been outraged by the male stereotypes depicted? Could they have hit just a bit too close to home?"[6]

What happened in *The Charleston Gazette* was part of a nationwide network of spirited talk. The film became such a force that the June 24, 1991, edition of *Time* addressed the great debate on its cover. "Why *Thelma & Louise* Strikes a Nerve" was plastered under the freshly photographed faces of Geena Davis and Susan Sarandon. Positioned above their heads, a secondary, smaller headline provided ironic commentary, though the content of "Volcanoes: Predicting Eruptions" was unrelated. The national weekly purported to supply answers and it kept its promise thanks to film critic Richard Schickel, who penned the cover story article. Schickel returned to the discussion with a good deal more to say about the fuss stirred by a "very enjoyable little movie."

His extended comments made considerable sense. Despite all the attention the film received, Schickel informed readers that *Thelma & Louise* hadn't earned a heap of money in its three and half week release. Mainly, the picture was doing well in big cities and college towns where "opinion makers are ever on the alert for something to make an opinion about." By not aiming to make history, the filmmakers provoked a national conversation simply because they hadn't intended to do so. The "best thing" about the great debate, in Schickel's opinion, was that the movie irritated viewers who failed to appreciate the precepts of art and expected *Thelma & Louise* to be "realistic" or "ideologically correct." Because of the dramatic nature of film, most of the questions being asked regarding role models, violence, feminism and male-bashing appeared "weirdly inappropriate," to the critic for *Time*, as they assumed that the fictional women and their story should be taken literally.

To Schickel, all the flack about whether the film was good or bad for relations between the sexes muddied the conversation. Putting Louise's Texas experience into explicit terms would have quieted critics who charged the film with male-bashing but "cheapened" the picture. As is, he felt, "the film implies that all forms of sexual exploitation, great or small, are consequential and damaging." Employing violence to retaliate against rape "ironically restores" equality between the sexes, at least within the action-adventure genre. Only "literalists" and the "humor-impaired," he laid out, could find the final showdown with the trucker objectionable.

In regards to whether or not the movie is good or bad for society, Schickel concluded that *Thelma & Louise* "advances the women's movement only a few hesitant steps" because the title characters die. Whether one appreciates the film's suicide ending or not, he contended, it sends the message that there is still a need for feminism, though *Thelma & Louise* should not be held to speak for all feminists. Finally, Schickel topped off his commentary with a levelheaded observation noting that the very existence of the great debate indicates that the movie is well-made and worthwhile.[7]

Directly following Schickel's piece, within the same edition of the magazine Margaret Carlson ignored her co-worker's thoughts and provided a counterpoint opinion under the headline "Is This What Feminism Is All About?" Less persuasive, her views encapsulated the minority opinion. Despite Schickel's statements, his gender and her own, Carlson separated responses to the movie by gender: women "for," men "against." Still, she argued that the film "can hardly be called a woman's movie or one with a feminist sensibility." Yet it is precisely because feminism "never happened" for women like Thelma and Louise that the film provides an expression of feminism. Implying the need for a feminist movement is the most basic feminist message from which all others spring.

After basing her perspective on wobbly legs, Carlson revived the notion espoused by the salon.com commentator and others that Thelma and Louise act as if they were Ted and Larry in lipstick. Like so many, Carlson downplayed the gender-sensitive issue of rape at the core of the film. To support the idea that the lead characters act more like men, Carlson stated that Thelma and Louise avoid "intimacy," which is not only incorrect but also sexist. Both men and women can be sensitive and equally involved in close personal relationships, or cold and removed. In any case, the suggestion that the women aren't intimate is nonsensical. Among a plethora of actions that demonstrate their closeness, Thelma and Louise girl-talk about their men, become criminal accomplices, pursue a desperate goal, frantically tour the southwest, sweat, kiss and finally die. What could be more intimate than facing death together?

A literalist, Carlson had trouble "rooting" for Thelma because she decides to have sex with J.D. so soon after her traumatic encounter with Harlan. Carlson read Thelma's consensual desire as reinforcing "one of the most enduring and infuriating male myths," that good sex cures all ills, which induced her to wonder if Callie Khouri wasn't "fronting for Hugh Hefner." But this position is also forgetful of the facts in that the film explores the opposite outcome. The best sex of Thelma's life doesn't "make everything all right," as Carlson protested. Temporarily, it works to soothe her nerves, widen her experience and bring a tremendous smile to her face. But soon afterwards, when J.D. takes off with the cash, Thelma's one-night stand makes everything much worse. Although Carlson recognized the film's impact on Hollywood hiring practices, particularly for women over 30, she failed to appreciate the title characters and didn't expect *Thelma & Louise* to affect the culture as much as *Fatal Attraction* did.[8]

When *Newsweek* jumped back into the game mid–June, editors dumped pro reviewer Jack Kroll in favor of fresh blood. In "Women Who Kill Too Much" (in a bow to John Leo, subtitled, "Is *Thelma & Louise* Feminism or Fascism?"), Laura Shapiro (aided by colleagues Andrew Murr and Karen Springen) sided more with the likes of Richard Schickel than Margaret Carlson. In the process, Shapiro added a few good points to the argument that the film is pro-women. "Contrary to every law of God and popular culture," Shapiro teased, Thelma and Louise "have something on their mind besides men." What angered opponents is that the women don't hate men, but they don't need them, either. "The most revelatory aspect" of *Thelma & Louise*, Shapiro breezily elucidated, "is its unmistakably female point of view." Compared to the prostitute Julia Roberts played in *Pretty Women*, "yes," Shapiro nodded decisively, Thelma and Louise are "fabulous" role models. And "of course they're feminist," she added, but not because of their violent crimes. Shapiro was able to see the title characters despite the confusing banter surrounding their freedom flight. "This is a movie about two women whose clasped hands are their most powerful weapon," she assured readers.[9]

For the most part, while focusing on the film's key issues of gender and violence, second wave reactions avoided the tricky terrain of feminism by name. About two weeks after she reviewed the picture, Janet Maslin of *The New York Times* told readers to "Lay Off *Thelma & Louise*" for reasons similar to Laura Shaprio's. According to Maslin, violence wasn't the problem since it accounts for a "remarkably small" portion of the film. Instead, the real issue at the center of the controversy was gender. A double standard is needed to blame the film for failing to exhibit "exemplary behavior," Maslin pointed out, because good deeds are something male buddy movies ignore.

In contract to critics who barked up various trees to find fault with the film, Maslin believed it was the secondary position accorded to men in Khouri's screenplay that truly fueled the raised "hackles" of the great debate. Although they "engage" the women, Maslin said, "men in the story don't really matter."[10]

Because many saw the great debate as a must-cover, big story, between July 1 and July 17, two regular columnists and an editor who stepped in for a special occasion film commentary broadcast their views in *The Christian Science Monitor*. Building to a climax, the newspaper saved the most supportive and incisive response for last, which can be deduced from the series of headlines: "The Movie *Thelma & Louise* Isn't Just About Trashing Men," "Wanted: a Better Response to Abuse" and "Why We Cheered *Thelma & Louise.*" The first two pieces were written by literalists, while the third watched the picture in a theater near Harvard Square with an audience consisting of college types versed in abstraction and identified by *Time*'s Richard Schickel as the film's main constituency.

Adopting a previously unseen twist, in "The Movie *Thelma & Louise* Isn't Just About Trashing Men," M.S. Mason corrected that what's wrong with the picture "isn't so much its male bashing as its female bashing" due to the women's portrayal as "childish, stupid, violently reactive, amoral, etc." Mason ignored the brighter aspects of the women's character, as a more balanced view of Thelma and Louise would also include attributes like hard-working, upbeat, loyal and resolute. She also overlooked the distinction between what Thelma and Louise should do to make society happy and what they choose to do as renegades and antiheroines. According to Mason, the title duo "keep going" over the cliff "because they cannot face the consequences of their own actions." Fans might argue in response that the women bravely face the ultimate consequence. On her own, however, Mason sensed that she was adrift. Switching tactics, she noted the double standard detected by Janet Maslin and others, then in sweeping fashion called for viewers to "reconsider the whole violent genre" of movie-making.[11]

Holding the picture to unrealistic expectations, in "Wanted: a Better Response to Abuse" Marilyn Gardner reminded readers of the obvious. "For the relatively few women who in desperation pull a gun on abusive men, adopting the Thelma and Louise approach," Gardner wrote, "there is nothing liberating about a prison cell," which the fictional women "conveniently avoid." Despite her headline's request, however, Gardner couldn't offer a better solution to abuse. Instead, she recognized improved reactions to the problem thanks in part to the film. Like many of the first wave reviewers, Gardner contradicted herself over the picture's worth, at first chastising its shortcomings then giving it credit. Though she personally preferred advances in attitudes among police, judges and women in the real world over art like *Thelma & Louise*, begrudgingly Gardner was willing to applaud the release for "forcing audiences" to "imagine" more constructive ways of handling maltreatment.[12]

With the guidance of deputy editor Ruth Walker, *The Christian Science Monitor* finally advanced the newspaper's discussion into fruitful territory. To set the scene, Walker sarcastically called her movie-going experience a "research project" to answer the question, "Why had the emotional response to this flick on the grapevine film-review circuit been so strong?" Her findings were based on viewing the film with a crowd that cheered three times: when Louise pointed the gun, when she murdered Harlan, and when she and Thelma blow up the trucker's rig. Though rowdy, the audience was nevertheless thoughtful. The second round of outbursts were "tempered by the realization that Louise has gone too far," Walker related, even though the crowd sympathized with the women. Walker concluded that a theater full of "thirtysomething professionals," who were enjoying richer lives, greater options and more "sound and wholesome" relationships with men than Thelma and Louise do, cheered at the film for good reason. In her words, *Thelma & Louise* "made explicit" the seriousness of abuse and attack. "Some kinds of behavior aren't just bad manners that need to be tolerated with a minimum fuss," Walker pointed out; instead, "they are acts of aggression that need to be stopped." Substantiating a link between verbal and physical abuse, the movie demonstrated the connection between Harlan's manhandling and the trucker's bad manners. As a result of her quick study, Walker, unlike her colleagues, recognized the drama's societal and cultural relevance as a piece of art that engenders thought, not a literal prescription for living.[13]

Outside of big cities, the great debate roared on in smaller newspapers, rarely giving one author as much space as Richard Schickel was accorded in *Time*. In "Changing Easy Riders' Gender Isn't the Answer," Jill Thompson of *The Oregonian* disputed the title's television advertising line, "Every woman will love it and every man must see it." Disappointed by the picture's "traditionally male solutions" of aggression and death, she contended that the "movie made for women to love doesn't leave them with much to keep." Expecting social policy from Hollywood, like so many other critics Thompson held *Thelma & Louise* to a separate standard. She lamented that film's violence furnished "small consolation for the many women who will walk out of theater to face actual insensitivity and violence from men." Limiting the release to a childlike "fantasy," as if art held little use for adults, she wanted the comedy-drama to provide "workable" answers instead of entertainment.[14]

Despite the contrary views of con critics Sheila Benson, Margaret Carlson, Marilyn Gardner and Jill Thompson, over and over, across the country, newspapers proved that reaction to the film did not follow gender lines as the promotional tag heard on the West Coast promised. What some women objected to, others embraced. A reader, a wife and mother of two, pressed *The Arkansas Gazette* with her views, which grew out of a memorable and meaningful viewing experience. Not accustomed to shielding her children from reality, she took her 12-year-old son and 10-year-old daughter to see R-rated *Thelma & Louise*. "I must admit that our giant box of popcorn jumped about six inches straight up in the air" as Harlan "slumped downward," she recalled. Initially, she worried about what her offspring would think, but her own gleeful reaction to the murder did not confuse her children, who shared the spirit of her response. Apparently, "sermons around the kitchen table" about "due process," "gun control" and the "vulgarity displayed by some men toward women" helped rear thoughtful, mature minors who understood the difference between reality and fiction. The family valued art for the way drama can enlighten one's approach to life. Thanks to *Thelma & Louise*, the reader hoped that her son would learn the lesson Louise taught Harlan, about rape not being any "fun" for women. To her daughter she offered sage advice: *Thelma & Louise* teaches that she "stay sober and alert to the miscalculations men often make of women whose minds and actions are altered by alcohol."[15]

Unfortunately, con critic Frank Gabrenya of *The Columbus Dispatch* missed the dinner table conversations in Arkansas or any equivalent instruction about art appreciation. Listing "twenty-six ways in which people in the movies differ from people in real life," on July 28, Gabrenya's twelfth observation was the only one to name a particular film. Gabrenya didn't want to grant *Thelma & Louise* recognition in the form of a follow-up op-ed piece, so he wedged his post-review thoughts into the newspaper indirectly.

> People in the movies have amazingly short memories. In *Thelma & Louise*, Thelma invites a handsome stranger into her motel bed less than 24 hours after nearly being raped and seeing her attacker shot at point-blank range. A real-life Thelma would still be curled up in a corner, too terrified to move.[16]

As someone who didn't think much of the women or their story, Gabrenya prioritized the thought of Thelma remaining actively traumatized while the filmmakers allow her to deal with her victimization and move forward.

Two views printed in *The Rocky Mountain News* adopted a more head-on approach to the great debate. John Horn, an Associated Press entertainment writer, mixed commentary and an interview with Callie Khouri. Clearly exasperated, Khouri directed attention to other films in order to put things into perspective.

> You look at a movie like *Beverly Hills Cop 2*. All of the women in that film were strippers, hookers or villains who deserve to die and do in the end. And I don't remember everybody sitting around, going, "So, did you mean this to be an anti-woman film? Was this a woman-bashing film? Was this supposed to be a masculinist film?"

After Khouri expressed her views about the great debate, Horn added his own stand, which was sympathetic to the screenwriter's. Following Khouri's lead, Horn created a scenario to illustrate the double standard in operation. To perk reflection, he quizzed, "Seen a ditzy, know-nothing spouse in a movie lately? Well, that's exactly what Thelma's Darryl is, except he's the husband, not the wife."[17] Male commentators like Horn further contradicted the "She likes it" vs. "He Hates It" theory.

Elaborating on the idea of a double standard, Mary Voeltz Chandler had fun with great debate. Jabbing at both sexes, she used the film and the flack to exercise her wit.

> The movie *Thelma & Louise* has left some fuming over its portrayal of men as furniture and love muffins, decorative objects and emotionally stunted fools. In other words, meat on the rack. Welcome to the stereotype train, fellas. Glad to have you on board.

Once she boarded both genders onto the "stereotype train," Chandler aimed her sarcastic remonstrations at women who feel superior to men and "see the doings of these outlaws-ettes as a betrayal to the utopian and altogether impossible notion that women are the softer, sweeter, nicer half of humanity." Chandler didn't buy the theory that women would run a kinder, gentler world if given the chance.

After equally running down both genders, Chandler broached the pertinent and intersecting issue of class. In most cases, with so much going on in the film to discuss, class considerations didn't receive much attention, yet Chandler understood that Thelma and Louise, as have-nots, "don't know the word feminist." Phrasing her distinction bluntly, she clarified that the fictional women "act" rather than analyze, which is a virtue only the "highborn" can afford.[18] Despite her sarcasm, Chandler hit on a relevant thought. One thing no doubt playing in the back of Louise's mind and influencing the decision to run is her inability to hire a high-priced lawyer. In similar financial straits, if Thelma had a job and money of her own, she might have left Darryl and befriended office co-workers instead of Louise. Had either woman attended college, the two might never have met.

During the second wave of commentary, great debaters became more entrenched in their attitudes about *Thelma & Louise*, even if their opinions were unsupportable and unpersuasive. In Baltimore, pairing up for a united front against the film, con critic Stephen Hunter was joined by co-worker Alice Steinbach, who also decried *Thelma & Louise*. In the June 3 issue of the *Baltimore Sun*, Steinbach took it upon herself to report on the picture's worthlessness. She told readers that the film's characters were fashioned to represent only the worst in both sexes by depicting all women as "dumb" and "violent" and all men as "dolts, louts, brutes, deceivers and bullies." Strongly committed to the minority opinion, Steinbach corralled pro critics in order to give the group a mental whipping. In her outlook, which she shared with a small group of journalists, the film was void of anything praiseworthy.[19]

A year later, in August 1992, Hunter analyzed selected films as either "conservative" or "liberal" and brought up *Thelma & Louise*. In "No Escaping Politics in Movies," Hunter didn't hide his personal slant to the right. "Today, with an economy going nowhere," he declared at the beginning of the Clinton era (which brought record employment and a balanced budget), "we seem to be in another period of liberal ascendancy." Under the title "pernicious" liberalism (which wasn't weighted by a conservative pejorative), Hunter cited "lack of responsibility" as a key component of the "worst" liberal pictures. Hunter's assessment of *Thelma & Louise* devalued rape from a "minor plot point" to nonexistence.

> Thelma and Louise were oppressed only if marriage and work are slavery; and if so, there are two things known as divorce and quitting that would go a long way toward relieving those states of oppression. But the movie labors clumsily to illustrate how nothing is their fault....[20]

Down South, Barbara Green of *The Richmond News Leader*, who thought the film was "wonderful" and "exhilarating," pushed the opposite sentiment. She supported the picture because Thelma and Louise do take responsibility for their choices. At the same time, she polarized reaction to the film by gender, telling readers that while "people are talking about it practically everywhere I turn," women "love" *Thelma & Louise* and "many men hate it." Like so many voices that took part in the second wave of the great debate, to support her point about men who railed against the movie in print she quoted John Leo (as well as Richard Johnson of the *New York Daily News* and Ralph Novak of *People* magazine). Unfortunately, this popular tactic gave contrary reviews and sexist divisions more attention than they deserved, further stoking the flames of contention and confusion.[21]

Maintaining his original stance, Harper Barnes of *The St. Louise Post-Dispatch* couldn't understand why other men wouldn't like the movie.

> It's a great road movie, funny, exciting, terrific acting, terrific cinematography, a first-rate rock 'n' roll soundtrack, a wonderful script, the best ending I've seen in years. And it stars a couple of beautiful, feisty women on the run in a vintage Thunderbird. It's filled with car chases and gunplay. What's there for men not to like?

Like Janet Maslin and other supporters, Barnes neutralized the pervasive male bashing charge hurled at *Thelma & Louise*, reminding readers that except for the hero and his friends, the men who play minor characters in action movies are typically "slimeballs." Furthermore, those who think that the film simply inserts female characters into a typical male-led violent scenario aren't familiar with male adventure movies or they're applying a double standard. Completely confident in his appraisal of the film, Barnes decreed that *Thelma & Louise*, destined to be a "classic," doesn't really need any defense.[22]

In contrast to Barnes, Jay Conley of *The Tulsa Times* disliked the film so

virulently he considered renouncing his citizenship. In his view, *Thelma &*
Louise, which features a "couple of dumb bunnies," is an "affront to anybody
with reasonable intelligence living in this part of the country." Like Chuck
Davis of *The Oklahoman*, Conley protested the film's depiction of the "sticks"
and what he saw as a slight to Oklahoma, although very little of the film purported to deal with the state. Conley also objected to "bad" acting, "beyond
bad" dialogue and "hideous and embarrassing" accents, for which he rudely
singled out "this Sarandon woman." The fact that it rained in Oklahoma City
contradicted his sense of "accuracy" and "realism." (The only time I've driven
through town, my road trip partner and I encountered a torrential downpour.)
Adamantly rallying against the idea that film was worthwhile, Conley refuted,
"If these are the independent women of the future, then Minnie Pearl is the
next president."[23]

One trip to the dump wasn't enough, as Conley's load of criticisms against
the picture was hefty. The following year, around Oscar time, in "This Movie
Deserved the Oscar Snub," Conley related a promise he made during a recent
speech given to some "very prominent people." If *Thelma & Louise* won "an
important" Academy Award, he vowed, "it might be time to leave this country in favor of one where the creative people were not so stupid." When the
awards were handed out, Conley rejoiced: Ridley Scott didn't win the Best
Director award and neither of the leads won Best Actress. Again, he referred
derogatorily to "the Sarandon woman." Untrue to his word, however, rather
than becoming an expatriate Conley weathered what he considered a loss —
Callie Khouri's win for Best Original Screenplay — by depreciating his own
profession. Acquaintances told him to disregard his pledge, as he phrased it,
because "who would ever consider winning an award for writing to be important?"[24] Commentators such as Conley became so turned around they got
stuck in their own muck.

The popularity of the great debate inspired editors to search out new
angles in order to widen the story and keep *Thelma & Louise* alive. With the
help of Alan Katz, who penned "Movie Rides Roughshod Over Truckers,"
The Denver Post covered the controversy from a unique perspective: defending truck drivers. By July 8, six weeks after the movie debuted, a "hundred
newspaper stories and magazine articles" had argued the picture's merits and
detractions including violence. But "nobody seems to care about the film's
depiction of truck drivers," Katz sympathized. In yet another literalist reading of the drama, Katz apprized readers that *Thelma & Louise* represents truck
drivers as "moronic, filthy, swaggering, oversexed, beer-drinking, tattoo-
wearing, male-chauvinist bozos." To balance the film's depiction of truck
drivers, he interviewed a few real life truckers, all of whom were reportedly
accustomed to Hollywood's negative portrayals of the profession, at an area
truck stop off of Interstate 70. Two denied that they had ever acted like the
trucker in the film. A third who gave his name admitted, "I haven't done any-

thing like that in years," not out of respect but because "you get in trouble for stuff like that."[25]

For some newspapers, such as *The Christian Science Monitor*, a review and one op-ed stirring up the controversy for local readers wasn't enough. Between June 16 and July 2, *The Times Union* of Albany, N.Y., published three op-eds and one news feature addressing the picture. In "Movies and Madness," Dan Lynch, managing news editor for the capital city's newspaper, confessed he hadn't seen *Thelma & Louise*. However, like one of the readers in Charleston who responded to Rheta Grimsley Johnson, that niggling detail didn't stop Lynch from leading his newspaper into the great debate. "Movies seem to have the capacity to make women just a little bit crazier than men," he wrote. Despite his unfamiliarity with the picture, he summarized its message, which he felt concerned violent retribution with a gun toward someone whose "genitalia differs in configuration from your own." Lynch picked up on the film's elevation of gender, but he belittled the film's relevance, describing *Thelma & Louise* as "*Death Wish* in drag."

To elucidate his point, Lynch shared a smug lecture about murder (it's not "nice") and a couple of anecdotes intended to sway readers. His first story concerned female co-workers who cheered when Louise shot Harlan and later reiterated their anti-social feelings at the office, "only pretending to be kidding." Next, showing little regard for the opposite sex's humanity, Lynch compared an incident involving a fight over a parking spot with Thelma's near rape. A woman who parked her vehicle in his clearly labeled spot rudely reasoned that a customer's needs should come first. At the time Lynch said nothing but for purposes of his article he figured he should have killed her. Based on his premise that movies make women crazy (but not men), Lynch expected very little good from the one-time fairer sex. He deduced sarcastically that it would have required "just one woman on the jury who'd seen *Thelma & Louise*" for him to get off with "justifiable" homicide.[26]

Lynch's piece successfully stirred a local fire around the film. According to Fred LeBrun, many women in the *Times Union* office and beyond went "crazy" after reading Lynch's column. Because of strong reaction to "Movies and Madness," LeBrun checked out the picture to "see what all the fuss was about." Copying Lynch's attitude in his opening, LeBrun related how he caught the film with seven random women of varying ages and "lived." However, deeper into his June 23 piece, "It Isn't Movies or Hormones," LeBrun carefully dissented from the managing news editor's stance. The implication that "one half of the population is a hairbreadth away from psychotic behavior" is "pretty scary," he reasoned. To LeBrun, the film's subtext suggested something more understandable and less apocalyptic having to do with the fact that "every" woman has had to deal with the likes of the trucker. In short,

LeBrun respected the opposite sex and better understood the role of drama than his boss did.[27]

On the same day as Fred LeBrun's "It Isn't Movies or Hormones" appeared in the *Times Union*, Catherine Clabby delivered a survey of viewer responses regarding the picture. Like her co-worker, Clabby sought to balance the managing editor's ill-conceived thoughts. "Viewers See Positive Side of *Thelma*" engaged female academics, the director of a rape crisis center, a male member of a pro-feminist men's group and regular viewers, male and female, young and old, to expound on the meaning of the movie. None of the regular viewers interviewed disliked the film. Two teenage males "scoffed at the notion the movie was in any way irresponsible," Clabby reported.[28]

Despite attempts to balance the newspaper's coverage, at *The Times Union* feelings against the film and feminism, whether conscious or unconscious, ran deep. While Dan Lynch's sexist views may have been well intended, co-worker Ralph Martin was undoubtedly far less generous. Evening *The Times Union's* record, two "for" *Thelma & Louise*, two "against," Martin's "Feminists Making a Big Deal" blatantly basked in misogyny. Combining two issues, the lawsuit arguing to admit women at the Virginia Military Institute and the great debate over *Thelma & Louise*, Lynch erroneously blamed "militant feminists"—rather than angry columnists or rabid viewers—for the uproar surrounding the film. Unable to support his contention in a convincing manner, he borrowed from *Time's* June 24 coverage the brief quote of one lesbian activist who commented that *Thelma & Louise* "is the downright truth." Otherwise, Martin based his perceptions solely on his own harangue.

Instead of aiming his remarks at specific critics who discussed in print the film's depiction of men, of whom there were many, Martin attacked a nebulous and pernicious notion of feminism. Martin never used the word without attaching a negative denotation. More interested in name-calling than fair and precise reporting, he derided feminism with slurs multiple times in his essay. He denigrated unspecific "crusading feminist types," whom he blasted as a "militant minority," and to reinforce his rant, Martin resorted to the phrase "fire-breathing feminists" twice. The journalist's agenda was clear: the destruction of any sympathy for feminism. He assured readers that "equality for all" is "not what all women want," just an "itsy-bitsy fraction." He continued his angry march, saying, "To believe that everyone acts like the dastardly creeps in the film is silly and absurd," though he didn't produce anyone who claimed to think that all real world people act like the film characters except himself. Spitting into the wind, Martin argued that, together with what turned out to be victorious legal efforts in Virginia, feminists were "making issues out of non-issues," which evidently required his utmost attention. Ironically, he "enjoyed" *Thelma & Louise* but only as "escapism."[29]

Not all newspaper writers who took part in the great debate were as reactionary as Dan Lynch and Ralph Martin in upstate New York. On the Gulf

Coast of Florida, between May 29 and July 7, *The St. Petersburg Times* followed Hal Lipper's laudatory but still conflicted review with at least three more articles engaging the great debate. A second essay from Lipper combined interviews with the leads and a few of his second wave thoughts about the picture. An additional female commentator submitted a second entirely pro review, and a syndicated journalist investigated the trend of female artists creating "loathsome" male characters. Coming from a newspaper that respected and appreciated the film if not deeply at least to a sizable extent, each of these articles offered a wider, more relaxed perspective than *The Times Union*, as none sought to pigeonhole women or men.

In the avalanche of coverage surrounding the film nationwide some articles gave readers a glimpse behind the scenes. Lipper's May 29 piece, "Taking Charge," identified the title characters as "feminists whom even piggish males can embrace." After talking with Davis and Sarandon, Lipper provided readers with information about the creative process that delivered the picture. Crediting Thelma's "metamorphosis" as the story's "crux" (thereby downplaying Louise's character), Lipper informed readers that Scott shot the picture in chronological order to help the players better portray their changing characters. Davis told Lipper that as Thelma, "My personal journey is finding my strength and taking responsibility for my life and being in charge of it." Sarandon explained the movie's theme of responsibility and "self-determination" in borrowed terms. "The point of the film is that you get what you settle for," she recited, reiterating Louise's dialogue from the film. Sarandon's view of the film was similar to her character; standing in contrast to a host of observers, she said that *Thelma & Louise* is about "taking responsibility and not blaming anybody else."

Stories about Hollywood told by major players have long provided fans with irreplaceable perspective. In her interview with Lipper, Sarandon discussed the process of collaboration between the filmmakers, which she believed resulted in a final product that was "probably more interesting than if it had been directed by a feminist." To make Khouri's script come alive, Scott determined the visuals and the actresses completed their characters, sometimes by altering the script. Sarandon described the situation as a true team effort: "We did his stuff, and he did our stuff, and it was an interesting example of what people can do coming [into the project] with completely different agendas." Less than a week after the film's release, Sarandon, a Hollywood veteran unafraid to speak her mind, foresaw the direction Hollywood would take if *Thelma & Louise* was profitable. The accomplished actress forecasted a "rash" of movies with women driving around and "knocking people off." Her prediction was fairly accurate considering the eventual rise of female action-adventure roles following *Thelma & Louise*.[30] Doing his part as a supportive critic, at the end of 1991, Lipper included *Thelma & Louise* as number eight in his end of the year ten best list.[31]

Perhaps benefiting from the mistakes of her predecessors, Anne V. Hull's review, "A Journey to Freedom," didn't mix attributes and detractions. Instead, Hull recognized contradictory responses in her own reaction, as opposed to a lack of balance and cohesion in the film. Submitting a heartfelt critique, she began, "I can't remember seeing something so powerful as *Thelma & Louise*." Hull was moved by the story's violence, which she read as "redemption" for "all" women, yet her reaction to the murder was complicated, as it made her feel both "rewarded" and "shocked." After taking in the film Hull stopped to reflect, which meant asking questions. To make sense of the story, on behalf of Florida readers she asked, "When all peaceful efforts have failed, must women take back the night and fight — against abusive husbands, against laws that don't always protect us, against our daily feelings of disappearing in a man's shadow?" Despite her keen interest, Hull didn't come up with an answer. Instead, like Virginia Woolf, she located smaller nuggets of truth about which she could discuss more confidently. She realized the gun Thelma brings along "buys their power" but that it also "buys their trouble." Beyond the plot's refusal to over-simplify modern life, as so often happens in movies, Hull found considerable solace and meaning is the women's voyage of self-realization. "We could all use a road trip," she contended, "a journey that allows us to feel awake and alive and in control of our lives."[32]

Moving away from personal reaction toward a bigger picture, newspapers that dug more deeply into the great debate urged readers to consider larger issues. "Women Writers Create Contemptible Male Characters," written by Nancy Shulins of the Associated Press, addressed the film's cultural impact and questioned the line between "man-bashing" and "art." Citing writers Sandra Cisneros, Mary Gaitskill, Kaye Gibbons, Jane Hamilton, Kathryn Harrison, Joyce Carol Oates, Nancy Price, Anita Shreve and Amy Tan, along with Callie Khouri, Shulins allowed readers to judge for themselves. With the help of interviews, mostly pro and one con, she presented the case for fiction revealing the reality of rape, incest, physical abuse, sexual exploitation, molestation and alcoholism better than crime statistics. Commentator Camille Paglia stood as the sole dissenter by speaking out against a culture of "victimology," which inflates reality instead of expressing it. One academic countered Paglia's perspective by describing the development of unflattering male characters as an understandable outcome springing from greater awareness about family dysfunction. Feminism's empowerment and shifting power between genders have opened new outlets for expression, as women pick up the pens previously held primarily by men. In her discussion of *Thelma & Louise*, Shulins quoted Susan Sarandon when she reasoned that the great debate existed only because of the title characters' gender. Originally expressed to Jay Carr of *The Boston Globe*, Sarandon's comparison was widely reprinted. To combat the notion of the film reveling in male bashing, the actress retorted, "I didn't hear anyone talking about female-bashing when

Arnold Schwarzenegger put a bullet through a women's head in his film," *Terminator 2.*[33]

Trying to appeal to the entire country of likely newspaper readers, *USA Today*, like its competitors, filed a few stories directly engaging the great debate. In the process, the number one nationwide newspaper sided more with the moderate to liberal voices found in *The St. Petersburg Times* than the centrist to conservative commentators who appeared in *The Times Union*. On June 6, Susan Wloszczyna's piece, "*Thelma & Louise* Shoots Hole in Stereotypical Roles," located the revolutionary nature of the film's casting. Adding her own take to the great debate, Wloszczyna explained that the film "rises above the crowd by shining the spotlight on two women." *Thelma & Louise* casts all the men in supporting roles, she continued, which is "a mirror image of what usually happens in those *Lethal Weapon* ripoffs." Like Richard Schickel of *Time*, after taking time to reflect Wloszczyna wisely analyzed the picture and its effect. She felt the real test of the movie's strength would be whether or not it "strikes any blow for female equality" in Hollywood.[34] This study believes that the film has made a positive contribution.

As the nation's most successful coast-to-coast newspaper, *USA Today*'s relaxed stance toward cultural issues reinforces the theory that newspaper readers as a whole lean left rather than right. On June 21, the full-color daily slanted strongly towards the film and feminism when Barbara Reynolds decried traditional religious views, in the process eliciting at least one angry reader's response. In "Male Clergy: See *Thelma & Louise,*" Reynolds directed her incendiary comments at the leader of the Catholic Church in New York City. Responding to a Father's Day sermon he gave, which was paraphrased in *The New York Post*, Reynolds sparred with centuries of religious dogma, using Callie Khouri's creation as a weapon.

> I don't do confessions, but if I did, I would force New York Cardinal John O'Connor to skip the Hail Marys and do penance by sitting through continuous showings of *Thelma & Louise*, the feminist, bad-girls cult movie. If he sees the movie, which destroys the view of women as passive, obedient cogs, maybe he will understand that women aren't buying a message of men as the center of the universe or the standard of humanity, let alone as the role model for God.... *Thelma & Louise* has a message for the men who run the churches. Even imperfect decisions by women are more liberating than watching men in the churches create God in their own image.[35]

USA Today editors printed one customer's equally vehement reply, which sought to offset the newspaper's strongly liberal commentary. A week after Reynolds' reordering of religion, a male from Louisiana countered her blow to male superiority. "Women are appreciated and adored," the reader patronized, but "feminists will never be."[36]

Though the newspaper didn't employ any writers who came down hard on the picture, over the course of June and July, *USA Today* allowed both sexes and a variety commentators to have their say about the film. CNN talk show host Larry King recommended the title as one all men should see for instructional purposes,[37] while columnist Joe Urshel made light of the great debate in "Real Men Forced Into the Woods." According to Urshel, the summer of 1991 was a bad time for male viewers at the movies because of their portrayals in *City Slickers*, *Thelma & Louise* and *Terminator 2*. In the face of cultural climate changes, Urshel tapped into feelings of uncertainty, anger and resignation by sulking.

> Summer movies are not for guys anymore. We're not suppose to sit around smoking cigars and playing poker all night. Watching football is a now a co-ed event. There are women all over the golf-course. Drinking is verboten, and most of us are two old for it anyway.[38]

Finally, in *Newsday*, two critics of the film who found themselves on the wrong side of the year's biggest argument tried to make amends. Columnist Liz Smith humbled herself and film reviewer Jack Mathews repeated his contrary views in hopes they would somehow gain greater credibility. Ten days after her June 4 column in which she advised against sending "impressionable young women" to see the film,[39] Smith acknowledged her position on the losing team. "Obviously, *Thelma & Louise* has struck a nerve among many women," she conceded, "and it is a big box office hit, despite the disparaging remarks of yours truly." Admitting that she missed the mark (with both her opinions and box office facts), Smith waved a white flag. "So much for column 'power.'"[40]

Mathews was not willing to accept to defeat in "On the Movies: Reaching (Too Far) for an Audience." Again, he claimed to be "enchanted" by the film until the final showdown with the trucker, which occurs nearly at the end of the movie. Holding onto his position like it was a life preserver, Mathews objected to the "irrelevant slapstick" of the scene. He complained that the explosion was a marketing decision needed to sell the movie to suburban audiences, among whom, he reported, the movie was playing "badly" anyway. Still refusing to relinquish, Mathews desperately nitpicked that he would have preferred the trucker "strip to his socks and hug a cactus." Mathews insinuated that he would rather see the women push the trucker to prick his penis (talk about "slapstick") than blow up a symbolic representation of his manhood. Ironically, Mathews "reached too far" for a defense.[41]

Throughout the post–*Thelma & Louise* decade, newspapers stayed with the story and kept the great debate alive. Today, discussion about the film continues online at websites like the Internet Movie Database (www.imdb.com) and amazon.com, where regular reviewers take the time to share their views. As of August 2003, over 12,000 registered visitors at www.imdb.com had cast a vote regarding the picture's worth. Replicating the breakdown of reactions found among media professionals, users had granted the film a mean of 7.3 and a median of 8 out of ten possible stars. While under 14 percent of respondents allowed five stars or less, almost half gave *Thelma & Louise* seven or eight stars. Over a quarter bestowed the controversial classic with top ratings of nine or ten stars. Between July 1998 and August 2003, 114 people took the extra time to compose reviews. People exchanged thoughts about the title on message boards specifically devoted to *Thelma & Louise*. Thread titles such as "Stupid Choices," "Women's Rights and Estrogenal Powers!" and "Conservative Hissy Fit" suggest that regular viewers mull over the same issues as members of the press.

At the same time, amazon.com, which sells copies of the film in all available formats, listed 75 user comments since December 1998. In total, Amazon users rated the film with four and half stars out of a possible five. One reviewer, a male from New Jersey, admitted that he didn't know how to react to *Thelma & Louise* at first but eventually came to value the film. His evolution from confusion to clarity shows the role passing time can play in settling disputes.

> I didn't get an opportunity to appreciate this movie when I first saw it on the big screen. First, I was stunned by the ending. Then, with all the media controversy surrounding this movie I didn't know just how to feel. I watched this film again on DVD after all these years and loved every minute of it — including the ending. Now, I wonder what all the fuss was about.

Over the course of the post–*Thelma & Louise* decade, instead of falling by the wayside a forgotten film, which would have validated the position of con critics, Callie Khouri's creation accumulated fans.

8. Deep Impact

In the fall of 1991, nearly six months after the film was released, *The Hollywood Reporter* referred to the present as "*Thelma & Louise*'–happy times."[1] Buoyed by the first and second waves of the great debate, the film became more than just another movie. Accumulating reviews, commentary and common talk, *Thelma & Louise* morphed into an event and soon achieved cult status. Mountains of references found in newspapers and media outlets across the country between 1991 and 2001 provide evidence of the picture's deep impact and ongoing influence. The controversial title touched individuals, society, gender issues, popular culture, business ventures, current events, travel, fashion, sports, entertainment and politics with unprecedented reach. Charting attitudes toward *Thelma & Louise* over time is one way of studying changes in attitudes toward women, men and feminism.

Fluctuating between comedy and drama with ease, *Thelma & Louise* became symbolic in that it had meanings that shifted from user to user. A couple stranded at the airport after the terrorist bombings on September 11, 2001, labeled their quest to make it home "our Thelma and Louise adventure."[2] A biblical scholar traced the figure of Judith, "sexual warrior," from the beginning of recorded history to *Thelma & Louise*.[3]

When not stirring ideas, the movie exercised emotions. Diehard fans wore the picture close to their hearts. Some people sported actual outerwear that advertised the movie. One fan of singer-songwriter Nanci Griffith threw a package on stage at a concert containing an oversized T-shirt that promised, "Thelma and Louise live forever!" Motivated by the combined effect of the film and Griffith's songs, the woman broke from an abusive husband, returned to school and reported that she's "doing well."[4]

The hope and belief that "Thelma and Louise Live" spread. Nearly a decade after the film's release, in 2000, *The Las Vegas Review-Journal* profiled a local feminist and Democratic supporter. The Nevada newspaper summarized the woman's character by listing her collection of bumper stickers: "Friends don't let friends vote Republican," "Keep abortion, safe, legal and accessible," "I'm a feminist and I vote" and "Thelma and Louise Live." Asked how her banner views play locally, she responded, "I've gotten one finger and about twenty thumbs up."[5] In 1997, northwest of the neon strip, a reporter for *The San Francisco Chronicle* spotted a pick-up truck driving around the Bay area with an amusing though ironic battery of mottoes: "Practice Peacemaking" and "My Kid Beat Up Your Honor Student," plus the often-seen refrain purporting that the title characters remain a vibrant force, at least in people's minds.[6] Those who stand behind the slogan "Thelma and Louise Live" refuse to let the film slip into oblivion.

There seems to be no end to the wide array of people who have invoked *Thelma & Louise* for their own purposes. In 1994, syndicated radio personality Don Imus spoke with President Clinton in an on-air telephone interview. The irascible host suggested that the president and first lady go on TV's "American Gladiator" to battle Harry and Louise, a fictional couple who starred in insurance industry commercials criticizing the Clinton administration's plans for health care reform. "You know, I wouldn't mind that actually," the president quipped. The commander in chief commented that at first he "thought they were Thelma and Louise."[7]

From Charleston to Seattle, back to Baltimore, down to Austin and in many places in between, to be a part of the "in" group, America embraced, reformatted and stretched *Thelma & Louise*, though not always in a complimentary fashion, to make it fit an array of positions. Some had nothing to do with issues raised in the picture. Like Mike Mayo in *The Roanoke Times*, L.T. Anderson of *The Charleston Daily Mail* complained about Geena Davis' accent. "Actors unfamiliar with southern or hillbilly speech invariably render 'anything' as 'any-thin,'" Anderson reproved in June 1991. The reporter explained in frustration, "We say 'nuth-un' for 'nothing,' but we don't say 'any-thin.'" Despite this criticism, the West Virginia columnist engaged the film in order to keep up with current trends.[8]

Perhaps influenced by other voices in the great debate or moderated by additional reflection, syndicated columnist Clarence Page's view toward *Thelma & Louise* changed over time. Like so many others, Page molded and shaped the film like putty. Under his watch, the movie supported multiple theses. In June 1991, Page defended the film against charges of excessive violence and male-bashing. "The violence in this movie is no more senseless than that to which we are exposed in Sylvester Stallone and Arnold Schwarzenegger movies," he asserted, labeling the film an allegory. At first, when the film debuted, in "*Thelma & Louise:* A Reel-Life Tale of Women and Power," Page used the film to talk about individuals who can't take criticism — in this case, white males.[9] Six months later, sporting a new tone, he manipulated the same film to represent a completely different point of view. Complaining about what he saw as a national tendency to gripe, Page named the "grouchy" movie *Thelma & Louise* to support his grievance about "grouchy times." In

"Patrick and David Can Duke It Out for Grouch of the Year," Page grumbled about two "outraged abused women, mad as Howard Beele in *Network* and not going to take it anymore." Once laid back in his attitude toward the women, Page grew dismayed by a duo who "terrorize men across the countryside, only to resolve their problem in ultimate grouch fashion." For whatever reasons, by the time winter rolled around Page no longer saw the film as a "working-class version of liberation and empowerment" as he had in the summer.[10]

One way people can engage in public debate is through the creation and use of slogans, bumper stickers and buttons. "Thelma & Louise Live" was a popular sentiment that sprang up in reaction to the film's ending, in which the characters "keep going" off a cliff. Button available through the National Organization for Women's website (now.org).

Whether for or against it, all over the country people wanted to talk about how *Thelma & Louise* reflected their pet issues. Many found a hook they could use, particularly relating to sexuality and gender. Some such fans held formalized discussions, immersing themselves in the deeper questions raised by the film. The American Studies Association met in Baltimore in 1991 for its annual conference to address the theme "The Question of Rights" and to investigate what it means to be an American. A *Baltimore Sun* reporter overheard one workshop leader raise the provocative question, "What would happen if Thelma and Louise could have kept on kissing and coming instead of committing suicide?"[11] In Salt Lake City in 1992, the festivities of a "weeklong celebration of women" at the University of Utah combined academic speakers with a screening of the film. According to *The Salt Lake Tribune*, in 1989 only 17 percent of full-time, tenure track professors at the school were women compared to a nationwide average of 28 percent.[12] The same year Utah feted the film, during Women's Mental Health Awareness Week at the University of Northern Colorado, the scheduled events included four showings of the film followed by a discussion group. *Thelma & Louise* shared the stage with such topics as "Sex Role Stereotyping," "Life After Rape" and "Women, Depression and Suicide."[13]

Newspaper archives contain vast amounts of copy recording the many waves of the great debate. Whether a major outfit like *The Boston Globe* or a smaller press like *The Dayton Daily News*, each publication displayed its own general posture toward the film primarily indicated by how much the title was either engaged or comparatively ignored. Beyond the amount of coverage given, differences in attitude within a single newspaper resulted because of variances between journalists. In Chicago, Clarence Page's dislike of the film grew over time. In Austin, *The Austin American-Statesman*'s attitude fluctuated depending on which journalist penned an article. In 1992, Jeff Nightbyrd roasted the film's title characters to help illustrate how women's attitudes about growing older were changing for the better. Pushing healthy nutrition and regular exercise to maintain appearances, Nightbyrd served the good news with a saucy twist: in the Austin area, women were "looking at their peers and realizing that their 40s and beyond are not a Thelma and Louise step from the brink of destruction."[14] Nearly a decade after Nightbyrd's rejoinder, in 2001, while criticizing "chick flicks," *The Austin American-Statesman* congratulated the movie for not upholding the myth that above all else women must marry in order to feel complete. Author Susan Smith believed that most Hollywood releases — with notable exceptions *Thelma & Louise* and *9 to 5*—clobber viewers with the sexist message that single women in their thirties obsess on single men and matrimony. Apart from characters such as Thelma and Louise who do not single-mindedly seek fulfillment at the altar, according to Smith the film industry supports the falsely inflated man short-age scare (detailed in Susan Faludi's *Backlash)* by telling women (but not men) that "happily ever after means being a we, not a me."[15]

At the same newspaper, one commentator viewed the women as sink-ing ships and another saw Thelma and Louise as stalwart symbols of inde-pendence; one can only guess why their opinions differed. Perhaps the characters earned a more biting reaction in the 1992 *Austin American-Statesman* piece because of Louise's negative attitude toward the state, which may have insulted some loyal Texans. As for the later article, evidently the writer simply appreciated the film more. With so much happening in one story, everyone remembered *Thelma & Louise* in their own way.

Symbol of liberation and power or sad tale of missed opportunity? What-ever general view a commentator assigns, *Thelma & Louise* quickly rises to the surface. Seven years after the film's release, in 1998, American Greetings, manufacturer of greeting cards, purchased a number of full-page ads in major national magazines such as *Newsweek* and *Life*. Reveling in the great debate's male-bashing charge, the ad promoted a card that celebrated women's cama-raderie in the context of "us vs. them" battle against the opposite sex. In the company's sarcastic view, the bond between Thelma and Louise is based on mutual hatred of men. American Greetings marketed anti-male sentiments hoping to cash in on the *Thelma & Louise* phenomenon.

To advertise the *Thelma & Louise*-inspired card, American Greetings went all out with a free giveaway. The company glued a full-size copy of the greeting onto a bright red, can't miss background. Next to the card, boldly written in white, the ad copy announced, "This is the card Thelma got from Louise before they headed out on the road." To further attract attention, the words "Thelma" and "Louise" were printed in noticeably larger type than the other words. Next to a 1950s image of woman smiling over a steaming cup of coffee, the card's cover stated dryly, "Men are always whining about how we're suffocating them." Inside awaited the punch line: "Personally, I think if you can hear them whining, you're not pressing hard enough on the pillow." For marketing purposes only, below the punch line the advertiser included a personal note signed "Louise," who has lovely, somewhat sentimental handwriting according to the card maker. "Men may come and go," her message reminded, "but friends are forever!" A spokesperson for American Greetings commented that the greeting invoking the film "happened to be on of our highest selling cards in 1998."[16]

The *Fort Worth Star-Telegram* covered the American Greetings campaign, reporting that the All New American Way line was designed to attract women under 45. Women buy 90 percent of greeting cards, yet younger women don't purchase traditional greetings as much as their mothers and grandmothers do. However, what a company spokesman called "tongue-in-cheek humor,"[17] syndicated columnist John Leo called male-bashing. Although Leo's response to the film back in 1991 was widely referred to as the leading example of too-angry, negative criticism, given some time to calm down and collect his thoughts he eventually made at least one good point. "Would American Greetings print a card with the sexes reversed," Leo asked, "so the humor came from men joking about suffocating a woman?" Probably not, since American Greetings markets cards to women, not men. He missed his own bias back in 1991, yet later in the decade Leo fairly asserted that "a double standard has emerged in the gender wars." His essay ran under the headline "Pervasive Male Bashing Not Good for Cultural Health" in Terre Haute[18] and Provo.[19] According to a second American Greetings spokesperson, although the card sold well, the company pulled the *Thelma & Louise*–inspired greeting from production due to negative press.

To bolster their own interests and engage in popular culture's closest approximation of a discussion about feminism, everyday people, business leaders, academics, entertainers, politicians and journalists all tugged after a piece of the film. One way *Thelma & Louise* remained on people's minds was through the very popular habit of naming other duos, including animals, after the women. In St. Petersburg, Florida, a town that couldn't seem to get enough of *Thelma & Louise*, an animal trainer christened a couple of travelling lion clubs after the pair.[20] The zoo in Charleston bestowed the names Thelma and Louise on two bobcats.[21] Moving down the feline chain of command, two New Jersey calico cats dubbed Thelma and Louise housed at the Humane Society of Bergen County lost their shelter due to a fire.[22] Not to be outdone by cats, in Lancaster, Pennsylvania, two street dogs were rescued and spotlighted in the *Sunday News*.

This week's featured pets are Thelma and Louise, two female dogs found wandering the streets together. These two dogs are done looking for excitement and are ready to settle down. Thelma, an 8-year-old terrier mix, was groomed at Petsmart because her time on the road left her a little matted. Louise, a 4-year-old beagle mix, is a happy, friendly soul. All they want is a home together, but really any permanent home will do.[23]

Observers across the country chuckled at the thought of animals carrying on the title characters' names. At the Southern Nevada Women's Correctional Facility, a University of Nevada horticulturist worked with inmates to build a greenhouse and habitat for two desert tortoises who were named Thelma and Louise by prisoners. Unfortunately, the turtles didn't adopt the characters' attitude toward friendship. "Louise had to be relocated by one of the local desert tortoise societies after the animal spent most of its time picking fights with Thelma," the *Las Vegas Review-Journal* relayed.[24]

In an advice column for the *San Francisco Chronicle*, a veterinarian commiserated with a reader who wanted to keep predatory birds out of her garden while welcoming non-predatory birds inside. The doctor felt the same about protecting her two bantam chickens from hawks. "Two plump pullets," called Thelma and Louise, "each possibly a romantic dinner for two, and no rooster to raise the alarm," the animal doctor sympathized. Despite fond feelings for creatures that might become another animal's meal, the consultant concluded there was nothing to be done to solve the reader's problem. In nature, hawks must find food to survive. As their natural habitats disappear, they are forced to prey on birds, domestic or wild. Applying the doctor's response to the film, men who prey on women can't rely on the same excuse because they benefit from a greater range of options.[25]

Blurring the distinction between entertainment and news with the aid of a sensationally named reptile, an Associated Press story about a "rare two-headed female corn snake" bared its fangs in numerous newspapers. Like the *St. Petersburg Times*, *The Tulsa World* ran the grabber first line, "Thelma and Louise are being held at the San Diego Zoo."[26] No doubt a portion of journalists and subscribers fancied the idea of the women, or at least their animal representatives, being detained.

Stories about animal stand-ins for the film characters also altered the film's ending. These reports speak for various wants, from keeping the women alive to trapping them. In the fall of 1996, two scarlet macaws escaped from Busch Gardens in Tampa. *USA Today* included the tale in their column "Across the USA: News From Every State."[27] *The St. Petersburg Times* also reported the story. Calling the tropical birds "true to their names," the Florida newspaper announced with fanfare, "Thelma and Louise flew away Friday and haven't been seen since."[28] A day later the newspaper regaled the birds' successful return under the headline "The Girls Are Back."[29]

Does the name make the bird, or the bird make the name? Bizarre coincidence, or not very surprising? The next spring in San Francisco, in preparation for an upcoming Earth Day event, two additional scarlet macaws named Thelma and Louise, along with a pal known as Blaze, escaped a practice flight. The birds were eventually recovered, but things grew tense, according to *The San Francisco Chronicle*, "when two hawks came in and went after" the trio, at which point the scared birds fled for their lives.[30] Apparently, the message here was that all species bearing the names Thelma and Louise are prone to being attacked and fleeing.

Besides animals, people and things were frequently named with a nod to *Thelma & Louise*. Sometimes newspapers bestowed the title; other times everyday people claimed "Thelma and Louise" for themselves. Because of the dearth of famous female friends, across the country, when two women teamed up the film came to mind, even when the two sets of friends held little in common besides biology. In Maryland, *The Baltimore Sun* recognized a "hard-hitting" female trainer and her jockey as the "Thelma and Louise of Maryland horseracing."[31] Oklahoma produced possibly the most philanthropic case of *Thelma & Louise* naming. *The Oklahoman* profiled two volunteer hairdressers who donated their time to the American Cancer Society-sponsored "Look Good" program, which fits wigs for cancer survivors who've lost their hair. "Friends often refer to them as Thelma and Louise," the newspaper shared.[32]

One week after the September 11, 2001, terrorist attacks, two elderly women in Montana who were traveling together in a 1977 Midas motor home without their husbands were called the "senior Thelma and Louise of the Northern Rockies" by the *Seattle Times*. Enjoying their golden years together, the women wore identical outfits ("red shorts, sleeveless plaid shirts and white sun hats"), as well as oxygen tubes to offset the effects of emphysema. The Washington State newspaper asked, "What do little old ladies do in times of war?" These two were searching for an American flag.[33]

In 1997, *The Las Vegas Sun* focused on a pair of elementary school teachers and close friends who inadvertently followed one another from one public school in Florida to another in Nevada. The newspaper began, "They've been dubbed 'The Florida Girls,' though some call them 'Thelma and Louise.'" The newly reunited women previewed plans to team-teach. According to the Las Vegas newspaper, they recited a credo that also applies to the film: "We're friends till the end."[34]

The *San Franscico Chronicle* labeled two female journalists "Thelma and Louise" in an article about the personal and professional relationship between an author and her friend, who represented the departed on a book tour. The living writer "made sure her friend's final byline didn't go unnoticed," the Northern California newspaper concluded.[35] The same newspaper featured women-run Internet start-ups including one company run by a pair of women crowned "*Thelma & Louise*' of the Net."[36]

On the opposite side of the country, a pair of Tampa photographers nicknamed a spontaneous trip to the Grand Canyon "Thelma and Louise Caravan '92." *The St. Petersburg Times* couldn't resist telling readers that this duo "didn't shoot any people, but they did shoot dozens of photos."[37] Further north, two sisters who launched a specialty greeting card company earned the title "Thelma and Louise of Gay Greeting Cards" from *The New York Times.* The Big Apple's mightiest newspaper inquired, "Does the pair have the hard edge needed to succeed?" Showing support for the film's main characters, the newspaper predicted, "If their choice of icon is any indication, yes."[38]

Based on the above examples of *Thelma & Louise* naming, in New York and parts of Oklahoma, *Thelma & Louise* served as a positive symbol of strength. Meanwhile, Baltimore recognized the two women as icons of dedicated teamwork. Both St. Petersburg and Seattle detected friendship at the heart of the film and Las Vegas agreed, preferring tokens that reflect western motifs. True to form, San Francisco celebrated all of the above aspects of the film's infamous characters.

Although the above incidents share a similar upbeat tone, not all *Thelma & Louise* naming sprung from positive anecdotes, and more than just animals and people honor the characters' memory. As reported in *The Houston Chronicle,* in California, home of Hollywood, Thelma and Louise remain alive — at least in people's crankier thoughts. In the wake of power shortages, "more cynical" Californians christened the Golden State's "most battered" utilities, Southern California Edison and Pacific Gas and Electric Company, Thelma and Louise. According to outsiders who in this case may have been delighted to direct the *Thelma & Louise* spotlight away from Louise's dreaded Texas, Californians recalled the women, though not happily, while they checked out "the morning weather, traffic and blackout reports."[39]

In Madison, Wisconsin, *The Capital Times* wanted to assure readers that two female attorneys "are no Thelma and Louise" just because their brochure on job stress boasts a State Historical Society photograph of a "western-style woman" bearing guns. The ad was a darkly humorous approach to solving work-related issues, and according to the Midwest newspaper, the copy coinciding with the snapshot advised, "Don't just fantasize about ways to solve your employment problems." *The Capital Times* adamantly refused to extend *Thelma & Louise* any kudos. However, the authors of the pamphlet, who urge people to seek their services, enthusiastically adopted imagery that even harsh critics readily related to the film.[40]

Despite some cantankerous objectors, many mentions of the movie entrusted *Thelma & Louise* with the power to usher in trends. Supporters of the film saw it leading the future, though one person's idea of advancement may be another's depiction of chaos. During the first year of the *Thelma &*

Louise decade, a rash of articles across the country connected women and guns. In September 1991, an article attributed to *The Hartford Courant* showed up in Albany and Tulsa under the headlines "More Feminine Hands Firing Guns" and "More U.S. Women Buying and Using Firearms."[41] The story cited gun-toting Thelma and Louise (as well as Kathleen Turner in *V. I. Warshawski* and Linda Hamilton in *Terminator 2: Judgment Day*) as realistic reflections of the female mindset. In the words of the Connecticut newspaper, though "Hollywood isn't always the most accurate of America's social barometers, this time it's on the money."[42]

While some believe there's more hype than fact behind this so-called trend of women buying more guns for protection, after the release of *Thelma & Louise* the firearm industry increased its marketing toward women. Later that fall, an article addressing women and gun ownership appeared in *The Miami Herald* under the headline "A New Target for Gunsmiths," subtitled, "Lines of Firearms Made with Women in Mind." According to Smith & Wesson, which has marketed and manufactured guns to gals since the 1800s, there were millions of women nationwide who didn't own guns but might be interested. To better target their marketing efforts and attract female buyers, the company hired a consultant. Smith & Wesson told the South Florida newspaper that their expert on women and guns, Paxton Quigley, taught Geena Davis how to shoot for her role in the film.[43]

The biggest bang connecting *Thelma & Louise* to women and gun ownership was the duo's appearance on the premiere newsstand issue of the Second Amendment Foundation's *Women & Guns*, which debuted in September 1991. "Some believe the terms 'women' and 'guns' are mutually exclusive," editor Sonny Jones contended. She countermanded that "an estimated 12 million women own guns," which would put female gun ownership at one out of every nine women in America. Jones also penned the cover story, whose headline asked, "What's So Scary About *Thelma & Louise?*" Like everyone else, her take on the film followed her personal predilections.

> The film is really about dominance and submission. The big debate over
> whether the female leads are exemplary feminist role models is interesting only
> in that it separates the panty-waists from the real women. Any real woman,
> placed in the same circumstances, would probably take the same course of
> action that Louise did. Recognizing Harlon [sic] as a cleverly disguised mad
> dog, one that would eventually attack other women, Louise eliminated him — a
> preemptive strike, if you will. Louise knew that she was sacrificing herself, but
> she did so with the sublime knowledge that she was saving other women from a
> horrible fate.[44]

There is slim evidence to support this picture of Louise as determined superheroine and selfless martyr, as she appears to be more privately motivated with no family or friends other than Thelma and no signs of charitable philanthropy outside their relationship. Still, Louise tells Harlan, "When

In September 1991, the first newsstand issue of the Second Amendment Foundation's *Women & Guns* featured *Thelma & Louise* on the cover. A link between women and weapons was one of many trends attributed to the film. (Courtesy of *Women & Guns* and the Second Amendment Foundation.)

a woman is crying like that, she isn't having any fun," then blows him away. Reasonably, she could be seen as a savior for women, although I would argue that she speaks out of personal experience and pain only. Louise doesn't appear to consciously shoot Thelma's attacker on behalf of future victims. Rather, she subconsciously shoots him in response to her own past, but Jones interpreted Louise's actions as she saw fit.

While some believed the time had come for women to arm themselves in greater numbers in order to fend off would-be aggressors, others took a less fatal approach to boosting the image of women's strength and the film. According to *The Baltimore Sun*, women were "pumped up on iron or attitude instead of the old sugar and spice" in response to renewed indignation towards battering, date rape, catcalls and sexual harassment. The opening of "Good Women Gone Bad" recalled the scene in which Thelma forces a New Mexico police officer into the trunk of his squad car at gunpoint. Because Thelma utilizes the handgun as a symbol of her power and will but does not fire, the newspaper viewed her actions as commanding rather than criminal. This same newspaper, which printed Frank Gabrenya, Stephen Hunter and Alice Steinbach's fiercely con reviews, championed a positive connotation of bad women, "being unafraid of being tough, either mentally or physically." Unlike the staff journalists who criticized the film's violence, syndicated writer Jean Marbella lauded Thelma's decisiveness. In *The Baltimore Sun*, three months after the picture was derided, Thelma represented "a dame in charge rather than a damsel in distress."[45] The same article appeared in Albany as "Bad Women No More Sugar, Spice,"[46] in Tulsa under the designation "It's Good to Be Bad"[47] and in Charleston as "Dame in Charge Rather Than Damsel in Distress, Bad Becoming Beautiful For American Women."[48]

After the film simmered for a couple of years, *USA Today* covered women's changing attitudes and behavior from yet another angle in "Women a Big Market for 'Legal' Drug Pushers." In 1993, the national daily reported that women were being "calmed down in record numbers" thanks to Miltown, Valium, Librium, Thorazine and the newest "mood sweeteners for women," Prozac and Klonopin. Perhaps women had built up brawn and brain but found few opportunities in which to use them, so instead of nurturing muscle mass and outfitting arsenals, large numbers of women were said to take tranquilizers. According to *USA Today*'s article, the push to drug women was "an interesting part of the backlash" expected to increase as women become "more direct" and drug company profits rose. Writer Joan Lester disdainfully called such drugs "general anesthesia" to contain women's rage. To balance this disturbing trend, *USA Today* reported, "fortunately, the niceness compulsion" historically attributed to women "has been wearing off, as the commercial success of Roseanne and Thelma and Louise attest."[49]

Whether considered positive or negative, it's difficult to deny the film's profound influence. Looking back on 1991, in 1995, *The Roanoke Times* contended that Callie Khouri, through *Thelma & Louise*, "unleashed a national war of the sexes."[50] Three years before, *The Rocky Mountain News* didn't go that far but did mention *Thelma & Louise* and its scribe in a February 1992 article titled "Oldest Battle on the Planet Still Rages On" and subtitled "On Valentine's Weekend, All's Fair in Love and War, Because the Two Are So Impossible to Tell Apart." The Colorado newspaper alluded to Khouri soon after *Thelma & Louise* was nominated for the Best Original Screenplay Oscar. "If you ask a few dozen people for their slant on the war between men and women," the newspaper suggested, "a feminist screenwriter will tell you that contemplating killing a man can be a surefire spur to creativity." Reminding readers how *Thelma & Louise* was "debated with odd passion on talk shows and in national magazines," the newspaper grouped the film with other recent, high-profile battles that pitted men against women. The battle between Supreme Court nominee Clarence Thomas and Anita Hill, the rape charges against William Kennedy Smith by Patricia Bowman, as well as the rape charges against Mike Tyson by Desiree Washington took their places beside the fictional *Thelma & Louise*. According to *The Rocky Mountain News*, the group of newsmakers constituted evidence of the "multi-millenia male-female saga." Undeniably, most movies come and go without making such a strong impression or mixing so vitally with the real world.[51]

The film made an undeniable mark, representing to many women's will and resolve while to others the title characters symbolized troublemakers. To some, Thelma and Louise instilled a mock sense of fear and respect. In the summer of 1992, *USA Today* commented on *Esquire*'s annual "Women We Love" feature, reporting that the magazine apologized to feminist authors and fictional film characters "Susan Faludi, Naomi Wolf, Thelma, Louise" for its "patronizing and objectifying exercise."[52] Others took women's strength more seriously. A 1991 doctor's advice column in *The Oklahoman* addressed relative longevity for men and women. According to the doctor, before the 20th century the risks related to pregnancy and childbirth resulted in men outliving women, but that trend has since reversed. Apart from medical advances, women live longer because they are not necessarily the weaker sex psychologically. Even though the film failed to play well in the Heartland, the medical expert mentioned the title characters in his column: "Thelma and Louise remind us: No force stronger than a woman wronged." More definitive than *The Roanoke Times*, which attributed the film's release with starting a war, the doctor reckoned that the picture itself *was* the war. Attributing to *Thelma & Louise* a power and reach far greater than most Hollywood releases, which seek to set the box office on fire, not ignite public debate, Dr. Randy Eichner pinpointed the movie as "the latest war between the sexes." Like West Virginia and Wisconsin, Oklahoma may not have supported the film as strongly as other states, but people there still wanted to talk about how *Thelma*

& Louise related to the larger culture in order to play a part in the country's preoccupation with the film.[53]

While *Thelma & Louise* became a one-size-fits-all symbol of the so-called gender war, when the fight got too rough and weary the film easily switched gears to represent the rosier side of women's friendships. Tamara Traeder, co-author of *Girlfriends: Invisible Bonds, Enduring Ties*, the first in a series of *Girlfriends* books, explained to *USA Today* in 1995 that women's friendships with other women are "their true long-term relationships," not marriages. Contradicting Peter Rainer and Margaret Carlson who criticized the film for lacking intimacy, Traeder pointed to films like *Thelma & Louise*, *The Color Purple* and *Fried Green Tomatoes* as welcome outlets for a woman's need to share personal stories with members of their own gender.[54] As Traeder and co-author Carmen Renee Berry express in their book, "We believe we redefine our womanhood within the context of our relationships with women — with our girlfriends."[55] According to the authors, sisterhood doesn't "seem to get much attention elsewhere."[56] Decades after Virginia Woolf, over a quarter century since Molly Haskell's *From Reverence to Rape*, and just a few years after *Thelma & Louise*, Wild Canyon Press bet on the existence of an audience still hungry for stories of female friendship.

Some of those friendships put the pedal to the metal in homage to *Thelma & Louise*. *Thelma & Louise* revitalized and reinvented the American road trip by playing up the fun and freedom of the open road. It's impossible to know how many non-journalist types donned scarves and sunglasses to cross the country Hollywood-style, but associating interstate travel by automobile with the film was definitely popular among writers. In 1993, one Washington, D.C., girlfriend talked her travel mate out of a trip to Cancun and into a tour of Graceland; she called their adventure "our own Thelma and Louise Tour of the South." As her article in *The Washington Post* regaled: "We ended up buying a cowboy hat. (All right, I did.) We got stopped by the cops. (All right, she did.) We didn't, however, kill any men ... At least none that we know of."[57] Another journalist from Austin described the road trip she took with a woman friend to Key West in 1997 in similar non-destructive terms while still regaling the film: "We felt like *Thelma & Louise*—complete with dark sunglasses and head scarves blowing in the wind — except we obeyed the speed limits."[58]

In *The Bad Girl's Guide to the Open Road*, published in 1999, Cameron Tuttle introduces her defiant and lighthearted topic with an obvious allusion to the film. The first line of her off-beat reference advises, "Despite what you've seen in the movies, you don't have to kill a man to go on a road trip." Tuttle elaborates, "Just wanting to kill someone is enough." Very fond of Thelma and Louise, Tuttle encourages any woman who feels "overwhelmed, depressed, crazy, bored, exhausted, or all of the above" to "hit the road."[59]

Covered in plastic as if to resist motor oil stains and colored pink to leave no doubt as to its audience, Tuttle's glove compartment-sized book relies heavily on a slice of culture saturated in *Thelma & Louise*, which is listed among recommended "road movies." When choosing travel companions, *The Bad Girl's Guide to the Open Road* suggests pairing up with someone not totally familiar, "someone who will surprise you along the way," evoking the initial distance between Thelma and Louise. Tuttle encourages the selection of a "road sister" who has "no scruples about bending the law when necessary." Although she relishes the criminal element of the film, the author lists several "non-gun weapons" that could be employed in case of a threat, such as a high-heeled shoe and car keys.

Nods to the film abound throughout the book, which mixes humor with actual pointers. According to Tuttle, one liberating persona "road sisters" can adopt is based on *Thelma & Louise*, with a look described as "rugged yet feminine," consisting of "jeans, cowboy boots, and a sleeveless shirt." Beyond clothes, women who travel in the spirit of the film's anti-heroines beam an attitude that says, "Treat me nice or I'll blow you away," yet they aim for a trip that allows for a return to work instead of a trip to jail, after the trip's conclusion. Instead of sky diving without a seat belt (which would prevent readers from buying subsequent *Bad Girl Guides*), Tuttle's imaginary spin-off Thelma and Louise head for "FBI headquarters for the tour and a little target practice." After counseling road trippers to consider the possibility of serial killers before picking up hitchhikers, in the case of an appealing roadside stranger *A Bad Girl's Guide to the Open Road* calls for a "Brad Pitt stop" to allow for a "closer look" without "commitment."

Mention "automobile," "road trip" or simply "driving" and more than one person will think of *Thelma & Louise*. In 2000, commemorating Seattle's one hundred year "autoversary" (one hundred years of cars in the city), *The Seattle Times* revved up enthusiasm by touting automobiles as "America's economic engine and our engine of adventure, from *Sullivan's Travels* to *Route 66* to *Thelma and Louise*."[60] In San Francisco, the "term road trip conjures up a vision for everyone," especially "Thelma and Louise ripping up the freeway with the top down and independence raging."[61] Like St. Petersburg and the city by the bay, Seattle is another town that couldn't seem to talk enough about the film. Bemoaning potholes and requesting nominations for the city's worst, on June 16, 1997, *The Seattle Times* "pothole of the week" first prize was awarded to a "chasm" that "felt like Thelma and Louise exploring the Grand Canyon."[62]

No other women rule the road like Callie Khouri's creations. Recalling "marathon" roadtripping with her father, a columnist in Arizona complained, "Maybe Thelma and Louise could get him to stop for a break." She said resignedly, "I seldom can."[63] Ten years after Thelma and Louise flew off a cliff, *The Baltimore Sun* featured the maiden voyage of eight "heady twentysomethings" in a "cast-off school bus painted green." Although reporter Jaimee Rose made ostensible and almost obligatory comparisons to the film, echoes of *Thelma & Louise* also rang in the words of the travelers, who were young teenagers in 1991. "We don't know where we're going, we don't know what we're doing," a 22-year-old male admitted. "You could say it's a rite of passage," he posited, "or you could say we're nuts." Like Louise coming to terms with Texas and Thelma separating from Darryl, he summarized the trip by saying, "We're all looking for epiphanies." A 22-year-old female member of the group said, "I guarantee we're going to get pulled over in every state at least once." Too young to directly recall the great debate, the young woman's words were probably influenced by *Thelma & Louise*. She went on to predict darkly, "We're gonna die on this trip," something that didn't happen on the road to Odysseus, Lewis, Clark, Bing Crosby, Bob Hope, Jack Kerouac's characters, Ken Kesey or the Merry Pranksters.[64]

Whether soul searching or simply looking for something to wear, people turned to the film for direction. In July 1991, as *The Oregonian* explained via a Newhouse News Service article, "Cultural commentators aren't the only ones talking about *Thelma & Louise.*" The syndicated piece named the film in nine out of 16 paragraphs, explaining that it was "making news in fashion circles, too." Like Cameron Tuttles' *The Bad Girl's Guide to the Open Road*, *The Oregonian's* article "Rags for the Road" described the *Thelma & Louise* look: "tight jeans, cowboy boots, sleeveless blouse, denim shirt knotted at the waist, a small kerchief knotted around the neck."[65] Two months later, in August, *USA Today* reported that "the hot look for gals is a muscle T-shirt (or a T with sleeves cut off); no bra; dirty jeans or army pants; pilot sunglasses; uncombed, messy hair; and no jewelry at all," as inspired by Linda Hamilton in *Terminator 2* and Geena Davis and Susan Sarandon in *Thelma & Louise.*[66] At a September fashion show in Charleston, as detailed in *The Charleston Gazette*, the emcee bragged "that leather brings out the 'Thelma and Louise' in everyone." Evidently, the commentator didn't want to bypass the opportunity to connect her event to the film, which was a practice definitely in vogue. Apparently, however, she hadn't seen *Thelma & Louise*, which casts its lead women in denim.[67]

During the summer of 1991, the film's fashion influence extended beyond outerwear to hair color, as reported by *USA Today*, which pointed to the fictional women as hot examples of the trend to go red.[68] Three-quarters of the way through 1992, *USA Today* continued to credit *Thelma & Louise* with the power and persuasion to define popular looks. "Risque Clothing Ads Show That Sex Sells" designated a 48-page *Details* magazine insert advertising Request jeans — "*Thelma & Louise* meet *9½ Weeks.*" According to Elizabeth Snead, who wrote all three articles linking the film to fashion for the national newspaper, the promotion evoked Hollywood because it included "a hitchhiker, two girls, guns, ropes and a motel room."[69]

Eventually, each aspect of the women's costumes from hairstyle to footwear were admired and copied. Memorial Day weekend 1992, *The Richmond Times Dispatch* credited the holiday with kicking off "sunglass season." According to the Virginia newspaper, Sunglasses Hut was accustomed to people inquiring about sunglasses spotted in movies, including Sarandon's retro tortoise shell eyewear, which in conjunction with a scarf wrapped over the head and around the neck caricaturized the essence of a reserved but proud Louise.[70]

In a culture enamored with appearances, fashionable influences affect not only tangibles, such as clothing ensembles and personal accessories, but also postures and pastimes. Soon after the film's release, some felt it encouraged gun sales, elevated female friendship, reinvigorated road trips and popularized a road-commando sense of style. Three years after Thelma and Louise took matters into their own hands while wearing cowboy gear, *The Houston Chronicle* examined the national trend to appropriate "western heritage" evident on television, in movie theaters and at book and music stores. Western migrations, increased rodeo ticket sales and nationwide interest in line dancing also supported the Texas newspaper's theory. Among movies mentioned, including *Tombstone* (1993) and *Wyatt Earp* (1994), *The Houston Chronicle* spotlighted *Thelma & Louise* as its lead example of western movies. The Lone Star State publication didn't single out the film for its gender bending exercises but for its take-no-prisoners attitude.

> Though set in modern times, it was a classic cowboy movie. A man harasses you? Blow up his truck. In a society where inappropriate or criminal behavior generally is seen as a sad consequence of social misfortune, such deal-with-it action can be awfully appealing.[71]

As the post–*Thelma & Louise* decade progressed, the film's considerable impact on tastes and trends remained strong. Cultural commentators found real-life women emulating the film's tough characters and major advertisers borrowed the *Thelma & Louise* mood to cash in on the film's popularity. In 1994, *The St. Petersburg Times* chronicled a host of new Diet Coke television commercials. Like *USA Today* discovered in *Details*, the Gulf Coast newspaper detected the *Thelma & Louise* spirit within the soft drink advertisements.

> True to Diet coke's target audience, the ads don't forget to show women with a sense of freedom and control. In one spot, a young woman pulls up in front of a pool hall and unloads her boyfriend's possessions from the trunk of her convertible. The boyfriend emerges, and as the Band's "The Weight" plays in background, she tosses his suitcase toward him, drop-kicks his baseball glove and stomps on his cowboy hat. Then she smirks, jumps back in the car, scratches the head of her dog and drives off.

Figuratively speaking, according to the Florida newspaper, the commercial was "a scene straight from Thelma and Louise."[72] As one of the world's premiere advertisers, the Coca-Cola Company's flattery of and confidence in the film strongly underscore the film's selling power.

Like the fashion host who remembered leather in a film whose leads actually wore jeans, *Thelma & Louise* so impressed people and empowered women, things were taken away from it that never appeared on screen. Up the eastern seaboard from Florida, a handful of states to the north, *The Record* picked up an article from *The Dallas Morning News*, which the New Jersey newspaper entitled, "Chick Is Chic Again — Just Watch Who You Say It To and When." As reported, the nineties' "chick" (as opposed to the sixties' "chick") was promoted from sidekick to center stage. "Just look at *Thelma & Louise*, the saga of two Nineties' chicks on a bizarre road trip," Colleen O'Connor pointed out.[73] Never mind that the word "chick" is never used in the film. In the years since its release, *Thelma & Louise* has come to represent much more than sum of its parts.

9. The *Thelma & Louise*-ing of American Culture

It's impossible to know just how far and wide the film has affected American culture, but indications suggest that the allure of *Thelma & Louise* befits a film whose characters dive into what is imagined to be the Grand Canyon. *Thelma & Louise* became so deeply ingrained in our popular mindset, people automatically thought of the film when any one of a host of cues were invoked: sticky gender issues, perky duos, women on the verge of breakdown, women on the rebound from victimhood, women taking charge, female friendships, breakout road trips and dusty road wear. In some cases, like the Diet Coke commercial noted in Florida, the film was copied for its representation of resilience and independence. To others, *Thelma & Louise* touted nothing more than vigilante justice.

When country music crossover artists the Dixie Chicks debuted their 1999 album *Fly*, a song about two women who decide an abusive husband must be killed elicited numerous comparisons to the film. *The Houston Chronicle* was one newspaper that mentioned the film and the song in relation to one another: "'Goodbye Earl' is a *Thelma & Louise* tale of two women who conspire to murder an abusive husband and get away with it."[1] *The Atlanta Journal-Constitution* interpreted the song as a "*Thelma & Louise* ballad of an abused woman who decides to kill her husband."[2] Though many recognized a connection between "Goodbye Earl" and *Thelma & Louise*, not everyone offered a neutral reaction. According to a local priest published in *The Telegraph Herald* of Dubuque, Iowa, because the "murderesses" don't emit sadness or guilt, the two women in "Goodbye Earl" plus "their culture and admirers of the song" sank even lower than Thelma and Louise, "who at least got rough justice by means of their semi-suicidal deaths."[3] Not moved by any measure of empathy, the Heartland commentator wasn't willing to fully credit Khouri's anti-heroines with their own deaths. Where the first two references out of Texas and Georgia accepted Thelma and Louise as cultural symbols without question or comment, the third reference from Iowa, eight years after the film's release, passed judgment and found the lead characters guilty.

America's breadbasket may be the place to go if morality is the question, but for more in-depth artistic analysis New York City still leads the pack. Arriving at the same conclusion as *The Houston Chronicle* and *The Atlanta Journal-Constitution*, the *Village Voice* provided additional information and greater reflection regarding the Dixie Chicks' song and its intersection with *Thelma & Louise*. Not only do the two women in "Goodbye Earl" murder an abusive husband, afterward they "happily partner up," taking female friendship a step beyond that in the film. Cued into the controversy surrounding both releases, the *Village Voice* elucidated, "To the heartland, Earl's fate seems like over-the-top manhating," much like some people viewed the movie's treatment of the trucker. "To cooler complainants," however, the Dixie Chicks' song is nothing more than "*Thelma & Louise* redux," according to Eric Weisbard. Conveying a nonplussed attitude toward the earlier cinematic release, he nonetheless recognized the film's place in cultural history. Moreover, Weisbard was interested in varied responses to creative endeavors. Regarding the Dixie Chicks' lyrics, he pointed out that "what's hardly wild to rockers"—lesbianism—"is beyond the pale in country." The distinction that separates country audiences from rock lovers is similar to the way *Thelma & Louise* played to enthusiastic crowds in what MGM management considered more "sophisticated" areas, such as New York City, while it received a cooler reception from locales in the interior, like Dubuque.[4] In the U.S., despite the designation "one nation under God," citizens hold conflicting opinions about art and entertainment, as well as politics and moral values.

Whether or not songwriter Dennis Linde wrote "Goodbye Earl" with *Thelma & Louise* in mind, singer-songwriter Tori Amos informed audiences that her ballad "Me and a Gun" was intended as a "reaction" to the rape scene in the film, according to *The Richmond Times Dispatch*.[5] With Amos' tribute added to a sea of other nods, clearly the movie attracted a significant but varied following. Like those who wanted to buy the same sunglasses as the weary waitress, some fans viewed *Thelma & Louise* as superficial outerwear. Others recalled the film's more serious social content, such as Amos and the Nanci Griffith fan who changed her life rather than her appearance.

Unless proven wrong by evidence found within the picture, all readings of the film are valid, even if wacky or irreverent. Held at the Pyramid Breweries, the Berkeley Saturday Night Outdoor Cinema Festival, which *The San Francisco Chronicle* called "one of the liveliest outdoor movie festivals in the West," featured *Thelma & Louise* as part of their 1998 summer series. That year the Northern California film festival projected other renowned titles such as *Easy Rider* (1969), *Raiders of the Lost Ark* (1981) and *Monty Python and the Holy Grail* (1975). Seven years after the women made a name for themselves, according to Pyramid some of the screening's more jocular attendees donned head scarves and carried guns in tribute to the film's leads.[6] *Thelma & Louise* was also shown at the Fremont Outdoor Cinema in Seattle in 1998, which treated film fans to a host of "classic summer selections," including *Terminator 2: Judgment Day*. The downtown Seattle venue attracted viewers who brought their own seating arrangements, from low back lounge chairs to full-size couches.[7]

Despite the preponderance of males employed in the field and the mistaken notion that *Thelma & Louise* is a "women's film," even sports writers turned to the picture as a metaphor. Reveling in the excitement of spring training, in 1992, *The St. Petersburg Times* profiled "The Philly Four," a group of women who annually leave their husbands behind and head south to Florida for some serious baseball watching. "In a way, they are Thelma and Louise and Louise and Louise," Tom Zucco quipped. One of the women expressed the realities of gender inequities, and shared a comment that evokes Geena Davis' next film, *A League of their Own* (1992): "If I were a guy, I'd be playing, but I can't." Sounding like Thelma near the end of her journey, another one of the "Philly Four" interjected, "I don't want to go back. None of us do."[8]

More recently, in 1998, *The Richmond Times-Dispatch* bemoaned the lackluster performance of the Washington Wizards, a nearby NBA team. "Once simply hard-luck losers and hopeless bumblers," the newspaper opined, "the Wizards this season were a metaphor for all that's wrong with the NBA." Not only were players overpaid underachievers prone to posturing, they encountered "more scrapes with the law than Thelma and Louise." According to the Virginia newspaper, team members were involved in brawls and charged with driving under the influence of drugs and alcohol. Players were also accused of sexual assault, which makes a comparison between the Washington Wizards and the film's title characters rather ironic and insensitive.[9]

"Popular culture is full of dynamic duos," *The Charleston Gazette* elaborated in 2001: "Batman and Robin. Abbott and Costello. Thelma and Louise." Highlighting Kentucky Wildcats guard Keith Bogans and forward Tayshaun Prince, the article focused on the pair's friendship and strong working relationship, thus remembering the film in a more appropriate fashion than *The Richmond Times-Dispatch* did in its article on the Washington Wizards. "The common bond the pair share as stars has forged a relationship that will likely last far beyond their stay" at the University of Kentucky, surmised the West Virginia newspaper with the help of the Associated Press. The two college players expressed sentiments that recalled Thelma and Louise's willingness to share resources and not withhold tough feedback: "We don't focus on who gets more attention," Prince reported. "If he sees me doing something wrong," Bogans explained, "he can scream at me and I know he's doing it to help me." Their comments echo the way Thelma criticizes Louise's plan to drive around Texas and how Louise scolds Thelma for blabbing their plans to J.D.[10]

While some observers held *Thelma & Louise* in low regard, the film enjoyed considerable esteem within Hollywood circles. As the head of MGM, the studio that produced the film, Frank Mancuso knew how to weave good publicity into a dramatic speech. Comparing the film industry with Thelma and Louise on their decline, he cautioned competitors and other executives, "We've lost our sense of restraint" by flooding the market with movies and megaplexes. "Like Thelma and Louise, we're heading for a cliff," Mancuso warned, but "will we stop before we go over the edge?" In early 1997, the industry leader advocated a reduction in the number of films produced, spreading releases evenly throughout the 12 month calendar year and following "instinct, not formula," as MGM did by greenlighting *Thelma & Louise*. He also suggested building new theaters in "underserved towns" (like Oklahoma City, for instance) and launching a collaborative advertising campaign to promote movie attendance, similar to the dairy producers' "Got Milk?" campaign.[11]

Unfortunately, film industry insiders missed the lesson to be learned by MGM's success with *Thelma & Louise*. Rather than increase marketing costs, as suggested by Mancuso, Hollywood producers might simply release a greater number of high quality women-led films. Rather than mimicking the film in a superficial manner, producers might do well to make movies that feature accomplished actresses appearing in well-told stories that might appeal to a wider audience than the usual "chick flick." As commonplace commodities, murder and sex didn't attract men and women to *Thelma & Louise*. The controversy of the great debate certainly helped ticket sales, but ultimately the characters' personal stories drew an audience and a created a fan base.

Because of *Thelma & Louise*'s well-written and clearly individualized female characters, the film's notoriety hasn't eroded with time. Imitation is the highest forms of flattery, and the film has been parodied extensively. In late 1991, *The Carol Burnett Show* came out of retirement for a CBS special and spoofed the women's quest.[12] Among theatrical film releases, according to the Internet Movie Database (imdb.com), *Thelma & Louise* was also spoofed in *Wayne's World 2* (1993), *Naked Gun 33⅓: The Final Insult* (1994), *Long Kiss Goodnight* (1996), *Spy Kids* (2001) and *Bridget Jones's Diary* (2001). The imdb.com website lists over 20 additional titles that have referenced the film, including *Made in America* (1993), *Boys on the Side* (1995), *Set It Off* (1996), *Bandits* (1997) and *Scary Movie* (2000). Even cartoon characters got into the act. In 1993, Marge Simpson and a neighbor took off on *Thelma & Louise*-inspired wild ride on the Fox Network's *The Simpsons*.

When TBS acquired the rights to show the film, the cable station tried to wring the most out of *Thelma & Louise*. In 1998, the film was mocked in one of the Superstation's short, 60-to-90-second "Monkeyed-Movies," which featured chimp actors reviving readily recognizable film roles. On *Dinner & a Movie*, an innovative TBS program that offered the makings of a complete date, *Thelma & Louise* played while the show's hosts prepared a recipe with the catchy title "Two Hot Peppers on the Lamb." The directions instruct: "For each serving, fling two hot peppers into a fiery pool of tomatillo sauce, garnish with a cilantro sprig and never look back."[13] Even death couldn't keep the popularity of *Thelma & Louise* down. In 1993, *The Hollywood Reporter* confirmed that the television arm of MGM was considering an hour-long weekly drama based on *Thelma & Louise* despite the namesakes' commitment to an earthly demise.[14]

Outside of Hollywood, dead or alive Thelma and Louise maintain their stature as industry icons. In 2000, *The Seattle Times* credited *Thelma & Louise* with launching the careers of actor Brad Pitt[15] and singer-songwriter Kelly Willis, who wrote the film's opening song, "Little Honey."[16] Two years prior, the same newspaper hailed the film as "the great grandmama" of female buddy movies and cited other female buddy movies such as *Beaches* (1988) and *Romy and Michele's High School Reunion* (1997) as "variations" of *Thelma & Louise*.[17] *USA Today* considered *Crouching Tiger, Hidden Dragon* (2000), *Charlie's Angels* (2001) and *Lara Croft: Tomb Raider* (2001) the "daughters of *Thelma & Louise* — except they're wiser and stronger and not about to plunge off a cliff, unless it's on a bungee wire."[18] *The Rocky Mountain News* named *Thelma & Louise* one of the ten best movies filmed in Colorado, along with *Butch Cassidy and the Sundance Kid*.[19] Film critics drew comparisons to *Thelma & Louise* with regularity, contrasting it with films such as *V.I. Warshawski* (1991), *Leaving Normal* (1992), *The Hand That Rocks the Cradle* (1992), *Fried Green Tomatoes* (1992), *The Gun in Betty Lou's Handbag* (1992), *To Wong Foo, Thanks for Everything! Julie Newmar* (1995), *Waiting to Exhale* (1995), *The First Wives Club* (1996), *Manny & Lo* (1996), *Set It Off* (1996), *Walking and Talking* (1996), *Freeway* (1997), *Double Jeopardy* (1999), *Bandits* (1999), *Freeway 2: Confessions of a Trickbaby* (1999) and *Baise-Moi* (2000), a controversial French film whose title translates to "Rape Me."

At large chain bookstores, mass-market books about movies often focus on personalities rather than product and meaning, but store shelves usually offer a few titles about breaking into the industry. Syd Field, who writes about screenwriting, considers *Thelma & Louise* "an extraordinary film," and discusses it at length in two of his books.[20] In *The Screenwriter's Problem Solver*, Field refers to Khouri's first effort as an exemplary screenplay numerous times: when discussing character motivation (referring to the women's need to escape),[21] developing character through action (citing the packing sequence),[22] novelist Henry James' notion about character determining incident and incident determining character (discussing Louise's rape experience in Texas, which Field guesses happened in her teens),[23] cross-cutting as a successful means of transition (exemplified by the cross-cutting between the women escaping and the police chasing them),[24] whether or not to utilize flashbacks (according to Field a flashback revealing what happened to Louise in Texas "would have been redundant and surely not be as effective as the way Callie Khouri originally conceived it"),[25] necessary set-ups (Thelma's packing the gun that later Louise uses to kill Harlan)[26] and good pacing (the build-up to Harlan's murder).[27]

In Field's *Four Screenplays, Studies in the American Screenplay*, he describes in shorter form his initial reaction to the film, after returning from a trip abroad.

> Suddenly I understood what everybody had been talking about. This film was fresh and funny, the relationships insightful, the humor laced believably through the dramatic situation. Every moment took me deeper and deeper into the characters and story. I experienced the film scene by scene, and I trusted the screenwriter and director to take me where they wanted me to go — the ending. I don't see too many films like that.[28]

While Fields believes that *Thelma & Louise* is an extraordinary screenplay based on its structure, plot, detail, and dialogue — not the gender of its characters — other authors (including myself) concentrate on the film's unusual female focus. *Chick Flicks: A Movie Lover's Guide to the Movies Women Love* defines the chick flick genre as "any movie that makes a special connection with a female audience."[29] Because the film appealed to a wider audience including males, *Thelma & Louise* classifies as more than just a "chick flick." Still, author Jami Bernard writes that *Thelma & Louise* is a "gloriously empowering movie for women," which she includes in a chapter entitled "Female Bonding."[30]

Gabrielle Cosgriff, Anne Reifenberg and Cynthia Thomas saw the film as more than something good to talk about; they credit *Thelma & Louise* with spawning their careers as film critics. The controversial movie was *the* inspiration behind their cable television program, which appeared on Access Houston Community TV, as well as their subsequent video guide, *Chicks on Film: Video Picks for Women and Other Intelligent Forms of Life.*

> This is the movie that planted the seed of an idea for our *Chicks on Film* TV show — not the movie itself, but the reaction to it. When (male, of course) critics called it "male bashing," my jaw dropped to my knees. Even though women get bashed and beaten in movies by the hundreds, nobody ever suggests that there's something the least bit wrong with this. What do they call movies where chicks are stalked and slaughtered? "Thrillers."[31]

More assertive than *Chick Flicks, Chicks on Film* puts *Thelma & Louise* in a chapter emblazoned with the title, "Uber-Chicks." Thomas leads her co-chicks and summarizes unequivocally that *Thelma & Louise* is "*the* pivotal movie for chicks in the movies." Thomas's co-critic, Cosgriff, aims her comments with an intention to sting. Compared to *Butch Cassidy and the Sun-*

dance Kid, "Thelma and Louise actually agonize over killing somebody, over breaking the law." Riled up, Cosgriff adds that the women "weigh the consequences" and as a result "their last defiant act is not a cop-out." Instead, she explains, the women's suicide is a "deliberate 'fuck you' to society and its sexist demands." Rounding out the review, Reifenberg chides, "Boys, it's time you got a grip." She sides with her co-authors and refers to a double standard toward violent films, something pro commentators noted with regularity.[32]

Though Syd Field, Jami Bernard and the authors of *Chicks on Film* support the movie, not every literary reference to *Thelma & Louise* lavishes praise. In *Girls on Film: The Highly Opinionated, Completely Subjective Guide to the Movies*, co-authors Clare Bundy, Lise Carrigg, Sibyl Goldman and Andrea Pryos are Vassar graduates not inclined to discuss feminism. The film is included in a list of "25 Action Films to Rent!" and reviewed as one of Ridley Scott's artful additions to the genre, not Callie Khouri's Oscar-winning script. According to *Girls on Film*, *Thelma & Louise* illustrates Scott's ability to "create a beautiful mood even when he leaves the lights on." Still lacking any comments aimed at the script, they add, "*Thelma & Louise* is sometimes self-consciously but impressively shot." *Girls on Film* pays no special attention to the film's female leads or its cultural impact.[33]

In *Brave Dames and Wimpettes: What Women Are Really Doing on Page and Screen*, Susan Isaacs rails against what she calls the film's "damsel-in-distress, movie-of-the-week mentality," which portrays women as "the demonstrably weaker sex" and "noble" victims.[34] According to Isaacs, Thelma and Louise "cannot take control of their lives, so they simply escape them." Unlike *The Baltimore Sun*, which remembered Thelma as "a dame in charge rather than a damsel in distress," Isaacs concludes that Thelma and Louise are not "brave dames." To the contrary, the women are "wimpettes," to whom she bids "good riddance." Like Detective Slocumbe when he interrogates J.D., Isaacs harbors no positive feeling for the women. Instead, she's annoyed by *Thelma & Louise* and seeks to discredit the picture's main characters.[35]

The problem with Isaacs' method is over-simplification. She separates "brave dames" from "wimpettes" by listing the philosophies of each (in her view) mutually exclusive group. Yet Thelma and Louise, like complex real-life individuals, exhibit characteristics found in both categories. Meeting Isaacs' definition of a "brave dame," renegades Thelma and Louise do stand up to injustice. They also "face moral and physical challenges" and remain true friends.[36] Because they choose not to betray one another and do take responsibility for their actions, Thelma and Louise fail to meet Isaacs' standards for "wimpettes."[37] Isaacs' too-rigid framework doesn't fit real women, nor does her theory best appraise the film. In *Brave Dames and Wimpettes*, Isaacs' claims regarding *Thelma & Louise* exemplify an approach that doesn't give enough consideration to the contents of the film.

In America, little is deemed sacred or spared from the public eye. Affecting backyards and big business, the *Thelma & Louise*-ing of American culture transpired in numerous forms creating a bottomless well of sometimes startling connections. Among others, newspapers in St. Petersburg, New York, Richmond and Houston summoned *Thelma & Louise* in the aftermath of O.J. Simpson's infamous 1994 slow car chase on the San Diego Freeway.

In June, police pursued a suicidal Simpson, who was being driven around by his friend Al Cowlings. The result was a 90-minute drama televised nationwide. The surreal scene transpired after the bloody murders of Nicole Brown Simpson, Simpson's wife, and Ron Goldman; Simpson later stood trial for the murders and was acquitted. Describing the "spectacle" as "ghoulish" with "raw narrative appeal," a *New York Times* piece reprinted in *The St. Petersburg Times* commented on commentators who came up "with movie analogies to try to describe the Simpson phenomenon." Labeling the media's coverage of the event "raucous," Michiko Kakutani noted that numerous journalists, "helping to blur the lines between reality and fiction," compared the bizarre happening to movies including *Thelma & Louise*. Kakutani joined his colleagues by adding *Butch Cassidy and the Sundance Kid* and *Bonnie and Clyde* to the list, which already included, he noted, *The Fugitive* (1993), *Dog Day Afternoon* (1975) and *The Sugarland Express* (1974). *The New York Times'* writer claimed that these movies identify with the "beleaguered hero" and "help nurture" rebellion. Discussing *Thelma & Louise* along with French Existentialists, writer Norman Mailer and the Revolutionary War, the Big Apple editorialist reminded readers in Florida and New York that a fascination with outlaws extends beyond Hollywood to literature and history.[38]

The Richmond Times Dispatch didn't fall into the trap of seeing the present only in terms of Hollywood movies as insinuated in the *St. Petersburg Times* and the *New York Times*. To make sense of the event, John Hall cited *Thelma & Louise* and Victor Hugo and Dostoyevsky while he sang "The Ballad of O.J.," which chimed "the stuff of nightmares and literature." In his column "No Apologies for Watching O.J.'s End Run to Nowhere," Hall displayed his familiarity with fine arts as well as popular culture to help legitimize his viewing pleasure. Like Kakutani, Hall also compared what transpired to Dr. Richard Kimball of *The Fugitive*, Edward G. Robinson in *Little Caesar* (1930), Humphrey Bogart in *The Treasure of the Sierra Madre* (1948), John Updike's *Rabbit* novels, Shakespeare's *Macbeth*. According to Hall, Simpson's story was about "Flight," with a capital "f," about fleeing from "reality, shame, life, death, oppression, responsibilities." Intellectually, Hall refused to harbor guilt for his fascination, yet in an attempt to assuage his lingering feelings of self-doubt he determined that attraction to watching someone trapped "with no way out" wasn't just a "male thing." Hall surmised, "Did we not hear female voices cheering in the theater for *Thelma & Louise?*" Using imagery reminiscent of the film and describing the same feeling many felt following the women's escape, the columnist sympathized with the criminal on the run.

> The only off ramp available to Simpson led to surrender, jail and whatever now may await him in the courts and beyond. The nation watched, hypnotized, knowing full well this was the only acceptable and logical outcome, but on the edge of our seats as always in the presence of an old, painful story. No one ought to feel unworthy for that experience.[39]

Instead of feeling for criminals, *The Houston Chronicle*, along with other newspapers across the country, focused on Al Cowlings and highlighted the display of true friendship. Knight-Ridder's Ellen Creagar explained to readers that literature, drama, television and film all ask the question, "How far would you go to help a friend in trouble or in an emergency?" After sharing real life stories of friends willing to take a risk to prove their loyalty, "Some Go the Extra Mile for a Friend" named examples of famous friends, mostly from television and film. "Think of friends," the article said, "and you think of Norm and Cliff, Lucy and Ethel, Hawkeye and Trapper John, Thelma and Louise, the Three Musketeers, the Three Stooges."[40]

There was no limit to the film's flexibility or American culture's willingness to review reality in terms of fiction, primarily Hollywood fiction. Using the film characters as a means to discuss current national events and to discuss law, *The St. Louis Post-Dispatch* connected Thelma and Louise with the bombing of the Alfred P. Murrah Federal building in Oklahoma City in 1995.

> If tragedy can ever have its moment of comic relief, in the Oklahoma City bombing it was surely provided Robert Jacks and Gary Alan Land, two motoring drifters who were briefly in custody after authorities stormed their motel in Neosho, Mo. Embarked on a beery, meandering odyssey, they seemed refugees from a bad movie.

Four years after the fictional women became famous, *The St. Louis Post-Dispatch* suggested that Jacks and Land seemed like "Thelma and Louise dumbed down." The comparison oddly elevated *Thelma & Louise*, as the compliment was a bit off-handed. In "Two Drifters Offer a Real-Life Lesson in the Meaning of Liberty," William F. Woo employed both real-life and imaginary individuals to highlight the Fourth Amendment's probable cause clause, which prevents law enforcement officials from holding suspected criminals indefinitely without an arrest warrant. In doing so, Woo linked Jacks and Land and Thelma and Louise to American colonists and the framers of the U.S. Constitution. Cognizant of different approaches to the same story, in the Missouri newspaper Woo added that *The New York Times*, "seeking a higher tone," described the men as "Rosencrantz and Guildenstern."[41]

Thelma & Louise has been recognized, legitimized and its lead characters memorialized — gleefully, scornfully, with deep purpose, minus much forethought and for a myriad of causes. To many, the film became a dynamic symbol that exhibited amazing flexibility and was a lens through which to view other seemingly unrelated things. In the heady summer of 1991, *The Charleston Gazette* analyzed "American values." After discussing excess and individualism, Richard Reeves touched upon violence. Sarcastically, he investigated aggression as a "legitimate and logical solution" to problems, then quickly turned to popular entertainment. Two weeks after the film was released to an immediate sensation, to prove that the entertainment industry sells what people want to buy, Reeves pointed to *Thelma & Louise*. Squeezing into the great debate, he called the film "provocative" and came down on the side of those who thought the women acted like men. Getting back to his thesis about values, Reeves criticized the American public as well as the federal government. He delineated that while "Thelma and Louise, like Rambo and Dirty Harry, are make-believe, at least to most adults," the "U.S. invasion of Panama and the Gulf War are real examples of the same inclination" to assert right with might.[42] Comparing real-life geo-political events to Hollywood dramas, on behalf of the Charleston newspaper, Reeves considered *Thelma & Louise* an instructional, cautionary tale warning others what not to do.

The film made a giant impression not only in cultural circles, from spurring road trips and being used to describe athletes to interpreting current events, but also created waves within important social spheres. In the wake of a 1993 U.S. District court ruling in favor of a group of Colorado State women's softball players, *The Rocky Mountain News* teased readers and evoked feminism, albeit with palpable hesitation and nervous titters. "Gender Equity is neither the hottest new grunge band from Seattle, nor the working title for the sequel to *Thelma & Louise*," the newspaper said. That school year, 48.2 percent of all CSU's students were female, yet only 37.7 percent of those who played for the college's organized sports teams were women. Listing some of the disparities female athletes face at the college level, the newspaper sided with the ruling yet consciously avoided the f word. Clearly, "resources and opportunities should be provided equally to men and women," the Colorado newspaper opined, concluding that equality is "not just the law, it's the right thing to do."[43] Remembering the film in conjunction with meaningful social progress is just the kind of positive reverberation that inspires artists like Callie Khouri to take chances and push boundaries.

Drawn to power and publicity, politicians also got into the habit of naming duos after Thelma and Louise. Back in 1991, during the pre-primary presidential election season, *The Los Angeles Times* questioned whether "outsider" candidate Jerry Brown and his political advisor Patrick H. Caddell had embarked on a "*Thelma & Louise* spree." Hendrik Hertzberg took a dim view of the pair's chances for success. Seeing the men's loftiest roles as potential messengers rather than likely winners, Hertzberg set up a comparison between the "unemployed" Brown and "troublemaker" Caddell and Thelma and Louise, particularly in terms of their denouement. Without "real solutions" voters nationwide could embrace, unless the political pair gave the country and the Democratic Party a powerful wake up call, Hertzberg predicted that Bown and Caddell would "touch off yet another downward cycle of hope and disillusion." This article, by the senior editor of the *New Republic*, conveyed the author's negative view of Thelma and Louise.[44]

Due to the way in which candidates from both major political parties were either assigned or adopted *Thelma & Louise* metaphors, the 1992 election year seemed to rise out of the dust stirred up by the women's death leap. In its political editor Susan Yoachum's 1998 obituary, *The San Francisco Chronicle* credited her with the distinction of dubbing U.S. Senate candidates Barbara Boxer and Dianne Feinstein, both Democrats from California, "The Thelma and Louise of American politics." In November 1992, the two politicians became the first set of female senators to represent the same state.[45]

On the other side of the political isle, *The Washington Post* reported that George Bush's deputy campaign manager Mary Matalin and press secretary Torie Clarke had been crowned "The Thelma and Louise of the GOP" due to their "cheeky style and take no-prisoners approach." Matalin was described as "gun-shy," refusing to be interviewed for the story after the fluff press she received as the love interest of Democratic strategist James Carville. Undaunted, Clarke responded, "I just want to be the one that kills the guy." Enjoying the exchange, *The Washington Post* pointed out that "presumably" Clarke meant Bill Clinton and "presumably" she was "speaking figuratively." Matalin and Clarke became notorious not shooting bullets, but for "attack faxes" sent to news organizations. One fax was headlined "Bill Clinton: He Calls Himself Elvis — But on Free Trade, He's the Great Pretender." According to "The Bush Women, Calling the Shots," it wasn't clear who was responsible for nicknaming Matalin and Clarke after the film's title characters, as if the application of the title was inevitable.[46]

The rush to jump in the green Thunderbird with *Thelma & Louise* even extended to Ross Perot's independent bid for election as president. As a successful businessman by trade rather than a politician, Perot recognized a hot commodity. Spotlighting Margot Perot, his wife, *The St. Petersburg Times* relayed that "her husband regales audiences by comparing her and Salvation Army sidekick Ruth Altshuler to Thelma and Louise when it comes to strong-arming the business community" for donations to the charity.[47]

Not to be outdone by the national spotlight, in 2002, *The Arizona Republic* reviewed the 45th State Legislature. The desert newspaper passed the word to readers that peers bestowed Representative Laura Knaperek, a Republican, and Senator Ruth Solomon, a Democrat, with the Thelma and Louise label for their hard work balancing Arizona's budget. "Strange bedfellows, Thelma and Louise have spent most of the year in a depressing, humor-and-health-sapping search for ways to balance a pair of $930 million gaps in this year's budget," the Southwest newspaper detailed. Although the two congresswomen exhibited distinct approaches, according to *The Arizona Republic*, Knaperek and Solomon "negotiated a bipartisan joint budget this year that enraged everybody but was the most politically feasible way to get out of the mess." Like the film characters did, the two politicians forged a working relationship despite their differences.[48]

Well-spun stories don't necessarily play out fairly. More than candidates running for the U.S. Senate, more than women married to men running for president of the United States or male multi-millionaires running national presidential campaigns, political outsiders Gloria Steinem and Florence Kennedy most closely reflected Thelma and Louise's marginal positions within society. Traveling the lecture circuit together for 20 years speaking on behalf of women's rights, they worked as a pair. Yet, as feminists, Steinem and Kennedy received little press when they adopted the popular moniker for themselves. It took Kennedy's death at age 84 for one Midwest press to notice leading feminists who had connected themselves to a film that had become famous for its gender issues nine years before. Kennedy's 2000 obituary, found in *The Capital Times* of Madison, Wisconsin, finally shared Steinem's recollection of the two women as "the Thelma and Louise of the '70s."

Of course this lack of coverage isn't at all surprising when one considers how little attention mainstream media pays to professed feminists. As Linda Brazil editorialized in *The Capital Times*, putting political beliefs into action as Kennedy did is difficult, especially "when women's stories still get less ink." Unfortunately, "women's actions are considered crazy instead of acknowledging that the situations that spurred Flo Kennedy's activism are the crazy part," she added. Applying Brazil's stance to the film, Louise might be "crazy" for killing Harlan and sidestepping the law, but society is also out of whack due to attitudes toward rape, which often blame the victim. Some viewers looked for a lesbian relationship between Thelma and Louise; when men who attended their speeches asked if Steinem and Kennedy were lesbians, Kennedy was said to retort, "It depends. Are you my alternative?"[49]

Covering the 20th anniversary of the National Women's Political Caucus, a group dedicated to increasing the number of women in public office, *The St. Louis Post-Dispatch* noted that Democratic representative from Colorado Pat Schroeder had become frustrated with the inadequate amount of federal funds allocated to women's health research. In 1991, the Missouri newspaper quoted Schroeder as saying, "I'm about ready to turn into Thelma and Louise, I'm so angry."[50] Far from despairing or criticizing their means, Schroeder empathized with the fictional women and understood the desperate path they chose to make themselves heard. Because of her less marginal, more mainstream position in society compared to Steinem and Kennedy, as a U.S. Congresswoman Schroeder didn't have to wait for her funeral to see her allusion dispersed via the press.

Forging a bond between *Thelma & Louise* and women's issues clearly made sense. Diane Mason, columnist for *The St. Petersburg Times*, associated the film with the f word in two essays written six months apart, one in July 1991 and the next in January 1992. She used her allotted space to summarize the mood many feminist activists felt during the immediate wake of the movie's release. In "A New Radicalism in NOW," Mason detailed how *Thelma & Louise* "kept popping up" at the annual convention of the National Organization for Women held in New York City — not in person or as an official theme, Mason emphasized, but "from the heart." Though I failed to find widespread coverage of the event in newspapers outside of the area, Mason reported that Steinem and Kennedy spoke, calling themselves "the Thelma and Louise of the 70s" soon after the picture debuted. Mason added that attendees bought buttons reading "Thelma and Louise Live" and T-shirts announcing "Graduate of Thelma and Louise Finishing School."

According to Mason, Louise's murderous, unfurled rage and Thelma's sudden change of attitude from object to subject infiltrated the proceedings and encouraged other women to act on their anger. "Whatever this radical spirit is that women are tapping into, whether in movie theaters or convention halls, it's got power — and women can feel it," Mason charged, though she later wondered if the emotional pitch was "too high." After Thelma and Louise get the best of a few men through extreme means, executive vice president Patricia Ireland announced that for the first time in its 25-year history, NOW officially called for civil disobedience. Mason quoted one feminist in her twenties who felt that if women could "harness" their energy "without blowing something up" they could "do anything."

Redirecting the group's explosive energy, Gloria Steinem spurred imaginations with a query: "Can you imagine what would happen if every welfare mother, every underpaid waitress, every sexually harassed secretary had two years of military training?"[51] By channeling women's renewed fire into service of country, Steinem's fantasy scenario provided conference attendees with a positive way to push forward. Uniting the young woman who recognized women's rekindled power and feminist leaders who grew tired of "sedate" means, Steinem indirectly addressed the desire for Thelma and Louise to actually live on. If the two fictional women were to each receive an extra life, they might battle together on behalf of worthwhile social causes. This time crusading with greater dignity, respect for rules and military-issued weapons, such a sequel could be entitled *Daughters of Thelma & Louise Take On Terrorists.*

Though Mason wondered if the rhetorical pitch at the NOW convention had gotten out of hand, by winter and the new year she fully sided with the righteous. In "A One-Way Trip Across the Line" (which referred to

Thelma's comment, "Something in me crossed over and I can't go back"), Mason reflected on the film's impact and renewed her feminist roots.

> Looking back, I think 1991 really started to take shape around May. The month Thelma and Louise came out. That's when women first began to remember who we are. And from then on, women just kept remembering and remembering. Even women who really hated the film (and many did) still walked out of the theater with something all stirred up inside. This story of two Arkansas women on a road chase to freedom got inside all of us, to that place deep inside where we store the truth about ourselves, and the longing to take control of our lives.

In her second piece, Mason elevated women who deserved to be angry, such as one woman who contacted her after "fending off" sexual harassment throughout her life. Mason sympathized with an array of abused women including those who looked back at "rough sex" and realized they'd been violated or raped, those who admitted that they'd been battered in "too intense" relationships, and those who "allowed themselves to remember" childhood incidents of incest and molestation. When she wondered what would be done with these newly stirred memories, Mason concluded that job was "for next year's heroines to decide," but she hoped that women would adopt Thelma's attitude regarding permanent and forward motion.

Optimistically, Mason assumed other fictional women in film would follow in the spirit of *Thelma & Louise*. She encouraged female writers, politicians, activists and any women with stories to confront abusers and "claim our own experiences." Similar to Congresswoman Pat Schroeder's impassioned view of the film, Mason's focus and tone were very different from those, like Henrik Hertzberg, who saw *Thelma & Louise* as a tale of loss and hopelessness. For Mason and others, Thelma and Louise were just as real and powerful as neighbors and news figures.

> 1991. The year we remembered. The year we got heroines. Never mind that Thelma and Louise plunged their car into a canyon, and Anita and Patricia were judged not credible by the political or legal systems that evaluated them. They stood for themselves — and dared to tell and live the truth about their lives. And we did too.[52]

In the film, Thelma and Louise assume that authorities would distrust or ignore claims of rape. In real life, a pervasive attitude that blames women for sexual violence committed against them may have also won out in the Patricia Bowman vs. William Kennedy Smith rape trial, during which the accused was acquitted. The same year, because many discredited her veracity and the seriousness of sexual harassment, Anita Hill's testimony before the Senate did not stop Clarence Thomas from winning a lifelong appointment on the Supreme Court bench.

To defend Hill, *Newsday* reasoned after a 1992 speech that she didn't seem the type to invent her story or bask in attention. The New York area newspaper felt that "admirable" as Hill was for exhibiting the courage to tell her story, she made a "rather bland, plodding speaker," unlike Gloria Steinem who introduced her. "Given to understatement and explication," the Long Island newspaper said, Hill was "the last person, it would seem, to go off on flights of fancy."

Perhaps the courts, politicians and the greater public demonstrated a poor understanding of the crucial difference between dramatic fiction and real life when Thelma and Louise were seen as wanting heroines and Anita Hill's and Patricia Bowman's testimonies were dismissed as unimportant or far-fetched. Society needs fictional characters and complex dramas so that people can learn through mistakes committed by character who are safely sequestered in make-believe worlds. The stories real women tell also need to be heard and, unless discredited by fair and reasonable means, they deserve to be validated and believed.[53]

The mood of righteous indignation induced by the film affected feminists of all ages. The "Graduate of Thelma and Louise Finishing School" slogan Mason first noticed in St. Petersburg in 1991 showed up on buttons distributed at Hill's sold-out speech the next year. Given at Manhattan's Hunter College where the student body is predominantly female, Hill's speech addressed a "Who's Who of women politicians, activists and writers," according to *The Houston Chronicle*.[54] *Newsday* reported that at the same event vendors trafficked T-shirts picturing Sarandon and Davis pointing "machine guns" and bearing the caption "William Kennedy Smith — Meet Thelma and Louise."[55]

Any feminist interpretation of the film and its impact risked belittlement as does any effort that proudly hoists the f word. That was the case when *USA Today* semi-seriously covered a 1992 gathering of Riot Grrls. Born in the early 1990s in Washington State and fronted by bands such as Bratmobile, Mecca Normal, Bikini Kill and L-7, the Riot Grrls movement hung out with punk rockers and drew third wave feminists including men. As their name suggests, Riot Grrls signify a thoughtfully formed growl based in part on adolescent angst. Naturally, one seminar during the Riot Grrl convention discussed what the national newspaper called the "bosom buddy" movie, *Thelma & Louise*.

Inside the pages of *USA Today*, *Thelma & Louise* was acceptable so long as proponents didn't draw a connection between the film and feminism by name. Due to the Riot Grrls' aggressive language, the newspaper's coverage of the event perhaps inadvertently attempted to undermine any positive outcome. The lead sentence of "Feminist Riot Grrls Don't Just Wanna Have Fun" teased, "Better watch out, boys," feeding to the public more imagery of a divisive war between the sexes instead of an opportunity for social change that might benefit all. After setting the stage for battle, *USA Today*'s first incli-

If you're raped, you might as well "relax and enjoy it." because no one will believe you.

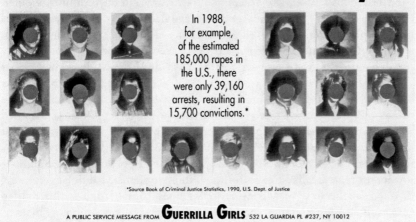

In 1988, for example, of the estimated 185,000 rapes in the U.S., there were only 39,160 arrests, resulting in 15,700 convictions.*

*Source Book of Criminal Justice Statistics, 1990, U.S. Dept. of Justice

A PUBLIC SERVICE MESSAGE FROM **GUERRILLA GIRLS** 532 LA GUARDIA PL #237, NY 10012

Instead of reporting Harlan's criminal actions to the police, Thelma and Louise decide to flee the Silver Bullet parking lot and head for the Mexican border. "Everybody did see me dancin' with him all night," Thelma admits. "They woulda made out like I asked for it." Fearing that no one would believe their story because of the "kind of world" women must either live in or escape, Thelma and Louise choose death over dealing with the criminal justice system. The 1992 Guerrilla Girls' poster "was inspired by William Kennedy Smith and all the other guys who get it away it." (Copyright 1992, 1995 by the Guerrilla Girls, Inc. Reprinted with permission.)

nation was to demean. "From hundreds of once pink, frilly bedrooms, comes the young feminist revolution," sometimes-fashion writer Elizabeth Snead sneered. She elaborated that the Riot Grrls political movement wasn't "pretty" and that it didn't want to be, "so there!"

Snead's focus and language, a mix of empathy, reasonable criticism and belittling sarcasm, undercut Riot Grrrls's validity. While Snead understood why the group was rebelling — date rape, sexism, violence against women, "unattainable" body images dominating the media, "disappearing" abortion rights — she still disparaged movement members. She explained that many of the girls grew weary of conversations centered on "clothes, boys, makeup and boys," though she heard "no talk of political action" to replace it. Branding the Riot Grrl men "male feminist sympathizers" and calling them "ardent, if slightly confused," the article patronized male feminists who purportedly "trailed after their Riot Grrrlfriends." *USA Today*'s coverage was short on quotes because most of the 150-plus attendees refused to talk to the press. Perhaps not as dumb and self-centered as the article made them out to be, attendees were evidently cognizant of how poorly feminists and their viewpoints are usually treated in the media.[56]

Less than one year after *Thelma & Louise* first ignited tempers and engendered heated discussion, *The St. Louis Post-Dispatch* ran the headline "Women Rush to Seek Office." Although the article avoided the f word, the movement's influence was undeniable. Speaking in terms of "blame" (whether seriously or jokingly, it was unclear), the newspaper first set the historical record straight. "Some blame it on the Clarence Thomas hearings," the Midwest newspaper stated, and others blamed "last summer's hit *Thelma & Louise*," which was designated a "male-bashing movie that touched a nerve among many." *The St. Louis Post-Dispatch* chose not to further investigate the issues that riled women. Instead, the newspaper cautioned, "Whatever it is, experts say a lot of angry women are out there," and furthermore warned that "many are running for office." Although the rest of the article skipped editorial commentary and instead detailed figures for the number of female candidates running for office in the state of Missouri, Jo Mannies' initial language discredited women. Following Mannies' tone and the customary connotation of "blame," Thelma and Louise and their real-life sympathizers equaled a force to be feared and a threat that required warning (even if mockingly), particularly when such women focused their energies on politics and social change.[57]

The *Thelma & Louise*-ing of popular cultural was still alive and kicking in the fall of 1997, when *The Las Vegas Sun* furthered the cause of objectifing women with a derogatory blurb about the appearances of Attorney General Janet Reno and Secretary of Health and Human Services Donna Shalala that was intended to be funny. Reno was vocal with reporters about her plans to take off on the open road after she and President Clinton left office. According to the newspaper, Shalala said, "I told her I'd drive." "Yes, it sounds idyllic," *The Las Vegas Sun* joked. Insinuating that the women were acting like men, the newspaper imagined "a post–Clinton *Thelma & Louise* road trip, both of them singing 'We've got a mighty convoy' as they motor across America."

The newspaper's true feelings became clear when it facetiously counseled Reno to avoid driving overseas after a gag printed in a foreign newspaper. Apparently, Reno's head was glued to a sensual figure, which coincided with a sarcastic statistic. Rather than counter the joke and defend Reno, *The Las Vegas Sun* joined in the merriment.

> Just don't drive to Japan, Janet; you may be mobbed. According to the Weekly World News, 78 percent of Japanese men would rather be stranded on a desert island with her than with "any other lady on the face of the Earth." Even Donna Shalala? Says one source, "To the Japanese male, Janet Reno is a vision of beauty — and by far the sexiest women in the world." It's easy to see why:

the editors have superimposed Reno's head onto a shapely, bathing-suited body.

No wonder the public buys action pictures portraying sexualized views of women. In concert with world-wide practice, *The Las Vegas Sun* agreed that women serving in politics are worth a laugh.[58] Avoiding thoughts about the women's performance as public servants, Nevada journalists evaluated Reno and Shalala on the basis of their physical attractiveness to heterosexual men. This focus implied that women more suitably equal eye candy rather than law enforcement or policy leaders, and that only those females deemed attractive in bikinis are worthwhile. If the men in the film had followed the newspaper's sense of humor, Harlan would not have raped a woman with crossed eyes and crooked teeth, and would not have shared his rude comments with women who shop at Lane Bryant because women who fail to look like supermodels aren't worth a rapist's effort or a stupid jerk's time. Though lightly dealt, the carelessness of the newspaper's coverage reveals misogynistic leanings. Newspaper stories like this one make clear the continued need for a feminist movement and the worthiness of studying *Thelma & Louise*.

Although *Thelma & Louise* evoked a full array of comments from serious to supercilious, from regard to disrespect, the most impressive attribute of the great debate was the way it revitalized attention toward important social, cultural and political issues. As *The Washington Post Magazine* concluded, "More people had more gut-level discussions about the anger between men and women after seeing *Thelma & Louise* than after reading any gray Op-Ed piece in any paper or watching any balanced report on *Nightline*."[59] Few films make such powerful, long-lasting impressions.

10. Thelma and Louise Reunite — In Jail

According to newspaper reports, a small number of women admitted they were moved to commit crime, including murder, after seeing *Thelma & Louise*. Much more serious than the other vagaries of the great debate, copy-cat offenses were clearly the most disturbing and misguided reaction to the film.

A year after the film's theatrical debut, *The St. Petersburg Times* reprinted a Scripps-Howard News Service story that described a couple of perpetrators who expressed a connection between watching the film and their own criminal acts. "Two teenage girls arrested in Dublin, Calif., for committing as many as a dozen burglaries tell police they were inspired by *Thelma & Louise*," the brief relayed. The girls were "bored," according to the report, and "decided to try a life of crime after watching the hit 1991 flick."[1] Undoubtedly, this type of response is not what the filmmakers had in mind.

In 1993, two Virginia women, Pamela Sayre and Carolyn Dean, were charged with robbery and capital murder for the hold-up of a cab company and the death of William L. Woodbridge, who was beaten to death with the handle of a hammer. While high, the pair devised a plan to steal money in order to buy more crack cocaine. After her capture, Pamela gave a statement to police. According to *The Richmond Times Dispatch*, she explained that her accomplice suggested they "go adventuring like the characters in *Thelma & Louise*." Pamela went along with Carolyn's plan mimicking the way Thelma follows Louise. It's regrettable that Pamela and Carolyn didn't simply opt to dress like the women instead.[2]

Around the same time in New Jersey, Peggy Kosmin and Tammy Ann Molewicz conspired to murder Peggy's ex-husband, William Kelly, Jr., in retaliation for years of domestic abuse. Because it was premeditated, Peggy and Tammy's crime sounds more like the murder committed in *Mortal*

Thoughts, also released in 1991, starring Demi Moore, Glenne Headly, Bruce Willis and Harvey Keitel, once again playing a police detective. Still, newspapers in New Jersey, Texas and Colorado linked the neighbors to *Thelma & Louise*. The widespread urge to label criminal pairs after the memorialized fictional females was especially popular among journalists and law enforcement officials. The fact that people liked to bandy about the women's names supports the notion that titles matter. Had Callie Khouri's creation been called something else, perhaps *Over the Edge* or *Don't Look Down*, the title of the B.B. King soundtrack selection, the film's notoriety and allure may not have been so strong.

In the New Jersey case, the victim was housed safely in jail and charged with aggravated assault after repeated arrests for beating Peggy and breaking her nose. Unlike Thelma and Louise, who do not premeditate events in the Silver Bullet parking lot, Peggy and Tammy concocted a grave plan while drinking "large quantities of alcohol." The women decided to bail Kelly out of jail, shoot him in the head with a .32 caliber handgun, store his body in the trunk of a car, dump him in a state forest and later torch the transport vehicle. Focusing on the relationship between the assailants, *The Record* asserted that Peggy and Tammy both said that "the other pulled the trigger," quite unlike Thelma and Louise and the loyal friends they were.[3] Like the pair in *Mortal Thoughts*, Peggy and Tammy turned on one another, meeting Susan Isaacs' definition of "wimpettes."

Two years after the film first caused a sensation, newspapers outside the Garden State also hyped a sensational *Thelma & Louise* angle to the Peggy and Tammy story. *The Houston Chronicle* initially covered their criminal acts under the headline "*Thelma & Louise*, New Jersey Women Accused of Killing Abusive Ex-Lover Turn On Each Other."[4] Two months later, the same newspaper followed with "Judge Unmoved by Killers' Tears, *Thelma & Louise* Given 8 Years." Recalling the wide array of reactions to the film, the second article portrayed conflicting opinion regarding Peggy and Tammy's crime. The Lone Star State newspaper recounted, "Their lawyers called it a desperate act to stop a violent man. The psychiatrist called it a classic battered-woman case. The judge didn't buy it." Apparently, readers in Texas appreciate dramatic crime coverage.

Like Louise admitted to Jimmy over the phone, "I did it and I can't undo it," in the courtroom Peggy asserted through tears, "I totally take responsibility for this crime." As a result of their misdeeds, Peggy and Tammy were sentenced to serve at least eight years of a 25-year sentence for voluntary manslaughter.[5] To the northwest, *The Rocky Mountain News* shared *The Houston Chronicle*'s lively coverage of the New Jersey case filing the story under the headline "No Dramatic End to *Thelma & Louise* Saga." Using popular fiction to punctuate reality, the Colorado newspaper contrasted the film's surprise ending to Peggy and Tammy's reckoning in court.[6] The article was subtitled "Prison, Not Theatric Leap, in Store for Two Women Who Bailed Abuser Out of Jail, Then Killed Him."

Thankfully, most criminal incidents that revived *Thelma & Louise* involved lesser offenses than murder. Furthermore, journalists and police attached the sobriquet to criminals much more often than the criminals did themselves. Occasionally, as with an event briefly described in *The Seattle Times*, the handle "Thelma and Louise" attached itself to female criminals anonymously, as if the coupling were obvious and natural. "The FBI said the second suspect in a female robbery duo nicknamed for movie characters *Thelma & Louise* has been arrested," the Northwest newspaper perfunctorily reported in the fall of 2000.[7]

One particularly memorable case of naming criminals after the characters was profiled on television's *Dateline, Unsolved Mysteries, A Current Affair* and *America's Most Wanted*. Despite the extensive coverage this story received, one fact remains unclear: whether the press or the police renamed Rose Marie Turford and Joyce Carolyn Stevens after Thelma Dickerson and Louise Sawyer. Although local journalists claim the police were responsible for tagging the duo Thelma and Louise, *The Houston Chronicle* followed the story from June 30, 1995, to January 27, 1998, publishing a total of 35 articles. Thirty-four of those articles referred to the pair as Thelma and Louise, beginning with the headline of the second piece: "The *Thelma & Louise* Robberies: Was It Coercion or Collusion?" Other headlines involving the movie title included: "*Thelma & Louise* Sought in Canada," "Local *Thelma & Louise* Catch National Eye Again," "On the Run in Canada, *Thelma & Louise* Spotted in a Resort Town Near Montreal," "Long Run Ends for *Thelma & Louise*," "*Thelma, Louise,* Appear in Canadian Court," "*Thelma & Louise* Fugitives in Houston," "*Thelma & Louise* Back Together—In County Jail," "*Thelma & Louise* Prosecutor Wants Competency Examinations," "*Thelma & Louise* Trial," "Woman Gets 10-year Term in Robberies, *Thelma & Louise* Suspect Pleads Guilty," "*Thelma & Louise* Trial, Act II, Is Set to Begin Today," "Male Victims Were 'Losers,' Diaries Playing Key Role in *Thelma & Louise* Trial," "Lonely Guy Tells of Date Gone Bad, He Looked for Love and Found *Thelma & Louise,*" "Fear for Kids Led Her to Crime, Turford Says, *Thelma & Louise* Defendant Testifies," "Who Was Thelma and Who Louise? Prosecutor: Turford in Charge," "Defendant Was Victim, Lawyers Say, *Thelma & Louise* Deliberations Begin," "*Thelma* Skirmish Settled" and "*Thelma & Louise* Hit with Big Penalties." All together, the title appeared in 21 headlines, four times on page one. Apparently, *The Houston Chronicle* felt use of the movie title would help sell the story and increase circulation of their daily edition.

Putting all the arguments and commentary surrounding the picture into proper perspective, pitted against *Thelma & Louise* the far more outlandish tale of Rose Marie and Carolyn proves the old adage that truth is stranger than fiction. The Houston duo first earned hometown notoriety when they jumped a half a million dollars' bond posted by Rose Marie's parents against multiple counts of aggravated robbery, which resulted from a dating service scam. The women victimized at least 10 men, targeting foreigners and married men less likely to report the crime to police, in total stealing $250,000 in cash and goods. Instead of Mexico, Rose Marie and Joyce, who goes by Carolyn, fled to Canada, where Rose Marie is a citizen and once lived. One the married mother of three and the other the daughter of a minister, the pair met while working at Spring Shadows Glen, a private psychiatric hospital, where Rose Marie worked as a nurse and Carolyn an aide. Finding the real-life story eerily reminiscent of the film, "puzzled" investigators tried to locate the women's whereabouts while marveling at how two individuals with "decent jobs" and no criminal background "could get into such trouble."[8]

As their story unfolded, incredible details emerged. A character named Avery who never materialized purportedly controlled the two women from a distance through letters and threats. He supposedly forced Rose Marie and Carolyn to engage in sadistic lesbian sex acts, schedule dates with victims and commit robberies on his behalf, though some investigators eventually came to believe that Carolyn invented Avery and wrote the letters in an attempt to brainwash Rose Marie. At the insistence of the shadowy Avery, the accomplices climbed Pike's Peak and kicked Rose Marie's husband out of the house. Surface wounds that appeared on Carolyn, a car wreck and the brief kidnapping of one of Rose Marie's boys were also attributed to the remote figure. To meet his odd demands, crime scenarios were scripted. The women supposedly watched *The Real McCoy* and *Thelma & Louise* for inspiration.

On the lam in Canada, the Texas team was spotted dressed as both nuns and strippers, which moved the *Toronto Star* to proclaim in a headline "*Thelma & Louise*–Nuns on the Run." Their bail bondsmen back in Houston printed T-shirts with the women's likenesses and sent them to Canadian officials, taxi drivers and hotel employees in hopes of recapturing the pair. Hiding out in Montreal, Rose Marie was admitted to a hospital for depression, escorted by a police officer who failed to run a background check. After a four-month fugitive trek, authorities retook Rose Marie and Carolyn in Toronto where they were working at a telephone sex service. The arresting officer claimed that Rose Marie "seemed to be relieved to see us," as if "she was glad it was over," which recalls Louise's needy calls to the police.[9]

Back in Houston, an attorney for one of the women's victims won a court order preventing the two fugitives from earning any movie profits from the sale of their story to Hollywood. "These women have paraded themselves about as being like the characters in the movie," he argued, and charged Rose Marie and Carolyn with originating the film comparison. *The Houston Chronicle* spelled out the movie in question within its headline "*Thelma & Louise* Lose Shot at Hollywood Riches; Restraining Order Blocks Movie Profits."[10]

A judge later lifted the ban and ordered that any proceeds resulting from negotiations with any film producers or book publishers be deposited into a special fund for potential payment to victims. Claiming the women had nothing to do with the popular reference, Carolyn's attorney responded, "This *Thelma & Louise* business is nonsense" and a "creation of the media." He relieved the police of blame and placed responsibility for his client's nickname on journalists. He added that the women weren't making any deals with producers, which is reminiscent of the way that Louise promised Thelma she wouldn't make any deals with the police. While Louise keeps her promise, it's unclear whether or not Carolyn's attorney told the truth.[11] Two years later, in early 1998, a $3.2 million civil judgment was awarded to two of Rose Marie and Carolyn's victims. According to prosecutors, 20th Century Fox vice president Tarquin Gotch was in the process of developing a script based on the women's lives, potentially providing funds for restitution.[12]

Unlike Thelma and Louise, Rose Marie and Carolyn didn't stick side by side or try to keep a lid on their criminal deeds. Faced with three counts of aggravated robbery, Carolyn negotiated a guilty plea in exchange for a 10-year sentence. In a seven-page confession, she named Rose Marie her partner in crime and handed prosecutors an additional weapon to use against her former lover. Like the couple in Steven Spielberg's *The Sugarland Express* (based on a true story also set in Texas), Rose Marie and Carolyn relished media attention. Diaries attributed to Rose Marie further hurt her defense with some entries outlining possible book titles such as "Pleasure by the Minute," "Phonemate Fantasies" and "The Naked Truth." The journals also included imaginary news accounts portraying the women's escapades as a "sordid tale of events," which "only could be described as bizarre."[13] In court, Rose Marie was asked if she still believed in Avery's existence. In response, she broke down and cried, "I don't know who's who anymore." Comparatively, by the end of movie, Thelma and Louise each have a pretty clear idea of what brought them to the edge.[14]

The central question at Rose Marie's trial became who invented Avery. "Prosecutors and defense attorneys continued their tug of war," *The Houston Chronicle* informed, "over which of the duo of robbers dubbed *Thelma & Louise* called the shots." Rose Marie's attorneys attempted to demonstrate how their client evolved "from a kindly suburban housewife into a pistol-packing criminal" due to duress resulting from Carolyn's influence. Unmoved, the jury convicted the former housewife and nurse of a single count of aggravated robbery, rejecting claims that threats against her family drove to her to commit crime and flee justice.[15] Rose Marie was sentenced to 30 years in prison—five years more than Peggy and Tammy Ann received in New Jersey for manslaughter and 20 years more than her accomplice. Her lengthy sentence prompted *The Houston Chronicle* to exclaim in a headline "Jury Gamble Doesn't Pay Off."[16] Rose Marie's harsh sentence makes the film characters' decision to forgo civilized justice and choose their own punishment seem more levelheaded. No wonder Louise wanted to avoid Texas.

The question of whether Rose Marie or Carolyn more closely matched Louise's lead was addressed in the courtroom through the 20-year difference in prison sentences awarded to the women. A dubious honor, Rose Marie earned the title of ringleader and landed twice as much time behind bars for her supposed scheming. However, the opposite may have been true, that a mentally disturbed Carolyn overpowered a naïve Rose Marie, who believed that her biggest mistake was feeling responsible for trying to help her cohort. After spending a few years in prison, Rose Marie told a reporter from the Canadian magazine *Saturday Night*, "I'm the type of person who brings a stray dog home to Mom and tries to nurse it back to health."[17] Like Thelma and Louise in the film, real life criminals aren't necessarily unremittingly bad individuals. Some find themselves in felonious situations due to poor decision-making and bad luck rather than anti-social attitudes.

While friendships are usually rewarding, the odd tale of Rose Marie and Carolyn reminds onlookers that making smart choices when picking associates is always key. Where Thelma and Louise grow closer over time, mostly rejoicing over rather than despairing their alliance, Rose Marie and Carolyn became adversaries. Still, both pairs of fugitives egged each other on, becoming seriously and inextricably entangled until death or imprisonment parted them. When *Thelma & Louise* enticed a great debate, some participants discussed worthwhile issues and others reacted in angry disbelief, yet there's no need to fight so vehemently over art when the actual culprit is reality.

Along with journalists in Houston, journalists in Albany, St. Petersburg, Spokane, Charleston and St. Louis were all guilty of doling out Thelma and Louise badges to female criminals. In the fall of 1991, *The Times Union* pressed police for a connection between the film and the arrest of Allison Jones and Jean Horn for the robbery of a convenience store. According to the upstate New York newspaper, a sheriff's investigator "declined to speculate on whether the women were inspired by the movie *Thelma & Louise*, which depicts a pair of notorious female robbers." As journalists rushed to push a connection between a local story and the film, sloppy editing failed to catch the difference between fictional characters and actual "notorious" criminals like those portrayed in *Bonnie and Clyde*.[18]

In 1998, a "*Thelma & Louise*–style car chase through three counties ended with the arrest of three women," declared *The St. Petersburg Times*. According to the account, police cruisers from each jurisdiction pursued two getaway cars. Tamika Simon crashed a Toyota Corolla through a railroad-crossing gate after trying to rob a flea market. While the police chased Tamika, a Buick driven by Harley Kirkland was chasing them. "Police couldn't explain why two women wanted for armed robbery and car theft would pursue a police cruiser," the Gulf Coast newspaper relayed. Perhaps, like Thelma and Louise, the women wanted to stick together. A third woman, Jamila Reese, a passenger in the Buick, admitted to waving a pellet gun at the flea market in an attempt to steal a woman's purse.[19]

Not everyone who earned the title did so by making dumb moves. In 1999, *The Spokesman-Review* strained to draw a comparison between the film characters and two clean air environmentalists who filmed wheat stubble burning for an educational video. "A Spokane veterinarian and the mother of an asthmatic daughter may be miscast as *Thelma & Louise*," the newspaper surmised of the two women, who faced criminal trespass charges for their pursuit of documented illegal activity.[20]

The Charleston Gazette thought of the film when it detailed the antics of a woman in Seattle who was kicked out of a bar for repeatedly pinching a waiter in the rear, threatening to punch him and using foul language. "I suppose you could call it the *Thelma & Louise* effect," the newspaper suggested.[21] As with other types of appropriation, a wide latitude of behavior from murder, robbery, fleeing justice, environmental activism, cursing, creating a disturbance and sexual aggression all earned female criminals Khouri's infamous tag.

Calling a pair of Great Britain seniors an "aging *Thelma & Louise*," *The St. Louis Post-Dispatch* detailed the story of Winnie Barstow and her sister Jane Payne, who joined their nephew, his girlfriend, her daughter and a dog named Sandy on a criminal holiday beginning in 1992. Travelling across Europe, the trip "turned into an extraordinary life of crime involving forged checks, false names, bogus bank accounts, house purchase fraud, the police of seven countries, the Italian Riviera and talk of enlisting the help of Interpol." People once close to the women were surprised at their actions. Like the waitress at the Silver Bullet who tells Slocumbe that Thelma and Louise aren't the type to commit murder, friends disbelieved the growing charges. They wondered if Winnie and Jane had been "drugged or brainwashed."[22]

Journalists weren't the only ones to connect the film characters to real-life female criminals. In 1991, after back-to-back robberies by the same pair (the second attempt unsuccessful due to the lack of surprise), the manager of a convenience store twice told *The Minneapolis Star Tribune* the same anecdote. As if it were a point of pride as well as an amusing retort, he repeated, "The police asked me, 'What were their names — Thelma and Louise?'"[23]

Two years before Rose Marie and Carolyn arrived on the scene, in 1993, *The Houston Chronicle* took care to explain that "police dubbed" Stephanie Narro and Melissa Lynn Wall after Thelma and Louise on account of their 12-day crime spree. Both women pleaded guilty to three counts of carjacking and one count of using a firearm during a violent crime. At her sentencing, after apologizing to the court and her victims, Stephanie received 15 years in federal prison. Instead of targeting men like Houston's more infamous Rose Marie and Carolyn, Stephanie and Melissa Lynn preyed on women, first asking them for rides, then robbing them at gunpoint. Their unsisterly attitude contradicted the notion of female solidarity prevalent in the film, a fact that authorities in Texas overlooked, paving the way for area journalists to do the same.[24]

In a move Louise would not condone, Cheryl Lynn Stevens and Jennifer Joyce Davis drove a stolen 1986 Toyota from Maryland to the Texas panhandle where they robbed a truck stop in 1994. Instead of avoiding Texas as Louise insists in the film, Cheryl Lynn and Joyce purposely headed for the Lone Star State's border. As the Shamrock, Texas, chief of police recalled, "It was just like in the movie," the name of which *The Baltimore Sun* spelled out in its account of the story: "Two Baltimore women were charged with attempted capital murder yesterday in Texas after a convenience store robbery, high-speed chase and shootout that law enforcement officials compared to the movie *Thelma & Louise*." Although the film title rolled off his lips with ease, the Shamrock chief of police was more familiar with the famous moniker than the actual movie. To support his comparison, he explained that one of the women "was leaning out of the passenger window, firing and firing at us," something neither Thelma nor Louise actually do.[25] In Tulsa, the story was dispatched under the headline "Real Life *Thelma & Louise* Face Charges." However, *The Tulsa World* didn't credit the Shamrock chief of police with the task of dubbing the duo. Instead, *Thelma & Louise* appeared in the headline as if bestowed by common folklore without any need of explanation elsewhere in the article.[26]

Although Long Island authorities arraigned a total of five suspects including two males for a series of robberies committed in 1994, police still believed that Shirley Muller and Darlene D'Angelis reenacted "Thelma and Louise all over again," according to *Newsday*. Upholding the ongoing cultural battle between New York and Los Angeles, *Newsday* celebrated regional flair, followed the police's lead and cashed in on the movie's popularity all in one shot, crowning the tale "Thelma and Louise, LI Style."[27]

In 1997, *The St. Petersburg Times* quoted a Tampa police officer who viewed Starsena Giles and Charlene O'Ladgun in terms of Hollywood. "They are like a teenage Thelma and Louise," the officer piped, referring to a troubled pair who robbed a beauty salon and held up a woman in the parking lot of a grocery store with the aid of a handgun. At 17 and 13 years of age, Starsena and Charlene were approximately 11 and seven when *Thelma & Louise* hit the big screen. While it's unlikely that the teenagers saw the R-rated film in theaters, in intervening years they may have heard about the picture through other channels or may have actually seen it. Whether or not the girls were familiar with the story, the Florida newspaper seemed to elect every opportunity to relive a classic favorite.[28]

In 1999, law enforcement officials in Louisiana added a new dimension to the trend of naming criminal duos after the film by comparing *Thelma &*

Louise to a trio of escaped male convicts who documented their flee across state lines into Arkansas and Texas. The men presumably took Polaroid pictures like the women do at the outset of their trip. "It was almost like *Thelma & Louise*," commented a sheriff's investigator. As detailed in *The Houston Chronicle*, Christopher Holman, Robert Cassidy Vince and James Lawrence "drank, partied, swam" and "cooked out on the grills." The men photographed themselves standing outdoors beside water and enjoying cocktails at a nightclub. Thelma and Louise aren't able to squeeze in that much recreation. Still, the arresting authorities readily recognized that Christopher, Robert and James desired a taste of freedom redolent of the women's doomed fictional flight.[29]

A surprising take on Thelma and Louise-style criminals occurred in New Mexico, where in the film the women lock a state police officer in the trunk of his squad car. In 1995, *The Albuquerque Journal* profiled two former detectives who were transferred out of the Criminal Investigation Division's child abuse unit for failing to update their supervisor regarding a case. Unaware that the man was actually an informant in a federal racketeering case, the policewomen arrested a suspected kidnapper and child rapist. Even though film's partners are wanted for *crimes* committed within the state, peers at the Bernalillo County Sheriff's Department South Valley sub-station "took to calling deputies Jeannie Web and Janet Barela *Thelma & Louise*," the high desert newspaper said. The film made such a strong impression, even law enforcement officials who might have been appalled by the criminal protagonists labeled their own after *Thelma & Louise*.[30]

In 1998, *The Columbian* of Vancouver, Washington, relayed that police in Portland, Oregon, referred to a couple of unnamed thieves using a *Thelma & Louise* metaphor. Portland authorities utilized the film title while reporting on what the FBI considered a growing trend: women robbing banks. A comparison was made to the film despite the fact that the movie characters never enter any banks. The article explained that hold-ups by women were "unusual" but becoming more common, according to federal officials. Appearing under the headline "*Thelma & Louise* Robbers Join Growing Ranks of Female Suspects," an interview with an FBI special agent did not provide an explanation for the recent rise in numbers. While some fans copied the women's fashion and attitudes, it is possible that other impressionable viewers may have imitated the film's criminal element and escalated from convenience stores to savings institutions.[31] For misguided women, taking the wrong road to liberation means a dead end in a jail cell.

One year after hits on the West Coast, Theresa Hayes and Susan DeAngelo were arrested on suspicion of robbing seven area banks north of Boston, Massachusetts. The area's first pair of female bank robbers were "nicknamed *Thelma & Louise* by their pursuers," *The Boston Herald* proclaimed. Police jockeyed the nickname "in reference to the film of the same name in which

Before their wild weekend begins, the women pose side by side for a photograph. Susan Sarandon and Geena Davis star as Louise Sawyer and Thelma Dickerson in MGM's *Thelma & Louise* (1991).

two women are chased cross country by lawmen after a murder and bank robbery," the newspaper reported incorrectly in March 1999.[32] Like reporters in Washington State, following the lead of police authorities the East Coast newspaper got the facts wrong, at least the facts about the film. Thelma holds up a liquor store, but neither woman in the movie robs any banks.[33]

Whether or not fiction influences real life, in some cases fact induced an incorrect memory of the film. On screen, Louise compares the women's crime spree to a growing snowball propelled by momentum; in the real world, police authorities and members of the press were responsible for inflating the hype surrounding the picture. Two days after the first story, in an article entitled "Cops Think They Have *Thelma* and/or *Louise*," *The Boston Herald* corrected its error and stated that the fictional women flee "after a killing and robbery." The next day, Massachusetts' second largest newspaper got right back into the act of sensationalizing the news by running a third story, "Friends Say 'Thelma and Louise' Were at Dead End." Even though *The Boston Herald* wasn't immediately familiar with the picture, editors relished the opportunity to use the provocative title in their headlines, even if they tripped over themselves in the process. Whether originated by police or journalists, the attention paid to "Thelma and Louise" criminals in the media may have inspired more copycat crime than the movie itself.

Once a trend gains momentum, it's largely impossible to accurately pinpoint all sources of the movement. Of course strides recorded in the media are the easiest to track. In 1998, two women and three teenage girls were arrested in Olympia, Washington, after a bank hold-up styled after the movie *Set It Off* (1996), a film which many critics saw as a knock-off of *Thelma & Louise*. A copy of the later movie was found in a house shared by the five females. Reports indicated that the group watched *Set It Off* repeatedly in preparation for their real-life heist.[34] That same year, *Set It Off* encouraged another group of women on the opposite side of the country, in Manhattan, to kidnap a man at gunpoint and rob him of $500. The crime was committed "after watching a flick about female bank robbers," police told *The New York Post*. "They did it for kicks," described one detective, who added that the women "were mimicking the movie." *The New York Post* pointed out that one film critic called *Set It Off* "a kind of *Thelma & Louise* times two," bringing the circle of influence back to the earlier release.[35]

Regardless of how many criminal acts the picture may have inadvertently encouraged, *Thelma & Louise* clearly amused law officials and journalists across the country. The authorities, who are accustomed to dealing with desperate and violent members of society, had fun with the title to take the edge off of their dangerous jobs. Businesses first and foremost, newspapers were delighted to use *Thelma & Louise* to enhance their product. Although the cases contained in this chapter are a subjective grouping, police authorities and journalists equated criminal behavior with the film far more frequently than offenders. Because of the huge amount of spin generated by the great debate, it's difficult to ascertain which influences were more damaging — mistaken readings of the film or the hype surrounding it.

More importantly, the truth is that artists can't control the reception of their work. Speaking philosophically, *Thelma & Louise* may have inspired Pamela and Carolyn, Peggy and Tammy Ann, Rose Marie and Carolyn, Allison and Jean, Tamika, Harley and Jamila, Winnie and Jane, Stephanie and Melissa, Cheryl and Jennifer, Shirley and Darlene, Starsena and Charlene, Theresa and Susan, Christopher, Robert and James and others.

The co-existence of art and self-agency may cause serious friction if viewers can't tell right from wrong or separate drama from real-life. While it is sobering to think that Khouri's creations may have played a small part in some true crime stories, an individual's freedom still comes with responsibility. Because drama is such a great teacher when handled properly, rather than censor expression, the nation would greatly benefit from better arts education.

PART III. CASE STUDIES

11. Middle of the Road — Dayton: *The Dayton Daily News*

Despite ubiquitous strip malls and homogenous suburbs, the nation's cultural outlook varies noticeably from area to area. A survey of newspaper archives in Dayton, Detroit, Chicago, Salt Lake City, Atlanta, Washington, D.C., Los Angeles, Boston and Kansas City shows that distinct attitudes were apparent in the manner and frequency in which local presses referred to and appropriated *Thelma & Louise* between 1991 and 2001. Comparatively, views toward the film displayed during that time period exhibited subtly distinct and sometimes starkly divergent takes on the great debate as published in *The Dayton Daily News, The Detroit Free Press, The Chicago Tribune, The Salt Lake Tribune, The Atlanta Journal-Constitution, The Washington Post, The Los Angeles Times, The Boston Globe, The Boston Herald* and *The Kansas City Star*. Representing the Midwest, Inner Mountain West, South, Mid Atlantic Coast, West Coast, New England and the very center of the Heartland, the following in-depth case studies reveal the particular flavor of coverage unique to each newspaper.[1] Each city used and replayed the film in its own way often revealing the character of the area as much or more than character of the movie.

America is a big country, so to get a complete taste of nationwide responses to the film, a broad survey of print news media is necessary. In the Midwest, where ticket sales lagged behind the East and West coasts, *The Dayton Daily News* followed national trends by naming petty criminals and a professional baseball team after Callie Khouri's creation but overall generated no original fanfare and little enthusiasm for the film. Unlike Seattle, St. Petersburg or San Franscico, Dayton didn't take to *Thelma & Louise*. As reflected in the newspaper's relatively short and superficial collection of articles that mentioned the film, the area saw the characters as dead-end criminals, not models of strength, friendship, fashion or freedom. Although an archive search for the title between 1991 and 2001 returned over 150 listings, over half of *The Dayton Daily News* results had nothing to do with the film. Obituaries and other pieces naming women "Thelma Louise so-and-so" outnumber relevant articles; a surprising number of senior citizens in the Dayton area came by the title first by birth. Movie reviews and a dozen top video sales lists in 1992 when *Thelma & Louise* was released in secondary formats largely fill out the selection.

Journalists in Dayton largely avoided the picture. In 1995, a brief article entitled "Teen Girls Lead Police Chase, Cruisers Follow Pair In Stolen Car From Lima" encapsulated the story of two females, ages 13 and 14, from Lansing, Michigan, who stole a stepsister's 1988 Oldsmobile Ciera. The pair drove south until they were caught driving erratically by the Ohio Highway Patrol in downtown Dayton. "They might seem a junior version of Thelma and Louise," the newspaper tentatively opined, representing one few of references to the film generated in-house.[2]

Not once in the intervening years after the film's release did *The Dayton Daily News* cast the women as positive icons, though the newspaper did grant *Thelma & Louise* a dubious place in film history. In October 1997, when the Cleveland Indians lost in the eleventh inning of Game Seven of the World Series to the Florida Marlins, the next day sports columnist Gary Nuhn dramatized the "Famous Final Scene." Comparing a crucial missed play to "Butch and Sundance charging out of the barn," "Thelma and Louise gunning the engine," and "Charleston Heston finding the Statue of Liberty on the beach," Nuhn preferred cultural references to films over literature. Getting into this particular game late, *The Dayton Daily News* used the title as a metaphor for sad endings and promoted *Thelma & Louise* to the ranks of two "classic" films from the 1960s, including *Planet of the Apes* (1968).[3]

A majority of *Dayton Daily News* articles that mentioned the movie were derived from outside sources. In addition, whether generated in or out of house, most of the references made were lightweight or derogatory in nature. In 1992, during the presidential campaign season, in his column "Campaign Notebook," Charles Stough replayed a "Top Ten List" from NBC's *Late Night with David Letterman*. Number seven on the list of "Top Ten Things Overheard on the Clinton-Gore Campaign Bus" was "I forgot again — am I Thelma or Louise?"[4] In 1999, a list of recent criminal activity indicated that on June 10 someone reported missing a trio of female Rottweilers, including two named after the famed duo.[5]

Appearing in the entertainment section of the newspaper in January 1992, "Directors Guild Nominee A Surprise" named the recent Directors Guild of America nominees for outstanding directorial achievement for the previous year. Along with Barbra Streisand for *The Prince of Tides*, Barry Levinson for *Bugsy*, Jonathan Demme for *The Silence of the Lambs* and Oliver Stone for *JFK*, Ridley Scott appeared on the list for his direction of *Thelma & Louise*. However, the newspaper slighted his achievement, calling the nod a "surprise." Because questions of male-bashing and excessive violence led the great debate, the newspaper caught wind of the spin surrounding the movie but forgot about the film's director, as if the sensation over content cancelled out all other possibilities such as merit. "While Scott won some praise for directing *Thelma & Louise*," *The Dayton Daily News* allowed, "most of the attention surrounding the film focused on stars Susan Sarandon and Geena Davis and screenwriter Callie Khouri." Instead of speaking directly about the great debate and discussing what actually received attention, the newspaper spoke in generalities, avoiding controversial terms like "feminism" or "rape." (Jonathan Demme eventually won the Directors Guild award for *The Silence of the Lambs*.[6])

In *The Dayton Daily News*, there was little sign that the film found fans within the newspaper's circulation area. Apart from one case of recalling the film in conjunction with crime and Gary Nuhn comparing the women's suicide leap to the losing Cleveland Indians, very few staff members at the Buckeye State newspaper approached the film. When individual journalists did recall *Thelma & Louise*, they tilted the newspaper toward an overall negative opinion. Covering television in the "Lifestyle" section, Tom Hopkins downplayed the movie as a means to uplift a television show in "Fabled Highway Series Gears Up." In 1993, Hopkins told readers that NBC was remaking the 1960s program *Route 66*. "Hit the road, Jack," Hopkins began. "That's a popular TV theme," he added, "certainly not hindered by the success of Thelma and Louise." Hesitant to applaud the big screen release, Hopkins didn't come right out and say that the film inspired subsequent creative endeavors, nor did he weave the picture into any other part of his piece. While some journalists readily credited the title with reinvigorating on the road stories, Hopkins' cold nod insinuated that the genre maintained popularity despite *Thelma & Louise*. Evidently Hopkins didn't warm to the picture, but he was excited about the small screen remake starring an actor born in Cleveland.[7]

When *Thelma & Louise* was embraced within the pages of the Buckeye State newspaper, independent commentators were responsible for making clearly positive comments. In 1998, "Corporations Make Giving Into An Art" reviewed dwindling government resources available to arts organizations. Employing the film to help tell his story, the head of a local theater troupe shared his experience raising funds from corporate and small business donors. The executive director of The Human Race Theatre solicited a commitment from a health care provider to AIDS patients to stage the play *Angels in America*, which concerns the epidemic. He described the decision to go ahead and produce the controversial script as "our Thelma and Louise moment." Instead of representing loss, as the film's closing scene did for sports columnist Gary Nuhn, the dive symbolized embarking on a journey in search of a positive outcome for a member of the local art community. "We just decided to drive that car over the cliff, and hoped we'd land on something soft," Kevin Moore explained, adding that the gamble paid off.[8]

While some newspapers rushed to jump on the *Thelma & Louise* band-wagon, *The Dayton Daily News* didn't run any stories about women's anger, women's travel, women's friendship or women's fashion and connect them with the film in the process. In September 1991, the Miami Valley newspaper directed attention to the opposite sex. In contrast to coverage of the new "bad" woman in Baltimore, Albany, Tulsa and Charleston, the Midwest newspaper purchased an article from *The San Francisco Chronicle* that described men as "bad." According to the piece, supposedly women "reward" men for poor behavior which ensures more of the same. "For men spelunking in the murky caves of 90s romance," contended Shann Nix, "survival may demand lessons on how to be a little less nice." Opposing thoughts published elsewhere in the country, the feature suggested that women wait for men to make a move and show them little or no respect. If readers bought this premise, polite manners were wasted on women in the nineties. Although a "gentle-manly" approach works for J.D., who successfully woos Thelma with the help of "yes, ma'am" and "thank you," by extension Nix argued that women preferred men like Harlan and the obnoxious trucker. In Nix's "Nice Guys Finish Last: At Least with the Opposite Sex," an editor from *Men's Health* magazine summarized the plight of the well-mannered man, labeled the "Alan Alda" guy.

> I cooked dinner, I volunteered to clean the house, I went to see Thelma and Louise with her, and she dumped me for the body builder at the health club. Where did I go wrong?

In this view, only women enjoy the film, while men simply endure it.[9]

In the summer of 1991, *The Dayton Daily News* ran one op/ed piece that focused solely on the season's biggest sensation. Brad Tillson asked readers, "*Thelma & Louise:* Is It a Movie or a Cause?" Confirming the movie "satisfying" entertainment but denying the film's cultural importance, Tillson revealed underlying assumptions that belied his tepidly supportive tone. Namely, he operated under the premise that Hollywood films about women and explorations of feminism are both suspect endeavors.

> Sociologists and psychologists are debating it. And ordinary people across the land are weighing in with their opinions. Sometimes the debate degenerates from the scholarly to the personal. It is dividing families and turning husbands and wives against each other.
>
> This debate is not over some revisionist theory of the Gulf War in which

Saddam Hussein is a good guy. It is not about whether the recession is over. It is not about the civil rights bill or abortion. It is not about the sad state of the Reds' pitching rotation.

Despite his dramatic flair, an incredulous Tilson refused to accept *Thelma & Louise* as a significant piece of art. At the same time, he did recognize "fear and some loathing" among men and women in light of feminism's impact on society but declined to mention any positive advances attributed to the movement.

Surprised that a film could cause such excitement, Tillson got caught up in his own amazement and assumed readers would, too, as he never names or quotes any sociologists, psychologists or "ordinary people" regarding their views on *Thelma & Louise*. No married couples were interviewed to support his theory about the movie leading to marital discord. While "a few" believed *Thelma & Louise* is about "machismo run amuck," Tillson touted, "many more" believe it is about "feminism run amuck." Again, Tillson never bothered to back his claims with actual evidence. *The Dayton Daily News* affiliated itself with the great debate but declined to credit the film with the start of a worthwhile discussion. Tillson praised the actors, cinematography and story but otherwise limited his probe, concluding that "psychoanalyzing" a film's attraction is "not" to be taken "seriously."[10]

As low ticket sales in the region predicted, journalists in Montgomery and Greene counties did not heartily engage in the *Thelma & Louise*-ing of American culture. A piece by satirist Mark Russell also appeared in 1991, representing the newspaper's habit of publishing reprints from out of town newspapers, syndicated columnists and national news services. A commentator on National Public Radio, Russell exhibited the kind of cultural savvy one might expect from someone who pokes fun at national politics and persuasions. "What's the difference between the United States and the New Russia?" he asked. "Russia has an Equal Rights Amendment," he answered, then delivered the punch line, "The framers of their constitution were Thelma and Louise."[11]

Although *The Dayton Daily News'* staffers declined to go below the surface of the great debate, Russell wasn't as reticent. Only men signed the Declaration of Independence, meaning that women in the United States have been fighting for equal legal rights ever since. Russell's jest implied that perhaps it takes the kind of firepower Thelma and Louise deliver to reorder the status quo. In this country, which boasts "liberty and justice for all" yet has relegated women to second class citizenship for the better part of 200 years, it's no wonder *Thelma & Louise* struck a sensitive nerve, one that Russell danced around. Through his cracks, Russell nudged his audience to make deeper connections. Whether readers were actually inclined to do so is a decision outside the messenger's control.

In 1992, Russell returned to the film in "Candidates Have a Ticket to Ride." Like David Letterman had done on his show, Russell called on *Thelma & Louise* to help him poke fun at the Clinton presidential campaign, in this instance by way of the candidates' wives. Playing on the Democratic ticket's show of friendship, the columnist roasted the role of political spouses and people living in the interior. Clinton and Gore were "like brothers," the columnist argued facetiously. Russell joked that Hillary Clinton and Tipper Gore were "even starting to look alike" and complained that he couldn't "tell who is Thelma and who is Louise."

Russell noted the region's appetite for folksiness over sophistication. "Bonding for votes while their spouses twirl batons may work in the Heartland," Russell allowed, "but I'd like to see if that bus [carrying the campaign] could have made it through a few big-city neighborhoods and remain right side up." To close his bit, Russell highlighted the difference in attitude between Americans inhabiting urban centers and those who make their home in the spaces between airports, far from the sea. Besides voting patterns, the divide between "red" and "blue" perspectives also affects the public reception of art and feminism.[12]

Compared to Russell's wit and appreciation of women's issues, *The Dayton Daily News'* review of the film demonstrated far less acumen. As if any picture that put women behind the wheel should automatically be discredited, critic Terry Lawson admitted that he nearly felt "guilty" about liking the film. Hesitancy and confusion may explain his subsequent zigzags and questionable turns in judgment. To Lawson, *Thelma & Louise* was "nothing more" than a "sex-reversed" *Butch Cassidy and the Sundance Kid.* In his view, the characters were "likable" although they "may not be original either," and the film was "smart," "funny," and "engrossing." However, he also believed that *Thelma & Louise* didn't appear to be "particularly authentic," and instead thought it was "thoroughly predictable." Meanwhile, Thelma is certainly shocked when Louise shoots Harlan, as Louise is awestruck by Thelma's emergence as a criminal. If the film hadn't caught so many people in the audience off guard, the great debate never would have erupted.

Just as maintaining their freedom and staying alive becomes an impossible balancing act for the women to pull off, "Film Puts Women in the Driver Seat" never reconciled Lawson's contrasting arguments of "engrossing" and "predictable." He conceded that "even when we know where this movie's going," viewers enjoy tagging along. Then a few sentences later, after condescendingly calling the first 15 minutes "an amiable little comedy about female trouble," Lawson changed up. Revealing the rape in his review, he turned "predictable" into "a disturbing turn." He later stated that Thelma and Louise's methods of escape as fugitive females are "decidedly different," despite his charges of replication.

Worse than giving a schizophrenic reaction to the story, Lawson disseminated mistaken information about the film. He assumed that the film operates on an "anti-man bias," and so he was surprised that *Thelma & Louise* was "written and directed by men." Perhaps the main reason Lawson discounted the effort, which he attributed solely to Ridley Scott, was because he recognized "more male-bashing in this movie's two-plus hours than in a month of Oprah and Sally Jesse." If Lawson's muddied sympathies weren't enough to place his review in doubt, retro misogynistic leanings even shined through his account of the picture's largest male role. "The most positive character without breasts in the movie is a cop, played by Harvey Keitel," he crudely (and incorrectly) intimated. According to the critic, Slocumbe is kind to Thelma and Louise "only because he wants to put them in jail." Lawson failed to recognize both the biology and humanity in Keitel's character, and he also reduced Thelma and Louise to mammary glands. Lawson managed to objectify women and denigrate men all in the same breath.[13]

Checking in with Lawson's 1992 review of *Leaving Normal*, a film which many reviewers compared to *Thelma & Louise*, readers see that *The Dayton Daily News* staffer made a point of finally getting straight the gender on the earlier picture's scriptwriting credits. In contrast to *Thelma & Louise*'s "bumpier road map," Lawson informed readers that *Leaving Normal* "was written by a man." In his review, "It's an Amiable Trip," Lawson also found the later buddy/road movie "predictable." Yet, while some critics delivered harsh reviews, Lawson went relatively easy on *Leaving Normal*. The Heartland critic sensed that *Dayton Daily News* readers would prefer its "cheery, unthreatening tone" to "last summer's favorite argument starter."

> For all those who might have admired Thelma and Louise for their sass, spunk and independence, but thought shooting people and blowing up trucks might be a rather extreme way of asserting self-esteem, we have *Leaving Normal*, a movie that rolls the same highways and pays the same tolls, but far more politely. When the ladies of *Leaving Normal* switch lanes, they always put on their turn signals, and never, ever give anyone the finger.

While appraising the later film, Lawson tailored his views for an audience critical of *Thelma & Louise*, one more likely to welcome a tamer if "less engaging" tale that employs "likable fellows," in his words, rather than "sexist predators." However, in reducing *Thelma & Louise* to a sloppy approximation of its raw exterior, Lawson continued to mishandle the production. One of the main themes of the earlier, stronger piece concerns good manners. Even when they punish Harlan and the trucker for their disrespectful displays, Thelma and Louise force the men to watch their vulgar language and check their obscene gestures. When the duo detain the police officer, their speech is littered with "please," "sorry," and "thanks," even as they hold a gun to his head and lock him in the trunk of his squad car. Although Louise does flip off the trucker after a distasteful run-in, Lawson's discussion regarding politeness and "the finger" flattens the women's quest and oversimplifies the film's complexity.[14]

Unimpressed by the picture, on its own *The Dayton Daily News* never positively aligned *Thelma & Louise* with women's rights or the need for social progress. Commentators in Dayton belittled the film's relevance, even when focusing on an important issue addressed in the movie. In 1997, Mary McCarty filed a story about the abduction and rape of a local 16-year-old girl. It was one of very few articles nationwide to link the film to violence against women, but, nevertheless, McCarty reduced the picture's ability to influence people's thinking. In effect, she denied art its important place in the real world.

> Thelma and Louise may be therapeutic on some primitive level, but here's the reality: The rapist is still out there. We can't yell at him, tell him how despicable he is, how he has harmed one young woman and robbed countless others of their sense of safety and freedom.

What McCarty ignored is that *Thelma & Louise* provides a safe opportunity for society to face — not on a primitive level but intellectually — a serious issue that doesn't receive enough attention. It's not the filmmaker's fault that real rapists exist and walk freely. Louise's loss of temper and Harlan's death shouldn't lessen the power of one of the few films willing to deal with the problem of sexual violence from a woman's perspective. Indirectly referring to *Thelma & Louise* in closing, McCarty alluded to the film's pull but continued to devalue the picture's worth. In reaction to rape, McCarty responded, "Rage is what we feel; caution is what we urge." She continued, "Vigilantism is what we fantasize about; vigilant is what we become."[15]

Despite the newspaper's overall unwillingness to appreciate the film, during Women's History Month in March 1994, while listing "milestones in the history of women" the following germane events were chronicled (with the help of *Ms.* magazine) to highlight 1991:

> Anita Hill testifies against U.S. Supreme Court nominee Clarence Thomas to an all-male U.S. Senate committee. She accuses him of sexual harassment. Thomas survives the hearing and is sworn into office. Many women angered by the hearings run for political office. The film *Thelma & Louise* strikes a national chord with its portrayal of women who strike back against abuse.[16]

Beyond this timeline, *The Dayton Daily News* didn't assign much additional space or analysis to the intersection of the film and the culture at large.

Due to its conservative cultural outlook, land-locked Dayton didn't welcome a film with a feminist message. Compared to other newspapers relatively few articles in *The Dayton Daily News* referenced the title and fewer still promoted it. In 1996, in the wake of the impressive showing of *First Wives Club*, a story reprinted from *The Milwaukee Journal Sentinel* simply entitled "Revenge" briefly mentioned *Thelma & Louise* as an example of comeuppance mixed with humor. Advancing the perception that feminism's preeminent precept of equality still hadn't permeated the Dayton area, the article reinforced the old image of an endless war between the sexes primarily prolonged by one side. "Increasingly," the newspaper drew readers in, "women (and some men) are taking out their checkbooks for The Big Payback."[17]

Dayton did offer one original and positive addition to the long list of nicknames inspired by the movie. In 2000, Liz Carpenter, former press secretary to Lady Bird Johnson, visited town for the Erma Bombeck Conference on Popular American Humor convened at the University of Dayton. Carpenter referred to herself and the late Bombeck as "the Thelma and Louise of the ERA (Equal Rights Amendment)," an acronym that *The Dayton Daily News* felt it should spell out. According to "'Soul Mate and Friend' Remembered," Carpenter and Bombeck met at the Lyndon Baines Johnson Library while attending a conference on how to encourage women to run for legislative office. Afterwards, the two traveled together for several years attempting to win support for the addition of a few lines to the U.S. Constitution, which would finally make women undeniable legal entities.[18]

One article that briefly mentioned *Thelma & Louise* and perhaps best represented the Midwestern mindset operating in Dayton spotlighted the rivalry between Chevrolet and Ford owners. Originating from the Cox New Service, owners of *The Dayton Daily News*, "Chevy vs. Ford: Quarreling Is Job 1" ran in 1999. Comparing the competition between automobile owners over car brands with the on-going match between Pepsi and Coke products, the article referenced *Thelma & Louise* as a big screen example siding with Ford because of Louise's 1966 Ford Thunderbird convertible. Like buying the beer their fathers drink, people follow their parents' lead and remain loyal to one company or the other, according to a Chevy fan and a Ford dealership owner interviewed for the piece. This kind of consumerism, displaying sentimental attachment to one global competitor over another based on emotion rather than reason, summarizes the friendly yet unsophisticated view Mark Russell associated with the middle of the country.[19]

12. Detroit:
The Detroit Free Press

Approximately 200 miles to northeast of Dayton, the city of Detroit is home to nearly one million people. Although Dayton entertains a much smaller population, registering less than 200,000 people in the 2000 census, *Thelma & Louise* fared about the same in terms of the amount space that *The Dayton Daily News* and *The Detroit Free Press* allotted the film. Both newspapers ran nearly 80 articles mentioning the title between 1991 and 2001. Outside of two female journalists who wrote extensively about the film mainly in the summer of 1991, the Knight-Ridder–owned Motown newspaper, like the Cox chain newspaper in Dayton, displayed a similar, low-level of involvement and lack of sympathy for the women and their story. Many of *The Detroit Free Press* articles referencing the film occurred without comment in the entertainment section and simply listed the film as part of an actor's or filmmaker's credits while conducting a review or an interview. Michigan's leading newspaper brightened towards the film only when *Thelma & Louise* crossed paths with the automobile industry.

Sticking to superficial references, in the second half of the decade *The Detroit Free Press* twice partook in the popular habit of comparing local crimes and criminals to the film. One time journalists applied the title; in the other instance police did. Unimpressed by *Thelma & Louise*, the newspaper namedropped the movie both times without exhibiting in-depth knowledge or genuine interest in the film. In 1996, a Bay City woman, allegedly working with a female accomplice, was arraigned locally on federal bank robbing charges for a series of coast to coast heists. "FBI Nabs Woman Believed Part of Bank-Robbing Duo" suggested that the pair's spree was "reminiscent of the movie *Thelma & Louise*," even though no banks are held up in the picture and the women don't adopt robbery as a profession. Far from trying to stay low, the woman from Bay City (near Michigan's thumb) was caught because she bragged about her actions to a concerned citizen who alerted the police.[1] At least Thelma had the sense to tell her story to another criminal who was unlikely to seek out the authorities on his own.

Three years later in 1999, local police spun the picture for fun. According to the newspaper, two women "likened by Waterford Township police to the movie characters *Thelma & Louise*" were sought in connection with the robbery of a couple of gas stations a mile apart, which the women hit up over the course of two days. To explain law enforcement's comparison, "2 Women Sought in Gas Station Thefts" informed readers that in the film two fictional women "staged robberies while fleeing the police." Bypassing rape and murder, the newspaper used the film for its main characters' names and remembered it for its lesser criminal element — going on the lam. Cued by local law enforcement and the national press, *The Detroit Free Press* portrayed the film characters as no more than petty thieves, which didn't represent the actual picture very well. Much more serious than ripping off a gas station (and returning later to buy 50 cents worth of gas, as reported of the Michigan pair), Harlan's murder and the attempted murder of a police officer would rightly carry far stiffer charges, yet Thelma and Louise represent so much more than their felonious actions. Although history does tend to remember bad deeds first, like rival newspapers that were unconcerned with the screenplay's various elements, *The Detroit Free Press* reduced the fictional women's rap sheet in order to fit the popular metaphor more snugly to the local crime. In the process, once again the misdeeds perpetrated against Thelma and Louise were ignored.[2]

A less than adoring attitude toward the women and their story extended throughout the relatively few *Detroit Free Press* articles collected. Rarely did the film title appear in the newspaper regarded with genuine esteem or enthusiasm, greatly contrasting super-fan newspapers like *The St. Petersburg Times* and *The Boston Globe*. In 1992, the tri-county newspaper did pass along Pat Shroeder's appreciation of the film when she bestowed the appellation on a pair of state politicians. At an appearance in Ypsilanti, the lawmaker from Colorado dubbed Democratic U.S. Congressmen Bill Ford and John Dingell "the Thelma and Louise of good-guy issues" for their support of "family issues." Coming from a non-native, this early reference to the film didn't reflect Great Lake State attitudes nor did Schroeder's comments appear to greatly influence area perceptions.[3]

From 1991 to 2001, the only reference made in *The Detroit Free Press* that accepted Thelma and Louise as an uplifting symbol occurred in connection with another crime: O.J. Simpson's slow motion escape from authorities on Southern California freeways. Ellen Creager's 1994 Knight-Ridder column including Thelma and Louise among famous friends originated in Detroit.[4] Otherwise, similar to *The Dayton Daily News*, *The Detroit Free Press* declined to connect the title with Anita Hill, the 1992 political season or any women's issues that happened elsewhere across the country.

Five articles published in *The Detroit Free Press* between 1993 and 2001 perhaps best reflected local attitudes toward the film, which perked up when *Thelma & Louise* symbolized road movies and car culture. In 1993, "Attitude Overhaul Repair Shops Promote Better Service to Women" featured car repair shops that cater to female customers. Comparing the treatment women encounter when they get their vehicles fixed with their treatment in other segments of society, a specialist in insurance from the National Organization for Women equated the lack of respect many women encounter from mechanics with unequal pay on the job. According to staff writer Sharon Andrews, who consulted out-of-state sources and attitudes, a mother and daughter team in Arizona, owners of Sherry & Lois Auto Repair, invoke the "'we're-not-taking-it-anymore' spirit of the film duo Thelma and Louise."[5]

Seen as partners united against a shared adversary, this view of Callie Khouri's creations posited a traditional "us vs. them" battle of the sexes void of common ground. Yet contrary to *The Detroit Free Press* story, many women *and* men feel as though auto repair shops take advantage of customers. Many people regardless of gender lack knowledge about how cars work and don't know how to fix them when they're broken. Male or female, the uninformed wonder if disreputable mechanics rip them off by overcharging for maintenance and conducting unnecessary repairs. Considering her fierce independence and distrust, after she was traumatized and left Texas for good, Louise may have learned to change her own oil.

As one might expect given the city's nickname, the U.S. automobile industry drives the Detroit economy and greatly influences *The Detroit Free Press*. Plugging the 1995 North American International Auto Show and the art of car design (not the art of movie-making), art critic Marsha Miro headlined her article, "Put the Art Before Horsepower." Rendering the Motor City invaluable, she implied that Louise's 1966 Ford Thunderbird sold the picture and accelerated the women's story more than the contributions of the screenwriter, director or actors.

> The Norman Rockwell Award for Vehicle Most Likely to Travel the Middle-of-the Road, Never Offend Jesse Helms and Be Car of Choice for Orphanages-of-the-Future: Chevrolet Corsica: Drive this anonymous Chevy, and no one will ever accuse you of upstaging the boss, overrunning your budget or living on the wild side. *Thelma & Louise* would never have made it at the box office or to that cliff if they had been fleeing in it. But there must be something to be said for predictability.[6]

By 1996 Terry Lawson had moved from Dayton to Detroit to become *The Free Press* movie critic. His piece, "Detroit and Hollywood: You Can't Have One Without the Other," is a good example of the way newspapers twist topics to fit local preoccupations. Squeezing in a little cultural criticism between the grease, Lawson contended that "unlike women or blacks, cars have never lacked good roles in the movies." Getting back on the same track as Miro, Lawson insisted that "cars were there at the inception" of Hollywood. Citing author David Robinson's *From Peep Show to Palace: The Birth of American Film*, Lawson explained how movie studios adopted "Ford-style production lines" by designing, assembling and manufacturing movies in an "on-site, orderly process," thus creating better efficiency and greater prosperity.

Working for a newspaper that devotes considerable time and space to the automobile industry, Lawson may have pleased area residents with his argument that "Hollywood didn't make the car" but rather "the car made Hollywood." However, it's a stretch more difficult to accept than Thelma's consensual rendezvous with J.D. In a company town, displaying loyalty may be more important than supporting viewpoints. Lawson listed *Thelma & Louise* as a road movie and a "loosely" qualifying chase film starring Sarandon, Davis and a "Thunderbird."[7]

Four years later, in 2000, an article that circulated Knight-Ridder newspapers identified car movies including classics like *Thelma & Louise*. Khouri's creation received first billing but didn't land a spot on Matt Nauman's top 10 list, which did include *The Love Bug* (1968), even though it "seems uncomfortably racist and sexist," and *Chitty Chitty Bang Bang* (1968). One of two female-led "car movie classics" largely outnumbered by movies starring men, *Thelma & Louise* was epitomized with the slogan, "I am woman, hear my car roar." Like Marsha Miro and Terry Lawson, Nauman demoted the women to a rank below their automobile. Clearly catering to the mainstay of the local economy, the syndicated piece ran in Detroit under the headline "Fender Flicks, Cars Are the Biggest Stars in Some Classic, and Trashy, Films."[8]

Apart from using the title to boost local egos, *The Detroit Free Press* did not remember the film fondly nor did journalists and editors recall specific details from the picture. In 2001, five years after retiring the make in 1997, Ford revived the Thunderbird by introducing a two-seater convertible. What's difficult to fathom is how *The Detroit Free Press* covered the new model in part by referring to the film but failed to mention Louise's 1966 Thunderbird. *The Free Press'* Lawrence Ulrich noted the car's "relaxed sportiness" tested the car on California's Highway 1 near Big Sur "where jagged roadside cliffs promise a *Thelma & Louise*–style ending for anyone who strays too near the edge." However, Ulrich misfired when he forgot to name the car the women drove over the edge, which was an earlier model of the car under consideration in the article. This certainly qualifies as an error, especially in an article promoting "Ford's Pretty Little Roadster Is Back."[9]

Exerting more effort than *The Dayton Daily News*, in 1991, *The Detroit Free Press* featured the film in a handful of articles. To join the great debate, *Free Press* movie critic Kathy Huffhines penned a preview, an opening weekend review and an op/ed piece. While she liked the film, Huffhines never took a bold stand regarding its feminist nature. Staff writer Judy Gerstel showed more guts promoting the film's worth to Hollywood and society multiple times that summer. Eventually, however, the newspaper's most ardent and thoughtful follower went sour on *Thelma & Louise*. Unlike the connection made between the picture and cars, which lasted throughout the decade, *The Detroit Free Press* quit associating *Thelma & Louise* with women and women in Hollywood after 1993.

Prior to the picture's May release date, Huffhines credited Julia Roberts' box office success with turning viewers and producers onto women-led films. "New for '90s: Female Buddy Movie" saw this development as a welcome change from the 1980s. A month before opening weekend, Huffhines promised readers that *Thelma & Louise* would be a "funny" thriller. She anticipated a female buddy picture, "more original, offbeat and gripping" than Shelley Long and Bette Midler in *Outrageous Fortune*. Relying on trailers and marketing pieces that conceivably mispromoted the film, Huffhines' first mention of *Thelma & Louise* may have misled viewers by emphasizing the runaway wife over her emerging independence. In her preview, Huffhines relayed the film's attraction without mentioning its intellectual and physical edginess.

> Like Moore and Headly [in *Mortal Thoughts*], they face a bad husband problem and solve it with violence. Going even further, Sarandon and Davis decide the experience is such a treat, they'll take the act on the road in a wild, crazy, cross-country trip.[10]

If MGM had more clearly marketed the film as a mind-quaking, expectation-busting comedy hybrid that mixes death with rebirth, viewers might have been less freaked out by *Thelma & Louise* and newspapers like *The Detroit Free Press* might have handled the picture with greater consideration throughout the subsequent decade.

On May 24, Huffhines' review, "*Thelma & Louise* is an American Original," bought into the film's fun-time marketing just as strongly as the actual, more sobering viewing experience. Calling the actresses a "terrific pair of travelin' ladies," she wrote that Americans "who can't appreciate Sarandon and Davis in these roles ought to go back to square one." Elaborating on the cliché, Huffhines explained that "our national birthright is the on-the-road outlaw career goal." Following the lead of studio sales staff, Huffhines pushed the idea of *Thelma & Louise* as a party film without consequences. She hinted at events in the Silver Bullet parking lot and Thelma's conversion from submissive wife to outlaw minimizing any gravity of the change. Impressed by the film's "sockeroo visuals," Huffhines believed that Sarandon and Davis were "terrific and irresistible," exhibiting "the ranginess, cheekbone spread and matching personalities" to prove that being an outlaw on the lam was "an equal opportunity field," but that's the closest she came to using the f word. While she appreciated the actresses and singled out Ridley Scott's touch, Huffhines ignored Khouri's contribution and the film's controversial ending.

Skimming over deeper issues, as she endorsed the picture Huffines didn't recognize any mixed emotions regarding her viewing experience.[11]

While Brad Tillson's *Dayton Daily News* op/ed tolerated *Thelma & Louise* as entertainment but refused to grant the picture the power of meaning and representation, *The Detroit Free Press* was more willing to accept the film as art but was still guarded about its worth. Perhaps the metro Detroit newspaper was also afraid that strong commentary might offend readers. Written by Huffhines following her review, "Film Heroines' Independence Triggers a Fight" first addressed the controversy surrounding *Thelma & Louise* by presenting angry evidence of the on-going great debate outside of Detroit (citing John Leo in *U.S. News and World Report*, Richard Johnson in *The New York Daily News* and syndicated gossip columnist Liz Smith). *The Detroit Free Press* highlighted the controversy as it appeared in other newspapers and magazines rather than assume what ordinary people were saying about the movie, as Tillson did in Dayton, yet editors in Detroit felt compelled to substantiate the great debate before entering the discussion. After validating the national controversy surrounding the film, the newspaper felt somewhat more comfortable adding an in-house opinion, yet Huffhines continued to sidestep the film's central tensions surrounding female friendship and gender strife.

In an article devoted to controversy, Huffhines declined to stake out her own position regarding the film's expression of feminism. Hiding behind the words and ideas of others, she discredited the movie by sharing Sheila Benson's view from *The Los Angeles Times* (wishing for a more "responsible" and "sensitive" reflection) as well as Margaret Carlson's opinion from *Time* ("the characters don't confide in each other as real-life women would"). To direct readers to a more "feminine" film, Huffhines suggested *City Slickers* since its male leads "learn to confide in each other." For Huffhines, the central question of the great debate shifted. Instead of questioning whether the picture was pro– or anti–either gender, the Midwest critic wondered where a supposed lack of intimate sharing "put" Sarandon and Davis "in the 'real-life woman' sweepstakes." Instead of allowing the movie and its lead female characters to exist on their own turf, Huffhines limited *Thelma & Louise* to existing standards and outdated gender role expectations.

Despite Detroit's slight advance over Dayton in that it provided specifics instead of relying on assumptions, Huffhines engaged in the disturbing habit of pitting women against each other. She expected one character to top the other despite the even-handedness of the title. Ignoring Khouri's script, Huffhines claimed that the "tone of director Ridley Scott's movie is much more Thelma than Louise," although Louise's murderous reaction and decision to flee drive the picture as much as Thelma's disastrous interaction with men. The film's powerful impact ultimately overpowered Huffhines, who sought to divide both the title characters and the lead actresses to lessen their combination blow.

After quoting both Sarandon and Davis speaking out against the film's "man-bashing" critics, Huffhines found a "divergent tone" amidst their "similar answers." She concluded that Sarandon was "dangerous because she's straightforward" while Davis was "even more dangerous because she's daffy." However, this analysis doesn't logically spring from the quotes. While Sarandon's comment was shorter and more concise, Davis' response was not cartoonish. Both thespians conveyed essentially the same idea pointing out a double standard in the way people considered the picture's violence. Sarandon directed attention to *Raiders of the Lost Ark* and that "Schwarzenegger thing," referring to *Terminator 2*. In a *People* interview, Davis argued:

> It's kind of humorous that people would all of a sudden go, "Oh, poor men." Let's get real here for a second. Ninety-nine per cent of all other movies are about women either having shallow, one-dimensional caricature parts or they're being mutilated, skinned, slaughtered, abused or exploited with their clothes off. Even if this film did convey some horrible man-bashing message — "Let's us gals all get guns and kill all the men" — it couldn't even begin to make up for all the antiwoman movies people don't even talk about.

Perhaps unconsciously, Huffhines assumed that there could only be one smart female in a crowd and only one manner in which to portray intelligence. Inadvertently, she limited women to token positions — the smart one and the wacky one — when she might have envisioned a greater spectrum of possibilities.

Huffhines enjoyed the movie; however, she seemed to hold back, as if she felt compelled (perhaps by peer pressure or editorial guidance) to downgrade the production. Using a questionable gauge, Huffhines found the film characters not so much flawed as incomplete. As if they lacked sufficient personhood on their own, Huffhines wanted to combine Sarandon and Davis to form a "new composite heroine."

> Why can't women be stronger? We are — in the best way — when we have Sarandon's sense of responsibility and moral consequences. Why aren't women more logical? We aren't — in the best way — when we act on Davis's giddy urge to change the rules of the game.

After quoting the actresses, Huffhines failed to make a distinction between the real women and their fictional roles and also mislabeled the title characters. While Thelma (not Davis) mistakes murder and armed robbery for assertiveness and freedom, Huffhines used "heroine" for its opposite. Operating on the wrong side of the law, the film's title characters (not its lead actresses) better constitute anti-heroines rather than all-around role models. If more film critics were clear about the difference between classic heroines who rise to the occasion and modern anti-heroines who make mistakes that we can all learn from but who still sink, viewers might have better accepted the film's symbolic nature and deeper relevance.[12]

Despite the cold response exhibited by *The Detroit Free Press*, evidently there was plenty of reason to connect the film to local concerns beyond the automobile industry. Judy Gerstel, the newspaper's number one *Thelma & Louise* proponent, touched upon "friction" between Detroiters in "Who Says Women Are Too Violent? Men, That's Who." Like Dayton suggested women want disrespectful men, Detroit claimed that women are too violent. Interestingly, amid tales of physically aggressive women, Gerstel bucked the trend posited at the top of her article. In contrast to the message in her headline (which are generally assigned by editors), Gerstel related the story of an assault she endured downtown at the Fourth of July fireworks. Gerstel got caught in traffic while traveling to the Motor City from Windsor, Ontario. Trying to maneuver her way through, she angered a male traffic attendant who pounded on the hood of her car. Her car was overheating, so she had ignored his instructions to stop. When he threatened to alert customs and have her vehicle searched, she yelled back, "Go ahead!" As Gerstel told it, the attendant "reached in, grabbed my seat belt and yanked it hard with a snap across my neck so I was pinned to my seat." After intimidating her, he left. Gerstel felt the incident would not have happened to a man or would not have transpired at all if her husband had been present. Arguing that men felt threatened by assertive women, which caused them to react and assert their physical stature, she called on "Thelma and Louise" six times without mentioning any other film characters.[13]

Her piece purporting that woman were acting inappropriately according to "worried" men said a lot about the area's conservative social attitudes, but Gerstel had more stories to tell. Maybe her ready mouth explains why her articles disappeared after July 1993. During a phone conversation in early 2004, Gerstel explained from her current desk at *The Toronto Star* that she was eventually squeezed out as a film writer at *The Detroit Free Press* and decided to leave the newspaper.

Back in 1991, Gerstel claimed in print that she "actually sat across a desk from a male editor who mapped the Southern states to prove that the movie was no good." More concerned with geography than rape, the guy couldn't accept the film because Louise says, "I think it's the god damn Grand Canyon" after departing from Arkansas and heading for Mexico. Not afraid to speak, Gerstel reportedly replied, "It's called suspension of disbelief, buddy." Giving her sarcasm a distinctively Detroit flair, she added, "Nobody asks how Robocop breathes." Despite his profession, the editor demonstrated his ignorance of the concept of the unreliable narrator who might not take the most direct route just because that would be the most sensible thing to do. Not enamored with uppity women or familiar with the precepts of fiction, no wonder the newspaper stuck to thoughts of *Thelma & Louise* stuffed safely within cars. Locating the film's "feminist bent" as the cause of fear, Gerstel analyzed, that "sadly, most men don't even realize they're responding in this primitive, infantile way to women and to movies like *Thelma & Louise*."[14]

Mourning a lost opportunity, Gerstel followed her July 1991 piece with a late August article, "Were Empowered Women in Film Just a Flash in the Pan?" Bemoaning the lack of roles allotted to women that tested their character apart from their love lives, Gerstel's sympathies and her answer were clear from the start: "Farewell, Thelma. Good-bye, Louise. Thanks for the ride." While the leads in 1991 summer releases like *City Slickers* and *The Doctor* struggle to become "real men, masters of the universe," Gerstel complained that too often women wait on men and serve as sidekick. Craving more female characters like Thelma and Louise who are "whole people who screw up and grow and change for the better," Gerstel called for a revolution in attitudes and practices to match the quantum change from silent black and white films to talking color. Gerstel returned to the picture to close her piece and bookend her ideas with *Thelma & Louise*. "As we leave Thelma and Louise poised over the Grand Canyon in their dramatic leap to freedom," Gerstel looked forward to "another dramatic leap"—advancing women in film and their reception. Because her hard-hitting articles invoking the film ceased at this point, it seems editors at *The Detroit Free Press* weren't prepared to accept the combination of Judy, Thelma and Louise.[15]

Safer than analysis and risking angry rebuttal, questions were the focus of the feature articles about the film in Dayton and Detroit. Gerstel's September follow-up piece queried, "How can one person's epiphany be another person's pile of excrement?" Four months into the great debate, in "No Middle Ground, It's Amazing How Some Movies Stir Such Passionate, Opposite Reactions" the picture's controversial reception was alluded to but never directly addressed, as if Gerstel was punished for being pro–*Thelma & Louise* and so duly silenced. The notion espoused in the article, that the "movies people love to hate most are sometimes the movies that affect them deeply," clearly implied the season's most hotly contested picture but obliquely, which was not Gerstel's style. Gerstel analyzed *The Fisher King, Barton Fink, Dead Again* and even mentioned "those who despise *Bambi* because the little deer's mother dies," but for some reason she avoided more talk about *Thelma & Louise*. Yet no other film opened that summer to a more fiery reception.

As if to apologize for this obvious shortcoming and still appease reactionary readers, Gerstel explained herself in contorted, whitewashed terms. "Sometimes, a powerful, unexpected statement that people aren't prepared for and don't know what to make of, or something they find very offensive or too invasive of their private emotional space incites a really angry reaction," she belabored. It looks like editors made Gerstel step so far around the film that in a piece focusing on recent cinema she named, without any explanation, James Joyce's *Ulysses* instead of *Thelma & Louise*. What an odd time to provide a literary example. In a sidebar, *Thelma & Louise* was included as number 27 in a list of 30 films that "people adore or abhor" along with *The Color Purple, Driving Miss Daisy* and *Miracle on 34th Street.* If the *Detroit Free Press* is an accurate indicator, before the summer of 1991 ended, by command *Thelma & Louise* and the great debate largely faded from the minds and lips of most Detroiters.[16]

The last time Gerstel discussed *Thelma & Louise* for *Detroit Free Press* readers, in 1993, they were, according to the title of her piece, "Out of the Picture." Avoiding her own opinions, Gerstel defined "real women's roles" with the help of Jeanine Basinger's *A Woman's View: How Hollywood Spoke to Women 1930–1960.* Following Basinger's lead, Gerstel blamed the lack of recent women's roles on the near disappearance of "real women's movies." Disappointingly, Gerstel's assessment of *Thelma & Louise* underwent a change as lurching and dramatic as Jessica Lange's shift in *Frances* before and after the title character's lobotomy. Conceding that the picture was close to being a real women's film (addressing problems that are inseparable from gender) and one of few modern examples of a real women's film, nevertheless Gerstel belittled *Thelma & Louise.* In two years' time, Gerstel went from advocating the film's feminism to complaining that *Thelma & Louise* was "pretty much *Butch Cassidy and Sundance Kid* in drag."

Even though Gerstel turned her back on *Thelma & Louise,* otherwise she continued to support women. The majority of her essay summarized Basinger's historical account of the roles given to women acting in Hollywood throughout its golden era. To provide a ray of hope, Gerstel added a post–1960s update highlighting "small, low-budget, non-mainstream, mostly foreign movies lacking American stars," such as Maggie Greenwald's *The Ballad of Little Jo* (1993), an 1800s western tale about a woman passing as a man in order to escape rape and other female hardships. Gerstel felt that in the absence of better opportunities for women within the mainstream industry, movies made outside of Hollywood provided most of the interesting roles produced.[17]

After the post–*Thelma & Louise* decade ended, of its own accord *The Detroit Free Press* finally copied the popular trend of likening real-life, non-criminal, positive female duos to the film's protagonists in 2002. Eleven years after the film's release and two years before the state elected its first female governor, Democrat Jennifer Granholm, the appointment of a new team of local nighttime television news anchors, who were both female, was characterized as "rare" due to the "unwritten rule" requiring at least one man be propped up in front of the camera. According to "Coming Up at 10," the "pantheon of famous female duos" preceding southeastern Michigan's pioneering women of television news was slight including Lucy and Ethel, Mary and Rhoda, and Thelma and Louise.[18]

During this period, area news coverage in Dayton and Detroit suggested that Midwesterners didn't care for *Thelma & Louise* and likewise didn't readily take to feminism — by name or otherwise. Unlike newspapers elsewhere as we shall see, neither *The Detroit Free Press* nor *The Dayton Daily News* used the term in conjunction with the film's positive effects. Ideally, at some point in the new millenium area attitudes towards social advancement will change for the better, although the 2004 passage in both Ohio and Michigan of unconstitutional anti-gay bans on homosexual marriage doesn't augur much hope.

13. Chicago:
The Chicago Tribune

Sitting confidently on the shore of Lake Michigan, Chicago offers more worldliness than Muncie and warmer temperatures than Duluth. Home to over eight million people, metropolitan Chicago houses twice the population of greater Detroit and is the largest city in the Midwest. Compared to *The Dayton Daily News* and *The Detroit Free Press, The Chicago Tribune*'s coverage of the *Thelma & Louise*'s relevance and impact parallels Chicago's status as the region's leading metropolitan area. Even while Midwesterners as a group failed to support the film wholeheartedly, the Windy City newspaper treated *Thelma & Louise* as an undeniable cultural icon, which, in the view of editors, affected politics, business and gender theory. The newspaper published approximately 200 articles that mentioned the film in the decade following its release, over twice as many as the other regional newspapers combined.

The expansive array of *Chicago Tribune* articles that broached *Thelma & Louise* included interviews with Callie Khouri, Geena Davis and Susan Sarandon; opinion pieces on violence in Hollywood and the Navy's Tailhook convention scandal; investigations into the so-called "Year of the Woman" in 1992; various entertainment articles featuring topics such as films that move on "wheels, wind or water"; and travel stories like "60 Hours on the Dog," which described a Greyhound bus adventure. In Chicago, news reporters, columnists, book reviewers, music reviewers, film critics, fashion writers, sports writers, automobile writers, travel writers, artists, actors and even a clergywoman all name-dropped *Thelma & Louise*.

Differing from the prevalent mood in other areas of the Midwest, many *Chicago Tribune* commentators expressed admiration and generally positive feelings for the film. In 1996, Alan Solomon was sent to explore "the 48 contiguous United States in 48 days." His assignment was to photograph every state welcome sign on the way. Solomon "felt silly," but for the sake of his job he endured truckers who honked their horns while he stood roadside trying to focus his camera. Upon his return, Solomon commiserated with the women's plight. Offering the fictional characters best wishes as if they were real entities and still alive, he included in his piece a special nod: "Bless you, Thelma and Louise."[1]

The Chicago Tribune's wealth of articles began in 1991 with an assortment of reviews and opinion pieces tackling the great debate. Compared to The Dayton Daily News and The Detroit Free Press, The Chicago Tribune printed more critiques of the film, providing readers with a wider spectrum of views. The majority of these pieces supported the picture but not all commentaries offered praise. After comparing the "chaotic comedy-drama" to Smokey and the Bandit, Chicago Tribune film critic Clifford Terry gave the film two stars. While it is "enormous fun to watch" Geena Davis and Susan Sarandon, Terry found Callie Khouri's script "incredulous," Ridley Scott's directorial touch "cliched" and the ending a "mess."[2] Meanwhile, in the Tribune's rival, The Chicago Sun-Times, the area's more famous film critic Roger Ebert graced the film with three and a half stars.[3]

Along with members of the media, everyday individuals from the Chicagoland area jumped into the great debate with vigor. Two Chicago Tribune guest reviewers from local high schools were more generous with their praise than Terry and more emboldened in their appraisals than The Detroit Free Press' Kathy Huffhines. On May 31, 1991, Lina Chern granted the film three and a half stars. Packed with appeal for both genders, Thelma & Louise concerns not only female liberation, she explained, but "liberation in general." The Main East student believed the film was "whimsical and shockingly funny," but recognized that the women's trip was doomed. In Chern's view, the filmmakers created a well-balanced blend of comedy and drama that avoids preaching and asks viewers to make up their own minds about Thelma & Louise and its unusual female leads. "When it is over," she suggested, "you don't know whether to laugh or to keep silent with a deep look on your face."[4]

Vincent Schleitwiler from Math & Science Academy showed even more enthusiasm for the filmmakers' effort. On June 7, 1991, he awarded Thelma & Louise four stars and called it "the best new film I've seen all year." Siding with Chern, Schleitwiler said the picture was "deep." Even though Schleitwiler demographically falls into a category of moviegoers that generally prefers special effects and male-action adventure stars with sexualized women served on the side, he understood the film's subtext and wasn't put off by it. He thought Thelma & Louise was "both subtle enough and daring enough to draw some fairly damning conclusions about the possibilities for women in our society." His review, despite being extremely positive overall, did come with a sarcastic warning. Like Clifford Terry, who took offense at the soundtrack, Schleitwiler cautioned viewers to be prepared for a "dangerous amount" of country and western music. Contradicting the notion that males in general didn't like *Thelma & Louise*, and despite his distaste for score, the high schooler concluded, "I don't say this very often but: See this movie."[5]

Counting the input from readers, two out of three *Chicago Tribune* reviews embraced the film and urged readers to go see it. Additionally, in the summer of 1991, the newspaper ran four editorials advancing the picture. All four appeared while the film was still showing in theaters, and all four pledged support. While *Chicago Tribune* film critic Gene Siskel filed the picture in his end-of-the-year movie wrap-up under "You liked it; I didn't," overall six out of eight commentators at *The Chicago Tribune* joined Roger Ebert at *The Chicago Sun-Times* to give *Thelma & Louise* an encouraging thumbs up.[6] If a majority if Midwesterners didn't like *Thelma & Louise*, it probably wasn't because film critics in Chicago newspapers turned them against the picture.

In addition to a rousing group of local voices, *The Chicago Tribune* gathered opinion pieces from around the country to present to its readers. In "Her Say, At Last, a Film Worthy of the 'F' Word," a freelance journalist from Los Angeles wrote about the controversial release in radioactively glowing terms minus any detractions. Focusing on the positives of sisterhood and personal growth, Nancy Randle touted the film as a boost for feminism's needed renewal amid too much female apathy. Not long after the women's breakout Randle, a super fan, related the film to her own life. To Randle, *Thelma & Louise* embodied the basic need for individual freedom.

> I think about Thelma and Louise every day. They inhabit the corners of my mind, stirring reminders of a road I chose to take a long time ago. They invite me to remember the beauty of independence. They warn me of the inherent danger in denying my need to go my own way. Wheeling that T-Bird into the majestic Southwestern landscape, these two women from Arkansas seem to say life's possibilities are limitless and worthwhile, even as they pay the price.[7]

Given the coverage found in Dayton and Detroit, it's difficult to imagine either *The Dayton Daily News* or *The Detroit Free Press* purchasing Randle's views.

In his first op/ed based on the film, Chicago-based syndicated columnist Clarence Page sought to balance the super-charged, often-cited, extremely disgruntled reviews of John Leo. Page pointed out that rather than advocating criminality, glorifying violence or undercutting feminism, *Thelma & Louise* throws two working-class women into an "allegorical tale." It illustrates "what happens when freedom truly becomes what Janis Joplin sang, just another word for nothing left to lose." In "*Thelma & Louise:* A Reel-Life Tale of Women and Power," Page presented his view that the lead characters' actions are hungry and desperate more than manipulative and aggressive. Not a huge fan but receptive to the picture's underlying meaning, Page felt that the film was "cartoonish" and "simplistic" more than destructive. Critics who complain that all the men in the film are painted the same overlooked Harvey

Keitel's sympathetic Detective Slocumbe, Page reminded readers. In counterpoint to Leo's contention that some women also disliked the film's extremes, Page rebounded with images of women who identified with the film's depiction of rape. Moreover, he chided those who can't accept fair criticism. Like commentators who "overreacted" to the portrayal of black men in *The Color Purple*, "white men" who couldn't accept the portrayal of their kind on screen struck Page as the most entertaining aspect of the film's heated reception.[8] (Nevertheless, six months later he described *Thelma & Louise* as "grouchy.")

Originally printed in *The San Francisco Examiner*, Stephanie Salter's piece ("Loving *Thelma* Do You Have to Be a Woman to Appreciate This Film?") focused on divergent reactions to the film, which she saw split along gender lines. Salter argued that in order to appreciate *Thelma & Louise* viewers must be women or empathize with women, two criteria not all filmgoers were equipped to meet. Salter assumed the need to inform those critics who rejected the film's "strange and disturbing hybrid," which outfitted Geena Davis and Susan Sarandon in trappings usually associated with Arnold and Sylvester. For them she elucidated the "paradox" many inhabit: women begrudgingly acknowledge male-dominated culture while choosing to love and live with men anyway. Thelma and Louise so easily cross over because of deep familiarity with the way the other half (men) live. Evidently, Salter's address wasn't aimed at a lesbian audience. Still, even for heterosexual women, Salter noted that the film wasn't easy to digest but was undoubtedly moving.

> Despite its rollicking, action-packed previews, *Thelma & Louise* turned my stomach and made me cry. It scared me, caused me to squirm, made my heart soar and brought forth laughs that were so hard and loud, I was startled at the sound of my own voice.

Because reactions to the film were so strong, Salter decided that people saw the movie through their own biased eyes, yet like all critics who engaged in the great debate Salter's eyes were also slanted. Ignorant of black male reviewers such as Page, she assumed that "male reviewers" bring a "white, male take" to movies, which prevented some from seeing *Thelma & Louise* as (white?) women did. Referring to "several" male reviewers who were aghast over Thelma's actions, Salter differentiated between what happens in the parking lot and Thelma's decision to engage J.D. so soon after Harlan's attempted rape. The attack concerns "violence, humiliation and power," Salter believed, while the one-night stand equals consensual sex. The two men enlivened a dichotomy in behavior, one Salter assumed women recognize "instinctively." Apparently, the San Francisco commentator was unfamiliar with Sheila Benson's dismay in Los Angeles over Thelma's "perky bounce-back." Like those critics who had trouble identifying with the film's female perspective, ironically Salter's contribution to the great debate might have been stronger had she not maintained a rigid view of the audience.[9]

Finally, a guest editorialist from Brown University, Shea Dean, informed syndicated columnist Liz Smith that despite her warning young women went to see the film anyway. Even though she humbly denounced her own authority on film and feminism, 21-year-old Dean wasn't afraid to voice her views about *Thelma & Louise*, as if the movie was an old friend she knew well. A woman after Stephanie Salter's heart, Dean read the story as "symbolic of women defying convention" while "trying to break the mold of roles society has imposed on them." Prepared to use the f word where Thelma and Louise were not, Dean sympathized with the fictional women more so than an Ivy League student might commiserate with an uneducated, single waitress and subservient, naïve housewife in real life. Locating the women's problems outside of their control, Dean hinted at the "emotional trauma" from the past that "stymies" their plan. No matter their educational background, geographic origin, class or race, among women the threat of sexual violence and rape transcends all divides. Optimistically calling the film "a landmark for the women's movement in America," Dean believed that the film holds the power to "change a lot of attitudes." Even if the picture's ability to revolutionize the culture was limited, at least it got people talking, the college student concluded.[10]

In smaller, less cosmopolitan Midwestern cities than Chicago, newspapers avoided the connection made elsewhere between the controversial film and national politics. Outside of reviews and op/eds, in the first half of the decade many of the references to *Thelma & Louise* made in *The Chicago Tribune* were topical and connected to current issues such as Clarence Thomas' nomination to the Supreme Court, abortion activism, NOW conventions, the political scene in Washington, D.C., and the Democratic Party platform in California. The newspaper even managed to include the fictional women within a profile of English royalty. Although the role *Thelma & Louise* played in these articles was limited with effects that are difficult to measure, the film and the great debate were not viewed as inconsequential.

In the fall of 1991, a handful of area residents on both sides of the divisive issue were interviewed for their reaction to U.S. Senate's 52–48 vote confirming Clarence Thomas to the Supreme Court. "Across Chicago, U.S., the Debate Continues" included comments from five area males and two out-of-town females. Though national polls showed that a preponderance of Americans supported Thomas, the majority of *The Chicago Tribune*'s sampling voiced disappointment in his nomination proceedings.

Though no women on the streets of Chicago were consulted for their views, the story described a protest rally attended by approximately 75 people, most of them women. The event was held outside the Kluczynski Federal Building where "one poster carried by a demonstrator pictured the title characters from the movie *Thelma & Louise*." According to the newspaper, the sign bore the sentiment, "Orrin Hatch and Arlen Specter meet Thelma and Louise." Evidently editors felt that one aggressive *Thelma & Louise* crack — which readers might presume (minus a photograph) came from a female because of the protestors' feminist politics — equaled the statements of five area men. With the help of Hollywood, demonstrators "threatened political reprisals" against the Republican senators from Utah and Pennsylvania who "led the attempt to discredit" Anita Hill. Interpreting the reference on page nine within the news section, the article explained that some people view the film characters as feminist icons. Because of the action of a sole demonstrator and this article, *Chicago Tribune* readers may forever remember Clarence Thomas in terms of *Thelma & Louise*.[11]

The most serious and far-reaching connection made between the film and politics occurred two years after the film debuted, when the *Harvard Law Review* published a Northeastern University law professor's treatise on sexual harassment. "The Woman's Ghetto" featured Cynthia Grant Bowman and her work "Sexual Harassment and the Informal Ghettoization of Women," which defined street harassment in an effort to change public attitudes toward unwanted advances. Bowman was inspired to review current harassment law and draft her proposal after she was interviewed on the topic, saw *Thelma & Louise* and endured salacious comments from two guys in a truck waiting next to her at a red light. According to *The Chicago Tribune*, Bowman "was surprised by the audience's positive response when the Sarandon and Davis characters blow up the truck of an abusive male jerk." After a similar personal experience, Bowman spoke with other women. She learned that disturbing and threatening street harassment was common. Although the first amendment makes passage of any effective laws difficult, Bowman believed that a few high-profile cases could spotlight the problem and bring about change. According to Bowman, the trucker harassed Thelma and Louise on public highways, meaning he should have been held liable by law. In her treatise, Bowman defines street harassment:

> Street harassment occurs when one or more unfamiliar men accost one or more women in a public space, on one or more occasions, and intrude or attempt to intrude upon the woman's attention in a manner that is unwelcome to the woman, with language or action that is explicitly or implicitly sexual.

As detailed in *The Chicago Tribune*, "Sexual Harassment and the Informal Ghettoization of Women" argues that lewd tongue actions like the trucker's be deemed a misdemeanor and subject to a $250 fine. However, Bowman's language as reported was sexist, implying that men are never subject to unwanted public intrusions by females, but this is a matter that could be easily fixed. With greater public support and enforcement of stricter laws against unwanted advances from strangers (such as the trucker's comment, "I'm your Captain Muff Diver"), relations between the genders could move forward, Bowman implied. Whether new laws are necessary or not, when more people respect women, audiences will be more likely to accept women as lead characters.[12]

In the early years of the post-release decade, two *Chicago Tribune* articles covering abortion activism invoked *Thelma & Louise* (though briefly) as if the film substantiated a liberal political outlook. One article informed readers about the gag rule against abortion counseling at government sponsored family planning clinics, which was upheld by the Supreme Court in 1991.[13] The other detailed the "Freedom of Choice" rally on Washington, D.C., in 1992, organized by NOW.[14] In both pieces, celebrities taking a stand included Callie Khouri, identified as screenwriter of *Thelma & Louise*, who lobbied congress and marched in support of a woman's right to control her own reproductive life. Whether Khouri demonstrated prior to her fame or fame gave her the courage to step forward is interesting on the personal level, but, as New York Redstocking Carol Hanisch's 1970s saying goes, the "personal is political." Khouri's appearance may have encouraged others to assert themselves as her screen characters do. Of course, in what way others might be moved can never be controlled, as copy-cat criminals who take inspiration from movies attest.

Two more articles that included *Thelma & Louise* focused exclusively on NOW. In 1991, the parent organization of the country's oldest nationwide feminist association held its annual conference in Chicago over the Fourth of July weekend. Participants made plans for addressing the upcoming election year and the nomination of Clarence Thomas, which the group opposed. According to the newspaper, comic Judy Carter led a well-attended session on how to handle serious issues with humor. As retold in "'92 Agenda Set," when Carter was questioned about her response to hecklers, she replied, "I just think, 'What would Thelma and Louise do?'" The picture was still in theaters when this article portraying the title characters in conjunction with NOW was published.[15]

The newspaper's coverage of women organizing for social progress clearly recognized a relationship between the film and feminism, which may have alienated some Midwestern viewers. Less than two months later, when readers were still able to catch *Thelma & Louise* at the local cineplex (though evidently many in the area did not), a shorter blurb advertised the upcoming anniversary of Illinois NOW, in existence since 1966, at the time boasting 8,500 members statewide. Workshops at the Saturday event were to include a discussion of *Thelma & Louise* and "how violence against women can be brought to the attention of the public," according to "Then and NOW: A 17-year Fight for Equity Issues," which ran on page two.[16]

Not all political references to the film in *The Chicago Tribune* involved serious issues, though all blurbs did revolve around women's lives. Gossiping from the nation's capital in 1992, the newspaper told readers back home that the "hottest" new T-shirt in this "capital" of political T-shirts announced, "Thelma & Louise Finishing School Graduate." The T-shirt was attributed to NOW, which marketed the T-shirt, though it was designed by Fern Narod

and copyrighted by Not So Subtle Tees, and the newspaper claimed that the design resembled a Miss Porter's Finishing School T-shirt.[17] Less than a month later, the newspaper published a response from Miss Porter's School in Farmington, Connecticut. A representative from the institution pointed out that finishing schools "disappeared" decades ago. With graduates at top colleges and universities, she continued, Miss Porter's is "neither in name nor in educational mission" primarily concerned with upholding sexist attitudes and teaching a curriculum concentrated around needlepoint and table manners. Apparently, Miss Porter's had no major problem with *Thelma & Louise* or the T-shirt, just the newspaper's inaccuracy regarding the school.[18]

Fern Narod and Not So Subtle Tees got into the great debate by printing T-shirts. "Thelma & Louise Finishing School Graduate" satirically suggests that women adopt the film characters' aggressive approach to problem solving. T-shirt available through the National Organization for Women's website (now.org).

On a more imperial note, in 1994, the newspaper compared Sarah, the Duchess of York, and Diana, Princess of Wales, to Thelma and Louise because of the media tsunami that followed them. Much like Callie Khouri's creations, the two royal women inhabited a "class by themselves," *The Chicago Tribune* noted. As Paul Galloway wrote, Sarah and Diana were "beauteous and vital and unconventional enough to have been written about by the rabid, ravenous British tabloids from time to time as though they were the monarchy's Thelma and Louise."[19]

Though no pair of fictional women is more notorious, eventually a cultural icon exerts its influence and recedes into the background. After a few years, connections between the film and political issues dried up in the Illinois newspaper. In 1995, the last mention of the film within a national political context occurred via "Affirmative Action Splitting Democrats," in which California Democrat Bob Mulholland warned against inside party fighting over affirmative action. The state's Democratic campaign adviser cautioned Golden State members, "If we spend 1996 battling among ourselves over affirmative action, we would be like the last scene in Thelma *& Louise.*"[20] Before evidence of the picture's political influence disappeared in *The Chicago Tribune*, *Thelma & Louise* served as a threat against re-election, symbolic bridge between middle and lower class women, royal metaphor, cautionary tale, motivation to write new laws, inspiration to take civic action, comic relief and food for thought.

Throughout the decade studied, the newspaper covered the film broadly rather than limiting *Thelma & Louise* news items to little more than criminal activities. In addition to political concerns, *Thelma & Louise* found a place within a diversity of stories and features, particularly regarding business, society and entertainment. While *The Detroit Free Press* believed its Motor City readers were mainly interested in automotive connections to the film, in 1991, *Thelma & Louise* popped up in a *Chicago Tribune* article addressing product placement in Hollywood movies. According to "Products Compete for Movie Roles, Too," a trend was set in 1982 when Universal's space alien E.T. ate Reese's Pieces, providing Hershey U.S.A. with free world wide promotion. Ever since, major national advertisers have paid film producers for the right to include their brands on-screen. Milwaukee's Miller Brewing Co. (a regional company) "nearly steals the bar scene" in MGM-Pathé's *Thelma & Louise*, the Cook County–based newspaper asserted, which is a stretch considering the music, smoke, characters and action that also vie for attention. Like *The Detroit Free Press*, *The Chicago Tribune* wanted to show support for an area business, yet the more prominent newspaper targeted a wider slice of the U.S. economy. In addition to Wm. Wrigley Jr. Co. of Chicago gambling on a Hollywood blockbuster, the article also discussed cinematic marketing efforts by Subway, Pizza Hut, Inc., and American Dairy Queen Corp., headquartered in Connecticut, Kansas and Minnesota.[21]

Claiming that "more than half of adventure travelers are women," a 1996 *Chicago Tribune* feature detailed vacation possibilities such as whitewater rafting, wilderness survival and sea kayaking that are stimulated by action movies. With the help of a CNBC business correspondent, the newspaper again covered national trends and business ventures popular outside of its circulation reach, exhibiting a broad-minded attitude toward local newsworthiness. In the minds of editors, people in greater Chicago should know or would be interested to know that Hollywood inspires trips and promotes destinations. Five years after the film's anti-heroines cruised into cultural history, the newspaper shared how *Thelma & Louise* "boosted" travel to Utah where the picture was filmed.[22]

The film maintained more steam as a sales pitch than a political cause in the city's major newspaper — very fitting given Chicago's status as an anchor city and economic leader. Eight years after *Thelma & Louise* first gunned its engine, a technology report out of Silicon Valley's *San Jose Mercury News* reviewed the computer industry's attempt to address sagging profits through the manufacture of designer personal computers. Aiming for the consumer that buys designer clothes, a sub-brand of Toshiba began fabricating laptops with carrying cases to match stereotypic lifestyles. Each version was identified by a grabber name such as Working Snob, Tank, White Box and Jackie K, and the new models were marketed accordingly, explained "PC-Makers Add Style to Profit Strategy." With the help of West Coast journalism, *The Chicago Tribune* relayed that the Jackie K "portrays women lounging on a large convertible and clothed in little more than lingerie." Associating the film with stylish women and sexy cars, the article suggested that the Jackie K ad could be subtitled "Thelma and Louise get a laptop."[23]

Back in 1992, the picture itself was the product. After the film was released on video, *Thelma & Louise* potentially played before more people parked at home on their couches than it did in 1991 playing on the big screen. While MGM tallied strong videocassette sales overall for *Thelma & Louise*, one video store manager in suburban Chicago interviewed by *The Chicago Tribune* confirmed that the rental version of the film scored well locally despite low first-run ticket sales at area box offices. With two years' experience managing operations and noting customer trends, Sinda Shapiro drew a distinction between what people pay to go see ("big films") and what they wait to rent ("small films"). Refuting the idea that Midwesterners didn't take to the release, the Video Adventure manager said in the newspaper's "First Person" column that "*Thelma & Louise* was our big winner in 1992."[24] Supporting the notion of the film's local popularity at least within select crowds, in 1993, Women and Children First, a Chicago-area feminist bookstore, reported that *Thelma & Louise* was the second best renting title after the musical performance *k.d. lang: Harvest of Seven Years*.[25]

Because there is more than one way to see a movie, box office receipts alone do not give an accurate picture of viewing patterns. Given the amount of coverage *The Chicago Tribune* devoted to *Thelma & Louise*, perhaps it was no coincidence that people in the metropolitan area rented the video and adopted the title for their own purposes. At the end of 1992, "Boxer Helps Women Fight for Fitness" featured a local female fighter and her trainer. Calling themselves the "Thelma and Louise of real life," the pair taught other women self-defense techniques.[26] In contrast, the scant times that *The Dayton Daily News* and *The Detroit Free Press* reported instances of *Thelma & Louise*-naming within the post-release decade the phenomenon originated elsewhere; either the person appointed the title themselves or the individuals receiving it lived outside the area. Momentum for the film never appeared to gear up in Dayton and Detroit, indicating a symbiotic relationship between newspaper coverage and public reception.

Not all Chicagoland women thought of the duo in an upbeat fashion, however. "Oh No, Not Another Story about Butts" presented the story of women taking up cigar smoking. Two women at a special event catered to women held at Morton's of Chicago commented, "We don't want to go as far as Thelma and Louise." Trying out some new things but cautiously, the two sisters-in-law spoke while smoking their first cigars and sipping debut martinis.[27]

Mixed among references that casually mentioned *Thelma & Louise*, *The Chicago Tribune* articles occasionally analyzed the film's lasting resonance with greater depth. Exploring the film's social relevance, a lengthy opinion piece on revenge appeared in 1994. The article cited a slew of diverse sources and covered the topic much more seriously than the similar but much shorter article that materialized almost three years later in *The Dayton Daily News*. While the smaller town newspaper assumed that women are more interested in retaliation, the big city newspaper weighed the evidence more closely before arriving at any conclusions to the question, "When it comes to getting even, is female really deadlier than male?" Looking for answers, *The Chicago Tribune* turned to *Thelma & Louise* as well as other films including *Fatal Attraction* (1987), *Sleepless in Seattle* (1993), *The Godfather* (1972), *Misery* (1990), *Gone with the Wind* (1939) and *Fried Green Tomatoes* (1992). In addition to big screen Hollywood products, author and professor of English and feminist theory at the University of Connecticut Regina Barreca studied fictional depictions on television, in Greek mythology and in literature. To investigate revenge, she also referenced the Romans, current events and the Bible. Treating her topic seriously, Barreca called on Michelle Pfeiffer as Catwoman, *The Mary Tyler Moore Show*, mythical Medea, antiquity's Juvenal, popular culture's Lorena Bobbitt and Amy Fisher, biblical Judith, Shakespeare's Lady Macbeth and literature's Cathy from *Wuthering Heights* in support of her argument. The philosopher Nietzsche, painter Paul Gauguin, author Nathaniel Hawthorne, talk show trailblazer Phil Donahue, filmmaker Alfred Hitchcock, fictional sleuth Sherlock Holmes, playwright Oscar Wilde, singers Laura Nyro and Connie Francis, and early feminist Elizabeth Cady Stanton also played a part in Barreca's short study.

At the end of her far-reaching inquiry, Barreca concluded that women aren't more likely to engage in aggressive payback. Instead, society focuses more on women and revenge to fit assumptions about gender. Most likely, both sexes seek retribution in equal numbers, Barecca suggested, though she detailed how women and men approach revenge differently because of the imbalance of power between them. In *The Godfather* series, for example, mafia men commit murder to seek ultimate, bloody revenge. In *Fried Green Tomatoes*, a heated Kathy Bates purposefully bangs her car into a younger woman's vehicle in order to exert her will and make a stand, but Bates only seeks to teach a lesson, not annihilate an adversary. A year later, writing again for *The Chicago Tribune*, Barreca analyzed lust in the same detailed manner. To illustrate the idea that lust isn't restricted to those who are attractive, she pointed to the truck driver in *Thelma & Louise*.[28]

In 1996, Barreca was also responsible for bringing up *Thelma & Louise* in *The Dayton Daily News* article "Revenge." Barreca located revenge in "nearly every great work of literature," but she wasn't given the space to provide specifics. Using Callie Khouri's creation as a conversation starter, she described the film's expression of retaliation as "anger channeled into something that basically has to do with humor." Although "Revenge" consulted one academic's point of view, the article primarily stuck to shallow surfaces by profiling sardonic self-help books and passing along urban legends intended to entertain readers. Conversely, in her *Chicago Tribune* piece, Barecca's "Payback Time" provided a more complex, historical look at human emotion.

> The desire for revenge can be transformed into forgiveness — but only if there is belief that justice will prevail. Swords can be turned into plowshares only if there is a belief in closure coupled with an assurance that the balance of power is guaranteed. Balance, however, can only be achieved if everyone has equal access to power; the powerless are fearless because they have nothing to lose. If the world were anything like what it should be, revenge would be as difficult for the ordinary person to understand as nuclear fission. The world being what it is, revenge flickers on our screen, fills up our pages and lights bonfires in our imagination.[29]

According to a *Dayton Daily News* article (reprinting one that originated in Milwaukee), revenge was little more than a mean-spirited joke, an act for "those who believe it's best to wound all heels." Inside the pages of *The Chicago Tribune*, revenge was a meaningful, sometimes appropriate, sometimes misguided response to injustice, imagined or real. The difference in weight accorded to the topic in Chicago and the rush in Dayton to attach sexist attitudes to revenge replicates the diverging views shown by the two newspapers regarding the film. In essence, editors in Dayton dismissed *Thelma & Louise* as the story of two inconsequential women who lose control; in Chicago, editors afforded the women greater consideration and respect.

Although few staff members were intent on jumping into the great debate, *The Chicago Tribune* made room for outside commentators willing to explicate the repercussions of *Thelma & Louise*. If sex, religion and politics are taboo topics best ignored in polite conversation, then printing a pro-*Thelma & Louise* plug penned by a Presbyterian clergywoman was risky business, particularly if a considerable portion of the newspaper's readers consider God a "He" and believe that the Divine's ministers should likewise be male. Braving a possible backlash, if not from *The Chicago Tribune* then perhaps within her congregation, a pastor from Minnesota shared one of her favorite movie scenes found in the film. In a 1995 essay titled "Cherish Lover, Lest You Lose Her," Kristine M. Holmgren recalled, "Be sweet to your wife." The words Thelma offers as advice to the New Mexico police officer before she closes the trunk lid on him — "My husband wasn't sweet to me, and look how I turned out"— serve as a reminder for husbands to be more "demonstrative," said Holmgren. According to the minister, wives need assurance that they are "important and loved." Referring to research that says even working women do more chores around the house than their mates, Holmgren urged husbands to not necessarily help out by making the beds and doing laundry but to give their wives much needed words of "approval."[30]

A more progressive and incisive view of women's roles in society followed two years later. Seeking to redefine the battle between the sexes mindset, a British think-tank's study on women, summarized by *The Chicago Tribune* in 1997, predicted that "a widening gap, not between men and women but between different types of women" would evolve in the new century. The study indicated that the future would challenge the women's movement by further stratifying women. Dividing women into types for purposes of evaluation, movie characters Shirley Valentine and Thelma and Louise represented "Frustrated Fran," one of five stereotypical caricatures.

> Frustrated Fran, like the movie characters Shirley Valentine or Thelma and Louise, has grown up believing that feminism should by now be delivering the results. But she is still struggling to cope, juggling a job and motherhood, usually little money and often with an absent husband. Rather than being supported by her "sisters," she finds herself increasingly marginalized by the success of those who have the education, support and determination to make it. Thirty-one percent of women surveyed say they suffer from poor self-esteem, and 23 percent, especially in lower classes, say they feel angry much of the time.

As "The Future for Women: To Each Her Own" elaborated, lower class women feel alienated from women like Shea Dean, attending Brown University, and Regina Barreca, teaching at the University of Connecticut. As individuals "connected to people, technology and their feelings," both Dean and Barreca appear to fit the profile for "Networking Naomi." Diversity among women like Thelma, Louise, Shea and Regina may delay progress toward gender equality, the report by think tank Demos warned, because differences between women may seem greater than similarities. This supposed schism between women replicates the dramatic difference in the way the film performed in various areas of the country. Ironically, while viewers in affluent, well-educated urban areas like Chicago and especially Boston embraced *Thelma & Louise*, viewers in suburban and rural areas who might have identified more directly with the film characters displayed less enthusiasm for their story.[31]

By devoting space to voices that sought to widen the discussion surrounding gender issues, the Chicago newspaper demonstrated its intrigue with the status of women as a reflection of society and culture. In terms of relating *Thelma & Louise* to gender, *The Chicago Tribune* far outperformed *The Dayton Daily News* and *The Detroit Free Press*. The newspaper was also more willing to discuss Hollywood and particularly women's experience work-ing there in association with the film. Exercising a progressive perspective, the newspaper summarized *Entertainment Weekly*'s December 18, 1992, fea-ture, "If Women Ran Hollywood" the day before the issue appeared on news-stands. The wishful thinking that Thelma and Louise would "live at the end" and "get away with it" topped a list of fanciful feminist musings listed in the article. Furthermore, both media outlets promoted the idea that if the oppo-site sex wielded control, "There would be a new TV series based on the movie," as MGM once considered. Reprinting other ironic remarks such as "Jodie Foster would make $10 million a picture" and "Julie Christie, Jacque-line Bisset, Helen Mirren, and Faye Dunaway would be allowed to be middle-aged sex symbols," the leading Midwestern newspaper encouraged its readers to reflect on gender bias in the film industry. While readers in the hinterlands may have remained in the dark about these issues, "Cast Changes; Entertain-ment Weekly Imagines a Hollywood Run by Women," with the help of bor-rowed sarcasm, informed readers in Chicago about the earnings imbalance and age discrimination that Hollywood actresses endure.[32]

On a much lighter but still complimentary note, ten years after the film debuted, in the spring of 2001, "Great Pairings in Hollywood a Rarity" took a nostalgic look at memorable screen duos of the past. Along with Jean Har-low and Clark Gable, Boris Karloff and Bela Lugosi, Spencer Tracy and Katharine Hepburn, Elizabeth Taylor and Richard Burton, and Robert Red-ford and Paul Newman, Susan Sarandon and Geena Davis made the retro-spective of famous pairings as the only female set of renowned stars on the list. *Thelma & Louise* "proved" two women could star in a "buddy picture," the newspaper declared. Forwarding a story from *The Baltimore Sun* (a news-paper that worked a diversity of angles toward the film), the Chicago news-paper credited the "resulting furor"— not the women's performance or Callie Khouri's script — as the reason Sarandon and Davis earned their Best Actress Oscar nominations.[33]

Though the reprint from the Mid-Atlantic region devalued Sarandon's and Davis' achievements, overall *The Chicago Tribune* displayed an open if not activist attitude toward women's issues, especially compared to lower-profile newspapers in the region. In a 1992 Valentine's Day piece on celebrity romance, which admitted that recent times had been hard on relations between men and women, the newspaper engaged in a sarcastic tribute to Eros. A quiz tacked onto "Love Hurts" asked readers to pair "fun couples" to their appro-priate tag. The correct response for Thelma and Louise was an often-repeated quote, though the newspaper didn't credit the author. Given the nation's lack of knowledge and concern for women's history and feminism, *The Chicago Tribune* didn't bother to unravel the mystery of who first said, "A woman without a man is like a fish without a bicycle."[34]

Returning to the world of academic analysis, in the summer of 2001,

"Giving Women the Power to Fight Back" promoted *Reel Knockouts* by Martha McCaughey and Neal King, who edited a selection of essays analyzing aggressive women in films. Speaking as a university professor, McCaughey expressed how each instructor discovered that screening images of violent women in class "messed with our students' assumptions" regarding gender. Even among society's better educated, in her words the exercise "scared the men" while it "empowered the women." As a teacher in the business of forcing students to reevaluate preconceived ideas, McCaughey added, "We liked that."

King claimed that the first two *Alien* movies, *Terminator 2* and *Thelma & Louise* reign as the most influential films to counter the "damsel-in-distress stereotype," though he later stipulated that Ripley from the *Alien* movies was the only truly "mean" woman of the group. King described women's on-screen violence as more rare than men's. He elaborated that violence enacted by women is "more likely to be framed with special explanations" (such as Louise's secret experience in Texas) and "more likely to come at the end of a lot of provocation" (such as Harlan's attempted rape of Thelma). In *Thelma & Louise*, the women don't depart from home with excessive aggression in their hearts. Instead, they develop their tough attitudes on the road. After the physical threat he wields subsides, Harlan dies because of his words, not because he poses any immediate danger. A form of street harassment, Harlan's verbal mockery prompts Thelma's friend and protector to pull the trigger, which aligns with King's theory.[34]

After the post–*Thelma & Louise* decade, Callie Khouri returned to the limelight in 2002 crowned by *The Chicago Tribune* the "doyenne of the chick flick" due to her "headline generating" screenplay for *Thelma & Louise* and her directorial debut, *Divine Secrets of the Ya-Ya Sisterhood*. Repackaging an article from *The Los Angeles Times* written by Rachel Abramowitz (author of *Is That a Gun in Your Pocket? Women's Experience of Power in Hollywood*), the Midwest newspaper continued its coverage of *Thelma & Louise* and issues concerning women in film and their fans into the next century.

"Forget Old Rules About Chick Flicks; Weepiness Is Out; Girl Power, Attitude Are In" paraphrased the opinions of frustrated Columbia chairman Amy Pascal. When a film starring women does poorly, it's derogatorily called a "chick flick," yet when blockbuster movies such as *Erin Brockovich* and *Titanic* feature female protagonists, they're perceived as "everybody movies." To combat this stereotype, according to Abramowitz more recent films starring women advocated "girl power" and physical bravado minus any "old-school feminist politics." While Hollywood generally steers clear of the f word, Pascal pointed to Columbia's 2000 hit *Charlie's Angels* (what might be called an example of "new school" feminist politics), as the kind of film she was looking to produce. She explained, "I wanted to make a movie about girl empowerment," no doubt catering to Hollywood's young audience. Describing *Charlie's Angels* as a film that delivers a message "without hammering it over people's heads," Pascal made an ironic statement about a production that gave its female leads little to do and even less to think about other than karate chopping bad guys and wearing skin-tight, revealing clothing.[35]

The success of *Charlie's Angels* doesn't mean that all women in Hollywood's potential audiences decline to use their minds while sitting in the theater. In 1996, after *First Wives Club* came out, "A Lucid Thought: Middle Age Sans Female Rage" compared Mir astronaut Shannon Lucid to female film characters who resort to revenge. Writer Mary Schmich preferred Lucid's entry into the headlines, "making news because she has done something bold and interesting, not because she's mad as hell about what some man has done to her." Although the writer believed that women, including Thelma and Louise, have reason to be angry, Schmich, like Judy Gerstel in Detroit, looked forward to the day when Hollywood makes movies about women who achieve by "marching boldly into middle age." According to Schmich, when Hollywood delivers stories like Lucid's, "we all will have grown up."[36]

14. Salt Lake City: *The Salt Lake Tribune*

Originating from the state capital, *The Salt Lake Tribune* worked Utah's unique *Thelma & Louise* angle and also partook in national trends, mainly with the help of soft-hitting articles purchased from outside sources. Serving a population slightly larger than Dayton, *The Salt Lake Tribune* mentioned the film more often than *The Dayton Daily News* or *The Detroit Free Press*, over 100 times between 1991 and 2001. Coverage in Salt Lake was heavier because the feature was shot within the Beehive State, but the tone and weight afforded to the production did not significantly improve or increase. From the Midwest to the Inner Mountain West, the center of the country was not impressed by the film. At *The Salt Lake Tribune*, *Thelma & Louise* commanded attention as a local product more than a symbol of cultural tension or change.

As detailed in numerous *Salt Lake Tribune* reports, most of the movie was filmed within a 100-mile radius of Moab in southeastern Utah, near the intersection of Colorado, New Mexico, Arizona and Utah, in an area referred to as the Four Corners. Three towns in Utah — La Sal, Cisco and Thompson Springs (as well as Paradox, Colorado, across the state line to the east) — were utilized for filming the women's pit stops. While viewers were led to believe that the women drive through Monument Valley on their way to a Grand Canyon finale in Arizona, the film production stayed mostly within Utah. Scenes were also shot at Arches National Park, Canyonlands National Park and Unaweep Canyon in Colorado. In terms of actual locations, the women never make it to the Grand Canyon. After ditching the state cop in New Mexico, they flee to the northwest. What looked to Louise like "the god damn Grand Canyon" was actually Utah's Shafer Trail below Dead Horse Point State Park.

Nearly one tenth of *The Salt Lake Tribune* articles communicated the state of Utah's contribution to the film's production, as well as the production's contribution to the state of Utah. In "*Thelma & Louise* Heats Up," which ran in August 1991, the director of the Moab Film Commission, Bette Stanton, proclaimed, "This is the first movie filmed here that's been this big a hit since the John Ford days," referring to the director of *Stagecoach* (1939) and *The Searchers* (1952). Stanton was happy to announce that the *Thelma & Louise* film crew infused $3.5 million into the local economy during August and September 1990, but that figure was just the start of a profitable relationship. Because of the film's impact and popularity, before the following summer ended the regional film commission received numerous calls, which generated additional revenue attributable to the high-profile release. Inquiries came from filmmakers scouting locations for their own projects and fans interested in making pilgrimages to locations seen on screen. Thanks to the sensation created by the great debate, which directed viewers towards a beautifully filmed feature, fashion and magazine photographers "looking for eye-popping backdrops" turned to Utah. In addition, according to the commission spokesperson, at least one fan who felt the film was the "best she'd ever seen" traveled from Texas to visit sights found in *Thelma & Louise*.[1]

Due to the film's positive impact on tourism and the state's economy, Utahans were proud to claim the movie as an impressive example of what the area offers geographically. "*Thelma & Louise* put us on the map as a great venue," the director of the Utah Film Commission, Leigh von der Esch, declared in the summer of 1991.[2] Capitalizing on a hit, residents took the opportunity to promote Utah and its citizens. Once known as "Chicken Corner," the spot overlooking the Colorado River where Louise's Thunderbird leaps and dives was renamed "*Thelma & Louise* Point" by locals.[3] When the owner of the Silver Grill in Thompson was quoted in a 1993 article concerning local elections, the newspaper identified her restaurant as "a locale for the movie *Thelma & Louise*," as if the coincidence gave her views greater weight.[4]

Area residents gladly adopted the film for their own purposes. Demonstrating state pride, in 1994, the members of a West Valley City neighborhood watch-group were said to use aliases borrowed from the movie.[5] When the picture's popularity extended into other Western states, *The Salt Lake Tribune* passed on the news to its readers as if *Thelma & Louise* and its fans affirmed Utah's worth. In 1996, a woman from Denver attending the nineteenth gathering of the National Widowed Persons Conference in Salt Lake City swore, "If either one of us gets a terminal illness" (speaking about her new husband), "we're going to do something like Thelma and Louise."[6]

Tragically, the sarcastic expression often credited to moms about jumping off a bridge (or a cliff) because someone else did isn't the unlikely notion it might seem to be. Despite criticism over the film's ending, in 1999, "Mission Impossible: To Film Prohibited BASE Jump" detailed director John Woo's wish to film a *Mission Impossible 2* stunt at *Thelma & Louise* Point. The Dead

Horse Point State Park manager consulted for the story commented, "After that *Thelma & Louise* sequence, we got calls from Grand Canyon about how people wanted to know where they could drive their car" into the famous depression.[7] Sadly, in 2000, *The Salt Lake Tribune* reported that although *Thelma & Louise* was not actually filmed at Grand Canyon National Park, the natural wonder became the setting for a "copycat" suicide. According to a park spokesperson, one woman tried to replicate the film's finale. When her car became stuck, she got out, stepped to the edge and leaped to her death. "That is one unfortunate thing that came out of the film," the park's spokesperson replied.[8]

Although Utah reaped millions from film productions in the 1990s as a result of *Thelma & Louise*, the film's stars didn't always receive the same respect from *The Salt Lake Tribune* as did the dollars that poured into the state due to production spending and the film's release. When the American Film Institute and Blockbuster Video parked their mobile movie memorabilia museum in Salt Lake City in 1998, the newspaper informed locals that they could enjoy the only stop on the 27-city tour with a separate special exhibit — a privilege extended to Utahans because the state has played a big role in cinematic history. To promote the event, *The Salt Lake Tribune* asked readers, "Wanna ogle John Ford's director's chair or the swan-dive Thelma dummy from *Thelma & Louise*?" After joking that the dummy in question was "not Christopher McDonald," who played Darryl Dickerson, the newspaper extended the same type of humor (in part derisive to actors, in part derisive to women) to Geena Davis, though she received a far larger helping. Bordering on misogyny, the newspaper wondered, "If the dummy filled in for Davis full-time, would anybody notice?"[9] Worse than Kathy Huffhines in Detroit calling Davis "daffy," staff journalists in Salt Lake City felt compelled to ridicule Davis, who is, ironically, a member of Mensa, a worldwide affiliation of individuals who rank in the top two percentile of the general population on standardized IQ tests.

A few years later, "Museum to House Movie Memorabilia" related that the Thelma dummy, "fished from the Colorado River," would become part of a collection to be displayed at the privately-owned Red Cliff Lodge, then under construction along the river in Moab. (No word on what became of the Louise dummy.) With plans to build a special space to house objects documenting the area's film making history, the former director of the Moab Film Commission (which had been taken over by the county) was delighted about plans to educate the public about moviemaking. "Sure, some of these things are made of paper or plaster," Betty Stanton told *The Salt Lake Tribune*, "but that's what movies are about." She continued, "They're illusions." While phony fronts displayed on screen are designed to deceive, hatred toward women is more readily detectable and far less appropriate, as seen in the newspaper's derisive comment about Davis' intelligence.[10]

Not as daring as editors in Chicago, apart from feting the film's significant financial impact on the state, editors in Salt Lake City hesitated to enter the great debate and talk about the film's meaning. The newspaper never published a single piece directed solely at the content of the feature. Articles like "*Thelma & Louise* Heats Up" largely focused on Utah's logistical connection to the picture. Still, the newspaper understood that "controversy can be good for business," so it granted one modest paragraph to the nationwide discussion.

> The movie stars Geena Davis and Susan Sarandon as two women who, on a whim, travel from Arkansas to the Grand Canyon, fending off male chauvinists at every turn. It has been called a ground-breaking feminist manifesto by some, a betrayal of womanhood by others. Fans of the movie say it is a rare Hollywood product, creating strong female characters. Detractors counter that the difference between violent, dime-a-dozen macho male movies and *Thelma* is only skin deep.[11]

Instead of taking its own stand, for the most part *The Salt Lake Tribune* let journalists in other areas, writing for other newspapers, articulate *Thelma & Louise.*

The handful of articles written by *Salt Lake Tribune* staff that did talk about the movie's content offered the best glimpse of local attitudes. The newspaper didn't publish much of a review of the film on May 24, 1991, just a quick nod in "The Movies Heat Up," which previewed a few releases from the upcoming season but very briefly. Apparently state residents are far more interested in revenue from films than in films themselves. The article grouped women-led films separately after the top movies led by men, and Sarandon and Davis in *Thelma & Louise* followed Julia Roberts in *Dying Young. The Salt Lake Tribune* announced, "Pretty women Geena Davis and Susan Sarandon promise to add a new dimension altogether with their female buddy picture, *Thelma & Louise*, opening today."[12]

Although the blurb didn't make clear what *The Salt Lake Tribune* thought about the film when it debuted, at the end of the year *Thelma & Louise* did make the cut, scoring the number 10 position on the newspaper's list of the 10 best movies of 1991. Taking an unassuming approach to the 10 best list, film critic Terry Orme listed his favorite films alphabetically. Orme's quick summary retold *Thelma & Louise* with a particular slant that preferred Ridley Scott's direction over Callie Khouri's script while highlighting Utah's natural beauty.

> Susan Sarandon and Geena Davis likely will be competing against each other at the Oscars with their loopy, yet tough portraits of women who rebel against the manipulative, violent and spineless men in their lives. The red rocks of Moab offer the perfect backdrop for a seamless mix of politics and adventure.[13]

Because newspapers distribute a variety of voices printed collectively,

each newspaper's overall attitude toward the film was balanced by any journalists who contradicted the majority and their opinions. After *Thelma &
Louise* challenged assumptions about buddy flicks, road movies and women
in film, *The Salt Lake Tribune* published a small number of pieces written by
staffers that maintained an unsurprising pro–*Thelma & Louise* stance considering the area's connection to the release. However, the Utah newspaper balanced those pieces with demeaning references and one tentative *Thelma &
Louise* naming, watering down the media outfit's overall editorial position.
At *The Salt Lake Tribune*, articles that praised the picture's economic benefits
overpowered an anti–*Thelma & Louise* outlook. Still, a negative cultural view
of both the film and women held strong.

In a country that prefers passive viewing over studying literature, newspapers often publish light fare, particularly outside of hard news. The pervasive practice in place across much of the country is to entertain while
attempting to inform a sometimes undemanding and apathetic readership.
At *The Salt Lake Tribune*, *Thelma & Louise* fared best in the hands of local
journalists who kept a safe distance from confounding world events and controversial national issues. To celebrate the Valentine's Day in 1992, "Can't
Afford Roses? Try a Video Valentine," co-written by Terry Orme and Sean
Means, suggested that "cheap" readers rent *Casablanca* (1942), *Say Anything*
(1989), *sex, lies and videotape* (1989), *Moonstruck* (1987), *The Tall Guy* (1989),
When Harry Met Sally (1989) or *An Affair to Remember* (1957). Indicating what
staff entertainment writers thought about locals' viewing habits, Orme and
Means assumed that readers hadn't gotten around to seeing the movie when
it played in theaters. For a "cautionary" Valentine, *Salt Lake Tribune* customers were counseled to "check out" *Thelma & Louise*. Referring to Thelma's
admonition, "Be good to your wife," the writers ventured, "Ann Landers
couldn't have said it better." Characterized as "wisdom for the lovelorn" in
The Salt Lake Tribune, Thelma's quip to the New Mexico police officer became
possibly the most widely quoted line in the film.[14]

Reading one article at a time rather than looking at the whole group,
whether the Salt Lake City newspaper came off sounding feminist-friendly,
misogynist or somewhere in between depended on the writer, or writers,
responsible for the piece. In July 1994, a pair of columnists pointed out the
clash of irony between a bumper sticker spotted on pickup truck and its mud
flaps. While the bumper sticker advocated "Teach respect for the Earth and
all living creatures," the truck's mud flaps recalled *Thelma & Louise*. As recognizable as Harley Davidson biker gear, the tire protectors in question
objectified women's bodies through the sexist silhouette of a female figure.
Salaciously contrasting with the more generous message on the bumper sticker,
the female form seen on the mud flaps defied nature with unlikely "large
breasts," an impossibly "tiny waist" and fairy tale "flowing long hair," as
described in the column "Rolly & Wells." Recognizing sexism and putting it

on their "priority list," Paul Rolly and JoAnn Jacobsen-Wells asked rhetorically, "Where are *Thelma & Louise* when you really need them?"[15]

In contrast to the supportive articles penned by Orme and Means and Rolly and Wells, before the harsh "dummy" dig aimed at Geena Davis in 1999, another derogatory reference, this time aimed at the female film characters, occurred in the fall of 1995. Discussing the Mormon practice of home teaching, whereby the priesthood visits member homes monthly, a guest columnist from the Mormon Church penned "Halloween Teaching Not For Timid." Women take part in home teaching, too, Robert Kirby assured readers, but while it "accomplishes the exact same thing," no reason was given as to why the practice is labeled differently when females minister to church members. When undertaken by a woman, "home teaching" becomes "visiting teaching," or, more cuttingly, "visiting screeching, which is the term used by the priesthood," according to the author. Kirby added that his own visiting teachers for the month of October were Thelma and Louise. Reading the article, it's not clear if he meant the visiting teachers were dressed up in blue jeans and sleeveless shirts for Halloween, or if in his opinion the female ministers who arrived at his door "screeched" like a couple of women.[16]

Intent on presenting the film with accolades, perhaps to offset the likes of Robert Kirby, *The Salt Lake Tribune*'s "'Best' Movies That Didn't Make It" in 1998 "pruned" some of the AFI's choices for the top 100 American films. Although Sean Means set out to do a good deed, his article elevated *Thelma & Louise* while restricting its detractors, and, by extension, circumscribed the movie's fans, too. He gallantly removed *Easy Rider* to make way for *Thelma & Louise*, *Little Big Man* (1970), and *Malcolm X* (1992), which feature non-traditional Hollywood subjects, women, Native Americans and African Americans, respectively. His attempt to include more minorities among the AFI's list was honorable, but when Means described the female buddy picture he displayed an attitude that extended compassion to marginalized groups but still maintained an avenue for hate and divisiveness.

> Susan Sarandon and Geena Davis hit the road, defend themselves from rednecks, and wind up as outlaws. What sets this gutsy story of friendship and female empowerment apart is how it was misread as a feminist bromide (by men who didn't get it) or as a lesbian manifesto (even though the only sex scene involved Davis and Brad Pitt).

Means must have gleaned his view about the film serving as a "lesbian manifesto" from personal experience or invention rather than research. If the film was relegated as such, the action wasn't acknowledged in the mainstream press. The only commentator who equated the film with sexual preference was found in Charlotte, North Carolina, in response to Rheta Grimsley Johnson's op/ed and originated in one reader's angry response. Even journalists who supported the film sometimes failed to realize that reactions to the movie weren't defined by gender, sexual orientation, race or creed. Both women and men denounced the film's expression of feminism. Liking or disliking the movie didn't align with any one group other than fans and detractors.[17]

When you can't beat 'em, join 'em. Bud the Silver Naked Trucker is a response to the silhouette of a buxom female figure found on the trucker's mud flaps and at least one vehicle in the Salt Lake City area. Decal produced by Rachel Bachman and She Shoots, She Scores! Available at oneangrygirl.net.

As the post-release decade developed, using the designation "Thelma and Louise" as a metaphor for criminals and nothing else crossed the line of good judgment. *The Salt Lake Tribune* was sensitive to this possibility but, in 1994, "*Thelma & Louise* Duo?" reluctantly tested the title on a pair of local female perpetrators. The newspaper gingerly applied the famous names to two 14-year-old girls who were booked for car theft, aggravated assault and felony evasion after they allegedly stole a 1972 Pontiac Firebird, fled the police and crashed the vehicle. Cautiously approaching the intersection of the popular film and the gravity of *Thelma & Louise* Point, the newspaper reassured its clientele. Unlike the fictional team, the young girls were not seriously injured.[18] During this period, for no other purpose did the newspaper find any other instance of local *Thelma & Louise* naming more appropriate. On its own, *The Salt Lake Tribune* appeared more comfortable reiterating the picture's benefit to the local economy and less comfortable associating the film's content with area attitudes about gender and society.

Buying syndicated articles allows a newspaper to lower its costs and at the same time widen its horizons more safely. A number of *Salt Lake Tribune* stories that cited the film during this period originated in other newspapers, such as *The Detroit News*, *The Los Angeles Times* and *The Orange County Register*, which could be credited for article content. Additional profiles were purchased from news services such as the Associated Press. Presenting out-of-town views, these articles covered the established gamut of great debate topics and even added a couple of new angles. An article (marketed by the Knight-Ridder News Service) about cigarette smoking in the movies used the film as an example of developing character by way of lighting up. "Susan Sarandon smoked, Geena Davis didn't, and that by itself told you a lot about who those women were," claimed "Smoking in the Movies? Don't Expect Films to Kick an Old Habit." More concerned with cultural currency than analytical accuracy, no one at Knight-Ridder or *The Salt Lake Tribune* detected writer Rene Rodriguez's error. In the film, Thelma adopts Louise's smoking habit (albeit without much dedication) because she erroneously believes that holding a cigarette makes her look more mature.[19]

Within articles acquired from other sources between 1993 and 2001, *The Salt Lake Tribune* stretched some extra mileage out of the film. *Thelma & Louise* became a metaphor for fighting female spirit, an example of female opposites teaming up, a display of reckless cliff diving and a show of "dynamic duos." The movie was mentioned in connection with Susan Douglas's book examining women's presentation in the media, *Where the Girls Are: Growing Up Female with the Mass Media*, and was briefly mentioned therein. The picture was credited with influencing a renewal of female friendships on television and cited as beacon for female friendships in real life. It also served as an example of top-down fun on the road and was observed ushering in the trend of women traveling together. Although local reception of the film's content was mixed and often distanced from the film's core messages, most out of town and syndicated views purchased by the newspaper supported the title. However, like the Knight-Ridder article focused on smoking, most did so in a superficial manner.

One *Salt Lake Tribune* expenditure did provide more in-depth information. In 1991, four months after the film came out, an Associated Press story revealed to readers in Utah the practice of "secret" research screening, which gives movie audiences the power to influence film stories. "Film Guinea Pigs Decide How Movies Are Made and Marketed" arrived with built-in appeal for newspaper subscribers who lived in the vicinity of *Thelma & Louise* Point. After a preview screening in Chicago, John Horn explained, the original ending of *Thelma & Louise* was changed. At first, when Thelma and Louise drove away "on the canyon floor, unhurt, their car undamaged," Midwestern audiences found the conclusion "unrealistic," cueing filmmakers to think again. Therefore, a happy ending that would have left open the possibility of a sequel was canned in favor of a compromise. The revised ending shown in theaters hinted at a more realistic wrap-up, but the filmmakers still refused to show the bloody truth of what would have happened to Thelma and Louise if the action didn't freeze and the camera had instead panned down. As Horn put it, the original ending served up "a Hollywood cliché crafted out of thin air." Inspired to wax poetic, he added, "The ending was changed, and now thin air is all we see."[20]

Most but not all of the articles that appeared in *The Salt Lake Tribune* bearing outside bylines promoted the film. A piece out of Southern California's *Orange County Register* patted Hollywood on the back while denigrating the feature. Extolling that American movies "almost always" give the impression that families will "endure," Jim Emerson espoused the universal "search" for family, "for a feeling of belonging and of being loved." After mentioning *Home Alone* (1990), *Fatal Attraction* (1987) and *The Prince of Tides* (1991) as Hollywood films that in the end reinforce strong traditional family units, Emerson categorized *Thelma & Louise* apart from most releases because the pair roam high and low for themselves, not marriage or children. Neither woman says one word about bearing offspring, which might have upset those who are pro-family but only in the most rigid way. Though the women do create a family bond together, Emerson incorrectly presumed in absolute terms barring any flexibility that "Nobody would argue that Thelma and Louise, for example, make a better couple than either did with her male mate."[21]

Clearly, not everyone would agree.

Of the newspapers analyzed so far, *The Chicago Tribune* most fully recognized *Thelma & Louise* as a newsworthy cultural icon. *The Salt Lake Tribune* gave the film credit with hired help that *The Dayton Daily News* and *The Detroit Free Press* elected not to employ, though the Utah newspaper better embraced *Thelma & Louise* because of the money the film production pumped into the state's economy and less so because of a genuine appreciation for the story. In 1995, a Knight-Ridder article that appeared in *The Salt Lake Tribune* written by television critic Mike Duffy asserted that *Thelma & Louise* "was one of those signature movies that ring the chimes of the American cultural zeitgeist." Whether Americans heard those reverberations depended on where they lived and what, if any, newspapers they read.[22]

15. Southern Exposure — Atlanta: *The Atlanta Journal-Constitution*

In the case of *Thelma & Louise*, ticket sales tell one story (*Thelma & Louise* was not a blockbuster), while newspapers as a group present another (*Thelma & Louise* shook up Hollywood and the culture at large). The picture's release inspired a truly great story that refused to stand still. As for the great debate, city by city, region by region, there were multiple accounts and definite trends but no steadfast rules about whether a commentator liked or disliked the film and why. Supporters and detractors could not be pinned down to men, women, feminists, journalists, whites or lesbians.

Thelma & Louise demanded that viewers actively address issues instead of relying on stereotypical thinking, but not everyone is willing to engage in the kind of entertainment that requires intellectual interaction. Given the diversity of the American public, some people loved the picture, some felt mixed emotions, some hated it and some didn't care. Opinions between the public and the press sometimes diverged, as opinions within each of those groups clashed, too. Journalists in Chicago and Salt Lake City endorsed the film out of responsibility and pride, yet newspaper subscribers may have discounted the upbeat attitudes presented in *The Chicago Tribune* and *The Salt Lake Tribune*. Certainly, non-newspaper readers ignored all newspaper coverage, good, bad or indifferent, which is not to say that newspapers have lost all influence. Editors in Dayton and Detroit seemed to avoid *Thelma & Louise*, acting at times uninterested or overwhelmed by its themes. As a result, *The Dayton Daily News* and *The Detroit Free Press* may have cued local response, accurately reflected it or both. With such a large country and massive population, there was plenty of room for many competing views of *Thelma & Louise*. Where ticket sales were strong, stray critics who disliked the film didn't deter the film's following. In areas where ticket sales were pronounced weak, even though some journalists feted the film, their words failed to ignite hotter box office receipts. Then again, box office receipts aren't everything, as enthusiastic newspaper coverage may have energized later video rentals.

While it may look like the great debate was a phenomenon restricted to journalists, letters to the editor and newspaper stories featuring everyday people who identified with *Thelma & Louise* vouch for the film's wider appeal. Naturally, newspapers that raised the film to cult status and inculcated the title into their lexicon were more likely to give space to readers who supported and adopted the film, yet because it was only a moderate box office success public involvement was limited, even if voracious in certain circles. Signs indicate that *Thelma & Louise* appealed to moviegoers who were more likely to read major newspapers and their reviews.

However, if *Thelma & Louise* is a good indicator of the relationship between movie reviews and box office, good press — even heated controversy — doesn't guarantee a bonanza because not enough people read newspapers and act on what they read. The 2002 report of the Newspaper Association of America analyzed nationwide daily and Sunday circulation. In an attempt to attract movie advertisements, the results proudly claimed that 68 percent of regular weekday subscribers and 73 percent of regular Sunday subscribers attended a movie in the previous six months. However, figures for newspaper readership over the last few decades are in decline and going to the movies twice a year isn't all that much. If critical acceptance did insure a film's financial success, *Thelma & Louise* would have out-earned *Terminator 2* and become one of the biggest selling movies of all times.

In terms of overall regard, the discussion of the film found in *The Atlanta Journal-Constitution* reveals an editorial stance most similar to the one found in *The Chicago Tribune*. Although the Southern newspaper serves a much smaller city, with just under a half a million residents and approximately four million people living in the greater metropolitan area, both newspapers ran multiple upbeat reviews showcasing *Thelma & Louise*, in addition to numerous articles that positively referenced the title. However, in terms of frequency of coverage, Atlanta outdid Chicago. The Peach State newspaper published close to 250 mentions of the film in the 10-year period from 1991 to 2001, while its competitor to the north published closer to 200, but numbers don't tell the whole story. Although *The Chicago Tribune* published fewer mentions, throughout the decade the Illinois newspaper was more likely to reference it in terms of politics, business and theories about gender. Meanwhile, especially after 1992's "Year of the Women," the Georgia newspaper was more inclined to revel in the film's warm, fuzzy feelings of female friendship, independence, cruising and fun. In the process, *The Atlanta Journal-Constitution* straddled between progressive social views and a traditional perspective that sees women as protected entities in the tradition of *Gone with the Wind*. To appease readers perhaps less progressive than staff journalists, coverage in the South's premiere city was half Scarlett O'Hara, half Melanie Wilkes, with a tone that wavered between adoration and uneasiness. Still, the newspaper gave the film received time, space and attention fit for a big story.

No one at the newspaper thought more of *Thelma & Louise* than Eleanor Ringel. As film editor for *The Atlanta Journal-Constitution*, she strongly supported the release on more than one occasion. Reviews infrequently glow, yet on May 24, 1991, before the controversy surrounding the film erupted, the headline of Ringel's review promised viewers "a breathtaking journey of identity." Calling *Thelma & Louise* a "breakthrough film," Ringel perceived that the production had challenged its filmmakers and would also require audience members to be flexible in their outlooks. Ringel also anticipated the great debate and expected negative reactions to the story. As a fan, Ringel recognized the film's "feminist undertones," but she warded off resistance with positive thoughts about *Thelma & Louise* as a whole: "Male-female issues are important, but the film is about so much more: friendship and growth, loss and liberation, living on the edge instead of edging into life."

To address potential unrest, she described the film's social consciousness as "ever-present and uncompromising," but announced that politics come second after a "whopping good story." Sounding like a movie marketer (or a reviewer truly impressed with the picture), Ringel tagged the leads "heroines for our times," Callie Khouri's script a "marvel" and Ridley Scott's visuals "extravagantly rich." To Ringel, the surprising and vivid tale of *Thelma & Louise* was a "mythopoetic odyssey" with gravity and consequence.

In her review, Ringel made only one negative comment about the picture, which she later considered a balk and recanted. Unlike those who complained about male-bashing, Ringel delved into the partnership at the film's center. Taking the idea of female relationships seriously, Ringel at first felt that the women's friendship and behavior were almost irritating. She wondered how "uptight, compulsive" Louise becomes close with Thelma, "an irresponsible child-woman." But Ringel didn't stay mad long. *Thelma & Louise* moved Ringel to change her mind about the main characters and their interaction because viewers, herself included, "make the same journey these women do"—one of self-discovery and acceptance. Unlike so many Hollywood movies, *Thelma & Louise* stimulates the intellect, which the newspaper's film authority found refreshing. While other critics called the filmmaker's work "manipulative," Ringel considered their effort commanding and confident.

> *Thelma & Louise* is an incredibly sure-footed film that irritates us when it wants, enlightens us when it wants, disturbs us when it wants, makes us laugh when it wants. Exuberant and provocative, this remarkable movie boldly goes where no so-called "women's picture" has ever gone before.[1]

Thelma & Louise encouraged critics to aim at other critic's opinions and

Thelma and Louise argue, as the women often do over the course of their trip. Geena Davis and Susan Sarandon star as Thelma Dickerson and Louise Sawyer in MGM's *Thelma & Louise* (1991).

instigated a debate about the story's meaning and worth. Two months after her initial review, Ringel's essay addressing the controversy asked, "*Thelma & Louise*, Why Is It So Hard for Us to Handle?" If not seeing the film equaled not "handling" it, the "us" in question referred to a few obstreperous movie reviewers and a considerable portion of the movie-going public. Conceding that *Terminator 2* made more money in five days than *Thelma & Louise* earned in six weeks, Ringel contended that despite its modest financial success the film "won't go away" because of audience support and members of the media, who "can't let it alone." That group of professional fans included Ringel, who doted on the release again in her December 29, 1991, piece commenting on the year's films. *Thelma & Louise* popped up three times in Ringel's year-end review, within talk of "female rage," "fun couples," and "A Dozen or So Movies I'm Especially Glad I Saw (This Year or Any Other Year)."[2]

Back in July, Ringel had responded to biased attacks directed at the film including one carp from a "respected" critic who complained that the lead women were "conveniently childless." Ringel rebounded that similar charges of childlessness weren't lobbed at "say, a *48 Hrs.* movie." To open clouded minds, she applied similar logic to the accusation of male-bashing and instead revealed an anti-female bias. According to Ringel, three other major summer releases, *Backdraft*, *What About Bob?* and *Hudson Hawk*, only offered women "tangential" roles like those allotted to men in *Thelma & Louise*. Calling for balance, Ringel noted that Linda Hamilton's character in *Terminator 2* elicited positive comments about her "pumped-up figure and gun crazy attitude." Yet the response to Hamilton's Sarah Connor stood in sharp contrast to the reaction drawn by Thelma and Louise for their far more comedic antics, which Ringel compared to television's Lucy and Ethel. Unlike critics did with Khouri's creations, "not one" critic "tsked-tsked" over Hamilton's "misguided and inappropriate identification with male violence," she noted wryly. Ringel figured that's because in *Terminator 2* Hamilton is paired opposite a male. The presence of Arnold Schwarzenegger in effect condones the film's violence for an audience of critics and viewers conditioned by sexism. As the stereotype goes, men in film are supposed to carry guns and explode with anger, but women aren't. Surveying the criticism surrounding *Thelma & Louise*, Ringel lost her patience with the film's detractors: "And as for those self-righteous howls that glorifying women with .38s is just another form of subordination to a male-dominated society, get real. And get fair."

Ringel appreciated the film's unique strength. She suggested that for decades while watching the likes of *One Flew Over the Cuckoo's Nest* (1975) and *Butch Cassidy and the Sundance Kid*, women have identified with Jack Nicholson, Paul Newman and Robert Redford as the subjects of stories, instead of Katherine Ross or Louise Fletcher, who merely attend male leads as girlfriends or nurses. As feminist film theorists have conveyed for decades, while mainstream female viewers are accustomed to identifying with lead male characters, mainstream male viewers have rarely been given (in Hollywood films) and seldom taken the opportunity (by watching independent and foreign films) to respond in turn. Some men, including professional critics (a field dominated by males), aren't comfortable identifying with leads who happen to be female.

Talk of male bashing overshadowed the main reason why the film attracted so much attention, Ringel insinuated, joining a consort of like-minded critics. *Thelma & Louise* earned acclaim due to its focus on women, not by bashing men but by moving them aside into the marginal positions women in film usually occupy. Putting the film into perspective, Ringel applauded *Thelma & Louise* for its messy, life-like, female leads.

> *Thelma & Louise* is a movie, not a manifesto. At its most political it's one small counterbalance to the zillions of faceless bimbos, whores, wives and girlfriends who gave their T- and A- to further careers of so many male stars.

Ringel rested her case by siding with Geena Davis, to whom she gave the last word: "If you're feeling threatened, you're identifying with the wrong character."[3] For some, the film's revolutionary casting equaled a negative appeal. For others, *Thelma & Louise* was long overdue.

During the first half of the decade between the film's release and its ten-year anniversary, at the *Atlanta Journal-Constitution*, *Thelma & Louise* stood as a marker to measure the progress of women acting in Hollywood. Particularly from 1992 to 1996, Eleanor Ringel and her colleague Steve Murray returned to the film when assessing the industry's record regarding the box office appeal of women-led films, the quality of roles awarded to women and employment in Hollywood by gender. Recognizing a "blast of recognition" for female thespians, Murray reported that at the 1992 Oscars Jodie Foster and Callie Khouri won their respective awards (Best Actress and Best Original Screenplay) but not for any feel-good reason. Hollywood welcomes women-led films as long as they make money, he explained, which *Fried Green Tomatoes*, *The Silence of the Lambs* and *Thelma & Louise* all managed to do.[4]

A list accompanying Murray's piece included *Thelma & Louise* among recent examples of "good" films with "three-dimensional" female characters. *Silence of the Lambs*, *Bugsy*, *Cape Fear* and anything by Woody Allen were a few of the others mentioned. *Basic Instinct*, *JFK*, *Wayne's World*, *Radio Flyer* and *Ruby* rounded out the list of "bad" films featuring "trite" female stereotypes. Typical of the schizophrenic attitude that affects women's advancement (women can advance as long as they behave and let men continue to run things), *The Hand That Rocks the Cradle* made both lists. *The Atlanta Journal-Constitution* deemed it "good" for the female friendship between Annabella Sciorra and Julianne Moore, but "bad" due to Rebecca DeMornay's evil home wrecking.[5] Unfortunately for fans of women in film, *The Hand that Rocks the Cradle* and *Basic Instinct* outsold both *Thelma & Louise* and *Fried Green Tomatoes*. *The Silence of the Lambs* earned over $100 million in domestic ticket sales, making it a blockbuster, but *Bugsy* (with Annette Benning) tallied less in the theater than *Wayne's World* (starring Mike Myers and Dana Carvey) banked in video rentals. Even as studios were starting to produce more films with complex women leading stories, the public continued to give more support to films featuring male leads and one-dimensional female sidekicks.

The remainder of articles from 1993 to 1996 that mentioned the film in conjunction with women in Hollywood told a depressing story. Many fans hoped that Louise's Thunderbird dissipating into thin air on its trajectory into movie history would result in decisive, sweeping change, but, unfortunately, it didn't. "After the unexpected success" of *Thelma & Louise*, Ringel explained in 1993, people anticipated a "mini-boom" of stories with women at the center, but instead "there were about 2½."[6] Two years later, the outlook for actresses in Hollywood remained grim. Along with *Silence of the Lambs*, *Thelma & Louise* had "caused a mild flurry of projects with action heroines," Ringel noted in 1995, but nothing earth-shattering or meaningful in the way of lasting change or memorable roles came about as a result of the shake-up. At the time, the most successful avenue for women, according to Ringel, involved "gender-bending an established male icon." Sarah Jessica Parker in *Miami Rhapsody* modeling Woody Allen and Sharon Stone in *The Quick and the Dead* mimicking Clint Eastwood exemplified this trend. Ringel rejoiced in the fact that there was at least one way for women acting in Hollywood to find meaningful work.[7]

According to the newspaper's appraisal of the film industry, Hollywood practices selective hearing. Film studios listened most closely to the comparisons between *Thelma & Louise* and *Butch Cassidy and the Sundance Kid* and largely ignored the remainder of the great debate. As a result, subsequent big-budget film productions copied the most superficial aspect of *Thelma & Louise* (women appropriating traditional male roles) and forgot about the women's friendship and how their characters separately grew and changed. The problem is, from a business standpoint, that course of action was and still is prudent. As Murray relayed, by 1996, the summer movies that offered viewers "ordinary" women with "down-to-earth problems," such as *Manny & Lo* and *The Spitfire Grill* (both low budget productions), failed to make money. Once again, a "female buddy-pic trend" following *Thelma & Louise* simply "didn't happen."[8]

To the chagrin of fans of women in film, the frustrating fact is that both women and men embraced *Thelma & Louise*. A theory emerged from the film's success: if Hollywood made quality, complex, adult-orientated films starring women, mature audiences would come, though perhaps not in droves, like their younger counterparts attend films produced for them. Between July 1991 and July 1992, a period of time when Hollywood experienced difficulty attracting mature moviegoers, five of the local adults profiled in *The Atlanta Journal-Constitution*'s weekly "1-Minute Profile" named the controversial picture as the last movie they'd seen. A female editor of *The Atlanta Business Chronicle*,[9] a female commissioner from Dekalb County,[10] a female college president,[11] a male restaurant owner,[12] and a female cosmetologist/beauty store manager[13] all chose to see *Thelma & Louise* over countless other possibilities in theaters and video stores at the time. These adult consumers tuned out mindless fare and tuned into *Thelma & Louise* instead.

Though professional journalists dominate the press, readers sometimes get to squeeze their ideas into the hometown newspaper, too. At dailies open to *Thelma & Louise*, interview subjects, guest commentators and letters to the editor joined the fray. Some splashed around with the title for fun; others considered the film's deeper meaning and impact. Like Eleanor Ringel, one *Atlanta Constitution and Journal* reader responded to lop-sided criticism levied at *Thelma & Louise*. Before *The Atlanta Journal-Constitution* entered the great debate, a subscriber from Marietta replied to critics who objected to the film's violence. A month prior to Ringel's opinion piece and a week before *Time* magazine put Sarandon and Davis on its cover, the reader identified the same double standard later elaborated upon by the newspaper's film editor. Flip-flopping the usual focus on the violence committed by the women, she countered, "Something tells me that the critics didn't take exception to the scene where Thelma was beaten and almost raped by a cowboy." Men can commit murder and rape without comment because viewers are used to their ungovernable ways, but women who act aggressively are somehow a different story.[18]

Though academics often lead public perceptions (usually without receiving credit for their efforts) and journalists are paid to keep watch on the culture, it doesn't take a doctoral thesis or a press pass to detect bias. Regardless of the lowest common denominator approach undertaken by many media outlets, mature movie audiences and avid newspaper readers don't necessarily operate with the equivalent of 12-year-old minds. While many vocalized worries about whether the film hated men, the reader from Marietta was correct. In print, far less concern was paid to rape than murder.

Hollywood's disappointing response to the great debate meant that movie producers, reinforced by consumer trends, continued to devalue women. Despite this lack of development, throughout the decade following the film's release *The Atlanta Journal-Constitution* helped keep the memory and various meanings of *Thelma & Louise* alive by volleying the film around throughout various sections of the newspaper. The film's relevance to people's lives adequately impressed editors of *The Atlanta Journal-Constitution* who allowed regular mentions of the title within current events, features and sports coverage, though overall most nods occurred within easy-going features. Apart from Eleanor Ringel's views, at first the newspaper seemed to prolong the great debate more because the topic remained relevant and the film's rightful place couldn't be denied, rather than because of a sense of stewardship. *Thelma & Louise* coverage was evidently good business. But editorial attitudes progressed, so the publication's appreciation grew warmer and more genuine over time.

Moving toward the new millennium with the invaluable help of *Thelma & Louise*, *The Atlanta Journal-Constitution* waded through contemporary events that were often confused by a collision with gender. In June 1991, *Thelma & Louise* was compared to a Virginia court case where the defense claimed premenstrual syndrome caused an orthopedic surgeon to drive drunk. "Suffice it to say," columnist Doug Monroe advised, the film heroines "didn't need to sail into that canyon to avoid the cops." Instead, he surmised sarcastically that going to court and pleading PMS might have gotten the women off and paved the way for a sequel. Less than three weeks after the film's release, on June 12, Monroe "didn't want to spoil the ending," but may have fanned curiosity by calling the film a "feminist cult spectacle." Such strong language probably fostered the attendance of certain crowds and confirmed the absence of others.

Painting a rowdy picture of moviegoers reminiscent of arena sporting events held at the Roman Coliseum around the time of Christ, Monroe's piece, "If Man Drives Drunk, Maybe Its Just Midlife Crisis," accentuated the women's retribution as if seeking to heighten the squabble surrounding the film. "Women viewers howl with approval and slap their dates every time Thelma or Louise plugs some louse," he reported, perhaps engaging in little hyperbole. Though he was sensitive enough to keep the ending a secret, Moore made the filmgoing experience sound as if Thelma and Louise kill repeatedly while audiences clamor for more and more blood. (When I first saw the film at a suburban theater west of Boston, surprise and awe fueled the crowd's more thoughtful reaction.)[19]

Other references to the film in 1991 were less rambunctious; they were also either written by women, shared a woman's point of view or were directed at females. Two columns by Patricia Carr addressed female friendship and the women's movement. A general rebuttal to the great debate came from Callie Khouri, and an encouraging though patronizing compilation of tips underlined the need for women to work hard in order to achieve success in business. Apart from Ringel's review and op-ed, four of five 1991 pieces including Doug Monroe's ran within one eight-day period in June, when the newspaper bounded between begrudging regard and tempered enthusiasm. By the end of the summer, the newspaper eventually built back up to a solid pro–*Thelma & Louise* stance, but over the decade the film would have to stay its course and sometimes wait for the newspaper to regain a strong positive outlook.

Standing as *The Atlanta Journal-Constitution*'s version of a he-sort-of-hates-it/she-rather-loves-it point/counterpoint, Carr's first piece and Moore's column ran on the same day. In "The Best of Friends," Carr retold the story of a pair of female friends from Georgia Tech who compared with "zest" an incident in a grocery store to a scene from *Thelma & Louise*. While vacationing in Florida and shopping in the "Crisco aisle," the women encountered a flasher whom they chased, temporarily lost and three nights later once again spotted at a beach front bar, where they turned the perpetrator in to the police. "You're such a sicko!" the friends recalled shouting to the man, who was surprised that his victims chose to pursue him.

According to Carr, the experience reminded the college women of how Thelma and Louise treat the unsuspecting trucker. The college friends would no doubt continue to travel regardless, but they might not have acted so boldly in the face of an aggressor if not for the example set by *Thelma & Louise*.[20]

Two days later, on June 14, "Feminists Are Outlaws, Too" poised "women" versus "critics" as if the two categories were entirely separate entities, despite the fact that the newspaper employed a female film editor. *The Atlanta Journal-Constitution* acknowledged, "While women have flocked to see *Thelma & Louise*, many critics have been aghast over the violence and question whether the pair should be seen as feminist role models." Less than a month after the film's release, the newspaper quoted Callie Khouri, who addressed the charges against her effort. The scope of the discussion encircling the film surprised its creator. She sounded irritated by the enflamed public reaction, as if she wished to diffuse the uproar and distance herself from the argument.

There's so much talk about whether it's a feminist screenplay, whether it's a male-bashing movie. It's none of those things. I am a feminist, so clearly it's going to have my point of view. But this is a movie about outlaws, and it's not fair to judge it in terms of feminism.[21]

Five days after the newspaper printed Khouri's comments, on June 19, "Good Luck Is Spelled W-O-R-K" assumed a motivated and reinvigorated climate for women. *The Atlanta Journal-Constitution*'s "Business Report" opened with a conversational but firm tone, quoting Louise when she warns Thelma, "You get what you settle for." Applying the film's message to the work world, the newspaper counseled women who want to succeed to "keep on trying." The article was based on the words of one woman who created her own good fortune through dedication and effort. The Georgia newspaper encouraged women to "never stop trying," as if otherwise they might take the film's ending literally and jump off a cliff, and men in business prevail by different means. Assuming that women needed a special boost and advice (as opposed to societal acceptance and access to affordable child care), the newspaper shared a list of to do's and contact information for business networking in the area.[22] By the conclusion of a *Thelma & Louise* saturated week at *The Atlanta Journal-Constitution*, the film was seen as a motivating force for women (but not men), which induced much needed action and advocacy. This focus on one gender's reaction to the film implied that women operate in a separate, segregated world and men need not take part in any societal changes.

Running in late August, Carr's second piece connected the film to the controversy over women in the military, the William Kennedy Smith trial, *Ms.* magazine going advertising free and the release of Naomi Wolf's *Beauty Myth*, which together, she claimed, were "heating up the women's movement." Situated within the bigger, more important picture of real life events, the Hollywood film was downplayed from star to team player. Still, Carr insinuated that women were reacting to *Thelma & Louise* by taking stands in their private lives. That summer, women were creating a "cultural flap" over political issues such as reproductive rights that benefited from synchronistic timing.[23]

Discussing the movie's effect on women was certainly reasonable and welcome, yet it would have been nice to find more inclusive coverage among the lot of articles archived in Atlanta. Weren't any men who saw the picture moved on behalf of their wives, girlfriends, daughters, sisters, mothers and aunts to take action against rape?

One year in which to highlight the film's cultural contributions wasn't enough for the Georgia newspaper. When the film was released on video in January 1992, Steve Murray condensed Eleanor Ringel's praise for the film and directly addressed what had become the great debate, even within individual newspapers. His article, "*Thelma & Louise* Tart-tongued, Provocative, Funny and Available," informed readers that Khouri's "tough and funny script" is "actually easier on the menfolk than you may have heard." Following the film's lead, Murray's piece moved between larger and smaller issues with ease. The short tract also exemplified variances in musical taste that mirrored the film's overall reception, which ran from very hot to very cold. Contradicting unfavorable reviews from up north, such as the one by the teenager from Chicago, down south the film's largely country-western soundtrack was considered a "bona-fide dashboard-banger."[24] An additional notice running on the same day in the same section of the newspaper circumscribed fans by labeling *Thelma & Louise* a "cult hit." Nevertheless, Murray considered the release "perhaps the most talked-about film of the summer."[25]

Because of the ongoing controversy surrounding its relevance and meaning, long after its release the film continued to be seen as a hot commodity, particularly in a cultural climate that prefers celebrity gossip and entertainment coverage to serious news. In 1992, the film cropped up in a short article about "less news" and "more trends" gracing the covers of *Newsweek, U.S. News and World Report* and *Time* (recall that Davis and Sarandon appeared as themselves on the cover on June 24, 1991). To *The Atlanta Journal-Constitution*, movie stars appearing on the cover of newsweeklies embodied the industry trend toward "lifestyle, culture and thought pieces" and away from politics — what one unnamed commentator called "men in suits."[26]

Bridging the split between "less news" and "more trends," in Atlanta Callie Khouri's inspiration engaged both politics and culture, particularly in 1992. The year after the Clarence Thomas U.S. Supreme Court confirmation hearings, *The Atlanta Journal-Constitution* proposed that "Anita Hill's treatment may have fanned the response" to *Thelma & Louise*, although the film opened in May and the Oklahoma law professor appeared before the Senate in October, when the film was leaving theaters. Given these facts about timing, the opposite may have been true: *Thelma & Louise* may have fanned responses to Anita Hill's story. In any case, in "Lessons from the Hill: What Have We Learned a Year After the Thomas Hearings," *The Atlanta Journal-Constitution* recognized that women were angry and declared 1992 the "Year of the Woman."

Similar to newsweeklies that promote celebrities on their covers, *The Atlanta Journal-Constitution* connected entertainment with societal trends. Bo Emerson argued that there was a causal relationship between public response to the film and real-life politics. Emerson suggested that after watching *Thelma & Louise*, looking at their own lives and considering the Hill/Thomas proceedings, real women "began to get mad." Like the film's female protagonists, who "lived the dark fantasies of many angry Americans," women were fed up over sexual harassment, lack of power, and the demands of working inside and outside of the home.

Presuming that *The Atlanta Journal-Constitution* and other newspapers were correct, a portion of the nation's women were looking for change in the form of new leaders, role models and seats in local and federal government. The period was fertile for developing alternative methods and fresh momentum. If the Senate confirmation hearings had been broadcast on prime-time network television instead of C-SPAN and watched by half as many viewers as the Super Bowl, women in all walks of life might have publicly adopted Hill's reserved and articulate manner instead of Thelma and Louise's demonstrative anger. The polar difference in style between the law professor and the film characters alludes to the fact that communicating women's issues is difficult work. No matter what form the message takes, people resist feminist expression. Painting old-guard male institutions as the opposition, Emerson quoted Geraldine Ferraro, former candidate for vice president, who testified that all-male committees on Capitol Hill, such as the one that judged Hill, "still don't get it."

Pushing the idea that retribution is cathartic, Emerson configured the controversial film as an example of women taking action when talk doesn't work. "Instead of giving in passively to male brutality," Emerson proposed, describing Hill's initial reaction to Thomas, Thelma and Louise "blew the jerk away." Thelma and Louise's angry firepower does achieve their short-term personal objectives, but many complained that their taste of victory doesn't last long. For some viewers, inverting traditional roles constituted an unconvincing argument and an unpleasant metaphor, so Thelma and Louise failed to win their sympathy. Over time, due to Hill's public testimony (though she became an object of derision) a still-resistant America did learn about the dangers and inequities of sexual harassment in the workplace. Unfortunately, there is no simple solution to the problem of re-educating people about gender. Hill's restrained integrity didn't impress everyone, and bully power didn't sway all viewers to root for the film. In order for a majority of men and women "to get it," the feminist message requires delivery in a variety of forms. Under the headline "Lessons from the Hill," *The Atlanta Journal-Constitution* ran a series of six articles on October 5, 1992. Examining the "aftermath of Anita Hill," the newspaper discussed personal relationships between men and women, attitudes in Washington, D.C., toward gender, a heightened focus on sexual harassment in the business world, policy-making on college campuses regarding sexual harassment, sexual harassment and the entertainment industry and Hill's scheduled appearance on NBC's *Today*.[27]

Two additional editorials that mentioned the film happened to hit newsstands the same week in 1992. Like Bo Emerson, neither author credited *Thelma & Louise* for its contributions to female friendship or fashion. Instead, both articles focused on the way the film called on society to affect change. One article posited that the film influenced society negatively; the other hoped for eventual improvement. In the first article, the author judged that the movie made modern life worse. On May 24, exactly one year after the film's launch, "Pay Heed to Message" supported Vice President Dan Quayle's criticism of television's Murphy Brown, who chose to become a single mother. Lumping all films and filmmakers together, Durwood McAlister asked, "Is the entertainment industry acting responsibly or is it contributing to a dangerous decay in moral values in this country?" Ironically, despite his own similar approach the editorialist argued that Hollywood fails to make distinctions by blurring the line between "the guys in white hats" and "the bad guys." McAlister's terms as well as his outlook were in need of some updating. Perhaps seeking gender parity in his examples if not his attitude, McAlister argued that characters Thelma and Louise and actors Arnold and Sylvester, in various roles, all engage in "vindictive violence" and "unrestrained bloodletting." McAllister made no distinction between one-time fictional characters and movie stars with numerous bloody credits. The author's general approach paid too much heed to the over-simplified message that *Thelma & Louise* only concerns violence by women against men.[28]

As it had in 1991, the Atlanta newspaper again clustered talk of the film in bursts. Three days later, "Men Must Participate in Defining Masculinity" served a different purpose, though its author also saw the film in dark terms. Short on solutions but long on analysis, Nicolaus Mills targeted "gender panic" among men. According to Mills, in the search for a new definition of masculinity in light of the women's movement, one popular view identified "man as the enemy." Alice Walker's novel *The Color Purple* and Callie Khouri's *Thelma & Louise*, in Mills' view, both send an "unmistakable" message that "there are few limits to men's crudity." Apparently, Mills didn't read or didn't agree with Northerner Clarence Page. Mills' argument that the film condemned all men contrasted Page's opinion in his *Chicago Tribune* column, "*Thelma & Louise:* A Reel-Life Tale of Women and Power." A year prior, comparing nervous reaction to *Thelma & Louise* with a similar response to the film adaptation of *The Color Purple*, Page virtually laughed at men who were offended by the 1991 sensation.

> I am most amused to see white men overreacting to this film's unflattering portrayal of white men the same way other social critics overreacted to the portrayal of black men in *The Color Purple*. Some of us can't bear to see our worst sides portrayed on the screen without getting our wid-dow feel-wings hurt.[29]

Page saw the film addressing some negative aspects of white male behavior, while Mills felt that *Thelma & Louise* sought to vilify the entire gender. Despite his negative outlook toward the picture, Mills' heart was in the right place. In the end, as men seek to redefine themselves, he hoped they would "change and feel easy with masculinity" so that society can achieve the ultimate goal of the women's movement. He aptly described that goal as "more intimacy than ever between the sexes."[30]

After a couple of years of heady consideration, by 1993, the Georgia newspaper decided the time was right to cut loose and start enjoying *Thelma & Louise*, even if it did so at the film's expense. Although the national dispute over how to view the movie was still unsettled, at *The Atlanta Journal-Constitution*, *Thelma & Louise* fell into a place as an icon, sometimes of questionable esteem, sometimes deserving respect. Primarily, the movie was called upon when women sat behind the wheel or existed in pairs. In May 1993, a professional auto racer and journalist worried that the picture's title might be applied to her and a friend should anyone have spied them when they became "mired" in an "anti-pavement adventure." Although the film characters purposefully drive off a cliff, Linda Sharp's profession made her more sensitive to *Thelma & Louise* name-calling.[31] A couple of months later, in a July 1993 piece on twins, two senior citizen sisters were said to have been together "longer than Thelma and Louise." Conveniently, the newspaper disregarded the fact that the women's adventure lasted only a weekend and instead implied that the fictional women had been a team for a lot longer.[32] Like the advent of cable television, the Internet and DVDs, for good or bad there was no looking back once Thelma and Louise flew that Thunderbird into the realm of history.

In 1994, editors ran two pieces that, when viewed together, debated the film's impact on feminism and its relevance to the Lorena and John Bobbitt story. In retribution for his abusive behavior, including sexual assault, in June 1993, Lorena Bobbitt severed her husband's penis while he slept. Both husband and wife eventually stood trial for marital assault and malicious wounding, respectively. He was acquitted; she was found innocent by means of temporary insanity. A January 1994 column imported from the *Philadelphia Daily News* written by Sandy Grady around the time of Mrs. Bobbitt's trial claimed that unnamed feminists "canonized" penis-snipping Lorena, who they viewed as a "living version of the *Thelma & Louise* beat-up-the-boys movie."[33] The same year, in May, when Callie Khouri delivered the commencement address at Sweet Briar College, the Atlanta newspaper printed excerpts from her speech, which also drew on the Bobbitt drama. Once the fires surrounding her debut effort died down, Khouri defended feminism and encouraged women to use the f word. Directly contradicting Grady's comments, Khouri joked darkly, "It makes as much sense to include Bobbitt in a discussion of feminism as it does to include Jeffrey Dahmer in a discussion of vegetarianism."[34]

Ping-ponging back and forth between connotations that teetered forward and backward, in 1994, two female friends in their sixties who did things the right way by staying home and publishing a cookbook together served as a counterpoint to the film characters. They were described as "remarkable sidekicks" who are "nothing like Thelma and Louise." Indirectly, the Southern newspaper indirectly pressed the idea that it takes all kinds of women to define the gender. The Georgian women pushed the envelope in their own way, not in the movies, but in the kitchen. The two senior citizens presented a recipe from *Sharing Our Favorites*, their mutual effort. "Strange Bedfellows," a gelatin salad concocted with crushed pineapples, maraschino cherries and green olives, sounded gut-wrenching, which is the way some viewers perceived Thelma's rendezvous with J.D.[35]

That same year a publicity still from *Thelma & Louise* accompanied a special section on "Wheels for Women." The piece intended to educate and aid females regarding every aspect of car ownership from purchase decisions to maintenance plans. Like the 1991 article counseling women with aspirations in business, this piece assumed that women (but not men) still didn't "get it" when it comes to cars. The one-day series included 11 related articles under headlines such as "Car Advertisers See Women as a Very Green Market" and "Vital Car Fluids."[36]

By the end of the decade, *Thelma & Louise* came to impress the staff and readers of *The Atlanta Journal-Constitution* with its stature as a classic, both comedic and tragic. Though journalists revealed lingering blind spots regarding gender issues, the film was remembered as a favorite story featuring memorable characters who bear Aristotelian flaws. Displaying a new twist, in 1997, Thelma was listed as an offender in an article about adulterers in the entertainment world. Harlan, Thelma's would-be rapist who admits he has a wife, was not mentioned.[37] Later that same year, a woman who wanted to escape "adulthood" by taking a road trip in a decked-out old convertible couldn't decide which title character she would like to be. She didn't spell out her feelings on murder, but she did make clear that she had no plans to copy Thelma's infidelity. "I adore my husband and two children, so I can't stay gone for long," Mary Anne Carroll Gordon said. Eager to return to her loving home, Gordon just wanted to "cruise around Conyers for an hour or two." Looking for a brief break rather than a new life, she found inspiration in Thelma and Louise and forgave them their imperfections.[38]

Taking part in the widespread habit of renaming entities in honor of the film, in 1998, an editorial in the newspaper nicknamed the Atlanta Regional Commission and the state Department of Transportation the "Thelma and Louise of transportation planning" due to the agencies' failure to curb dependence on automobiles and control resulting air pollution. "Hellbent on driving their car off the cliff at top speed" despite legal restrictions, in the words of the newspaper the two groups kept "planning new highways" and "plotting more asphalt." Revealing fonder feelings for the film characters than the government offices it spoofed, the editorial mentioned the renowned characters three times.[39]

In 2000, author and consultant Robert McKee conducted a screenwriting seminar in Atlanta. He named *Thelma & Louise* as an example of a great script along with *The Silence of the Lambs* and *American Beauty.* Once stripped of their surfaces, he explained, these films are not based on formula. According to McKee, films that fail to find a unique voice don't enjoy staying power, although additional qualities such as masterful filmmaking and star power are also necessary for financial success.[40] In his book, *Story: Substance, Structure, Style, and the Principles of Screenwriting,* McKee points to the film as a example of a classical "archplot," which he defines as "a story built around an active protagonist who struggles against primarily external forces of antagonism to pursue his or her desire." Dramatic stories like *Thelma & Louise* proceed chronologically, build to a climax and end in "absolute, irreversible change," according to McKee.[41] Unique in his acceptance of their final act, McKee commends Thelma and Louise for their "courageous choice to take their own lives" during what he calls their "crisis decision."[42]

McKee's view of the film's permanence was illustrated in 2001 when a reader from Stockbridge shared how she used her tax refund sent by President George W. Bush and the U.S. Treasury to "pull" a pleasant and well-behaved "*Thelma & Louise*." Regardless of serious studies like McKee's, which define the movie's elements in classical terms, in common vernacular the film title now meant "to go on a road trip," in this case to Tybee Island. By its tenth birthday, to some viewers *Thelma & Louise* had transformed into a pastime minus any pejorative connotations.[43]

Later that year, a loss by Georgia Tech's football team to the University of Virginia resulted in a heartfelt, sentimental nod to the film. After taking many twists and turns in attitude, by the end of the decade *The Atlanta Journal-Constitution* looked to the film as an endearing metaphor. "Picture, if you will," the newspaper requested politely, "the general direction Thelma and Louise were traveling at their journey's end." Likening football to film, the article's tone and sympathies reiterated Eleanor Ringel's original commendation of the film. Over the course of the decade, *The Atlanta Journal-Constitution* came full circle in its criticism and commentary about the film. "Sometimes you just get beat," the newspaper solemnly stated, and sometimes "you get extinguished in ways painful and profound and, yes, classic."[44]

Through its persistent coverage, *The Atlanta Journal-Constitution* overpowered individual journalists who hesitated to give *Thelma & Louise* the credit it deserves. Atlanta's tribute adds to the mountain of copy in Chicago and other big cities such as Washington D.C., Los Angeles and Boston, plus towns of all sizes in between. The result is that although you can't make someone like *Thelma & Louise*, no one can rightfully deny the film its place in American culture.

16. Coast to Coast —
Washington, D.C.:
The Washington Post

Like *The Detroit Free Press* assiduously covers the automotive world, *The Washington Post*, with its home base in Washington, D.C., features politics as its specialty. Unsurprisingly, when the Beltway newspaper mentioned *Thelma & Louise*, which it did about 250 times in the decade following the picture's release, the discussion was sometimes ensconced within political stories. Exhibiting the topic's flexibility as well as the newspaper's willingness to engage the great debate, *The Washington Post* joined *Thelma & Louise* to stories about the Clarence Thomas confirmation hearings, a political talk show featuring the female point of view, women serving in government, females athletes breaking new ground, the Lorena Bobbitt story, the Clinton administration's strategy for the war in Kosovo, a lengthy profile of Hillary Rodham Clinton's life with the president, the possibility of an all-female shuttle crew and the real-life story about Americans "on the lam" in Mexico. Like other media outlets, the newspaper wove talk about the picture within crime coverage, entertainment news, the travel section, fashion pages, car talk, columns about local sports teams (in this case the Washington Redskins) and features concerning friendship (including local groups the Wednesday Night Bridge Club and the Canasta Girls). As with other newspapers that regularly referred to the title and its controversial characters, at *The Washington Post Thelma & Louise* and its associated meanings became part of the newspaper's cultural jargon.

In their cornucopia of stories, *Washington Post* journalists thought of *Thelma & Louise* sometimes endearingly, sometimes sarcastically. The first half of the decade saw more mentions of the film than the later half, with a rush of references coming in 1992 due to the film's release on video and the annual Oscar awards. *The Washington Post* just about matched the number of mentions in *The Atlanta Journal-Constitution*, yet the mid–Atlantic newspaper's attitude toward *Thelma & Louise* was noticeably different compared to either the Southern newspaper or the North's *Chicago Tribune*. Often, *Thelma & Louise* references seemed less warm and generous when Washington, D.C., journalists tossed around the title. In many instances the capital newspaper sounded either more dramatic or more acerbic. When churning *Thelma & Louise* talk, *The Washington Post* was sometimes chatty and upbeat, but it was occasionally more cutting, too.

Journalists didn't appear to hold back mention of the film whenever thoughts of it arose. In 1992, "The 'A' Word Confronts Bush Campaign" introduced a newly formed political action committee, the WISH List (Women in the Senate and the House), comprised of Republican women united in support of abortion rights. *The Washington Post* determined that the group presented trouble for President George Bush's unsuccessful re-election campaign, which was anti-abortion, because WISH List women were "decidedly unmilitant" and not "radical feminists" who could be easily discounted. To imagine the group, Jack Anderson and Michael Binstein urged, "Think of *Thelma & Louise* meet Miss Manners."[1]

Not worried about restricting its coverage to one area, *The Washington Post* scattered opinions about the film liberally throughout the newspaper. To provide an enticing backdrop for a review of two new books, one a speculation that recent concerns over date rape were overblown (Katie Rophie, *The Morning After: Sex, Fear and Feminism*) and the other a defense of men presumably against feminism (David Thomas, *Not Guilty: The Case in Defense of Men*), reviewer Cathy Young pitted the print releases against *Thelma & Louise*, as if the film largely defined the era's expression of feminism. "Whether or not the 1980s were the backlash decade," Young contended, tentatively summarizing Susan Faludi's argument in *Backlash*, "the 90s have emerged as the decade of the sex wars: Anita Hill, the date rape crisis, *Thelma & Louise*— all symbols of the evil that men do to women."[2] Reducing Hill's somber testimony and the film's multiple facets to oversimplified and inflamed terms encouraged pugilistic and snappy views of the entire landscape of gender relations.

In 1994, *The Washington Post* printed a travel piece simply titled "The Grand Canyon," which provided readers with information and tips such as avoid the south rim in the summer. With a sense of macabre, the newspaper didn't avoid the dark side of visits "to peer into the mammoth hole in the ground." If not for the suicide story out of Salt Lake City, it might seem like travel writer James T. Yenkel ventured over the edge of objectivity into speculation when he postulated on the inspiration behind numerous deaths attributed to falls.

You do have to be cautious on park ledges and trails. As many as 10 visitors a year plunge to their deaths in the canyon.... A few are suicides, a problem perhaps exaggerated by the movie *Thelma & Louise*, which featured a purported Grand Canyon suicide incident. Some tumbles are attributed to carelessness as a result of too much booze. And three deaths last year occurred when the victims fell from an unsafe rock or ledge while friends were snapping their photos.[4]

Another helpful reminder thanks to *Thelma & Louise*: grave danger awaits friends fooling around at the edge of enormous chasms.

According to editors at *The Washington Post*, who give generous consideration to a story's newsworthiness, even seemingly frivolous topics contained notable connections to *Thelma & Louise*. The many times *Thelma & Louise* was drawn into completely unrelated discussions and used to more creatively explain the goings-on of the world helps account for the newspaper's numerous mentions of the film. In 1999, "Fingernail Fashion Choices" investigated cultural attitudes toward nail polish by combining the views of a 12-year-old girl with those culled from a couple of fashion historians. While long nails were no longer signified "elite," in the words of the newspaper, many working class women still fancied them. The article arrived at the obvious, that nail polish choices reveal self-expression. Colors like Rebellious, Wanted ... Red or Alive and Gun Metal were lassoed and branded, "Finally, polishes for Thelma and Louise."[5]

Similar to the Knight-Ridder article that erroneously connected cigarette smoking with the film, a 1994 column in the financial section of *The Washington Post* reported that smokers and non-smokers were debating online in at least one specialty newsgroup. Though participants could "sharpen" their debate skills and "learn" from one another by taking part, as the Washington, D.C., newspaper said, some discussions were decidedly silly, such as the one about compiling films (including *Thelma & Louise*) in which the main characters light up.[6] Yet despite its criticism of levity, in 1993, *The Washington Post* purchased an article from the Universal Press Syndicate that detailed things we can't live without; refrigerator magnets, takeout food, disposable diapers and Post-It notes were among items listed. The next time readers withdrew cash from an automated teller machine or utilized any number of handy, recent inventions, the newspaper reminded them to stop and think: Americans should "count our blessings" for twist ties. According to "Diversions: How Did We Ever Get Along Without ...," twist-ties were "as inseparable from trash as Laurel is from Hardy or Thelma is from Louise."[7]

The Washington Post didn't invent all the commentaries about the film published on its pages. In some cases, the newspaper simply published articles on current events as others termed them. In 1995, the newspaper teased students at Altholton High School, which held a Jell-O wrestling tournament to ease the financial burden of going to the prom. Approached with same flair for dramatics that characterizes the World Wrestling Federation, the event was a success, complete with costumes and comical personalities. "Slick Way to Get to The Prom" included a photograph of a referee declaring wrestlers "Thelma and Louise" the winners.[8]

Within the entertainment section of *The Washington Post*, *Thelma & Louise* proved to be just as nimble. The picture popped up in Ellen Goodman and Art Buchwald columns as well as features on singer Tori Amos and country singers Wynonna Judd and Pam Tillis. The title was name-dropped when the newspaper covered musicians Kelly Willis and Chris Whitley, who both performed songs on the movie's soundtrack. Interviews with Susan Sarandon, Geena Davis, and Callie Khouri referenced the picture. *Thelma & Louise* was also wedged into approximately 25 reviews of other films. Staff film critics made the connection between the explosive 1991 release and later films like *Ruby in Paradise* (1993), *Walking and Talking* (1996) and *To Wong Foo, Thanks for Everything Julie Newmar* (1995). The controversial release appeared in articles aimed at Hollywood, which addressed a variety of topics, including black directors, violence in movies, the Cannes Film Festival, the Oscars and the America Film Institute.

To cover Hollywood, *The Washington Post* sought out many voices and provided an array of opinions. The newspaper saw the movie's relevance to the film community in diverse terms — mostly positive, but sometimes neutral and occasionally negative, depending on the speaker. The picture was named in a 1991 feature on a 68-year-old local cineplex usher who retired after dedicating over 50 years of his life to taking tickets and maintaining a clean, orderly lobby. "The End: After 54 Years, Credits Roll for Usher Phil Ahern" informed readers that although the senior citizen thought modern movies lacked substance and depended too much on blood and violence, he'd seen *Thelma & Louise* twice at a competing theater.[9]

Representing the newspaper's film staff, in November 1991, Rita Kempley reviewed the English film *Antonia & Jane* as a sympathetic fan of the earlier, American female buddy picture. She announced that the later film "is dedicated to the unassertive women of the world, the unsung sisters now eating the dust of recently martyred *Thelma & Louise*."[10] In April 1994, Joe Brown, another supporter of *Thelma & Louise* and a colleague of Kempley, reviewed *The Favor* with Elizabeth McGovern, Harley Jane Kozak, Bill Pullman and Brad Pitt. The film was completed and shelved in 1991 after its production company, Orion, went under. Full of compliments, Brown's review asserted that the "orphaned" film is a "frisky, frank, and funny female-buddy film — as if *Thelma & Louise* had stayed in the suburbs, making girl-talk about sex and satisfaction, married vs. single."[11]

Like commentators at *The Chicago Tribune*, most of the many *Washington Post* journalists who reviewed *Thelma & Louise* endorsed the picture, but at least one staff critic, Hal Hinson, did not. At the end of December 1991, Hinson shared a "wish list" for the upcoming year. For his part, he hoped that "*Thelma & Louise* don't land on the other side of the Grand Canyon in *Thelma & Louise 2.*"[12]

In late winter of the next year, Hinson bemoaned the way modern movies fail to "reflect the real lives we live." In response, according to Hinson, moviegoers were forced to lower their expectations. Hollywood pictures were "no longer at the center of our culture," he felt, because movies no longer spoke to viewers the way they did in the past. Although many viewers thought *Thelma & Louise* reflected real life and spoke to them, Hinson did not share their opinion and filed the film under "the raging current of feminist payback." Not in the mood to cut the production any slack, he accused the filmmakers of using "genre cliches" to distribute their message.[13] Still irritated a year later in April 1992, in his review of *Leaving Normal*, Hinson retorted, "If you wondered where Thelma and Louise landed after they went over that cliff, now you've got your answer." Unlike Terry Lawson in the Midwest, apparently Hinson didn't care for either picture, as "The Déjà vu of 'Normal'" complained that the *Leaving Normal* film rehashed the *Thelma & Louise*.[14]

Hinson wasn't anti-female, however; he was just anti–*Thelma & Louise*. In March 1993, he elaborated upon the sad fate of women directors in Hollywood and focused on four independent features directed by female first-timers. Aware of the low employment figures for women across the job spectrum in Hollywood, Hinson set the stage for his article by allowing that no critics, including himself, call pictures directed by men "men's pictures," while almost all critics consider pictures directed by women in terms of gender. We look at women's film differently, he suggested, because we're trying to figure out what it means to be a woman independent of gender bias. In the process, we're learning that there are "many styles" of women and so many styles of art created by women. Comparing Alison Anders's *Gas, Food Lodging* (1992) to *Thelma & Louise*, he believed that the newer film conveys a flat reality, "a sense of ongoing life," while the earlier film, with "all that dramatic tension and resolution, all those guns and cars and explosions," plays like a series of "boys' games in drag."[15] Although Hinson's general perspective toward women in Hollywood was sympathetic, the widely-held notion that Thelma and Louise act like they're Ted and Larry reflected a biased perception. Commentators like Hinson reacted as if one gender owns the right to take off, drive, shoot, flee, command and enjoy. To this way of thinking, the women borrow or steal what is rightly men's to begin with.

To kick off the decade, *The Washington Post* printed two laudatory reviews of *Thelma & Louise*, neither written by Hinson. Walking the line between snobbery and plain talk, Desson Howe's critique was aimed at a well-read readership. He commented that the film's "humor is mixed adroitly with existential ominousness." At the same time, to the great relief of East Coast intellectuals, "you don't have to be a mental pygmy to find things funny," he assured readers. Toning down his rhetoric while maintaining his upper crust attitude, Howe conceded that "*Thelma* is unabashed, streamlined entertainment ... and you won't hate yourself in the morning for liking it." As a pro critic, he recognized the film's "stirring undertones about oppressed women," the screenplay's distinction between helpful and harmful male characters and the soundtrack's "great" music ranging from "blues to reggae." Howe welcomed the film's direction, writing, cinematography, acting and the way the production approached the buddy movie genre. Howe's review was even more consistently glowing than Eleanor Ringel's in Atlanta, and he did not hesitate in his appreciation of the film.[16]

In contrast, in his review of *Amos & Andy* (1993) a couple of years later, Howe lumped the film with *Tango & Cash* (1989) and *Turner & Hooch* (1989), then advised against seeing movies with ampersands in the title. "With exceptions, you should consider '&' the equivalent of a skull and crossbones," Howe cautioned. "After bumping heads for the whole movie," he explained, buddies in the "&" genre "learn how to value each other's obnoxious qualities and anticipate the sequel." His conclusion in this case: "It ain't no *Thelma & Louise*."[17]

Rita Kempley penned the second opening weekend review of *Thelma & Louise* for *The Washington Post*. She delved more deeply into the movie's cultural tension and approved of what she discovered, although she did find fault with the film's ending. "This liberating adventure has a woman's perspective," she assessed, "but one that aims to give moviegoers of both sexes an ungirdled good time." To prepare those who might hold stereotypical expectations, Kempley elaborated, "This is one chick movie that isn't about to whine, bitch or back-seat drive." Her disappointment stemmed from the "inappropriately dire" ending that she felt "fails the characters, the movie and the audience." Kempley dismissed the suicide as a "borrowed ploy," but she didn't give away specifics about the ending to the audience. Instead, she only revealed that it's as if Khouri and Scott "ran up against a roadblock." Not ready to condemn the whole based on one bad part, her displeasure with the ending didn't stop Kempley from supporting the film, which she believed resurrected feminism in Hollywood despite its misstep.[18]

Due to Hal Hinson's dissent, *The Washington Post* film staff could not agree on the picture's merit, so the newspaper presented conflicting views and let readers decide for themselves. At the end of 1991, Desson Howe rated *Thelma & Louise* his fifth most enjoyable film of the year, describing the women's trip as "a runaway train of a movie, barreling along on the turbo-gasoline of character." To Howe, only *The Commitments*, *The Silence of the Lambs*, *My Own Private Idaho* and *The Vanishing* bettered *Thelma & Louise*.[19] Rita Kempley compiled her list alphabetically, so that *Thelma & Louise* fell between *Strangers in Good Company* and *Truly, Madly, Deeply*. *Thelma &*

Louise did not make Hinson's ten best list, but it didn't make his ten worst list, either. Speaking for the film's status as the most talked about movie of the year, of all the movies discussed in Hinson's year end wrap up (which included both his and Kemply's lists), the one picture accompanying the article was from *Thelma & Louise*.[20]

Considering nationwide professional reaction to the film, which leaned toward the positive, *The Washington Post* printed a fair selection of commentaries. When the film was released on videocassette, which happened to be the day that Hinson's and Kempley's year-end lists were published, another additional *Washington Post* reviewer presented her positive take on the film. Jami Bernard (author of *Chick Flicks*) extolled the film's entertainment value, stamping the much-talked about title "funny" and "sexy." Aware of the movie's pulled-taffy condition, she tagged the picture a "litmus test for everything from feminism to drunk driving," though Bernard preferred to think that filmmakers simply told a "skillful" and "exuberant" story.[21] Less than a week later, Rita Kemply reduced her earlier review into a shorter plug, this time saying that the film was "off the shoulder and ahead of its curve." Kempley restated her positions on the great debate and the movie's conclusion, both of which still disappointed her but didn't wreck her enjoyment of the picture. Although none of the men the duo encounter along the way could be confused with "Mr. Goodwrench," she stated frankly for the benefit of non-believers, "That's not to say that Thelma and Louise are male-bashers or that the movie is a load of spiteful feminism."[22]

Taken together, Howe, Kempley and Bernard's pro reviews set a welcome tone toward *Thelma & Louise*, which other staff entertainment writers refused or strained to uphold. At both ends of the *Thelma & Louise* decade, the film featured prominently if not ecstatically within *Washington Post* articles concerning women in Hollywood; Mrs. Dickerson and Miss Sawyer narrowly held their ground as symbols of powerful though ultimately defeated female characters.

With so little competition to knock it off its perch, the picture reigned, though ineffectively, as the powerhouse film showcasing strong women. Pat Dowell's "Reel Redemption: This Summer's Movies Demonstrate That White Males Can Suffer Adversity and Still Triumph" looked back at recent Hollywood releases. "Despite the attention they've gotten, pistol-packin' mammas like Thelma, Louise, and V. I. Warshawski are one-night stands for the movie industry," Dowell lamented. Instead, a glut of films such as *Regarding Henry*, *City Slickers*, *Doc Hollywood* and *Life Stinks* showed how "born-again guys," particularly "white guys," earned second chances to become better "yuppies, lawyers, doctors and landlords." Despite the many voices that entered the great debate, all together handing the film a huge amount of publicity, *Thelma & Louise* became a nearly isolated phenomenon and to some, including Dowell, a one-trick pony.[23]

Nationwide, the women's internal development was often overshadowed by their criminal flair even when commentators rooted for them. Ten years after the film's release, in 2001, Jennifer Frey took a supportive stance toward a trend she said spent a long time in development due to financial disincentives derived from a mostly male teenage audience. Female action heroes had finally arrived on screen. "Babes of Steel: Hollywood's Powerful Fantasies" traced the development of *Lara Croft: Tomb Raider* through the *Alien* and *The Terminator* series. In between Sigourney Weaver's Ripley and *Charlie's Angels* characters, according to Frey, progress moved slowly. The Bond women needed the lead character to save them, and "we knocked off Thelma and Louise." Taking responsibility for their demise as if society was to blame, Frey thought the women would be better off alive, so that they might function literally instead of figuratively. Glancing from Dowell to Frey, according to the District of Columbia newspaper, on one end of the decade the women's firepower was outnumbered by an onslaught of male-led movies; on the other, their forcefulness was undermined by their deaths and nearly forgotten with the passage of time.[24]

Despite the variety of inroads to *Thelma & Louise* trafficked by *The Washington Post*, the newspaper's most unique selection of articles mentioning the film concerned politics and current events, and in this regard, it covered all angles from right to left. Monitoring the pulse of the nation from the capital, with a penchant for theatrics, in October 1991 *The Washington Post* related the scene outside the Senate Caucus Room before and after Anita Hill testified to Congress against Clarence Thomas. "Dozens of backers" supporting Supreme Court nominee Thomas "lined the hallway" of the Russell Senate Office Building, the newspaper reported, setting the scene as "part political convention, part heavyweight championship."

In attendance that morning as part of the exuberance that eventually died down after Hill "calmly recounted" her story, leading anti-feminist Phyllis Schlafly told the newspaper that women who oppose Thomas are "like Thelma and Louise." She charged, "They hate men." Brimming with steam, she further lambasted that "they hate anybody who stands in their way and they're willing to kill anyone who gets in their way." Though Schlafly did side with the majority in support of Thomas, her extraordinary views about the film and Hill supporters placed her in a one-person minority, at least among those who spoke publicly. Wearing a button emblazoned "Pro-Woman/Pro-Thomas," Schlafy, like others across the country, appropriated the film to further her own agenda. In her case, she twisted the characters and real-life women into gross distortions. Though many people saw women as angry, Schlafly looked at the same scene and shouted unfounded accusations equating political sympathy with a willingness to commit murder.[25]

Schlafly was among those who read the film on a literal level only, therefore ignoring art's metaphoric mode of expression. Far worse, she sponsored the outrageous notion that large numbers of real women were willing to kill for their feminist beliefs, a far-fetched sentiment that the newspaper was willing to repeat. In direct opposition to Schlafly's claims, Thelma certainly enjoys J.D.'s company, and Louise cares enough about Jimmy to protect him. So that he won't become an accomplice to murder, she refuses to tell her boyfriend anything about the trouble she and Thelma are in and why they need money. Earlier in the year, shooting down Schlafly's words with her own, Callie Khouri made clear to *Time*, "I don't hate men." She continued, "Most guys don't relate to the truck driver or the rapist, and if they do," Khouri added when *Thelma & Louise* made the cover of the magazine, "their problems are bigger than this movie."[26]

During the next year, 1992, the so-called "Year of the Woman," *The Washington Post* called on *Thelma & Louise* to characterize the female camaraderie and hard-edged banter among panelists on Maryland Public Television's *To the Contrary*. The show was designed to offset the mostly male talking heads seen on political pundit shows such as *Inside Washington, Washington Week in Review* and *MacNeil/Lehrer NewsHour*. According to the show's producer, women are included on these programs, "but it's usually one seat, and one voice, that is often overshadowed." The newspaper backed that perspective with statistics from Women Are Good News, based in San Francisco, which found that women represented only 15 percent of guests on PBS's public affairs programs. In contrast to Phyllis Schlafly's accusations, *To the Contrary* and Women Are Good News exemplified a willingness to work — not murder — to change outdated social structures and sexist attitudes, although the television show's panelists didn't always make that difference clear for the trope-impaired.

As anyone who has accidentally misspoken or had their words misconstrued can corroborate, the debate over gender issues requires care. Comments intended to be humorous differ in flavor from angry boasts fired in the heat of a tense moment, but hearsay and gossip blur this distinction. Because temperaments surrounding gender issues are often touchy, inflammatory language such as Schlafly's can cause all sorts of trouble. One lesson to be learned from the screenplay, and perhaps the Thomas/Hill hearings as well, is that sarcasm can be dangerous.

When she hears Thelma's attempted rapist retort brazenly, "I should've gone ahead and fucked her," Louise loses her mind. When she returns to her senses after killing Harlan, she immediately regrets her reaction but by then it's too late. *The Washington Post* reportedly overheard on the set of *To the Contrary* the quip, "This man was awful to her. This man needed to die! He needed killing!" Toted as a humorous solution to "man-problems" that could have originated "from the script of *Thelma & Louise,*" private jokes like this, when leaked to the public, can be taken out of context and come back to haunt the speaker.[27]

Not an advocate of settling disagreements through violence, Khouri expressed to *The New York Times,* "I don't want anybody doing anything they saw in this movie." Her characters "are outlaws who should be punished and are." She stated unequivocally the week after the film hit theaters, "I do not justify their actions." The idea was to learn from the mistakes made by Thelma and Louise and Harlan, not to repeat them.[28]

Due to greater resources and higher expectations, high-profile newspapers like *The Washington Post* provide more in-depth coverage and analysis (though not necessarily more objective reporting) than smaller-profile newspapers such as *The St. Louis Post-Dispatch.* Both newspapers ran stories on the record number of women running for Congress in 1991. Unlike the comparatively brief article featured in the Missouri newspaper, the first installment of a two-part series ("Women on the Verge of a Power Breakthrough") in the District of Columbia newspaper detailed some minute but meaningful aspects of the U.S. House of Representatives, which could only be ascertained by actually being there. Surveying the "floor" in the spring of 1992, the newspaper reported that there were "so many men, so many suits," all in dull colors. In contrast, when women enter the chamber, the newspaper dramatized, they bring color. According to *The Washington Post,* Susan Molinari, R-New York, who was said to drive around town listening to the soundtrack of *Thelma & Louise,* wore red. Displaying a striking contrast to the more mundane outfits worn by most congressmen, colors and patterns ascribed to congresswomen included turquoise, paisley and bright orange.

More important than fashion sense is what these choices in clothing represented. The women's brighter colors reflected divergent approaches and previously quieted female experience. Because differences between congressmen and congresswomen included inflicting versus receiving gender-biased slights, reporter David Finkel was induced to label Congress "a place somewhere on the continuum between the Flintstones and true enlightenment." For congresswomen, slights could mean the need to ward off sexual overtures or "overlook" demeaning remarks based on gender. Finkel relayed that a visitor thought it would be amusing to scribe "Dick Hurtz of 131 Penis Drive" in one congresswoman's guest book.

Although the treatment of women serving in the federal government is "less crude" than before, according to the capital newspaper, it's fair to say that in the United States there's still room for the anger expressed in *Thelma & Louise.* Finkel sympathized with congresswomen: "Their workplace still fosters a culture of female lobbyists, visitors and trophy wives, who teeter and click their way along, as if the best way to approach a congressman is on stiletto heels." In other words, individual congressmen may be no better behaved than the disrespectful trucker in the film. According to the Center

Thanks to the Guerrilla Girls, Hollywood filmmakers were able to drive by this reminder on their way to the 2003 Academy of Motion Picture Arts and Sciences annual Oscar ceremony in Los Angeles. (Copyright 2003 by the Guerrilla Girls, Inc. Reprinted with permission.)

for the American Woman and Politics at Rutgers University, whose figures Finkel referenced, in 1992, out of 11,238 members of Congress since 1789, only 131 were women. In light of these numbers and ongoing sexist slights, complaints about the handful of wayward male characters that Thelma and Louise must deal with sound sorely out of touch.[29]

With a flair for show business, an eye on world affairs and its finger on the cultural pulse of America, *The Washington Post* continued to make regular references to the film throughout the decade. Conditioned by political displays and so drawn to drama, the newspaper in August 1992 wondered facetiously if female marathoners running through Barcelona "had done something terribly wrong." The sirens, five helicopters, and 16 motorcycle cops that proceeded runners turned out to be a matter of security. However, at first the newspaper imagined that the scene looked "like the ending of *Thelma and Louise*."[32]

In 1993, an editorial taking a stand on "Toni Morrison and the 'Anti-Male' Rap" appeared in the newspaper. Cataloguing the male characters in Morrison's *Beloved*, as well as those in *Thelma & Louise* and Alice Walker's *The Color Purple*, Amy E. Schwartz checked into the on-going argument debated in more intellectually inclined newspapers about whether or not female artists unfairly pick on men. Joining *The Chicago Tribune*'s Clarence Page and *The Atlanta Journal-Constitution* Nicolaus Mills, Schwartz analyzed the subject using sensible criteria based on a "varied-characters test." The determining factor as to whether or not a work of art beats up on either gender isn't so complicated as the debate makes it sound, Schwartz implied. Individual characters should have integrity, not kowtow to an agenda. According to Schwartz, if within a single work all men are all bad and all women all good, then charges of bias may be fair.

> If the question is whether men are seen as simplistically evil or women simplistically good, a novel like *The Color Purple* may be vulnerable, if not to charges of cartoonishness then at least to the observation that the author does seem to believe that men are women's only enemies.

In Schwartz's view, though Alice Walker's novel may be accurately charged with male-bashing, *Beloved* and *Thelma & Louise* pass the test and rise above bias. Schwartz points out that the female characters Sethe and Beloved in Morrison's novel are "upsetting," while men like Paul D and Stamp Paid serve to comfort and aid the people closest to them. Likewise, according to Schwartz, among the "sexist, insensitive creeps" in *Thelma & Louise*, Jimmy delivers the money to Louise when she asks, even though he doesn't know what's going on, and Detective Slocumbe tries to "save the women's lives" in the film's last scene. Schwartz doesn't necessarily endorse *Thelma & Louise*, but she does defend female artists.

> That a writer is supposedly "anti-male" has nothing to do with her use of stereotype, or implausibility, or absence of depth in the characters portrayed, or any such artistic flaw. Just offer the reader or the viewer a single negative, a single case where a man acts nastily or a treats a woman badly, and the whole thing is written off as prejudice. This isn't literary criticism but that old socialist standby — the demand that literature be reduced to cheery propaganda.[33]

Associating *Thelma & Louise* with gender politics outside of Hollywood turned out to be the newspaper's subspecialty, as *The Washington Post* featured an array of speakers from Phyllis Schlafly to Amy E. Schwartz. An educational consultant whose firm specialized in seminars about rape and masculinity for men told the newspaper that debate surrounding Lorena Bobbitt reminded him of *Thelma & Louise*. "I'm a man, and I certainly don't support penises being cut off," he expressed, "but I hope this will not be a smoke screen to really mask the incredible violence that men are doing to women." Providing the kind of real life response to rape many would like to see, the consultant commiserated with assaulted women, both real and fictional. "Arguably," he added, "there are some men who deserve this." Like the great debate surrounding the film, in the words of *The Washington Post*, "sentiment" in the Bobbitt case crossed gender lines.[34]

While some men recognized serious issues within the film, others batted it around as if it was a favorite joke worth repeating. Between January 1992 and January 2001, sports columnist Tony Kornheiser dragged *Thelma & Louise* through seven of his columns, none of which were about movies,

politics or women. Exemplifying the kind of journalist who became fasci-
nated by the women's adventures though not in a very meaningful way, Kornheiser alluded to the film's crashing denouement in six out of seven articles.
Enamored by the image of the women driving off the cliff, over and over he
described sinking hopes and mismanaged plays in terms of the film's close.
In 1993, no doubt reacting to an understandable ploy aimed at keeping players keen and fans interested, Kornheiser nevertheless objected to the Washington Redskins' coach pushing playoff talk with an abysmal 2–6 record. Still,
"What's he suppose to say?" Kornheiser commiserated. He added teasingly
"'We've gone over the cliff like Thelma and Louise'?"[35]

Concerned with the quality of hard news reporting, editors at *The Washington Post* admitted when they made a mistake. In the 1994 column, "Unconventional Wisdom," the newspaper debunked the myth of women and guns
with the help of the University of Chicago's General Social Survey, which
determined that reports published across the country claiming increased gun
ownership among women were wrong. The only place gun ownership was
"surging," according to the University of Chicago as paraphrased by *The
Washington Post*'s Richard Morin, "was on the pages of America's leading newspapers and magazines," including *The Washington Post, The New York Times,
The Wall Street Journal, USA Today, The Los Angeles Times, Newsweek* and
Time." Culled mostly from the 1990s, more than 90 stories printed in newspapers and magazines were analyzed by researchers. Many articles asserted that
ownership figures were climbing and claimed that from 17 to 20 percent of
women packed heat. Investigators at the University of Chicago found that
gun ownership levels had actually remained stagnant since 1980 and that only
11.6 percent of women owned weapons.

The University of Chicago uncovered evidence that print media stretched
the facts after the persuasive film due to preoccupation with Callie Khouri's
characters and interest in anything sensational that might sell more newspapers. According to the survey, women and gun articles tended to paint an inaccurate profile of the typical female gun owner. Often she was depicted as a
single city-dweller aiming to protect herself, while married women living outside of cities, predominantly in the South or the West, were more likely to
own guns for hunting. Those groups that might gain from images of either
a gun-enthusiastic or a gun-crazy population were blamed for "stupid stats,"
in Morin's words. Echoing researchers, *The Washington Post* also blamed the
news media, including itself, for passing along inaccurate data and "exaggerated" results and turning them into "tales resembling Thelma and Louise."[43]

Describing sports endeavors that fail in ways reminiscent of the film
characters' final leap and forging thoughts of an angry female majority intent
upon firepower suited the newspaper's lively perspective. In 1998, *The Washington Post* came up with a new way to weave the film into a feature on all-
women travel escapes. At end of the article, the newspaper concluded that

for most excursions there's a "time to come home," but added in a conspicuous aside, "for everyone but Thelma and Louise." [44]

Clearly, the film, especially its final images, permanently impressed a
number of journalists who wrote for the newspaper, yet other commentators
purposely sidestepped the ending. Seven years after the women run low their
last tank of gas, columnist Phylicia Oppelt based an article "Wheel Love," on
her love for the film. Oppelt sided with staff writers who appreciated the film
and opposed journalists like Hal Hinson and Tony Kornheiser who either
hated it or loved trashing the title. Analyzing her attraction to a red convertible, Oppelt decided "Perhaps I loved the movie *Thelma & Louise* for the
same reasons I loved being ensconced in that car." Forgiving or perhaps forgetting Thelma and Louise's final decision, Oppelt related how the convertible became the women's "vehicle to self-realization, pride, and, yes, freedom."
Connecting cars with romance and men with cars, she shared a short personal history of their intersection. Oppelt closed with revelations worthy of
the film, as a writer sounding more reminiscent of cerebral Louise than action-
oriented Thelma.

> I'm older now. My hair is short. My manner is more composed. I still crave
> excitement, but these days I want to be the one to create the sense of adventure.
> I want a relationship with a convertible, not a relationship with a man who
> owns one. [45]

The Washington Post was not alone in its impassioned use of the film as
a symbol. Showing incredible bounce, in 1999, *Thelma & Louise* helped
assess an international life and death situation. An article that also appeared
in *The Salt Lake Tribune* mentioned the picture in a story about the war in
Kosovo. Three U.S. soldiers were captured by Yugoslav president Slobodan
Milosevic's troops after they allegedly crossed into enemy territory. In reaction, the Clinton administration reiterated its plans, in the newspaper's words,
to "increase" the war's scope and "pound" Yugoslavia, until Milosevic
accepted NATO's terms. Because the bombing campaign drew disapproval,
a senior administration official explained to *The Washington Post* that the
president and his advisors "constantly" reviewed their decision "to examine
other options." However, like Thelma and Louise find no better alternative
than to "just keep going," the White House had found "no better course."
Still, the unnamed official insisted, "We are not *Thelma & Louise*." The newspaper completed his analogy by adding "going off a cliff." Insinuating that
the women were out of control and the government wasn't, the Clinton
administration official protested, "We're driving this car. It's just a bumpy
road." [46]

Perhaps *The Washington Post* more cleverly disguises its gossip than other
newspapers, which designate special columns for the purpose of running down

individuals. With the help of *Thelma & Louise*, in the spring of 1999, a lengthy essay entitled "The Hillary Dilemma" analyzed Hillary Clinton's life with Bill Clinton. Of the three women — Mrs. Dickerson, Miss Sawyer and Mrs. Clinton — Hillary received the harshest treatment. The feature spanned 25 years, from Mrs. Clinton's decision to move to Arkansas for the launch of Mr. Clinton's campaign to obtain a seat in the U.S. House of Representatives, to the aftermath of his public confession of his affair with Monica Lewinsky, a confession made while he was president of the United States.

A confidant from the past told the newspaper that she was "deeply opposed" to Mrs. Clinton's decision to hook up with Mr. Clinton but nevertheless accompanied her friend to Arkansas. "Rather than Thelma and Louise," the newspaper surmised of the road trip that led Mrs. Clinton to her future, "the two women were more like Thelma and June Cleaver, though it's hard to say which woman was playing whom." To suit a *Leave It to Beaver* metaphor, the profile limited itself to Mrs. Clinton's position as wife and only superficially considered her other roles as mother, lawyer and public speaker.

Criticizing the first lady like others criticized the film characters, author Liza Mundy chided Hillary Clinton for "distorting" feminism by talking one way on the lecture circuit and acting another way within her marriage. Addressing audiences around the world, she worked to "shore up choices" for women, but at home, by sticking with her man, she symbolized "a narrow idea of how women should behave." However, Mundy upheld the limitation of women through her own restricted perspective. Seeing Clinton mainly through the lens of her marriage, a private rather than public affair, Mundy characterized her subject's choice to stay married as "traditional" and one that relinquished "equality." Meanwhile, others might consider Mrs. Clinton's decision not to divorce to be more about resolve, commitment or even good strategy, qualities that are not incompatible with also being liberal-minded. "Hillary Clinton symbolizes not choice but the limitations of choice," Mundy contended, because of "the actions of Bill Clinton," to whom she chose to stay married, like Thelma and Louise chose to take their own lives.

No matter what she might do, stay with her cheating husband or leave him, in many eyes Hillary Clinton couldn't win. As Mundy put it, Mrs. Clinton's experience teaches us that "we are inevitably the product of other choices we've made." Furthermore, what applied to the president's wife applied to everyone. "Once we make a choice," we "lose" other choices, the article pointed out, but this is old news. No one can escape the fact that some choices are "lousy," Mundy continued, and even worse that choices "sometimes clash." For example, some viewers felt suicide clashed with liberation. *The Washington Post* decided that Mrs. Clinton's marriage clashed with her public life, but outsiders hold no right to opine on a supposed dilemma involving an ongoing marriage. Mundy mistakenly claimed that Mrs. Clinton "did not choose to end up where she is now," but because every choice brings both good and bad, she did exactly that. Like Louise says, "You get what you settle for." Her motto applies up to the point where luck and happenstance overtake personal accountability. Thelma didn't settle for rape, yet Hillary did decide to stick by Bill, for better or for worse.

In selecting only tough times to emblematize Mrs. Clinton's married life, the newspaper took a wrong turn. Like Thelma and Louise equal more than their violent aggression and unfortunate suicide, Mrs. Clinton's world contained much more than a "blemished" family life, a future "marred" by scandal and a public persona "clouded" by suffering, as her later election to the U.S. Senate confirmed. Just as critics of the film harped about pervasive male-bashing and other misrepresentations, looking at only negatives *The Washington Post* distorted Mrs. Clinton's life as well as the lessons her example offers. Confusing "choice" with the more intricate and mature realms of circumstance and compromise, *The Washington Post* ignored the probability that Hillary Clinton's decisions have brought her both positive and negative outcomes. Worse, Mundy discredited the fact that as a professional, wife and mother, Hillary Clinton does symbolize the widening of choices for women delivered by feminism.[47] Apparently, Mundy had not heard the future senator's speech delivered a year before in Seneca Falls, New York, for the 150th anniversary of the first women's rights convention. Celebrating women like Elizabeth Cady Stanton and Susan B. Anthony and others like them, the First Lady encouraged women to support one another in the choices each make. "Will we admit once and for all that there is no cookie-cutter model for being a successful and fulfilled woman?" she asked. Her words evidently fell on deaf ears at *The Washington Post*.

Although the idea of a strong woman occupying either the driver's seat or the White House makes some people uneasy, as the century drew to a close no one could deny women's gains against the considerable forces of history and custom. Still, room for improvement exists. In 1999, *The Washington Post* reported that NASA was considering an "all-woman" shuttle crew. Though the issue was characterized as receiving more talk than action, the notion prompted the headline "Thelma and Louise in Space?" Working its vivid imagination and enduring fascination with the film's ending, the newspaper urged the sight of Thelma and Louise continuing their ascension off the cliff and into the galaxy. Within the space agency at the time, a single woman ranked among top commanders, only 32 of 144 astronauts were women and little of NASA's research had focused on the effects of weightless on women's bodies.[48]

Skyrocketing into pop culture history, *Thelma & Louise* continued to defy gravity by maintaining a presence in the leading press long after the movie left theaters. In 2001, *The Washington Post* sustained its captivation with the film, this time focusing on the women's thwarted plans for a life in Mexico, which the newspaper called "one of the oldest stories in American crime." At the time, the capture of American fugitives in Mexico was on the rise as a result of Mexican president Vicente Fox's resolve to "improve law enforcement cooperation" with the United States, the newspaper reported. Meanwhile, the former head of Interpol in Mexico complained to *The Washington Post*, "I blame Hollywood" for the problem of people trying to escape to a mythical Mexico. In the newspaper's view, along with real life fugitives from England's Great Train Robbery in 1963, *Butch Cassidy and the Sundance Kid*, *Thelma & Louise* and *The Shawshank Redemption* (1994) exemplified the trend to equate Mexico with freedom. However, it's "getting harder to fade into the Mexican sunset," the newspaper warned, in essence due to NAFTA. According to *The Washington Post*, American fugitives who make it to Mexico "often take jobs using their English skills," for example by working in the tourist trade. It turns out Thelma's dream of getting a job at Club Med wasn't so crazy after all.[49]

Although Thelma and Louise must eventually crash despite the filmmakers' attempt to dissolve the bloody truth waiting at the bottom of the canyon, signs indicate that there is no end to the film's afterlife. Reclaiming the duo for the umpteenth time, and looking beyond the *Thelma & Louise* decade, in 2002, a mother-daughter road trip undertaken in a reliable Honda versus a vintage Ford convertible paralleled one of the movie's warmer messages about tightening interpersonal bonds. Written from a mother's perspective, the article noted that experience encouraged new levels of awareness for one mother-daughter team.

A comparison between mother-daughter relationships and the partnership between Thelma and Louise sprung repeatedly from the article, which touched on role models, growth and connection. Similar to the way Thelma looks up to Louise as an example of womanhood, the daughter, to the mother, was a "lady-in-waiting." Like Thelma towers over Louise, the writer's road companion stood "two inches taller than I am." M.L. Lyke concluded that her maturing child was "someone to get to know, all over again." Her sentiments evoked the tension evident between Thelma and Louise during the many bumpy times the two continually surmounted.

Pointing to the "easy intimacy of the road, the breezy bond that forms over the slap of rubber on pavement," the author related, "we were our own Thelma and Louise, two against the world," exchanging and sharing all the way. Like Louise leads Thelma out of the house and Thelma drags Louise into a life of crime, the author introduced her daughter to winery tours and the California Redwoods. In turn, daughter initiated mother to mosh pits and the joys of water-slide parks. In an oblique nod to both *Thelma & Louise* and a later Susan Sarandon film in which she plays mother to a teenage daughter, the article's duo chose not to pick up a hitchhiker who carried a sign begging "anywhere but here." In this case, unlike Thelma and Louise, the travelers picked up only the hitchhiker's message. In Lyke's eyes, on the road her daughter transformed into a "near-woman." Rather than kid about or denounce the picture, over ten years after its release, Lyke's account in "Goodbye, Girl" reinforced belief in the film's positive message of inspiration.[50]

Overwhelmingly, most of the voices who mentioned the film in *The Washington Post* remained polite even if they were not enthusiastic supporters. Outside of Hal Hinson and Tony Kornheiser, few journalists at the newspaper downed the film with gusto. Purposely printed to present an opposing viewpoint, two additional pieces heavily criticized the fictional duo. Like Phyllis Schlafly maligned the characters' view of men, a 1996 piece on women and violence recalled *Thelma & Louise* as a film that relished physical aggression. Missing the movie's salient points about violence being regrettable and agency being gender blind, "the hunger of women to celebrate their more violent side was reflected in the success of films like *Thelma & Louise*," asserted an opinion piece entitled "The Amazons Among Us." Referring to the "long-disguised violent feminine impulse" exemplified by both talk and action, Harold Bloom suggested that women have purposely hidden their violent nature like mythical Amazons lobbed off their left breasts to better handle bow and arrows.

Bloom's essay stretched pretty far to make its point. Bloom claimed that besides actually committing murder, women "encourage killers in others ways" such as "by falling in love with warriors and heroes," thus mitigating a man's responsibility for his own actions. Applying Bloom's thesis to the film, Thelma and Louise should have picked more blood-thirsty men to bed up with and let Darryl and Jimmy's replacements do the women's killing and entombing for them. Bloom's article didn't touch on rape, yet he suggested by extension that Harlan's wife might have somehow encouraged her husband's aggression against Thelma.

Like those who complained about and bungled the number of sympathetic males in *Thelma & Louise*, Bloom's essay ran adrift of what was pertinent. His too-easy conclusion that it was "useless for women to blame violence on men" as it is "futile for men to blame violence on women" overlooks the more crucial message that criminals of both genders must repay society for their crimes. This more difficult and timely aspect of the colliding issues of women and violence was apparent in the two real-life criminal cases during the 90s: the state-sanctioned execution of Karla Fay Tucker, a female death row inmate in Texas, who used a pick-axe to murder Jerry Lynn Dean and Deborah Thornton; and society's indictment of penis-snipping Lorena Bobbitt, who was no heroine to anyone interested in a peaceful society. Meanwhile, as offered in Bloom's article, references to violent behavior among female gorillas at best reinforced the animal nature of humans — all humans. Our beastly condition is an uncontested notion when it is compared to whether or not the state can carry out the death penalty, a husband can force his wife to have sex with him or individuals have the right to choose their own deaths.[51]

Finally, fending off possible charges of bias toward the film, author Susan Isaacs presented her minority opinion and anti–*Thelma & Louise* stance to Washington, D.C., readers. In a 1999 *Washington Post* article, she reiterated her brave dames and wimpettes thesis, which originated in her book. "Too often" in the 1990s, characters like Hildy Johnson of *His Girl Friday*, Mary Richards of *The Mary Tyler Moore Show* and Norma Rae and Karen Silkwood "gave way" to wimpettes like Thelma and Louise, Isaacs argued. Labeling them victims of "slobby," "brutish," and "violent" men, Isaacs conceded that the women "fought back" but didn't approve of their methods or recognize any positives in their portrayal. "They went on a shooting, stealing and burning spree in revenge," she argued, "then drove off a cliff rather than accept the consequences of their actions."[52] Meanwhile, free to speak their mind thanks to the long line of female forerunners and leaders before them, other viewers like Phylicia Oppelt and M.L. Lyke saw the film quite differently. The women's decision to commit suicide constitutes acceptance of their fate but with consequences they devise.

17. Los Angeles:
The Los Angeles Times

Attracted to controversy, most newspapers across the country felt obligated to discuss *Thelma & Louise* to some extent. Captivated by memorable characters who meet an unforgettable conclusion, major newspapers in the East and elsewhere elevated the film. Even though the picture was filmed primarily outside of the state, in Southern California *Thelma & Louise* equaled both a nationwide, headline-generating, cultural phenomenon and a hometown product. While few viewers could accurately identify the film's Utah locations, everyone in the world knows that major movies are produced in Hollywood. Because of the picture's popularity, *The Los Angeles Times* couldn't very well avoid *Thelma & Louise*, although in some respects not long after "True of False: Thelma and Louise Just Good Ol' Boys?" the newspaper did try to stay out of the great debate, which resulted in conspicuous absences of coverage. Stories and trends evident elsewhere, like associating women and guns and tying local criminals to the film, did not appear in *The Los Angeles Times*. Replicating the area's many diversities and geographic sprawl, the newspaper's extensive coverage of the film was all over the place with the exception of blackout zones. Hollywood's hometown newspaper lacked a predominant guiding vision toward the movie despite heavy coverage. As a result, the story of *Thelma & Louise* and *The Los Angeles Times* is more fragmented than any other newspaper surveyed. In Southern California, a wide and conflicting collection of voices refused to unify.

The cacophony began with the newspaper's entertainment staff. Opposing Sheila Benson and Peter Rainer, film critic Kenneth Turan joined the pro–*Thelma & Louise* crowd. According to Turan's surprised but enthusiastic review, the once "exclusively masculine preserve" of adventure and discovery on the road was "changed" by *Thelma & Louise* "forever." Unlike those commentators who reacted with anger and dismay, and felt others should,

249

too, Turan trounced the view that *Thelma & Louise* mucked up gender relations. Optimistically, he believed just the opposite, that the film furthered understanding across gender divides. In his perspective, *Thelma & Louise* does not weigh itself down with male-bashing or relentlessly beat the audience over the head with a leaden agenda. Rather, the story presents an opportunity for people to widen their outlooks.

Instead of resisting identification with the lead characters or feeling threatened, Turan sympathized with the film's female point of view. Watching the women get into the "worst trouble of their lives" while surprisingly empowering themselves posed too much of a stretch for some people, but for Turan the story was a "great and paradoxical pleasure." Watching Thelma and Louise, viewers meet marvelous characters who grow and learn; simultaneously, viewers are asked to judge crazed criminals who screw up and lose. The film provides a complex layering of character so often absent in Hollywood films, particularly those starring women, and seems very much like real life. Turan opined that by living vicariously through the main characters viewers "gain a realization not only of the different needs of the sexes, but also of how deeply society pigeonholes men and women." Turan implied that society helped program both Thelma and Harlan by encouraging some women to act irresponsibly ditzy and pushing some men to behave violently chauvinistic.

Not completely lost in his praise, Turan criticized the "regrettable" interlude with a "Neanderthal" trucker, but otherwise alleged that *Thelma & Louise* "makes its points while scrupulously avoiding being preachy." At ease with the overall depiction of males in the film, Turan felt that the production manages to "seamlessly blend political concerns with mainstream entertainment" and to never forget the audience or get off track. He commended Callie Khouri's "exceptional ear" and "enviable understanding of character." Turan credited Ridley Scott's "panache" and "good sense." To Geena Davis and Susan Sarandon, he awarded hearty approval for the "gamut of emotions" they showed, in what Turan guessed would be the "most satisfying" women's roles of the year. His forecast was accurate. Few films inspire similar high grades and gushing praise, particularly films that are also so strongly disliked by contemporaries and co-workers.[1]

Validating the considerable coverage *Thelma & Louise* received in the press, on the West Coast, as was the case elsewhere, the film captured the attention of newspaper readers as well as journalists. Between June 8 and June 23, 1991, *The Los Angeles Times* shared numerous letters written to the editor in response to the controversy, heightened locally by Peter Rainer and Sheila Benson's May 31 joint effort. Reacting to a variety of issues brought up by the film, collectively *Los Angeles Times* readers discussed *Thelma & Louise* with depth and intellect. Subscribers considered the film in terms of sexual violence toward women, the limitations women face in society, feminism, the filmmaker's alleged deception and profiteering, the connection between the film and real life politics, class issues, the role of film reviewers, bias toward the film, women's anger, women acting as their own worst enemies, the film's value as a reflection of society and inspiration for change, socially aware film reviews and the public's preference for unassertive women. The ratio of letters printed in support of the film versus those that criticized *Thelma & Louise* roughly paralleled the breakdown of journalists for and against the picture found in the newspapers consulted nationwide. Following the overall trend, more readers offered praise than criticism, yet all who wrote did so passionately.

On the positive side, a woman from Malibu focused on the violence perpetrated against the women and felt that "whether or not we agree with the artistic merits of what was put on screen, at least something that weighs heavily on all women's minds was explored in a thought-provoking way."[2] A man from Los Angeles sided with Kenneth Turan's sentiments and instructed Peter Rainer and Sheila Benson to see the film again. He added, "And this time, try to see a beautifully crafted, inexorable tragedy about two hapless friends who discovered what they would do to be free."[3] Explaining that "in every area women are being pushed back to a repressive time," another writer from Los Angeles addressed the film's political impact then drew a comparison between *Thelma & Louise* and recent happenings in the Supreme Court and Congress. Conscious of gender issues and open to a story told through a woman's point of view, she noted the low percentage of women in government. She concluded, "Since we seem to have little power by the ballot, it is heartwarming to live vicariously by Thelma and Louise's bullets."[4] A class- and gender-conscious reader from Santa Barbara pointed out why the film garnered a "fevered" critical response: because the title characters are "working-class" women. Turning a critical eye to film reviewers, he wondered, "What business is it of the critics to judge this movie on the basis of its uplifting moral value?"[5] One woman from Los Angeles also questioned the special treatment the film was receiving. Asking why *Thelma & Louise* was "scrutinized in minute detail for its attention to political correctness" when other films aren't, she praised the film for raising "some interesting questions."[6] Another reader from Los Angeles joined those voices that criticized the critics. She responded that Rainer and Benson "missed the boat." Defending the film's emotional complexity, she argued that "a feminist movie doesn't have to put forth a utopian view of society."[7] A reader from Glendale identified himself as someone involved in filmmaking who was "tired" of seeing racial and gender groups stereotyped on screen, yet he wasn't bothered by the depiction of men in the film, as some were. While he looked to *Thelma & Louise* as a possible vehicle to "inspire change," he was conscious of the suicide's great cost. "Perhaps," he offered, the film's "only fault is that, in the end, the only place society has for a strong female is at the bottom of the Grand Canyon."[8] Lastly in the proverbial "thumbs up" column, a letter from a Los Angeles reader dismissed the film's detractors by sarcastically contrasting "anxious" reactions to the women's aggressive behavior with Julia Roberts' effusive popularity based on her "Bambi-like quality."[9]

As with any controversial topic, not all letters to the editor that were printed pledged support. However, in keeping with the hype surrounding *Thelma & Louise*, the following readers did write in earnest. A woman from North Hollywood decried the film's "non-feminism" and stated that "the use of women in leading roles serves only as a hook for these director-producers to propagate the values they take for granted as males in a male-dominated industry."[10] Like Terry Lawson in Dayton, she was apparently unaware of or ignored Callie Khouri's contribution as screenwriter and co-producer. A woman from Long Beach shared a comment that might please Ford Motor Company. She found the movie to be nothing more than a "silly, beautifully photographed car commercial." She felt the film actually concerned "two gals victimized by their own stupidity," not gender relations. Without mentioning the attempted rape directly and evidently not impressed with the story's personal element, the same reader perhaps inadvertently insinuated that Harlan gave Thelma exactly what she deserved.[11] Lastly in the "thumbs down" category, a man from Los Angeles commented that Rainer and Benson's criticisms were "more thoughtful" than the film they critiqued.[12] Unfortunately, his letter as printed did not include specifics that might have supported his view. What these readers have in common with the professionals who did not appreciate the picture is an unwillingness to empathize with film's main characters. Con critics refused to see the world through the eyes of women, in particular Thelma and Louise, who are both exemplary and flawed.

In the first wave of the great debate, Los Angeles served as a heightened microcosm of the entire nation. Regarding the divisive case of *Thelma & Louise*, what was bitter to some tasted like honey to others. Later in the summer of 1991, a reader wrote in response to a *Los Angeles Times'* travel piece, one of many published nationwide that was happily modeled after the film. "Sara and Martha weren't the only two inspired by Thelma and Louise," a woman from West Hollywood shared. Paralleling positive aspects of the fictional women's journey, her story also capped off with a bittersweet though less destructive ending.

> [W]hen Becky and I put our convertible's top down, it stayed down ... through thunderstorms, red rock canyons, night stars, forested mountains and 1,700 miles of unending, open, untainted-by-man space.... Basically, our only wrong move was in returning to L.A. We had gotten used to the open road and it was good to us.[13]

While *Thelma & Louise* served as a beloved inspiration it also appalled viewers. In April 1992, a reader from Arleta contributed harsh words in reaction to the film and a recent report that founding second wave feminist Betty Friedan, author of *The Feminine Mystique*, had "applauded" *Thelma & Louise* at a Women in Film Academy Awards viewing party. The reader couldn't understand how Friedan could support the movie after devoting her life to the "cause of women achieving their potential." Sarcastically, she wondered what Freidan enjoyed the most: "the "near-rape," the "killings," or the "fiery explosion." Although the upset subscriber noted Friedan's explanation — that she appreciated the women's friendship — the reader was apparently unprepared to accept her answer.[14]

The opinion pages of *The Los Angeles Times* indicated that people from Huntington Beach to Santa Barbara, in addition to critics from East to West, were deeply impressed, for good or for bad, by the film. *Thelma & Louise* made people think and in some cases fume. In late July 1991, writing in response to a sexual molestation trial involving a 12-year-old victim, a reader chastised a local judge for his demeaning remarks towards the child. He allegedly called her a "tart" and "harlot" and insinuated that the girl "shared responsibility" for the abuse she endured. The judge's choice of words "should come as no surprise," the reader felt, "since adult victims of rape and other sexual abuse continue to be blamed for their victimization in courts nationwide." Recognizing a critical reflection of reality on screen where others saw mere car commercials, the reader concluded that the judge's "beliefs and actions lend new meaning" to *Thelma & Louise*. Unlike those who dismissed the women as stupid or violent, the reader connected Louise's distrust of the judicial system with actual case history that validated her fear.[15]

Of course, to take an honest stand on the movie, people needed to first see the picture. Those who didn't catch the film at theaters in the summer of 1991 but heard about the controversy traveled in droves the following winter to merchants like Blockbuster Video, Video 4 You and Plaza Video. Whether they supported, were ambivalent about, or hated the film after watching it, many people rented *Thelma & Louise* from their neighborhood video store, according to the Ventura County edition of the newspaper. "What's hot in the local video rental market?" *The Los Angeles Times* asked at the end of January 1992. "Let's just say those wild women on wheels just keep rolling along," was the reply. Three weeks out of the gate, *Thelma & Louise* was the top pick at each of the three rental outlets highlighted, located in Port Hueneme, Thousand Oaks and Ventura.[16]

Adding fuel to the eventual rental fire, the year *Thelma & Louise* came out, *Los Angeles Times* columnists stoked the great debate. Back in July 1991, two months after the film opened in theaters, *Los Angeles Times* columnist Patt Morrison logged in her pro–*Thelma & Louise* opinion, emblazoned with the headline, "Get a Grip, Guys: This Is Fantasy." Like many viewers, Morrison addressed the film's conclusion and gave her own impression of the title characters' final choice. Thelma and Louise "finished up not as Joan of Arc martyrs," Morrison analyzed, "but as tank-top samurai whose code left them the option of dying on their own terms." She spoke like an interpreter, as if the *Thelma & Louise* was something she well understood and others apparently did not, which was a common tone among great debaters. Morrison explained that *Thelma & Louise* is "the way you win when your adversary insists that you play by his rules." The ending, with its allowance for ambivalence, didn't make the columnist feel just one way about the picture. As a result of the viewing experience, she admitted to crying (which she hadn't done since *Old Yeller*, 1957) and noticed other women doing so also. Morrison wept because the ending was "triumphant," "sad," and "liberating," as well as rewarding and cathartic. Not the picture of a woman undone by emotion, Morrison didn't let tears prevent her from generating a response to the critics who worried that female viewers would follow the film's lead and commit violence.

> When *Butch Cassidy and the Sundance Kid* made train-robbing look like something you could get a merit badge for, no one wrung their hands for fear that insurance agents would shred their actuarial tables, strap on a pair of colts and go chase down the Southern Pacific. *Pretty Woman* came out, and I heard nobody fretting that their women would pull on spike-heeled boots to wobble out onto Hollywood Boulevard and into Richard's Gere's life.[17]

The newspaper printed two replies to Morrison's piece, both written by male readers who voiced similar humanist sentiments but in voices far more formal than the article to which they responded. Typical of the point/counterpoint, one commiserated with her outlook and the other didn't. The first reader joined Morrison to denounce mistreatment of women. Inspired by *Thelma & Louise*, he accepted the film as a fantasy and added encouragingly, "Women and men need each other, to share hopes and dreams, to help each other make their dreams come true or just to get a job done."[18] In contrast, after discrediting Morrison's "approval" of the film's "violent" nature, the second reader labeled *Thelma & Louise* "misguided" entertainment that achieved a "new level" of male-bashing. Objecting to all on-screen violence, except rape, which the author of the reply ignored, he concluded, "If we are to realize our potential as a species, then we must question our actions as human beings."[19] A careful screening of the film shows that before their demise Thelma and Louise do question their actions, each in their own way, but some viewers couldn't see that fact or reflect calmly through their dismay.

While *Los Angeles Times* readers located serious issues within the film to spur discussion, some of newspaper's columnists took a lighter, even selfish approach to the controversy. In 1993, Patt Morrison wrote two additional pieces mentioning the title, but neither stimulated weighty concerns. In January, Morrison's column, "Big Screen, Small Idea," denounced the idea of interactive movies that charged viewers admission and then asked them to determine the story's conclusion, in effect replacing screenwriters and directors who get paid for their work — a no-no in an industry town. Guessing what the general populace might do with *Thelma & Louise*, Morrison figured that in the hands of regular, everyday people, the women would surrender and Louise's "fab" car would get sold at police auction.[20] Later, in October, Morrison penned the "Name of the Game," pointing out cheekily that when debating nature versus nurture readers shouldn't "underestimate nomenclature." Addressing the question of what's in a name, the columnist believed that *Thelma & Louise* was "swell" because of the film's "tough names, tough women, no diminutives, no bull."[21]

While Patt Morrison sided with Kenneth Turan, syndicated columnist Art Buchwald sat closer to Sheila Benson and Peter Rainer, yet he also took a more irreverent approach to *Thelma & Louise*. Unlike viewers who wanted to delve into the film's deeper relevance, Buchwald, in 1991's "Highway Robbery After the Movie," expressed mock distress at the way the film encouraged debate. "The trouble with the film is that if you go with your wife," Buchwald warned, "she wants to discuss it all night and you can lose a lot of sleep." The columnist then reproduced the conversation he supposedly had with his wife about the picture. Conveniently, Buchwald attributed more reasonable comments to his side of the argument. After he contended that being ripped off isn't a good reason to reciprocate and commit armed robbery, his puppet wife chimed in, "If someone steals money from you, I don't see any reason why you shouldn't take money from somebody else."

Eventually, Buchwald's daffy banter narrowed in on his problem with *Thelma & Louise*. "I feel that its success is because the playing field is tilted toward the female perspective," he complained to his wife, "and that's bad for better relations between the sexes." However, Buchwald wasn't really interested in presenting a fair match, for he didn't provide his wife with a formidable response. Her reply, "It's not tilted," put up a weak protest.

A veneer of humor and a flippant tone didn't hide Buchwald's obstinate position or the meaning behind his words. In his view, it's not okay for art to highlight the imbalance between genders by reversing the usual power structure for fear that the same thing might happen in real life. According to his theory, if it's wrong that men stay ahead in the game of life, then it's equally wrong for women, too, even in fiction. However, Buchwald employed a metaphor that revealed the prejudice underlying his argument. In real life, professional "playing fields" are the province of men and require some "leveling" in order to achieve equilibrium between genders. Leaving things as they are and expecting wrongs to right themselves has not worked. The filmmakers' effort has enlivened a discussion that could lead to change while Buchwald's column belittled that aim.

In closing, Buchwald depreciated his partner and took the last word, placing even more doubt upon his already-suspect interest in a truly balanced arena. As determined by the columnist, his wife's idea of what all women want is "to be treated like men" (which would include winning access to "playing fields"), but Buchwald spoofed that goal's dramatic representation. Buchwald kidded, if *Thelma & Louise* is what women really want, he would "stay off the highways in Oklahoma and Arizona until they get it."[22]

Nearly two years later, Buchwald sought to either rectify or sarcastically reinforce his disparaging view of the title characters. The headline of his second column announced, "Thelma and Louise Make House Calls." Injecting the title with a medical twist, in this scenario the women weren't guilty of questionable logic. Instead, "after administering nuclear waste proposals for the Department of Energy," the women found themselves employed in the "watchdog division of the Reduction in Medical Bills' Agency," where they put their skills to work sifting through requests for healthcare. While a discussion regarding government involvement in healthcare reform was contemporary at the time, in terms of *Thelma & Louise* this column was even more idiosyncratic than Buchwald's previous effort. Outside of Buchwald's quirky imagination, there was no apparent connection between the film and the topic. By putting Thelma and Louise in position to solve tough problems, it seems the writer sought to further lambaste the women's intellect or demonstrate his possible remorse for dismissing them as silly. Whatever the case may have been, Buchwald's attempt to successfully associate the film with healthcare reform failed to elevate either the women or the issue.[23] But, to be fair, Buchwald wasn't the only one to maintain a twisted view of the film. In October 1993, an article on Hollywood-inspired Halloween costumes quoted one reveler who told the newspaper, "My girlfriend and I are going to be Thelma and Louise after the fall." The whimsical response favored by Buchwald was also apparent among members of the public.[24]

As if to project an air of sensibility emanating from far-out Los Angeles, Buchwald's co-worker Dianne Klein intended to set things straight, but as a result of her personal interests and family matters, the women didn't fare well in "Wasn't Hitting Boys How Thelma and Louise Got Started?" either. In her 1992 column, Klein connected *Thelma & Louise* with an incident her child had at school. Concerned by her young daughter's poor behavior, Klein equated rash, violent outbursts with the film characters. In response to her daughter's actions, which were both Thelma *and* Louise, Klein adopted a stance of disapproval and took a firm stand among con critics. As if to publicly placate her daughter's teacher, the columnist disagreed with the notion that girls and women should fight back like boys and men do. Denouncing violence as a means to an end, Klein reproached, "This is 1992," implying that society had progressed beyond such barbaric solutions to conflicts.

For self-serving purposes, Klein's commentary unabashedly assumed that Thelma and Louise began acting out as youngsters. "And about Thelma and

Louise," she commiserated, "I'm sure their parents tried their best." To build her case, she urged readers, "Think of 'Thelma and Louise: The Early Years.'" Like Buchwald gave himself a more commanding role when debating the film with his wife, Klein stretched the facts to ease her own worries over a first-grade daughter who "hit" a classmate named Fred. Looking carefully at the film, however, Thelma is decidedly "sedate" and passive at the start making her an unlikely candidate for a disorderly girl gang. The only evidence of Louise as a child happens via a quickly seen photograph taken on her birthday as she stands alone wearing a ballerina costume and smiling sweetly for the camera. In contrast to Klein's assumption, the story shows viewers how two fully-grown women dramatically change over the course of the film. Importantly, Thelma and Louise do not begin as delinquents.

In actuality, *Thelma & Louise* delivers the same message as the elementary teacher who sought to punish all forms of violent reaction, whether provoked or unprovoked. Because it is intended for a mature audience, the film offers more complexity than the basic colors that denoted the severity of misbehaving in Klein's daughter's classroom. Hearing the disturbing news that her daughter was on orange, the columnist used her space in the newspaper to divert attention from troubles on the home front. In doing so, she simplified and teased *Thelma & Louise*, using the film characters as cover and treating them like children. To some, making fun of the movie became a hip thing to do. In Klein's case, she reprimanded the women as if rape, murder and armed robbery could be corrected with a time-out.[25]

After the initial wave of reviews, letters to the editor and columns, *The Los Angeles Times* ceased mirroring the nation's split reaction to the picture and instead began a decade of unique coverage that spanned an array of the established categories. Feeling burned (an emotion explained in detail later in the chapter), the newspaper largely declined to link *Thelma & Louise* with politics or current events but more readily related the film to gender issues and popular culture, particularly Hollywood, which comes as no surprise. Like Detroit stood out for matching the film to the auto industry, Salt Lake City promoted the film's Moab locations and Washington, D.C., touted the film's political relevance, Los Angeles excelled at connecting *Thelma & Louise* to women in film, but *The Los Angeles Times* only did so throughout the first half of the decade.

As insiders worked for improved conditions and small gains for women in Hollywood were made, the California newspaper spearheaded coverage, monitored developments and gave credence to the effort. Well versed in the issues, the newspaper discussed the title while investigating an extensive list of topics including Hollywood's dearth of parts for older women; women and blacks as "special interests" who rarely have the opportunity to tell their own stories; a weak demand for strong women on television and in movies; Women in Film's first Academy Awards viewing party; 1992's post–Oscar celebrations including Callie Khouri, who joked about her inspiration for the script's male characters; an optimistic view of the "untapped" women's market; a columnist's musings about the way *Sleepless in Seattle* turned its back on the advances of *Thelma & Louise*, which he preferred; the return of westerns; "girl" movies versus "boy" movies; "tough gal" films; the 1994 conference of Women, Men & Media, a research and outreach project at the USC School of Journalism started by Betty Friedan (that year the organization could not find a suitable film for its "Breakthrough" award); a 1995 piece bemoaning the motion picture academy's slight to Robin Swicord's *Little Women*; Hollywood's failure to reflect real women's lives; an optimistic profile of female screenwriters despite depressing Writer's Guild statistics; a Jack Mathews piece on Hollywood's gender "gap," in which he spotlighted the challenges facing women in film and credited *Thelma & Louise* with closing the "Grand Canyon–size gash" between women and men in Hollywood; the financial realities for women in film when Julia Roberts was the top earner at $12 million per film; proof that an audience for female-driven films does exist as exemplified by *Thelma & Louise*'s success; the lack of female film critics and female film marketers; marketing for Callie Khouri's second film, *Something to Talk About*, which failed to mention *Thelma & Louise*; and a Valley Edition columnist's reaction to *First Wives Club* (although man-bashing was in, he didn't understand all the fuss about it or *Thelma & Louise*). As was the case at *The Atlanta Journal-Constitution*, while the film continued to resonate in other areas, articles referencing *Thelma & Louise* largely dried up in the film section of *The Los Angeles Times* after 1996. The newspaper's comprehensive coverage of women in Hollywood carried on without *Thelma & Louise* by name, though the picture's undeniable influence continued to spread throughout the film community and beyond.

Apart from expert analysis of the local economy's star product, most entertaining and telling in *The Los Angeles Times* were those articles that couldn't have sprung from anywhere else. Well ahead of newspaper readers elsewhere in the country, in October 1991, *Los Angeles Times* readers learned that *Thelma & Louise* would be released on videocassette on January 8, 1992. The studio had been debating whether or not to release the title in time for Christmas gift giving, which would have meant greater competition from other summer 1991 releases. George Feltenstein, MGM/UA's vice president of sales and marketing, told the newspaper that January represented better timing because of the winter month's traditionally strong rental sales. Plus, the "10-best lists will be out by then," he enthused. "This movie is bound to make some of those lists," he added. The company's plan, which was successful, called for using any such plugs to boost the film's chances of receiving Oscar nominations.[26]

Another aspect of newspaper coverage unique to Los Angeles is the obituaries for entertainment industry figures that appear among *Los Angeles Times* archive search results. Costume designer Elizabeth McBride,[27] co-producer Dean O'Brien[28] and stuntman Bobby Bass[29] all passed away during the *Thelma & Louise* decade. They each received mention in the newspaper, which listed *Thelma & Louise* among each's life credits.

While the debut of new automobile designs and problems plaguing American automobile manufacturers make the news in Detroit, threats of legal recourse and government intervention aimed at the film industry attract copy in Los Angeles. Although the Catholic Church was successful in forcing the movie industry to adopt a "code of decency" in the 1930s, recent attempts to curb on-screen violence have failed to substantially change Hollywood practices. Still, some have blamed filmmakers for copycat crimes and unsuccessfully sought accountability in court. Ironically, by the end of the post–*Thelma & Louise* decade, one grieving family supported the film on the very grounds upon which the great debate first arose.

According to *The Los Angeles Times*, in the spring of 2001, a Louisiana judge rejected a lawsuit against director Oliver Stone that held *Natural Born Killers* (1994) accountable for an homage crime spree. Sarah Edmondson and Ben Darras told authorities they modeled their actions after repeated viewings of Stone's film, which tells the story of two serial killers who become media stars. Edmondson and Daras killed a man and paralyzed a woman from the neck down, but the judge declared that Stone did not intend to provoke viewers in such a way and that the U. S. Constitution's First Amendment sheltered both the filmmaker and the distributor, Warner Brothers. While the prosecuting attorney representing the family of victim Patsy Byers promised an appeal, he delineated the difference between two Hollywood releases, *Natural Born Killers* and *Thelma & Louise*. According to *The Los Angeles Times*, the lawyer explained that "in the latter film the two outlaws drove over a cliff and received their punishment." In contrast, said the Byers family representative, the duo in *Natural Born Killers*, "drive off in a motor home with their two little kids." The Byers family lawyer believed Stone's film sent the message that crime does and will go unpunished. In comparison, the way filmmakers handled the violence in Callie Khouri's script — an issue that caused so much controversy a decade earlier — was deemed responsible and respectable. It took ten years, but in at least one legal opinion *Thelma & Louise* was finally vindicated.[30]

Other mentions of the movie that were unmistakably Southern Californian in nature included the offbeat and bizarre. In the fall of 1991, Nathalie Dupree introduced a recipe for homemade caramel candy by sharing her movie-going experience. "I took my mother and her cousin to see it," Dupree set up, "and they hated it as much as I loved it." Because seeing the film was her idea, the author felt obliged to treat her companions. At the concession stand she ran out of money before she had the chance to buy herself any candy, so when she returned home she learned how to make caramels. Some journalists like Dupree and columnist Dianne Klein went far out of their way in order to take part in the flurry of talk surrounding the film. "How Sweet It Is" ran just in time for Halloween.[31]

Los Angelinos concerned about their appearance might have skipped Dupree's recipe in favor of an October 1995 piece focused exclusively on abdominal workouts. One example of a fluff piece particular to the region, "Ab-session" (subtitled, "For Many Guys, Nothing Says They're Lean, Mean Fitness Machines More Than a Washboard Stomach") in the "Body Watch" column took health and beauty matters seriously. "While washboard stomachs are stereotypically linked with fitness," the newspaper explained, "it's not always the case." The article encouraged readers to give the look a try. Men tend to hold weight around the middle, said one fitness experts consulted by *The Los Angeles Times*. He counseled that "a man could be very lean, have a fairly athletic body fat percentage and still have a little abdominal fat." Besides the obvious dietary change, the key to reducing a beer belly is to cut body fat and build muscle. Brad Pitt was one of 22 celebrity males added to a fitness guru's best male abdominals list. To reinforce the importance and appeal of a ripped mid-section, a photo caption that ran with the article read, "Brad Pitt's abs starred in *Thelma & Louise*."[32]

Another prime example of an article peculiar to Southern California ran at the end of 1992. A couple of years before O.J. Simpson pulled a stunt that many newspapers compared to *Thelma & Louise* (but *The Los Angeles Times* did not), the newspaper published a piece that eerily forecasted later events. Columnist S. J. Diamond gave a name — "freeway fliers" — to people who flee the police by driving away. Although this was not a new trend, live television coverage of "freeway fliers" was new. Diamond interviewed a spokesperson for the California Highway Patrol who claimed that Los Angeles didn't host more incidents of televised police chases compared to other metropolitan areas, even though personal observations may have indicated otherwise. Instead, due to viewer interest, supposedly more television stations in the area were willing to interrupt programming in order to broadcast such events. Recently, a maroon Ford Escort had raced at speeds of 95 mph from Barstow to the San Fernando Valley (a 180 mile span) keeping a large audience "riveted for hours," according to the newspaper. Along with the CHP spokesperson, a psychiatrist at UCLA's Neuropsychiatric Institute voiced concern about people copying what they see in the movies. Worried that the hope of stardom might influence further "freeway fliers," the researcher brought up *Thelma & Louise*, in particular the ending. He told the newspaper that people who choose flight "have a sense of continuing mobility, a sense they can drive off forever, like Thelma and Louise, who end up in mid-air."[33]

When the salacious trucker refuses to apologize for his lewd behavior, Thelma and Louise shoot out his tires and accidentally blow-up his rig. Susan Sarandon and Geena Davis star as Louise Sawyer and Thelma Dickerson in MGM's *Thelma & Louise* (1991).

Not all of the articles found in Los Angeles upheld the area's reputation for being air-headed and flighty, though much of the copy generated around the title did support a picture of media obsession. *The Los Angeles Times* also offered more sober, less sensational *Thelma & Louise* coverage, especially in regards to women's issues. However, most of the journalists who wrote about the film and feminism for the newspaper were independent observers who failed to make clear sense of the great debate, as if smog blurred their vision. Articles mentioning *Thelma & Louise* in an unmistakably L.A. fashion, like the stories about steely abdominals and "freeway fliers," represented the newspaper better than pieces that supplied personal perspectives and tried to dig deep. When *The Los Angeles Times* noted trends and covered local happenings in conjunction with *Thelma & Louise*, its presentation was interesting and fun; when analyzing the women question apart from Hollywood most times the newspaper fell short of convincing and instead sounded confused.

When in doubt, stick to the basics. In the fall of 1991, the Southern California newspaper looked at women working in radio and reported that in the Los Angeles area listeners wouldn't hear "in any substantial capacity" female disc jockeys during radio primetime, often referred to as "morning drive time," from five a.m. to ten a.m. An industry observer quoted in "Radio Drive Time Isn't Prime Time for Women" maintained that this fact was true across the country. As in the *Terminator* series, where Linda Hamilton needed Arnold Schwarzenegger to legitimize her hardcore approach, most women on-air in the morning served as sidekicks to men. As for the reasons for gender bias in radio, Claudia Puig uncovered a few possibilities. Like the bias against women in movies, there was no one cause and both women and men played a part.

> Those who make their living in radio offer no single explanation for this disparity. Rather, they postulate a variety of theories ranging from an inherent male bias on the part of those in charge, to women not being socialized to aspire to the job of wacky morning deejay, to the notion that both men and women prefer the sound of a male voice in the mornings.

Even within an aural medium, a woman's "image" is often restricted to her sexual nature. Once told not to mention a pregnancy on-air for fear of alienating male listeners, former disc jockey Cynthia Fox shared her frustrations about not being able to simply be herself and get paid for it. Fox wasn't interested in projecting herself as a purely sexual persona, "putting on some bedroom voice," as she described it. Yet she told the newspaper that in 1987 she was "advised" not to discuss her condition during her shift. "I was told that guys would no longer find me a fantasy figure," she explained. Female disc jockeys, sporting provocative names like Rita Wilde and Caroline Fox, and particularly those with the "throatiest voices and most suggestive deliveries," are hired for late-night slots, *The Los Angeles Times* assessed.

Perhaps the most disturbing force preventing women's advancement is women limiting themselves. One of radio personality Rick Dees' sidekicks, Ellen K., admitted to the newspaper that she prefers "turning on the radio and hearing a man." She supposed, "I guess it's just something with authority." This attitude recalls moviegoers preferring to see films starring men. Giving credence to the idea of anti-female bias supported by women, the female disc jockey elaborated, "I think if I turned" on the radio, and "I heard just a woman I would think she was sort of masculine." Listening to radio, like watching televised sports and viewing big-budget films, the public has trouble accepting females who lead. Scanning the future of women in radio, Cynthia Fox wondered, "Where are the *Thelma & Louise* of morning radio?"[34]

A week later, a *Los Angeles Times* reader and local AM deejay wrote a response pointing out what she felt Puig's piece overlooked. In the process, Tracy Miller added to the discussion about women on air and replied to Cynthia Fox's *Thelma & Louise* metaphor. Although Miller didn't use the film to make her point, she did inform the newspaper that KFI-AM's "TNT in the Morning with Tracey Miller and Terri-Rae Elmer" featured "two women in the spotlight backed up by two men," which she labeled a "ground-breaker for women." Puig mentioned the program in her article, but she had neglected to discuss the show. To apprise readers of women's advancement in radio, Miller stated that on-air she and her co-host were allowed to be "informative" and "creative" individuals. Because of a "more sophisticated" AM listening audience compared to "wild and wacky" FM morning programs, Miller's pregnancy became a "nine-month running segment" on KFI-AM. Furthermore, Miller claimed that after she gave birth, management arranged for her to broadcast the show from home. Because of her experiences, Miller concluded that women are making "greater strides" both in the work place and in their personal lives. She believed:

> [M]en are not entirely to blame for the lack of women on morning radio, but I will take it a step further by saying that if women want to really get ahead in radio, we'll have to start doing something men have been doing all along: supporting each other.
> As for the answer to the article's question, "where are the Thelma and Louise of morning radio?" I'm not sure, but I do know one thing—they're not on KFI. After all, we know what happened to those two.[35]

Outside of its bearing on Hollywood, *The Los Angeles Times* didn't directly assign heavy-duty relevance to the film. As exemplified in Claudia Puig's piece, in regards to women's issues especially, for the most part external commentators such as Cynthia Fox and Tracy Miller along with staff editorialists and guest commentators presented personal perspectives about the film and its impact. Apart from random comments and purchased views, the newspaper as an entity espoused more of a hands-off approach. News editors declined to connect *Thelma & Louise* to developments such as the 1992 national political season and the wave of women entering politics, though one staff writer reported that *The Washington Post* did. As if it were a matter of evolving policy, *The Los Angeles Times* seemed to back away from the ongoing great debate, yet the Southern California newspaper didn't mind when individuals occasionally brought up the film.

At the start of the decade, the newspaper set its pattern of coverage—mentioning the title but leaving hard-hitting remarks to others who could be quoted directly. In 1991, while covering local abortion rights rallies *The Los Angeles Times* surveyed a crowd in attendance on the lawn in front of the federal building in Westwood. Among the people gathered, the Southern California newspaper highlighted "flamboyant ACT UP/LA activists," elected officials, a rabbi, and "the screenwriter for *Thelma & Louise*." The article, "Rallies Try to Put Abortion Issue Back in Spotlight," did not name Callie Khouri, as if she'd already received too much press that summer due to the film's high-profile reception. As is usually the case in Hollywood, the newspaper disregarded the screenwriter, following the custom of directors, producers, other moguls and studio executives, who traditionally view writers as underlings.

The newspaper name-dropped a controversial product but declined to advertise its creator or take any further stand.[36]

In stark contrast to the newspaper's miserly reporting, later that year during the infamous fall of 1991, Howard Rosenberg wrote an involved though convoluted commentary on "mixed messages" that he believed perplexed "even some men who respect women as equals in every way." Given the timing and subject matter of his piece — the tension between men and women — a discussion of the season's top political story would have been incomplete without a nod to *Thelma & Louise*. Rosenberg contended that Anita Hill's demeanor and style of dress matched her purported conservative politics, but newswomen and actresses who appeared on news magazine shows wore too-revealing "micromini" skirts. Taken together, these images were confusing, Rosenberg maintained. In his view, women on television who chose to wear what the author pegged "provocative" outfits that could have "stopped the presses" muddled the issue of sexual harassment. However, what was actually muddled in Rosenberg's piece was the distinction between women, as if Hill or any other woman aren't full-fledged individuals but one in a herd. Revealing clothing had nothing to do with Hill or the veracity of her testimony, Rosenberg stressed, yet it had "everything to do with the way men view women, and everything to do with mixed messages." But whose fault is that?

Televised images are important, he argued, because so many people watch and absorb them. Still, the medium's two-dimensional portraits are problematic. In the business of earning high ratings and accumulating advertising revenue, the television industry oversimplifies ideas and jumbles thoughts, which Americans might not bother to wade through. Rosenberg pointed out how the small screen repeatedly ran "side-by-side pictures" of the two key players in the Hill vs. Thomas showdown. This reduction of ideas to mug shots served to heighten viewer anticipation for who might lose rather than foster concern about sexual harassment and its effects on society. Rosenberg explained that although "gender inequality" would not end with the outcome, Americans might be most impressed with idea of a "winner take-all war of the sexes, he representing the dominant male establishment, she Thelma and Louise." In his analogy, the Hill-Thomas encounter played like a football game with the film characters acting as mascots for the underdog's team.

If Rosenberg's "mixed message" theory was correct, Thomas' victorious ascension to the Supreme Court meant that due to non-germane issues — clothing prerogatives and the pressure for females seen in the media to look a certain way — Hill and her supporters were trounced in the eyes of the general public. In short, the wardrobe decisions of a relatively few women may have determined society's view of the entire gender's legal rights. Perhaps sexual harassment failed to be taken seriously because of a non sequitur involving the whims of fashion where they didn't belong. Forecasting a loss for the women's team, Rosenberg claimed that "hot pants" wouldn't change Hill's rights under the law, but they would definitely influence attitudes. Although Hill didn't wear "hot pants," Rosenberg felt that other Americans, in addition to himself, might have trouble keeping separate issues straight.

Like Nicolaus Mills' piece on masculinity published in Atlanta, Rosenberg's essay didn't offer any solutions. The author simply stated his view, defending the "confused" male without looking at the situation from any other point of view. Rosenberg alluded to but did not name the "female TV interviewer" whose "somber" tête-à-tête with a male "political figure" wrapped up with a shot of her dress and revealing hemline, yet he didn't try hard enough to get to the bottom of the problem. Rosenberg still didn't judge the show's camera operator, television director or audience, just the "female TV interviewer." Ready to pounce, he was less cautious regarding the identities of the two actresses wearing short skirts whom he did name, yet Rosenberg didn't consider the pressure women are under to attract viewer attention by way of their looks. Instead, he implied that all females in the public eye should wear more conservative clothing to prevent confusion — never mind that the public spends big bucks on scantily clad women. Anita Hill and any woman who dresses provocatively are too easily interchangeable for people to keep straight, he contended. Conspicuously, Rosenberg didn't mention any trouble separating thoughts of Clarence Thomas' alleged behavior from men such as Larry Flint and Howard Stern, who've built lucrative careers around giving consumers exactly what they want: objectified and demeaning images of women.[37]

When associated with women's issues, *Thelma & Louise* didn't fare well in the newspaper's editorial section. Within the next year's so-called "Year of Women in Politics," Elaine Ciulla Kamarck examined the women of the Republican Party who played key roles in the 1992 presidential election. Profiling the combined efforts of Mary Matalin, Leslie Goodman, Katherine Murray, Chris Seeger, Condoleeza Rice, Barbara Bush and Marilyn Quayle, Kamarck's article, "GOP Women Serve Grit, Not Tea," looked at gender "under the big tent." Commenting rather than straight news reporting, the author presented her theory that the Republican Party put all their women up front to "deflect attention," in Kamarck's words, from a "position on abortion that constitutes cruel and unusual punishment to women." She determined that the prominence of women at that year's Houston convention was due in large part to hype rather than true commitment to inclusion.

Although she didn't find it necessary to directly draw the film into her discussion, Kamarck did cover another newspaper that jumped at the same opportunity. To add punch to her contention, parenthetically Kamrack added that *The Washington Post* was responsible for calling Matalin and Torie Clarke the "Thelma and Louise of the GOP," as if the East Coast newspaper had added its own spin to the Republican Party's misleading front. Meanwhile, across the country the capital newspaper presented the nickname as common vernacular, like *The Los Angeles Times* covered Brad Pitt's celebrated abdominal muscles.

Kamarck wanted to discuss *Thelma & Louise*, but skirted doing so directly. She asserted that Republican women were needed during the presidential campaign season because the "men of the macho party" were "exhausted and confused," much like Howard Rosenberg claimed to be. Kamarck affixed to the GOP a western scenario similar to *Thelma & Louise* but denied giving the film its due credit.

> If they were to make a Western movie about the GOP circa 1992, it would feature an attack on the homestead that left the men wounded and in danger of dying. It would end with the women hitching up their skirts, taking the men's weapons and saving the day. At least that's what the women of the macho party hope to do.[38]

More straightforwardly but with enervation and audacity, two opinion pieces published during this period related *Thelma & Louise* expressly to the women's movement. In one case this was accomplished through Callie Khouri, but in both instances independent voices poked out from underneath the umbrella of the newspaper's masthead. Nineteen ninety-three's "A Woman's Place" (subtitled, "It's No Longer Likely to Be in the Home") accepted women's advancement as the new status quo, while 1994's "The Trouble with Male-Bashing" (subtitled, "It Used to Be a Political Statement, but Now It's Just Name-Calling") bucked some recent developments.

The first essay assumed that the world was completely changed by feminism and totally explicable in sarcastic terms. Jonathan Gold's essay described the "endemic" trend of professional women marrying artists and activists, reversing the *Leave It to Beaver*, Ward and June Cleaver scenario. In Los Angeles, unemployed husbands were "available for lunch" while their wives had places to be. Gold was one of those husbands, and, with time on his hands, he admitted to "gender guilt." The author saw *Thelma & Louise* whether he wanted to or not, as if watching the movie was a requirement for all evolved males. On behalf of Southern California men, Gold proclaimed with mock pride, "We have read *A Room of One's Own*," even "if we haven't actually purchased male-shame-inducing Bikini Kill records or seen *Thelma & Louise* through more than once."

Happy to let a woman support the household, Gold testified that MTV-generation males did not believe their gender entitled them to anything. In a droll, self-deprecating tone, he added that "unlike our fathers," his contemporaries had "no problems working for women bosses," but would prefer not to work at all. Gold didn't seem to share Howard Rosenberg's confusion. Instead, while surveying the terrain of women who've "got to work overtime and follow the rules and make connections if they want to succeed," he was affected by malaise, for the West Coast filled the absence of a newly invigorated masculinity that Nicolaus Mills searched for in Atlanta.[39]

A year later, Deanne Stillman wrote a long and winding essay that at its core blamed a nebulous image of feminism for rampant male-bashing. Although she gave the women's movement due credit for the good it has achieved, including abortion rights and gains toward equal pay, Stillman empathized with men in the face of so much verbal abuse "facilitated" by the women's movement. She downplayed Anita Hill's testimony, as if women were wasting the public's time and money by fighting over minor issues. She roasted women who championed the likes of Lorena Bobbitt and pictured a sea of women siding against men, presumably with bloody knives in hand. Stillman belabored her point that women were the problem but offered few facts to support her claims, didn't detail any statistics, and didn't paint any women in a positive light. Based solely on sweeping generalities and personal anecdotes about friends who left their low-income, infertile husbands, Stillman called for an end to male-bashing. Observing the situation in white and black terms, without any gradation, she insinuated that women's attitudes were in need of overhauling, not society's.

Insinuating that feminists were self-involved, Stillman, with the help of an interview found in Naomi Wolf's *Fire with Fire*, highlighted Callie Khouri's purported worry for her career after publicly adopting the f word. As recorded in *Fire*, Khouri and Wolf discussed closeted feminists who are afraid to voice their thoughts, as Stillman put it, "because they work in a company town" such as Los Angeles. Stillman argued that it's not just feminists in Hollywood who keep their beliefs secret. She stated that "no one in Hollywood shows their beliefs too openly for fear of saying the wrong thing," but Stillman was mistaken, as evidenced during the 2003 U.S.-led war against Saddam Hussein in Iraq. Despite receiving considerable flack, many Hollywood personalities, including Susan Sarandon, Sean Penn, Jessica Lange, Martin Sheen, Mike Farrell and Madonna, stepped forward to take a stand against Operation Iraqi Freedom.

Amid her twisted logic and meandering prose, in which she utilized the same flawed approach as the problem she identified, Stillman made at least one good point. Most convincingly, Stillman believed that absolute statements such as "all men are jerks" advocate an "us-vs.-them philosophy that only serves to continue the baring of fangs and keeps everyone in their own caves." Similar to John Leo's assessment of the *Thelma & Louise*–inspired American Greetings card, Stillman correctly pointed out that many would be offended by the phrases "all women are jerks" or "all blacks are jerks," even though throughout her article she implied that all women are jerks. Urging all parties to move forward, in the spirit of conciliation Stillman proclaimed, "We all possess the jerk chromosome."[40] If we put Stillman's best argument in terms of the movie, *Thelma & Louise* reminds us that both sexes can screw up.

As if Hollywood truly is the only game in town, in the years following the film's release *The Los Angeles Times* failed to offer readers persuasive and insightful commentary regarding gender issues and *Thelma & Louise*. A couple of years after Stillman's disjointed and contradictory piece, a former member of the board of directors of the National Organization for Women in New York City sought to reveal the double standard he found underlying the 1996 film *First Wives Club*, which was based on Olivia Goldsmith's 1992 novel. More like Art Buchwald and Howard Rosenberg than Jonathan Gold, in "First Wives Club: Thelma and Louise Exhale," Warren Farrell objected to the destruction of "a few men in general just to make a broader point." Though he didn't share what he thought that point might be, Farrell was plainly offended by women's revenge. Meanwhile, he had nothing to say about husbands who dump their wives for younger, thinner models.

Farrell wasn't interested in allowing fictional women from various backgrounds their chance to act out frustrations, so he tried to hide the real problem he had with their deeds. Diffusing his foggy argument regarding sexism with a misleading discussion of race and class, Farrell complained that *First Wives Club* used "upper-middle-class white women" as "*Waiting to Exhale* used upper-middle-class black women" and "*Thelma & Louise* used middle-class white women." All three films jockeyed stereotypes, according to Farrell, "to symbolize the plight of all women whose dream of being swept away was swept away." Trying a second bent to discredit the movie, Farrell juxtaposed the nationwide success of *First Wives Club* to local support directed at convicted murderer Betty Broderick, who killed her ex-husband and his second wife in bed as they slept. But, to reiterate Deanne Stillman, not all women are jerks, and, more specifically, not all women are ready to engage in destructive retaliation or back real-life women who do. Farrell's empty discussion regarding race, class and crime simply hid what lurked behind, which was similar to John Leo's 1991 argument against *Thelma & Louise*. Though "First Wives Club: Thelma and Louise Exhale" failed to provide a cohesive thesis, reading between the lines reveals that Farrell and others weren't comfortable with artistic expression. In modern times, emerging female characters sometimes fight to redefine gender roles, reject poor treatment and demand the power to control their own lives. These actions stoke anger rather than quell it, and result in stories that people who read art only in literal terms may find disturbing.

After his first two avenues of attack fell short, Farrell undertook a third equally shaky strategy. The true heart of Farrell's essay — empathetic rhetoric explicating men — elucidated real problems, but whether his analysis was correct or even pertinent remained unclear. Stipulating that "failed marriages hurt both sexes," which is a reasonable contention, he listed histrionic examples of unhappy men who balanced out each unhappy woman. In dramatic terms, he detailed the plight of the driven, workaholic father whose family deserts him because he worked too much, yet "the women's crisis centers do not invite his call." Opposite "each single mother," he singled out the "single dad" whose worth becomes reduced to child support payments "for children who have been turned psychologically against him." Turning his attention to wrongs done to men, Farrell argued that women, with the apparent support of law enforcement and the courts, unfairly denied fathers their rights in direct proportion to the number of fathers who abandoned their families: "For each woman faced with a deadbeat dad, there is a desperate dad, desperate to love his children, but told that if he comes any closer, she will accuse him of being a child molester or a wife beater."

Farrell looked at feminism through the lens of a few special films and found real-life women totally blaming men for all their problems. He wanted to redirect this blame and aim it right back at the opposition. One problem with Farrell's case was that he offered no evidence to back his supposition about the numbers of unhappy spouses matching up. He shared his opinion that women commit crimes of the heart and fail to support their husbands emotionally and sexually in equal numbers to "deadbeat" dads and wife-jilting husbands, but without the burden of statistical evidence. Farrell asserted, "For each 40-year-old wife turned in for two 20s, there is a 40-year-old husband caught between a sexless marriage and his moral scruples," which may or may not be true. Farrell could never prove his hypothesis. When people tried to figure out the number of sympathetic males in *Thelma & Louise*, many lost proper count even though there are less than ten males with speaking parts in the film. Still, Farrell demanded that it is necessary to see all of the destructive acts men and women commit at home as occurring with equal regularity.

Rather than evaluating individuals on a case-by-case basis, which makes the most sense, Farrell wanted to spread guilt uniformly between genders. He implied that an even slate would make men feel better and more equal to women. Ironically, despite his call for balance, Farrell accused women of engendering a one-sided "war." In conclusion, Farrell called for mutual empathy and repeated the old cliché about walking a mile "in each others' moccasins." Unfortunately, he didn't address how his revisionist ledger would actually lower the incidence of criminal abuse, neglect or broken families.[41]

Since issues affecting women deserve greater attention than they have received in the past, early in the post-release decade features like the Claudia Puig piece concentrating on the dearth of women in radio served the newspaper's readership well. Unfortunately, a majority of the articles filed throughout the time were less useful. To our detriment as a country, matters most central to gender strife, shown in crimes such as rape, receive the least time and space of all. Nationwide, few articles turned to *Thelma & Louise* when covering the crime, probably due to a low number of stories dedicated to it. Reflecting Southern California's proximity to Mexico, early in 1997, the article "Mexico Murder Trial Puts Women's Rights in Spotlight" detailed a criminal case where life did seem to imitate art. Instead of circling revenge or pacing before calls of male-bashing with cluttered opinion, the article purveyed a news story involving actual rape, self-defense and murder south of the border. Here, *The Los Angeles Times* moved into otherwise unseen and uncharacteristically weighty territory in terms of associating *Thelma & Louise* with relevant current events. Pushing comparisons to the film in the first line of the article, the newspaper reasoned that the "machismo of Mexican society leaves little room for strong female characters, a la the movie *Thelma & Louise*." According to the Southern California newspaper, which cited the film a second time within the piece as if to justify the first instance, women's rights supporters "acknowledge" that the murder of Juan Miguel Cabrera had "chilling echoes" to a scene in the film.

As retold by *The Los Angeles Times*, Claudia Rodriguez and Victoria Hernandez spent the night drinking and dancing with Cabrera. Outside the Meson Tarasco bar, just prior to sunrise, Cabrera ignored Rodriguez's resistance to his advances and attempted to rape her. To stop him, Rodriguez fatally shot Cabrera with a .22-caliber pistol, which she carried as a result of two recent attacks. In the article's words, the difference between Victoria and Claudia and Thelma and Louise is that the Mexican women "did not flee afterward." (Already in Mexico, where could they go?)

Although Mexican law allows for deadly force in pleas of self-defense, at first the judge blamed the attempted rape victim, who was a married mother of five, for being out late. Though rape clearly affects women, naturally the crime also touches families and society. Cabrera was also married and the father of two children. Disregarding Cabrera's free will and a father's equal responsibility to his offspring, the magistrate purportedly argued that Rodriguez "provoked" Cabrera "to attack her so she could shoot him in some vital part of his body."[42]

Six months later, after protests from local women's rights supporters and scrutiny from similar groups around the world, the prosecutor dropped the murder charge against Rodriguez,[43] who was found guilty of using excessive force, fined nominally and freed.[44] No doubt Louise would be pleased and perhaps amazed by this advance in attitudes toward rape victims who fight back (even though Rodriguez found justice only because of the role feminist activists played in the outcome of her story). More beneficial to women than *The Los Angeles Times*' attempts at feminist discussion, reporting on current events such as this helps spread the word and advance gender justice.

In most cases, *The Los Angeles Times* continued to let essayists and guest commentators include *Thelma & Louise* in their opinion pieces rather than cover it forthrightly outside of space dedicated to editorials. Occasionally, however, as the decade elapsed, when ideal opportunities presented themselves editors took a stab at uncovering greater relevance. In 1998, the newspaper ran a feature on Mavis Leno, wife of Jay Leno. The piece was tagged "Stealing Back the Lives of Women" and focused on her work as a board member for the Feminist Majority Fund. Contrary to the assertion of leading members of the religious right such as Pat Robertson and Jerry Falwell, feminists don't encourage terrorist attacks against the United States. In fact, the opposite is true. Three years before the September 11 attacks, the Lenos donated $100,000 to help "increase awareness" of women living under the Taliban. The Los Angeles newspaper described how the host of *The Tonight Show* wrestled Hulk Hogan to raise money for a charity championed by his wife.

As reported in the article, The Feminist Majority's Campaign to Stop Gender Apartheid began its crusade in 1996 in an attempt to make the public aware of the atrocities occurring in Afghanistan and to put pressure on the country's ruling party to restore women's rights. Mavis Leno explained in earnest, "Saving these women is in the interest of every woman on the planet." In an article subtitled "Mavis Leno Is Leading the Charge Against Afghanistan's Taliban, Who Are Subjugating Women and Girls," *The Los Angeles Times* commented with appropriate sobriety that third-world religious discrimination against women "is not a glamorous issue, nor is it easily remedied."

In Los Angeles, people are apparently clued in and caring when they can see what's going on. To make a serious global issue more attractive to local readers, "Stealing Back the Lives of Women" attached a touch of sparkle to the facts. Providing a quick glimpse behind the scenes, the newspaper described the Feminist Majority's headquarters in West Hollywood as "an odd pinkish building with reflective glass doors and windows" complete with an "enormous signed poster from *Thelma & Louise*" and "Price Club–sized bottles of Rolaids and Motrin."[45] Not big on providing clear analysis when it came to feminism, *The Los Angeles Times* urged readers to decide what this assortment of information may have meant.

The global mistreatment of women is no laughing matter, but comparatively, women in the western world can afford to relax and smile. Most women in the United States enjoy far easier lives than women in Afghanistan, as the numerous articles found in newspapers across the country regarding women who spent their leisure time and extra money traveling together proved. When *The Los Angeles Times* covered the trend late in the decade, like so many others, it did so with a little help from *Thelma & Louise*. In 1998, a new column dedicated expressly to women's travel opened with lines from the film. Written by a fan, Susan Spano, the column called on Thelma to christen its debut. Writing in the relatively calm wake of the great debate, Spano was able to discuss the movie in her own terms while avoiding the orig-

inal turbulence caused by the controversial release. Under her care, the film
was a tainted artifact that embodied a few good traits amid detractions.

> "I always wanted to travel. I just never got the opportunity," says Geena Davis
> in *Thelma & Louise*, a movie about two girlfriends on a wild car trip that
> doesn't end happily. Still, I love the film because it touches on two things that
> make my life worthwhile: travel and women friends.

Believing that "women define themselves in relationships," Spano collected "anecdotal evidence" about the numbers of women vacationing
together. Though she didn't attribute the trend of women travelling together
to the film, she found a renaissance of female-only trips to be in "full spring."
To historically ground her piece extolling the popularity and joys of women-
only excursions, Spano harked back to George Eliot instead of Virginia Woolf.
"What do we live for," Spano quoted, "if it is not to make life less difficult
for each other?"[46]

Perhaps after scanning the archives for other *Los Angeles Times* columns
that touched on the title, two years later, in 2000, Spano returned to the
film but with an even warier attitude. Though she evidently studied and
appreciated women's lives, perhaps by this time societal pressure to criticize
(exemplified in programs like *The Tonight Show*) got the better of her efforts.
In a column called "Seeking Lessons in Life from Stars Who Traveled Across
the Silver Screen," she expressed how movies "shaped" her as a traveler. Spano
recalled Bette Davis' newfound verve in *Now, Voyager* (1942) and Dorothy's
transformative slippers in *The Wizard of Oz* (1939), and also listed travel role
models as well as trips to avoid. Although her heart still rooted for *Thelma
& Louise*, this time around her words offered more bite and a taste of ambivalence, as if she had come to her senses. Spano asked emphatically, "who
would want to end up" like Thelma and Louise? Instead of risking imper-
fection, she ordered up a hand-tailored mannequin to meet her specifications.
Once safely divorced from the "harm" Mrs. Dickerson inflicts on the police
officer, the columnist added Thelma's "steel" into her mix of an ideal traveler.[47]

If *Thelma & Louise* is a reliable measure, in Southern California hard
news and movies don't often mix, perhaps in an effort to separate professional
journalism from the glitter of Hollywood. At least in terms of its coverage of
Thelma & Louise, from 1991 to 2001, *The Los Angeles Times* was less overtly
political than other major newspapers. In 1991, *The Los Angeles Times* produced the Hendrik Hertzberg article (from its Washington, D.C., desk) comparing presidential candidate Jerry Brown and his advisor Patrick H. Caddell
to the film characters. Reprinted around the country, "Is Brown and Caddell
Race a *Thelma & Louise* Spree?" constituted the West Coast newspaper's sole
incidence of renaming people after the film.[48] Otherwise, *The Los Angeles*

Times' newsroom was hesitant to associate the film with politics in any original or forceful way.

Occasionally, like films made by or starring women do well at the box
office, individual idiosyncrasies snuck through the newspaper's screen. Much
like journalists in Washington, D.C., journalists in the City of Angels understand the power of putting on a good show especially when running for president of the United States. Soon after the November 1992 election, editorialist
Frank Kosa admitted to readers that he needed a "12 step" recovery program
to withdraw from his campaign jokes. To account for his addiction, Kosa primarily blamed Ross Perot's dramatic display and the third party candidate's
creation of a "concept for which he'll go down in history," that being the "far
center." Kosa proudly testified that he "loved" the election season so much,
he abandoned his friends and "went flying off the cliff—like Thelma and
Louise."[49]

Apart from personal comments like Susan Spano's and Frank Kosa's
printed in the travel and political sections, for the most part *Los Angeles Times*
editors outside of entertainment and fashion ignored or downplayed the film
to a self-conscious degree. In 1995, a long article featuring Democrats Barbara Boxer and Dianne Feinstein discounted the *Thelma & Louise* label that
other newspapers embraced. Though the fictional women received prominent mention, they appeared only briefly in the dismissive headline "Forget
the Thelma and Louise Thing." The article was subtitled "Barbara Boxer and
Dianne Feinstein Are Way Beyond the Election-year Road Show," as if seeking to distance show biz from politics. Later in the piece, when the author
might have continued the comparison with the film characters while specu-
lating "whether California's two very different female senators get along," the
author and editors chose not to do so.[50]

Speaking on its own behalf, *The Los Angeles Times* news desk was more
comfortable with an easy-going approach to remembering the film. In 2001,
the West Coast newspaper covered out-going Attorney General Janet Reno's
much-discussed plans for a drive across the country, granting the movie a tiny
nod within a generous feature. "A sort of *Thelma & Louise* road trip," the
newspaper said, as did countless others, here with Reno stipulating that there
would be "no Louise." As the country's top lawyer and someone opposed to
the death penalty, which she judged a means to "vengeance" rather than a
tool to combat crime, no doubt Reno found Louise's charge of murder more
objectionable than Thelma's charge of armed robbery.[51]

An earlier *Los Angeles Times* article published in 1993 reflected on the
way controversial newsmakers "cope with the humiliation that accompanies"
public scrutiny. "The Agony of Humiliation Behavior" glanced over the manner in which Richard Nixon, Anita Hill and William Kennedy Smith handled the press after notoriety's onset. Ironically, since he was least important
to national matters, the latter was portrayed as having the most difficult time

slipping under the cultural radar. Gossiping as much as reporting, the article told readers that the omnipresent T-shirt warning "William Kennedy Smith, Meet Thelma and Louise" was seen hanging in the window of a feminist bookstore in Albuquerque. According to the newspaper, the bookstore was located near the University of New Mexico, next door to a coffee shop, which was frequented by Smith, who was a medical student in residency.[52] Embodying the split between hard news and lifestyle coverage uncovered in *The Atlanta Journal-Constitution*, when it came to *Thelma & Louise*, *The Los Angeles Times* gravitated toward fluff.

It's no surprise that many mentions of *Thelma & Louise* made by *The Los Angeles Times* in this period popped up in light features dealing with the film industry apart from the "special case" of women in Hollywood or that entertainment features that referenced the picture stayed on the sunny side and radiated a breezy tone. In 1993, *Thelma & Louise* appeared in a Peter Rainer piece about date movies, which contained much less passion than "True or False: *Thelma & Louise* Just Good Ol' Boys?" from 1991. "Trying to Pick a Romantic Movie?" noted the genre's demise and listed whether films were "good" or "bad" for women and men. Leaving room for dissent, the article rated *Thelma & Louise* "good" for women, "if you think it's high time women took control of their own destiny and empowered themselves with the privileges of the patriarchy," and bad for men, "if you're not Brad Pitt." For a change, Rainer reduced the presence of men in film to their looks, a situation women in film have endured for decades.[53]

Recalling the article about men's abdominal muscles (or lack thereof) and the quip about Brad Pitt's flat stomach starring in *Thelma & Louise*, according to *The Los Angeles Times*, if anyone was objectified in the film, it was definitely J.D., not Thelma or Louise. In 1999, announcing the opening of a country-western style bar and restaurant, the newspaper proclaimed the return of the cowboy, L.A.-style. One of many fashion and style features to mention the film, the piece explained, "We're not talking about those big-butted men in tight Wrangler jeans and Garth Brooks–American flag shirts," but "that sexy breed of booted boys" strutting down Sunset Boulevard and "epitomized by Brad Pitt in *Thelma & Louise* or John Travolta in *Urban Cowboy*."[54] In 2001, Pitt's on-screen look was again regaled, this time in an article about the return of the mullet, a much-mocked hairdo.sometimes called "the ape drape" or "the squirrel pelt" for its short sides and long back. According to the newspaper's lifestyle pages, a website dedicated to the hirsute style, which purported to quote Pitt, claimed that the haircut he wore in *Thelma & Louise* helped propel the actor's career.[55]

As if a following a special decree, *The Los Angeles Times* hesitated to suggest that *Thelma & Louise* was relevant outside of Hollywood. However, in 1996, the newspaper implied that films could contain important messages, but instead of taking a stand and risking charges of bias or frivolity, it asked independent voices to tackle more serious commentary about the film for "The Reel America: The Films That Show Us Who We Are." The newspaper surveyed artists, journalists, academics, cultural spokespersons and political leaders for their views about meaningful movies, asking each respondee to supply three movies that "best sum up the national persona." Even among the cultural elite, the results reflected the movie-going audiences' preference for male-led films. Among almost 40 published responses, few of the films selected featured female leads, but Pulitzer Prize–winning author Francis Fitzgerald (*Fire in the Lake: The Vietnamese and the Americans in Vietnam*) named *Thelma & Louise*, as well as *Mr. Smith Goes to Washington* (1939) and *Mississippi Masala* (1992). In Fitzgerald's view, *Thelma & Louise* is a prototypical American "road movie."

> Anyone can drop out, disappear and become an outlaw — civilization is that thin. European "road movies" tend to be pilgrimages — they are going to some place, as in *The Canterbury Tales*. The American road movies are stories of escape and going toward the unknown. The point is never the goal but what happens along the way. In those movies there is no tragedy of separation and no desire to return.[56]

After this foray into cultural analysis, the newspaper's ambivalence toward the film's contribution resumed in a brief article listing "escapist movies," which pushed video rentals. Late in 1997, *The Los Angeles Times* encouraged readers, "If you can't get away for the weekend, rent a movie that did." Short on reflections, in contrast to Francis Fitgerald's analysis, this article paired *Thelma & Louise* with the suggestion, "Don't try this at home."[57]

Although editors in Detroit underappreciated *Thelma & Louise*, they weren't completely off-base when they published articles overestimating the automobile's contribution to Southern California, Hollywood and the movies. Like the Motor City, Los Angeles is cemented in long boulevards and driven by automobile travel. In 1998, commenting on the ease of filmmaking with roofless vehicles, *The Los Angeles Times* spotlighted the role of convertibles in the movies. A quiz accompanying the main article, "Just Can't Top This," tested reader knowledge of movie stars who "went topless and still retained their dignity." Unlike the comparable piece that ran in *The Detroit Free Press*, *The Los Angeles Times* didn't elevate cars over stars, no doubt acting on the same urge, to bolster local egos. But, like editors in Detroit were unfamiliar with the film's specifics, editors in Los Angeles also failed to detect copy errors relating to *Thelma & Louise*. "Lights! Camera! Top Down!" brazenly and mistakenly stated, "OK, so we all know it was a blue 60's Ford Thunderbird convertible driven to distraction and destruction in *Thelma & Louise*," even though Louise distinctly identifies her 1966 Thunderbird as "green." Improving its track record after getting the car's color wrong, the newspaper associated the vehicle with the more important characters riding inside and asked readers whether the car belonged to Thelma or Louise. Cognizant of the power of appearances, the editors ran a still from the film with both the main article and the sidebar. Two shots from *Thelma & Louise* ran alongside glimpses of *Ferris Bueller's Day Off* (1986), *Pink Cadillac* (1989), *Two for the Road* (1967), and *Hud* (1963), and provided the only images of females commanding the wheel.[58]

Among the landslide of articles in *The Los Angeles Times* between 1991 and 2001, one thing really stands out: reviews of other films are largely absent from the approximately 200 articles mentioning *Thelma & Louise*. In contrast to reviewers at other newspapers, staff film critics nearly already avoided the movie when assessing subsequent releases. A search of the archives for the film delivers only four reviews that reference it: *V.I. Warshawski* (1991), *Gay Night* (1993), *Baise-Moi* (2001) and *Beautiful Creatures* (2001). Interestingly, however, book reviewers for the newspaper showed no reserve and referred to *Thelma & Louise* more often than their counterparts covering movies. Since Los Angeles is not known for book publishing or reading, it doesn't make sense for the newspaper to talk more about the film's impact on books than its impact on movies, yet during the post–*Thelma & Louise* decade, the film appeared in approximately 13 book reviews. However, since book lovers don't necessarily like to mix literature and cinema, these mentions may have disenchanted potential readers. Reviewers risked estranging their audience because the film was so controversial; they may have spoken about the film in such a way as to repel both detractors and fans. In this case, for the hardworking author fighting for a spot under the microscope, even good press may have been bad press.

Not long after the film hit theaters, *Los Angeles Times* literary critics began seeing new books in terms of the film, as in the case of Joyce Walter's review of Nora Johnson's novel *Perfect Together*. In August 1991, to introduce her subject Walter contrasted her fatigue for weepy women broken by love with "*Thelma & Louise* envy," which she defined as a "craving for let's-kill-all-the-men stories." Though Walter recommended Johnson's novel, her review didn't sound as though she liked the film.[59]

The same year, after the fall equinox, Carolyn See reviewed Maxine Chernoff's *Plain Grief*, which she said "lurches, lunges and offers a conclusion both satisfying and surprising." See compared a husband who "stays home and sulks" to Darryl Dickerson. To meet anticipated objection, immediately after her comment about the dejected and forlorn husband, she felt it was prudent to clarify, "Remember, a woman wrote this book, a woman fed up with the configuration of women having to settle for unhappiness and persecution as their lot in life." Unlike Walters, See appeared to approve of *Thelma & Louise*, though not all of the film's fans would tolerate her explication of gender issues.[60]

Later in the fall of 1991, Anne Thompson's appreciation for the picture clouded her outlook of the novel she was assigned to review. She figured that Erika Taylor's heroine in *The Sun Maiden* "may own some debt to pistol-packing mamas like the movies' Thelma and Louise," even though the book was no doubt completed prior to the picture's release. This type of leap in logic may have annoyed readers.[61]

Emily Levine contended in 1992 that "women all across America watched *Thelma & Louise* and experienced the same exhilaration." Yet by pigeon-holing the film's audience, Levine may have shut out women who didn't feel that "same exhilaration" regarding the women's retaliation. In this instance, the critic ignored the great debate out of convenience. To give base to her review, Levine expressed that the "mother lode of emotion into which the movie tapped" remained "nameless." Meanwhile, other commentators had overwhelmingly assigned a nametag to the urge: male-bashing. No matter, according to the book reviewer, since Judith Levine's *My Enemy, My Love: Man-hating and Ambivalence in Women's Lives* revives the opposite of misogyny, "misandry," in order to dig more deeply into the conflicting emotions women feel towards men. [62]

The next year, in 1993, Karen Stabiner succinctly recommended Cynthia Heimel's collection of columns, *Get Your Tongue Out of My Mouth, I'm Kissing You Good-Bye!*, which includes Heimel's "Problem Lady" mock advice column which first appeared in *Village Voice*. In this brief review, it was easier for Stabiner to show above-average restraint and focus on the humorist because the nod to the film came directly from within the book. Stabiner commented that she was taken with Heimel's "barbed wit." Rather than reveal her own take on the picture or give away Heimel's punch lines, Stabiner enticed readers by saying she wanted to extend the columnist's piece and hear her "long-form analysis" of *Thelma & Louise*.[63]

In 1994, as if in flashing neon lights, the film appeared in the headline of Pauline Mayer's review of Shelby Hearon's *Life Estates*. "Thelma and Louise, 30 Years Later" outdid the four *Los Angeles Times* film reviews that cross-referenced the picture, none of which elevated the film to title status. Because a message can never be fully controlled, the danger here was that inserting the film into the title may have moved readers to draw conclusions without ever perusing the review or the book. [64]

The great debate about *Thelma & Louise* lived in community with shared words, opened eyes, stubbornness and blindspots. In 1997, Celeste Fremon described how she had eagerly anticipated *Locas* by Yxta Maya Murray. She expected that the novel would become "Thelma and Louise in the barrio," which to her meant a work of complexity and compassion. To Fremon's dismay, she discovered that the book presents "caricatures of cartoon villainy." Though she may have distracted potential readers with her movie-based argument, Fremon was genuinely worried. If seen as "ethnographic reality," she believed that Murray's careless images would make girl gang members look inhuman to the uninitiated. "Imagine publishing a novel that depicts Native Americans as pitiless savages during the Indian-hating 1850s," she said, switching modes of art.

Ironically, Fremon could have been talking about *Thelma & Louise*, as her words matched those of commentators who complained about the film's handling of gender and accused the picture of making matters between the sexes worse. "Such a book, no matter how skillfully crafted," she stressed, "could not help but become part of the problem." A fan of the movie, Fremon was disappointed that *Locas* didn't replicate its employment of metaphor. She wanted the novel to contain "mythical" outlaws and cast its characters on a "symbolic path to self-hood and empowerment" like *Thelma & Louise* did, in her opinion. Fremon readily assumed a unified reaction to the earlier release, one steeped in art education, yet in a nation with alarmingly low active literacy rates, many people viewed the film in literal terms only.[65]

The only male in this subjective serving and one of only two male reviewers to cite the title during this time period was Paul Dean. His remarks about the film and the book under consideration were both uncomplimentary. "By very nature of its theme," he stated in 1998, *How to Dump a Guy* is a "pretty sexist work" that upholds the unhelpful view of a war between the sexes. In his estimation, "Most men are presented as unfeeling, putty-minded clods" by authors Kate Fillion and Ellen Ladowsky. Dean labeled the co-writers a "Thelma and Louise duet," which espouses the idea that the film was also sexist. While some fans of the film might have enjoyed his appraisal of a book "filled with more impersonal wisdoms than a divorce lawyer," they might not have appreciated the way he lumped the film's women with the authors.[66]

Apart from the sensible and pertinent coverage of women in radio, the story of rape and self defense in Mexico, and the Feminist Majority's campaign to fight the Taliban, too often in the post–*Thelma & Louise* decade the Southern California newspaper floundered when its writers tried to navigate the intersection of the film and gender issues. Like the title of one of the newspaper's columns "Only in L.A.," the most amusing articles that mentioned *Thelma & Louise* could not have originated anywhere else in part because of their over-the-top nature. Articles located outside of the entertainment and obituary sections that were still distinctly L.A. in style represented not only the newspaper's most memorable selections but also its most flavor-filled coverage. According to the stereotype, people in Los Angeles are prone to superficiality and acutely concerned with images, including credits. Not every Los Angelino fits that mold, of course, but sometimes the description is apt. Only in L.A. would a television producer take the time to write a rebuttal regarding a metaphor that favored a film over his own work. Only in L.A. do personalities, politics and Tinseltown meet.

The reason why *The Los Angeles Times* was hesitant to associate *Thelma & Louise* with women in politics or any other heady concerns ("Forget the Thelma and Louise Thing," November 1995) may stem from the October 31, 1992, article "U.S. Senate Candidates Crisscross State for Votes," which discussed that year's fast-approaching election. In 1992, Californians enjoyed the unprecedented chance to send two female senators to the United States Senate. A week before voters headed for the polls, staff journalists quoted Dianne Feinstein cheer at a rally — "It's a one-two punch — a Thelma and Louise for California" — referring to herself and Barbara Boxer.[67] Whether the comparison truly helped or not is unknown, but in November Feinstein won a seat in the U.S. Senate left vacant by Pete Wilson's election to the governor's office. At the same time that Feinstein beat her Republican opponent, U.S. Senator John Seymour, to win a special two-year term, Boxer was victorious in her regular race against Republican Bruce Herschensohn. As a result, the Golden State made history.

Four months after the election, a March 8, 1993, article, "Senators Reverse Styles to Match New Roles," outlined the manner in which Boxer and Feinstein had collaborated to become the first all-woman U.S. Senate delegation. Based on Feinstein's earlier comment, *The Los Angeles Times* reported that the women "ran historic campaigns together as the 'Thelma and Louise' of politics."[68]

A problem arose later that month on March 21, when *The Los Angeles Times* printed an objection submitted by Barney Rosenzweig, executive producer of the 1980s television show *Cagney & Lacey*, to the March 8 article. Rosenzweig incorrectly assumed that the newspaper was responsible for the *Thelma & Louise* nametag. Acting out of hubris and an angry ego, he sought to set the record straight, though this study did not find any evidence to support his claim.

> In telling the world that U.S. Sens. Dianne Feinstein and Barbara Boxer are the "*Thelma and Louise*" of politics, you did more than miscalculate. Throughout the state, throughout the nation, indeed even in a banner headline in the Nov. 5 edition of the venerable *London Times*, these two officials have been designated as the "Cagney & Lacey" of politics.... *Thelma & Louise* may be a lot of things, including a very fine film and a commercial success, but it is not the first Hollywood female "buddy" project and it is not the correct political label for the new senatorial team from California.[69]

Nine months later, in a December 20, 1993, article, editors put Rosenzweig in his place. When *The Los Angeles Times* concluded their occasional series on the two politicians with "Feinstein and Boxer Carve Distinct Niches in Senate," editors were careful to make clear in the first sentence that the two "entered the U.S. Senate as the *self-dubbed* 'Thelma and Louise' [italics mine]," yet the question of who originated the nametag waged on for some time.

Meanwhile, according to the article, the senators grew tired of the media "particularly *The Times* ... contrasting their performance in office." Apparently, the film metaphor representing the women's alliance had hit a wall. In reaction to press coverage that looked for a catfight between the women, Feinstein complained to a reporter, "It is as if you are trying to drive a wedge between us." Boxer was quoted from her autobiography, *Strangers in the Senate:* "The press kept waiting for us to turn on each other, and they still are." Both women objected to excessive comparisons and contended that the same scrutiny isn't applied to male senators who are from the same state. "They write stories that treat us as though we are joined at the hip," Boxer wrote, and "when we differ, they act like it's a big deal." Still lingering in the early years of enjoying feminism's bounty, society is unaccustomed to powerful women working cooperatively. Too often people can't get beyond still-new developments to see women as individuals apart from their gender. If the entertainment draw of two women sparring doesn't fit under the microscope, the problem of lumping all women together often crops up. This same problem of individuation vs. group identification also affected the reception of the film's supporting male characters.[70]

Though not responsible for coining the term, *The Los Angeles Times* eventually indicated that it might have overworked the *Thelma & Louise* metaphor. Seizing political opportunity, Michael Huffington, Feinstein's Republican competitor in 1994, picked up the *Thelma & Louise* assignation after Feinstein and *The Los Angeles Times* let it go. Covering the race on March 13, 1994, the newspaper carefully informed readers of who said what first and who then repeated what was originally said. "Taking advantage of a line the California senators used in the closing days of their 1992 campaign," the newspaper introduced, Huffington turned what was originally intended as a positive into a negative. Referring to his opponent, Huffington derided, "She and Mrs. Boxer, who is not known as moderate, are the Thelma and Louise of the United States Senate." Huffington assumed that the designation would deter voters, whereas Feinstein and Boxer thought it could work to their advantage.[71]

In a speech published verbatim two and a half months later on May 29, 1994, Huffington intended to hammer home his message and malign the women with the label, which was no longer in use to describe Feinstein and Boxer by either the Congresswomen themselves or the newspaper. Once again Huffington denounced Feinstein and Boxer as "the Thelma and Louise of the United States Senate." Like Feinstein and Boxer had complained of *The Los Angeles Times*, Huffington packaged and sold only the most superficial aspects of the metaphor — that both of the politicians were women and therefore must be alike. Ignoring the differences between the two Democrats, as well the differences between the film characters, Huffington claimed that Feinstein and Boxer acted as "almost identical twins in the Senate." He objected (though the newspaper computed a somewhat lower percentage) that they voted "95 percent the same," which may not be so unusual for two politicians from the same party.[72]

Conversely, an environmentalist quoted in the December 20, 1993, article on Boxer and Feinstein adopted the essence of *Thelma & Louise* metaphor with greater subtlety. Perhaps subconsciously recalling the film, he described Feinstein as "cautious" and "cerebral" (like Louise) and called Boxer a "gut-instinct politician who just will instinctively jump on an issue and go for it" (reminiscent of Thelma). Likewise, by the time *The Los Angeles Times* penned "Forget the Thelma and Louise Thing" in 1995, the newspaper made a point of showcasing the senators' separate styles.

After Rosenzweig's protest, the newspaper took greater care handling the film title but didn't bypass the opportunity to gloat about its one-upmanship over the television producer. In September 1994 (weeks before Feinstein's re-election battle against Huffington), when *Cagney & Lacey* co-creator Barbara Avedon died, *The Los Angeles Times'* obituary conspicuously recalled Rosenzweig's conceited complaint.

> With Barney Rosenzweig and Barbara Corday, Ms. Avedon created single, ambitious and attractive policewoman Chris Cagney and played her off Mary Beth Lacey, a dedicated police officer, wife and mother. *Cagney & Lacey* was set in the grand tradition of *Butch Cassidy and the Sundance Kid* and other male-dominated action epics, and until *Thelma & Louise* came along it was considered a singularly successful sample [sic] of women as both caring and cantankerous friends.

In Los Angeles, even death doesn't guarantee a reprieve from competition and comeuppance. Utilizing Avedon's passing for other business, the newspaper established a timeline of famous fictional female duos, purposefully recognizing nuances between women who work together. However, the newspaper's intention seemed to be to get back at Rosenzweig and maybe even placate Feinstein and Boxer, not celebrate Avedon.[73]

In other parts of the country, the press and police authorities sometimes disagreed over who pinned the Thelma and Louise label on local female criminals. In California, the battle over who christened Feinstein and Boxer "Thelma and Louise" was fought up and down the state. In this case, Boxer and Feinstein came out winners. Up until election day in 1994, the loser, Huffington, refused to let the contentious comparison fade away. "And you remember what happened at the end of the movie," he told a crowd gathered in Monrovia.[74] Jay Leno picked up on the minor debate in his *Tonight Show* monologue, replying that such name calling "has got to be tough" on Feinstein and Boxer, "being attacked by the Forrest Gump of American politics."[75]

After being accused of wearing the *Thelma & Louise* label thin early in the 1990s, *The Los Angeles Times* shied away from likening the film to other interests outside of entertainment. Instead, the newspaper preferred to let independent commentators make those connections; the *Times* would simply serve as the conduit for those thoughts. Upholding the tradition of inflated egos and monster-sized budgets (two things that Los Angeles is famous for), among all the *Thelma & Louise* naming that took place nationwide, Southern California's giant metropolis, home to nine and half million people, claimed the largest examples. The biggest objects to receive the notorious appellation were a couple of tunnel-boring machines that cleared the way for a subway system between Studio City, in the San Fernando Valley, and Hollywood, on the other side of the Santa Monica Mountains, an expanse of about two and a half miles. Learning from past experience, in each of many articles discussing the project *The Los Angeles Times* was always careful to make clear that constructions workers, not journalists, nicknamed twin digging machines Thelma and Louise. To avoid over-sensationalizing the issue, never did editors repeat the full movie title in the headlines accompanying the nine articles researched like *The Houston Chronicle* did for its criminal coverage. However, when spokespersons for tunneling operations tried to bury the reference to help downplay delays and direct attention away from a bleeding budget, the newspaper continued to report the facts, including the catchy nicknames given by project employees.

In July 1996, *The Los Angeles Times* informed readers about what was happening 220 feet below Fredonia Drive in the Cahuenga Pass. While workers took off for the long Fourth of July weekend, sedimentary rock settled and put pressure on the giant digging machine below, in the process trapping the equipment and bending the tunnel liner.

> The entrapped tunnel-boring machine, nicknamed Thelma by construction workers, is now just 960 feet along its 2.3 mile journey beneath the mountains from Studio City to Hollywood.... A twin digging machine, nicknamed Louise, has been delayed in its mission to excavate a tunnel for trains headed in the opposite direction while engineers modify its cutter head to match conditions encountered by Thelma.[76]

Later that same month, when residents of the Hollywood Hills with the help of state senator Tom Hayden protested the construction of the subway due to environmental concerns, *The Los Angeles Times* sought screenwriter and area resident Callie Khouri's opinion about the project's appropriation of her title characters. Evidently, Khouri was aware that her creation had been used and misused to suit an infinite number of causes.

> [S]he said she objected "in a good-spirited way" to naming the tunneling machines after her characters...." I haven't been offended by almost any use of the names — and that includes a zoo that named its two-headed snake Thelma and Louise," said Khouri. "But the point of the movie is that my characters never really get mired down or hit bottom — and that's what these machines have done."

In response to the situation underground, which some felt could have been avoided with better planning, Hayden suggested that the machines be renamed Abbott and Costello.[77]

In a subsequent article detailing on-going engineering problems, like a child repeating a curse, *The Los Angeles Times* frequently and happily utilized the pet names.[78] However, that carefree attitude eventually wore out, just like it had with politicians Feinstein and Boxer. After Thelma had been bogged down all summer costing taxpayers more and more money, an editorial published in late August wondered, "Did workers have to tempt fate by naming the two tunnel-boring machines Thelma and Louise?" At this point editors were more inclined toward negative connotations of the film rather than Khouri's more upbeat point of view.[79]

By Labor Day, in the San Fernando Valley edition, the newspaper's enthusiasm for the Hollywood-inspired designations had degenerated even further. In the "Valley Newswatch" column, "Boring Nicknames" suggested that maybe "those cute nicknames" weren't "all that funny." In an apparent attempt to subdue negative spin, public relations officials for the project tried to remove the popular titles. "Mimicking a phrase normally associated with descriptions of the rock star Prince," the newspaper relayed, "the spokesmen now tell reporters of the progress of 'tunnel boring machines Nos. 1 and 2, formerly known as Thelma and Louise.'" [80]

The failed retraction attracted even more critical attention and revived the newspaper's appreciation for the metaphor. The next year, in May 1997, when news of a time capsule to be buried outside of the MTA's new headquarters reached *The Los Angeles Times*, Steve Harvey, in his column "Only in L.A.," requested that readers send in their ideas about what should go inside. Without any concern for the wishes of transit authority officials, he noted that there "probably wouldn't be room for Thelma and Louise, the MTA's two tunnel-digging machines famed for getting stuck in an MTA tunnel."[81]

In October 1997, over a year after the first report of the tunnel digging troubles, "Beleaguered MTA on Verge of Tunnel Triumph" signaled a wrap. "When the mechanical mole claws through the final feet of its almost 2.4-mile subterranean journey, a city famous for its love affair with the car will have a 17.4-mile subway tunnel from downtown Los Angeles to North Hollywood," *The Los Angeles Times* celebrated. Optimism was limited though, as planned extensions looked doubtful due to lack of public support and high costs. While the newspaper included mention of the original nicknames within the article, it only did so once, subsequently referring to the two giant-sized pieces of equipment as "the huge digging machine" and "the other machine." In an accompanying text box, however, the controversial nicknames, which sprung from an already controversial film, were repeated twice. Respectful of Metropolitan Transit Authority wishes to a limited degree within the main body of coverage, editors righteously clung to their original sources in the sidebar.

> Two tunneling machines, nicknamed Thelma and Louise, are chewing through the mountain range. Thelma, in the east tunnel, dug through 64 feet of rock between Monday and Tuesday mornings. Louise, stalled in the west tunnel, is about 500 feet behind.[82]

Building a subway takes time and forces other entities to move out of the way. In Hollywood that meant relocating 222 Hollywood Walk of Fame stars. When *The Los Angeles Times* apprised readers of the return of stars Connie Stevens and Barry Manilow to the sidewalk along Hollywood Boulevard between Vine and Gower streets in 1998, the newspaper also provided an update on the subway construction news, including problems with sinkholes. "To those in Hollywood," the newspaper elaborated, "the subway project has often resembled a low-budget movie being made with a very fat bankroll." In its discussion of problems with the project, the newspaper reminded readers of the work stoppage in 1996. Reviewing the incident, the newspaper explained, "Tunnel workers had dubbed the two drilling machines *Thelma & Louise*," and then added that the designation "proved grinding to some Hollywood nerves." Reviving comments printed two years before, this time *The Los Angeles Times* credited the suggestion to call the machines Abbott and Costello to Khouri.[83]

In the end, the MTA was not successful in its attempt to undo the Thelma and Louise nicknames, which the newspaper considered permanently attached to the agency's tunneling machines like the "Hollywood" sign remains in place over Los Angeles despite earthquakes and mudslides. In 2000, "Timeline for the Red Line" reiterated the appellation without hesitation. Like a precocious youngster, once the newspaper learned the lesson about clarity, attributing without question who designated the label, it showed little reservation about repeating the title when given by others.[84]

With all this in mind, once again, a cautious but stubborn approach to the *Thelma & Louise* mark was exercised in 2001 during a period of electricity shortages and rotating blackouts in California. Not until state lawmakers initiated the reference did *The Los Angeles Times* print the reappearance of a title that had given the newspaper a few headaches. In this case, "legislators have nicknamed Edison and PG&E *Thelma & Louise*," the newspaper detailed, as did *The Houston Chronicle*. Referring to the possibility that the companies might go bankrupt, an assemblyman sponsoring a bill designed to help solve the state's energy woes commented, "If Thelma and Louise drive off the cliff, this problem gets significantly harder for the state government to resolve." Ten years after her first screenplay debuted, especially in the monster metropolis of Los Angeles, Callie Khouri's creation had roamed far from her control.[85]

18. The Hub — Boston: *The Boston Globe*

Of all the cities surveyed for this study, none beat Boston's heady captivation with *Thelma & Louise*.[1] The area's number of colleges and the city's perch on the Eastern seaboard far from the Southwest explain to some extent why *The Boston Globe* outdid all other newspapers in its appreciation of the film: more intellectual inclinations and an interest in distant Western motifs. The differences between Boston and other cities are remarkable, and the variance in frequency and depth of coverage between a larger city from the Midwest like Detroit, whose metropolitan area totals four and half million residents, compared to a smaller city in New England like Boston, with a million fewer people living in the vicinity, is striking but perhaps not surprising. According to the 2003 figures from the Newspaper Association of America and Crain Communications, among the top 50 newspapers in terms of circulation, *The Boston Globe* ranks fourteenth, serving a smaller population than *The Detroit Free Press*, which ranks twenty-first. (The rest of the newspapers surveyed that made the list ranked as follows: *The Los Angeles Times* fourth, *The Washington Post* fifth, *The Chicago Tribune* eighth, *The Atlanta Journal-Constitution* seventeenth, *The Kansas City Star* thirty-third and *The Boston Herald* fortieth.) In the case of *Thelma & Louise* worship, geography and size didn't necessarily count but intellectual climate did play a part in whether or not a newspaper and a city took to the film. Although this project was completed in suburban Detroit in the midst of *Detroit Free Press* country, it's no surprise that I was struck by a need to write an entire book based on Callie Khouri's creation while living within *The Boston Globe's* circulation reach.

En masse, the newspaper's journalists began paying the film a good deal of serious attention from the moment it debuted. Before *Boston Globe* columnists Diane White and John Robinson vociferously bickered in the nationwide "great debate" with their June 14, 1991, point/counterpoint, on May 24, *Boston Globe* film critic Jay Carr wrote an opening-day review that kicked off the newspaper's noteworthy fascination with the film. That summer, Carr and his film critic colleague, Matthew Gilbert, banded together to write four articles trumpeting the new release. Ellen Goodman, syndicated *Boston Globe* columnist, extended enthusiasm for the picture from the Living Arts section onto the editorial pages, where she included the fictional film women in three columns during July and August.

More effusive in his praise than White ("It's only a movie, and a comedy at that"), Carr had good things to say about the movie in his review, "*Thelma & Louise:* Buddies with Heart." He also offered the filmmakers criticism designed to humble, though his cuts were more soberly and constructively delivered than Robinson's tirade ("enough is enough, and somebody has to say so"). In his first article pertaining to the picture, Carr was restrained. He rooted for it but remained firm and in control of his passions. Well before Labor Day, in a follow-up opinion piece, Carr shed his guard. By the end of the year, he no longer bothered to hide his affection and let his strong feelings for the film flow unabated.

Overall, the praise in Carr's initial offering outweighed the shortcomings he detailed. To begin with aspects of the movie that at first riled Carr, the sex scene between Geena Davis and Brad Pitt is "blatantly orchestrated." At times Ridley Scott's direction relies too heavily on his advertising past, Carr chided, "backlighting his heroines in the manner of a shampoo commercial." The main characters as written confront a string of no-win situations that are "pretty blatantly manipulative," and the men, while not bashed, are "drawn pretty simplistically."

Over a short period of time, it wasn't difficult for Carr to shed his objections because they were so flimsy. His points are solidly based, but simple explanations exist to address and ease each one of them. Despite the film's sticky plot twists and jarring character points, as part of a well-crafted, highly-polished, major Hollywood movie, of course the sex scene between Thelma and J.D. is choreographed, even when Pitt's character recklessly clears a table top. Likewise, the fact that the heroines are lit attractively, even when grime builds up in their hair, isn't surprising, either. What Hollywood does best is make pretty pictures.

While dreaming up her screenplay, Khouri searched for an action that would send a couple of women on a crime spree, and she found her inspiration in one of the world's oldest crimes, one not often or easily talked about: rape.

> I started asking: Why would they go on a crime spree? What would that be like? What two women would go on a crime spree? What would drive them to go on? And I wanted positive women — women who had problems and weren't perfect, but weren't evil and manipulative and psychotic. So, basically, two average women end up on a crime spree.[2]

Khouri gave her characters backstories so that what has happened in the past affects the future. Once the women cross Harlan's path, a chain of events takes over. What some might call fate or destiny kicks in. When Harlan harms Thelma, Louise comes to her rescue, reacts instinctively and the women's crime spree begins. Like a line of dominoes, once the process starts, it doesn't stop until all the dominoes fall down; for Thelma and Louise, the end comes when they reach the end of the road. What Carr calls "manipulative," Louise calls "a snowball effect."

Carr also complained about the film's men initially. As minor characters the male characters are necessarily cut with less dimension than the leads because that's the nature of smaller parts. Khouri explains:

> [W]hen you show men as secondary characters, a certain fragment of the male population has a very difficult time with that concept. I've had a lot of guys come up to me and say, "I wanted to know more about Darryl, Thelma's husband."[3]

But the movie isn't about Darryl, as the title indicates. Lead characters rightly receive the most backstory, attention and screen time. How many times have viewers gone to the cinema and come away wishing they knew more about the wife, or the daughter, or the dead girl? The same principle is at work here, yet the minor male characters in *Thelma & Louise* fare better than many minor women's roles found elsewhere.

Split between the picture's writing and direction, the initial detractions Carr listed did give some credence to the criticisms of viewers who didn't like the film at all. Still, the drawbacks he detailed didn't prevent Carr from embracing and supporting the picture as a whole. Even in the reviewer's first take, the female leads emanate soul, which is accessible to both genders and impossible to miss. Right from the start, for Carr the lead actresses make the film work. "You'd have to be dead inside to remain untouched by the chemistry between Sarandon and Davis," he avowed.

Like other critics, Carr anticipated strong objections to the film along gender lines, yet as a man Carr didn't have any trouble with the film's female center. Despite his less than spot-free critique, on Memorial Day weekend, Carr counseled readers, "You don't have to be a woman to love *Thelma & Louise*." He also held the actresses in high esteem, calling leads Sarandon and Davis "two terrific women." Instead of fighting the flow, he got into the very thing that makes the film so unique: the female characters and their ever-growing relationship. Carr didn't question Thelma's transformation from mousy to confident. He recognized and delighted in Louise's acceptance of her friend's growth. Some viewers dismissed the film's protagonists, as if women claiming new territory was necessarily a bad thing or a trifling ploy. Carr found that *Thelma & Louise* achieves a "more mature, more emotionally generous outlook than this sort of movie usually gets when guys are running it." Far from objecting to the manner in which the film treats men, he noticed how the women "react humanly and in some cases humanely" to the males they encounter. Carr's open attitude toward Thelma and Louise allowed him to see the film for its true worth.

Though he found that the picture "isn't perfect," Carr nevertheless commended the filmmakers. Cutting through the roadblocks that waylaid other critics, he defined the ending as a "moral victory if not exactly a triumph" and accurately predicted that *Thelma & Louise* was "certain to be the summer's most talked about" release. Noting variance and subtlety, he credited Khouri's "shrewd" decision to make Detective Slocumbe "the nicest guy" in the picture because it "takes the man-bashing onus off" *Thelma & Louise*. For Carr, Scott's directorial vision "giddily inhales the open spaces of the American West" in a "visually super-charged manner," despite the director's excessively slick approach during select scenes. Like Eleanor Ringle in Atlanta, Carr wasn't afraid to take a stand and, in effect, simply say this picture is really good.

Immediately, without instructions from organizations like the AFI, Carr considered *Thelma & Louise* a classic. Connecting the film to *Easy Rider, Butch Cassidy and the Sundance Kid* and *The Sugarland Express* (and *Bonnie and Clyde* later), in "Buddies with Heart" Carr asserted the picture "breathes new life" into both the "existential road" movie and the "outlaw buddy" movie. As many commentators have noted, all four films share numerous similarities, including elements of character, plot, structure, theme, sound and script. Three of the four are set in or bound in some way to the state of Texas, but *Thelma & Louise* is most like *The Sugarland Express* in terms of emotional motivation. The violence in both films comes as a huge surprise to no one more than the lead characters. In the earlier Steven Spielberg film, a married couple scraping the bottom find themselves in the midst of growing absurdities and high crimes when all they wanted in the first place was to take command of their derailed lives.

Unlike some of his peers, Carr didn't fret over an association between women and criminal violence, nor did he feel that the film simply turned the women into superficial men. Thelma and Louise, Carr figured, "never just set their adversaries up to be offed," as male characters would do in their place. Their precursors Butch and Sundance (played by Paul Newman and Robert Redford) are an exception; they also display unusually good manners for criminals and maintain their affable charm (especially Butch) no matter the circumstances. Although Sundance runs a little cold, even more so than Louise, overall both pairs take care and show genuine concern when committing assault. In reality, the New Mexico state cop would perish if locked inside a car trunk in the middle of the desert, regardless of air holes blown into the hood, but in the movie, it's clear that Thelma and Louise mean no bodily harm to those who don't harm them. In a similar fashion, in William Goldman's screenplay, Butch strikes up an odd kind of regard for Woodcock, the man in charge of protecting the Union Pacific Railroad and Mr. E. H. Harriman's money. The Hole-in-the-Wall gang repeatedly hijack the company's locomotives, blow up its safes and steal the cash but leave the train's passengers relatively unharmed. At worst, Woodcock incurs scrapes and bruises but remains alive in order to take on Butch and Sundance the next time. Likewise, the New Mexico state cop doesn't die after Thelma and Louise get through with him, either. Instead, he serves as a sight gag when a pot-smoking biker stops by the patrol car to flaunt his illegal cigarette. Pursued by a herd of police cars, the women by this point are pretty much finished, but thanks to Thelma and Louise the biker is free to exercise his free will without directly hurting anybody or worrying about the law.

Faults and all, in "Buddies with Heart" Carr enjoyed *Thelma & Louise* a good deal just the way it is. Even when the women's "initial larkiness gives way to something darker and more desperate," Carr reasoned gracefully without spoiling the show, "the film still carries you along." Though the tone of this comment contradicts his charge that the movie is also "manipulative," over a short period of time Carr changed his mind about the picture without bouncing back and forth.[4] Comparatively, knowing ahead of time how things end up for historical figures Clyde Barrow and Bonnie Parker, Arthur Penn's picture (starring Faye Dunaway and Warren Beatty) leads viewers to squirm in uncomfortable anticipation for the inevitable bloody end to all that machine gunfire. In contrast, as Carr might agree, *Thelma & Louise* dazzles and stuns without nearly as much graphic violence.

Eventually, movies must end and wrap up their characters' lives. Watching *Thelma & Louise*, viewers zoom closer to the title duo as the film gears up to a final stop that appears increasingly doomed. But fans don't want to see the women surrender, get captured or die. Aiming to reclaim their son, the couple from *The Sugarland Express*, Lou Jean and Clovis Poplin (played by Goldie Hawn and Ben Johnson), lead Texas authorities on a slow-speed chase across the state. At Lou Jean's insistence, Clovis breaks out of jail just a few weeks before his scheduled release. Reunited, the couple attempt to recover their child, baby Langston, who became the ward of foster parents due to his birth parents' incarceration. The heart of the film is a daffy dash to Sugarland, Texas, festooned with interested onlookers and gaudy media attention. Comedy aside, Lou Jean and Clovis find themselves in a serious bind with no easy escape. In the end, Lou Jean's hopeless plan makes its final wrong turn when Clovis is shot by police and dies at the Mexican border. Interestingly, *The Sugarland Express* is based on a true Texas story. Before the credits roll, viewers read that the real Lou Jean served a short sentence and was eventually successful in reclaiming her son, Langston. Amazingly, truth is still stranger than fiction.

Of course there's only one way out of this world. The partners in these criminal buddy movies face nothing but a bad conclusion. An old friend tells Butch and Sundance, "It's over, don't you get that? It's over and you're both gonna die bloody, and all you can do is choose where." Pursued to the end by a relentless Texas Ranger with a grudge to settle, Bonnie and Clyde are riddled with bullets and rendered pulp. Injured but still kicking, Butch and Sundance go out shooting. Before *Thelma & Louise* and its conclusion, *Butch Cassidy and the Sundance Kid* ended with a freeze-frame sparing viewers the sight of the characters' implied bloody death in Bolivia. Surrounded by authorities and perched at the rim of what looks like the Grand Canyon, Thelma and Louise must also go down somehow. Despite the crime buddy genre's bleak tradition, the picture's fresh hybrid makeup encourages viewers to expect a new take on established endings, which the picture delivers. Wishing to grant the title characters symbolic, ever-lasting life, the filmmakers end *Thelma & Louise* with fantasy (dreaming of heaven) and amnesia (forgetting all troubles).

Judging by the newspaper's rapt attention to *Thelma & Louise*, Boston loves to watch, read and talk about women in film noticeably more than other cities. On Sunday, May 26, 1991, two days after *Thelma & Louise* opened, *The Boston Sunday Globe* ran a piece in its film section spotlighting "the violent vengeance of women against abusive men." Written by Jay Carr's co-worker, Matthew Gilbert, "The New Fatal Attractions: The Current Crop of Film Heroines Strike Back at Abusive Men and Win Our Sympathy" drew attention to new roles for Hollywood women: center stage, rejecting victimization and bearing aggression. Gilbert's discussion included *Mortal Thoughts*, *A Kiss Before Dying*, *Sleeping with the Enemy*, *Drowning by Numbers* and *Switch*, but he prioritized *Thelma & Louise* by labeling it the "most persuasive," as if his article came together with the release.

Some critics attacked the film's extension of violence toward men enacted by women, but *The Boston Globe* took the opposite stance. It championed women who have been "pushed to an extreme" and "driven to self-protective attack" against the "unpleasant" men in their lives. Some viewers identified Thelma and Louise as criminals and nothing more. Displaying his sympathies, Gilbert felt that the new women in film were "anything but clear-cut villains." He surmised that the collective filmmakers responsible for these fresh characterizations want audiences to find the men guilty to give the films "moral complexity."

In Gilbert's view, what put *Thelma & Louise* ahead of the competition was the movie's effectiveness. The picture successfully blurred the line between victim and aggressor and in the process achieved the highest sense of "spiritual liberation."

> As Davis and Sarandon become unlikely outlaws on the run, as their actions become less socially acceptable, they gain a euphoric acceptance of themselves

and each other. Amid the violence and crime, Thelma and Louise become fully realized women, experiencing moments of sheer epiphany. This tension between what is legal and what is moral informs most of these movies.

Gilbert reasoned that murder is such an integral part of our culture's notion of entertainment, killing has become legitimized, at least in fiction. Through its omnipresence and role in countless films, murder has become an acceptable act representing the ultimate expression of anger. Since people like the movies for the "vicarious satisfaction" they offer, Gilbert weighed, "If you can't keep men from hurting you, at least you can now see *Thelma & Louise*."[5]

While most newspapers revisited the film with opinion pieces after publishing reviews, few matched *The Boston Globe*'s level of coverage and analysis. A little over a month after Jay Carr first reviewed the film on May 24 and two weeks after "The Great Debate Over Thelma and Louise," which appeared on June 14, Carr returned with more to say on June 30. Few journalists relished the film's impact or lavished it with as much second-serving acclaim. Although "Out There: Movies Seek Interior Truths in the Wide-Open Spaces" also discussed *City Slickers* and *Robin Hood*, more time was devoted to *Thelma & Louise*. Like Gilbert's first piece, this article feels like an excuse to bask in talk about the picture.

Initially, in his review "Buddies with Heart," Carr believed that Ridley Scott's advertising background resulted in too much polish on the picture, while Callie Khouri's storyline manipulated the women and limited the men. After taking time to reflect, Carr intensified his original reaction and resolutely changed his mind about what at first bothered him. He decided the film is "provocative" with "big, bold panoramic images" that "mythify the themes it taps with surprising potency." Furthermore, compared to *The Silence of the Lambs*, *Sleeping with the Enemy*, and *Mortal Thoughts*, to Carr, in a month's time *Thelma & Louise* transformed into "a depth charge, exploding at some subterranean level, freeing a lot of societal lava waiting to blow, providing an exit for huge masses of anger hitherto unarticulated in mass culture terms." Unlike most American films, *Thelma & Louise* gives audiences "something to talk about," to quote the title of Khouri's follow-up screenplay. Addressing liberation, rape, class struggles, tension between genders, finding one's own "spiritual elbow room" and violence, to Carr *Thelma & Louise* fulfilled the intellectual needs of a nation "starved for vigorous discourse."

Earlier he played the reproachful guardian, but later Carr became the devoted admirer. Pledging his support, Carr was prepared to defend the film against its detractors. He decided that "it doesn't matter if some of the men" the women "humble are little more than political cartoons." Criticism of the title pair acting like superficial males did not address "the main issue," just as flack over Thelma's choice to have sex with one man after narrowly escaping rape by another was "beside the point." Sharing Gilbert's view, Carr argued that *Thelma & Louise* is about the lead characters becoming complete and true selves. What grabbed Carr before (Thelma and Louise) eventually entranced him. "They're not just emptying the cash register of a convenience store," Carr charged. "[T]hey're destroying forever yet another male monopoly." Men who felt threatened by the women's "declaration of independence" and "orthodox" feminists who discredited the picture because of its role reversals missed the vibrancy and timeliness of the story's "primal" impact, Carr rallied. Brimming with life both messy and thick, the lead characters' "journey of transformation" attacked viewers' sensibilities. Without redoubt, Carr elevated *Thelma & Louise* from Hollywood product to art.

> In this age of potentially suffocating political correctness, it's worth remembering that a work of art is not a moral tract. Nor should it be. If it makes contact with human behavior on some illuminating level, or at least compels fuller examination of important forces and issues, it has done its job. No matter what you think of *Thelma & Louise*, it's the year's wide-open-spaces movie where flight is farthest from mindless escapism.[6]

Still lingering in a *Thelma & Louise*–soaked summer, Matthew Gilbert presented his second say about the film. Though their perspectives were quite similar, Gilbert sought an even *Thelma & Louise* scorecard between himself and Carr. *Boston Globe* editors didn't deter their fascination, so neither critic got to write more often about a deserving film, one of few recent releases with grit to chew. Competition or not, both critics located within *Thelma & Louise* a rich vein of worthwhile ideas that inspired ruminations beyond the usual Hollywood movie.

On August 11, Gilbert submitted "Greetings from Screen City, There and Back Again: Postcards from One Critic's Trip Across the Country of Cinema," an inventive conceptual piece written in epistolary style. The journalist conducted a one-way correspondence with a newfound friend in Wyoming ("J.W.") who didn't have access to cineplexes or Eastern newspapers. "Well, after a month touring the country's back roads (and stumbling onto generous souls like you)," Gilbert set up, "I find that the East Coast feels like a hurricane of cinema and culture." To exemplify his contention, he contrasted gaily, "If we were play acting *Thelma & Louise* last month, then this month I'm doing the Woody Allen." As Gilbert reviewed the season's cinematic offerings, he brought up *Thelma & Louise* five times, more often than any other summer film. Gilbert credited *Thelma & Louise* above all other releases with stirring up the cerebral scene back home in Boston.

Declaring his allegiance from the start, Gilbert's initial reference to the film occurred in his first postcard when he alluded to a recently concluded road trip with friends touring the countryside in homage to the film. Recalling the West's natural screen filled with big sky and majestic mountains, Gilbert apologized to J.W. for his assumption about the universal appeal of moving pictures. With the critic's capacity for poetry and rhetoric refreshed by distant vistas, Gilbert continued undeterred as silent J.W. failed to protest the content of the postcards. In his second fantasy mailing, Gilbert named *Thelma & Louise* "the best of all the summer movies."

> The two stars are women, so there's been a lot of chest-pounding about sexual politics — but truly the movie is more than that. It's about liberating yourself, or finding yourself, on the road. A journey home, in a way. An authentic awakening.

In his third postcard, Gilbert began with additional humble words about the worthiness of films compared to nature's glory, but nothing was going to stop him from talking about the meaning of movies. Gilbert contended that *Thelma & Louise* "set the theme for the summer," which was in his opinion "private apocalypse, or almost-apocalypse." He elaborated, "[T]he end of the hero's world threatens to occur — and, as a result, he finds the meaning of life" and changes "radically." In "Out There," for which Gilbert's co-worker also reviewed a similar thematic landscape, Carr focused on the means of change (escape to the West's open spaces) embarked upon by the lead characters in films such as *City Slickers*. In his piece, Gilbert discussed the act of change itself. Investigating more widely than Cynthia Heimel of *Village Voice* and Jeff Simon of *The Buffalo News*, who compared *Thelma & Louise* to films from the 1970s, Gilbert noted the evidence of a retro trend in a number of 1991 films.

> We're getting to basics all over again. Personal transformation, that touchstone of the New Age movement, has gone mainstream.... Or maybe it's just nostalgia. In "City Slickers," Billy Crystal's wife urges him to "Find your smile." Was that an allusion to the smiley faces of the '70s? Is there a 70's revival happening?

Finally, in his fifth missive-length postcard, Gilbert emphasized one of the most important and overlooked aspects of the film's reception: the fact that it employed two lead females. Gilbert recognized that *Thelma & Louise* was an island. "Women, you see," he lamented to his attentive friend, "do not figure largely in this summer's films." Considering the lack of lead roles written for women and the public's blasé acceptance of the situation, it's ironic but not surprising that *Thelma & Louise* caused such an uproar regarding its treatment of men. To Gilbert, speaking for the culture at large, if Hollywood movies were a reliable measure, "the conflicts of male identity" seemed "foremost on our minds." Overturning the usual focus on men explains in large part why *Thelma & Louise* bruised so many egos.[7]

In addition to Carr and Gilbert, *Boston Globe* syndicated columnist Ellen Goodman recognized *Thelma & Louise* as something more than a whim to be forgotten before the summer's end. In Goodman's view, the movie brought to the screen at least one very important issue: physical safety. Goodman said that for women, "It seems the most deeply felt constriction on daily life may be fear." One of the film's central themes concerned violence, but not just the violence committed by Thelma and Louise. Unlike few of her peers from other newspapers, Goodman was impressed by the violence committed against the women. "Where women go, what we do, and how comfortable we feel doing it," she pointed out, "are often limited more by a sense of danger than by legal discrimination." Goodman was particularly struck by what reactions to the film said about society's view of men and women when retaliatory murder garnered more attention than the near rape that precipitated it.[8]

More so than other columnists such as Art Buchwald and Dianne Klein in Los Angeles, Goodman weighed all of the important and often confounding issues touched upon by the film. In many of her essays, Goodman demonstrated that she's not confused by characters who are both victims and criminals, like Thelma, Louise and scorned lover and convicted murderer Jean Harris. Goodman was not undone by characters who are both criminals and female, like Thelma, Louise and knife-wielding Lorena Bobbitt. Goodman made the distinction clear where many others were muddled or refused to tread. "Abuse may mitigate a woman's guilt," she allowed in 1994, when she drew *Thelma & Louise* into "Bobbitt Babbling," but it "rarely makes her innocent."[9]

Brandishing a thoughtful feminist approach, Goodman often expounded on male-bashing, a deduction some critics too-easily arrived at after discounting rape. She believed that recipients of the charge are often more accurately described by other terms, such as Hollywood rarities. In 1996, when she reflected on *Thelma & Louise* coming before *First Wives Club*, Goodman explained that few films star women who "fight back." Though there are many films in which women are abused and mistreated, inevitably movies with strong, righteously angry women (including *9 to 5*, which came first) are labeled "male-bashing" even when no blows are actually struck. "Maybe fighting for yourself constitutes male-bashing these days," Goodman pondered in frustration.[10]

Between July 1991 and September 1996, Goodman nodded to Thelma and Louise in seven different columns about gender. In July 1991, less than a month after the film debuted, she picked up on a thread begun by Carr and Gilbert when she recalled the fictional women in an article decrying Hollywood's current view of men. While representations of both genders were unsettled, it seemed to Goodman that wherever women tread on new ground previously dominated by males, a backlash occurs. Men can drive cars, fire weapons, hurt people and grab our attention, but women? When the male lead in *Regarding Henry* is shot in the head thus beckoning a slew of positive changes in his personal life, the impetus for those changes is ignored. Meanwhile, Goodman reflected, "Sitting in the theater, it occurred to me that if Thelma or Louise had shot Henry, this movie would be on the cover of magazines and on talk shows featuring learned lectures on the perils of male-bashing." Since a random male conducting a routine hold-up shoots Henry, this stroke of violence is absorbed without question to better focus on the good brought about by the action. Thelma and Louise did not enjoy the same nonchalant attitude, except when it came to Thelma's near rape.[11]

Later that summer, in August 1991, Goodman shared a story to reinforce why the film was so pertinent to modern lives. Reminiscent of Patricia Carr's anecdote in Atlanta about the two college women who bagged a flasher, in Goodman's tale two women were the victims of a drive-by attack of "lewd suggestions" and "vague threats" perpetrated by a "car loaded with young men." Afterward, the columnist revealed, one woman said to the other, "Where are Thelma and Louise when you need them?" Recounting the season's onslaught of stories, real and fictional, all pertaining to sexual misconduct spanning from minor verbal assaults to major physical assaults such as rape, Goodman summarized, "To the degree that women lead more equal lives, they are more angry when the new terms are violated." Despite the right to work and earn a decent living, feminist gains are mitigated when a woman can't walk down the street without fearing violence. While Goodman's column ran in Boston under the headline "A World of Caution," on Long Island in *Newsday* it appeared under the tag "Thelma and Louise, We Really Need You!"[12]

Goodman, aware of the gravity of the fictional women's story, waited less than a month before mentioning the film again. Annually, to celebrate the anniversary of women's suffrage, in her column she recognizes "those who have tried the hardest" to "set back" women's progress. Goodman's award was rendered with sarcasm, but that didn't obliterate the serious nature of the transgressions she revealed. Like *Thelma & Louise*, Goodman used a laugh to separate right from wrong.

[T]he Blind Justice Award—so many judges, so little time—goes to US District Judge E. B. Haltom, who dismissed a sexual-harassment suit in Alabama because "at the time of the alleged sexual advance," the women "wore little or no makeup, and her hair was not colored in any way." To him we send a certificate for a beauty seminar led by Thelma and Louise.[13]

A year later, in August 1992, again celebrating the passage of the 19th Amendment, Goodman found additional cause to repeat and recommend the title:

The Battle of the Sexes Award, which we had hoped to retire in the post–Cold War era, goes to those Navy Pilots who turned the Tailhook convention into a sexual harassment maneuver. To these officers and gentlemen we send a courier who will collect all their tapes of "Top Gun." We will replace them with "Thelma and Louise."[14]

In "Clemency for Prisoner 81-G-0098," advocating the release of Jean

Harris on the grounds of her good conduct behind bars (where she purportedly organized programs and taught classes to other prisoners), Goodman attempted to give readers "an idea of how long ago" the former headmistress was locked up. Writing in January 1993, Goodman recounted that Harris was incarcerated "before Charles married Di" and "before Thelma met Louise," which was less than two years prior. Perhaps mocking short attention spans, Goodman insinuated that the film's infusion into the cultural mainline was so mind-blowing that *Thelma & Louise* erased memory of the time before the film existed.[15] A similar time-tripping tribute occurred in Atlanta, when *The Atlanta Journal-Constitution* profiled elderly twin sisters.

The next winter, in January 1994, Goodman analyzed the supposed gender wars in light of the Bobbitt case. In addition to questionable charges of male-bashing, she found further inequities in the way violent issues are termed when women are involved. "After centuries of male fantasies about castrating females," the columnist elaborated sarcastically, "we finally have one." Thanks to the public's blood thirst, Lorena Bobbitt became the "universal" symbol of the latest go-round in the often-cried "battles of the sexes," which Goodman discounted. She wondered why it's only called a "battle" when women "are caught fighting, or fighting back." When a guy shoots the lead in *Regarding Henry* in the head, tired cliches are not bandied about. When men commit aggressive acts against either sex, there's no conflagration. Goodman surmised, "If John had only abused Lorena, we would have called it violence but not a war."

Male aggression is considered business as usual. Only women's actions bring out claims of male-bashing and battles as if "all is fair in love and war" applies exclusively to one side. Goodman compared this phenomenon to the press *Thelma & Louise* received. "Just a few years ago, with slasher movies filing the cineplexes with female blood," Goodman recalled, *Thelma & Louise* "became the topic for worried gender-watchers." Refuting the view that feminists hate men, she noted that goal behind equality is "to lead lives that [are] more alike." Agreeing with Nicholaus Mills in Atlanta, the goal is for men and women to "get closer," Goodman reminded readers, not fight to the death.[16]

When Goodman entered the fray over *First Wives Club* in September 1996, she championed the cause of women fighting back when struck down, not as means to prolong the supposed battle, but to assert their rights. "Every once in a while in the history of womankind," she promised, "a doormat rises off the floor and, breaking all evolutionary speed records, develops a pair of legs to stand on." This brave strike, in Goodman's view, invariably precipitates the question, "Why is she so angry?" That naïve query is a clear indication that the reactionary charge of male-bashing is soon to follow just like it did with *Thelma & Louise*. If the genders were considered equally, Goodman implied in her collection of columns, female-bashing would cause just as much concern as male-bashing and fewer film commentators would have by-passed rape when discussing Khouri's creation.[17]

To give an idea just how *Thelma & Louise*-happy the Massachusetts newspaper was, apart from Diane White and John Robinson's "great debate," Jay Carr's review and follow-up analysis, Matthew Gilbert's two entertainment op-eds and Ellen Goodman's collection of 1991 columns, the remainder of meaningful coverage published in *The Boston Globe* in 1991 and 1992 outnumbered the total coverage analyzed in *The Detroit Free Press* for the entire decade. Furthermore, when the contents of articles mentioning the title are compared, distinct regional profiles emerge. If major newspapers are fair gauges, while Detroit builds cars, Boston trades in ideas. Located in the vast middle of the country, the Motor City was most interested in the Ford Thunderbird convertible in which the women snaked their way around the Southwest; along the Atlantic seaboard, the Hub was captivated by what the women's travels represent — to themselves and the rest of us. Considering the ticket sales in each area, *The Detroit Free Press* and *The Boston Globe* appropriately catered to, accurately reflected and most likely influenced readers in their reach. *The Detroit Free Press* wasn't taken with *Thelma & Louise* and neither were people in Detroit, at least not compared to Boston, where both journalists and moviegoers welcomed the release.

Serving an area that includes Harvard University and some 70 other colleges, *The Boston Globe* addressed an audience that values learning and holds intellectual pursuits in high regard. Like *The Washington Post* provided more in-depth analysis of political issues than cities further removed from the action on Capitol Hill, *The Boston Globe* wrote more analytically about *Thelma & Louise*-related subject matter than newspapers serving locales not as invested in education as an industry. When *The Boston Globe* looked at current cultural roles for men in July 1991, as *The Dayton Daily News* did in September of the same year, the depth of each newspaper's probe differed greatly, as did the content of the two articles. In fact, the two newspapers investigated conflicting trends.

Ignoring one of the messages underlying the biggest entertainment story of the summer (that women deserve and demand respect from the men in their lives), in Dayton, "Nice Guys Finish Last" hypothesized that women want a man to treat them badly. Drawing on subjective sources with similar points of view, thus delivering a one-sided conclusion (and what some might call evidence of a backlash), the Dayton article cited a Roper Organization Poll, an editor at *Men's Health* magazine and two authors, including Robert Bly, whose book *Iron John* called for men to return to their primal selves. Operating on the level of stereotypes and sweeping generalities, at *The Dayton Daily News* women were quoted saying things like, "Nice guys are doormats," and men responded in frustration, "You watch the jerks getting all the action."

A light, entertaining tone dominated the piece, which opened with the line, "Listen up, ladies."[18]

Anchored in abstraction rather than singles' bars, in Boston, "The New Male Bimbo" by Mark Muro investigated current images of the "so-called New Man" in advertising. The article discussed the meaning behind marketing campaigns for Calvin Klein, Giorgio Beverly Hills and Yves Saint Laurent as found in *GQ* and *Vanity Fair*, in which male bodies were displayed as objects much like females bodies have been for centuries. In contrast to Dayton's offering, the Boston article was twice as long, consulted twice as many pundits and, importantly, allowed those voices to conflict and present more than one side to the issue. Where "Nice Guys Finish Last" simplified its thesis by not allowing any strong dissent, "The New Male Bimbo" didn't try to contain the outcome to match a cute headline. Cultivating a wider perspective, the Beantown newspaper analyzed, "What the ads mean depends on how you think they work, and who you think they're aimed at." Possibly the ads were aimed at women who buy cologne and the idea of a more docile, caring, family-orientated man, or they were intended for men and women who want to gaze at beautiful male bodies, or they were designed to allure the androgynous self and appeal to everyone. This multiplicity of possible reactions represents the heart of liberalism: recognizing and supporting a peaceful and fair diversity of thought and action.

Where *The Boston Globe*'s article read like a lunchtime consortium of academics, *The Dayton Daily News* sounded like a gossipy advice columnist in a high school newspaper. "Nice Guys Finish Last" reduced Robert Bly's contention that men should connect with their inbred, natural "fierceness." In more common terms, the Midwest newspaper counseled male readers that "a thin skin of wimp-be-gone will impress no one for long." After 24 paragraphs heralding the insensitive tough guy, at the end of the article writer Shann Nix squeezed in an unconvincing about-face with the help of one pundit, "who literally wrote the book on the subject," an advice book called *How to Love a Nice Guy*. In a quickly tacked-on conclusion, Nix advised that "nice guys shouldn't try to be jerks" because doing so might attract a superficial girlfriend. Thus the Dayton article presented two types of women: those who want insensitive men and those who are insensitive.

One litmus test for separating subjective fluff from more steely investigative journalism involves the willingness to recognize an important development like feminism. Though Nix consulted experts on men, the article in the Dayton newspaper avoided the f word and chose not to consult the opinions of any individuals who referred to themselves as feminists. Conversely, in its piece about male gender roles, the Boston newspaper consulted two professed feminists, making clear that they each held separate points of view. Without feeling the need to define the term, the East Coast newspaper also quoted a third woman who referenced "the first postfeminist films of the early

'70s" as well as "postfeminist wives and girlfriends." (Some use "postfeminist" to separate the second and third waves of feminism in the United States.)

Though both articles mentioned *Thelma & Louise*, in Dayton the film was shrugged off as the in-touch, sensitive man's rote duty. If seeing *Thelma & Louise* didn't work to appease women, what will? The film was used to get a laugh and dismissed as a joke. The film popped up in Boston when writer Mark Murro asked, "What does a woman want?" Even though the Massachusetts newspaper also name-dropped the film, Murro aimed for timeliness as well as levity, and, in the process, displayed a more progressive attitude. A woman certainly does not want "those smarmy, muscle-bound lug-heads lined up and humiliated in *Thelma & Louise*," Murro quipped, ironically describing the kind of guys *The Dayton Daily News* implied that women did want. In *The Dayton Daily News*, one of the pundits quoted in the piece patronized *Thelma & Louise* as an icon representing women's fickle taste. Despite the ongoing debate surrounding the representation of men in the film, whether he personally like the picture or not, *The Boston Globe's* journalist better understood what *Thelma & Louise* expressed. Murro's article better identified why the title characters had so much pent-up rebellion and anger.[19]

Although *Boston Globe* articles pertaining to *Thelma & Louise* delved more deeply into various issues than articles found elsewhere, not every piece referencing the film portrayed the area as an exclusive enclave inhabited by highly evolved individuals who seek only lofty pursuits. As if to prove that the region is populated by more than just blue-bloods and intellectuals, at about the same time as "The New Male Bimbo" was printed, a far more irreverent reference to the film occurred in the sports section within a story about the poor behavior of local sports fans. In July 1991, columnist Dan Shaughnessy reacted to reports of Red Sox enthusiasts, specifically those sitting in the Fenway Park bleachers, making lewd gestures with inflatable female dolls. Feigning indignation at the story, which his tone suggested was overblown, Shaughnessy joked that the tasteless display attracted protesters from the fictitious group "Women Who Love Real Men Who Love *Thelma & Louise*."[20] Less than two weeks later, *The Tulsa World* printed an article written by another journalist from *The Boston Globe*, Steven Stark, who wrote, "Is Snob a Synonym for Liberal?" which appeared in *The Salt Lake Tribune* in January 1992. Stark's 1991 piece, "Ball Park Rudeness Part of Old World Culture," also mentioned the blow-up female substitutes seen at Fenway Park. "Threatened by *Thelma & Louise*? Bring your inflatable doll to the stadium," Stark suggested satirically. Bearing jocularity mixed with edgy awareness, both writers recognized the film characters as the latest symbolic incarnation of what constitutes a strong, modern woman, though Shaughnessy goofed on men and women who championed the film and Stark roasted those who couldn't handle it.[20]

Apart from these excursions into popular, lowbrow culture, the remainder of *Boston Globe* articles that referenced the film in 1991 credited it with greater relevance. A newspaper that comfortably used the f word should have been more apt to connect the picture and rape. In August 1991, within the newspaper's opinion pages, "Rape and the Culture of Silence" examined the crime in the aftermath of the charges made against William Kennedy Smith. Legal reforms such as rape "shield laws," which prevent defense attorneys from bringing up a victim's sexual history, don't always hold up in court, *The Boston Globe* informed readers. However, they do exist and ideally encourage the public to see the act as criminal aggression, not a consequence a woman invites. As Renee Loth explained, escalating degrees of rape, which distinguish "simple" rape from "aggravated" rape, were intended to make juries more likely to convict rapists, especially those who commit the most severe acts. Loth also mentioned "products of popular culture" that have helped to "ease the stigma" surrounding rape, including *Thelma & Louise*, "A Case of Rape" (a 1975 television movie starring Elizabeth Montgomery) and *The Accused*, based on the 1984 bar rape of a 22-year-old woman in New Bedford, Massachusetts.[21]

Throughout the time period studied, *Thelma & Louise* was used as a lens through which to consider various creative outlets including new ventures in theater, dance, music and literature. "Texas Women: Sass, Brass ... and Steel," which appeared in *The Boston Globe*'s "Focus" section in early September, went beyond the usual limits of associating the film with any project that featured two or more women bearing attitudes. Specifically, the piece discussed Lone Star State women. Like *The Atlanta Journal-Constitution* separated Thelma from her friend to talk about adultery (though more briefly and with less focus), here Louise stood alone in the limelight. Recalling the complaints of California senators Dianne Feinstein and Barbara Boxer, who grew tired of constant comparisons that overlooked their unique personalities, it's refreshing to find the fictional women seen as individuals.

To get his piece rolling, David Nyhan first swung through a chatty but informed introduction. He touched upon former Texas governor Ann Richards, as well as Wanda Holloway, the woman outside of Houston who hired a hitman to take out another mother whose daughter rivaled hers for a spot on the cheerleading squad. After setting the stage, Nyhan shared the "best single explanation of Texas women to cross" his path, Patricia Browning Griffith's *The World Around Midnight*. To summarize the novel, Nyhan stated that the lead character's story is a "grown-up version of *Thelma & Louise*." He continued, "If Texas was where a bad thing happened to Louise, it's where some good things happened to a very real character named Dinah." Despite Nyhan's slight regarding the maturity of Callie Khouri's creation, *The Boston Globe*'s on-going assessment of the film and its characters didn't sidestep the women's point of view or avoid rape in favor of complaints about male-bashing. John Robinson's protracted whine was the exception, but it was too over-the-top to be taken seriously.[22]

To recuperate from its summer of indulgence, *The Boston Globe* laid off *Thelma & Louise* through the fall until the end of December when both Jay Carr and Matthew Gilbert plus a third writer for the newspaper included the film in year end summaries. Both *Boston Globe* film critics rated *Thelma & Louise* the number one film of 1991. Carr capped off his trio of commentaries about the picture by calling it "the year's most exhilarating studio movie," though he added that considering the dearth of similarly "exhilarating" Hollywood products, his was "faint praise."

> In the year of Clarence Thomas' elevation to the Supreme Court, Susan Sarandon's and Geena Davis' seizing of male prerogatives — not in any aggressive way, but merely to maintain some dignity — remains a shining exception to the flow of demographics-oriented factory product neither reflecting nor containing nourishing values.

As the year progressed, Carr was less concerned with the depiction of males in the film and more enthralled with Thelma and Louise.[23]

On the same day, Gilbert also reiterated his views on the picture's worth and meaning. For him, by year's end the women had become so large, they spiritually outgrew the continental United States.

> *Thelma & Louise*, the year's best picture, inspired thunderous chest pounding about sexual politics. But Ridley Scott's liberation fable is more than lifestyle fodder — way more. It's about people, male or female, breaking out of societally imposed chains. As Thelma and Louise fly their renegade T-bird into the apocalyptic Southwest dawn, they come nearer and nearer to the spiritual homeland they couldn't find in America. Scott drew affecting performances from Sarandon and Davis, then paved their trail with dust and smoke and dusk and fire.[24]

Finally, in *The Boston Globe*'s Sunday opinion section, a tribute in "1991: Year of the Paper Tiger" constituted the third mention of the film on December 29. *Thelma & Louise* was the only motion picture included in a compendium that closed the year. The newspaper couldn't let the year end without heavy-duty waves of goodbye to 1991's most important artistic and cultural marker. To *The Boston Globe*, *Thelma & Louise* was an issue and a news event. The picture was important enough to mention along with the release of hostage Terry Anderson, the fall of the Soviet Union and the explosion of Mount Pinatubo.

To summarize the film's impact, *The Boston Globe* returned to the ground of its "great debate" by encapsulating the two most popular arguments surrounding the film. Along with Robert Bly's *Iron John* and Patricia Bowman's charges against William Kennedy Smith, the film was portrayed as stoking the never-ending "battle of the sexes," despite Ellen Goodman's argument against use of the term. "The movie *Thelma & Louise* became a symbol of exhilarating feminist retribution or male-bashing, depending on your perspective and chromosomal makeup," Renee Loth commented, ignoring the gender and dedication of *The Boston Globe*'s film critics.[25]

The *Boston Globe*'s nearly unwavering recognition of the film didn't wane in 1992, when the newspaper almost matched its 1991 output of coverage. More important than the number of times the film was mentioned, however, was the nature of the articles in which the title appeared. Few of the thirteen articles studied located the film outside of current events and inside light features, yet to begin year two of the *Thelma & Louise* decade *The Boston Globe* did start off with a soft touch. The newspaper included the film in a requisite January 1 article (shelved in the "Living" section) about what was "in" and what was "out" going into the new year. According to the newspaper's cultural barometer, *Thelma & Louise* was still "in," not having lost any ground since its last nod three days before.[26]

Though most of the newspaper's frontline journalists who brought up the picture adored it, not everyone on staff found the effort lovely and amazing. Two days later, on January 3, the film's video release was announced with a fresh twist. Instead of criticizing the story's depiction of men, as happened so frequently around the country, Michael Blowen called into question the film's portrayal of "local desert dwellers" and the last act's "black jogger [sic] smoking dope." The East Coast newspaper's reviewers and columnists collectively mulled over the "great debate" and decided that the male-bashing charge didn't fit, but intent upon finding a flaw Blowen figured other politically correct concerns might. As a result, within the short blurb "*Thelma & Louise*: A Volatile Mixture" the first objectionable characterization was considered patronizing and the later "pointless" and possibly "offensive."[27]

Before the end of the first quarter, *The Boston Globe* got its final breezy mention over with when its "Sunday Magazine" briefly previewed spring fashions. Like it had been elsewhere, the film was roped to the "cowgirl" look. In particular, what was in, according to the newspaper, was "not the debutante kind Ralph Lauren has turned out for years, but something more like Annie Oakley by way of Thelma and Louise."[28] (It's a shame that in modern times the story of a real-life female as intriguing and accomplished as Oakley hasn't been told outside of the silly musical *Annie, Get Your Gun*. Oakley was born in 1860 and performed as a sharp shooter in Buffalo Bill's Wild West Show.)

Other newspapers stopped at superficial references, but *The Boston Globe* continued to espouse a more thoughtful approach to the film. From February through November 1992, the movie was linked to new horizons in women's sports, gay and lesbian activism in Hollywood, an editorial on Hollywood's recent discovery of women, Senator Arlen Specter's re-election battle against Lynn Yeakel, the Hunter College conference featuring speaker Anita Hill, a lengthy piece on women's swelling "ire," the political "Year of the Women," the women's gun magazine (*Women & Guns*), and Susan Faludi's local tour to promote the paperback edition of *Backlash*. The year's collection of articles clearly presented a pro-feminist editorial stance that accepted *Thelma & Louise* as a legitimate symbol of the woman's movement. The newspaper considered the film a noteworthy commentator on social progress as well as an accomplished piece of art.

The *Boston Globe* demonstrated that in at least one city of the United States there existed men who were honestly excited about women's expansion into uncharted territories previously known only to males. To tell the story of the first women's biathlon held at the 1992 Winter Olympics in Albertville, France, Thelma and Louise were called into action three times. Replicating the sense of drama evident at *The Washington Post*, staffer Michael Madden didn't bother to tone down his exuberance as a witness to history in the making.

> We came to this with visions of Thelma and Louise on skis instead of in their convertible. Women have touched many a frontier in recent decades, and this was the latest, women skiing 7.5 kilometers cross-country and, in the interim, stopping twice to pull their rifles from over their shoulders, take as many deep breaths as possible to still their heartbeats racing at 180 beats a minute, and then start firing.

As the article progressed and Madden's respect for the athletes grew, the fictional women took a back seat. "Thelma and Louise were small-towners to these women," Madden expressed with admiration. Holding college degrees and brighter outlooks for the future, and giving people a reason to rejoice, not react, "Thelma and Louise they most certainly aren't," Madden went on to say regarding the American athletes who shot for sport, not retribution. His comment also recalls the rift between socioeconomic classes of women discussed in previously reviewed articles identifying "Frustrated Fran" in *The Chicago Tribune* and differing attitudes toward fingernail style in *The Washington Post*. If Thelma and Louise had access to higher education and enjoyed the riches of a more upwardly mobile lifestyle, they too might have found more productive and positive outlets for their energies. While some of the references that used *Thelma & Louise* as a negative comparison read like digs in light of a newspaper's overall attitude toward the film, Madden's comments in *The Boston Globe* rooted too strongly for women to raise suspicions of misogyny. The frequency and familiarity with which he brought up Thelma and Louise made them sound no worse than wayward relatives for whom one cares but can't help.[29]

The intellectual largesse that *The Boston Globe* extended to women was also offered to homosexuals. In "Beyond Villains and Buffoons," subtitled "Gay and Lesbian Activists Want Hollywood to Broaden Its Portrayal of Them on Film," the curator for the Boston Gay and Lesbian Film Festival explained why members of the gay community embraced *Thelma & Louise*. There are so few "normal" homosexuals portrayed in Hollywood movies, gay audiences must "invent their heroes," the newspaper quoted. In the case of heterosexual Thelma and Louise, "Just the idea of two women being together and empowering each other is enough," the festival curator commented. The newspaper's attitude toward minority groups went beyond superficial gloss, which better describes its coverage of fashion trends. Like the 1991 article investigating the "New Male," this later piece consulted a variety of spokespersons from *The Advocate, Queer Nation, Gay Community News* and *GLAAD. The Boston Globe* presented a multifarious gay community, much like its presentation of feminists, understanding that homosexuals and feminists are individuals with similarities and differences. People who identify as either or both are not interchangeable or unilaterally identical. Pressing beyond the headlines and uncovering bias, the article shared Hollywood history informing readers that the Hollywood Production Code from the 1930s through the 1950s "forbade" screen depictions of homosexuality.[30]

The Boston Globe paid the same attention to historical detail when covering the plight of women in the movies but took its concerns further. Within the parameters of this study, no other newspaper elevated the case of gender inequality in Hollywood to a hallowed spot on its editorial page, as if the topic was no less important than the global warming or world peace. "Hollywood's Latest Discovery" realized that women "have always had a share of leading roles in films," if not an equal share, but reminded readers that in the past, parts for women were usually restricted to "romantic or selfless partners to men." In the summer of 1992, "for the first time in Hollywood's history," the newspaper proclaimed, filmmakers were creating "beefier roles for women in their own right" and importantly casting those parts "in big budget, highly visible flicks." Without pointing to any other film, *The Boston Globe* credited *Thelma & Louise* with this historic change.

> After the success of last summer's *Thelma & Louise*, Hollywood quickly adjusted its former equation of X plus Y equals blockbuster hit. X still equals adventure, but Y now symbolizes a strong, female character.[31]

Recognizing the film as a landmark, the newspaper's editorial board congratulated filmmakers who grant female characters individuality and verve. In lieu of petty comparisons to thieves, the newspaper called on Thelma and Louise to serve as cultural cues and simply be themselves.

"Hollywood's Latest Discovery" wasn't the only time *Thelma & Louise* graced *The Boston Globe*'s editorial pages in 1992, nor was it the only time the film was mentioned up front in the hard news section of the newspaper. In the spring, political cartoonist Dan Wasserman adapted the film to spoof U.S. Senator Arlen Specter's re-election battle against newcomer Lynn Yeakel, which was heating up in Pennsylvania. Yeakel was moved to run for office after watching Specter and the other members of the Senate Judicial Committee grill Anita Hill during the Clarence Thomas Supreme Court nomina-

Media pundits dubbed the 1992 political season the "Year of the Woman" due to the unprecedented numbers of female candidates running for political office. Some women, including Lynn Yeakel in Pennsylvania, were spurred into action by the way members of the Senate Judiciary Committee, including Sen. Arlen Specter, grilled Anita Hill when she testified during the Clarence Thomas Supreme Court nomination hearings. Dan Wasserman's cartoon, which appeared on April 30, 1992, in *The Boston Globe*, used *Thelma & Louise* to spoof Specter, who was challenged by Yeakel for his seat in the Senate. (Dan Wasserman, copyright 1992 Tribune Media Services. Reprinted with permission.)

tion hearings. As reported in *Time*, Yeakel declared, "I looked at those fourteen men and I thought, these are not the people I want running my life and my children's and grandchildren's life." In the magazine's words, Yeakel wanted "to make the fall campaign in part a referendum on Specter's memorably merciless questioning of Hill."[32] To create his caricature, Wasserman replaced the film's obnoxious truck driver bearing bad manners with Specter, who reacted, "Oh, No!! It's Thelma and L ... L ... Lynn Yeakel!!"[33] Specter, a Republican who was first elected to the Senate in 1980, narrowly defeated Yeakel to retain his seat.

Other newspapers avoided the women's movement in their discussions of the film. When *The Boston Globe* provided extensive coverage of Anita Hill's April 1992 address ("Women Tell the Truth: Parity, Power and Sexual Harassment") at Hunter College in New York City, it added to the list of slogans generated by the movie. Aiming to please the crowd back home, Jolie Solomon reported that "Thelma and Louise in '92" was popular among attendees. On a more serious level, "NYC Feminists' Rally Roars for Ballot-Box Power in '92" included a discussion of the "Maggie Thatcher factor," as Solomon phrased the concept. Here, the newspaper dug deeper than some event attendees. According to Solomon, the issue of whether or not women should automatically support other women received "limited" but "urgent" attention at the sold-out conference. In response to calls for gender parity in government, Solomon pushed readers to reflect, asking, "Should women support and vote for other women, even if they disagree on the issues?"

The question readily applies to the concerns of women in Hollywood and their fans. Should interested viewers patronize films starring and made by women even if the movies aren't appealing or don't look like they'll be any good? To address the question's political application, *The Boston Globe* summarized Bella Abzug's response of "selectivity," as well as Geraldine Ferraro's opposing argument based on Harvard psychologist Carol Gilligan's work, *In a Different Voice*. In Solomon's article, Ferraro argued that women "in general might bring less confrontation and more cooperation" to Congress, which is a point that *Rocky Mountain News* journalist Mary Voeltz Chandler and others might argue.[34]

Theoretically, in terms of movie production, greater box office support for women in film would inspire Hollywood to create more female roles but without any guarantees regarding quality. As an artist, personally, although I'm torn between the need to bolster women in film and my preference for quality work, ultimately I come down on the side of Abzug's "selectivity." Wishing the female stars I grew up admiring received more big screen time, I supported Susan Sarandon and Goldie Hawn's *The Banger Sisters* (2003) but immediately felt ripped off and disappointed. Not all movies led by women, including respected players, are necessarily worthwhile.

Three days after Jolie Solomon's piece, a title that recalled a duet by Barbra Streisand and Donna Summers commanded the reader's attention. "Enough Is Enough, They Say" detailed numerous reasons why women as a political group were acting up in 1992. As Renee Graham explained, like Lynn Yeakel many people and not just women were irked by the Anita Hill–Clarence Thomas hearings. Other circumstances that purportedly had people riled up included gender tensions at the Harvard Law School, disturbing news about silicone breast implants, blasé attitudes toward ongoing violence against women and even an athletic magazine's annual swimsuit issue. Graham reported that less than halfway through the year in Massachusetts 10 women had been murdered by their husbands, boyfriends or former mates. In addition, according to a study conducted by the National Victims Center and the Crime Victims Research and Treatment Center, 13 percent of women in the United States had been the victim of rape.

Women are angry; it's as simple and complicated as that. From the teen-ager who has only lived in times of legalized abortion and believes that right may be compromised; to the working mother who cannot afford child care; to the woman employee who must endure sexual comments and advances from male co-workers for fear she will lose her job; to the abortion foe who feels not enough attention has been paid to the development of contraceptives; to the ailing, elderly woman who finds her health concerns are ignored because she's a woman, their anger rages like an unchecked fire.

Beyond itemizing problems, Graham's article addressed what feminist activists were doing to improve conditions. Taking a stand against the little fires that feed the global furnace of bias and abuse, a letter to the editor published in *Sports Illustrated* called for coverage of women in sports, *The Boston Globe* relayed, not uncoverage of their bodies. Representing a much larger front, NOW's April 5 march on Washington, D.C., brought out more than 500,000 protestors, according to the organizers. As a result of Clarence Thomas's confirmation to the Supreme Court, membership in EMILY's List doubled. (EMILY's List, which stands for Early Money Is Like Yeast, is a political group dedicated to the election of Democratic women who support abortion rights. Each member pledges to donate at least $300 per year to political campaigns.)

Real or fictional, female leaders in the entertainment industry sometimes serve as role models and spokespersons whom the public looks to for leadership. Echoing feelings of anger and frustration that clicked with audiences, in Graham's words *Thelma & Louise* was "aggressively embraced by women who saw themselves in the film's titles characters." Supporting women's issues without fear, Jodie Foster was noted for her use of the f word when she accepted the Best Actress Oscar for her work as Clarice Starling in *The Silence of the Lambs*. The newspaper recalled that Foster thanked the Academy of Motion Picture Arts and Sciences "for embracing such an incredibly strong and beautiful feminist hero." The same evening, Callie Khouri urged women to "fantasize about accomplishment and fantasize about equality until it's a reality." Far from Brad Tilson's attitude in Dayton, in Boston analyzing films and listening to Hollywood were both fine ways to pass the time.

Articles denouncing feminism often fail to include the opinions of everyday women, as if only college-educated, professional females (a group the British think tank Demos labeled "Networking Naomi") care about gender equality. "Enough Is Enough, They Say" sought out the views of a dozen local women, ranging from a dental assistant, a schoolteacher, a Harvard Law professor, a women's health advocate, a receptionist, two women who started a local chapter of NOW in reaction to Clarence Thomas' confirmation to the Supreme Court, a paralegal, a teenager and a political activist. While feminism is often associated with abortion rights, Graham also included the views of two anti-abortion feminists who stressed the common ground women share apart from reproductive issues, such as concerns for the numbers of women and children in poverty. To reinforce the concept of sisterhood, which was prevalent and celebrated in the film, Graham interviewed a broad coalition of women including NOW president Patricia Ireland. The argument that feminism was dead was given space and put to rest. Ireland referred to the "concerted campaign to discredit not just the word, but the philosophy." In defense of feminism against ongoing resistance, she added, "You don't put irrelevant, dead movements on the cover of *Time* magazine." The article closed with the words of one local woman who recast "women's issues" as "people issues" and wondered why everyone wasn't angry.[35]

The devil may exist in the details, but so does a newspaper's interest in impeding, ignoring or assisting social change. Unafraid to give cultural currents a name or use the names already given to them, *The Boston Globe* commanded in November 1992, "After all its frenzy subsides, this election will be marked as the Year of the Women." Although other big city newspapers raised the same designation, "Sex Looms Large in 'Year of Women'" provided greater historical perspective. Martin F. Nolan researched a biography of Eleanor Roosevelt and claimed that "the first election after suffrage, 1920, was the first scheduled Year of the Women." As regular readers of *The Boston Globe* were apprised, the dearth of homosexuals in Hollywood movies stretches back for decades and women have been fighting for legal equality for longer than any living person can imagine. (The article quoting Hillary Clinton's remarks in Seneca Falls, New York, originated in a Mary Leonard piece written for *The Boston Globe*. The newspaper celebrated the 150th anniversary of the feminist movement with a prime spot on the front page.)

Not all newspapers covered the latest so-called "Year of the Women" in relation to *Thelma & Louise*. Some newspapers shied away from sponsoring direct and forceful *Thelma & Louise* talk, especially in political circles, but *The Boston Globe* showed little reserve. Without any immediate stake in the outcome of the election in California, Nolan passed along Dianne Feinstein's "It's a one-two punch, Thelma and Louise for California!" To tie the West Coast campaign to Massachusetts, Nolan claimed that in the "trendsetting" Golden State, "the Lexington and Concord of this revolution" have been the campaigns of the state's Democratic senators, Feinstein and Barbara Boxer. Interested in the debate over women's issues, the East Coast newspaper even gave Boxer's Republican opponent, Bruce Herschensohn, time to complain that talk about female candidates was biased. Nolan reported to New England readers that Herschensohn objected to Feinstein's rallying reference to the movie. Boxer's opponent argued that if he said the same thing, he would be labeled sexist. Siding with the women, Nolan quieted Herschensohn's remarks by concluding, "But men have enjoyed a double standard for decades."[36]

Diane White, who stood opposite John Robinson in the newspaper's "great debate," appears in the lifestyle features section of the newspaper, while

Ellen Goodman calls the opinion pages home. Throughout *The Boston Globe* during the post–*Thelma & Louise* decade, women's issues were labeled "feminism" without stuttering or apology, and both columnists understood that the need for a women's movement adversely affected everybody. Introducing the Second Amendment Foundation's magazine *Women & Guns* in her piece "Gun-Toting Women," White surmised in early 1992 that combining feminism and firearms was "sure to fuel some men's worst *Thelma & Louise* fantasies." Aware of the larger debate surrounding women's issues, including internal resistance from women, she added that a lot of women were "bound to be disturbed by the idea that equal opportunity ... can be construed to mean equal opportunity to carry guns." After *Women & Guns* pictured Geena Davis and Susan Sarandon as Thelma and Louise on the front of its debut newsstand issue, White reported that the representation of female gun owners had come "under fire, so to speak." In this case, the controversy exemplified conflicts between women. The magazine's readers voiced concerns about "too tough" and "too sexy" cover models such as actress Linda Hamilton. Paraphrasing editor Sonny Jones' response, White said that "all women," whether mini-skirted or muscle-bound, "have the right to protect themselves."

In contrast to the magazine's pro-gun perspective, White shared her own view regarding firearms with shades of *Thelma & Louise* standing in the background.

I believe handguns should be far more difficult to acquire than they are now. But I can also understand why someone might want a gun for protection, especially if that someone is a woman who has already been a victim of violent crime. Whether that sense of security is founded in reality is open to debate.[37]

Thinking it would help protect his possessions, Thelma's husband Darryl bought the gun that Louise uses to kill Harlan. What was supposed to be a good thing provided the sole means for the women's undoing and Harlan's unnecessary death.

Getting ready to close out the year in the fall of 1992, *The Boston Globe* accorded a generous amount of space to feminist author Susan Faludi and the promotion of *Backlash*'s paperback edition. Evidently, sales for the hardcover edition of the feminist classic in the Boston area warranted an additional tour stop to tout Faludi's work. To its credit, like *The Washington Post* printed stories that criticized in-house staff, *The Boston Globe* was also willing to print scrutiny of its own pages. When Faludi disapproved of actions taken by the newspaper, *The Boston Globe* validated her opinion with coverage. "Susan Faludi Lashes Back" paraphrased the author's cynicism in response to all the talk about 1992 being "The Year of Women," a trend in which the newspaper took part. "'What's next?' Faludi muses. 'The Month of the Woman? The long weekend? Sixty minutes with Thelma and Louise?'"

In response to the slogan that represented more hype than hope, Faludi voiced sober concerns about whether or not the year would actually bring about monumental, lasting change. To support her doubts, she pointed out to a large crowd gathered at the Cambridge Public Library that the biggest story of the year wasn't "the newly found strength and voices of female politicians, but the shaming and silencing of one political wife," referring to Hillary Clinton.[38] In effect, Faludi argued that greater attention should be paid to the setbacks women were encountering when real and fictional individuals like Hillary, Anita, Thelma and Louise received so much flack for daring to take action.

Though it's beyond the scope of this study to know whether or not any newspaper premeditated overall coverage of the film, looking back it seems as though the Beantown newspaper suddenly became self-conscious. After the surprise sensation of the summer of 1991 and the super-charged political season of 1992, in the period between 1993 to 1995, *The Boston Globe* slowed down the frequency of its *Thelma & Louise* references. Maybe editors were embarrassed by the demonstrable crush that most staffers (though not all) seemed to have on the film. Perhaps the newspaper decided enough was enough. Whatever the explanation may be, in 1996, *Thelma & Louise* momentum geared back up with key mentions occurring in each of the subsequent years reviewed. While entertainment writers at *The Atlanta Journal-Constitution* and *The Los Angeles Times* cut back on the amount of historical credit accorded to the title, *The Boston Globe* deepened its show of respect.

Even though the number of times the picture appeared by name decreased after 1992, the New England newspaper continued to distinguish itself by the critical way it remembered *Thelma & Louise*. In Boston, alongside the performances of symphony orchestras and ballet companies, movies are an art form. In 1993, a John Ford weekend at the Brattle Theater, located in Cambridge's Harvard Square, warranted a good size article, "Reprinting the Legend at the Brattle, John Ford Gets Another Shot at the American Imagination." Like *Thelma & Louise*, two of Ford's films, *She Wore a Yellow Ribbon* (1949) and *The Searchers* (1956), were filmed in Monument Valley, which Martin F. Nolan designated "the archipelago of basilicas in the Southwest." The acclaimed director staged his movies there so many times, Nolan quipped, the area "is so Fordian that it seems profane" when other films utilize the location. After a dash to connote emphasis, he added, "even *Thelma & Louise* riding through the night." Nolan presumed that Ridley Scott's picture was worthy of classic stature, though perhaps not in the same category as the Ford retrospective, which also included *The Man Who Shot Liberty Valance* (1962).[39]

Also in 1993, Susan Bickelhaupt submitted a piece on Mary Matalin's and Jane Wallace's cable television show *Equal Time*, which was produced by CNBC. Bickelhaupt previewed the program as a "blend" of *Wayne's World* and PBS's "Crossfire" with a "dash" of *Thelma & Louise*. The *Wayne's World* mix-in came by way of the offering's "free-wheeling spirit," while the *Thelma & Louise* sprinkle was derived from the format: two women, previously unfamiliar with one another, brought together and asked to talk. Not only did *The Boston Globe* consider *Thelma & Louise* a classic, to staff journalists and editors the controversial film had also become a cultural condiment.[40]

On March 9, 1994, the front page of *The Boston Globe* announced "Barbie's Birthday." "America's teen-age fashion model turns 35 today, although she doesn't look a day over 18," the newspaper teased, setting the tone for an article that chose to consult academics who questioned "whether Barbie has been good for girls" over enthusiasts and collectors. Rather than sing "Happy Birthday" or send well wishes, Alice Dembner reported that ever since Barbie's debut feminists have "criticized" her "physical extremes." Specifically, many believe that Barbie's figure set "an impossible ideal, fostering eating and shopping disorders instead of dreams." Two University of Massachusetts academics humorously dubbed "Barbiologists" concluded that if the doll morphed into a real woman, her measurements would make her "anorexic, or at least seriously skinny." Within the article, a reporter at *Newsday* who was working on a book about the doll discussed the difference between Barbie's advertised image and the way children actually play with her. Likening girls' imaginative play to "the popular film" *Thelma & Louise*, M.G. Lord painted a scenario where "Barbie drives the car and drives round with other Barbies" while "Ken is out of the picture." Another academic voiced concerns about race and gender myths ensconced within the doll's milieu. Lord predicted that despite criticisms, "Barbie will be around forever, literally, since she's not biodegradable."[41]

Although memories of *Thelma & Louise* are intangible and subject to disappearance, *The Boston Globe* did its part to keep thoughts of the film fresh, tasty and relevant. Despite its appetite for Thelma and Louise, however, the newspaper largely avoided the widespread tabloid-like practice of linking the fictional women to real-life criminals, but not completely. Although it declined to originate any such stories regarding local perpetrators, the Boston newspaper did reprint a newswire article involving Thelma and Louise naming out of New Jersey.[42] In addition, three months after Barbie's birthday, in June 1994, *Boston Globe* sportswriter Bob Ryan couldn't pull himself away from the television coverage of the O.J. Simpson chase to watch the basketball game he was supposed to cover. Transfixed by the drama of a former football star threatening suicide while cruising Southern California highways, Ryan wondered, "How could I leave the press room to see the Knicks play the Rockets when CNN was showing me, live and in color, '*Thelma & Louise* Meets *Dog Day Afternoon*, and Featuring O.J. Simpson'?" Like Callie Khouri's creation's surprised viewers, Ryan commented in amazement, "There has never been such a scene involving anyone with the remote stature of O.J. Simpson as that shot of the Ford Bronco proceeding along those California highways with all those police cars trailing behind."[43]

Replete with *The Boston Globe*'s flair for unique detail, two features on travel in 1995 conjured the kind of carefree nods seen more frequently elsewhere, but the New England newspaper took the theme a good distance further. Retelling her story for readers in January, Cheryl Charles "eagerly offered" to drive across country with a girlfriend who was changing jobs from waitress in Harrisburg, Pennsylvania, to blackjack dealer in Las Vegas, Nevada. Charles had excitedly agreed to tag along with her close friend because she imagined "*Thelma & Louise* with a better ending." Similar to what happens in the movie, however, one woman was portrayed as confident and the other as "easily flappable," and, like Thelma and Louise, ended their first night "barely speaking." Still, the road trip was successful, eventually bringing them closer together. Modeled after Thelma and Louise, each woman eventually claimed her own errors and forgave her friend's mistakes.[44]

Exercising an urbane, even continental perspective (that is, a more "open" attitude toward marriage), the second piece focused on married couples vacationing separately. "Separate Vacations: The Pause That Refreshes" pushed the notion of independence revitalizing unions. According to *The Boston Globe*, separate vacations made marriages stronger as long as plans were "discussed" in advance, "agreed upon" and "reciprocal," rather than routes to escape. Echoing the idea of Barbie gangs cruising the highways minus any Ken figure, Doreen Iudica Vigue designated one independent travel consultant's excursion without her husband a "*Thelma & Louise*-type car trip through various U.S. states."[45]

Following a few years in which the newspaper quelled its passion for *Thelma & Louise*, 1996 saw a significant resurgence of references, perhaps because the film was still desperately needed to help the nation focus on gender issues. A salute to the picture made perfect sense to *The Boston Globe* in a handful of stories — some serious, some lightweight — involving women. According to the newspaper, when Susan Sarandon was presented with the Hasty Pudding Theatrical's Woman of the Year award in Harvard Square in February 1996, her presenters were confused about whether she'd played Thelma or Louise; five years earlier when the film came out, the college students were still in high school. Apparently, not everyone in the Boston area was truly enraptured by the film, but the muddle was okay to Sarandon, who replied generously, "If you stop making mistakes, you're either boring or dead." Since the R release drew an adult crowd, the perplexity shown by Harvard students is not surprising when one considers their ages when the film was released, though one may wonder why the nation's elite didn't better prepare themselves.[46]

Although Southern cities like Nashville are better known than Boston for their appreciation of country music, "Sisterhood Finds a Place in Country Music" noted the emerging trend of female country singers touring together without any male country singers headlining the bill. Similar to the situation of women acting in Hollywood films, as Mary Chapin Carpenter explained to *The Boston Globe* in August 1996, there was a time when "women artists were not selling as many records as men," so promoters would naturally think that shows featuring female singers only wouldn't be as profitable. A change in attitude was evident in the current tour featuring Carpenter, Trisha Yearwood and Kim Richey. The show wasn't devised as a "gender gimmick act" or a performance restricted to songs written by women, Steve Morse assured readers, but simply a union of artists who felt an affinity for one another's music. Drawing on one of the newspaper's stock metaphors, Morse portrayed one of Yearwood's songs, "Hello, I'm Gone" (written by Kevin Welch), as "a sort of *Thelma & Louise* tale about a woman who leaves her boyfriend and hits the road."[47] Some con critics failed to grasp how the film reminded people of the need to be responsible and stand on their own two feet. For women who've made bad choices in mates, in part because of heavy societal pressure to be married, taking charge may entail leaving home.

A month later, Diane White returned to feminism and the film sounding even more divisive than she did during 1991's great debate. In September 1996, White wondered why men such as Warren Farrell in Los Angeles weren't laughing at *First Wives Club*. She chuckled, at least until "the plot line expires." Framing the film as a "knee-jerk feminist revenge comedy, kind of a *Thelma & Louise* Meet Annie Hall," White conceded the limits to her summary. In *First Wives Club*, she deadpanned, "nobody ends up dead," except the suicidal friend.

Analyzing a possible "humor gender gap," White inquired if it's true that men and women crack up over different stimuli. Investigating the thesis currently bandied about — that women laugh self-reflectively while men laugh at other people — she turned to her relationship with a male friend as anecdotal evidence. Though they both laughed about her being fat, in the columnist's words, only White laughed about his comb-over. If the theories floating around at the time were correct, as a woman White's idea of humor revealed a masculine nature. A second joke in White's column also contradicted the so-called "humor gender gap" when the columnist defended the star power and comedy talent of *First Wives Club* leads Bette Midler and Goldie Hawn but insulted their co-star. "How can you hate a movie" with Midler and Hawn, White asked incredulously, then added with blasé derision, and "Diane Keaton too, if you like that sort of thing." Because of her aggressive remarks about others, White's column undermined the gender theory in question. Since there were zero steadfast rules that could accurately predict reactions to the picture 100 percent of the time, the impact of *Thelma & Louise* makes clear that psychological divisions and cultural stereotypes rigidly assigned by sex simply do not hold up. As society tries to move closer to liberty and justice for all, sweeping generalities like the "humor gender gap" hold back progress in attitudes.

To White, in "'Wives': Why Men Aren't Laughing," attacking men in movies was sometimes both humorous and appropriate. Unlike Ellen Goodman, White did trade in male-bashing but found that its practice in *First Wives Club* "is for the most part not funny" because the male characters aren't "interesting." Five years earlier, White grounded her reaction to *Thelma & Louise* by suggesting that the recent trend of aggression aimed at male characters in movies stemmed from women "getting really fed up with always being the bashees." Revealing her own frustration in 1991, White wished that someone had "nailed that little weasel" who stole Louise's nest egg and declared that Thelma's husband "cried out for a good bashing." Some people, regardless of gender, lean toward pacifism even in entertainment. Others like White appear more willing to engage in a fight or at least release a cathartic cheer from the sidelines when someone else does.[48]

As art, whether they're good or bad, motion pictures equal more than just entertainment. A second article about *First Wives Club* graced the op-ed page of *The Boston Globe* five days later when the film was analyzed in terms of "class warfare." Also in opposition to Warren Farrell's feelings about the picture (essentially decrying the film for male-bashing though he didn't use the term), Martin F. Nolan advised readers that *First Wives Club* offered viewers "two hours of sophisticated wit and anger." After a divorce, it is generally true that "men are richer," *The Boston Globe* sympathized (recalling Virginia Woolf's talk of money), "while women still encounter the glass ceiling." Like earlier Hollywood comedies such as *My Man Godfrey* (1936), *It Happened One Night* (1934) and *The Palm Beach Story* (1942), which enlivened tensions between rich and poor, according to Nolan, *First Wives Club* "is a box-office bonanza because it feminizes the class warfare that animated the screwball comedies of the 1930s." Once again, the newspaper sympathized with female characters and revealed avid interest in Hollywood history.

Nolan compared the possible male-bashing quotient in *First Wives Club* to *Thelma & Louise*, which he termed more "lethal," though Nolan understood the women's rage. Looking at the big picture of women in film, he aimed his sarcasm at the "male-dominated mind-set of Hollywood" where "Jane Austen hasn't made a dent" and "the Duke must have more cable channels than Rupert Murdoch." Nolan's assessment relied on considerable knowledge of film studies, which the newspaper deemed a worthwhile preoccupation, as it gave Nolan's article space in its front, hard news section. Nolan took the liberty of calling *First Wives Club* a "remake" of *The Women* (1939), which was directed by George Cukor and written by Anita Loos. Similar to *First Wives Club*, *The Women* assembles an all-female cast and revolves around "the then-touchy topic" of infidelity.

In a competitive culture, the tendency to compare women-led films solely with other women-led films because of their similar, almost redundant, particularly female storylines can become tiresome. However, due to unavoidable sexual politics and cultural persuasions, the habit is also very understandable. After comparing *First Wives Club* with *The Women*, Nolan came full circle in his essay and found screenwriter Loos both more "sardonic and inventive" than Bob Dole, a Republican running for president who presumably denounced *First Wives Club* without seeing it, hence the title of Nolan's article: "A Must-See Flick for the GOP."[49]

Perhaps the one article of all the many analyzed that best sums up why so many *Boston Globe* writers rooted for *Thelma & Louise* while viewers elsewhere responded with rejection and ridicule ran in October 1996. It compared the film characters to Hillary Clinton, but in a more positive light than *The Washington Post*. A month before the presidential election between incumbent Bill Clinton and his Republican challenger, Bob Dole, "A Massachusetts Mantra: 'Hail to Hillary'" demonstrated just how liberal the Commonwealth of Massachusetts is in its collective outlook. Though Hillary Clinton's popularity was described as "fragile" in states like Texas and Ohio based on poll numbers from Harte-Hanks, *The Cincinnati Enquirer* and *The Boston Globe*/WBZ-TV, "Hillary Clinton reigns supreme in the Land of the Bean & the Cod," according to David Nyhan. In one of the smallest but most influential states in the union, her favorable rating reached 62 percent, two points higher than her husband's. Her unfavorable rating was so insignificant, Massachusetts' most widely circulated newspaper didn't feel the need to include the figure in the article. Comparatively, in the Lone Star State, Hillary Clinton scored 50 percent favorable, 45 percent unfavorable. That doesn't sound too bad, except that one-third of those polled in Bush country claimed that they disliked Mrs. Clinton so much, in Nyhan's words, they were "less inclined to vote for her partner." In Ohio, a 2000 and 2004 "red" state and home to *The Dayton Daily News*, Clinton slipped to 38 percent favorable, 45 percent unfavorable, which matched the national ratings cited.

In the Midwest, where ticket sales for the film dipped, Hillary Clinton's public acceptance also wavered. In Nyhan's view, the disparity between those who favored Clinton and those who didn't illustrated a sharp difference in attitudes that closely paralleled reception of the film.

To the radio talk show hosts who turn the airwaves sulfurous with insults and castigation, Hillary is the Supreme Evil in the White House, the Wicked Witch of the West Wing. To the men enclosed in the paranoid world of pick-up truck radio, she's Thelma, she's Louise, she's your worst nightmare....

With flair and adequate reason for doing so, *The Boston Globe* merged perception of the First Lady with those of the film characters. Meanwhile, Nyhan portrayed inflammatory, mean-spirited radio talk show hosts and easily riled-up listeners as people who must live outside of Massachusetts or exist inside the state within a small minority. The newspaper recognized the wary reception of all three women in conservative areas of the country, in contrast to the acclaim they enjoyed within progressive strongholds. In the land of Wellesley College (Hillary's alma mater) and the Kennedy Compound, the president's wife raised millions of dollars for the Democratic Party in a state compact enough to drive across in less than two hours — which is another reason why Bostonites loved *Thelma & Louise* so much: size envy.

In general, while greater numbers of Midwesterners and Southerners purportedly disliked or discounted Hillary, Thelma *and* Louise, people living on the East Coast admired the three women for the very same reasons: who they are and what they represent. Detractors dumped upon the picture their frustrations and worries stemming from a society reordered by feminism; people did the same to Hillary. Fans smiled and cheered at the command of power shown and encouraged by Thelma and Louise; the same could be said of Hillary and her admirers. Sounding like he was appraising the film characters, Nyhan appointed Mrs. Clinton "a handy, ubiquitous symbol for all the casualties in the Battle of the Sexes." *The Boston Globe* cast Hillary Clinton as a "walking, talking, in-your-face reminder that a whole lot of male-female struggles have yet to be resolved," which equally well described *Thelma & Louise*.

Another male fan of powerful women, Nyhan assumed most people were sick of Bill Clinton and Bob Dole and would rather watch a debate between Hillary and Elizabeth, their wives. Despite its progressive outlook, *The Boston Globe* did show room for improvement in its attitude toward women. Nyhan provided the women's ages, but he declined to be so forthcoming about their husbands'.[50]

To cap off a varied and electric year of *Thelma & Louise* talk, after Columbus Day, *The Boston Globe* took the idea of women and wheels one step farther than the gluttony of their peers. Good-naturedly mocking Virginia Woolf, "A Varooooom of Their Own" shined a light on women on two wheels rather than four. For her profile of women motorcycle riders, Sally Jacobs interviewed columnist Art Buchwald's daughter, Jennifer Buchwald, a 20-year veteran of the road. According to the *Boston Globe*, the man who had little good to say about *Thelma & Louise* in *The Los Angeles Times* (and newspapers throughout the country) once offered to pay his offspring ten grand if she would give up her riding habit. She turned him down, and he eventually gave up his resistance. "I would rather she were a congresswoman, but what can I do?" the senior Buchwald admitted. In response, Jacobs pointed out that women could do both — ride *and* serve. Unlike her father in more than one respect, the representative of the next generation of Buchwalds bore an openminded, but still whimsical, outlook. As recounted by Jacobs, Jennifer Buchwald's black Gold Wing 1100 sported a "Thelma and Louise Live" bumper sticker, refrigerator, toy telephone and water pistol.[51]

Although 1997 was a slower year than 1996 in terms of the numbers, *The Boston Globe* articles that brought up *Thelma & Louise* did so with incredible panache. Even more startling than the newspaper appointing the nation's first lady Thelma *and* Louise, Indira A.R. Lakshmanan equated the film characters with India's notorious and very real Bandit Queen, Phoolan Devi, one of only three women *dacoit* leaders throughout country's long history. Of all the comparison's between the fictional women and women in real life, in August 1997, a story appearing on the front page among national and foreign news contained the most stunning suggestion.

> Imagine if Thelma and Louise, the movie outlaws who went on a crime spree to avenge attacks on them and all women, had surrendered to police, then been hailed as feminist folk heroes and elected to Congress.

Where other news organizations like ABC and *The Atlantic Monthly* drew on British folklore and compared Devi to Robin Hood, *The Boston Globe* did the same and then took its characterization of the illiterate Hindu another giant step forward a few centuries. As a gang leader, the lower-caste Devi directed higher-caste men through remote villages, "reputedly stealing from upper castes while leaving women and children alone," the newspaper alleged. She aggressively avenged those who had mistreated her in the past by reportedly massacring at least 20 upper-caste men primarily in retaliation for acts of rape.[52]

According to an extensive article in *The Atlantic Monthly*, at age 11 Devi was married to a widower in his thirties "in exchange for a cow." Fierce and brave despite the lack of respect and education accorded to women in her culture, at age 12 she left her husband and walked "across an area the width of Texas" to return to her home where she began a long fight to reclaim land stolen from her family. Upon her arrival, Devi's mother complained about the "disgrace" her daughter's actions had caused. Journalist Mary Anne Weaver, who traveled abroad and interviewed Devi as an adult, quoted the Bandit Queen as she retold her story.

"There is no alternative," Devi emphasized. "You must commit suicide," her mother commanded. "Go jump in the village well." Instead, Devi continued her bold defiance by swimming in the nude, taking lovers and earning a reputation. Years later, a jealous rival and male dacoit leader scornfully labeled her a "character-loose woman." After surrendering to authorities and spending 11 years in jail, Devi gained notoriety, attracted a following and won a seat in parliament. During this time, she learned to read. Bold, confident and commanding, Devi considered herself to be the reincarnation of the goddess Durga, representing power and strength. On the campaign trail, she reportedly ordered around her current husband, who was born into a higher caste, referring to him as "my wife."

During a testy interview during which the rebel and purported murderess requested that Weaver allow her to continue without interruption, Devi explained what it means to be a poor woman in India:

> You call it rape in your fancy language. Do you have any idea what's it's *like* to live in a village in India? What you call rape, that kind of thing happens to poor women in villages every day. It is assumed that the daughters of the poor are for the use of the rich. They assume that we're their property. In the villages the poor have no toilets, so we must go to the fields, and the moment we arrive, the rich lay us there; we can't cut the grass or tend to our crops without being accosted by them. We are the property of the rich. They wouldn't *let* us live in peace; you will never understand what kind of humiliation that is. If they wanted to rape us, to molest us, and our families objected, then they'd rape us in front of our families.

When questioned why she stood up for her rights, Devi replied, "Anger."[53]

As quoted in *The Boston Globe*, when Devi was asked by Lakshmanan at what point she felt most empowered, in an apparently more relaxed mood the Bandit Queen replied that "being in society" is "nice," but, she felt more powerful when she was a bandit. Devi confided, "Sometimes I think I shouldn't have surrendered."

On July 25, 2001, ABC news reported that Devi, "an Indian Robin Hood," at age 37, was assassinated outside her home.[54] When *Time* ran a short piece about the biopic based on her life, also called *Bandit Queen*, which was at first banned in India, the magazine veered from the routes taken by other news organizations to describe Devi as "part Joan of Arc, part Ma Barker," neither of whom were raped according to their popular legends. Ma Barker played the overly dutiful mother to her thieving, kidnapping, murderous sons, earning her J. Edgar Hoover's designation "Bloody Mama." Fighting the English to defend her French homeland, teenager and religious devotee Joan of Arc wore boy's clothes to protect her modesty, which hopefully worked, but no one knows for sure. Consequently, *The Boston Globe*'s characterization of Devi in terms of Robin Hood crossed with *Thelma & Louise* sounds most precise.[55]

For Westerners unaccustomed to third world realities, Devi's story illuminates the need for feminism to remain alive and well in order to reach beyond "civilized" countries to any place — from Delhi to Detroit — where women lack basic human rights. Reading Devi's account of poor women without access to plumbing in rural India, I remembered a Barbara Ehrenreich story in *Time* written during the so-called "Year of the Woman" about American women serving in a U.S. Senate chamber that didn't have a women's bathroom.[56] Recalling also the Feminist Majority's campaign to educate the American public about the plight of women in Afghanistan years before the September 11, 2001, terrorist attacks, the world-wide sphere of influence connected by *Thelma & Louise* is truly astonishing. From wall posters inspiring women's political action groups in Los Angeles, to *The Boston Globe*'s equation of the film with a flesh and blood figure of female power and rage, is there any other Hollywood film whose characters exhibited a greater effect on the' image, action and future of women? That *Thelma & Louise* has been honored, ignored and decried attests to the picture's power. The great debate illuminates the fury of resistance to improving women's status and the persistent need for feminism around the globe.

One of the many bumper stickers available through NOW quotes Harvard historian Laurel Thatcher Ulrich and her counsel, "Well-behaved women rarely make history." As more and more people came to understand gender bias, women in all ranks and stations were indeed acting on their anger. In Delaware, Ohio, three female relatives retaliated against an admitted child molester by means of abduction, torture and sodomy with a vegetable. In September 1997, *Boston Globe* reporter Michael Grunwald cast the "so-called cucumber case" as a "David Lynch version of *Thelma & Louise*." Law enforcement officials arrested Jewel Hosler, Mary Franks and Vickie Coulter, wife, mother and aunt of Rodney Hosler, for their actions. Like those in India who considered Phoolan Devi a hero, reportedly many living in Ohio felt the same way about the female avengers in their midst. Yet a return to "frontier justice," as *The Boston Globe* termed it, is not a civilized path to a more equitable future. Too bad few popular visions of women acting powerfully and legally exist. This dearth of uplifting female role models is particularly unfortunate in a culture that prefers to sit and watch portrayals in movies and on television rather than to read books. From the untold story of gun pioneer and show woman Annie Oakley to Hollywood's avoidance of real life feminists when it comes time to shoot a biopic, a healthy range of high quality women in Hollywood film is surely missed.

By appreciating art, we learn from the triumphs and mistakes of fictional characters. Within an imaginary scenario, rooting for the anti-hero is acceptable as part of well-balanced creative diet because no one really gets hurt. Although we note shortcomings, we can also recognize the anti-hero's symbolic worth. In reality, those who seek justice through violence are guilty, and so are the supporters who champion their acts — guilty of suspect reasoning at least. "Last month," Grunwald added, "a legal defense fund was established for the three women," yet no fund had been created for the Hosler girls. As innocents under the care of a "classic co-dependent mother," who married their stepfather after accusing him of child rape, the girls deserved public sympathy the most. Though American society is moving towards the eradication of gender bias more quickly than rural India, in the U.S. we are still progressing in bursts, ebbs and lulls. While dealing with a multitude of other issues, Americans are in the process of learning what it means to consider men and women equally. Fatigued by the pace of modern life and enervated by technological advances, our new understanding is tested by messy situations that leave us bewildered. Many viewers were consumed with the less important aspects of *Thelma & Louise*, like the size of the roles delegated to men, while they ignored more important details such as rape. In Ohio, distracted by the actions of the parents, observers forgot about the children.[57]

It's odd that people don't read more to help maintain equilibrium during the chaotic times in which we live. Not surprisingly for a college town, *The Boston Globe*'s book section rivaled its film section during the years studied. Returning to the realm of the imaginary and attesting to art's considerable influence, around the autumnal equinox of 1997, the newspaper commemorated the fortieth anniversary of Jack Kerouac's *On the Road* by toasting the Beat writer from Lowell and his famed novel. "*On the Road* Again, Jack Kerouac's 40-Year-Old Novel Still Holds a Uniquely Influential Place in American Culture" provided the most explorative piece found connecting Kerouac's book to Hollywood and *Thelma & Louise*. Involving the novel more than *The Baltimore Sun* travel piece about 20-year-olds kicking around the country in an old bus had, what was special about Mark Feeney's story was its total submersion in a modern literary classic. According to Feeney, the book's fresh attitude about the possibility of automobiles and the open road impacted literature, movies, television, music and advertising. "Try to find a beer commercial that doesn't trade on either highway imagery or male bonding," he suggested. Feeney argued that Kerouac's main characters Sal and Dean "don't just light out for the Territory," like Mark Twain's Huck and Jim. Instead, "they just light out period," opening Americans to exploration without an end location in mind, prioritizing interior discoveries over destinations, exalting driving from transportation to entertainment. In Feeney's view, the novel's reliance on music and mobility gave the Beat generation a name and maintains *On the Road*'s vibrancy. Although Kerouac originally meant "beat" as in "beaten," Feeney explained, "the term now seems to make the most sense ... as an allusion to rhythm and drive."

One the Road narrator Sal comments about his trip to Hollywood, "Everybody had come to make the movies, even me." Feeney located two key Hollywood elements derived from the novel: the sway of automobile culture and buddy movies. "For better or for worse," Feeney contended, "Kerouac's novel claimed for the car a place in American culture to rival its place in American society." Feeney reasoned that prior to *On the Road*, except for comedy teams male duos in the entertainment world contained "a clear superior and a clear inferior" as a result of ying-yang casts and the star system. After *On the Road*, first television then the movies picked up on the idea of uniting balanced pairs of men on a mission. Through Bill Cosby and Robert Culp in *I Spy*, to Dustin Hoffman and Jon Voight in *Midnight Cowboy*, women were excluded from this province in a show of "cinematic misogyny," Feeney expressed, until *Thelma & Louise* regenerated "*On the Road* in drag."

Feeney's helpful analysis of the book stops short of adequately explicating the film, though it's nice to see a critic recognize a balance between the two women. *Thelma & Louise* veers from *On the Road* in its expression of gritty self-protection. Early in the film, while the women still are not far from home, Thelma in particular learns that highway travelers face danger and need to watch out for themselves. In Kerouac's novel, Sal continually receives money wires from his kindly aunt while he safely thumbs rides from trusting and trustworthy strangers. In comparison, some 35 years later, strangers rape and rip-off Thelma and Louise, and at best cast them a wary eye. Feeney describes *On the Road* as "affirmative" rather than rebellious, whereas *Thelma & Louise* criticizes the divisiveness of American society.[58]

Although the number of references to the film in *The Boston Globe* eventually petered out, the Massachusetts newspaper never lost its remarkable edge. (The number of references dropped from approximately 50 in both 1991 and 1992, to somewhere in the teens from 1993 through 1996, and averaged under 10 per year in the remaining years studied.) In 1998, from sea to shining sea, many U.S. newspapers covered Attorney General Janet Reno's reported *Thelma & Louise* fantasy as she prepared to leave office with the exiting Clinton administration. The Massachusetts newspaper went beyond the usual limits of passing along one-liners and closely investigated the person behind the quip. Mary Leonard explained why Reno looked West to the open road: she would leave behind "those who made her life so difficult." In Washington, D.C., the president's "tight circle" of male advisors shut her out, Leonard elucidated, while Republicans criticized her job performance.

Recognizing the highs and lows of modern women more readily than other newspapers, *The Boston Globe* apprized Bostonians that Reno had "emerged as the role model for character, sobriety, and steel under pressure in an embattled Clinton administration that did not even want her around in a second term." Instead of running derisive jokes about her looks or calculating her measure as a sex object as happened in Las Vegas, Leonard portrayed Reno as just the kind of real-life heroine whom men, women, boys and girls could admire for standing up to opponents without inflicting physical pain. According to "Reno Fights Back After Citation for Contempt," the attorney general once shared, "[O]ne of the things I try to do is to make sure I don't let the pressure push me over backward or push me over forward." In the face of critical attack, Reno's plan was to stand tall and allow herself to sway but not break. Her real-life example is more stable and noble than blowing up rigs, jumping off a cliff, murdering out of revenge or raping molesters in retribution.[59]

That same year, *The Boston Globe*'s appreciation for female leaders who touched off thoughts of *Thelma & Louise* extended across the Atlantic to Ireland. In October, Kevin Cullen wrote a feature on the president of Ireland, Mary McAleese, who was portrayed as filling her "relatively obscure, mostly ceremonial post" with verve and vigor by speaking her mind and promoting the arts. Labeled a "maverick" by Cullen, McAleese won an election in which she couldn't cast a vote, and she did so by the widest margin ever seen in an Irish presidential contest. Under the Irish constitution, *The Boston Globe* informed, Northerners, such as McAlesse (who was born in Belfast, in Northern Ireland), are claimed as Irish citizens but denied suffrage.

Like Janet Reno held her ground and listened to her own voice, once in office the Catholic McAleese called for the ordination of women and upheld gay rights, upsetting the Catholic hierarchy. Trying to reach out to Protestants in a British Isle long known for its religious warfare, soon after her victory McAleese took communion at an Anglican church. Jean Kennedy Smith, then U.S. ambassador to Ireland and also a devout Catholic, did the same in what Cullen saw as a "show of solidarity." The newspaper that later broke the story of sexual misconduct and abuse among Roman Catholic clergy in Boston stated, "Despite finger-wagging by some of the more conservative Catholic clergy, the Thelma and Louise of ecumenism were hit with the Irish people." *The Boston Globe* compared the film characters to ambassadors of religious change. Ceremoniously, McAleese and Kennedy Smith unified two previously opposing factions and a bitterly divided country; artistically, *Thelma & Louise* brought together men and women from diverse backgrounds to oppose sexual violence and gender limitations.[60]

Returning stateside, exactly eight years to the day after Jay Carr wrote his first review of the then-new film, on May 24, 1999, *The Boston Globe* announced that Geena Davis had returned to Boston University, where she spent time as an undergraduate. As part of the school's commencement exercises, she received an honorary doctor of fine arts degree. According to the newspaper, college president Jon Westling complimented the actress for her contribution to *Thelma & Louise* and *A League of Their Own*. He commended, "Your luminous charms turn these eccentric roles into memorable characters, but you also etch unforgettable portraits of women at work, at play and at the end of their ropes." The only woman and the only entertainer within the group of honorees, Davis was honored alongside Henry Kissinger, esteemed academics and a community activist.[61]

Thelma and Louise fit right into a nation filled with so many odd pairings. Flip-flopping the trend in Detroit, where writers first tied the title to cars then years later adopted *Thelma & Louise* as a metaphor for female pioneers, *Thelma & Louise* popped up five times in two *Boston Globe* articles that appeared in the automotive section early in 2000. Even though *The Boston Globe* covered the film far more extensively in other sections, automotive editors at the newspaper were no more familiar with *Thelma & Louise* than their counterparts in the Motor City. Still, the way each town connected cars to the film followed their distinct characterizations. To Detroiters, domestically produced automobiles reign supreme; they are a way of life, the only mode of transportation imaginable and, for many, a paycheck. In Boston, where people also opt for public transportation such as buses, trains, subways, taxis and drive foreign models, cars are appreciated like fine wine and serve as conduits for whimsical thought.

In *The Boston Globe*, unseasonable weather and the sight of an attractive woman on the freeway inspired "Author Captures Convertibles and Their Siren Call to the Open Road."

> Three days into the New Year, air warm and sun glistening, she passed me on the interstate. The top of her Saab convertible was down and she had a scarf on her head, sunglasses wrapped across her eyes, as she bopped to music I could not hear. "Thelma or Louise?" I asked myself.

Serving as book critic and automotive writer, Royal Ford found the idea of a female reincarnated in either character's likeness attractive despite the women's criminal records and hazardous final bow. His breezy review of a book about the convertible's history closed with a toast: "[T]o unexpected warm days, and to the woman in the Saab — Thelma or Louise — and many miles in open cars on open roads."[62] The second article, "Yearning for the Movie Car — Until Another Comes Along," recited an ode to favorite cars appearing on the big screen. To add to a list that included cars driven by Grace Kelly and Ava Gardner, one reader voiced affection for the Pacer from *Wayne's World* and the Thunderbird in *Thelma & Louise*. Again, Royal Ford romanced the automobile.

> And so we fall in love, or like, with cars we see on screen. Sometimes it is because we want to own the car. Sometimes it is because the car represents something far larger — escape, freedom, rebellion ... But love is often in the air. Thelma and Louise, fleeing bad marriages, loved each other all the way to the edge of the Grand Canyon.

Of course, Louise is actually single and the picture was not shot at the Grand Canyon, but people who worship cars are apparently prone to idling other details when talk comes around to their beloved possessions. [63]

From car talk to theatrical productions, to close out the decade of *Thelma & Louise* coverage, in 2001, the newspaper conveyed how well the film had become affixed to vivid imaginations. A review of playwright Carter W. Lewis' "Women Who Steal," which was running on Cape Cod, noted the similarities between the film and the current stage production, which also featured a female duo who pair up and take off, in Lewis' version, behind the wheel of a Mercedes. In this case, *The Boston Globe*'s coverage of theater sounded like *The Houston Chronicle*'s coverage of convicted criminals Rose Marie Turford and Carolyn Stevens, branded "Thelma and Louise fugitives" in Texas. Less enthusiastic about the stage spin-off than the film, *The Boston Globe*'s Ryan McKittrick commented that the leads of "Women Who Steal," Peggy and Karen, "look like a faded copy of Thelma and Louise."[64]

PART III. CASE STUDIES

Similarly, three months later the memorable title appeared in a serialized novella, *Riptide*, by Elizabeth Benedict. One of Benedict's characters compared another's suggestion to "keep driving"—in this case, south on Interstate 93, through downtown Boston, heading for Wood's Hole, Martha's Vineyard and the Atlantic Ocean—to the fictional women's zigzag course around the desert Southwest. As readily as people associate consulting a mirror with Disney's *Snow White*, ten years after the film's launch commentators in Boston related the open road to *Thelma & Louise*.[65]

Callie Khouri's formidable screenplay was stretched in so many ways by so many people. As the post–*Thelma & Louise* decade wound down, encouraged by the area's top newspaper greater Boston's still vibrant appreciation for the film was evident from Boston University on Commonwealth Ave. out west to the suburbs. Near the end of the millennium, in late November 1999, a reader from Needham wrote a letter to the editor correcting a recent *Boston Globe* headline.

> It's quite a stretch to apply the headline "A turn for the better" to recent data about the health of our planet.... That's a bit like saying that things were looking up for Thelma and Louise as they headed for the cliff because they weren't pressing quite so hard on the gas pedal anymore.... What they needed wasn't a matter of pushing less hard on the accelerator or even easing off the gas entirely. They needed to apply the brakes immediately and forcefully while turning the car in a completely different direction. And so do we.

From global politics and religion, to crime, education, arts and environment, *Thelma & Louise* made a crater-size impact in Massachusetts and beyond providing a wide range of inspiration. Long after the release left theaters, people pointed to the film to help better understand and explain the world at large.[66]

19. The East vs. the Heartland: *The Boston Herald* and *The Kansas City Star*

Thelma & Louise was said to do better in "sophisticated urban areas," yet whether they are described as "liberal" or "conservative," particular regions are not of one mind. When studied more closely, most areas reflect a purple mix of attitudes rather than solid red or blue colorings. Known as a working class newspaper in comparison to *The Boston Globe* with its more intellectual standpoint, *The Boston Herald* mentioned the picture close to 150 times from 1991 through 2001, falling just a few dozen instances short of the cross-town competition. However, the two Boston newspapers handled the film in distinct ways, as we will see.

The number two Boston newspaper not only filed fewer stories including *Thelma & Louise* compared to *The Boston Globe*, but it also covered the film within a more narrow focus. Except for entertainment news, the tabloid-style newspaper once owned by the Hearst Corporation sold readers more shallow analysis. Outside of Hollywood, the film didn't hold much importance in *The Boston Herald*; it was more likely to pop up in gossip columns and trivia quizzes rather than in-depth cultural or political investigations. For example, in 1995, the column "Tuesday Celebrity" conveyed to readers that "feminist icon" Callie Khouri's follow-up release, *Something to Talk About*, featured Julia Roberts sticking by a disloyal spouse. Rather than discuss the film, the newspaper described Khouri as "more or less missing in action" since winning her Oscar for *Thelma & Louise*. Addressing the individual instead of her work, *The Boston Herald* tattled that Khouri "denied reports of a nervous breakdown, but confessed to a whopping bout of writer's block."[1] The next year, in the column "Wednesday Celebrity," the newspaper provided the answer to the previous day's trivia question: "Brad Pitt portrayed a hitchhiking cowboy named J.D. in what 1991 film?"[2]

Both newspapers treated the release as an undeniable presence, but they allocated different weight to the production. Though exceptions exist, in general *The Boston Globe* supplied longer articles, conducted more searing analysis and accorded the film more respect, while *The Boston Herald* played with the title more superficially. *The Boston Globe* chose not to use *Thelma & Louise* as one-size-fits-all phrase to describe local female criminals, while *The Boston Herald*, drawn to the sensational, jumped at the opportunity. When two female bank robbers ripped off area banks in Arlington, Boston, Everett, Lexington, Stoneham and Wilmington, editors at *The Boston Herald* fit the film title into three headlines and within the body of five pieces between March 19 and March 25, 1999. "Cops Think They Have *Thelma* and/or *Louise*" tipped off readers to the "*Thelma & Louise* bandits," who "represent the first known time that two women have paired up for heists." To *The Boston Herald*, a pair of real women committing crime was the surest evidence of the film's worth.[3]

Politics, culture, and women's history were merged in the Hub's collected coverage of *Thelma & Louise*. In Boston, lines were drawn between important female figures, both real and imaginary. *The Boston Herald*'s attitude toward Hillary Clinton was a reliable indicator of its editorial attitude toward *Thelma & Louise*, at least outside of the entertainment section. Indicating the newspaper's disparate perspective, in a discussion of Ken Burns' documentary *Not for Ourselves Alone: The Story of Elizabeth Cady Stanton and Susan B. Anthony*, *Boston Herald* columnist Margery Eagan labeled Hillary "nauseating." Eagan's disapproval landed her in a minority category among people in Massachusetts: those who didn't support the president's wife, a group *The Boston Globe* didn't address.

Though a feminist, Eagan showed signs of bearing a double standard in regards to gender. Her dislike for Hillary sometimes sounded as if it extended to all women, including fictional Thelma and Louise, who she deemed "killerettes." In her November 7, 1999, column, "Burns Is Haughty but Brilliant in Anthony, Stanton Portraits," *The Boston Herald* columnist admitted that she enjoyed the program but held some reservations. After watching the documentary featuring the country's first legendary feminist friends, she felt moved "to stand and give the sisterhood salute," despite Burns' objectionable "all-the-rage-on-Brattle-Street sensibilities." Although she found Burns' signature touch on previous works *The Civil War* and *Baseball* in turns "moving" and "brilliant," Eagan didn't appreciate the same style when applied to "somber ladies in lacy caps."

Addressing *Boston Herald* readers, Eagan distanced herself from the area's intellectual foment centered on Harvard Square in Cambridge (home to the art house Brattle Theater and the Hasty Pudding Theatrical, which awarded Susan Sarandon its Woman of the Year award mid-decade). Snipping at Burn's "PC in over-drive" tone but without substantive criticism, Eagan staked out separate territory from which to applaud the documentary about two individuals whose actions eventually led to women's suffrage. With her no-frills attitude bent on being ornery, Eagan sided with stereotypical South Bostonians and hawkers outside of Fenway Park across the Charles River. She conceded that Burns "is a genius at what he does," but through her snide tone poised a dichotomy between educated and street-smart sections of greater Boston reminiscent of the city's portrayal in *Good Will Hunting* (1997).[4]

Too many people are clueless about feminist history, whether the topic is present day conditions for women in film or the distant past, when women enjoyed few of the rights often taken for granted today. Three days prior to Eagan's hard-hitting perspective, *The Boston Herald* reviewed Burns' PBS documentary on November 4 and again reminded viewers to watch in a second mini-review that ran on November 5. Jeanette Johnston wrote both pieces, which incorporated an interview with the filmmaker. In Johnston's first article, "Herstory," Burns relayed his humiliation as an American history filmmaker who didn't know much about Stanton and Anthony prior to making his film. "I had no idea that they were the two most important women in American history," he admitted. Johnston informed readers of a Global Strategy Group poll which found that 93 percent of Americans fail to associate Stanton with women's rights and nearly three-quarters are unaware of when the 19th amendment passed. This lack of familiarity led her to wonder if the documentary would find an audience. To generate enthusiasm, Burns passionately explained that the birth of feminism in the United States "is just not women's history. It's everybody's history." Picking up on the filmmaker's ardor, Johnston elaborated that in the early 19th century women exercised fewer rights than a "lunatic."[5]

Johnston assumed that *Boston Herald* readers would fall into the majority who didn't recognize Stanton apart from a foggy link to the unpopular dollar coin. In her shorter follow-up piece, she wisecracked, "Didn't know who Stanton and Anthony were, huh?" Johnston commiserated, "Well, before making this film, Burns didn't either." While her brief blurb quickly adopted a more earnest tone and highly recommended the program, in comparison to *The Boston Globe*, *The Boston Herald* projected a far less progressive view of its readership.

Although *The Boston Herald* didn't grant *Thelma & Louise* a place in "everybody's history" as readily as *The Boston Globe* did, the newspaper did recognize the film's impact and related its formidable stature to Burns's historical documentary. "Daring Women," Johnston's second mini-review of *Not for Ourselves Alone*, rewrote the founding mothers of American feminism as "fiery, stubborn revolutionaries"; in other words, "Thelma and Louise in hoop skirts."[6] Enlarging the already large reach extended by the picture, *The Boston Herald* corseted Stanton and Anthony in yet another perhaps outlandish (and this author's personal favorite) instance of *Thelma & Louise* naming.

While *The Boston Globe* projected the spirit of the film characters into current political events, *The Boston Herald* looked backward. In at least one respect, due to separate methods and goals (in short, from the selfish to the selfless), it seems ridiculous to compare the movie's fictional women with real-life revolutionaries. After a cursory glance, the two sets of females appear to hold little in common besides biology and close friendship. Yet even though their drives diverge, because they hurdle similar roadblocks, the comparison does make sense. It's certainly understandable considering the dearth of famous female figures embraced by American culture. Historically speaking, in their distinct battles against biased attitudes, one staged in the public arena, the other captured on film, Elizabeth and Susan and Thelma and Louise mark separate points along the same continuum.

More than the *Herald*, the *Globe* embraced Hillary, Thelma, Louise, Susan and Elizabeth with greater ardor and appreciation. The newspaper also logged three pieces on the Burns documentary but overall provided readers with more copy regarding the filmmaker, his film, its reception, and Anthony and Stanton. Like Jeanette Johnston had done but in longer form minus the conversational jabs, Don Aucoin interviewed Burns and previewed his work in the arts section on October 31. In "The 'Family Drama' of Women's History," Aucoin cast Burns as a revved-up "man on a mission" out to rescue his subjects from "semi-obscurity." Neither woman lived to see the ratification of the 19th amendment, which lifted verbatim the wording drafted by Stanton and Anthony in the 1870s around the time of the historic Seneca Falls Women's Rights convention, but according to Aucoin, in excess of eight million women voted in 1920. The filmmaker charged that if Stanton and Anthony had been men, "there would be marble monuments in Washington with cherry blossoms around them" to celebrate and honor their invaluable contributions. Father to two daughters awash in a "culture of Victoria's Secret" Burns fervently protested the lack of a constitutional Equal Rights Amendment.[7] Over two hundred years after the country's inception, unlike men, women still are not specifically represented in, nor protected by, the U.S. Constitution.

In the "Living" section on November 5, Aucoin's review, "A Vivid History of Early Feminists," located the usual place for women's history: "relegated to the periphery." However, rather than play up the public's lack of familiarity with the roots of feminism in the U.S., *The Boston Globe* took the time to educate readers with summary sketches detailing Stanton and Anthony's lives. Stanton married, raised seven children, stayed home and wrote, while Anthony remained single, traveled extensively and delivered speeches. The two forged a formidable partnership, in Aucoin's appraisal, breaking "rules and ground for a half century," for which they were taunted and jailed.[8]

Following Aucoin's critique, "Viewing Parties Toast Women Who Changed History" appeared on November 9, after the film's two-night run. Attesting to the documentary's consequence and appeal, *The Boston Globe* reported on local gatherings in Walpole, Jamaica Plain, Brookline, Concord, Medfield and Cambridge, which centered on Burns' film. In contrast to the picture of viewer ignorance pushed by *The Boston Herald*, according to *The Boston Globe*, which assumed viewer interest in feminism, over a thousand similar events were held across the country. To drive home the significance of the two historical figures, the newspaper pointed out that women who watched *Not for Ourselves Alone* from the comfort of houses they owned owed a special debt to the women whose story they followed. Anthony and Stanton's work lead to changes in property law, which allow today's women to sign mortgages.[9]

In our fast-paced, sound-bite age, oversimplification undermines debate. Imprecisely, people lump nicotine, alcohol, heroin and marijuana together in a category loosely labeled "drugs" that should also include fast food and excessive, mindless consumerism. Likewise, frequent calls blame society's ills on an unwieldy collection of entities tied together and referred to derogatorily as "the media." Yet coast-to-coast newspaper coverage surrounding *Thelma & Louise* reminds us that not all mastheads and journalists are created alike. Extrapolating on the variances between *The Boston Globe* and *The Boston Herald* and applying those thoughts across the country, what might be fairly termed "socially conservative" in Boston, Massachusetts, still falls to the left of center in Grand Forks, North Dakota, Cedar Rapids, Iowa, and Kansas City, Missouri. Hillary Clinton's fictional sisters in feminism as christened by *The Boston Globe* received a tad more attention by article count in *The Kansas City Star* than *The Boston Herald*, but less enthusiastic coverage. *The Boston Herald* didn't appreciate the film as much as *The Boston Globe* did, but *The Kansas City Star*, which talked about the picture nearly just as much as the two Massachusetts newspapers, liked *Thelma & Louise* even less.

As the reception of Hillary Clinton, *Not for Ourselves Alone* and *Thelma & Louise* together tell us, society continues to mishandle women. Dead center in the continental U.S., at *The Kansas City Star*, Ken Burns' documentary wasn't awarded its own review space, and hometown journalists discredited *Thelma & Louise*. Although *Not for Ourselves Alone* played locally, in lieu of a plug for the piece on behalf of "everyone's history," the Show Me state newspaper preferred an article prioritizing local history. Within the "E" section towards the back, "The Forgotten Feminist" told the story of Clarina Irene Howard Nichols, a native of Vermont who moved west and attended the 1859 state constitutional convention that resulted in Kansas entering the union in 1861. She was the only woman to address the assembly, and as result of her efforts women in the newly admitted state were given unprecedented rights including the right to vote in school elections and the right to equal custody of children in cases of divorce. However, because Burns didn't include Nichols in his film, *The Kansas City Star* evidently felt slighted on behalf of its readers. Though it used the occasion to tell a very worthwhile story, the Heartland newspaper focused on Nichols' life instead of the documentary. Using either/or thinking instead of more open-minded plurality, as a result the newspaper relegated the 19th amendment to a brief parenthetical.[10]

In determining how well a newspaper covers women's issues and cultural reflections of women's lives, a progressive perspective is most important. Frequent mentions of *Thelma & Louise* didn't mean that a newspaper embraced the film. It was possible to engage the great debate but still dislike the picture, which happened in Kansas City. Local journalists were not supportive, but even more telling, essays generated in-house lacked cohesion. Any praise extended by *The Kansas City Star* was subject to wavering like a flag caught in strong wind.

Although the publication named *Thelma & Louise* in over 150 articles throughout the *Thelma & Louise* decade, the Knight Ridder–owned newspaper (part of a chain of newspapers including *The Detroit Free Press*) covered the controversy by relying in large part on journalists writing for other newspapers and outside news services, such as *Newsday*, the Associated Press, *The New York Times* news service, *The Chicago Tribune* and *The Los Angeles Daily News*. Obituaries appear under a *Kansas City Star* archive search for *Thelma & Louise*, accounting for approximately 20 of the listings; one such example is the obituary for Thelma Louise Jobst, from Independence, Missouri, who passed away in 1993. Never receiving the depth of analysis offered by *The Boston Globe*, the film made the newspaper's "Stargazing" gossip column 15 times.

In Kansas City, Robert W. Butler's May 24, 1991, review, "The Role Reversals in This Buddy-road Movie Really Sparkle," revealed a schism in the reviewer's perspective. Butler conceded two and half stars to *Thelma & Louise*, thus falling in the mixed column of critiques. He was impressed by the leads and Ridley Scott's technical prowess, particularly his carefully framed shots, but was not won over by Callie Khouri's "simplistic exclamation points." Setting the tone for what was to come in subsequent *Kansas City Star* articles, in contrast to the "sparkle" promoted in the headline, Butler couldn't fully appreciate the way the story moved females into traditional male territory. In theory he accepted the film's "role reversals" but later wondered "what feminist message is being sent when women ape the most violent tendencies of the opposite sex."

Straddling opposing responses, Butler believed that Khouri "borrows shamelessly" from previous films including *Badlands* (1974), whose numb, apathetic tone sharply contrasts the spirit of Khouri's work, and the more commonly compared *Butch Cassidy and the Sundance Kid*. Yet he admitted that "the picture's feminine emphasis imparts a fresh twist." Portrayals in the film "walk a fine line between reality and the patently absurd," according to his review, although Davis and Sarandon submit "convincing" and "terrific performances." Trying to sum up a picture he enjoyed but felt compelled to discount, Butler was torn between the picture's "engaging interplay" and a "downbeat ending." Unmoved by rape and abuse, which he did not address beyond brief summary, Bulter found the film "uneven" and only "modestly successful," which better described his review.[11]

Comparatively, Butler heaped three stars on 1992's *Leaving Normal*, which many critics panned, and lauded Edward Solomon's "meandering but often hilarious" script. "*Leaving Normal* is the film *Thelma & Louise* could have been had its makers not been so interested in turning the title characters into a distaff Butch and Sundance," Butler snipped, backhanding a slight to both the earlier film and the idea that women might walk in men's footsteps. As if there is only room for one set of female buddies in Hollywood, and Thelma Dickerson and Louise Sawyer aren't women enough to fill the bill, Butler's piece on *Leaving Normal* appeared under the headline "Meet the Real *Thelma & Louise.*"[12]

In June 1991, by way of an opinion piece subtitled, "No One Is Not Talking About *Thelma & Louise*," Virginia Hall dove into "the boiling pot" of commentary fired up because of the picture. In Hall's opinion, the great debate involved mostly "men and women of the media," which may have been the case in Kansas City, but the evidence from other cities tempers her outlook.

Despite the rush of talk, because "too much" had been "left unsaid," Hall shared her take, which came in a few contrasting forms. Her opinion varied as a result of seeing the film twice with two different people. Sitting in the theater, Hall was initially swayed by the story, but afterward she decided to dislike the picture based on principle and due to embarrassment. Later, after a second viewing, she was moved to cut *Thelma & Louise* some slack when she witnessed someone else doing so. Indirectly, Hall admitted that perhaps she was too quick to condemn the movie the first time around.

Juggling her perspective from the very start, at first Hall supported Liz Smith's worries about impressionable viewers. Counting herself among the impressionable as she sat and watched the show, Hall stated that she was "ready to cut loose, hit the road, Jill, give 'em what-for" when the picture ended. Outside of the theater, she "blathered at length" to her daughter about the "awfulness of it all," meaning the awfulness of the film's men, but her daughter's response changed her own. Hall's daughter blamed Thelma for Harlan's actions because she enters the bar, drinks swiftly, waves and flirts. Letting an attempted rapist completely off the hook, according to her mother, the daughter summed up, "I mean, she put herself in a position where something like that could happen," which is true but not the complete story.

Hall started to condemn Harlan's actions, but she decided not to because Hall didn't want "to make an issue ... when the kid plainly has a pretty good grip on how things too often are" when men assault women. Ironically, this conversion between mother and daughter reinforced the decision Thelma and Louise make to flee. The fictional duo assume they were right to run because otherwise people would have held Thelma solely accountable and totally forgiven Harlan's bad behavior. Without college degrees or impressive job titles, Callie Khouri's characters accurately forecast mistaken reactions like the Halls'. Providing a more thoughtful perspective, the reader of *The Arkansas Gazette* who counseled her daughter to beware shared a more appropriate response. As her letter to the editor expressed, physical assault is illegal and unacceptable, but since it happens anyway women should take precautions, use their brains and try to prevent the likelihood of attack. Over-simplifying the situation and only blaming the victim, the Halls unfairly released Harlan from his social responsibility. This reminder seems obvious but somehow the message tends to get lost: individuals have no right to commit rape no matter the circumstances.

Now prepared to deplore the "multiple misadventures of Thelma and Louise," Hall argued that the film was "anti-feminist" because the women go fishing. "Look," she emphasized, the women "set off on a traditionally male outing." Hall ended her paragraph there as if to say the leads' brazen whim was enough to prove her point. Deriving literal emphasis where the filmmakers employed metaphor (the title characters hold no real desire or actual intentions of fishing), Hall complained that Thelma and Louise "enter a male world where they become mock men in order to survive." As a result of their misguided venture on the wrong gender track, Hall assessed that things turn out "badly, to say the least."

Following Hall's rationale and tone, if only the women would have simply stayed home, Thelma with her inattentive, verbally abusive husband, Louise with a dead end job and unreliable boyfriend, then everything would've worked out better. She chose not to recognize the women's "journey of transformation," as Jay Carr called their adventures. Instead, Hall insinuated that a woman's place is in the home and nowhere else. If only Thelma and Louise had acted like good sports and accepted verbal abuse and second class status silently, they could have gone on living like before, perhaps taking up embroidery for fulfillment. To combat backward mindsets that restrict women, NOW markets a bumper sticker that boldly states, albeit with incorrect grammar: "A WOMEN'S PLACE IS IN THE HOUSE AND SENATE."

After her first viewing, Hall stood among the small minority of critics who, once they felt compelled to join the great debate, vociferously objected to the film. Luckily, Hall was drawn to the movie a second time. Moved by the reaction of an adult male companion, Hall later conceded within the same article that *Thelma & Louise* was "fascinating," "funny" and "sad." Hall was so blown away by the picture, even after two screenings she struggled to analyze her own response. When her male companion pointed out how poorly "co-dependent" Darryl and Jimmy fare without Thelma and Louise, Hall was induced to label the women "enablers." Hall's friend influenced her opinion, which fluctuated without a firm anchor. At first Hall wanted to like the film, but her daughter wouldn't let her, so dutifully the journalist panned the picture. "The 14-year-old at my side was saying to me what I, as a parent, should have been saying to her," Hall gulped. Later, when another adult found subject matter worth talking about, Hall rethought her position. She realized her first impression was hasty and that the film deserved more consideration, though her appraisal continued to side against the women.[13]

Viewers like Hall didn't know what to make of *Thelma & Louise* in part because they weren't properly prepared. Ignorance of women's history, lack of experience with feminist expression and poor art appreciation skills hurt the picture's reception nationwide. The movie's marketing campaign intensified the problem. Media hype moved Hall, perhaps recklessly, to take her young teenager to the theater to see the R-rated release without previewing it first. Inside, another patron caught her eye. She assumed that he had also expected to encounter laughs. Hall interpreted that the man felt misled and looked for comedy at the wrong time during Thelma's assault. Later in the film, when Thelma calls Darryl from the road and says, "We're in the mountains.... We're fishing," its very humorous in an ironic way, considering what the women are actually up to, but viewers who were blown away by any of the film's other elements may have missed the joke and taken Thelma's words at face value.

During the summer of 1991, journalists at *The Kansas City Star* failed to offer clear and persuasive commentaries about *Thelma & Louise*. The day after Virginia Hall's split response, "Violence and the New Woman" missed the film's figurative nature and instead harped on the "destructive" acts of two "dizzy gunslingers." Completely ignoring Harlan's deplorable actions and totally bypassing the positive aspects of the women's growing bond, George Gurley reiterated the views of his co-workers. Gurley decried the film's feminist appropriation of traditional male territory, including "male quests for self-knowledge."

One reason why Gurley had trouble grasping the film as a whole may have had something to do with his poor understanding of feminism. Sneering at the women's movement, Gurley defined "the ultimate feminist argument" as achieving equality with men by becoming "equally destructive." Too bad *The Kansas City Star* didn't review and recommend *Not for Ourselves Alone* to readers because Gurley's view of history could have used some balance. Feminists "have sought and won coed dorms, admittance to Skull and Bones, the privilege of participating in Bass Anglers fishing tournaments," he trivialized. Gurley surmised that women may not "feel truly indistinguishable" from men "until as many of them see combat, commit serial murders and go to the electric chair." Without hesitation, he reduced hard won rights such as the right to vote, which he skipped over, to purely negative reflections of women's advancement.

Like Hall, Gurley appeared dazed and confused by *Thelma & Louise*. After seeing the picture and encountering a bewildering mix of internal responses, Gurley turned his focus to greater society, hoping he'd find an easier target for his criticisms, but the Heartland cultural observer noted "bizarre" gender politics on the part of both men and women. Obliquely referring to Robert Bly as well as *Thelma & Louise*, Gurley complained that the "gropings of men and women for sexual identity make it embarrassing to be either one." With his bearings blown, Gurley tried to disappear into a neverland without gender or conflict. He condemned violence, calling it an "eternal attraction for lost, ineffectual souls," but also contested that no one would "be caught dead espousing caring, conciliation, cooperation and peace in these macho times." Gurley's dismantled views left him little room to move or think, especially about a story that combined gender tensions, sexual violence, dramatic retribution and sisterly cooperation.[14]

When *Thelma & Louise* was released on videocassette in 1992, Scott Herrick voiced his disapproval of the film, the fourth *Kansas City Star* staffer to do so. In "Buddies on a Rampage," he commented on how "unfortunate" the film and the great debate were. A film that "cast women in the kind of violent, renegade roles usually reserved for men was heralded last year as a triumph for women," Herrick wrote, dismayed. Without citing employment statistics for women in Hollywood or noting the lack of quality parts available to big screen actresses, *The Kansas City Star* columnist commented sarcastically, "Great. Now girls have adult female role models whose lives are so messed up that they break away from society and embark on a cross-country, lawbreaking drive into oblivion." Yet when Ken Burns offered upstanding, laudable, real-life female role models, the newspaper shunned them out of pettiness.[15]

In a 1993 profile of a local 12-year-old girl, *The Kansas City Star* once again displayed its sympathies. "A 'Prep,' So Close to 13" expounded on child rearing and adolescence in the suburbs. If one relied only on the newspaper's report, apparently parents in the greater Kansas City area didn't worry about movie ratings and instead allowed their underage children to watch *Thelma & Louise* "in the dark till midnight," as the girl was purported to do, followed by cartoons the next morning. Worried about the "subtle" messages that "practically beg young people" to experiment with illegal drugs, alcohol and sex, Elaine Adams reminded readers about the dangerous ideas contained in the girl's video rental choice, which was presumably authorized by her parents.

> Look no farther than Thelma and Louise. Those two ran away from home, got drunk, shot a person, robbed a store and, in the last frame, ended their lives in glorious suicide. And don't forget the one-night stand.

Despite Adams' concerns over the trouble Callie Khouri's creations get into, her subject was drawn to the film's positive elements. Referring to the pre-teen as a "modern woman," who "thinks for herself," Adams informed readers that although the girl winced at the film's violence she also understood *Thelma & Louise* "as a story of friendship that's loyal and true." Ironically, within the pages of *The Kansas City Star* the youngster was the only local to focus on the relationship between the title duo, recalling the maxim about wisdom and the mouths' of babes. In regard to Adams' glaring omission of rape within her summary of the film, I wonder if comprehensive sex education and women's history — "everybody's history" — will ever constitute a vital part of public school education in the area, which Adams also touched upon in her article. In an ideal world, before young women head out on their own, they should be exposed to a wide range of pertinent information including more than pregnancy prevention and a rudimentary knowledge of our founding fathers.[16]

There's no use criticizing outdated attitudes and questionable behavior without giving individuals who subscribe to them a chance to grow and change. To be fair, eight years after George Gurley analyzed *Thelma & Louise* with the help of female-contaminated "all-male asparagus" to propose that the sexes will always be in conflict due to biological differences, he showed signs of developing a more mature, broader outlook. Manning a book review column, his August 15, 1999, headline asked, "Does Anyone Really Miss Misogyny?" In other words, did anyone really miss the old George? Like ex-smokers who nag current smokers to quit, Gurley snickered at an "indignant" reader who accused the journalist of being homosexual because he recently claimed that women can do "anything as well as men, if not better." As if Gurley was addressing his former self, he chided, "Hmmm ... do those sound like the words of someone who's secure in his masculinity?" Surveying the literary history of "ill will toward women" (not including his own contribution), Gurley substantiated his new female-friendly position with a variety of references including the Book of Genesis and Shakespeare's *The Taming of the Shrew*. With the help of Marina Walker's *Six Myths of Our Time*, which drew on *Thelma & Louise*, Gurley proclaimed, "In spite of a long history of men trying to keep women in their place, the days of the 'weaker sex' are over." For whatever reasons, it just took some folks in Kansas City longer to catch on.[17]

One article produced in-house at *The Kansas City Star* remembered the film in tentative, lukewarm terms. "Women-only Ski Classes" in the fall of 1991 picked up on the trend to use *Thelma & Louise* as a symbol of female friendship, but the article did so very hesitantly and then retreated. Highlighting programs designed especially for female skiers, Claire Walter stressed that the new approach "is not Thelma and Louise and Martha and Jennifer on skis." Instead, she explained, "a women-only format seems to enhance skill

building, accelerated by mutual encouragement and female camaraderie."
What Walter was trying to say by contrasting a group of women against the
idea of women learning together wasn't clear. Whether Martha and Jennifer
also represented particular characters or were intended to stand for everyday
women and girls was also lost in a haze of imprecision. How would four
women, including Thelma and Louise, learning to ski necessarily deviate from
"mutual encouragement" and "female camaraderie"? Did *The Kansas City Star*
worry that women skiing without men but with Thelma and Louise might
seem too radical to its readers, which might explain its skittish metaphor?
Whatever the case, although the newspaper used the film characters creatively,
editors didn't feel safe doing so without watering down and refuting the reference.[18]

Outnumbering those written in-house, many articles in *The Kansas City
Star* that referred to the film relied on opinions from the East Coast and elsewhere, some complimentary, some not. Representing Universal Press, Joseph
Sobran reviewed *Thelma & Louise* together with Madonna's *Truth or Dare*.
To set his course, Sobran satirically adopted the *Random House Dictionary*'s
encouragement to avoid sexist language. "In that spirit," Sobran callously
logged in on a "pair of new films about womyn." In his summary of Khouri's
plot, he teased the picture's "only decent" male character, in the process sounding more like a schoolyard bully than an adult. Because the police officer on
the women's trail shows the type of humane concern George Gurley felt was
missing from society, Sobran sneered that Slocumbe "surely has the *Random
House Dictionary* on his desk." After giving away Thelma's near rape in the
parking lot, two paragraphs later Sobran wrote, "Nobody really gets hurt,"
tremendously downplaying the trauma associated with sexual abuse and the
beating Harlan directs at Thelma. Designating the film a "feminist manifesto" and juxtaposing Thelma and Louise against his bitter notion of "doc-
trinaire feminists," Sobran accused the filmmakers of having a plot (apparently
failed or delayed) to "carry the feminist message to the heartland." His own
message, that the film "doesn't trust you to react on your own," may have
been more persuasive if Sobran hadn't let his misogyny shine so blatantly.
Without explaining the pertinence of his contention, he criticized Geena
Davis for being "a little too luscious, like a Playboy cartoon." (Though no
surprise, if it is any conciliation to Davis, Madonna didn't fare to well in
Sobran's piece either.)[19]

Although syndicated columnist Donald Kraul's view of the film divari-
cated from Sobran's and the newspaper's staff, one wonders how readers of
The Kansas City Star weighed more harshly critical opinions of locals against
the ideas of more accepting outsiders, in this case arriving via Tribune Media
Services in June 1991. "Let me put this as simply as I can," Kraul spelled out.
He sounded as if he was surveying an audience of simple minds though his
point was to cut through all the media hype that confused viewers. "This is

a great film," Kraul admitted, but he didn't think *Thelma & Louise* was funny either.

> This is not a romp; even less of a high ol' time. When does it get sassy as a rest stop? Finally I realized I had been misled. It is none of those things. It is instead a brilliant exposition on the subject of rape; in both the literal sense and as a metaphor for the myriad ways men abuse women.

Kraul empathized with the serious heart of the film while overlooking its camp and sass. Still, feminists can't argue against his sympathies in regards to women and respectful behavior. He went on to describe a scene involving a female reporter for *The Washington Post* who was inappropriately "grabbed" and "pulled" across the lap of president George Bush's doctor at a dinner party in Washington D.C. "That incident and the absolute lack of shame it produced at the Bush White House, Mecca of Republican Family Values, says a lot about rape in our society," Kraul pointed out prior to the Anita Hill/Clarence Thomas conflict. "So does *Thelma & Louise,*" he concluded, urging readers to "go see it." Apparently, comparatively few readers in the area heeded his suggestion.[20]

Other newspapers in the heartland showed much less interest in the film than *The Kansas City Star*. Instead of printing kudos or complaints, surrounding newspapers simply locked *Thelma & Louise* outside their radar. According to NewsLibrary archives, *The Journal World* from Lawrence, Kansas, tipped its hat to *Thelma & Louise* all of eight times between 1991 and 2001, not including a film review. *The Gazette*, out of Cedar Rapids, Iowa, mentioned the title in 14 articles starting in 1992, the furthest back its NewsLibrary archives reach, but that count includes obituaries as well as Ellen Goodman columns. Further north, *The Grand Forks Herald*, serving Grand Forks, North Dakota, evidently didn't review the film either. In the decade studied, out of six articles listed in a NewsLibrary search, the North Dakota newspaper ran one travel article in 1996 tagged, "New Mexico, Move Over, Thelma and Louise: Sisters Hit the Road to the Land of Enchantment." Due to a lack of interest in both films and presumably feminism, the great debate did not draw many folks from the very middle of the country but was, as we have seen, a hot topic in metropolitan areas around the country.

Back on the East Coast, although not as progressive in its outlook as its local competitor, *The Boston Herald* displayed a more female-friendly front than *The Kansas City Star*. Like many of its peers across the country, *The Boston Herald* associated *Thelma & Louise* with a smattering of trends seen elsewhere, such as women and guns[21] and women and cowgirl fashion,[22] yet the East Coast newspaper also held up the film as a source of power to abortion rights defenders. Describing a "hastily organized" rally on Boston Common in 1992, the newspaper printed the warning, "George Bush — meet Thelma and Louise and thousands of their closest friends." The version of

"Abortion Clashes Wind Down in the Hub" available through online archives was unclear about whether the newspaper or demonstrators called in Thelma and Louise.[23]

For the most part, however, *The Boston Herald* adopted a tepid tone and stuck to the picture's surface. Picking up the trend late in the decade, the *Boston Herald* included the film in three articles about travel, none of which tilled new ground. One christened two women trekking together in honor of *Thelma & Louise*.[24] Informing local readers of what people in Salt Lake City had known for years, the other two articles discussed tourism in Utah. One piece mentioned that the picture was filmed within the Western state[25]; and the other explained that Fossil Point in Canyonlands National Park was renamed "Thelma and Louise Point."[26] Within the decade, *Thelma & Louise* appeared in *The Boston Herald*'s sport's section once. Toasting the Boston Bruins' head coach, "Burns, Baby, Burns" suggested that Pat Burns' dominion should be expanded to include the New England Patriots and the Boston Celtics. In January 2000, Steve Buckley sounded like *The Washington Post*'s Tony Kornheiser when he teased, "Send Burns out to the third-base coach's box and Red Sox baserunners wouldn't look like Thelma and Louise going over the cliff."[27]

Apart from general interest pieces, which are often instigated by stories circulating newswires and drummed up by reading competing newspapers, staff columnists sit closest to a publication's editorial heart, whether they are employed to buck the tide or define a position. Compared to supporters at *The Boston Globe*, who came close to campaigning for the canonization of Thelma and Louise, when *Boston Herald* columnists Don Feder and Margery Eagan mentioned the film, their views strongly contrasted Ellen Goodman's.

Both Eagan and Feder's attitudes toward Hillary Clinton matched their outlooks regarding the film characters. Bemoaning the "deep-seated contempt" for Christianity shown by the Harvard School of Divinity, in 1994, Feder mocked the school's calendar for including "a peace dance, meditation sessions, a Nigerian tribal drum performance, feminist symposiums and a showing of *Thelma & Louise*." Feder objected as if harmony, multiculturalism, women and film had no business mixing with religion.[28] Two years later in a column entitled, "You Know You're a Real Liberal If...," Feder warmed up the crowd by filling in the blank with a spread of anti-feminist bait: "You think sexual harassment is rampant, date rape pervasive, domestic violence common and Paula Jones is lying. You hate Hillary jokes." Feder followed up by conducting a litmus test that revealed his personal opinion of art: "You are convinced that Frank Capra films and Norman Rockwell paintings are lies and distortions but *Platoon*, *Dances with Wolves* and *Thelma & Louise* are realistic." Even more cutting than commentators in Kansas City, Feder lambasted the film and its followers. Although art's function is to reflect reality with a certain slant, meaning that artistic expression is bound to come in an array of styles, Feder didn't accept diversity in drama like he wasn't inclined to honor multiplicity in religion.[29]

Between August 1991 and June 1994, Margery Eagan included *Thelma & Louise* in her essays six times, nearly as often as *The Boston Globe*'s Ellen Goodman did through 1996. One difference between the two columnists was that Eagan resisted the film's appeal while Goodman readily welcomed it. Not attracted to the movie's capacity for symbolism, Eagan was wasn't willing to let the picture stand for more than what literally transpires, but instead claimed a preference for reality over imagination. "Truth beats fiction," she declared in "When the Going Gets Tough, These Women Get Tougher." Listing the 1991 trio of *Thelma & Louise*, *Terminator 2*, and *V.I. Warshawski*, Eagan argued that fictional "killerettes" hold "nothing" over their counterparts from real life such as Judge "Bloody" Mary Lupo and prosecutor Moira Lasch, who were both assigned to the William Kennedy Smith trial taking place in Palm Beach, Florida. Reversing her position against fantasy, Eagan (not knowing at the time that Smith would be acquitted)[30] envisioned a courtroom drama starring Linda Lavin as Judge Lupo and Sondra Locke as prosecutor Lasch.

In November 1991, Eagan demonstrated a lack of sympathy and patience with dumb individuals who make criminal mistakes. While discussing the desperate flight of a state representative who was under suspicion of embezzlement, Eagan found spin about his flee as relayed by his family to be a "voyeuristic" display designed to elicit pity. Comparing the "Runaway Rep's" escape to *Thelma & Louise*, the columnist was bored by the "mundane" nature of the desperate politician's "cross-country sojourn" after he threatened to kill himself and failed to do so. "I guess in the 90s we're all victims," she sarcastically commented in "O'Leary's Confession Plays Like a Made-for-TV Movie." Recalling the film but not deeply, like *The Boston Globe*'s Diane White, Eagan apparently enjoyed *Thelma & Louise* for the opportunity to make wisecracks but felt it offered little more.

> At least *Thelma & Louise* had some wild nights in raunchy roadside motels. They held up convenience stores, blew up a truck and, in the end, drove their great big, blue vintage Thunderbird, a convertible, of course, into oblivion. Their odyssey was summed up in a divinely inspired sunset scene in South Dakota's Badlands.

The shallow depth of Eagan's appreciation was revealed in her mistakes: calling the car "blue" when Louise calls it "green," reviving a sunset when there wasn't one and locating the final scene a few states northeast of both the Grand Canyon in Arizona (where many incorrectly assumed the film was shot) and Canyonlands National Park in Utah (where it was actually took place).[31]

In "The Clarence, The Willie, The Magic, The Wilt," on the last day of the year, Eagan surmised that "1991 must go down as The Year of the Man." Comparatively, women lost ground as evidenced by the film's conclusion.

"Thelma and Louise went over the cliff in their beautiful blue-green Thunderbird," Eagan despaired. (Evidently, someone corrected her color error although she only conceded the point in part.) The body of "Women Made Real Progress During 'Year of the Man'" discussed Naomi Wolf's *The Beauty Myth* and Susan Faludi's *Backlash*, the latter of which Eagan better promoted. She belittled Wolf's book because of the author's enviable appearance and background as a Rhodes Scholar and graduate of Yale. As if a pretty woman had no right to analyze the faults of the beauty industry, Eagan clamored, "Check in again, Naomi, when you're fat and 50." Supporting two old fashioned notions, that women deemed unattractive are worthless and women considered attractive can't also be smart, Eagan ironically upheld "The Year of the Man" in her column.[32]

Although both Eagan and Goodman identified with feminism, they judged things differently with Eagan preferring quick, hard-edged responses and Goodman delineating nuances. Eagan saw Thelma and Louise primarily as criminals, while Goodman viewed the women as victims of abuse who were also guilty of transgressions. In March 1992, probing a little deeper, Eagan softened and reconsidered her attitude toward the film, though cynically rather than earnestly. "Imagine if Women Had the Muscles and Guns" gave *Thelma & Louise* and *Terminator 2* a second glance. "Maybe Thelma and Louise had the right idea," Eagan theorized, but still not very seriously. She epitomized their story as, "Love 'em, leave 'em, and if they give you any lip, shoot 'em."

Looking around at the culture at large, Eagan broadly aimed her satire at reality as well as fiction. In her view, recent headlines seemed to warrant the need to take strong action in order to achieve equality, and to make her point, she denounced both a U.S. Senator accused of rape and sexual harassment. Ready to spar, Eagan also took on women who want to enjoy the benefits of feminism without adopting the label. Her sarcastic stand implied that women with guns should consider using them against other less politically-minded women.

Eagan was unhappy about the status of feminism in America especially as seen through the eyes of the "male-run press," yet she committed some of the same missteps that she criticized. Like *The New York Times*, Eagan wondered if NOW's newly-elected president Patricia Ireland was the best choice to represent women because of her bisexuality. Although Eagan applauded Ireland's "stupendous idea for a woman's version of 'America's Most Wanted' featuring average Janes' tales of abuse," she shared the media's tendency to prioritize Ireland's private life, which has unfortunately resulted in little being made of Ireland's suggestion. While mentioning *Thelma & Louise* the columnist consistently championed the cause of exposing and ending violence against women, yet at the same time she often undercut her own pro-woman position.

Like Thelma and Louise didn't really give a hoot about fishing, Eagan didn't really want to take up arms in "Imagine if Women Had the Muscles and Guns," but she was frustrated with reality's slow change of pace. Not afraid to use the f word, Eagan criticized the media for rushing to assert that the women's movement is dead and that achieving women are unhappy. To combat those notions, again she passed on to her readers the fruit of Susan Faludi's research. Eagan explained that when much publicized but unfounded anti-feminist theories are debunked, such as the trumped-up marriage scare aimed to keep women out of the workforce, "the press" turns its back, publishing corrections on back pages or not at all. Figuratively throwing up her hands to the whole mess, Eagan concluded, "Whatever, I now appreciate the Thelma/Louise perspective," as if hypothetically Eagan might terrorize women afraid of the f word with "karate maneuvers" and "mega-machines of destruction." Now a fan of fiction, Eagan would have loved "to walk a mile in the big, bad army boots of the Terminatrix," whom she described as a "gratifying if twisted heroine for our times."[33]

On a much more grave note, in April 1992, Eagan wondered what led male members of the *Harvard Law Review* to circulate its annual lampoon, "The Harvard Law Revue," containing a tasteless and very questionable parody of Mary Joe Frug's *Postmodern Feminist Legal Manifesto*. The special issue was distributed exactly one year after Frug was brutally murdered by multiple knife wounds to her chest and her inner thigh. Some Harvard Law students thought mocking commentary as if coming from a deceased Frug in the form of "He-Manifesto of Post-Mortem Legal Feminism" written by "Mary Doe, Rigor-Mortis Professor of Law" was a funny idea. In "Feminism Terrifies Men & Law at Harvard," Eagan opined that women within the ranks of "Harvard Law boys" made the men "nervous" by beating them out for federal clerkships. Possibly, Eagan surmised, sounding much more supportive in her assessment of the film, "they're still smarting from *Thelma & Louise.*"[34]

On screen, Thelma's beating by Harlan mirrors real world violence, but safely, through art. More disturbing is gender violence that occurs in life. According to the cumulative account of at least 20 stories published in *The Boston Herald* between 1991 and 1995 (compared to at least 30 in *The Boston Globe* over a shorter span of time), Frug, a 49-year-old professor at the New England School of Law and a Bunting Fellow at Radcliffe, died 200 yards from her home in an exclusive Cambridge neighborhood near Brattle Street on April 4, 1991. Though the suspected murder weapon was found, as of this writing Frug's murder has not been solved.

The Boston Herald reports detailed the ensuing controversy at Harvard after editors of the *Harvard Law Review* abolished the annual parody issue in light of the piece thoughtlessly involving Frug.[35] Eventually, 10 students came forward to apologize, nine of whom where slated for judicial clerkships and bright futures as possible Supreme Court justices. (Maybe Howard Rosenberg in Los Angeles had a valid point when he confused Anita Hill with women who wear hot pants. Fair or unfair, reading about the judicial angle to this story one can't help but think of Clarence Thomas.) Because of purportedly pervasive gender discrimination within the school, some called for the dean of the Harvard Law School to step down, which he declined to do. In 1992, as reported by *The Boston Herald*, Harvard Law School's instructional staff consisted of 53 white men, five white women and six black men.[36]

The great debate reminds us: art is not the problem; reality is. In light of this mockery of feminism at Harvard Law School, Don Feder's criticisms of Harvard Divinity, written two years later, seem heartlessly misdirected and direly out of touch. Likewise, I wonder what Virginia Hall and her daughter would make of Frug's murder. Frug wrote about the problems surrounding the pursuit of equality under the law as complicated by biological differences; perhaps her work drove someone to her murder. Yet Frug's controversial writings may have benefited George Gurley's 1991 commentary in "Violence and the New Woman" concerning *Thelma & Louise* more than his vegetable tangent. "Biological differences may keep the sexes forever in conflict and apart," Gurley cautioned, but his tone wasn't serious. "Consider the attitude of the folks who developed an all-male asparagus," who sued a supplier for "degrading its product through 'gross contamination with females.' "

With horrible coincidence, Eagan summarized in her column, Frug argued that statutes and their interpretation at times "reinforce and trivialize" violence against women.[37] According to "The Professor and the Murder," published by *The Boston Herald* a few days before the one year anniversary of the unsolved crime, on the night Frug was slain she quickly dressed in preparation for a five-block walk to buy some cookies in Harvard Square. The newspaper reported that the law professor "threw a wool coat over her black cashmere sweater and periwinkle-blue polka-dot cotton miniskirt." If Thelma's actions precipitated Harlan's, would commentators like the Halls also argue that Frug's feminine attire enticed her murderer?[38]

Reading the opinion pieces published in *The Kansas City Star*, replete with misplaced emphasis on ichthyology and paranoid fear of uppity women, it's tempting to think that journalism and critical thinking in the interior suffer from a lack of perspective and education, perhaps due to its land-locked location and distance from top-rated universities. However, Don Feder and the guilty members of the *Harvard Law Revue* plunder that possible thesis. Even those who enjoy the privilege of an Ivy League education and life in a world-class metropolitan area are subject to gross errors of logic and cruel miscalculations.

In 1994, Eagan resumed her downbeat tone toward the picture when she voiced mock disappointment that O.J. Simpson didn't "blow his brains out" on the 405 freeway. She allowed, "At least Thelma and Louise didn't keep us in suspense for two hours." Implying that the women's lives didn't matter that deeply after all, Eagan was thankful that the duo "put the pedal to the metal and sailed that beat-up T-bird into oblivion." In comparison, frustratingly, O.J. "refused to give us the perfect Hollywood cliché ending to his otherwise perfect made-for-TV tragedy," the columnist complained. Pointing out the public's blood thirst and complicity in the media frenzy surrounding the event, she calculated, "There may have been more cop cars trailing Thelma and Louise as they drove the T-bird into the canyon." However, in Eagan's analysis, "There were more helicopters hovering over O.J. from ABC, NBC, CBS and CNN." For Eagan, by mid-decade neither the film nor the lurid news event spoke well for the times.[39]

If *The Boston Herald* plumbed the meaning behind images of men pushed by advertisers or Hillary Clinton's value as a role model for women, the newspaper didn't employ *Thelma & Louise* to aid their quest. To *The Boston Herald*, *Thelma & Louise* was good for a chuckle or two, but otherwise, outside of the entertainment section of the newspaper, the film didn't deserve much thoughtful criticism. Margery Eagan's irritated analysis offered the most attention, though amid the realms of politics and society other staff journalists did grant the title a few condescending nods. In the fall of 1991, the newspaper rehashed the moniker given to Jerry Brown and his campaign manager, who appeared in *The Boston Herald* as "the *Thelma & Louise* of the Democratic party." Wayne Woodlief further defined both pairs as "outcasts from the party establishment, independent mavericks defying convention and, some would say, logic."[40]

Throughout the remainder of the decade, the other links forged by the newspaper between the film and current political news involved more isolated concerns with less widespread influence. When *The Boston Herald* news desk invoked *Thelma & Louise*, the newspaper often basked in salaciousness or just plain silliness. "Seeking Gramm of Truth" compared a 1970s "skin flick" financially backed by presidential hopeful Senator Phil Gramm (R-Texas) with the later film. Four years after his previous reference to the picture, Wayne Woodlief dubbed the female leads of *Truck Stop Women* "cheap forerunners of Thelma and Louise." Not inclined to draw any players in the piece positively, *The Boston Herald* described Gramm, one of the Republican contenders in the 1996 election, as a "sad sack." Woodlief thought Gramm was a marginal contestant and someone whose character and past were as questionable as the current president's "Clintonesque shiftiness."[41]

After Republican Paul Cellucci won the election for governor of Massachusetts in 1998, *The Boston Herald* told Massachusetts readers that he was a "rabid film buff" and that his campaign web site provided an annotated list of the incoming leader's favorites, which included *Thelma & Louise*. According to the newspaper, the man who chose Jane Swift as his running mate opined that the picture went "against the grain a little bit." By this, the governor-elect meant that the women "were in control." Incredulously, the newspaper declined to comment about the intersection of the governor's remarks and his choice for second in command of the Commonwealth. When Celluci stepped down in 2001 to become the Ambassador to Canada under President George W. Bush, Jane Swift became the first female governor of Massachusetts. Soon after her swearing in, she gave birth to twins. Although countless male politicians have fathered children while in office, Swift's dual position as new mother and governor came into question as people tried make sense of yet another development resulting from women's advancement.[42]

Providing the newspaper's second and final instance of *Thelma & Louise* political naming apart from Jeanette Johnston's reference to Elizabeth Cady Stanton and Susan B. Anthony as "Thelma and Louise in hoop skirts," "What Will Those Fun-loving Doles Do Now?" gently roasted Bob and Elizabeth Dole. Shifting the title from feminists to Republicans, Beth Teitell detailed the wacky antics of the "so-called *Thelma & Louise* of American politics." Teitell sarcastically listed the transgressions of a "cross-country spree" the couple reportedly undertook after Mrs. Dole withdrew her bid for president in the 2000 election. *The Boston Herald* claimed that as the primary approached the Doles were spotted "driving by various headquarters in their sedan, him at the wheel, her riding shotgun, tearing down bunting and spraying shaving cream."

Although the newspaper failed to attribute much cultural or social relevance to the picture, staff journalists Beth Teitell and Wayne Woodlief did use the film to get a laugh.[43] But there's a difference between someone laughing with you and being laughed at. The difference between *The Boston Globe*'s and *The Boston Herald*'s sense of humor was evident in the way each newspaper treated the fictional women in relation to political figures. A few years earlier, employing a movie with social ramifications to prod a Republican, *The Boston Globe*'s Martin F. Nolan wryly suggested that Bob Dole see *First Wives Club* before knocking the picture. Conversely, at *The Boston Herald*, Teitell warmly teased Bob and Elizabeth Dole by bringing up *Thelma & Louise*.

Although *The Boston Herald*'s view of *Thelma & Louise* was lighter and more derogatory than *The Boston Globe*'s, the city's second newspaper still demonstrated awareness of the film's historic impact, much more so than *The Kansas City Star*, *The Grand Forks Herald*, *The Gazette* or *The Journal-World*. Like many newspapers, *The Boston Herald* most enthusiastically discussed *Thelma & Louise* in terms of entertainment. Unlike *The Los Angeles Times*, *Boston Herald* film critics often revived the 1991 sensation within reviews of other films. Accounting for roughly a quarter of the newspaper's references, between the fall of 1991 and the close of 2001, *Boston Herald* movie reviews, primarily written by James Verniere, referred to *Thelma & Louise* while appraising such film as *Slacker* (1991), *Fried Green Tomatoes* (1992), *Leaving Normal* (1992), *One False Move* (1992), *Single White Female* (1992), *The Living End* (1992), *Reservoir Dogs* (1992), *Love Field* (1993), *Point of No Return* (1993), *Orlando* (1993), *The Getaway* (1994), *Bad Girls* (1994), *Boys on the Side* (1995), *Camilla* (1995), *Bandit Queen* (1995), *Something to Talk About* (1995), *Fargo* (1996), *Kansas City* (1996), *La Ceremonie* (1997), *Nothing to Lose* (1997), *Niagara Niagara* (1998), *Practical Magic* (1998), *Anywhere But Here* (1999), *Chocolat* (2000), *Beautiful Creatures* (2001), *Baise-Moi* (2001) and *The Business of Strangers* (2001).

In all of the above instances, *Thelma & Louise* served as the model against which other films and their characters were held. Only in one case, *Fargo*, written and directed by the Cohen brothers and number 84 on the AFI's list of top 100 movies, did Verniere deem that the newer portrayal surpassed the original. Assessing Marge, the pregnant cop played by Frances McDormand, Verniere praised, "She's Thelma and Louise without the awful boyfriends or bad attitude, a modern but miraculously well-adjusted American who is happy with her job, in love with her husband and not tormented by neuroses." Instead of distressing viewers by committing murder followed by suicide, Marge gives audiences a heroine who calmly solves heartless, bloody crimes. Recalling Janet Reno's modest style, Marge tracks down murderous culprits, in Verniere's words, armed with a Midwestern, working class, "maternal method."[44]

Of course, there are no rules or standards for film criticism, only different theories and distinct approaches. Where Robert W. Butler in Kansas City preferred *Leaving Normal* to *Thelma & Louise*, Stephen Schaeffer, Verniere's co-worker at *The Boston Herald*, did not. Anticipating comparisons between the two releases, he made clear at the beginning of his review that the two films should "not be confused." In Schaeffer's opinion, *Leaving Normal* features two women "on the road, but not on the run" cast in "collisions ... not necessarily with men as much as cliched stereotypes." In the Heartland, rather than reject *Leaving Normal*, as Schaeffer did, Butler discounted the men in *Thelma & Louise* as "caricatures of thuggish, beer-breathed boors" and later sympathized with the "bipedal oddities" in *Leaving Normal*, including two truckers who say grace and cry. What Schaeffer found "leaden" and "too-cutesy," Butler enjoyed. "You've got to admire a film that makes a running gag out of characters who can't tell the difference between 'phlegm' (the gunk in your throat) and 'flan' (the Spanish custard)," Butler enthused. A script that kept one "step ahead of our expectations" impressed Butler, while Schaeffer felt that director Edward Zwick "never demonstrates the controlling vision Ridley Scott has with his charming outlaws." One reviewer congratulated Christine Lahti ("at the top of her form") and Meg Tilly ("her best performance yet"); the other panned both actresses. Schaeffer reproved that Lahti is "fine as a last-minute replacement for Cher," although she is "never much fun," while Tilly "couldn't have been anyone's first choice" because she's "as welcome as a visit to the dentist." As divergent as baton-twirling contests and *Not for Ourselves Alone* viewing parties, which review readers might trust more represents a subjective decision.[45]

To the entertainment staff at *The Boston Herald, Thelma & Louise* was a tough act to follow. "*Love Field* is *Thelma & Louise* without Thelma," declared Verniere and consequently, "it doesn't challenge our preconceptions in the way *Thelma & Louise* did."[46] Although *Boys on the Side* "conjures up the ghost of *Thelma & Louise*" with a line about "not driving over any cliff," Verniere criticized "the irony is that film comes close to crashing and burning anyway." [47] Where *Thelma & Louise* "struck a hilarious, low blow against the male sex," Callie Khouri's next screenplay, *Something to Talk About*, delivered a mere "love tap."[48] At best, *Anywhere But Here*, starring Natalie Portman and Susan Sarandon, "begins on the road like a kind of *Thelma & Louise Jr.*," Verniere quipped, though the later drama never develops a distinct attraction.[49]

Verniere's co-worker Schaefer reviewed the French film *Baise-Moi*, which follows two women whose story also includes rape. Because *Thelma & Louise* became the standard against which other films were measured, Schaefer differentiated the "crassly exploitative" *Baise-Moi* from *Thelma & Louise* by stating that the French pair of "dysfunctional rage-aholics do what Thelma and Louise might have if they'd been homicidal maniacs." Pushing an idea some would object to, Schaefer contrasted the American pair with Nadine and Manu, who "embark on a killing spree." Not every viewer would agree that Thelma and Louise weren't also "homicidal maniacs," so clearly Schaefer, like Verniere, was a fan.[50]

Despite the newspaper's overall attitude toward the 1991 release, which wasn't very warm, movie critics at *The Boston Herald* recognized the film's full range of attractions even while other commentators, including co-workers in other sections, derided the film. Regarding *Thelma & Louise*, Verniere and Schaefer stood in contrast to the glut of *Boston Herald* staff journalists establishing a range of perspectives in the distance between columnist Don Feder and the newspaper's film reviewers. In this way the two Massachusetts newspapers were similar, as *The Boston Globe* employed John Robinson and his polar opposites, Jay Carr, Matthew Gilbert and Ellen Goodman. The *Thelma & Louise* decade indicates that although a newspaper might be fairly described as "liberal" or "working class," individual journalists sometimes oppose the predominant perspective, offering readers a wider selection of voices. Furthermore, although a majority of film reviewers nationwide posted "pro" critiques of the film, not all did. In Boston, film critics at both major newspapers toasted *Thelma & Louise*, but considering Robert W. Butler in Kansas City and others, it's not fair to make blanket statements about the profession's proclivities.

Apart from nods within movie reviews, *The Boston Herald* addressed the film in features about Hollywood trends and women in film, a practice not exclusive to California newspapers. Decrying an "era when movies have been proclaimed an endangered species," Schaefer registered *Thelma & Louise* as a "sleeper hit" and claimed that it was destined to become 1991's "most-talked about" movie. [51] Besides crediting *Thelma & Louise* with fresh energy, *Boston Herald* film critics exhibited the same sympathy for the plight of women in film as did their counterparts at other major newspapers. In December 1991, summing up the year in film, Verniere bemoaned that "for American women, the major roles were few and far between." Viewing the trend of physically strong and socially aggressive women in films as a defensive response from the left, Verniere came to this conclusion:

> Thematically, 1991 was the year of warrior women, redemptive fables and dysfunctional families. Amazons marched across our screens, perhaps in response to the fear that advances made by the feminist movement would be swept away in the neo-conservative '90s. In *Silence of the Lambs, Mortal Thoughts, Terminator 2, Thelma & Louise, La Femme Nikita* and *V.I. Warshawski,* women kicked butt and fired off a fusillade of snappy rejoinders. [52]

Aware of gender inequities within the film industry, *The Boston Herald* maintained a regular watch on the status of women acting in Hollywood. Throughout the first half of the nineties, the newspaper filed at least one report each year that included talk of *Thelma & Louise.* Following the trend set by most newspapers that covered the topic, as the decade progressed *Boston Herald* film staff increasingly looked to other films when discussing women in Hollywood. Earlier on, however, Verniere inserted the picture into a timeline of strong women's roles pinpointing *Aliens'* Ellen Ripley as "the spiritual mother of Thelma and Louise." [53]

Despite his optimistic view in 1991, Verniere's hopes soon died. A year after he credited Hollywood filmmakers as having pro-woman sensibilities that sought to counteract conservative politics, he witnessed a change in Hollywood. Like other critics across the country, reviewing 1992 releases Verniere discovered "an apparent *Thelma & Louise* backlash" that inspired *The Hand That Rocks the Cradle, Final Analysis, Basic Instinct, Innocent Blood* and *Single White Female.* [54]

In February 1993, Verniere designated a "post–*Thelma & Louise* era," when women began "striking out" but not in a positive direction. In "Trials by Fire," Verniere delved into the public's taste for watching characters who self-destruct and reject conventional values, then "go up in flames." After discussing Michael Douglas in *Falling Down* (1993), which he termed "racist, reactionary and misogynistic," Verniere touched on *Bad Lieutenant* (1992) with Harvey Keitel and *Taxi Driver* (1976) with Robert De Niro. Conversely, before women like Jessica Lange in *Frances* (1982) can do themselves in, "raging females" are punished by the culture at large, Verniere contended, "not just for breaking the law, but for threatening the social order." Still, even though *Thelma & Louise*–backlash films are "reprehensibly backwards," Verniere understood the confounding fact that box office hit *Basic Instinct* also provided Sharon Stone with a breakthrough role.[55] Unable to wrangle any overwhelming good out of the year, less than a month later, *The Boston Herald* was forced to declare that that lack of movies "carried" by women in 1992 was a "scandal." According to "Cast System," the year confirmed Meryl Streep's "bleak" predictions when she noted there were four times as many major film roles for men as women.[56]

Resigned to make the best of a bad situation, in 1994, Verniere high-lighted the "fashionable" trend of "bad girl" behavior. Not looking at the film's quality but the attempt to bolster women as leads, he found that *Bad Girls* copied the "main-baiting, gun-toting, post-feminist heroines" of *Thelma & Louise* and the *Alien* films. Another gushing fan of women on the screen, joining Jay Carr and others, speaking of Ripley, Thelma, Louise, and other "bad girls," Verniere beamed, "their virtue may be tarnished, but their hearts are pure, and their aim is true."[57]

Following *The Boston Globe*'s 1991 lead, the *Boston Herald* in 1995 ran a piece titled "Hollywood's Woman Woes" on page 27. Less compassionate than the competition's op-ed piece and featured further back in the newspaper, the article nevertheless took a stand, which may have swayed reader opinion from the likes of Don Feder. But, like Margery Eagan, Bonnie Erbe's view of women was mixed. "Hollywood women issue slews of complaints, some valid, some just caterwauling," she penned. Erbe, the host of PBS' *To the Contrary*, a PBS program featuring female perspectives that launched in 1992's "Year of the Women," believed that Meryl Streep "whined" when she compared the salaries of Julia Roberts (then at seven million a picture) and her own (hovering around five million) to those earned by Dustin Hoffman, Robert Redford and Jack Nicholson (which were substantially juicier at approximately ten million per film). As Eagan felt little pity for O.J. Simpson, Thelma or Louise, Erbe extended scant sympathy for performers who make millions of dollars regard-less of the great disparity between what top men and women thespians in Hol-lywood earn. The problem with Erbe's argument is that no matter how nitpicky the complaint may sound when paychecks are so large, fans of women in every arena still need to root for equal salaries in Hollywood. As Virginia Woolf taught us, unlike anything else — way beyond violence and criminal parity — achieving equal earnings across the employment spectrum will announce that roadblocks to women's advancement have finally been eradicated.

Erbe did however find ways to sympathize with other women. She decided that Streep's "much-substantiated" grievance about the "paucity" of good roles for women constituted a better argument, although the dearth of roles for women in Hollywood is irrefutably connected to their smaller paychecks. Analyzing the problems of films led by women attracting smaller audiences than films led by men, Erbe hit on the problem of foreign audiences preferring male action-adventure stars. Moved by women in Hollywood in so far as they are also underrepresented as producers, directors and writers, on behalf of *The Boston Herald*, Erbe posed an interesting question: "Since we helped" foreigners "develop a taste for blood and gore," she summarized sarcastically, "cannot we also push them toward developing a taste for liberated women?"[58]

For readers who absorbed the publication from front to back, throughout the decade *The Boston Herald* printed mixed messages about *Thelma & Louise*, as did every newspaper studied to some degree. Ten years after its release, when Margery Eagan doubted whether *Laura Croft* heralded "some sort of action-girl, tough chick, post-feminist film breakthrough," she remembered *Thelma & Louise*, but not fondly.

> [W]omen cheered wildly in theaters a decade ago when, in Ridley Scott's *Thelma & Louise*, Susan Sarandon brutally murdered, at close range, the would-be rapist of Geena Davis; when the gorgeous outlaw duo sadistically forced a whimpering cop in the trunk of his car; then blew up the 18-wheeler of a leering, tongue-wiggling trucker.
> It was pretty sick stuff.

Although Eagan continued to speak out strongly against male on female assaults, as someone who didn't appreciate *Thelma & Louise* she emphasized the acts of violence perpetrated by the women but ignored their friendship. Eagan didn't view the film figuratively or rejoice in its sisterly show of solidarity, determination, personal growth and camp. Busy with her snubbing, she had little to say about Harlan's attack. Still, Eagan was a helpful contributor to the great debate.

Like she questioned *Thelma & Louise*, Eagan questioned supposed gains for women contained in *Lara Croft*. A decade after Thelma Dickerson and Louise Sawyer surprisingly find themselves reborn as outlaws, Eagan noted the basest threads of *Thelma & Louise*, namely weaponry and sexual objectification, present and center stage in the current theatrical release. Speaking for others, she leveled, "If there's anything new about *Lara Croft* it's this: Jolie, tough and alone, is the box office draw, not her male action co-star. But we're not sure that big guns and big breasts, rolled into one, is necessarily progress."[59]

20. Conclusion:
Too Many Bogus Years

Despite the lightweight nature often attributed to big budget films (and rightly so), on occasion Hollywood renders classics that stretch beyond entertainment to engage both emotions and intellect. Watching *Thelma & Louise*, there's no sitting back and letting the filmmakers take over. In order to make sense of what happens, viewers must become involved in the picture.

While giving the audience a wild ride, *Thelma & Louise* explores personal choice embedded in a tale complicated by gender. When she was still a teenager, Thelma chose to marry Darryl. In the film, she leaves her husband and cozies up with Harlan. However, society is responsible for the gender bias that influenced each party's actions. If women weren't pressured to view marriage as a primary career, Thelma might have avoided Darryl and taken a different road altogether. If Darryl believed that men and women are equals based on communal values absorbed since birth, he might have treated his wife better. If Harlan respected women, he may not have ignored Thelma's "No!" and resorted to rape as a means of power and acquisition.

Essentially, great debaters tried to locate the relationship between individual and society. At what point does personal responsibility end and societal responsibility kick in? Privately, most of the characters in *Thelma & Louise* are guilty of something. Thelma becomes inebriated and loses control. Harlan doesn't heed acceptable manners or the law. Louise doesn't check her rage. J.D. rips off the women. Darryl takes his wife and marriage for granted. Jimmy comes through too late. Slocumbe's heartfelt sympathy and sincere police work do little good, yet the FBI's calculating, inhumane nature doesn't accomplish much either. The system's overall insensitivity is infectious.

Because of the film's complicated intersections, connecting all its characters in a web of influence, Louise's comment, "You get what you settle for," doesn't fully explain the big picture because more than one individual determines each stroke of fate. In human society, responsibility roots in the spaces between people, in the world of interactions. Thelma and Louise do not "settle" for rape, nor Harlan does not "settle" for death. Other people play roles in those unfortunate outcomes. Louise would not have been angry enough to shoot Harlan had she not been assaulted or raped in the past. Whoever traumatized Louise is not legally accountable for the fatality, but the parties involved represent an integral part of the story.

Viewers will never know exactly what happened to Louise in Texas, but details aren't necessary to understand how events in the past affected each character in the present. From a philosophical standpoint, there's no one person solely responsible for any of the criminal acts in *Thelma & Louise*. True in real life and in drama, responsibility is necessarily a shared commodity.

Outside of the fictional world of film, the relevance and impact of *Thelma & Louise* illuminate the important but too often overlooked role of the film viewer. Filmmakers and those individuals who support their work form a powerful alliance. Filmmakers together create a movie; in turn, moviegoers decide which pictures become popular. The cycle determines future production trends and connects those who produce a film with those who support it. Filmmakers and moviegoers share responsibility for the kind of films being made in Hollywood like tobacco companies and cigarette smokers share responsibility for health care costs stemming from nicotine use.

Because Hollywood is a business and not a cultural leader, it would be inappropriate to expect mainstream filmmakers to lead the way to a better future resplendent with more gender equality. Like fast food restaurants will never serve a strict diet of healthy, low-fat, low sodium, sugar-free meals while the public clamors for junk food, Hollywood isn't about to divvy up juicy roles and big salaries in a fairer fashion just because it's the lofty thing to do. To change the situation for women in film, the public must act — individually and collectively. The best way to pressure Hollywood to employ more women both behind the scenes and on screen is through ticket sales. The industry will only hire women and portray female characters with more regularity and greater integrity if the results are profitable.

In her book about the legendary American film *Citizen Kane*, published 30 years after the film's release, Pauline Kael values the story surrounding the film as much as the story itself. Kael, longtime film critic for *The New Yorker* magazine, provides an insider's glimpse illustrating the notion that filmmaking, like film viewing, is a collaborative endeavor, like it or not. Kael quotes director Orson Welles, who was purported to comment, "Theatre is a collective experience; cinema is the work of one single person." She responds:

> This is an extraordinary remark from the man who brought his own Mercury Theatre players to Hollywood (fifteen of them appeared in *Citizen Kane*), and

also the Mercury co-producer John Houseman, the Mercury composer Bernard Herrmann, and various assistants, such as Richard Wilson, William Alland, and Richard Barr. He not only brought his whole supportive group — his family, he called them then — but found people in Hollywood, such as the cinematographer Gregg Toland, to contribute their knowledge and gifts to *Citizen Kane*.[1]

In her essay "Raising Kane," found in *The Citizen Kane Book*, Kael outlines the power struggle/collaboration between Welles and Herman Mankiewicz. According to Kael, Mankiewicz wrote the screenplay based on his own ideas, which sprang from his newspaper past and personal relationship with William Randolph Hearst. Yet somehow Welles and Mankiewicz share the Oscar for screenwriting, the sole award bestowed on the project. To correct history, Kael reports, "Orson Welles wasn't around when *Citizen Kane* was written, early in 1940."[2] The popular belief that Welles single-handedly created *Citizen Kane*, Kael says, is a mistaken view, supported by "film enthusiasts" who "find it simpler to explain movies in terms of the genius-artist-director, the schoolbook hero — the man who did it all."[3]

Whether anyone in the past actually believed that one man could make a mountain of a picture alone, this kind of idolatry shouldn't hold up anymore. Accustomed to a multi-cultural world, the rise of feminism, the lure of special effects and the bravery of stunt artists, modern viewers face the cult of celebrity with more skeptical outlooks. Still, Kael explains the nature of film production (which is applicable to any period in film history) well:

> Extraordinary movies are the result of the "right" people's getting together on the "right" project at the "right" time — in their lives and in history. I don't mean to suggest that a good movie is just a mess that happens to work (although there have been such cases) — only that a good movie is not always the result of a single artistic intelligence. It can be the result of a fortunate collaboration, of cross-fertilizing accidents. And I would argue that what redeems movies in general, what makes them so much easier to take than other arts, is that many talents in interaction in a work can produce something more enjoyable than one talent that is not of the highest. Because of the collaborative nature of most movies, masterpieces may, like *Kane*, be full of flaws, but the interaction frequently results in special pleasures and surprises.[4]

When a quality film like *Thelma & Louise* is produced and enthusiastically received, many hands and minds are accountable, including filmmakers and audience members. Although the relationship between product and consumer is obvious, mass recognition of the power and responsibility of film patrons has yet to be seen in the modern era.

Louise says to Thelma, "We're fugitives now. Let's start behaving like that." Likewise, given the integral role moviegoers play in the filmmaking process, fans of women in film should act accordingly. Viewers concerned about women in film might review their overall box office habits and make appropriate changes. If you want to help, avoid pictures whose story, cast lists, credits, marketing and publicity indicate that women in the production are demoted to a rank below men. If women are employed primarily for their looks or are relegated to the periphery or largely absent, stay away. Seek out quality films created by women instead.

Making wiser, more conscientious choices when shopping at cineplexes should lead to more equitable conditions. Ideally, demanding renewed attention to thoughtful stories artfully told would improve depictions of both genders. What would the world be like if every consumer followed a strict entertainment diet consisting only of sexist pornography, live wrestling events, angry hip hop and violent video games?

Whereas *Thelma & Louise* begins with women leaving their husband and boyfriend, throughout much of the history of women in film, female characters have rotated around the men in their lives. While most movies have supported at best only one female protagonist per film, *Thelma & Louise* features two female protagonists who are able to count on each other. As throwbacks to the "I Am Woman, Hear Me Roar" 1970s as well as avant-garde anti-heroines, Thelma Dickerson and Louise Sawyer represented anomalies in 1991. Nevertheless, Callie Khouri's screenplay is the result of Hollywood's treatment of women over the 20th century, as Molly Haskell describes in the title of her groundbreaking book, "from reverence to rape."

In *From Reverence to Rape: Hollywood's Treatment of Women in the Movies*, first published in 1973, Haskell argues that women's inferiority is a "big lie." In her view, while not responsible for this myth's creation, Hollywood is partly responsible for its propagation. Haskell attributes the problem of women's diminishing stature in Hollywood films to the downfall of romance between the sexes and the subsequent rise in the male auteur filmmaker (such as Orson Welles) following the demise of the Hollywood studio system in the 1950s and 1960s. Attitudes toward romantic love and marriage increasingly changed as the 20th century progressed, and the status of the film heroine became ever perilous. Women were blamed and made to pay for the break-up of the family. If love wasn't the only game in town anymore, thanks to feminism, what good was a woman?

Questioning marriage and child rearing as life's only paths for females coincided with the break-up of Hollywood's monopoly over the production, distribution and exhibition arms of the movie business. Television's colossal rise as a major competitor added to the mix. When the men who made movies in this new fragmented Hollywood couldn't pigeonhole women as easily as before, male-controlled Hollywood stopped writing women into films as important, vibrant, commanding entities.

Separately, within the social and cultural arenas, second wave feminists sought to explicate the greater possibilities for women, but few pioneering, powerful women worked behind the scenes in Hollywood. Since the dissolution of the Hollywood studio system and the shakeups of the late sixties and early seventies, Hollywood's primarily male decision-makers along with the greater public have existed in a state of confusion regarding gender. According to Haskell, women were increasingly left out, in part, because the men in control of Hollywood, like men across the country, had no idea what to do with them.

The road to *Thelma & Louise* begins around the time Virginia Woolf wrote *A Room of One's Own*. In the 1920s, women were portrayed as virgins who waited obediently for their husbands, flappers who matured and eventually married or sexualized vamps who were caricatured as grotesque. Rarely were women depicted as freedom-fighting suffragettes or independent types who earned their own keep.

In the sophisticated screwball comedies of the 1930s, such as *It Happened One Night* (1934) or *My Man Godfrey* (1936), men and women hold equal ground, at least in terms of screen time and the number of lines. However, by the end of the film the institution of marriage always triumphs preventing the rise of bright, vivacious, self-reliant women. Before the Production Code of Decency went into effect in 1933 due to the successful efforts of Catholic consumers, Mae West got away with dropping sexual double entendres; afterward, Haskell outlines, women characters were "whitewashed" and restricted to wifely roles.[5]

Working-women films, primarily produced by Warner Brothers studio, were a positive by-product of the hart times of the Great Depression. Although Rosalind Russell talks up a storm in *His Girl Friday* (1940) playing opposite Cary Grant, she's forced to marry, pressured to give up her career and quieted before the credits roll. The only genre of the period in which women stood by other women were the gold-digger tales, exemplified by show biz stories and Busby Berkeley musicals. However, even in these narratives, if a girl found a guy, she dumped her career aspirations.[6]

World War II heavily influenced the roles Hollywood allotted to women. Replicating the situation in greater society, war pictures featured resilient gals like Rosie the Riveter, who performed a man's job while the troops faced the enemy. During this peak decade for the industry, pin-up girls catered to the GI and bobby-soxers reflected the rise of the young adult as consumer. Betty Grable's legs became famous, not her mind or accomplishments. As a child, Deanna Durbin could brandish power without representing a threat to the status quo. The peculiar world of so-called "women's pictures" and the appearance of the deadly femme fatale (essentially the vamp updated) constituted the most significant developments for women on screen in the 1940s.

Film historian Jeanine Basinger chronicles the women's film in *A Woman's View: How Hollywood Spoke to Women 1930–1960*.[7] After studying hundreds of examples, she attributes three main purposes to the genre: 1) to locate female protagonists in the center of their own world, 2) to reinforce women's limited conception as wife and mother, and 3) to create a brief escape, a hint of liberation and power, before returning the central figure to the home or killing her off for trying to break free. During this period, the only major (though still limited) respite from outside control or condemnation for trying to beat the system came in the form of Katharine Hepburn and Spencer Tracy pairings, such as *Woman of the Year* (1942).

Eventually, women in Hollywood were ghettoized. In a film like *Citizen Kane* (1941), number one on the AFI's list of the top 100 films, women occupy the sidelines while men run the world. The film's three actresses, Agnes Moorehead, Dorothy Comingore and Ruth Warrick, do not fill powerful, driving roles. Moorehead, who plays Charles Foster Kane's mother, appears in one early scene only. In effect, she sells her son to an East Coast bank, making them both rich and setting the heartless tone for Kane's subsequent life. Comingore portrays Susan Alexander, a nightclub singer with whom the adult Kane has an affair. (As Haskell explains, a female performing on stage has often insinuated a polite cover for prostitution.) According to Pauline Kael, Alexander's character was based on Marion Davies, who worked as an actress and served as mistress to William Randolph Hearst. Drawn unflatteringly, Alexander's character whines, can't sing and is depicted as brainless, which weren't qualities true of Davies. Lastly, Warrick stands as Kane's wife. The most striking thing about her role is Welles' cold and uninviting presentation of wifehood. A montage of peeks at the Kane's breakfast table conveys the couple's disintegrating marriage. This noteworthy sequence signifies the couple's lack of intimacy, adeptly illustrated through body language and compositional arrangement. Although *Citizen Kane* deserves adulation for the quality of the filmmaking that went into it, including Gregg Toland's cinematography, the minor roles dished out to women in the most celebrated American film — a wicked mother, a women of ill-repute and a rejected, sexless wife — speak for the contemptible treatment women have long endured in Hollywood movies.

In the 1950s, Hollywood once again changed with the nation. Rosie the Riveter was demoted from airplane manufacturer to cupcake baker and sent back home. Women then ruled on the small screen in shows like *Leave It to Beaver* and *The Donna Reed Show*, attired in a full-skirted, cinched-waist dress, pearls and two-inch heels just to do the dishes and vacuum. Theatrical attempts to combat the influx of television included silly Technicolor comedies and the vivid display of actresses with large breasts, such as Jayne Mansfield and Marilyn Monroe, who were on hand to counter the image of the girl next door. Because of the break-up of the studio system, fewer films were made meaning there were fewer parts of any quality for women.

As the 1960s and 1970s rolled around, power in Hollywood shifted to the "director as superartist," in Haskell's words.[8] Talented men such as Robert Altman, Hal Ashby, Peter Bogdanovich, Francis Ford Coppola, Dennis Hopper, George Lucas, Bob Rafelson, Paul Schrader, Martin Scorsese and Steven Spielberg guided the most interesting productions of the period, but they didn't spend much time investigating the lives of women. The situation even worse than in the previous decade, actresses began scrounging for roles in a glut of stories skewed toward men. The sexual revolution often meant that women such as Raquel Welch, who did find work in film, starred as sex-kittens rather than super-moms, scribes or senators. In a period marked by social change, according to Haskell, the memorable roles devoted to actresses required them to play "whores, quasi-whores, jilted mistresses, emotional cripples, drunks ... daffy ingenues, Lolitas, kooks, sex-starved spinsters, psychotics ... icebergs, zombies, and ball-breakers."[9] While the male anti-hero and the new sensitive male took center stage, Haskell regrets that "the new liberated woman was nowhere in sight."

> What we were offered as the "strong woman" of the seventies? ... In every case, we got not only less than we might have expected and hoped for, but less than ever before: women who were less intelligent, less sensual, less humorous, and altogether less extraordinary than women in the twenties, the thirties, the forties, or even the poor, palled, uptight fifties. There were no working women on the screen, no sassy or smart-talking women, no mature women, and no goddesses either. There were instead, amoral pin up girls, molls taking gruff from their gangster that would have made their predecessors gag, and thirty-year-olds reduced to playing undergraduates.[10]

Actresses Sally Field, Jessica Lange, Sissy Spacek and Meryl Streep recorded unforgettable performances in the 1980s, as actresses have each decade. Hollywood produces so many movies, over the years, despite patterns of restriction, memorable women's roles have been and remain a beloved part of film history. To name a scant few: Greta Garbo in *Anna Christie* (1930), Jean Harlow in *Hold Your Man* (1933), Norma Shearer in *Idiot's Delight* (1939), Bette Davis in *Petrified Forest* (1936), Carole Lombard in *Twentieth Century* (1934), Constance Bennett in *What Price Hollywood?* (1932), Gene Tierney in *The Ghost and Mrs. Muir* (1947), Irene Dunne in *I Remember Mamma* (1948), Elizabeth Taylor in *National Velvet* (1944), Katharine Hepburn in *The Philadelphia Story* (1940), Ginger Rogers in *Roxie Hart* (1942), Judy Holliday in *It Should Happen to You* (1954), Anna Magnani in *The Rose Tattoo* (1955), Shirley MacLaine in *The Apartment* (1960), Joanne Woodward in *Rachel, Rachel* (1968), Gena Rowlands in *A Woman Under the Influence* (1974), Anne Bancroft and Shirley MacLaine in *The Turning Point* (1977), Sissy Spacek in *Coal Miner's Daughter* (1980), Goldie Hawn in *Private Benjamin* (1980) and Meryl Streep and Cher in *Silkwood* (1983).

However, prior to *Thelma & Louise*, the most talked about film of the modern period associated a career woman with madness. The message contained in *Fatal Attraction* (1987) was that evil lurked behind a career, a great apartment, nice clothes and the single life. Produced by Sherry Lansing, who eventually rose to the top of Paramount Studios and become one of the most powerful women in today's Hollywood, and directed by Adrian Lyne (*Foxes*, 1980, *9½ Weeks*, 1986, *Indecent Proposal*, 1993, *Lolita*, 1997), *Fatal Attraction* features Glenn Close as a beautiful, smart, sexy editor who is prepared to slash her wrists, engage in animal cruelty, kidnap a young child and murder her adversaries when scorned. Reinvigorating the femme fatale (who, recall, began as the vamp) after the likes of Barbara Stanwyck in *Double Indemnity* (1944) and Joan Crawford in *Mildred Pierce* (1945), the film ushered in what Haskell dubs "crazy women" roles and paved the way for *Thelma & Louise* just a few years later.

To indicate how topsy-turvy attitudes had become, toward the end of the 20th century women co-opted violence (*Badlands*, 1974, *Black Widow*, 1987, *Body Heat*, 1981, *The Exorcist*, 1973, *Dressed to Kill*, 1980, *Mommy Dearest*, 1981) while men began taking on the role of caring homemaker (*Kramer vs. Kramer*, 1979, *Mr. Mom*, 1983, *Tootsie*, 1982) and desirable sex object (*American Gigolo*, 1979, *Urban Cowboy*, 1980, *Top Gun*, 1986). Counter to some of the actual improvements women enjoyed in society, women's representation in entertainment and popular storytelling suffered. For years until the rise of Julia Roberts, Barbra Streisand was the only bankable female star surrounded by a slew of popular and successful male actors such as Sylvester Stallone, Clint Eastwood, Robert de Niro, Al Pacino, Dustin Hoffman, Jack Nicholson, Robert Redford, Paul Newman, John Travolta, Richard Gere, Tom Cruise and Mel Gibson.

Although the press began referring to 1992 as "The Year of the Woman," it wasn't the first time the patronizing title was volleyed about, in essence implying but not making explicit the corollary notion that all other years revert back to the status quo and the on-going spotlight on men. The term has been around for a while, as *The Boston Globe*'s Martin F. Nolan uncovered, going back to at least 1920, when women in the United States were finally allowed to vote.

As part of an effort to understand and label cultural currents, commentators have appointed numerous years special ones for women's progress. In 1975, when women comprised 53 percent of registered voters but only 5 percent of elected officials, *Time* named "American Women" their annual "Person of the Year." Explaining that 1975 "was not so much the Year of the Woman as the Year of Women," the magazine cited advances made by a range of females, as well as the struggles still looming ahead. Singling out individuals like Susan Brownmiller and her book *Against Our Will: Men, Women and Rape*, editors pointed to the worlds of business, military, law, politics, education, sports, literature, journalism, religion and family to recognize that half the people were "not quite the subordinate creatures they were before." Despite backlash forces including women themselves (*Time* named Phyllis

Schlafly, a "conspicuously liberated woman," as the leader of the Anti-ERA lobby), the national weekly saw fit to give the women's movement front page coverage. At that point, though the magazine didn't pretend to be able to predict the future, *Time* noted serious changes in society.

> American women, if they have not arrived, are in the process of arrival. Just how far they will go — and how fast — is not totally clear, for women are themselves altering the destination, changing it from a man's world to something else.[11]

According to Molly Haskell, journalists covering Hollywood appropriated the "Year of the Women" a couple of years after *Time*, in 1977. Looking back on the designation in a 1983 edition of *Psychology Today* (not exactly a magazine mecca for filmgoers), Haskell analyzed current roles for women in film and highlighted their smaller paychecks compared to the day's leading men. In the absence of sustained progress, she restrained her excitement for recent advances.

> If I'm leery of so-called "breakthroughs" in women's roles, it's because I've heard this tune before. Back when 1977 was turning into 1978, critics and pundits made the somewhat belated discovery that something was missing from movies and acknowledged what that missing something was by dubbing 1977 "The Year of the Woman." That was the year of *Julia*, *The Turning Point*, *The Goodbye Girl* and *Annie Hall*, and what all that shouting meant was that there were finally enough women in leading roles to fill the five slots for the Academy Award nominees without voters having to upgrade supporting actresses for that purpose.

Pre-dating *Thelma & Louise* by nearly a decade, Haskell elucidated the ongoing dilemma of how to portray female characters in a turbulent age. Discussing a handful of films that turned out to be some of the best the decade delivered, such as *Sophie's Choice* (1982), *Frances* (1982) and *Norma Rae* (1979), Haskell drew the difficult to navigate line between depicting women "truthfully" (caught in a man's world) or "hopefully and progressively" (striving against the odds). Looking around, she wondered why there weren't more female "rite-of-passage" stories and more films reveling in female bonding.[12]

A decade and half after the 1970s' so-called special year for women in film, in the early 90s media pundits resurrected the title, trying either to make things look better than they were or reinforce the need for progress. (Conspicuously, the Reagan-era 1980s didn't entertain any special years for women, either superficially or more meaningfully wrought.) A 1991 article in *The Wisconsin State Journal* quoted a Hollywood analyst who surmised in advance of the pack that 1991 was "going to be the year of the women," mandated by the success of *Ghost*, *Pretty Woman*, *Misery* and *Thelma & Louise*.[13] Approximately 15 years after the last widely recognized special year for women, Hollywood officially adapted 1992's national "Year of the Women" for its March 1993

Oscar telecast. But the community drew criticism for an empty gesture, and 1992 didn't put an end to the trend.

Recalling the industry's "Tribute to Women in Film" debacle, five years down the road in January 1997, *Variety* ran an article entitled "Oscar's Year of the Woman." Repeating what had become an almost annual woe regarding the dearth of parts for women, the industry observer proclaimed "good" and "bad" news. While Hollywood still drew women as "bimbos, crones or special cases," concurrently the industry showed signs of improvement. A year prior, as has happened all too frequently, members of the Academy of Motion Picture Arts and Sciences were "starving" for five "worthy" Best Actress roles. Referring to performances including Courtney Love in *The People vs. Larry Flint*, Debbie Reynolds in *Mother*, Frances McDormand in *Fargo*, Diane Keaton and Meryl Streep in *Marvin's Room*, Laura Dern in *Citizen Ruth* and Gwyneth Paltrow in *Emma*, the entertainment daily felt that 1996 movies provided a "refreshing contrast" and a "feast" compared to 1995's offerings. Quoted in the article, Molly Haskell agreed, commenting that 1996 was a "real" year of the woman.[14]

In the new millennium, the resurgent trend of recognizing women's spotty progress continued, validating the existence of an entrenched double standard for the sexes. In 2001, reporting on the status of women in film on behalf of readers in the upper Midwest, Minnesota's *The Minneapolis Star Tribune* surveyed the year's Best Picture Oscar nominees. Film critic Colin Covert found that a majority of the stories (*Erin Brockovich, Crouching Tiger, Hidden Dragon* and *Chocolat*) centered on "women playing the hero." He calculated that nearly a quarter of a century had passed dating back to the second wave of feminism since the last time female-centered stories figured so prominently in the industry's top award.

> Since 1977, when the best-picture race featured *The Goodbye Girl, Julia, The Turning Point, Star Wars* and *Annie Hall* (the eventual winner), there have been only a handful of female-lead Best Picture nominees and four winners: *Out of Africa, Terms of Endearment, Driving Miss Daisy* and *The Silence of the Lambs* (and the latter two ranked their lead actresses beneath their male co-stars in the credits).[15]

Filing a variation on the "Year of the Woman" trend, in February 2003, *The Boston Herald* suggested to its New England readers that 2002 be called the "Year of the Middle-Aged Actress." Similar to the situation noted at *The Star Tribune*, again the field of potential Best Actress Oscar contenders presented real competition, a wider array of roles and cause for optimism. Meryl Streep, Nicole Kidman, Julianne Moore, Renée Zellweger, Kathy Bates, Selma Hayek and Diane Lane delivered strong performances in *Adaptation, The Hours, Far from Heaven, Chicago, About Schmidt, Frida* and *Unfaithful*. In "Women's Day; Finally! Hollywood Casts Veteran Actresses in Starring Roles," Lauren Beckham Falcone computed the ages of the year's Best Actress and

Best Supporting Actress nominees. With palpable enthusiasm, she arrived at a median age of 44. "All candidates are older than 33," she delighted, "and eight of the 10 highest-paid actresses in Tinsel town have blown out more than three decades of candles on their birthday cakes."

In the absence of decisive victory, fans of women in film have learned to survive on scraps and tidbits making the most of small increments toward parity. Hesitant to fully celebrate, Jeanine Basinger, who was interviewed for Falcone's piece, at first focused on the number of film credits actresses accumulated. In contrast to Falcone's upbeat mood, Basinger cautiously pointed out that during Hollywood's golden era, top female performers like Barbara Stanwyck and Joan Crawford enjoyed a far greater number of "juicy" roles than their modern counterparts, having made in their careers 50 to 60 movies across many decades. However, because she was motivated to note improvement, Basinger added that nevertheless the current year did offer a "hopeful" sign. Falcone readily agreed, as she pointed to progress in the fight against ageism. Ignoring the fact that most of the films she mentioned were not box office dynamos, Falcone surveyed the recent past in order to focus on the present good.

> Consider that only five years ago, Halle Berry, then 29, was paired with the 61-year old Warren Beatty in *Bulworth*. Harrison Ford, 57, and Anne Heche, 29, seemed a normal couple in *Six Days Seven Nights*. Jack Nicholson, 62, courted Helen Hunt, 34, in *As Good As It Gets*. And perhaps worst of all? Michael Douglas, 53, locked lips with his good friend's daughter Gwyneth Paltrow, 25, in *A Perfect Murder*.[16]

Back in 1992, the buzz surrounding the "Year of the Woman" centered on national elections, but as indicated by David Dahl of *The St. Petersburg Times*, momentum for a focus on women didn't gather strength solely in the political arena. On behalf of Floridians, Dahl opened his article "With Outsiders In, Female Candidates Have a Chance" by juxtaposing *Thelma & Louise* against U.S. congressional races. "Too bad Thelma and Louise went over that cliff," he lamented lightheartedly. Similar to *The Boston Globe*'s comparison of India's very real Bandit Queen, Phoolan Devi, to the film characters, Dahl declared that the fictional women — had they lived out the calendar year and made it to 1992 — might have driven their convertible "right up to Congress."[17]

Because of the great debate and the special spotlight on women's issues leading up to the national elections, film commentators applied 1992's "Year of the Women" to Hollywood. In July 1992, Lewis Beale wrote "Hollywood Hears Her Roar, The Year of the Woman, from Properties to Protagonists" for *The Washington Post*. In November 1992, Eleanor Ringel of *The Atlanta Journal-Constitution* checked in with "Year of the Woman? Not in Hollywood." Likewise, in December of the same year, James Ryan of the Entertainment Newswire appeared in *The Boston Globe* correcting, "It Wasn't the Year of the Woman in Hollywood."

The difference between Beale and the other two commentators is analogous to judging a glass half empty or half full. Beale played up the possibility of a brighter future. He based his sunny prognosis on a current interest in female authors such as Edith Wharton, whose titles *The Age of Innocence* and *Ethan Frome* were in production, along with works by Kate Chopin, the Brontë sisters, Jean Rhys, Ayn Rand, Frances Hodgson Burnett, Willa Cather and Beryl Markham.[18] Taking a different tack, Ringel and Ryan assessed the year's releases and arrived at more negative conclusions. Ringel counted few lead roles devoted to women and renamed 1992 "A Few Good Men."[19]

Like David Dahl in Florida, Ryan opened his article with *Thelma & Louise* talk. Name-dropping the title seven times in his piece, Ryan supported the picture's strength and influence. He recalled, "When *Thelma & Louise* became a red-hot critical and commercial success, in the summer of 1991, many predicted the resurgence of movies driven by strong female characters." The theory was what "Anita Hill did for American politics," Ryan explained, "Susan Sarandon and Geena Davis would do for Hollywood." However, that promise did not pan out. According to Ryan, as evidenced by the number and nature of roles actually created for women (not all of the productions Beale mentioned resulted in theatrical releases), 1992 was not a particularly special year for women in film. Instead, he argued that "it was one of the worst years in recent memory for interesting female performances." The year might actually be seen as a backlash to *Thelma & Louise* since "several" 1992 movies "featured women beating up on other women." Like James Verniere in *The Boston Herald*, Ryan cited *The Hand That Rocks the Cradle*, *Single White Female*, and *Death Becomes Her* as examples.[20]

In 1992, the year after *Thelma & Louise* was released, even hopes for women's progress in political spheres wore thin, explained Barbara Ehrenreich in *Time*. In mid–November 1992, she noted that women's issues failed to ignite the presidential campaign and that women's congressional races had begun to "sputter" as fall loomed. In Pennsylvania, Lynn Yeakel lost her fight against Arlen Spector, and in Illinois Carol Moseley Braun's Medicaid fraud charges urged the "the realization that women do not necessarily inhabit a loftier moral plane" than men, according to "What Do Women Have to Celebrate?" Combining a touch of optimism with hard reality, looking ahead Ehrenreich encouraged that 1994 need not be the "218th Year of the Man." She predicted that both progress and setbacks would inspire women to forge ahead in the future.[21]

Undaunted by mixed results from the fall elections, film critics kept pressing the inherent irony of yet another special designation into the new year. In January 1993, Jessica Seigel of *The Chicago Tribune* logged in with "And the Winner Is ... Year of the Woman? It's Still Named Oscar, Isn't It?" Allowing that the title might be apt politically, Seigel otherwise sided with Eleanor Ringel and James Ryan. Anticipating the upcoming Oscar gala, she informed readers that the theme for the annual event, "Women and the Movies," was selected because of the spin generated by national politics rather than a reflection of industry progress.[22] That same month, Caryn James shared her take in *The St. Petersburg Times*. She also uncovered a *Thelma & Louise* "backlash" in "Women Took Backward Steps in Hollywood."[23] Back in the Midwest, on the last day of January, Judy Gerstel joined the chorus and bemoaned the lack of "big, bravura" women's roles. In "Another Year, Another Dilemma for the Oscars; As Nomination Time Nears, Noteworthy Men's Roles Far Out Number Women's," she told readers of *The Detroit Free Press* an old story very familiar to film critics. Again, voting members of the Academy were hard pressed to fill the five slots for the Best Actress award.[24]

Usually Hollywood capitalizes on its winners, which Thelma Dickerson and Louise Sawyer as big-time Hollywood attention-getters ought to have been considered, but Jay Carr of *The Boston Globe*, writing in February 1993, suggested a drastically different summary of events. He believed that Hollywood launched the misleading "Year of Women in Film" as a "PR move to deflect last year's anger at Barbra Streisand's being denied a best director Oscar nomination for *Prince of Tides* and the fact that *Thelma & Louise* won only a screenplay award." In 1992, when the Academy rewarded 1991 films and filmmakers, Streisand was not nominated for Best Director, although *The Prince of Tides*, the film she directed, starring Nick Nolte, did receive a nomination for Best Picture. Conversely, *Thelma & Louise* did not earn a nomination for Best Picture, even though Ridley Scott was nominated for Best Director. To those with their eyes fixed upon the industry, it looked like Hollywood purposely carved around women to reward men.

In "More Losses than Gains in Hollywood's Year of the Woman," Carr sympathized with women, who he claimed as a group ("half the human race") had been "robbed." According to Carr, the "post–*Thelma & Louise* era of great women's roles" didn't materialize. Instead, few women directors other than Penny Marshall were landing jobs, and women on screen were "stigmatized as crazies." Instead of the "Year of the Woman," Carr detected a "year of men being more threatened than ever by women's competence and the few small gains women made in the face of escalating male hysteria." Going beyond James Ryan and James Verniere, Carr connected films like *The Hand That Rocks the Cradle*, *Basic Instinct* and *Single White Female* to the "rejection" of Anita Hill and "overreaction" to Hillary Rodham Clinton.[25]

As the 1993 Oscar telecast drew near, members of the press kept hounding the issue. *The Chicago Tribune*'s Jessica Seigel returned to the subject at the end of March. In her second attempt to spread the word, "Year of the Woman — Yeah Sure! Despite Oscar Salute, Men Still Wear the Pants in Hollywood," Seigel dug deeper into the conditions affecting women's employment in Hollywood. Detailing a list of problems, she analyzed the predominance of young males in the audience, a preference for films led by men and reluctance to buck anti-women trends.[26] John Horn, of the Associated Press covered the story the same week. In Salt Lake City, his piece ran under the title, "Women in Hollywood Find Little Reason to Celebrate,"[27] and in Los Angeles it appeared as "A Year to Bemoan the Plight of Women in Hollywood?"[28] After informing readers of on-screen employment statistics, Horn interviewed Hollywood insiders for their take on the problem. Midge Sanford, a co-producer of *Love Field*, which starred Michelle Pfeiffer, cracked, "The joke is that it's true that this is the year of the woman." Sanford deadpanned that unfortunately, "no one has told us who the one woman is."

At best an ironic plea, "Year of the Woman" in film talk sprung from the media's collective conscious, yet while the mainstream press volleyed the term, at least one of publications that serve Hollywood ignored the title. Not once in the entire Hollywood year from Oscar night 1992 to Oscar night 1993 did *Variety* use the designation, as if the specialty newspaper wanted to avoid angering its clientele, who knew enough to hide their heads over the issue. However, as we have seen, the 1993 Oscars' "Tribute to Women in Film" amounted to either a cover-up or amazing shortsightedness. Not a true beacon of promotion or support, the ill-chosen theme backfired by highlighting Hollywood's lost chances and continued maltreatment of women.

The "Tribute to Women in Film" primarily took the form of feature and documentary filmmaker Lynne Littman's four-minute-plus, truly startling collage of womanhood as seen in various Hollywood films. Introduced by Geena Davis, Littman's short was shown at the start of the Oscar telecast. As Littman explained in a phone conversation, she felt her purpose was not to say that the roles contained in the film clips she selected — or roles for women in Hollywood in general — are sympathetic to women. The truth about in women acting in Hollywood films, she expressed, is more often quite the contrary. Making the best of her assignment, the director of *Testament* (1983) instead used the snipped footage as tools to make her own statement about women's lives.[29]

Littman's story germinates in fantasy appropriated from Walt Disney's *Snow White* and *Cinderella*. Her film begins with the classic cartoon brunette singing, "Someday My Prince Will Come," while on screen a dainty foot slips easily into a highly impractical glass slipper. A mood of romantic hopefulness abruptly and purposefully comes to an end, cut short by a record needle scratch. The introduction of conflict eradicates reverie. With this bubble burst, thematically Littman's short film starts over. Switching from fairy tale to reality, Littman's collected images represent women in the real world: caught between work and relationships and destined to struggle in a male-ordered society. In a scene borrowed from *Adam's Rib* (1950), attorney Katharine Hepburn questions a male witness, "Do you believe in equal rights for women?" The man replies adamantly, "I should say not." His sentiments echo the feelings of Hepburn's attorney husband, played by Spencer Tracy, who wants a wife, not a "competitor." Diane Keaton protests in *Baby Boom* (1987), "I can't have a baby. I have a 12:30 lunch meeting."

Many of the snippets Littman collected deal with romance including the allure of the opposite sex, older women/younger men pairings and the trappings of being a sex object. Moving quickly through an array of engagements, Littman's brief documentary shifts topics and tone to reflect the intensity of mother/daughter relationships and the bottomless well of a mother's love. A swelling denouement closes the montage with a celebration of remarkable women replete with courage and reinforced by friendships with other women. Littman ends her whirlwind tribute with Sissy Spacek and Whoopi Goldberg uniting across racial lines in *The Long Walk Home* (1989), an upbeat clip from *Thelma & Louise*, Shirley MacLaine and Anne Bancroft arm in arm in *The Turning Point*, and the silhouette of Vivien Leigh, still standing proud and determined to rebuild her life in *Gone with the Wind* (1939).

Testimony to her breadth as an artist, Susan Sarandon appears in Littman's piece three times. In addition to her contribution as best friend to Thelma, Sarandon portrays an older woman loving a younger man in *White Palace* (1990), and she fills the role of a wife and mother working with her husband to find a cure for her son's disease in *Lorenzo's Oil* (1992). Among many others, Bette Davis, Jane Fonda, Barbra Streisand, Meryl Streep, Jodie Foster, Madonna, Jessica Lange, Michelle Pfeiffer, Sigourney Weaver and Jane Alexander were also featured in the piece, starring in clips from *All About Eve* (1950), number 26 on the AFI's list, *Coming Home* (1978), *The Way Were* (1973), *Yentl* (1983), *Sophie's Choice* (1982), *The Silence of the Lambs* (1991), *The Accused* (1988), *A League of Their Own* (1992), *Dick Tracy* (1990), *Terms of Endearment* (1983), *Frances* (1982), *Everybody's All American* (1988), *Batman Returns* (1992), *The Fabulous Baker Boys* (1989), *Alien* (1979), *Gorillas in the Mist* (1988) and *Testament* (1983).

Even after the Oscars were handed out, the buzz over the Academy's misleading tribute didn't let up. Reacting to the telecast in her syndicated column, *The Boston Globe*'s Ellen Goodman shared her reflections about the contrast between the program's theme and the actual status of women in Hollywood. Analyzing some of the high profile pictures that had come out in the past year, particularly *Unforgiven*, *A Few Good Men* and *Scent of a Woman*, Goodman located a traditional women's issue at the heart of each story — their respective leading men were "mustering out of violence." While Goodman applauded this shift, she too, like Molly Haskell and others, wondered where were the "complex, meaty roles for women who are changing our beliefs, our institutions, our country?"[30]

Later that month, journalistic coverage of the disingenuous "Year of the Woman" continued in Minneapolis. In "Females for Sale," Kristin Tillotson of *The Minneapolis Star Tribune* criticized the recent trend of "female body-bartering" evident in *Indecent Proposal, Honeymoon in Vegas* and *Mad Dog and Glory.*

Despite the major commercial and critical success of *Thelma & Louise* and *Fried Green Tomatoes*— both of which feature strong, inspiring women as main characters — and despite the declaration that this is moviedom's "Year of the Woman," the Hollywood wolf pack seems to be following the trail of profits led by *Pretty Woman*, in which the dreams of a prostitute come true after a wealthy businessman "buys" her for a week.[31]

Evidently, Kristin Tillotson tapped into a rich vein. In August 1993, *The Los Angeles Times* foregrounded the "ballyhooed" year in light of the Heidi Fleiss prostitution scandal, in which Hollywood filmmakers purportedly billed hired sex for male performers within production budgets, in effect re-enacting *Pretty Woman* on the mean streets of Beverly Hills and Hollywood. Carla Hall interviewed Callie Khouri regarding the controversy. In response to charges that studios financed prostitution, Khouri retorted, "I would feel guilty asking someone to wash my car." Joining in on the flak with barbed wit, *The Los Angeles Times* exercised its position as the industry's hometown newspaper. Alluding to the joke circulating among insiders, editors headlined Hall's article "Heidi Fleiss: Hollywood's Woman of the Year?"[32]

In the new millennium, women in film continue to push for recognition and screen time. "Casting Data Reports" released by the Screen Actor's Guild in 2000, 2001 and 2002 read much like their predecessors from the 1990s. In 2000, men received 62 percent of the roles cast in all television and theatrical productions (excluding daytime television, game or reality shows and cartoons). In 2001 and 2002, that figured remained unchanged, leaving women with 38 percent of parts. According to findings available on the Screen Actor's Guild website, men still capture "almost twice as many roles" and work "more than twice as many days as women," meaning the characters designed for men represent far more substantial parts, with more dialogue and more screen time. Furthermore, both the 2000 and 2001 reports featured the heading "Women Experience More Ageism." In 2002, the story for mature females brightened ever so slightly but overall the grim outlook stayed the same. "Older women continue to face greater challenges in finding roles than older men," according to SAG's Affirmative Action Diversity page, though women aged 40 and over did see a 2 percent increase among all female roles cast, from 27 percent in 2001 to 29 percent in 2002. Still, the numbers are entrenched in sexism. Among all roles cast, women aged 40 and over landed only 11 percent of parts, while men in the same age group grabbed over a quarter of the pie at 26 percent.

Martha Lauzen of the San Diego State University School of Communication has continued her work monitoring Hollywood. In her 2001 "Celluloid Ceiling Study," which analyzed the top 250 films of the year, Lauzen discovered that men directed nine out ten features. One-fifth of the films declined to hire women in any key production positions. Women served as cinematographer on only 2 percent of the films and as director on 6 percent. While the numbers for women directors and writers slipped "substantially" compared to previous years, the figures for women acting as executive producer and producer rose slightly. Women accounted for 19 percent of all executive producers, producers, directors, writers, cinematographers and editors, but the rate of women's participation dropped to 17 percent when looking at just the top 100 films. "Over the last 15 years," Lauzen wrote, "the percentages of women directors, writers, and cinematographers have increased one percentage point." In the same period of time, women editors lost one percentage point. "Since 1987," she summarized in 2001, "virtually all gains for behind-the-scenes women can be attributed to increases in the percentages of women executive producers and producers." Although women's creative talents aren't reflected much on the big screen, when women do direct, according to Lauzen, they hire "significantly greater" percentages of women in key production positions than do male directors.[33]

In 2002, Lauzen expanded her "Celluloid Ceiling Study" to include on-screen employment of women, in addition to her behind-the-scenes counts. Her data revealed numbers for women acting in Hollywood far worse than SAG's most recent tabulations. According to Lauzen's research, which analyzed the top-selling 100 films, "male characters outnumbered females by more than two to one (72 percent males vs. 28 percent females)." Lauzen's 2002 figures for the year's most successful pictures more closely match SAG's late 1980s results. Able to paint a scene far more grim than the actor's union due to the closer scrutiny it received, Lauzen claimed that 77 percent of "clearly identifiable protagonists" were male and 16 percent were female (6 percent were shared between men and women, leaving 1 percent for non-humans). While women over 40 played 9 percent of all characters, men of the same age group appeared over three times more often, comprising 30 percent of all characters.

Going beyond numbers, Lauzen's research team analyzed the quality of roles and found that in 2002 female characters were more likely to be identified by their marital status, fill occupations with little or no power, hold power over children only, flounder without goals and follow rather than lead. Comparatively, male characters were more likely to be identified by their occupational status, hold power over other adults, have identifiable goals and run society. All religious and media leaders observed were male. Nearly all military leaders (98 percent) and heads of government (94 percent) were male. There was little room for women to serve as business owners or public servants as males filled 90 percent and 85 percent of those positions. As in the previous year's study regarding women directors who were more likely to hire females in other key behind-the-scenes positions, films with women writers created more female characters than films without women writers by a margin of 11 percentage points.[34]

In Lauzen's 2003 edition of "The Celluloid Ceiling," there was no change in the percentage of women working behind the scenes in the top 250 domestic films. Again, men directed nine out of ten features and one in five films skipped female filmmakers altogether failing to employ any female directors, executive producers, producers, writers, cinematographers or editors. Only 4 percent of the top 100 films were directed by women, and only 11 percent of the top 100 films were written by women. In short, men continue to dominate and control Hollywood.

Lauzen's work focuses attention on the industry's image-producing, highly influential reach. In conjunction with her recent work, she told www.films42. com that "if you change media messages, you change the world." Regarding the reception of her research results within the Hollywood community, Lauzen described varying responses, from female filmmakers who are "happy" to see her compilations, to studio executives who become defensive or deny the data.[35]

In 2002, *Variety* backed Lauzen's research. "Film Femmes Walk Razor's Edge" described the situation bluntly: "Films toplined by women that really click with audiences are few and far between." Indeed, the *Variety* website lists the "Top 250 Films of All Time" in terms of domestic box office totals. Apart from 1997's *Titanic*, which still reigned number one six years after its release, in 2003, none of the top 25 pictures narrated stories about a female protagonist. Only about one-fifth of the films on the entire list featured complex roles for women, if you agree that films like *My Big Fat Greek Wedding* (2002), number 29, *Ghost* (1990), number 38, *Grease* (1978), number 55, *Pretty Woman* (1990), number 68, *There's Something About Mary* (1998), number 71, and *Chicago* (2002), number 81, all offered women meaningful, meaty parts. Fewer than 10 films, begetting odds worse than one in 25, featured primarily female casts. *Sister Act* (1992), number 126, *Charlie's Angels* (2000), number 166, *A League of Their Own*, (1992), number 221, *The First Wives Club* (1996), number 231, and *9 to 5* (1980), number 238, represented exceptions to the norm, in which parts for men far outnumbered parts for women, film by film. In the new millennium, while men like Tom Cruise, Tom Hanks, Harrison Ford and Jim Carrey continue to earn $20 million a picture, women like Meg Ryan, Sandra Bullock and Jodie Foster are believed to draw at least $5 million less. Cameron Diaz joined Julia Roberts in the women's $20 million club for *Charlie's Angles II*, but purportedly her salary slipped back down to $15 million for *The Sweetest Thing* (2002).[36]

As for female directors, Patrick Goldstein of *The Los Angeles Times* sought superlative terms to characterize the chances of a woman becoming as famous and beloved as Steven Spielberg. "In 21st century Hollywood," he charged in 2003, "it's a man's, man's, man's world." Even when women run the show, a male-centered perspective reigns.

The dearth of female directors at major studios is especially mysterious at a time when more women than ever are running studios. Five studios have top creative-decision-makers who are women, bearing the title of chair or head of production. But hiring records at studios run by women are virtually indistinguishable from studios run by men.

Unlike Lauzen's findings related to women directors and women writers, who were more likely to give other women jobs, Goldstein uncovered a less encouraging view of a possible budding women's club.

Goldstein reasoned that traditional attitudes and practices surrounding gender plus the high cost of filmmaking combine to explain the under-use of women as directors. In Goldstein's piece ("Good Women Hard to Find?"), Columbia chairwoman Amy Pascal alleged that women aren't interested in making action-adventure pictures like *Men in Black 2*. Goldstein noted that "chick-flick duds" directed by women further pigeonhole directors by gender. Compounding the problem, women shy away from the directing divisions of film schools like the University of Southern California's School of Cinema-Television. Looking at the situation logically, women give up hope of becoming the next Steven Spielberg due to the absence of working role models and possible mentors. Complicating matters to a dizzying degree, motherhood and directing don't mix well given the nature of location shooting, 18-hour days and seven-day weeks.

Putting the brakes on any threat of speedy advancement, when women do manage to secure high-level filmmaking roles, they are subject to special scrutiny from all sides. Because female directors are given less latitude for failure of any kind, reportedly they've been asked to audition before lead actors who hold more clout. According to Goldstein, director Nancy Meyers (*What Women Want*, 2000) first had to be "approved" by Jack Nicholson for *Something's Gotta Give* (2003), also staring Diane Keaton.[37] During his 40-year career, Nicholson had never before worked with a female director and evidently held reservations. He may have been unsure about working with a less experienced director, as most women directors are, or unimpressed by Meyers' previous work, including *The Parent Trap* (1998).

Early in her career, Meyers co-wrote *Private Benjamin* for Goldie Hawn; more recently she scored big with Mel Gibson and Helen Hunt in *What Women Want*, which earned $183 million domestically. *Something's Gotta Give* didn't do as well, but did earn over $100 million at U.S. box offices. However, criticism that Meyers' films rely on easy laughs and tired stereotypes ranks her work below *Thelma & Louise* in terms of quality. For their annual Good, Bad and Ugly awards, a grassroots group that supports women working in film, CineWomen NY (www.cinewomenny.org), voted *What Women Want* the number one "bad" film of 2001. (The film was released in mid-December 2000 and enjoyed most of its 25 week run in 2001.) CineWomenNY bestowed *What Women Want* with a Certificate of Demerit for "its dumb sex jokes and stupid women characters in a film that might have been an interesting comedy for women." *Something's Gotta Give* is promising but falters with interesting parts that are stronger than its whole, beginning with a perplexing title. To his credit, in the film Nicholson was willing to bare his ass in a hospital gown, re-evaluate life after a heart attack and eventually fall in love with a woman over 50. Although the picture's screenplay, pacing and score mire the overall effort, Keaton, appearing opposite Nicholson, is also given a decent part. She's a successful New York playwright who gets to have an affair with a young doctor, played by Keanu Reeves, before she hooks up with her senior citizen co-star at the end.

Despite a harsh climate, organizations dedicated to improving the situation for women in Hollywood and bettering images of women on screen continue to fight for audience awareness. The First Weekenders Group Weekly Update, www.50/50summit.com, encourages moviegoers to support films directed by women regardless of quality as soon as they reach theaters. Their newsletter rallies readers, "We can only make a change if we affect box office sales! You can buy a ticket over the phone in NYC and LA without actually being there!" This note was included in their Friday, June 7, 2002, e-mail address:

> Dear Friends,
> I'm writing to encourage everyone to see the DIVINE SECRETS OF THE YA-YA SISTERHOOD this weekend. Directed by Callie Khouri, the film stars Sandra Bullock, Ashley Judd, Ellen Burstyn, Maggie Smith, Shirley Knight and Fionnula Flanagan. Bring a friend, bring all your friends and let's be a show of force at the box office.
> The film, based on Rebecca Wells' novel, is a wonderful story of friendship, forgiveness, and the unique bond between mothers and daughters. It's about real life and real women!
> The most important thing is that we go out THIS WEEKEND![38]

If you're a fan of women in films looking for like-minded individuals, go online. In conjunction with a Martha Lauzen interview in 2003, www.films42.com featured "Spotlight on the Celluloid Ceiling." The website designed for heterosexual couples interested in seeing quality pictures together listed what moviegoers could do to "smash" the "unofficial" male-dominated system that restricts female filmmaking. Based on a presentation given to the Illinois chapter of the American Association of University Women, Jan Lisa Huttner, creative director of www.films42.com, implored concerned Hollywood patrons who visited the website to support films by women filmmakers, generate a positive "buzz" about films made by women, donate money to independent women filmmakers and to reject "Play-Doh" roles.

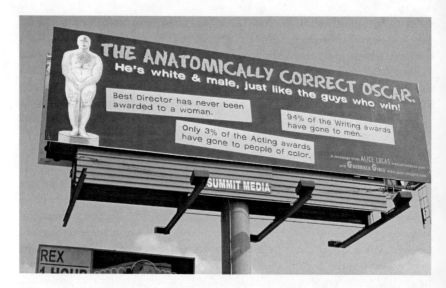

When the Guerrilla Girls make appearances, they wear gorilla masks to focus attention on issues. This billboard towering over the intersection of Highland and Melrose in Hollywood throughout March 2002 revealed the "Anatomically Correct Oscar." Just in time for the annual Academy Awards ceremony, the famous statue was reconfigured so he would more closely resemble the usual winners. (Copyright 2002 by the Guerrilla Girls. Reprinted with permission.)

> A Play-Doh part is a woman's role with only 2 functions: she is there so that the male lead can tell his sad story to someone sympathetic, and she is there so that the male lead can relieve his sexual tension. Otherwise, you know almost nothing about her. She has no backstory. She has no future of her own beyond the role she might play in the hero's future.... Now some guys in Hollywood have made some progress. Play-Doh used to just come in one form: thin, blonde, young and white. But in out newly liberal world, Play-Doh comes in all colors: African-American, Asian-American, Mexican-American, brunettes, redheads, whatever. It all stinks.[39]

Although many of the groups working in this area operate in cyberspace, one standout coalition of activists make public appearances wearing gorilla masks to focus on issues rather than personalities. Provocatively named to reflect their aggressive tactics, the Guerrilla Girls (*www.guerrillagirls.com*) produce and post signs that "expose sexism and racism in politics, the art world and the culture at large." Labeling themselves "your cultural conscience," the group has since 1985 held protests to confront the opposition on meaningful turf, like Los Angeles during Oscar time. In March 2002, the Guerrilla Girls erected a billboard at the intersection of Melrose and Highland displaying the Anatomically Correct Oscar: "He's white & male just like the guys who win!" Illustrating the disparity between ideal images and every day reality, the famous statue was rendered chubby with plenty of middle age paunch. To highlight Hollywood's gender inequities, the sign informed passersby that no woman has ever won a Best Director award. In another action aimed at the film industry, the Guerrilla Girls' mocking movie poster entitled "The Birth of Feminism" appeared in *The Nation's* April 2001 special film issue. Featured in the fake ad showing a lot of skin, Pamela Anderson, Halle Berry and Catherine Zeta-Jones star as Gloria Steinem, Flo Kennedy and Bella Abzug. The send-up announces the slogan: "They made women's rights look good. Really good."

In order to grow into content, responsible women, girls need appropriate direction. New Moon Publishing (www.newmoon.org), parent of *New Moon Magazine for Girls and Their Dreams*, in 2002, ran a contest for girls ages eight to sixteen. "If I Made the Movies" was a part of the organization's annual "Turn Beauty Inside Out" (www.tbio.org) campaign. That year, public service announcements read, "If the definition of beautiful gets any thinner, no one will fit." To widen views of what it means to be beautiful, girls recognized in the magazine's May/June 2002 issue, "25 Beautiful Girls," traveled to Los Angles where they voiced their opinions about images of girls and women in the media. Actresses Susan Sarandon, Kathy Najimy, Lindsay Wagner, Janeane Garofalo and Sheryl Lee, as well as filmmaker Julie Dash, endorsed the roundtable discussion with movie industry professionals.

New Moon counsels girls how to handle Hollywood, though its contest winners needed little help. Curriculum guides available at www.newmoon.org suggest that girls should watch movies with "good observation skills" and ask questions afterwards such as, "Do the female characters look like girls and women you know in real life?" and "Do the female characters have interesting jobs or adventures?" According to the *New Moon* girls' editorial board, a good movie "gives more girls and women a significant leadership role/character," while a good movie doesn't "use girls and women's bodies to draw in the audience." More emphatically, Emily Larson, age 11, first place winner in the "If I Made the Movies" 8 to 11-year-old division, addressed Hollywood with an open letter. "There is a saying in the Book of Psalms," Larson began, "'The beauty of the king's daughter lies within.'" However, she noted that Hollywood's portrayal of the main character, Mia, in *The Princess Diaries* sends the opposite message. If Larson made the movie, she would have focused much more "on how a princess should *act.*"

The oldest organization dedicated to work in this area is Women in Film (www.wif.org), founded in Los Angeles in 1973. According to the organization's publicity material, "On March 12, 1973, ten women representing various facets of the entertainment world," including the publisher and editor-in-chief of *The Hollywood Reporter*, Tichi Wilkerson Kassel, gathered to establish an organization of professional women in the industry. From its inception, WIF has aimed to advance the fair employment, depiction and position of women in film and television. WIF hosts the annual Crystal Awards luncheon honoring outstanding contributions by and for women in film and television. Part of Women in Film & Television International, Women in Film boasts chapters in many cities across the states, including New York Women in Film & Television and Women in Film & Video Washington, D.C.

A number of film festivals around the country also support women in film including Boston's International Festival of Women's Cinema, MadCat Women's International Film Festival in San Francisco, Moondance International Film Festival in Boulder, the Rocky Mountain Women's Film Festival in Colorado Springs, the Women Cinema Festival (part of the Seattle International Film Festival), and Women in the Director's Chair in Chicago. Organizations such as WIF and the Women's Image Network in Los Angeles also host women's film festivals to elevate women and educate the public about present inequities in the film industry.

Hollywood's production practices must be monitored, as film critics, the Screen Actor's Guild, Martha Lauzen and numerous groups, many of which meet on the Internet, are committed to doing. The good news is that things in Hollywood can and do change, even if advances for women trickle in slowly, through tiny, spotty increments. Depending on the figures consulted, following the release of *Thelma & Louise* women in film have increased their numbers a tad. There is still much room for improvement, but thanks to the reception of Callie Khouri's masterpiece, growth in independent filmmaking, hard work, dedication and the passage of time, recently movies offer fans of women in film a wider selection of entertainment possibilities. Much more so than in the 1960s, 70s and 80s, discerning viewers can choose quality movies made by women featuring better and more numerous roles for women.

Some of the movies released since *Thelma & Louise* that reflect the trend towards stronger, more diverse roles for women in Hollywood films include: *Fried Green Tomatoes* (1991), *Rambling Rose* (1991), *Enchanted April* (1992), *A League of Their Own* (1992), *The Joy Luck Club* (1993), *Love Field* (1992), *Lorenzo's Oil* (1992), *Mississippi Masala* (1992), *Sister Act* (1992), *This Is My Life* (1992), *The Ballad of Little Jo* (1993), *Household Saints* (1993), *Like Water for Chocolate* (1993), *The Piano* (1993), *The Remains of the Day* (1993), *Ruby in Paradise* (1993), *The Secret Garden* (1993), *What's Love Got to Do with It?* (1993), *Angie* (1994), *Blue Sky* (1994), *The Client* (1994), *Corrina, Corrina* (1994), *Crooklyn* (1994), *The House of the Spirits* (1994), *Little Women* (1994), *Mi Vida Loca* (1994), *Nell* (1994), *River Wild* (1994), *Quick and the Dead* (1994), *Bandit Queen* (1995), *Boys on the Side* (1995), *Clueless* (1995), *Copycat* (1995), *Dead Man Walking* (1995), *Dolores Claiborne* (1995), *Heavenly Creatures* (1995), *A Little Princess* (1995), *Mrs. Parker and the Vicious Circle* (1995), *Muriel's Wedding* (1995), *Now and Then* (1995), *Sense & Sensibility*

(1995), *Waiting to Exhale* (1995), *Antonia's Line* (1996), *Breaking the Waves* (1996), *Citizen Ruth* (1996), *Emma* (1996), *The English Patient* (1996), *Evita* (1996), *Fargo* (1996), *The First Wives Club* (1996), *Fly Away Home* (1996), *Girls Town* (1996), *Grace of My Heart* (1996), *If These Walls Could Talk* (1996), *Jane Eyre* (1996), *Marvin's Room* (1996), *Moll Flanders* (1996), *The Portrait of a Lady* (1996), *Secrets & Lies* (1996), *Set It Off* (1996), *The Truth About Cats and Dogs* (1996), *Walking & Talking* (1996), *Contact* (1997), *Kama Sutra* (1997), *Eve's Bayou* (1997), *G.I. Jane* (1997), *Mrs. Brown* (1997), *Selena* (1997), *She's So Lovely* (1997), *Smilla's Sense of Snow* (1997), *Soul Food* (1997), *A Thousand Acres* (1997), *Beloved* (1998), *Cousin Bette* (1998), *Elizabeth* (1998), *Ever After* (1998), *High Art* (1998), *How Stella Got Her Groove Back* (1998), *Living Out Loud* (1998), *Mrs. Dalloway* (1998), *Object of My Affection* (1998), *Shakespeare in Love* (1998), *Sliding Doors* (1998), *Stepmom* (1998), *The Theory of Flight* (1998), *Anna & the King* (1999), *Anywhere But Here* (1999), *Boys Don't Cry* (1999), *Election* (1999), *Girl, Interrupted* (1999), *Mansfield Park* (1999), *Music of the Heart* (1999), *The Other Sister* (1999), *Run Lola Run* (1999), *The Straight Story* (1999), *24 Hour Woman* (1999), *Tumbleweeds* (1999), *The Virgin Suicides* (1999), *A Walk on the Moon* (1999), *Erin Brockovich* (2000), *The Contender* (2000), *Crouching Tiger, Hidden Dragon* (2000), *The Perfect Storm* (2000), *You Can Count on Me* (2000), *Ghost World* (2001), *Monster's Ball (2001)*, *Moulin Rouge* (2001), *My First Mister* (2001), *Riding in Cars with Boys* (2001), *Songcatcher* (2001), *Tortilla Soup* (2001), *Adaptation* (2002), *Chicago* (2002), *Frida* (2002), *The Hours* (2002), *Kissing Jessica Stein* (2002), *Laurel Canyon* (2002), *Le Divorce* (2003), *Lovely & Amazing* (2002), *Moonlight Mile* (2002), *My Big Fat Greek Wedding* (2002), *Real Women Have Curves* (2002), *White Oleander* (2002), *Cold Mountain* (2003), *Girl with a Pearl Earring* (2003), *Into the Cut* (2003), *Lost in Translation* (2003), *The Missing* (2003), *Mona Lisa Smile* (2003), *Monster* (2003), *House of Sand and Fog* (2003), *Crash* (2004), *Garden State* (2004), *Maria Full of Grace* (2004), *Million Dollar Baby* (2004), *Vera Drake* (2004), *In My Country* (2005), *North Country* (2005), *The Upside of Anger* (2005) and *Friends with Money* (2006).

However, the fight is definitely not over. Most of these movies did not take home a prize or set fire to the box office because women in film still face a tough fight for equal recognition. Deservedly, Charlize Theron won the Best Actress Oscar for her incredible portrayal of serial killer Aileen Wuornos in *Monster*. Although the low budget movie, made for a paltry $8 million, turned a healthy profit, its minor league $34 million stateside take indicated the movie-going public's taste for something else. Even the follow-ups *Charlie's Angels: Full Throttle* (2003) and *Lara Croft Tomb Raider: The Cradle of Life* (2003) failed to make as much money domestically as their predecessors did. *Charlie's Angels* barely topped the blockbuster mark and *Laura Croft Tomb Raider* fell far short. The clincher, of course, is that both releases performed very well worldwide meaning additional series offerings may be in the works.

When hard times hit, no one is immune. Julia Roberts' recent starring vehicle, *Mona Lisa Smile* (2003), is set at Wellesley College in Massachusetts and supposedly based on Hillary Clinton's real life experience at the Ivy League institution in the 1960s. But the picture must have disappointed financiers, as it barely recouped its $65 million budget. Evidently the film disappointed fans, too, perhaps because Roberts broke from tradition to rely on her mind more than her trademark smile. In the film, Roberts' long locks don't co-star as they have in the past. Dressed in garb designed for a 1950s bohemian/intellectual, she plays an art history teacher imported from far-out Berkeley hired to teach the young female elite—but not too much. A stand-out liberal on conservative campus, she tries to widen her students' perspectives about the modern world and their own lives. Harking back to *Mystic Pizza* in terms of her character's inner compass, Roberts leaves behind a boyfriend, refuses his surprise marriage proposal, loses her job and dumps a second love interest, but she maintains principle and integrity. Apparently, audiences would prefer that Roberts simply look good and get her man.

There are signs that Hollywood is backing away from the myopic pursuit of blockbusters in order to reach a fragmented audience, though the financial figures for films led by women and the industry's production record don't support a very rosy picture. As *Variety* forecasted in early 2003 in "H'w'd Revels in Niches Riches," producers are becoming aware of regional and age driven tastes. Instead of expecting one size to fit all, studios are recognizing the wisdom of making films slated for a particular segment of moviegoers. [40] However, more than women in film, young women in film are reaping the benefits.

In the future, the challenge for fans of women in film is to make Hollywood aware that they exist in number too big to ignore like teenage girls have. After women starring in literary adaptations and women leading action-adventure pictures, the next wave of new roles for females includes a considerable number of stories directed at eight to 25 year olds. In these screenplays, girls endure high school, perform on stage, look for love and pursue fairy tales. In other words, in large order new narratives aren't being developed as much as existing ones are being rewritten and retold for a new generation.

Unsurprisingly, the audience for pictures focusing on young women isn't as big as the audience for the Harry Potter and *Lord of the Rings* series. Employing men and boys in major film productions is still the best way to launch a financial success. With each film in the *Rings* trilogy making near or over a billion dollars worldwide and each film in the Harry Potter series so far finding a spot on the list for the top 50 grossing films of all time, women of all ages face stiff competition for audience share. In 2001, MTV, successful purveyor of teenage wares, produced the bi-racial remake of *Flashdance* (1983). Compared to the billions reaped by the latest top-performing male quest stories, *Save the Last Dance*, with headliner Julia Stiles, turned a tepid $91 million in

U.S. box office receipts after relying on $13 million to start. In its own right the effort garnered a more than respectable draw but still paled in relation to worldwide mega hits, particularly in terms of its overseas take, which was slight.

But wait: add a male star to the mix and box office figures magically improve. When Drew Barrymore courted Adam Sandler in the romantic comedy *50 1st Dates* (2004), a $75 million budget returned $120 million stateside but added another $120 million in foreign ticket sales. Comparatively, take out the male and guess what happens. For a similar investment, Reese Witherspoon in *Sweet Home Alabama* pitted country versus city to draw $127 million in U.S. returns, but the picture collected relatively little from elsewhere around the globe.

From Hollywood's viewpoint, one major drawback of movies geared toward and featuring teenage girls is that they do not attract large foreign crowds, unless the film's sex appeal stands out. Part of a movement to bring R rated sensibilities to PG-13 rated films, in 2000, *Coyote Ugly*, populated by tightly-clad, hip-swinging barmaids, saw a slight national gain over its initial investment, earning $60 million on a $45 million budget, but the production tantalized another $40 million in non–U.S. sales.

Movies domestically marketed to girls include: *Clueless* (1995), *Freeway* (1996), *Slums of Beverly Hills* (1998), *Dick* (1999), *Drop Dead Gorgeous* (1999), *She's All That* (1999), *Ten Things I Hate About You* (1999), *Bring It On* (2000), *Coyote Ugly* (2000), *Crazy Beautiful* (2001), *Legally Blonde* (2001), *The Princess Diaries* (2001), *Save the Last Dance* (2001), *O* (2001), *Bend It Like Beckam* (2002), *Blue Crush* (2002), *Girlfight* (2002), *Good Girl* (2002), *Sweet Home Alabama* (2002), *Whale Rider* (2002), *The Challenge* (2003), *Down with Love* (2003), *Freaky Friday* (2003), *Honey* (2003), *How to Deal* (2003), *How to Loose a Guy in 10 Days* (2003), *I Capture the Castle* (2003), *Just Married* (2003), *Legally Blonde 2: Red, White and Blonde* (2003), *Lizzie MacGuire The Movie* (2003), *Thirteen* (2003), *Uptown Girls* (2003), *What a Girl Wants* (2003), *13 Going on Thirty* (2004), *Bring It On Again* (2004), *Chasing Liberty* (2004), *Confessions of a Drama Queen* (2004), *Ella Enchanted* (2004) *New York Minute* (2004), *The Prince and Me* (2004), *Perfect Score* (2004), *The Princess Diaries: Royal Engagement* (2004) and *Win a Date with Tad Hamilton* (2004). Amanda Baines, Mandy Moore, Lindsay Lohan, Hillary Duff, Mary Kate and Ashley Olsen and Anne Hathaway perform at the teenage end of this mini-spectrum. More established but still youthful actresses including Kirsten Dunst, Julia Stiles, Renée Zellweger, Reese Witherspoon, Kate Hudson and Jennifer Aniston fill roles that age-wise fall somewhere between young womanhood and the select parts for more mature women in film, meaning the over 40 crowd whose employment figures continue to lag. These special releases represent major studio offerings, smaller productions, films that saw a good return on their investments and even a few blockbusters. Many of the pictures package sex, emphasize appearance and reinforce the primacy of romance above all else. A few forge new stories giving screen time and attention to a fresh female perspective. A couple update Shakespeare. New female characters in film pursue sports and careers, as well as boys, though meaningful and well-told coming of age quests for girls and young women are still rare, with the better ones often produced outside of the U.S.

Since not all films starring women are necessarily worthwhile, as choices increase moviegoers need to balance the drive to support projects made by women with a discriminating palate. Writing for *The New York Times*, in 2000, Molly Haskell compared *Charlie's Angels*, the television show, which debuted in the banner year 1977, with anticipatory thoughts about *Charlie's Angels* the movie. She noted that the small screen program left little girls with the impression of "beauty before business anytime." A seasoned and wary professional, Haskell correctly doubted that nearly 25 years later the big screen depiction of *Charlie's Angels* would show much grit or evolution.

> The new movie will no doubt give us the real thing: powerful, enterprising women who haven't got time to look perfect, whose fingernails crack and whose roots grow, who give their Bosley (Bill Murray) not girlish giggles but power-grrrl guff.... And if you believe that, you'll believe that there's a vast new commercial frontier for women as heroines who play tough, crack wise and shoot straight, who make no concessions to glamour and are strangers to the hairdresser's art.[41]

Similar to Margery Eagan's complaints in *The Boston Herald* about *Lara Croft: Tomb Raider*, Haskell highlighted the dichotomy between what's big at the box office and more imaginative possibilities. Unfortunately, as is the case with all audiences, among films sold to young women and girls, those that appeal to the lowest common denominator of taste sell the most admissions. Rarely do original stories about remarkable women and girls who reorder the world make a lot of money, especially abroad. Featuring racy and provocative teenagers, the white school versus black school cheerleader movie *Bring It On* domestically mounted an impressive $68 million against a $10 million budget. Though the storyline included a few male cheerleaders, *Bring It On* failed to draw the interest of foreign audiences. Relying on a woman's traditional physical power in addition to an improbable Harvard law degree, *Legally Blonde* tallied almost $100 million in the states springing from a budget of less than $20 million. But the Reese Witherspoon effort, like Kirsten Dunst's *Bring It On*, didn't appeal to international tastes. Crowning this list of light fare, *The Princess Diaries*, in which an American teenager suddenly discovers that she's a European princess, ascended to blockbuster status and was crowned with $108 million in domestic ticket sales. However, the fantasy fell flat in Europe where moviegoers are familiar with actual royalty and apparently not interested in Disney's fairytale spin.

Meanwhile, more meaningful and inspired stories starring girls and young women given some marketing manage to achieve cult following and even international box office esteem but not blockbuster status. *Bend It Like Beckham* unfolds on the soccer field and concerns the clash of cultures and generations. *Whale Rider* is set in tribal society amid modern tensions. Both turned very handsome worldwide profits, especially against their small budgets, but not enough to shake up Hollywood. Produced in England for 3.5 million British pounds, *Bend It Like Beckham* kicked up $44 million around the globe and $33 million in the U.S. Made for $6 million in New Zealand with a Maori cast, *Whale Rider* earned less ($20 million in the U.S. and $17 million elsewhere).

Word of mouth advertising is always welcome and fringe media coverage is better than none at all. Still, greater marketing efforts would no doubt help worthwhile efforts. Directed by first-timer Karyn Kusma, *Girlfight* is a female boxer story that demands its own recognition apart from the established *Rocky* series. Though the low-budget feature drew the Best Director prize and the Grand Jury prize at Sundance in addition to praise from journalists, *Girlfight* nevertheless socked away less than $2 million at U.S. theaters.

To make the most money, mass-marketed men and boys are needed in films. About four guys and their sexual desires, the gross-out comedies *American Pie* (1999) and *American Pie 2* (2001) collectively jerked U.S. audiences for almost $250 million setting a high bar for teenage blockbuster earnings. Although the first offering didn't do much abroad, once word got around, the second outing took in $287 million worldwide.

Apart from Hollywood, without the aid of trite plot twists, oversexualized sheen or ever-fresh lipstick, women continue to strive for equality under the law and in people's hearts and minds. Sometimes action takes the form of simply but profoundly spreading the word about feminism and speaking the truth about women's lives. National Organization for Women founder and author of 1963's *The Feminine Mystique*, Betty Freidan told *The Charlotte Observer* in the fall of 1991 that the "shock reaction to *Thelma & Louise* just showed how widespread the 'new feminine mystique' was." During her interview, which was reprinted for Texans in *The Houston Chronicle*, Friedan voiced concerned over just how far society had strayed from the image of an "autonomous" and "independent" woman, which the 1970s' second wave of feminism delivered.

The hit movies that have anything to do with women recently have been the hooker.... Take *Pretty Woman*—her whole mission in life is to get a sugar daddy to buy her pretty clothes. And when women are shown on television practicing their professions they are shown in the kitchen. I mean, how can you be an architect if you spend 24 hours a day in the kitchen, like in *The Cosby Show?* I run a project called Women, Men and Media, which is sponsored by the Freedom Forum. And we saw that symbolic annihilation on the front pages of newspapers. Eight-five percent of the people mentioned, named, quoted, described or shown on the front pages are men. The same figure turns out to be the case for broadcast news.[42]

Over ten years later, in 2002, a commentator featured on Women's E News (*www.womensenews.org*) shared with readers her experience living life as a feminist in Nebraska. In an area of the country that didn't extend a warm reception to *Thelma & Louise*, labeling one's self with the f word "is nothing short of a major challenge." Because knowledge is powerful, Bonnie Coffey detailed the forces working against progressive attitudes toward gender in the Heartland state: a unicameral state legislature that passed a fetal homicide bill endorsed by the Catholic Church and the state's Catholic governor; a ranking of 50th among all states by the Institute of Women's Policy Research regarding reproductive rights; the refusal of the state's Catholic dioceses to allow altar girls (one of few dioceses nationwide to do so); discriminatory attitudes toward homosexuals as depicted in *Boys Don't Cry*; a high teenage pregnancy rate; a statewide refusal to include information about condoms or safe sex during HIV/AIDS education in public schools; and an "F" from the National Woman's Law Center due to the number of women living in the state without health insurance; an alarming infant mortality rate; the large number of women living in poverty and the state's considerable gender wage gap. Firm in her beliefs, Coffey claimed to carry on despite the negative and misinformed reactions she receives.

> Here, you will find the word "feminist" uttered with distaste and disdain; it is really the "F" word. Those who bravely assert their feminist beliefs are subjected to disparaging remarks as to one's patriotism or sanity. Letters to newspaper editors — from both men and women — reinforce the reality that feminists are generally not welcomed or wanted.[43]

Although backlash, anti-feminist forces have survived into the new millennium, women — ranging free of gender limitations, living outside of Hollywood in the real world, prepared to distinguish art from their daily lives — are not, in large numbers, resorting to criminal behavior and driving off cliffs. Female criminals may be on the rise as some seriously misguided individuals find new avenues for expressing themselves, but moreover women are accomplishing fabulous feats like violin teacher Roberta Guaspari, who inspired Meryl Streep's character in the 1999 flop, *Music of the Heart*.

If the situation for women in film is to improve, when deserving, worthwhile movies are made, audiences must support them. As well, it would be very beneficial for fans of women in films to embrace the f word without fear to help disabuse people of the misinformed notions about what feminism is not.

Does feminism mean leave your husband? Kill your friend's rapist? Threaten adversaries with firearms? When all else fails, jump? In *Thelma & Louise*, feminism concerns the responsibilities and limits of self-agency. The film *is* feminist because it reveals gender bias in hopes of improving society for all.

Epilogue

The year is 2006. Stereotypes — about gender, sexual orientation, ethnicity, race — are still in vogue and still not helping. Following the news, one hears that would-be Muslim terrorists are starting to use their skin color as strategy by adopting third world national profiles from places like Mexico.

As the world turns, the Dixie Chicks have graduated from echoing *Thelma & Louise* to stirring national political ire by criticizing the current president, son of the sitting president in 1991, when the film hit screens.

This world of art, politics and life is almost too much for words. Today, Hollywood is struggling with King Kong–sized production budgets and internet piracy, while the Screen Actors Guild continues to report the same stagnant rates for women's participation in film and television production. Arnold Schwarzenegger left Hollywood and is no longer the Terminator but now governor of California, where Barbara Boxer and Dianne Feinstein still hold office. Two other coastal states have followed to elect pairs of female senators; since the "Year of the Woman," Maine has elected two Republican female senators, while in Washington a triptych of women Democrats lead from the governor's office to Capitol Hill. Meanwhile, Hillary Clinton has graduated from most scorned First Lady to the most talked about (and still scorned) U.S. Senator. And Anita Hill is teaching law at Brandeis University outside of Boston, while Clarence Thomas sits conservatively on the Supreme Court — filling Thurmond Marshall's spot in terms of color and gender but not philosophy.

Thelma & Louise confused the public by mixing issues. Like commentator Howard Rosenberg did in Los Angeles talking about women and women in film, the Anita Hill/Clarence Thomas hearings confused the distinctions between questions of race and gender. Hill told an audience at Stanford University in 2002, "It was as if I had no race or that my race wasn't significant in the assessments that people made about the truthfulness of my statements." She continued, "How do you think certain people would have reacted if I had come forward and been white, blond-haired and blue-eyed?" Welcome to the

381

21st century, when women and men are still coming to terms with feminism and inequality of all forms.

Art exists in the eternal present. A finished film is cast in stone never to be altered — save for the addition of sound to silent pictures, the colorization of black and white films, and the release of special director's cuts. Once they became a part of our cultural conscious, Robert Redford and Paul Newman could not have swapped roles in *Butch Cassidy and the Sundance Kid,* like Clark Gable and Leslie Howard could not have filled each other's bill in *Gone with the Wind.* In the same spirit, as talented as Susan Sarandon and Geena Davis are, they could not have switched positions and convincingly played opposite roles. As the senior professional, Sarandon earned the role of Louise, just as Davis rightly filled the role of Louise's less experienced companion, and not just because of the real life age difference between the two women.

At the time *Thelma & Louise* was cast, Sarandon gravitated toward characters who exhibit street smarts and carry on despite emotional fatigue and road weariness, while Davis was drawn to upbeat, kooky characters who reveal their own unique brand of wisdom. However, the elasticity shown by Davis as an artist, growing from her award-winning portrayal of Thelma Dickerson to a supremely convincing *Commander in Chief* of the United States of America (the program aired on ABC-TV during the fall of 2005), brings this story about women's place in society and culture to a close better than any writer could imagine. Overhearing incessant talk regarding whether or not Hillary Clinton will run in 2008 for the highest office in the land, we can say for sure that the country is closer than it's ever been to accepting a woman president: first in art, then in reality. Reflecting upon the many individuals responsible for bringing us to this moment in history — including *Thelma & Louise*'s Callie Khouri, Susan Sarandon and Geena Davis — one must say: thank you.

With thespians there exists a correlation between fictional roles and real life personalities. Indubitably, the players involved in a film irreplaceably imprint that project. This connection of the real and the dramatic suggests a kind of mirror bouncing images and ideas back and forth between the two worlds. Hollywood, a fantasy factory, recycles and inspires American culture, for better or for worse. When audiences welcome violence, Hollywood reflects more violent images. This fluidity between fictional worlds and the world we live in validates the study of real women represented in make-believe Hollywood films.

The story of women's advancement stretches throughout time, which is why we look back to see recent history more clearly. Carolyn Heilbrun, formerly a professor of modern British literature at Columbia University who resigned in protest over the handling of women's issues on campus, taught and studied Virginia Woolf's work. Heilbrun wrote extensively on the topic of women's roles and built her career on the basis of accepting a symbiotic relationship between reality and imagination. In the following quote imagine that bracketed alterations have been added to bridge "fiction" with "film." Writing during the second wave of feminism, Heilbrun proclaimed,

> Literature is both the fruit and nourishment of the imagination. We must look to it not only for the articulation of female despair and constriction, but also for the proclamation of the possibilities of life. We must ask women writers to give us, finally, female characters who are complex, whole, and independent — fully human.... I shall move on a winding path between life and literature, refusing to separate them, to confine myself, as a woman, to one or the other. Women have too long imagined only a constricted destiny for themselves, allowing the imagination of possibility to be appropriated for the exclusive use of men.[1]

Empathetic to the challenge of comparing art and reality, a few generations earlier Virginia Woolf explained her view of the relationship between the novel and life. Again, picture brackets with alterations to link "woman and fiction" with its sister "women in film":

> If one shuts one's eye and thinks of the novel as a whole, it would seem to be a creation owning a certain looking-glass likeness to life, though of course with simplifications and distortions innumerable. At any rate, it is a structure leaving a shape on the mind's eye.... This shape, I thought, thinking back over certain famous novels, starts in one kind of emotion that is appropriate to it. But that emotion at once blends itself with others, for the "shape" is not made by the relation of stone to stone, but by the relation of human being to human being. Thus a novel starts in us all sorts of antagonistic and opposed emotions. Life conflicts with something that is not life. Hence the difficulty of coming to agreement about novels, and the immense sway that our private prejudices have upon us.[2]

The role of readers and moviegoers is similar: to wade through "private prejudices" and struggle past ingrained roadblocks in an attempt to judge fairly. For while trying to reach an understanding about art, we learn more about life.

Cast and Credits

Pathé Entertainment presents
a Percy Main production
Copyright 1991 Metro Goldwyn Mayer

Cast

Louise	Susan Sarandon
Thelma	Geena Davis
Hal Slocumbe	Harvey Keitel
Jimmy	Michael Madsen
Darryl	Christopher McDonald
Max	Stephen Tobolowski
J.D.	Brad Pitt
Harlan Puckett	Timothy Carhart
Lena, Silver Bullet waitress	Lucinda Jeney
State Trooper	Jason Beghe
Truck Driver	Marco St. John
Albert	Sony Carl Davis
Vagabond diner waitress	Carol Mansell
Mountain bike rider	Noel Walcott

Filmmakers

Writer	Callie Khouri
Director	Ridley Scott
Producer	Ridley Scott
Producer	Mimi Polk

Co-Producer	Callie Khouri
Co-Producer	Dean O'Brien
Director of Photography	Adrian Biddle, B.S.C.
Editor	Thom Noble
Production Designer	Norris Spencer
Music	Hans Zimmer
Casting	Louis Di Giaimo, C.S. A.
Costume Designer	Elizabeth McBride
Stunt Co-ordinator	Bobby Bass

Chapter Notes

Introduction

1. Virginia Woolf, *A Room of One's Own* (New York: Harcourt Brace & Company, 1929), p. 3.

2. Nick Madigan, "Minority Programs Try to Keep Hollywood Honest," *Variety*, Mar. 9, 2001.

PART I

Chapter 1

1. Virginia Woolf, *A Room of One's Own* (New York: Harcourt Brace & Company, 1929), p. 4.

2. Dade Hayes, "Acad Rave for B.O. Fave," *Variety*, Mar. 26, 2001.

3. Ted Johnson, "Studios Toe the $20 Mil Line," *Variety*, Dec. 30, 1996.

4. Martin A. Groves, "To Reach Hanks or Ryan, Type 'mail@awards.com,'" *The Hollywood Reporter*, Oct. 14, 1998.

5. Benedict Carver and Chris Petrikin, "Turtletaub and Hanks to 'Dance,'" *Variety*, Sept. 25, 1998.

6. "Ryan Takes Call to 'Hanging Up,'" *The Hollywood Reporter*, Jun. 26, 1998.

7. Roger Cels, "It's Moses vs. Hanks, Ryan, Shopping On Hold," *The Hollywood Reporter*, Dec. 18, 1998.

8. Johnson, "Studios Toe the $20 Mil Line."

9. Carrie Rickey, "Oscar's Year of the Woman," *Variety*, Jan. 8, 1997.

10. Martin A. Groves, "Summer Shape," *The Hollywood Reporter*, Jun. 7, 1991.

11. "Why Thelma & Louise Strikes a Nerve," *Time*, Jun. 24, 1991.

12. Michael Rechtshaffen, "Best Friend," *The Hollywood Reporter*, Mar. 12, 1998.

13. Brooke Comer, "A Woman's Touch," *The Hollywood Reporter*, Dec. 9, 1997.

14. Cari Beauchamp, *Without Lying Down: Frances Marion and the Powerful Women of Early Hollywood* (Berkeley: University of California Press, 1998), p. 11.

15. Lizze Francke, *Script Girls: Women Screenwriters in Hollywood* (London: British Film Institute, 1994), p. 6.

16. Cari Beauchamp, "The Women Behind the Camera in Early Hollywood," www.moviesbywomen.com, 2003.

17. Beauchamp, *Without Lying Down*, p. 12.

18. Comer, "A Woman's Touch."

19. "Tales from the Script," *The Hollywood Reporter*, Nov. 6, 2001.

20. Rachel Abramowitz, *Women's Experience of Power in Hollywood: Is That a Gun in Your Pocket?* (New York: Random House, 2000), p. 352.

21. Laura Fires, "Reel Models: The First Women in Film," www.variety.com. Posted May 30, 2000.

Chapter 2

1. Virginia Virginia Woolf, *A Room of One's Own* (New York: Harcourt Brace & Company, 1929), p. 40.

2. *VideoHound's Golden Movie Retriever* series, edited by Jim Craddock and published annually by Visible Ink Press is helpful in researching major motion picture trends by providing useful reference information with a relaxed, humorous approach.

3. wif.org, Sept. 15, 1999.

4. Woolf, *A Room of One's Own*, p. 82.

5. Andrew Hindes, "Auds Seeing Stars," *Variety*, Dec. 17, 1996.

6. Her *Music of the Heart* Best Actress nomination makes Streep tied with Hepburn for the most number of Academy Award nominations at 12. Keith Collins, "Nominations ... by the numbers," *Variety*, Mar. 1, 2000.

7. Ann Hornaday, "Movies That Matter," *The Baltimore Sun*, May 17, 1998.

8. Ted Mahar, "Buddies in the 90s," *The Oregonian*, May 24, 1991.

9. John Leo, "Toxic Feminism on the Big Screen," *U.S. News & World Report*, June 10, 1991.

10. Deborah J. Funk, *"Thelma & Louise* Fun Time in Boonies," *The St. Paul Pioneer Press*, May 24, 1991.

11. David Denby, "Road Warriors," *New York*, Jun. 10, 1991.

12. Jack Kroll, "Back on the Road Again," *Newsweek*, May 27, 1991.

13. William Arnold, *"Thelma & Louise:* All Roads Lead To a Solid Movie," *The Seattle Post-Intelligencer*, May 24, 1991.

14. Robert Denerstein, *"Thelma & Louise* Makes Bang-Up Buddy Movie," *The Rocky Mountain News*, May 24, 1991.

15. Linda Deutsch, "At Last, A Feminist Buddy Picture," *The Commercial Appeal*, May 24, 1991.

16. Jeff Millar, *"Thelma, Louise* A Must-See Movie," *The Houston Chronicle*, May 24, 1991.

17. Lou Cedrone, *"Thelma & Louise* A Good Road Film That Ultimately Goes Too Far," *The Baltimore Sun*, May 24, 1991.

18. Hal Lipper, "Women Hit The Road to Freedom," *The St. Petersburg Times*, May 24, 1991.

19. David Sterritt, "A Driving Movie With Women At The Wheel," *The Christian Science Monitor*, Jun. 17, 1991.

Chapter 3

1. Timothy Blake, "How to Win Roles and Influence Moguls," *Screen Actor*, Fall 1990, vol. 29, no. 2, p. 11–13.

2. "SAG Employment figures over the last five years show steady minority job growth; increasing opportunities for African American performers. Percentage of female lead roles also on the rise," SAG press release, Oct. 8, 1996.

3. "SAG Casting Data for 1997," mailed to me, no author.

4. Trey Graham, "Fans Speak," *USA Today*, Jun. 17, 1999.

5. "New Screen Actors Guild employment figures reveal decline in roles for Latinos, African Americans and Native Americans Indian Performers," SAG press release, May 3, 1999.

6. Bill Higgins, "Lion Crows Over 'Crown,'" *Variety*, Jul. 29, 1999.

7. Co-produced by WGBH and the BBC, originally broadcast in Boston, Jun. 17, 1999.

8. John Dempsey, "Playboy Adds Shade of Blue," *Variety*, Feb. 7, 2001.

9. David Finnigan, "Porn Biz Puts on Condom," *Variety*, Jul. 28, 1998.

10. Dempsey, "Playboy."

11. Josh Chetwynd, "Lights, Camera, Money?

Financiers Play a Growing Role in Movie Making," *USA Today*, Mar. 8, 1999.

12. John Dempsey, "PPV Delivers Roaring 90s," *Variety*, Dec. 1, 1999.

13. Brett Sporich, "Downsized VSDA Tries to Fit in As Chains Rule Vid Biz," *The Hollywood Reporter*, Jul. 10, 2000.

14. "Magazines Find Video Helps with Exposure," *The St. Petersburg Times*, Sept. 3, 1992.

15. Bruce Westbrook, "Playboy, Penthouse 'Bare' Down on Video," *The Houston Chronicle*, Mar. 6, 1992.

16. "Uncut 'Basic' Hits Homer for Top Adult Vid," *The Hollywood Reporter*, Jul. 15, 1993.

17. Scott Hettrick, "MGM/UA Video a Real Teaser for 'Showgirls,'" *The Hollywood Reporter*, Sept. 7, 1995.

18. Alan Waldman, "Self Starter," *The Hollywood Reporter*, Nov. 25, 1997.

19. Meryl Streep, "When Women Were in the Movies," *Screen Actor*, Fall 1990, vol. 29, no. 2, p. 15–17.

20. Gallup Poll #133223, Mar. 11–18, 2001.

21. Robert Sklar, *Movie-Made America; A Cultural History of American Movies* (New York: Vintage Books 1976), p. 270.

22. In 2001, three women ran Hollywood studios: Sherry Lansing at Paramount, Amy Pascal at Columbia and Stacey Snyder at Universal. (Anne Thompson, "What Women Want," *Premiere*, 2001 Women in Hollywood issue, p. 66.) These days, Hollywood is a state of mind, as well as a town. Though they're not all located in southern California, the top studios compete in the same national and international marketplace. Ranked by earnings, the top ten studios are: 1) Warner Brothers, 2) Universal, 3) Paramount, 4) Disney, 5) 20th Century Fox, 6) Sony, 7) Miramax, 8) New Line 9) MGM/UA and 10) Dreamworks. (Carl Diorio, "WB's billion-$ beat," *Variety*, Jan. 2, 2002.)

23. Bruce Westbrook, "'Terminator 2' Has Biggest Budget Yet as Hollywood Keeps Banking on Blockbusters," *The Houston Chronicle*, Jun. 30, 1991.

24. Stephen Galloway, "Star Salaries: Way, Way, Way Above the Line," *The Hollywood Reporter* Dec. 27, 1995; "3-pic Uni Pact Makes Stallone $60 Million Man," *The Hollywood Reporter*, Aug. 8, 1995.

25. Don Groves, "America's Pics Find Foreign B.O. Hit, Miss Puzzle," *Variety*, Dec. 16, 1999.

26. Dade Hayes, "Inside Moves: 'Titanic' Titan Takes Time Out," *Variety*, Dec. 18, 2001.

27. Don Groves, "America's Pics Find Foreign B.O. Hit, Miss Puzzle," *Variety*, Dec. 16, 1999.

28. John Dempsey, "WWF Reskeds for Viacom," *Variety*, Sept. 3, 2001.

29. Overton McGehee, "'Thelma and Louise' Film Characters Get Revenge for Author's Frus-

trations," *The Richmond Times-Dispatch*, Nov. 24, 1991.

30. William Froug, *Zen and the Art of Screen Writing, Insights and Interviews* (Los Angeles: Silman-James Press, 1996), p. 97.

31. Susan Douglas, *Where the Girls Are: Growing Up Female With the Mass Media* (New York: Random House, 1994, 1995), p. 278.

32. Chris Koseluk, "Teen Beat," *The Hollywood Reporter*, May 11, 1999.

33. Andrew Hindes, "'Pix' B.O. Blast Fails to Last," *Variety*, April 8, 1997.

34. Douglas, *Where the Girls Are*, p. 271.

35. Thea Klapwald, "Crystals Celebrate Humor, Achievement," *Variety*, Jun. 16, 1997.

36. wif.org, 9/15/99. Timothy Blake, "How to Win Roles and Influence Moguls," *Screen Actor*, Fall 1990, vol. 29, no.2, p. 11–13.

Chapter 4

1. Molly Haskell, *From Reverence to Rape: The Treatment of Women in the Movies* (Chicago: The University of Chicago Press, 1987), p. 371.

2. This is not to say they didn't deserve their Oscars. Foster and Hopkins won that year's Best Actress and Best Actor awards, Jonathan Demme won the award for Best Director and *The Silence of the Lambs* won the award for Best Picture. Although Davis and Sarandon were nominated for the Best Actress award that year and Scott was nominated for Best Director, *Thelma & Louise* was not nominated in the best picture category. *The Silence of the Lambs* made the AFIs top 100 list, at number 65.

PART II

Chapter 5

1. Mike Mayo, "One the Road with Thelma, Louise, Kowalski, Goldie" *The Roanoke Times*, Jan. 8, 1992.

2. Michalene Busico, "New Era Begins in fight Against Sexism At work," *The Houston Chronicle*, Aug. 4, 1991, and "Psychologist Sees Women Waking Up To Sexism," *The Times-Union*, Aug. 2, 1991.

3. Andrea Diconi and Tamara Ikenberg, "Milestones on the March to Equality," *The Baltimore Sun*, Apr. 2, 2000.

4. Knight-Ridder News Service, "U.S. Depends on Its Stars to Spark Debate," *The Salt Lake Tribune*, May 22, 1992.

5. Michael MacCambridge, "Magazines Explore Effects of Recent Events on Feminism Mainstream May Not Relate to Movement," *The Austin American-Statesman*, Feb. 22, 1992.

6. In 1992, four of 11 female candidates for the U.S. Senate won election bringing the total number of women serving in the 100-member body to six. Of the 106 female candidates running for the U. S. House of Representatives, 48 were elected, giving women 11 percent representation in the more populous chamber of the federal legislature.

7. Meryl Streep, "When Women Were In the Movies," p. 15.

8. Martha M. Lauzen, "The Celluloid Ceiling Study," 2000.

9. Paula Parisi, "MGM?UA Video on Fast-forward," *The Hollywood Reporter*, Feb. 8, 1993. Various sources peg the film's box office take anywhere from $44 to nearly $50 million. Notoriously, income from Hollywood films is difficult to pinpoint based on public reports.

10. Geraldine Fabriant, "MGM-Pathe's Surprise: A Low-Cost Hit," *The New York Times*, Jun. 3, 1991.

11. Anne Thompson, "Can 'Thelma & Louise' Continue to Defy Gravity?" *Variety*, Jun. 17, 1991.

12. James Ulmer, "'Thelma' Cruises in Foreign Theaters," *The Hollywood Reporter*, Oct. 15, 1991.

13. Paula Parisi, "MGM/UA Video on Fast-forward," *The Hollywood Reporter*, Feb. 8, 1993

14. Paula Parisi, "'Thelma' Vid Gets $2 Mil Campaign," *The Hollywood Reporter*, Oct. 15, 1991.

15. Paula Parisi, "MGM/UA Vid on Fast-forward," *The Hollywood Reporter*, Feb. 8, 1993.

16. Scott Hettrick, "MGM Vid Puts 'Thelma,' 'Rain,' 'Story' on Shelf," *The Hollywood Reporter*, Dec. 21, 1994.

17. Elizabeth Guider, "MGM, Brits Bond," *Variety*, Jan. 22, 1999.

18. Elizabeth Guider, "MGM Beams to India," *Variety*, Aug. 30, 2000.

19. Scott Hettrick and Michael Speier, "DVD Releases: A Pack of Pix o' Redux," *Variety*, Sept. 4, 2001.

20. John Dempsey, "Encore For Lion Pix," *Variety*, Oct. 23, 2001.

21. Anne Thompson, "Can 'Thelma & Louise' Continue to Defy Gravity?" *Variety*, Jun. 17, 1991.

22. John Robinson and Diane White, "The Great Debate Over Thelma and Louise," *The Boston Globe*, Jun. 14, 1991.

23. Quentin Bell, *Virginia Woolf: A Biography* (New York: Harcourt, Brace, Jovanovich, 1972), p. 226.

24. Despite a good deal of talk about bra-burning originating from a 1968 protest outside the annual Miss America pageant in Atlantic City, no bras were actually burned. Instead, women threw away bras and cosmetics into a trash barrel while carrying signs that equated the female body with butcher shop meat. To see footage from the event, see "Half the People," a PBS production. In *Where the Girls Are*, Susan

Douglas devotes an entire chapter, entitled "Throwing Out Our Bras," to the Miss America protest. According to Douglas, *Newsweek* is responsible for misrepresenting the facts about what actually happened to bras at the protest (p.159). As a result of biased anti-feminist coverage, over thirty years later people still refer to feminists in a derogatory fashion as "bra burners."

25. Sheila Benson and Peter Rainer, "True or False: Thelma & Louise Just Good Ol' Boys?" *The Los Angeles Times*, May 31, 1991.

26. For a discussion of 1970s films, see Peter Biskind's *Easy Riders and Raging Bulls: How the Sex-Drugs-and-Rock 'n' Roll Generation Saved Hollywood* (New York: Simon and Schuster, 1998).

27. Cynthia Heimel, "Problem Lady," *Village Voice*, July 9, 1991.

28. Anne Thompson, "Can *Thelma & Louise* Continue to Defy Gravity?" *Variety*, Jun. 17, 1991.

29. Steven Stark, "Is Snob a Synonym for Liberal?" *The Salt Lake Tribune*, Jan. 17, 1992.

30. Jay Boyar, "Creator of 'Summer Oscars' Picks 'Thelma & Louise' as Best Picture," *The Baltimore Sun*, Aug. 30, 1991.

31. Michael Lollar, "Stores Stock Up, See No Rush for 'Thelma, Louise,'" *The Commercial Appeal*, Jan. 3, 1992.

32. John Perry, "Art Films Find Market Tough in City," *The Oklahoman*, Jan. 10, 1992.

33. Jeff Strickler, "Movies," *The Minneapolis Star Tribune*, Jun. 28, 1991.

34. Karen Hollinger, *In the Company of Women: Contemporary Female Friendship Films* (Minneapolis: University of Minnesota Press, 1998), p. 124.

Chapter 6

1. "Crix's Picks," *Variety*, May 27, 1991.

2. A number of factors influenced the selection of newspapers included in this study. At the time I conducted my research a newspaper needed to offer on-line newspaper archives dating back to May 24, 1991. Secondly, I was less inclined to study in-depth those newspapers that charged the highest rate per article. Aiming for representative geographic coverage, I collected movie reviews from every newspaper possible while I dug deeper and profiled newspapers with more affordable rates.

3. Frank Gabrenya, "Female Buddy Film *Thelma & Louise* Filled with Miss-Takes," *The Columbus Dispatch*, May 24, 1991.

4. Stephen Hunter, "Superficially Correct, *Thelma & Louise* Has a Terrifying Theme," *The Baltimore Sun*, May 24, 1991.

5. John Leo, "Toxic Feminism on the Big Screen," *U. S. New & World Report*, Jun. 10, 1991.

6. Lou Cedrone, "*Thelma & Louise* a Good Road Film That Ultimately Goes Too Far," *The Baltimore Sun*, May 24, 1991.

7. Jack Mathews, "On the Run with *Thelma & Louise*," *Newsday*, May 24, 1991.

8. Betsy Pickle, "*Thelma & Louise* Sails Around Curves, Falls Victim to Plot," *The Knoxville News*, May 24, 1991.

9. Chuck Davis, "*Thelma & Louise* Interesting," *The Oklahoman*, May 24, 1991.

10. Julie Salamon, "Film: Hollywood-Style Firefighters; Ladies on the Lam," *The Wall Street Journal*, May 30, 1991.

11. David Sterrit, "A Driving Movie With Women at the Wheel," *The Christian Science Monitor*, Jun. 17, 1991.

12. Terrence Rafferty, "The Current Cinema: Outlaw Princesses," *The New Yorker*, Jun. 3, 1991.

13. Stuart Klawans, "Films," *The Nation*, Jun. 24, 1991.

14. J. Hoberman, "Borderline," *The Village Voice*, May 28, 1991.

15. Hal Lipper, "Women Hit the Road to Freedom," *The St. Petersburg Times*, May 24, 1991.

16. Tom Alesia, "Duo's Bright Talents Make This Buddy Picture Work," *State Journal-Register*, May 23, 1991.

17. Bob Curtright, "*Thelma & Louise* Compelling, Dramatic," *The Wichita Eagle*, Jun. 9, 1991.

18. Daniel Newman "A Road Show, But A Good One," *The Richmond Times Dispatch*, May 24, 1991.

19. Dennis King, "Thelma & Louise," *The Tulsa World*, Jun. 2, 1991.

20. Martin Moynihan, "Hit the Road, Jill," *The Times Union*, May 23, 1991.

21. Deborah J. Funk, "*Thelma & Louise* Fun Time in Boonies," *St. Paul Pioneer Press*, May 24, 1991.

22. Mike Mayo, "These Girls Offer a Great Time on the Road," *The Roanoke Times*, May 25, 1991.

23. Mike Clark, "*Thelma* Makes Road to Hilarity a Harrowing Ride," *USAToday*, May 24, 1991.

24. Jack Kroll, "Back on the Road Again," *Newsweek*, May 27, 1991.

25. William Arnold, "*Thelma & Louise*: All Roads Lead to a Solid Movie," *The Seattle Post-Intelligencer*, May 24, 1991.

26. Ted Mahar, "Buddies in the 90s," *The Oregonian*, May 24, 1991.

27. Robert Denerstein, "*Thelma & Louise* Makes Bang-Up Buddy Movie," *The Rocky Mountain News*, May 24, 1991.

28. Michael MacCambridge, "Wit, Wisdom from a Dynamic Duo: Acting Sparkles in *Thelma & Louise*," *The Austin American-Statesman*, May 24, 1991.

29. Robert S. Cauthorn, "*Thelma & Louise* Weaves Bewitchment," *The Arizona Daily Star*, May 24, 1991.

30. Richard Schickel, "A Postcard from the Edge," *Time*, May 27, 1991.

31. Janet Maslin, "On the Run with 2 Buddies and a Gun," *The New York Times*, May 24, 1991.

32. David Denby, "Movies: Road Warriors," *New York*, Jun. 10, 1991.

33. *Thelma & Louise* review, www.variety.com.

34. Phillip Wuntch, "*Thelma & Louise* Two Women on the Run Take a Wildly Joyous Ride," *The Dallas Morning News*, May 24, 1991.

35. Jeff Millar, "*Thelma & Louise* A Must-see Movie," *The Houston Chronicle*, May 24, 1991.

36. Bill Cosford, "Take a Wonderful Ride with *Thelma & Louise*," *The Miami Herald*, May 24, 1991.

37. Harper Barnes, "Female Butch and Sundance, in 90s Style," *The St. Louise Post-Dispatch*, May 24, 1991.

38. Linda Deutsch, "At Last, A Feminist Buddy Picture," *The Memphis Commercial Appeal*, May 24, 1991.

39. Jeff Simon, "The T-Bird Fugitives; *Thelma & Louise* in Great American Tradition," *The Buffalo News*, May 23, 1991.

40. Carole Kass, "*Thelma & Louise* is About Rare Birds," *The Richmond-Times Dispatch*, May 24, 1991.

41. Diane Carman, "*Thelma & Louise* an Exhilarating Taste of Freedom," *The Denver Post*, Jun. 22, 1991.

42. Jerry Bokamper, "Witty, Gritty Road Film," *The Arkansas Democrat Gazette*, May 26, 1991.

43. Kathi Maio, "*Thelma & Louise* Take Flight," *Sojourner*, Jul. 31, 1991, v.16, n. 11, p. 36.

44. Jeff Strickler, "SNOBS Will Hate *Thelma & Louise*," *The Minneapolis Star Tribune*, May 24, 1991.

Chapter 7

1. Rheta Grimsley Johnson, "3D *Thelma & Louise:* Women's Feel-Good Film," *The Charleston Gazette*, Jun. 21, 1991.

2. Robert Keith Smith, "*Thelma & Louise* is an Anti-male Film," letter to the editor, *The Charleston Gazette*, Aug. 2, 1991.

3. Leroy G. Schultz, "Any Issue Subject to 'Show-biz,'" letter to the editor, *The Charleston Gazette*, Aug. 7, 1991.

4. Donald Andrews, "Movie Shouldn't Threaten Any Man," letter to the editor, *The Charleston Gazette*, Aug. 10, 1991.

5. John R. Molloy, "Movie Reviewer Has Aversion to Males," letter to the editor, *The Charleston Gazette*, Aug. 12, 1991.

6. Lynne Douglass, "Movie Hit too Close to Home?" letter to the editor, *The Charleston Gazette*, Aug. 19, 1991.

7. Richard Schickel, "Gender Bender," *Time*, Jun. 24, 1991, p. 52.

8. Margaret Carlson, "Is This What Feminism Is All About?" *Time*, Jun. 24, 1991, p. 57.

9. Laura Shapiro, Andrew Murr and Karen Springen, "Women Who Kill Too Much," *Newsweek*, Jun. 17, 1991, p. 63.

10. Janet Maslin, "Lay Off *Thelma & Louise*," *The New York Times*, Jun. 16, 1991.

11. M.S. Mason, "The Movie *Thelma & Louise* Isn't Just About Trashing Men," *The Christian Science Monitor*, Jul. 1, 1991.

12. Marilyn Gardner, "Wanted: a Better Response to Abuse," *The Christian Science Monitor*, Jul. 9, 1991.

13. Ruth Walker, "Why We Cheered Thelma & Louise," *The Christian Science Monitor*, Jul. 17, 1991.

14. Jill Thompson, "Changing Easy Riders' Gender Isn't the Answer," *The Oregonian*, Jun. 14, 1991.

15. Barbara Middleton, "Pent Up Anger Released By Scene from Movie," letter to the editor, *The Arkansas Democrat Gazette*, Aug. 14, 1991.

16. Frank Gabrenya, "People in Movies Live By Other Natural Laws," *The Columbus Dispatch*, Jul. 28, 1991.

17. John Horn, "Runaway Debate Irks Film's Author," *The Rocky Mountain News*, Jul. 17, 1991.

18. Mary Voeltz Chandler, "*Thelma* Causes Stir Because it Hits Home," *The Rocky Mountain News*, Jun. 30, 1991.

19. Alice Steinbach, "A Movie in which Women Act Like Men," *The Baltimore Sun*, Jun. 3, 1991.

20. Stephen Hunter, "No Escaping Politics in Movies," *The Baltimore Sun*, Aug. 23, 1992.

21. Barbara Green, "Two Women on the Lam," *The Richmond News Leader*, Jul. 12, 1991.

22. Harper Barnes, "What's For Men Not to Like in the Movie *Thelma & Louise?*" *St. Louis Post-Dispatch*, Jun. 23, 1991.

23. Jay Conley, "Oh, Geez, Please, *Louise*," *The Tulsa World*, Jun. 15, 1991.

24. Jay Conley, "This Movie Deserved the Oscar Snub," *The Tulsa World*, Apr. 2, 1992.

25. Alan Katz, "*Thelma & Louise* Reaction: Movie Rides Roughshod Over Truckers," *The Denver Post*, Jul. 8, 1991.

26. Dan Lynch, "Movies and Madness," *The Times Union*, Jun. 16, 1991.

27. Fred LeBrun, "It Isn't Movies or Hormones," *The Times Union*, Jun. 23, 1991.

28. Catherine Clabby, "Viewers See Positive Side of *Thelma*," *The Times Union*, Jun. 23, 1991.

29. Ralph Martin, "Feminists Making a Big Deal," *The Times Union*, Jul. 2, 1991.

30. Hal Lipper, "Taking Charge," *The St. Petersburg Times*, May 29, 1991.

31. Hal Lipper, "A Three-way to Fame and Fortune," *The St. Petersburg Times*, Dec. 27, 1991.

32. Anne V. Hull, "A Journey to Freedom," *The St. Petersburg Times*, Jun. 1, 1991.

33. Nancy Shullins, "Women Writers Create Contemptible Characters," *The St. Petersburg Times*, Jul. 7, 1991.

34. Susan Wloszczyna, "*Thelma & Louise* Shoots Hole in Stereotypical Roles," *USA Today*, Jun. 6, 1991.

35. Barbara Reynolds, "Male Clergy: See *Thelma & Louise*," *USA Today*, Jun. 21, 1991.

36. Bobby Odom, "Letterline," letter to the editor, *USA Today*, Jun. 28, 1991.

37. Larry King, "A Triple Treat for Summer Filmgoers," *USA Today*, Jun. 17, 1991.

38. Joe Urschel, "Real Men Forced Into the Woods," *USA Today*, Jul. 26, 1991.

39. Liz Smith, "Just Say 'No' Gets New Shot," *Newsday*, Jun. 4, 1991.

40. Liz Smith, "Tine on Women and Facts," *Newsday*, Jun. 14, 1991.

41. Jack Mathews, "On the Movies: Reaching (Too Far) for an Audience," *Newsday*, Jun. 16, 1991.

Chapter 8

1. Matt Wolf, "'Death and the Maiden,'" *The Hollywood Reporter*, Nov. 12, 1991.

2. Michael Cabanatuan and Diana Walsh, "Train, Bus Stations Swamped as Travelers Hit the Road," *The San Francisco Chronicle*, Sept. 13, 2001.

3. Pamela Schaffer, "Judith and Her Story: Popular, Threatening, Co-opted," *National Catholic Reporter Online*, Feb. 5, 1999.

4. John T. Davis, "Griffith Keeps Going through Stages," *Austin American-Statesman*, Feb. 6, 1992.

5. Jane Ann Morrison, "Liberal Activist Back to Fighting in the Silver State," *Las Vegas Review-Journal*, interview with Harriet Trudell, Mar. 13, 2000.

6. Leah Garchik, "Personals—Bouncing a Dime Off Bob's Face," *The San Francisco Chronicle*, Nov. 7, 1997.

7. Associated Press, "Never Got to First Base," *The Star Tribune*, Feb. 18, 1994.

8. L.T. Anderson, "We Don't Say 'Any-Thin' for 'Anything' and We Don't Say 'Eye-ther,'" *The Charleston Daily Mail*, Jun. 7, 1991.

9. Clarence Page, "*Thelma & Louise*: A Reel-life Tale of Women and Power," *The Chicago Tribune*, Jun. 12, 1991.

10. Clarence Page, "Patrick and David Can Duke It Out for Grouch of the Year," *The Seattle Post-Intelligencer*, Nov. 22, 1991.

11. Jean Marbella, "Window on American," *The Baltimore Sun*, Nov. 4, 1991.

12. Lili Wright, "U. Celebration to Examine Women's Roles," *The Salt Lake Tribune*, Feb. 23, 1992.

13. "Women's Seminars Set," *The Rocky Mountain News*, Feb. 18, 1992.

14. Jeff Nightbyrd, "Women in their 40s Entering a Prime Time," *The Austin American-Statesman*, Jul. 30, 1992.

15. Susan Smith, "'Chick Flicks' Give Single Life a Bad Name," *The Austin American-Statesman*, Apr. 25, 2001.

16. Personal e-mail.

17. Margo Harakas, "Card Sharks, Some Say Thelma and Louise Greeting Goes Over the Edge," *The Fort Worth Star-Telegram*, May 13, 1998.

18. John Leo, "Pervasive Male-bashing Not Good for the Cultural Health," *The Tribune Star*, May 10, 1998.

19. John Leo, "Pervasive Male-bashing Not Good for the Cultural Health," *The Daily Herald*, May 3, 1998.

20. "Where the Wild Things Are for a Day," *The St. Petersburg Times*, Feb. 23, 1995.

21. "Logan Animal Exhibit More than Pork, Legislator Jibes," *The Charleston Gazette*, Sept. 15, 1995.

22. *The Record*, Mar. 9, 2000.

23. Megan Gallagher Clark, "Tired of the Road, Thelma, Louise Need a Home," *The Sunday News*, Jun. 20, 1999.

24. J.M. Kalil, "Nurturing Growth," *The Las Vegas Review-Journal*, Apr. 3, 2000.

25. Sophia Yin, "Birds Are Victors, Victims in Natural Game of survival," *The San Francisco Chronicle*, Apr. 18, 2001.

26. Associated Press, "'Thelma and Louise' Zoo Double Feature," *The Tulsa World*, Jul. 10, 1991.

27. *USA Today*, Oct. 22, 1996.

28. David Krup, "Busch Birds Thelma, Louise Hit the Road," *The St. Petersburg Times*, Oct. 21, 1996.

29. "The Girls Are Back," *The St. Petersburg Times*, Oct. 22, 1996.

30. Emelyn Cruz Lat and Ray Delgado, "Rare Birds Found After Attack," *The San Francisco Chronicle*, Apr. 20, 1997.

31. Ross Peddicord, "'Thelma,' 'Louise' Never Say Die," *The Baltimore Sun*, Oct. 7, 1994.

32. Carla Hinton, "Program Helps Patients," *The Oklahoman*, Feb. 8, 1999.

33. Alex Tizon, "Crossing America; 'Old Ladies Do What We Can,'" *The Seattle Times*, Sept. 18, 2001.

34. Teresa Hinds, "Wolfe Women Living the Buddy System," *The Las Vegas Sun*, Jan. 27, 1997.

35. Joan Ryan, "Thelma and Louise in Pursuit of the News," *The San Francisco Chronicle*, Nov. 2, 1997.

36. Jon Swartz, "Women Take on Cyberspace," *The San Francisco Chronicle*, Jun. 1, 1996.

37. Anne Plohr, "Tampa Pair Take Canyon by Storm," *The St. Petersburg Times*, Sept. 21, 1992.

38. Barbara Presley Noble, "The Thelma and Louise of Gay Greeting Cards," *The New York Times*, May 3, 1992.

39. David Ivanovich, "Power Crisis Ominous for Business," *The Houston Chronicle*, Jan. 28, 2001

40. "PSSSST!" *The Capital Times*, Dec. 6, 1996.

41. Jeff Wu, "More Feminine Hands Firing Guns," *The Times Union*, Sept. 6, 1991, and Jeff Wu, "More U.S. Women Buying and Using Firearms," *The Tulsa World*, Sept. 9, 1991.

42. Jeff Wu, "More U.S. Women Buying and Using Firearms," *The Tulsa World*, Sept. 3, 1991.

43. Lore Croghan, "A New Target for Gunsmiths, Lines of Firearms Made with Women in Mind" *The Miami Herald*, Nov. 22, 1991.

44. Sonny Jones, "*Thelma & Louise* Reality Meets Movie Myth," *Women & Guns*, Sept. 1991, p. 16.

45. Jean Marbella, "Good Women Gone Bad," *The Baltimore Sun*, Aug. 14, 1991.

46. Jean Marbella, "Bad Women No More Sugar, Spice," *The Times Union*, Aug. 16, 1991.

47. Jean Marbella, "It's Good to Be Bad," *The Tulsa World*, Sept. 1, 1991.

48. Jean Marbella, "Dame in Charge Rather Than Damsel in Distress, Bad Becoming Beautiful For American Women," *The Charleston Daily Mail*, Sept. 12, 1991.

49. Joan Lester, "Women a Big Market for 'Legal' Drug Pushers," *USA Today*, Jun. 29, 1993.

50. Mal Vincent, "There Will Always Be A Welcome Place for Southern Belles in American Movies," *The Roanoke Times*, Aug. 19, 1995.

51. J. R. Moehringer, "Oldest Battle on the Planet Still Rages On," *The Rocky Mountain News*, Feb. 16, 1991.

52. "Ode to Women in 'Esquire,'" *USA Today*, Jul. 10, 1992.

53. Dr. Randy Eichner, "Focus on Your Life: Health," *The Oklahoman*, Jun. 28, 1991.

54. Karen S. Peterson, "In An Unsteady World, Girlfriends Endure," *USA Today*, Dec. 5, 1995.

55. Carmen Renee Berry and Tamara Traeder, *Girlfriends: Invisible Bonds, Enduring Ties* (Berkeley: Wildcat Canyon Press, 1995), p. 8.

56. Carmen Renee Berry and Tamara Traeder, *Girlfriends: Invisible Bonds, Enduring Ties*, p. 13.

57. Christine Spolar, "Thelma and Louise Go South," *The Washington Post*, Oct. 3, 1993.

58. Carolyn Kelly, "Thelma and Louise Go to Key West," *The Austin American Statesman*, Dec. 14, 1997.

59. Cameron Tuttle, *The Bad Girl's Guide to the Open Road* (San Francisco: Chronicle Books, 1999).

60. Eric Sorensen, "Car Struck: Seattle Celebrates 100 Year 'Autoversary,'" *The Seattle Times*, Jul. 23, 2000.

61. Eileen Matthews, "Born to Be Mild," *The San Francisco Examiner*, Nov. 12, 2000.

62. Jean Godden, "Deep In and Nominate a Pothole," *The Seattle Times*, Jun. 16, 1997.

63. Bonnie Henry, "For Real Bladder Control Test, Try a Non-stop Drive," *The Arizona Daily Star*, Oct. 2, 1994.

64. Jaimee Rose, "These Twentysomethings Aren't Following Jack Kerouac's Route," *The Baltimore Sun*, Jun. 26, 2001.

65. Kristi Turnquist, "Rags for the Road," *The Oregonian*, Jul. 11, 1991.

66. Elizabeth Snead, "Interfacing with New Edge Fashion," *USA Today*, Aug. 15, 1991.

67. Connie Shearer, "Soft, Romantic Theme Prevails at Symphony Fashion Show," *The Charleston Gazette*, Sept. 26, 1991.

68. Elizabeth Snead, "Red Alert for Coif-conscious: Flaming Hair Color is Hot," *USA Today*, Jun. 18, 1991.

69. Elizabeth Snead, "Risqué Clothing Ads Show That Sex Sells," *USA Today*, Sept. 2, 1992.

70. Gary Robertson, "Sunglass Season is Coming Into Focus," *The Richmond Times-Dispatch*, May 26, 1992.

71. Cheryl Laird, "Wild About the West," *The Houston Chronicle*, Jan. 9, 1994.

72. Tom Zucco, "Diet Coke Ads Are a Real Break," *The St. Petersburg Times*, Feb. 2, 1994.

73. Colleen O'Connor, "Chick is Chic Again — Just Watch Who You Say It To and When," *The Record*, Jul. 16, 1995.

Chapter 9

1. Rick Mitchell, "Chicks Still Ruling the Roost with 'Fly,'" *The Houston Chronicle*, Aug. 31, 1999.

2. Miriam Longino, "Dixie Chicks Country's Future," *The Atlanta Journal-Constitution*, Jul. 26, 1999.

3. Rev. Richard Schaefer, "Music, Movies Portend Bleak Future," *The Telegraph Herald*, Mar. 9, 2000.

4. Eric Weisbard, "Formula Racing," *The Village Voice*, Sept. 15–21, 1999.

5. Mike Gangloff, "Tori Amos Stills the Crowd During Flood Zone Show," *The Richmond Times Dispatch* Sept. 16, 1992.

6. Peter Stack, "The Stars Come Out," *The San Francisco Chronicle*, Jun. 21, 1998.

7. Melanie McFarland, "Backstage Pass," *The Seattle Times*, Jul. 9, 1998.

8. Tom Zucco, "C'Mon Play Along," *The St. Petersburg Times*, Mar. 7, 1992.

9. "They May be Wizards, But Magic Was

Lacking," *The Richmond Times-Dispatch*, Apr. 21, 1998.

10. Steve Bailey, "Another Year for Kentucky Duo," *The Charleston Gazette*, Nov. 12, 2001.

11. Dan Cox, "Bigger Not Better," *Variety*, Mar. 4, 1997.

12. Faye Zuckerman, "Country Music Stars Light Up the Sky," *The Charleston Gazette*, Dec. 13, 1991.

13. superstation. com

14. Steve Brennan, "MGM TV Testing Syndie 'Limits,'" *The Hollywood Reporter*, Aug. 31, 1993.

15. Moira Macdonald, "Outtakes: Hollywood and Split Personalities," *The Seattle Times*, Jun. 23, 2000.

16. Patrick MacDonald, "Country-music Legend Survives Another Brush with Death and Emerges Clean and Sober," *The Seattle Times*, Feb. 10, 2000.

17. "Coming Attractions," *The Seattle Times*, Sept. 10, 1998.

18. Claudia Puig, "Hollywood Heroines Get Tough," *USA Today*, Jan. 23, 2001.

19. "Hollywood, Colorado," *The Rocky Mountain News*, Jun. 9, 1994.

20. Syd Field, *The Screenwriter's Problem Solver* (New York: Dell Trade Paperback, 1998), p. 186.

21. Syd Field, *The Screenwriter's Problem Solver*, p. 7.

22. Syd Field, *The Screenwriter's Problem Solver*, p. 60.

23. Syd Field, *The Screenwriter's Problem Solver*, p. 69, pps.168–170 and p. 194.

24. Syd Field, *The Screenwriter's Problem Solver*, p. 148.

25. Syd Field, *The Screenwriter's Problem Solver*, p. 245.

26. Syd Field, *The Screenwriter's Problem Solver*, p. 269.

27. Syd Field, *The Screenwriter's Problem Solver*, p. 320.

28. Syd Field, *Four Screenplays, Studies in the American Screenplay, An Analysis of Four Groundbreaking Contemporary Classics* (New York: Dell Trade Paperback, 1994), p. 4.

29. Jami Bernard, *Chick Flicks: A Movie Lover's Guide to the Movies Women Love* (New York: Carol Publishing Group, 1997), p. xii.

30. Jami Bernard, *Chick Flicks: A Movie Lover's Guide to the Movies Women Love*, p. 201.

31. Gabrielle Cosgriff, Anne Reifenberg and Cynthia Thomas, *Chicks on Film: Video Picks for Women and Other Intelligent Forms of Life* (New York: Avon Books, 1998), p. 62.

32. Gabrielle Cosgriff, Anne Reifenberg and Cynthia Thomas, *Chicks on Film: Video Picks for Women and Other Intelligent Forms of Life*, p. 63.

33. Clare Bundy, Lise Carrigg, Sibyl Goldman and Andrea Pryos, *Girls on Film: The Highly Opinionated, Completely Subjective Guide to the Movies* (New York: Harper Perennial, 1999), p. 214.

34. Susan Issacs, *Brave Dames and Wimpettes: What Women Are Really Doing on Page and Screen* (New York: Ballantine, 1999), p. 4.

35. Susan Issacs, *Brave Dames and Wimpettes: What Women Are Really Doing On Page and Screen*, p. 92.

36. Susan Issacs, *Brave Dames and Wimpettes: What Women Are Really Doing On Page and Screen*, p. 12.

37. Susan Issacs, *Brave Dames and Wimpettes: What Women Are Really Doing On Page and Screen*, p. 20.

38. Michiko Kakutani, "Simpson Drama Holds Primal Appeal," *The St. Petersburg Times*, Jul. 10, 1994.

39. John Hall, "No Apologies for Watching O.J.'s End Run to Nowhere," *The Richmond Times-Dispatch*, Jun. 23, 1994.

40. Ellen Creager, "Some Go the Extra Mile For a Friend," *The Houston Chronicle*, Jun. 28, 1994.

41. William F. Woo, "Two Drifters Offer a Real-Life Lesson in the Meaning of Liberty," *The Saint Louis Post-Dispatch*, May 21, 1995.

42. Richard Reeves, "American Values in the Summer of '91," *The Charleston Gazette*, Jun. 9, 1991.

43. Mark Wolf, "Colleges Must Find a Way to Assure Equity," *The Rocky Mountain News*, Feb. 25, 1993.

44. Hendrik Hertzberg, "Is Brown and Caddell Race a *Thelma & Louise* Spree?" *The Los Angeles Times*, Oct. 27, 1991.

45. Kenneth J. Garcia, "Political Editor Loses Her Fight with Cancer," *The San Francisco Chronicle*, Jun. 23, 1998.

46. Lloyd Grove, "The Bush Women, Calling the Shots," *The Washington Post*, Aug. 18, 1992)

47. Donnie Radcliffe, "The Unknown Perot," *The St. Petersburg Times*, Jul. 4, 1992.

48. Chip Scutari, Robbie Sherwood, Mary Jo Pitzl and Ashley Bach, "It's Time for Kudos to Some and a Boot to Party Poopers," *The Arizona Republic*, May 26, 2002.

49. Linda Brazil, "Flo's One-Line Wisdoms," *The Capital Times*, Dec. 28, 2000.

50. Margaret Wolf Freivogel, "Pride, Frustration Mark Organization's 20th Anniversary," *The St. Louis Post-Dispatch*, Jul. 12, 1991.

51. Diane Mason, "A New Radicalism in Now," *The St. Petersburg Times*, Jul. 8, 1991.

52. Diane Mason, "A One-Way Trip Across the Line," *The St. Petersburg Times*, Jan. 8, 1992.

53. Carole Agus, "Working to Fulfill a Fantasy," *Newsday*, Apr. 26, 1992.

54. Deborah Sontag, "Activists Laud Anita Hill as the Newest Heroine of Feminism," *The Houston Chronicle*, Apr. 26, 1992.

55. Carole Agus, "Working to Fulfill A Fantasy,"

56. Elizabeth Snead, "Feminist Riot Grrls

Don't Just Wanna Have Fun," *USA Today*, Aug. 7, 1992.

57. Jo Mannies, "Women Rush to Seek Office," *The St. Louis Post-Dispatch*, Apr. 1, 1992.

58. Scott Dickenshets, "People in the News: Janet Reno's Media Shower," *The Las Vegas Sun*, Nov. 24, 1997.

59. James Morgan, "The United States of Entertainment: What's the Difference Between *Thelma & Louise* and "Nightline"? Not a Whole Lot These Day," *The Washington Post Magazine*, July 25, 1993.

Chapter 10

1. Christine M. Holsten, "Celebrity Update: He's Too Much," *The St. Petersburg Times*, Jun. 6, 1992.

2. Andrew Petkofsky, "Murder, Robbery Charges Certified Against Two," *The Richmond Times-Dispatch*, Apr. 15, 1993.

3. Melanie Burney, "2 Women Admit Killing Abuser But Each Says the Other Pulled the Trigger," *The Record*, Oct. 26, 1994.

4. Associated Press, "*Thelma & Louise*, New Jersey Women Accused of Killing Abusive Ex-Lover Turn On Each Other," *The Houston Chronicle*, Oct. 27, 1994.

5. Maureen Graham, "Judge Unmoved by Killers' Tears, *Thelma & Louise* Given 8 Years," *The Houston Chronicle*, Dec. 17, 1994.

6. Associated Press, "No Dramatic End to *Thelma & Louise* Saga, Prison, Not Theatric Leap, In Store for Two Women Who Bailed Abuser Out of Jail, Then Killed Him," *The Rocky Mountain News*, Dec. 17, 1994.

7. "WSU Says Beating Result of Frat Feud, Not Racism," *The Seattle Times*, Oct. 13, 2000.

8. Mark Smith, "The *Thelma & Louise* Robberies: Was It Coercion or Collusion?" *The Houston Chronicle*, Jul. 7, 1996.

9. Mark Smith, "Long Run Ends for *Thelma & Louise*," *The Houston Chronicle*, Oct. 5, 1995.

10. George Flynn, "*Thelma & Louise* Lose Shot at Hollywood Riches, Restraining Order Blocks Movie Profits," *The Houston Chronicle*, Jan. 12, 1996.

11. George Flynn, "Judge Lifts Ban on Film About Duo, Suspected Bandits Must Pay Victims," *The Houston Chronicle*, Jan. 26, 1996.

12. George Flynn, "*Thelma & Louise* Hit with Big Penalties," *The Houston Chronicle*, Jan. 27, 1998.

13. Mark Smith, "Male Victims Were 'Losers,' Diary Playing a Key Role in *Thelma & Louise* Trial," *The Houston Chronicle*, Feb. 27, 1996.

14. Jennifer Liebrum, "Turford Details Twisted Demands of the Mystery Man," *The Houston Chronicle*, Feb. 29, 1996.

15. Jennifer Liebrum, "Attorneys Argue Over Who Called the Shots: *Thelma* or *Louise?*" *The Houston Chronicle*, Mar. 2, 1996.

16. Jennifer Liebrum, "Jury Gamble Doesn't Pay Off," *The Houston Chronicle*, Mar. 7, 1996.

17. Robert Hough, "Prisoner of Love," *Saturday Night*, May 1999, p. 60.

18. "2 Women Charged in Robbery of Store," *The Times Union*, Oct. 31, 1991.

19. James Thorner, "Women Lead Police on 3-county Chase," *The St. Petersburg Times*, Jun. 10, 1998.

20. Karen Dorn Steele, "Trial Opens Today for Clean-air Activists," *The Spokesman-Review*, Feb. 23, 1999.

21. James F. Dent, "Turn on the Light — and Duck!" *The Charleston Gazette*, Aug. 12, 1991.

22. London Observer News Service, "British Crime Spree Likened to Aging *Thelma & Louise*," *The St. Louis Post-Dispatch*, Jul. 7, 1993.

23. James Walsh, "2 St. Paul Women Arrested in 5 Robberies," *The Minneapolis Star Tribune*, Aug. 9, 1991.

24. Associated Press, "Partner in *Thelma & Louise* Carjacking Gets 15-year Term," *The Houston Chronicle*, Jun. 28, 1993.

25. Joel Obermayer, "2 Women Held After Chase, Shootout in Texas," *The Baltimore Sun*, Sept. 24, 1994.

26. Associated Press, "Real life *Thelma & Louise* Face Charges," *The Tulsa World*, Sept. 24, 1994.

27. Michele Salcedo, "Thelma and Louise, LI Style," *Newsday*, Nov. 24, 1994.

28. Babita Persaud, "Girls Identified as 'Teenage Thelma and Louise,'" *The St. Petersburg Times*, Jun. 29, 1997.

29. Steve Olafson, "Escaped Convicts Had Good Old Time On Trek, and Photos To Prove It," *The Houston Chronicle*, Sept. 3, 1999.

30. Carrie Seidman, "Reprimanded and Reassigned," *The Albuquerque Journal*, Dec. 3, 1995.

31. Associated Press, "*Thelma & Louise* Robbers Join Growing Ranks of Female Suspects," *The Columbian*, Jun. 5, 1998.

32. Jose Martinez and Ralph Ranalli, "Cops Think They Have 'Thelma' and/or 'Louise,'" *The Boston Herald*, Mar. 21, 1999.

33. Beverly Ford, "Police Close In On *Thelma & Louise*," *The Boston Herald*, Mar. 19, 1999.

34. The Associated Press, "Bank Heist Mimics Film; Women, Girls Are Charged," *The Boston Globe*, Aug. 13, 1998.

35. Philip Messing, "Women Abduct Man in 3-hour Terror Ordeal," *The New York Post*, Jan. 5, 1998.

PART III

Chapter 11

1. Every effort was made to access all pertinent articles that a featured newspaper may have

printed referencing the film. However, because of the nature of archive search engines and the issue of reprint rights, some articles may have been unavoidably missed or unintentionally overlooked.

2. Jim Bland, "Teen Girls Lead Police Chase Cruisers Follow Pair In Stolen Car From Lima" *The Dayton Daily News*, Jul. 9, 1995.

3. Gary Nuhn, "Cleveland Now Adds 'The Error,'" *The Dayton Daily News*, Oct. 28, 1997.

4. Charles Stough, "Campaign Notebook," *The Dayton Daily News*, Aug. 11, 1992.

5. Greg Simms Jr., "Crime & Safety," *The Dayton Daily News*, Jun. 17, 1999.

6. "Directors Guild Nominee A Surprise," *The Dayton Daily News*, Jan. 29, 1992.

7. Tom Hopkins, "Fabled Highway Series Gears Up," *The Dayton Daily News*, Jun. 8, 1993.

8. Kathy Whyde Jesse, "Corporations Make Giving Into An Art," *The Dayton Daily News*, Mar. 29, 1998.

9. Shann Nix, "Nice Guys Finish Last: At Least With the Opposite Sex," *The Dayton Daily News*, Sept. 23, 1991.

10. Brad Tilson, "*Thelma & Louise:* Is It a Movie Or A Cause?" *The Dayton Daily News*, Jun. 23, 1991.

11. Mark Russell, "Conservatives Make Sure Chappaquiddick Incident Surfaces Yet Again," *The Dayton Daily News*, Sept. 12, 1991.

12. Mark Russell, "Candidates Have a Ticket to Ride," *The Dayton Daily News*, Aug. 3, 1992.

13. Terry Lawson, "Thelma and Louise-Film Puts Women in Driver's Seat," *Dayton Daily News*, May 24, 1991.

14. Terry Lawson, "It's An Amiable Trip," *The Dayton Daily News*, May 1, 1992.

15. Mary McCarty, "Rape Revives Terrors," *The Dayton Daily News*, Dec. 17, 1997.

16. Merry Beth Hopkins, "Local, state And National Milestones In The History of Women," *The Dayton Daily News*, Mar. 22, 1994.

17. Jackie Loohauis, "Revenge," *The Dayton Daily News*, Nov. 18, 1996.

18. Katherine Ullmer, "'Soul Mate and Friend' Remembered," *The Dayton Daily News*, Mar. 31, 2000.

19. Joe Capozzi, "Chevy VS. Ford: Quarreling is Job 1," *The Dayton Daily News*, Feb. 26, 1999.

Chapter 12

1. Matt Helms, "FBI Nabs Woman Believed Part of Bank-Robbing Duo," *The Detroit Free Press*, May 14, 1996.

2. Brian Ballou, "2 Women Sought in Gas Station Thefts," *The Detroit Free Press*, Oct. 18, 1999.

3. Amy Wilson, "Family Bills Get Michigan Boost in Congress," *The Detroit Free Press*, Oct. 28, 1992.

4. Ellen Creager, "Al Cowlings: Friend to the End, People Reflect on How Far They'd Go to Help a Pal," *The Detroit Free Press*, June 23, 1994.

5. Sharon Andrews, "Attitude Overhaul Repair Shops Promote Better Service to Women," *The Detroit Free Press*, Apr. 1, 1993.

6. Marsha Miro, "Put Art Before the Horsepower," *The Detroit Free Press*, Jan. 11, 1995.

7. Terry Lawson, "Detroit and Hollywood: You can't Have One Without the Other," *The Detroit Free Press*, June 21, 1996.

8. Matt Nauman, "Fender Flicks Cars Are the Biggest Stars in Some Classic, and Trashy, Films," The Detroit Free Press, Apr. 13, 2000.

9. Lawrence Ulrich, "Fords' Pretty Little Roadster is Back Revived Thunderbird is Plush and Sporty," *The Detroit Free Press*, May 31, 2001.

10. Kathy Huffhines, "New for '90s: Female Buddy Movies," *The Detroit Free Press*, April 21, 1991.

11. Kathy Huffines, "*Thelma & Louise* Is an American Original," *The Detroit Free Press*, May 24, 1991.

12. Kathy Huffines, "Film Heroines' Independence Triggers a Fight," *The Detroit Free Press*, Jun. 30, 1991.

13. Judy Gerstel, "Who Says Women Are Too Violent? Men, That's Who," *The Detroit Free Press*, Jul. 5, 1991.

14. Judy Gerstel, "Who Says Women are Too Violent? Men, That's Who," *The Detroit Free Press*, July 5, 1991.

15. Judy Gerstel, "Were Empowered Women in Film Just a Flash in the Pan?" *The Detroit Free Press*, Aug. 25, 1991.

16. Judy Gerstel, "No Middle Ground It's Amazing How Some Movies Stir Such Passionate, Opposite Reactions," *The Detroit Free Press*, Sept. 29, 1991.

17. Judy Gerstel, "Out of the Picture," *The Detroit Free Press*, Jul. 25, 1993.

18. Julie Hinds, "Coming Up at 10," *The Detroit Free Press*, Mar. 29, 2002.

Chapter 13

1. Alan Solomon, "Welcome to America," *The Chicago Tribune*, Oct. 6, 1996.

2. Clifford Terry, "*Thelma & Louise* Rowdy Road Trip Slowed by Plot Holes," *The Chicago Tribune*, May 24, 1991.

3. "Thelma & Louise," www.suntimes.com.

4. Lina Chern, "*Thelma* Simply a Good Film," *The Chicago Tribune*, May 31, 1991.

5. Vincent Schleitwiler, "*Thelma* is the Year's Best," *The Chicago Tribune*, Jun. 7, 1991.

6. Gene Siskel, "The Best Movie of the Year," *The Chicago Tribune*, Dec. 22, 1991.

7. Nancy Randle, "Her Say, At last, a Film Worthy of the 'F' Word," *The Chicago Tribune*, Jun. 9, 1991.

8. Clarence Page, "*Thelma & Louise:* A Reel-Life Tale of Women and Power," *The Chicago Tribune*, Jun. 12, 1991.

9. Stephanie Salter, "Loving *Thelma* Do You Have to Be a Woman To Appreciate This Film?" *The Chicago Tribune*, June 30, 1991.

10. Shea Dean, "Fan Sees *Thelma & Louise* as Trailblazers," *The Chicago Tribune*, Sept. 1, 1991.

11. Steve Johnson, "Across Chicago, U.S., the Debate Continues," *The Chicago Tribune*, Oct. 16, 1991.

12. James Warren, "The Women's Ghetto," *The Chicago Tribune*, Mar. 14, 1993.

13. Linda P. Campbell, "Abortion Activists Shift Battle Into High Gear," *The Chicago Tribune*, Jul. 29, 1991.

14. Cox News Service, "Abortion Forces Gird for D.C. Rally," *The Chicago Tribune*, Apr. 5, 1992.

15. Linda Lehrer, "'92 Agenda Set," *The Chicago Tribune*, Jul. 21, 1991.

16. Nina Burleigh, "Then and NOW: a 17-year Fight for Equity Issues," *The Chicago Tribune*, Sept. 8, 1991.

17. Nina Burleigh, "Then and NOW: a 17-year Fight for Equity Issues," *The Chicago Tribune*, Sept. 8, 1991.

18. Carol Messineo, letter in "Voice of the People," *The Chicago Tribune*, May 28, 1992.

19. Paul Galloway, "Fergie Takes Five Close Up," *The Chicago Tribune*, Apr. 27, 1994.

20. Howard Witt, "Affirmative Action Splitting Democrats," *The Chicago Tribune*, Apr. 11, 1995.

21. Cara Applebaum, "Products Compete for Movie Roles, Too," *The Chicago Tribune*, Jul. 21, 1991.

22. Andrew Leckey, "The Thrill of it All, Movies Provide Impetus and Ideas for Action-packed Vacations," *The Chicago Tribune*, Jan. 4, 1996.

23. Deborah Claymon, "PC-Makers Add Style to Profit Strategy," *The Chicago Tribune*, May 10, 1999.

24. Phyllis Feuerstein, " Home-video Store Manager: 'Most of Our Customers Want a Recommendation They Can Count On," *The Chicago Tribune*, Dec. 20, 1992.

25. "Women's Issues," *The Chicago Tribune*, Jan. 28, 1993.

26. Julie Deardorff, "Boxer Helps Women Fight for Fitness," *The Chicago Tribune*, Dec. 23, 1992.

27. Joanne Cleaver, "Oh No, Not Another Story about Butts," *The Chicago Tribune*, Mar. 24, 1996.

28. Regina Barreca, "Lust's Allure," *The Chicago Tribune*, Jun. 25, 1995.

29. Regina Barreca, "Payback Time When It Comes To Getting Even, Is Female Really Deadly than Male?" *The Chicago Tribune*, Mar. 27, 1994.

30. Kristine M. Holmgren, "Cherish Lover, Lest You Lose Her," *The Chicago Tribune*, Sept. 17, 1995.

31. Veronique Mistiaen, "The Future for Women: To Each Her Own," *The Chicago Tribune*, June 22, 1997.

32. James Warren, "Cast Changes Entertainment Weekly Imagines a Hollywood Run by Women," *The Chicago Tribune*, Dec. 17, 1992.

33. Chris Kaltenbach, "Great Pairings in Hollywood a Rarity," *The Chicago Tribune*, April 5, 2001.

34. According to Gloria Steinem in a letter she wrote to *Time* in 2000, the line can be traced back to the 1970s and is attributable to Irina Dunn, an Australian feminist.

35. John D. Thomas, "Giving Women the Power to Fight Back, 'Reel' Examines Film Violence," *The Chicago Tribune*, Jul. 15, 2001.

36. Rachel Abramowitz, "Forget Old Rules about Chick Flicks; Weepiness is Out; Girl Power, Attitude Are In," *The Chicago Tribune*, Jun. 2, 2002.

37. Mary Schmich, "A Lucid Thought: Middle Age Without Female Rage," *The Chicago Tribune*, Sept. 27, 1996.

Chapter 14

1. Vicki Barker, "*Thelma & Louise* Heats Up," *The Salt Lake Tribune*, Aug. 9, 1991.

2. Terry Orme, "Film Production in Utah High, But Not Record-setting," *The Salt Lake Tribune*, Aug. 11, 1991.

3. Tom Wharton, "Four-Wheelin' in Utah," *The Salt Lake Tribune*, Apr. 18, 1995.

4. Christopher Smith, "Grand County Voters Return to Polls," *The Salt Lake Tribune*, Feb. 10, 1993.

5. Laurie Sullivan, "Thugs Be Warned," *The Salt Lake Tribune*, Jan. 15, 1994.

6. Hilary Groutage, "Widowed Share Tips, Tears at Meeting," *The Salt Lake Tribune*, Nov. 4, 1996.

7. Christopher Smith, "Mission Impossible: To Film Prohibited BASE Jump," *The Salt Lake Tribune*, Aug. 24, 1999.

8. Micheal Vigh, "Pictures, Map Lead Authorities to Park Suicide," *The Salt Lake Tribune*, Mar. 29, 2000.

9. Brandon Griggs, "Culture Vulture," *The Salt Lake Tribune*, Jul. 31, 1998.

10. Lisa Church, "Museum to House Movie Memorabilia," *The Salt Lake Tribune*, Apr. 21, 2001.

11. Vicki Barker, "*Thelma & Louise* Heats Up," *The Salt Lake Tribune*, Aug. 9, 1991.

12. Terry Orme, "The Movies Heat Up," *The Salt Lake Tribune*, May 24, 1991.

13. Terry Orme, "Best & Worst: The Cream & The Craftless of the Film Crop," *The Salt Lake Tribune*, May 24, 1991.

14. Terry Orme and Sean Means, "Can't Afford Roses? Try a Video Valentine," *The Salt Lake Tribune*, Feb. 13, 1992.

15. Paul Rolly and JoAnn Jacobsen-Wells, "Rolly & Wells," *The Salt Lake Tribune*, Jul. 6, 1994.

16. Robert Kirby, "Halloween Teaching Not For the Timid," *The Salt Lake Tribune*, Nov. 4, 1995.

17. Sean P. Means, "The 'Best' Movies That Didn't Make It; Dump 'Gump': Revising the Top-Movies List," *The Salt Lake Tribune*, Jun. 26, 1998.

18. "Thelma & Louise Duo?" *The Salt Lake Tribune*, Dec. 21, 1994.

19. Rene Rodriguez, "Smoking in the Movies?" *The Salt Lake Tribune*, Jul. 9, 1995.

20. John Horn, "Film Guinea Pigs Decide How Movies Are Made and Marketed," *The Salt Lake Tribune*, Sept. 16, 1991.

21. Jim Emerson, "U.S. Movies Celebrate 'Family' Values — Even in the Strangest Arrangements," *The Salt Lake Tribune*, Jun. 7, 1992.

22. Mike Duffy, "Female Bonding Gets Another Set of TV Buddies With 'Hope & Gloria,'" *The Salt Lake City Tribune*, Apr. 14, 1995.

Chapter 15

1. Eleanor Ringel, "*Thelma & Louise* a Breathtaking Journey of Identity," *The Atlanta Journal-Constitution*, May 24, 1991.

2. Eleanor Ringel, "Eloquent 'Silence,' A Beautiful 'Beast' Among Year's Best," *The Atlanta Journal-Constitution*, Dec. 29, 1991.

3. Eleanor Ringel, "*Thelma & Louise* Why is it so Hard for us to Handle?" *The Atlanta Journal-Constitution*, Jul. 14, 1991.

4. Steve Murray, "Hollywood's Vote of Confidence on Oscar Night Attests to Females' Increasing Clout in Cinematic Circles," *The Atlanta Journal-Constitution*, Apr. 9, 1992.

5. "From Role Models to Stereotypes," *The Atlanta Journal-Constitution*, Apr. 9, 1992.

6. Eleanor Ringel, "Hollywood's Way: Monkey See, Do," *The Atlanta Journal-Constitution*, Apr. 25, 1993.

7. Eleanor Ringel, "Male-ing It In," *The Atlanta Journal-Constitution*, Feb. 26, 1995.

8. Steve Murray, "Independent Girls," *The Atlanta Journal-Constitution*, Sept. 1, 1996.

9. Profile of Anita Sharp, "1-Minute Profile," *The Atlanta Journal-Constitution*, Jul. 11, 1991.

10. Profile of Sherry Diane Sutton, "1-Minute Profile," *The Atlanta Journal-Constitution*, Aug.15, 1991.

11. Profile of Dr. Ruth Schmidt, "1-Minute Profile," *The Atlanta Journal-Constitution*, Oct. 10, 1991.

12. Profile of Wade Wright, "1-Minute Profile," *The Atlanta Journal-Constitution*, Apr. 16, 1992.

13. Profile of Betty Ryan, "1-Minute Profile," *The Atlanta Journal-Constitution*, Jul. 23, 1991.

14. Janice L. Schraibman, "Letters to the Editor: *Thelma & Louise* Portrays Women Who Fight Back," *The Atlanta Journal-Constitution*, Jun. 20, 1991.

15. Doug Moore, "If a Man Drives Drunk, Maybe It's Just Midlife Crisis," *The Atlanta Journal-Constitution*, June 12, 1991.

16. Patricia Carr, "The Best of Friends," *The Atlanta Journal-Constitution*, Jun. 12, 1991.

17. "Feminists are Outlaws, too," *The Atlanta Journal-Constitution*, Jun. 14, 1991.

18. "Business Report: On Women: Good Luck is Spelled W-O-R-K," *The Atlanta Journal-Constitution*, Jun. 19, 1991.

19. Patricia Carr, "Current Issues May be Redefining the Gender Agenda," *The Atlanta Journal-Constitution*, Aug. 29, 1991.

20. Steve Murray, "*Thelma & Louise* Tart-tongued, Provocative, Funny and Available," *The Atlanta Journal-Constitution*, Jan. 9, 1992

21. "Inside," *The Atlanta Journal-Constitution*, Jan. 9, 1992.

22. Bo Emerson, "The Covers: Less News, More Trends," *The Atlanta Journal-Constitution*, Jan. 28, 1992.

23. Bo Emerson, "Lessons from the Hill: What Have We Learned a Year After the Thomas Hearings," *The Atlanta Journal-Constitution*, Oct. 5, 1992.

24. Durwood McAlister, "Pay Heed to Message," *The Atlanta Journal-Constitution*, May 24, 1992.

25. Clarence Page, "*Thelma & Louise:* A Reel-Life Tale of Women and Power," *The Chicago Tribune*, June 12, 1991.

26. Nicholaus Mills, "Men Must Participate in Defining Masculinity," *The Atlanta Journal-Constitution*, May 27, 1992.

27. Linda Sharp, "Off-pavement Driving not a Thrill for Everyone," *The Atlanta Journal-Constitution*, May 21, 1993.

28. Alan Patureau, "It Takes TWO: Twins Foundation Serves as a Resource to Help in Studying Genetic Mysteries," *The Atlanta Journal-Constitution*, Jul. 12, 1993.

29. Sandy Grady, "No Meaning in Bobbitt Melodrama," *The Atlanta Journal-Constitution*, Jan. 12, 1994.

30. "Around the South," *The Atlanta Journal-Constitution*, May 28, 1994.

31. Lessie Scurry, "Southern Cooks: Pals in the Kitchen, Pals for Life: Gainsville Women Publish Family Recipes," *The Atlanta Journal-Constitution*, Jul. 14, 1994.

32. "Wheels for Women: Special Section: Hit the Road" *The Atlanta Journal-Constitution*, Aug. 19, 1994.

33. Drew Jubera, "Gimme an A: Adultery," *The Atlanta Journal-Constitution*, Jun. 16, 1997.

34. Mary Anne Carroll Gordon, "Anyone Want to Join Me on an Escape from Old Age?" *The Atlanta Journal-Constitution*, Oct. 30, 1997.

35. Editorial, "Last-chance Road Block: We Can't Pave our Way to Clean Air in Metro Atlanta," *The Atlanta Journal-Constitution*, Nov. 11, 1998.

36. Bob Longino, "Screenwriting Seminar Gets the Dialogue Started," *The Atlanta Journal-Constitution*, Sept. 24, 2000.

37. Robert McKee, *Story: Substance, Structure, Style, and the Principles of Screenwriting* (New York: Harper Collins, 1997), p. 45.

38. *Ibid.*, p. 306.

39. Heather Ballew, "Reader Postcard: A Free Day, a Few Dollars and a Tybee Island Day Trip," *The Atlanta Journal-Constitution*, Sept. 9, 2001.

40. Steve Hummer, "Virginia 39, Georgia Tech 38: Game, Season both Get Away from the Jackets," *The Atlanta Journal-Constitution*, Nov. 11, 2001.

Chapter 16

1. Jack Anderson and Michael Binstein, "The 'A' Word Confronts Bush Campaign," *The Washington Post*, Mar. 19, 1992.

2. Cathy Young, "Boys Will Be Boys," *The Washington Post*, Sept. 19, 1993.

3. James T. Yenkel, "The Grand Canyon," *The Washington Post*, Jul. 3, 1994.

4. Vicki Vantoch, "Fingernail Fashion Choices," *The Washington Post*, Dec. 28, 1999.

5. John Schwartz, "Internet Newsgroup Intrusion has Tobacco Wags Smokin' Mad," *The Washington Post*, Aug. 22, 1994.

6. Andrew Nelson, "Diversions: How Did We Ever Get Along Without...," *The Washington Post*, Aug. 9, 1993.

7. Ivelisse DeJesus, "Slick Way to Get to the Prom," *The Washington Post*, Jan. 19, 1995.

8. Judith Weintraub, "The End: After 54 Years, Credits Roll for Usher Phil Ahern," *The Washington Post*, Jul. 1, 1991.

9. Rita Kempley, "Movies Shrink Rapping," *The Washington Post*, Nov. 9, 1991.

10. Joe Brown, "Surprisingly Funny 'Favor,'" *The Washington Post*, Apr. 29, 1994.

11. Hal Hinson, "Amid the Dogs and Doomsaying, A Surprising Number of Delights," *The Washington Post*, Dec. 29, 1991.

12. Hal Hinson, "Screening Out Life," *The Washington Post*, Mar. 8, 1992.

13. Hal Hinson, "The Déjà vu of 'Normal,'" *The Washington Post*, Apr. 29, 1992.

14. Hal Hinson, "Cool Chicks," *The Washington Post*, Mar. 21, 1993.

15. Desson Howe, "On the Loose: Comic Thelma," *The Washington Post*, May 24, 1991.

16. Desson Howe, "'A&A': Into the Ampersand Box," *The Washington Post*, Mar. 5, 1993.

17. Rita Kempley, "*Thelma & Louise*: In the Hammer Lane," *The Washington Post*, May 24, 1991.

18. Desson Howe, "The Best of the Year," *The Washington Post*, Dec. 27, 1991.

19. Hal Hinson and Rita Kempley, "Amid the Dogs and Doomsaying, A Surprising Number of Delights," *The Washington Post*, Dec. 29, 1991.

20. Jami Bernard, "Effect Keeps 'T&L' Rolling Along," *The Washington Post*, Dec. 29, 1991.

21. Rita Kempley, Richard Harrington and Joseph McLellan, "New On Video," *The Washington Post*, Jan. 2, 1992.

22. Pat Dowell, "Reel Redemption," *The Washington Post*, Aug. 11, 1991.

23. Jennifer Frey, "Babes of Steel: Hollywood's Powerful Fantasies," *The Washington Post*, Jun. 19, 2001.

24. John E. Yang, "Outside the Hearing, It was Cheers, Jeers Thomas's Supporters Were Most Vocal, Visible," *The Washington Post*, Oct. 12, 1991.

25. Janice C. Simpson, "Moving Into the Driver's Seat," *Time*, Jun. 24, 1991.

26. Fern Shen, "Forget The Girl Talk An All-Women News Show Takes on the Guys," *The Washington Post*, Apr. 2, 1991.

27. Larry Rohter, "The Third Woman of *Thelma & Louise*," *The New York Times*, Jun. 5, 1991.

28. David Finkel, "Women on the Verge of a Power Breakthrough," *The Washington Post*, May 10, 1992.

29. Martha Sherrill, "Together to the End — Almost: Yegorova Pulls Away in Women's Marathon," *The Washington Post*, Aug. 2, 1992.

30. Amy E. Schwartz, "Toni Morrison and the 'Anti-Male' Rap," *The Washington Post*, Oct. 15, 1993.

31. Maria E. Odum, "A Symbol of Shared Rage," *The Washington Post*, Aug. 12, 1993.

32. Tony Kornheiser, "Don't Say that Word, Please!" *The Washington Post*, Nov. 9, 1993.

33. Richard Morin, "Unconventional Wisdom," *The Washington Post*, Dec. 4, 1994.

34. Melanie Choukas-Bradley, "The Getaway All-Women's Gatherings," *The Washington Post*, Jun. 8, 1998.

35. Phylicia Oppelt, "Wheel Love," *The Washington Post*, Aug. 2, 1998.

36. Thomas W. Lippman, "Allies Level a Bridge, Hit Troops in Kosovo," *The Washington Post*, Apr. 2, 1999.

37. Liza Mundy, "The Hillary Dilemma," *The Washington Post*, Mar. 21, 1999.

38. Kathy Sawyer, "Thelma and Louise in Space? Idea of All-female Crew Could Redefine 'Unmanned' in NASA-speak," *The Washington Post*, Apr. 13, 1999.

39. Kevin Sullivan and Mary Jordan, "Fugitive's Haven No Longer," *The Washington Post*, May 22, 2001.

40. M.L. Lyke, "Goodbye, Girl," *The Washington Post*, May 12, 2002.

41. Howard Bloom, "The Amazons Among Us," *The Washington Post*, Apr. 1996.

42. Susan Isaacs, "A Look at ... Women on Screen," *The Washington Post*, Aug. 15, 1999.

Chapter 17

1. Kenneth Turan, "Smooth Ride for *Thelma & Louise*," *The Los Angeles Times*, May 24, 1991.

2. Janice Hickey, "*Thelma & Louise*: What's It All About?" letter to the editor, *The Los Angeles Times*, Jun. 8, 1991.

3. Andrew Christie, "*Thelma & Louise*: What's It All About?" letter to the editor, *The Los Angeles Times*, Jun. 8, 1991.

4. Peg Yorkin, "*Thelma & Louise*: What's It All About?" letter to the editor, *The Los Angeles Times*, Jun. 8, 1991.

5. Eric Dodson, "*Thelma & Louise*: What's It All About?" letter to the editor, *The Los Angeles Times*, Jun. 8, 1991.

6. Sue Horton, "*Thelma & Louise*: What's It All About?" letter to the editor, *The Los Angeles Times*, Jun. 8, 1991.

7. Carolyn Woolsey, "*Thelma & Louise*: What's It All About?" letter to the editor, *The Los Angeles Times*, Jun. 8, 1991.

8. Paul Arthur Hartman, "More *Thelma & Louise*," letter to the editor, *The Los Angeles Times*, Jun.15, 1991.

9. S.C. Dacy, "Roberts' Star Power," letter to the editor, *The Los Angeles Times*, Jun. 23, 1991.

10. Kristina Callahan, "*Thelma & Louise*: What's It All About?" letter to the editor, *The Los Angeles Times*, Jun. 8, 1991.

11. Stace Aspey, "*Thelma & Louise*: What's It All About?" letter to the editor, *The Los Angeles Times*, Jun. 8, 1991.

12. Richard Silverstein, "More *Thelma & Louise*," letter to the editor, *The Los Angeles Times*, Jun.15, 1991.

13. Kelly McKee, "On the Road," letter to the editor, *The Los Angeles Times*, Aug. 18, 1991.

14. Joy Trachtenberg, "So, This is What Betty Friedan Has Come To?" letter to the editor, *The Los Angeles Times* Apr. 26, 1992.

15. Irene Briggs, "Judge Wrong to Blame Girl in Abuse Case," letter to the editor, *The Los Angles Times*, Jul. 28, 1991.

16. Leo Smith, "Flicks, Film and Video File," *The Los Angeles Times*, Jan. 30, 1992.

17. Patt Morrison, "Get a Grip, Guys: This is Fantasy," *The Los Angeles Times*, July 22, 1991.

18. John K. Frieborn, "Women and Violence," letter to the editor, *The Los Angeles Times*, Aug. 1, 1991.

19. Phillip J. Festa, "Women and Violence," letter to the editor, *The Los Angeles Times*, Aug. 1, 1991.

20. Patt Morrison, "Big Screen, Small Idea," *The Los Angeles Times*, Jan. 24, 1993.

21. Patt Morrison, "Name of the Game," *The Los Angeles Times*, Oct. 24, 1993.

22. Art Buchwald, "Highway Robbery After the Movie," *The Los Angeles Times*, Jul. 25, 1991.

23. Art Buchwald, "Thelma and Louise Make House Calls," *The Los Angeles Times*, May 27, 1993.

24. Anne Louise Bannon, "Box Office Fuels Frenzy for Costumes Holiday," *The Los Angeles Times*, Oct. 28, 1993.

25. Dianne Klein, "Wasn't Hitting Boys How Thelma and Louise Got Started?" *The Los Angeles Times*, Oct. 18, 1992.

26. Dennis Hunt, "Thelma and Louise Hit Rental Road in January," *The Los Angeles Times*, Oct. 18, 1991.

27. "Obituaries; Elizabeth McBride, 42; Film Costume Designer," *The Los Angeles Times*, Jun. 19, 1997.

28. "Obituaries; Dean O'Brien; Movie, TV Producer," *The Los Angeles Times*, Oct. 7, 1999.

29. "Obituaries; Bobby Bass, 65; Legendary Hollywood Stuntman," *The Los Angeles Times*, Nov. 11, 2001.

30. Robert W. Welkos "Company Town; Judge Throws Out Lawsuit Against Oliver Stone," *The Los Angeles Times*, Mar. 13, 2001.

31. Nathalie Dupree, "How Sweet It Is," *The Los Angeles Times*, Oct. 24, 1991.

32. Kathleen Doheny, "Ab-session," in "Body Watch," *The Los Angeles Times*, Oct. 24, 1995.

33. S. J. Diamond, "The Human Condition," *The Los Angeles Times*, Sept. 24, 1992.

34. Claudia Puig, "Radio Drive Time Isn't Prime Time for Women," *The Los Angeles Times*, Oct. 13, 1991.

35. Tracey Miller, "A Real Ground-Breaker on KFI," *The Los Angeles Times*, Oct. 21, 1991.

36. Tracy Wilkinson and Jane Fritsch, "Rallies Try To Put Abortion Issue Back in Spotlight," *The Los Angeles Times*, Aug. 25, 1991.

37. Howard Rosenberg, "The Talk of the Electronic Town," *The Los Angeles Times*, Oct. 10, 1991.

38. Elaine Ciulla Kamarck, "GOP Women Serve Grit, Not Tea," *The Los Angeles Times*, Aug. 19, 1992.

39. Jonathan Gold, "A Woman's Place," *The Los Angeles Times*, Jan. 10, 1993.

40. Deanne Stillman, "The Trouble with Male-Bashing," *The Los Angeles Times*, Feb. 27, 1994.

41. Warren Farrell, "First Wives Club: Thelma

and Louise Exhales," *The Los Angeles Times*, Oct. 14, 1996.

42. Mark Fineman, "Mexico Murder Trial Puts Women's Rights in Spotlight," *The Los Angeles Times*, Feb. 7, 1997.

43. "Murder Charge Dropped in Alleged Mexico Rape Case," *The Los Angeles Times*, Feb. 9, 1997.

44. "World in Brief; Mexico; Woman Who Shot Assailant Freed," *The Los Angeles Times*, Feb. 12, 1997.

45. Mary McNamara, "Stealing Back the Lives of Women," *The Los Angeles Times*, Oct. 28, 1998.

46. Susan Spano, "Voyages of Inner, Outer Discovery as More Women Travel Together," *The Los Angeles Times*, Jun. 28, 1998.

47. Susan Spano, "Seeking Lessons in Life From Stars Who Traveled Across the Silver Screen," *The Los Angeles Times*, Aug. 13, 2000.

48. Hendrik Hertzberg, "Is Brown and Caddell Race a *Thelma & Louise* Spree?" *The Los Angeles Times*, Oct.27, 1991.

49. Frank Kosa, "Confessions of a Political Junkie," *The Los Angeles Times*, Nov. 15, 1992.

50. Nina J. Easton, "Forget the Thelma and Louise Thing," *The Los Angeles Times*, Nov. 15, 1995.

51. Eric Lichtblau and Ronald J. Ostrow, "'Cussed at, Fussed at,' Reno Shrugs, Survives," *The Los Angeles Times*, Jan. 16, 2001.

52. Michael Haederle, "The Agony of Humiliation," *The Los Angeles Times*, Feb. 9, 1993.

53. Peter Rainer, "Trying to Pick a Romantic Movie?" *The Los Angeles Times*, Jul. 21, 1993.

54. Heidi Siegmund Cuda, "Rounding Up A Good Ol' Time," *The Los Angeles Times*, Sept. 30, 1999.

55. Ann O'Neill, "The Most Unwelcome Comeback," *The Los Angeles Times*, Apr. 29, 2001.

56. Compiled by Kathleen Bueno, "The Reel America: The Films That Show Us Who We Are" *The Los Angeles Times*, Jun. 30, 1996.

57. "Just the Facts: Escapist Movies," *The Los Angeles Times*, Nov. 30, 1997.

58. Paul Dean, "Just Can't Top This," *The Los Angeles Times*, Jun. 25, 1991.

59. Joyce Walter, "A Novel to Take to Your Bed By," *The Los Angeles Times*, Aug. 25, 1991.

60. Carolyn See, "Attempting to Cope with the Impossible," *The Los Angeles Times*, Sept. 23, 1991.

61. Anne Thompson, "Alive and Armed in LA," *The Los Angeles Times*, Nov. 17, 1991.

62. Emily Levine, "The Body Politic," *The Los Angeles Times*, Jun. 14, 1992.

63. Karen Stabiner, "Nonfiction," *The Los Angeles Times*, Jul. 4, 1993.

64. Pauline Mayer, "Thelma and Louise, 30 Years Later," *The Los Angeles Times*, Mar. 6, 1994.

65. Celeste Fremon, "Homegirls," *The Los Angeles Times*, Jun. 15, 1997.

66. Paul Dean, "Speed Read," *The Los Angeles Times*, Mar. 14, 1998.

67. Dean E. Murphy and Douglas P. Shuit, "U.S. Senate Candidates Crisscross State for Votes," *The Los Angeles Times*, Oct. 31, 1992.

68. Glenn F. Bunting, "Senators Reverse Styles to Match New Roles," *The Los Angeles Times*, Mar. 8, 1993.

69. Barney Rosenzweig, "Senate Team," letter to the editor, *The Los Angeles Times*, Mar. 21, 1993.

70. Glenn F. Bunting, "Feinstein and Boxer Carve Distinct Niches in Senate Politics," *The Los Angeles Times*, Dec. 20, 1993.

71. Dave Lesher, "Will Huffington's Purse Strings Tangle the Senate Race?" *The Los Angeles Times*, Mar. 13, 1994.

72. "Special Report; Election Preview Decision '94," *The Los Angeles Times*, May 29, 1994.

73. Obituary, "Barbara Avedon; *Cagney & Lacey* co-creator, Peace Activist," *The Los Angeles Times*, Sept. 4, 1994.

74. Cathleen Decker and Gebe Martinez, "Candidates Seek Votes in O.C., Across the State," *The Los Angeles Times*, Nov. 7, 1994.

75. "Laugh Lines," *The Los Angeles Times*, Nov. 9, 1994.

76. Jon D. Markman, "Tunneling Machine is Stuck Under Mountains," *The Los Angeles Times*, Jul. 19, 1996.

77. Jon D. Markman, "Plan to Resume Tunneling Told," *The Los Angeles Times*, Jul. 24, 1996.

78. Jon. D. Markman, "Arch Replacement Delays Tunneling Again," *The Los Angeles Times*, Aug. 2, 1996.

79. "The Experts and Thelma's Plight," *The Los Angeles Times*, Aug. 21, 1996.

80. Martha L. Willman, Jon D. Markman and Jill Leovy, "Valley Newswatch," *The Los Angeles Times*, Sept. 6, 1996.

81. Steve Harvey, "Only in L.A.," *The Los Angeles Times*, May 13, 1997.

82. Richard Simon and Jeffrey L. Rabin, "Beleaguered MTA on Verge of Tunnel Triumph," *The Los Angeles Times*, Oct. 27, 1997.

83. Bob Pool, "Displaced Walk of fame Stars Stage Comeback," *The Los Angeles Times*, Mar. 17, 1998.

84. "Timeline for the Red Line," *The Los Angeles Times*, Jun. 18, 2000.

85. Carl Ingram and Nancy Vogel, "California Nears Crossroads in Power Crisis," *The Los Angeles Times*, Jan. 21, 2001.

Chapter 18

1. At the time of this study, *The New York Times* online archives dated back only to 1996, but from that point forward the parent company

of *The Boston Globe* maintained steady, heavy mention of the film.

2. William Froug, *Zen and the Art of Screenwriting*, p.99.

3. William Froug, *Zen and the Art of Screenwriting*, p 92.

4. Jay Carr, "*Thelma & Louise*" Buddies With Heart," *The Boston Globe*, May 24, 1991.

5. Matthew Gilbert, "The New Fatal Attractions," *The Boston Globe*, May 26, 1991.

6. Jay Carr, "Out There," *The Boston Globe*, Jun. 30, 1991.

7. Matthew Gilbert, "Greetings from Screen City," There and Back Again: Postcards from One Critic's Trip Across the Country of Cinema." *The Boston Globe*, Aug. 11, 1991.

8. Ellen Goodman, "A World of Caution," *The Boston Globe*, Aug. 1, 1991.

9. Ellen Goodman, "Bobbitt Babbling," *The Boston Globe*, Jan. 13, 1994.

10. Ellen Goodman, "First Wives Get the Last Word," *The Boston Globe*, Sept. 29, 1996.

11. Ellen Goodman, "Real-Men Guidelines," *The Boston Globe*, Jul. 14, 1991.

12. Ellen Goodman, "A World of Caution," *The Boston Globe*, Aug. 1, 1991.

13. Ellen Goodman, "Equal Rites, Double Standards," *The Boston Globe*, Aug. 25, 1991.

14. Ellen Goodman, "Potholes on the Road to Equality," *The Boston Globe*, Aug. 26, 1992.

15. Ellen Goodman, "Clemency for Prisoner 81-G-0098," *The Boston Globe*, Jan. 3, 1993.

16. Ellen Goodman, "Bobbitt Babbling," *The Boston Globe*, Jan. 13, 1994.

17. Ellen Goodman, "First Wives Get the Last Word," *The Boston Globe*, Sept. 29, 1996.

18. Shann Nix, "Nice Guys Finish Last," *The Dayton Daily News*, Sept. 23, 1991.

19. Mark Murro, "The New Male Bimbo," *The Boston Globe*, Jul. 30, 1991.

20. Dan Shaughnessy, "Hysteria at Fenway Park Blows Up In Our Faces," *The Boston Globe*, Jul. 3, 1991.

21. Steven Stark, "Ball Park Rudeness Part of the Old World Culture," *The Tulsa World*, Jul. 14, 1991.

22. Renee Loth, "Rape and the Culture of Silence," *The Boston Globe*, Aug. 4, 1991.

23. David Nyhan, "Texas Women: Sass, Brass ... And Steel," *The Boston Globe*, Sept. 8, 1991.

24. Jay Carr, "The Key Word: 'Dysfunctional,'" *The Boston Globe*, Dec. 29, 1991.

25. Matthew Gilbert, "It Was the Directors Who Stood Tall in '91," *The Boston Globe*, Dec. 29, 1991.

26. Renee Loth, "1991: Year of the Paper Tiger," *The Boston Globe*, Dec. 29, 1991.

27. Joseph P. Kahn, "What's In — What's Out," *The Boston Globe*, Jan. 1, 1992.

28. Michael Blowen, "*Thelma & Louise*: A Volatile Mix," *The Boston Globe*, Jan. 3, 1992.

29. "A Spirited Season," *The Boston Globe*, Mar. 8, 1992.

30. Michael Madden, "They're Straight Shooters," *The Boston Globe*, Feb. 12, 1992.

31. Matthew Gilbert, "Beyond Villains," *The Boston Globe*, Mar. 22, 1992.

32. "Hollywood's Latest Discovery," *The Boston Globe*, Aug. 22, 1992.

33. "Score Another for Anita Hill," time.com, May 11, 1992.

34. Dan Wasserman, political cartoon, *The Boston Globe*, Apr. 30, 1992.

35. Jolie Solomon, "NYC Feminists' Rally Roars for Ballot-Box Power in '92," *The Boston Globe*, Apr. 26, 1992.

36. Renee Graham, "Enough is Enough, They Say," *The Boston Globe*, Apr. 29, 1992.

37. Martin F. Nolan, "Sex Looms Large in 'Year of Women,'" *The Boston Globe*, Nov. 2, 1992.

38. Diane White, "Gun-Toting Women," *The Boston Globe*, Mar. 30, 1992.

39. Jospeh P. Kahn, "Susan Faludi Lashes Back," *The Boston Globe*, Oct. 13, 1992.

40. Martin F. Nolan, "Reprinting the Legend at the Brattle, John Ford Gets Another Shot at the American Imagination," *The Boston Globe*, Aug. 15, 1993.

41. Susan Bickelhaupt, "CNBC Takes Its Pols and Pony Show to Hub," *The Boston Globe*, Dec. 15, 1993.

42. Alice Dembner, "35 and Still a Doll," *The Boston Globe*, Mar. 9, 1994.

43. The article regarded Peggy Kosmin and Tammy Ann Molewicz and the murder of William Kelly, Jr.

44. Bob Ryan, "Following Simpson Saga From Afar An American Hero's Fall Overshadows A Ballgame," *The Boston Globe*, Jun. 18, 1994.

45. Cheryl Charles, "A Long, Long Road Trip Tests Friends," *The Boston Globe*, Jan. 29, 1995.

46. Doreen Iudica Vigue, "Separate Vacations: The Pause that Refreshes," *The Boston Globe*, Mar. 2, 1995.

47. Bruce McCabe, "Sarandon Stirs Up the Pudding," *The Boston Globe*, Feb. 13, 1996.

48. Steve Morse, "Sisterhood Finds A Place in Country Music," *The Boston Globe*, Aug. 15, 1996.

49. Diane White, "'Wives': Why Men Aren't Laughing," *The Boston Globe*, Sept. 23, 1996.

50. Martin F. Nolan, "A Must-See Flick for the GOP," *The Boston Globe*, Sept. 28, 1996.

51. David Nyhan, "A Massachusetts Mantra: 'Hail to Hillary,'" *The Boston Globe*, Oct. 6, 1996.

52. Sally Jacobs, "A Varooooom of Their Own," *The Boston Globe*, Oct. 29, 1996.

53. Indira A.R. Lakshmanan, "'Bandit Queen' of India Battles on Charges Renewed Against

Indian Politician," *The Boston Globe*, Aug. 11, 1997.

54. Mary Anne Weaver, "India's Bandit Queen," *The Atlantic Monthly*, Nov. 1996, vol. 278, no. 5, p. 89–104.

55. Satish Jacob, "Lost to Violence," abcnews. com, Jul. 25, 2001.

56. Richard Corliss, "Outlawed," *Time*, Aug. 14, 1995.

57. Barbara Ehrenreich "What Do Women Have to Celebrate," *Time*, Nov. 16, 1992.

58. Michael Grunwald, "Anger at Molesters, Court Wins Sympathy for Vigilantes," *The Boston Globe*, Sept. 8, 1997.

59. Mark Feeney, "'On the Road' Again," *The Boston Globe*, Sept. 21, 1997.

60. Mary Leonard, "Reno Fights Back After Citation for Contempt," *The Boston Globe*, Aug. 9,1998.

61. Kevin Cullen, "Mary McAleese's Mission," *The Boston Globe*, Oct. 15, 1998.

62. Rob Nelson, "AT BU, Kissinger Warns on Technology," *The Boston Globe*, May 24, 1999.

63. Royal Ford, "Author Captures Convertibles and their Siren Call to the Open Road," *The Boston Globe*, Jan. 8, 2000.

64. Royal Ford, "Yearning for the Movie Car — Until Another Comes Along," *The Boston Globe*, Aug. 19, 2000.

65. Ryan McKittrick, "Jumpy Script Hampers 'Women,'" *The Boston Globe*, Jun. 1, 2001.

66. Elizabeth Benedict, "Riptide," *The Boston Globe*, Aug. 29, 2001.

67. Rick Leskowitz, "Planet Earth: A Turn for the Better," letter to the editor, *The Boston Globe*, Nov. 29, 1999.

Chapter 19

1. "Tuesday Celebrity," *The Boston Herald*, Sept. 19, 1995.

2. "Wednesday Celebrity," *The Boston Herald*, Apr. 3, 1996.

3. Jose Martinez and Ralph Ranalli, "Source: Cops Think They Have Thelma and/or Louise," *The Boston Herald*, Mar. 21, 1999.

4. Margery Eagan, "Burns is Haughty but Brilliant in Anthony, Stanton Portraits," *The Boston Herald*, Nov. 7, 1999. Eagan's comment "all-the-rage-on-Brattle-Street sensibilities" refers to Brattle Street in Harvard Square, Cambridge, Massachusetts, near Harvard University.

5. Jeanette Johnson, "Herstory," *The Boston Herald*, Nov. 4, 1999.

6. Jeanette Johnston, "Daring Women," *The Boston Herald*, Nov. 5, 1999.

7. Don Aucoin, "The 'Family Drama' of Women's History," *The Boston Globe*, Oct. 31, 1999.

8. Don Aucoin, "A Vivid History of Early Feminists," *The Boston Globe*, Nov. 5, 1999.

9. Irene Sege, "Viewing Parties Toast women Who Changed History," *The Boston Globe*, Nov. 9, 1999.

10. Diane Eickhoff, "The Forgotten Feminist," *The Kansas City Star*, Nov. 6, 1999.

11. Robert W. Butler, "The Role Reversal in This Buddy-road Movie Really Sparkle," *The Kansas City Star*, May 24, 1991.

12. Robert W. Butler, "Meet the Real *Thelma & Louise*," *The Kansas City Star*, May 1, 1992.

13. Virginia Hall, "Road Warriors," *The Kansas City Star*, Jun. 21, 1991.

14. George Gurley, "Violence and the New Woman," *The Kansas City Star*, Jun. 22, 1991.

15. Scott Herrick, "Buddies Go on a Rampage," *The Kansas City Star*, Jan. 10, 1992.

16. Elaine Adams, "A 'prep,' So Close to 13," *The Kansas City Star*, Aug. 16, 1993.

17. George Gurley, "Does Anyone Really Miss Misogyny?" *The Kansas City Star*, Aug. 15, 1999.

18. Claire Walter, "Women-only Ski Classes," *The Kansas City Star*, Nov. 17, 1991.

19. Jospeh Sobran, "*Thelma & Louise* and Madonna," *The Kansas City Star*, Jun. 19, 1991.

20. Donald Kraul, "'Robust Romp,' My Foot," *The Kansas City Star*, Jun. 6, 1991.

21. Gayle Fee, "Wary Women Boost Gun Sales," *The Boston Herald*, Nov.17, 1991.

22. M.A.J McKenna, "Yippee-I-o! The Cowgirls are A-comin'," *The Boston Herald*, Apr. 28, 1994.

23. David Weber and Samson Mulugeta, "Abortion Clashes Wind Down in the Hub," *The Boston Herald*, July 1, 1992.

24. Tristram Lozaw, "The Beat Goes On, Comfortably, as London Rock Tours Take to the Air," *The Boston Herald*, Dec. 19, 1999.

25. Helen-Chantal Pike, "Kids Trips Navigate Way to a Rafting Vacation," *The Boston Herald*, Apr. 28, 1996.

26. Amy Abern, "Pretty as a Picture — Discover the Reasons for Hollywood's Love Affair with Southern Utah," *The Boston Herald*, Dec. 16, 2001.

27. Steve Buckley, "Burns, Baby, Burns," *The Boston Herald*, Jan. 14, 2000.

28. Don Feder, "Harvard Divinity Snubs Christianity," *The Boston Herald*,, Apr. 4, 1994.

29. Don Feder, "You Know You're a Liberal If...," *The Boston Herald*, Apr. 22, 1996.

30. Margery Eagan, "When the Going Gets Tough, These Women Get Tougher," *The Boston Herald*, Aug. 1, 1991.

31. Margie Eagan, "O'Leary's Confession Plays Like a Made-for-TV Movie," *The Boston Herald*, Nov. 19, 1991.

32. Margery Eagan, "Women Made Real Progress During 'Year of the Man,'" *The Boston Herald*, Dec. 31, 1991.

33. Margery Eagan, "Imagine if Women Had the Muscles and Guns," *The Boston Herald*, Mar. 3, 1992.

34. Margery Eagan, "Feminism Terrifies Men & Law at Harvard," *The Boston Herald*, Apr. 14, 1992.

35. Andrea Estes, "Harvard Review Scraps Parody after Uproar," *The Boston Herald*, Apr. 13, 1992.

36. Andrea Estes, "Cracks Form in Staid Harvard Institution," *The Boston Herald*, Apr. 20, 1992.

37. Margery Eagan, "Feminism Terrifies Men & Law at Harvard," *The Boston Herald*, Apr. 14, 1992

38. Alice McQuillan, "The Professor and the Murder," *The Boston Herald*, Mar. 29, 1992.

39. Margery Eagan, "We Waited for the Hollywood Ending, but it Never Came," *The Boston Herald*, Jun. 1994.

40. Wayne Woodlief, "Race for White House 1992," *The Boston Herald*, Oct. 1991.

41. Wayne Woodlief, "Seeking Gramm of Truth," *The Boston Herald*, May 28, 1995.

42. Jon Keller, "No Oscar if He Acts Naturally," *The Boston Herald*, Jan. 1, 1999.

43. Beth Teitell, "What Will Those Fun-loving Doles Do Now?" *The Boston Herald*, Oct. 22, 1999.

44. James Verniere, "Coens Return with a Vengeance with *Fargo,*" The Boston Herald, Mar. 8, 1996.

45. Stephen Schaeffer, "*Leaving Normal* Cluttered with Cliches," *The Boston Herald*, Apr. 29, 1992.

46. James Verniere, "A *Field* Swamped in Mixed Images," *The Boston Herald*, Feb. 12, 1993.

47. James Verniere, "Three for the Road," *The Boston Herald*, Feb. 3, 1995.

48. James Verniere, "Julia Roberts Stands by Her Man in Retro *Something to Talk About,*" *The Boston Herald*, Aug. 4, 1995.

49. James Verniere, "Portman Makes Her Mark *Here,*" *The Boston Herald*, Nov. 12, 1999.

50. Stephen Schaeffer, "These Natural Killers are a Turnoff," *The Boston Herald*, Nov. 30, 2001.

51. Stephen Schaefer, "Do Women Still Lack ox Office Clout?" *The Boston Herald*, Dec. 1, 1991.

52. James Verniere, "Films '91: Hype Outweighed Hits," *The Boston Herald*, Dec. 29, 1991.

53. James Verniere, (missing headline) "If this weekend's box-flice grosses prove anything...," *The Boston Herald*, May 24, 1992.

54. James Verniere, "Critical Difference," *The Boston Herald*, Jan. 1, 1993.

55. James Verniere, "Trails by Fire," *The Boston Herald*, Feb. 28, 1993.

56. Ivor Davis, "Cast System," *The Boston Herald*, Mar. 14, 1993.

57. James Verniere, "Violent Femmes in Hollywood," *The Boston Herald*, Apr. 24, 1994.

58. Bonnie Erbe, "Hollywood's Woman Woes," *The Boston Herald*, Mar. 28, 1995.

59. Margery Eagan, "*Tomb Raider* Falls Short as Film Breakthrough for Women," *The Boston Herald*, Jun. 24, 2001.

Chapter 20

1. Pauline Kael, *The Citizen Kane Book* (Boston: Little Brown and Company 1971), "Raising Kane," p. 8.

2. Pauline Kael, *The Citizen Kane Book*, p. 29.

3. Pauline Kael, *The Citizen Kane Book*, p. 48.

4. Pauline Kael, *The Citizen Kane Book*, p. 74.

5. Molly Haskell, *From Reverence to Rape*, p. 123.

6. Molly Haskell, *From Reverence to Rape*, p. 145.

7. Jeanine Basinger, *A Woman's View: How Hollywood Spoke to Women 1930–1960* (New York: Alfred A. Knopf, 1993).

8. Molly Haskell, *From Reverence to Rape*, p. 326.

9. Molly Haskell, *From Reverence to Rape*, p. 327–328.

10. Molly Haskell, *From Reverence to Rape*, p. 329.

11. "Person of the Year 1975: American Women," time.com, Jan. 5, 1976.

12. Molly Haskell, "Women In the Movies Grow Up," *Psychology Today*, Jan. 13, 1993.

13. Russell Evansen, "Women Take Top Billing," *The Wisconsin State Journal*, Jun. 16, 1991.

14. Carrie Rickey, "Oscar's Year of the Woman," *Variety*, Jan. 8, 1997.

15. Colin Covert, "Coming on Strong," *The Star Tribune*, Mar. 25, 2001.

16. Lauren Beckham Falcone, "Women's day; Finally! Hollywood casts veteran actresses in star-ring roles" *The Boston Herald*, Feb. 11, 1993.

17. David Dahl, "With Outsiders In, Female Candidates Have a Chance," *The St. Petersburg Times*, Apr. 30, 1992.

18. Lewis Beale, "Hollywood Hears Her Roar, The Year of the Woman, from Properties to Protagonists," *The Washington Post*, Jul. 26, 1992.

19. Eleanor Ringel, "Year of the Woman? Not in Hollywood," *The Atlanta Journal-Constitution*, Nov. 22, 1992.

20. James Ryan, "It Wasn't the Year of the Woman in Hollywood," *The Boston Globe*, Dec. 6, 1992.

21. Barbara Ehrenreich, "What Do Women Have to Celebrate?" *Time*, Nov. 16, 1992.

22. Jessica Seigel, "And the Winner is... Year of the Woman? It's still named Oscar, isn't it?" *The Chicago Tribune*, Jan. 10, 1993.

23. Caryn James, "Women Took Backward

Steps in Hollywood," *The St. Petersburg Times*, Jan. , 1993.

24. Judy Gerstel, "Another Year, Another Dilemma for the Oscars; As Nomination Time Nears, Noteworthy Men's Roles Far Out Number Women's," *The Detroit Free Press*, Jan. 31, 1993.

25. Jay Carr, "More Losses Than Gains in Hollywood's Year of the Woman," *The Boston Globe*, Feb. 18, 1993.

26. Jessica Seigel, "Year of the Woman— Yeah Sure!" *The Chicago Tribune*, Mar. 28, 1993.

27. John Horn, "Women in Hollywood Find Little Reason to Celebrate," *The Salt Lake Tribune*, Mar. 29, 1993.

28. John Horn, "A Year to Bemoan the Plight of Women in Hollywood?" *The Los Angeles Times*, Mar. 30, 1993.

29. At the time of our interview I was a student, and Littman was generous enough to mail me a copy of "Tribute to Women in Film" at her own cost for me to keep as part of my collection.

30. Ellen Goodman, "Stand Behind Your Man," *The Boston Globe*, Apr. 1, 1993.

31. Kristin Tillotson, "Females for Sale," *The Star Tribune*, Apr. 11, 1993.

32. Carla Hall, "Heidi Fleiss: Hollywood's Woman of the Year?" *The Los Angeles Times*, Aug. 18, 1993.

33. Martha Lauzen 2001.
34. Martha Lauzen 2002.
35. "The Celluloid Ceiling (2002): Jan Chats with Martha Lauzen," www.films42.com.
36. Charles Lyons, "Film Femmes Walk Razor's Edge," *Variety*, Jun. 9, 2002.
37. Patrick Goldstein, "Good Women Hard to Find?" *The Los Angeles Times*, Apr. 8, 2003.
38. First Weekenders Group e-mail, Jun. 7, 2002.
39. www.films42.com, August 2003.
40. Dade Hayes, "H'w'd Revels in Niches Riches," *Variety*, Feb. 23, 2003.
41. Molly Haskell, "Can *Charlie's Angels* Still Fly in a *G.I. Jane* World?" *The New York Times*, Sept. 10, 2000.
42 "America's Traditional Scapegoat," *The Houston Chronicle*, Oct. 31, 1991.
43. Bonnie Coffey, "A Nebraska Woman Says Aloud She Is an 'F' Word," *Women's E News*, www.womenenews.org, Jun. 19, 2002.

Epilogue

1. Carolyn G. Heilbrun, Reinventing Womanhood (W.W. Norton & Company 1979) p.34.
2. Virginia Woolf, A Room of Her Own, p.71.

Bibliography

Books

Abramowitz, Rachel. *Is That a Gun in Your Pocket? Women's Experience of Power in Hollywood.* New York: Random House, 2000.

Basinger, Jeanine. *A Woman's View: How Hollywood Spoke to Women 1930–1960.* New York: Alfred A. Knopf, 1993.

Beauchamp, Cari. *Without Lying Down: Frances Marion and the Powerful Women of Early Hollywood.* Berkeley: University of California Press, 1998.

Bell, Quentin. *Virginia Woolf: A Biography.* New York: Harcourt Brace Jovanovich, 1972.

Bernard, Jami. *Chick Flicks: A Movie Lover's Guide to the Movies Women Love.* New York: Carol Publishing Group, 1997.

Berry, Carmen Renee, and Tamara Traeder. *Girlfriends: Invisible Bonds, Enduring Ties.* Berkeley: Wildcat Canyon Press, 1995.

Bundy, Clare, Lisa Carrigg, Sibyl Goldman, and Andrea Pryos. *Girls on Film: The Highly Opinionated, Completely Subjective Guide to the Movies.* New York: Harper Perennial, 1999.

Cosgriff, Gabrielle, Anne Reifenberg, and Cynthia Thomas. *Chicks on Film: Video Picks for Women and Other Intelligent Forms of Life.* New York: Avon Books, 1998.

Douglas, Susan. *Where the Girls Are: Growing Up Female with the Mass Media.* New York: Random House, 1994.

Faludi, Susan. *Backlash: The Undeclared War Against American Women.* New York: Crown, 1991.

Field, Syd. *Four Screenplays: Studies in the American Screenplay.* New York: Dell Trade Paperback, 1994.

_____. *The Screenwriter's Problem Solver.* New York: Dell Trade Paperback, 1998.

Franke, Lizze. *Script Girls: Women Screenwriters in Hollywood.* London: British Film Institute, 1994.

Froug, William. *Zen and the Art of Screen Writing: Insights and Interviews.* Los Angeles: Silman-James Press, 1996.

Haskell, Molly. *From Reverence to Rape: The Treatment of Women in the Movies.* Chicago: University of Chicago Press, 1987.

Heilbrun, Carolyn G. *Reinventing Womanhood* (New York: W.W. Norton, 1979), p. 34.

Hollinger, Karen. *In the Company of Women: Contemporary Female Friendship Films.* Minneapolis: University of Minnesota Press, 1998.

Issacs, Susan. *Brave Dames and Wimpettes: What Women Are Really Doing on Page and Screen.* New York: Ballantine, 1999.

Kael, Pauline. *The Citizen Kane Book.* Boston: Little, Brown, 1971.
Khouri, Callie. *Thelma & Louise and Something to Talk About.* New York: Grove Press, 1991.
McKee, Robert. *Story: Substance, Structure, Style, and the Principles of Writing.* New York: Harper Collins, 1997.
Sammon, Paul M. *Ridley Scott Close Up, The Making of His Movies.* New York: Thunder's Mouth Press, 1999.
Sklar, Robert. *Movie-Made America: A Cultural History of American Movies.* New York: Vintage Books, 1976.
Tuttle, Carmen. *The Bad Girl's Guide to the Open Road.* San Francisco: Chronicle Books, 1999.
Wolf, Naomi. *The Beauty Myth.* New York: Doubleday, 1992.
Woolf, Virginia. *A Room of One's Own.* New York: Harcourt Brace Jovanovich, 1929.

Newspapers and Periodicals

The Albuquerque Journal
The Arizona Daily Star
The Arizona Republic
The Arkansas Democrat Gazette
The Atlanta Journal and Constitution
The Atlantic Monthly
The Austin American-Statesmen
The Baltimore Sun
The Boston Globe
The Boston Herald
The Buffalo News
The Capital Times (Madison, Wisconsin)
The Charleston Daily Mail
The Charleston Gazette
The Chicago Tribune
The Christian Science Monitor
*The Columbian (*Vancouver, Washington*)*
The Columbus Dispatch (Columbus, Ohio*)*
The Commercial Appeal (Memphis, Tennessee)
The Daily Herald (Provo, Utah)
The Dallas Morning News
The Dayton Daily News
The Denver Post
The Detroit Free Press
The Fort Worth Star-Telegram
The Hollywood Reporter
The Houston Chronicle
The Kansas City Star
The Knoxville News
The Los Angeles Times
The Las Vegas Review-Journal
The Las Vegas Sun

The Miami Herald
The Minneapolis Star Tribune
The Nation
National Catholic Reporter
Newsday
Newsweek
New York
The New Yorker
The New York Post
The New York Times
The Oklahoman
The Oregonian
Psychology Today
The Record (Orange County, New Jersey)
The Richmond News Leader
The Richmond Times-Dispatch
The Roanoke Times
The Rocky Mountain News
The Salt Lake Tribune
The San Francisco Chronicle
The San Francisco Examiner
Saturday Night
Screen Actor
The Seattle Post-Intelligencer
The Spokesman-Review (Spokane, Washington)
State Journal-Register (Springfield, Illinois)
The St. Louis Post-Dispatch
The St. Paul Pioneer Press
The St. Petersburg Times
Sojourner
The Sunday News (Lancaster, Pennsylvania)

The Telegraph Herald (Dubuque, Iowa)
Time
The Times Union (Albany, New York)
The Tribune Star (Terre Haute, Indiana)
The Tulsa World
U.S. News & World Report
USA Today
Variety

Village Voice
The Wall Street Journal
The Washington Post
The Washington Post Magazine
The Wichita Eagle
The Wisconsin State Journal
Women & Guns
Women's E News

Index